PSYCHOLOGY FOR TEACHING

10TH EDITION

A bear ~~always usually sometimes rarely never always faces the front will not commit himself just now faces the future is politically correct~~ is not a choirboy!

GUY R. LEFRANÇOIS
University of Alberta

Wadsworth
Thomson Learning™

Australia • Canada • Denmark • Japan • Mexico • New Zealand • Philippines
Puerto Rico • Singapore • Spain • United Kingdom • United States

For my first teacher, my father,
who taught me to love books and learning,
and
for my mother,
who taught me to love people and life.

Education Editor: Dianne Lindsay
Assistant Editor: Tangelique Williams
Editorial Assistant: Keynia Johnson
Marketing Manager: Becky Tollerson
Project Editor: Trudy Brown
Print Buyer: Barbara Britton
Permissions Editor: Susan Walters
Production Service: Hespenheide Design
Copy Editor: Jan de Prosse

Text and Cover Designer: Stephanie Greisen, Hespenheide Design
Cover Illustrator: Dianne Bennett
Cartoonists: Tony Hall, Jeff Littlejohn
Technical Illustrators: Teresa Roberts, Natalie Hill
Photo Researcher: Leslie Shapiro, Hespenheide Design
Compositor: Hespenheide Design
Indexer: Bob Marsh
Cover Printer: Phoenix Color
Printer/Binder: World Color Book Services/Taunton

Printed in the United States of America
3 4 5 6 7 03 02

For permission to use material from this text, contact us:
   Web: www.thomsonrights.com
   Fax: 1-800-730-2215
   Phone: 1-800-730-2214

For more information, contact
Wadsworth/Thomson Learning
10 Davis Drive
Belmont, CA 94002-3098
USA
www.wadsworth.com

International Headquarters
Thomson Learning
290 Harbor Drive, 2nd Floor
Stamford, CT 06902-7477
USA

UK/Europe/Middle East
Thomson Learning
Berkshire House
168-173 High Holborn
London WC1V 7AA
United Kingdom

Asia
Thomson Learning
60 Albert Street #15-01
Albert Complex
Singapore 189969

Canada
Nelson/Thomson Learning
1120 Birchmount Road
Scarborough, Ontario M1K 5G4
Canada

Library of Congress Cataloging-in-Publication Data
Lefrançois, Guy R.
    Psychology for teaching / Guy R. Lefrançois.—10th ed.
       p.   cm.
    Includes bibliographical references (p.) and index.
    ISBN 0-534-57447-5
    1. Educational psychology.   2. Teaching—Psycho-
logical aspects.   3. Learning, Psychology of.   I. Title.
    LB1051.L568   1999
    370.15—dc21   99-44849

BRIEF CONTENTS

TABLE OF CONTENTS

PREFACE

Edmonton, Alberta
At the turn of the 3rd millennium

Dear Reader:

The first **Bear**, *Psychology for teaching: A bear always faces the front*, appeared more than a quarter of a century ago. **Bear I** described itself as a book that presented educationally relevant theory and research in a clear and interesting way, that was substantive but not encyclopedic, and that made more use of humor and illustration than was typical of its academic cousins. It even included cartoons—a rare thing in books of that day. "Dick," one reviewer with knotted shorts grumbled to my editor, "don't publish that thing. It doesn't treat educational psychology with enough respect."

My grandmother said it more clearly: "That Bear book," she cracked, "It has more dog meat than choirboy in it."

But, in spite of all that, dang if the bear didn't survive to see daylight again three years later, and again three years after that, and again . . . and again, until, shoot, the millennium is upon us and still, **Bear X** is not ready for that long hibernation—or wherever it is that really old bears go.

One of the most often-asked questions about this book is: Why a bear? As my grandmother put it: Why not an owl? Or a crow, for crying out loud? Sadly, there isn't room enough here to answer that question. But there is a bit of an answer in the epilogue.

What's Old and What's New in Bear X?

This tenth edition is still anchored in the conviction that the best teaching decisions are based on sound psychological principles and research applied with enthusiasm and imagination and tempered with a love of children and teaching. Even in this enlightened age, teaching cannot easily be reduced to a handful of instructions to be followed like kitchen recipes. Children, and teaching, are too complex for such simple-minded approaches.

Good teaching is still far more than just telling. It requires motivating, organizing, previewing, showing, illustrating, explaining, evaluating, reviewing, inspiring, perhaps even standing on one's head or dancing little jigs while singing songs in foreign languages. *Psychology for Teaching*, Tenth Edition, tries to be a good teacher. It illustrates, shows and compares; it evaluates, reviews, and previews; maybe it even inspires a little. And on at least one occasion that I can think of, it almost stands on its metaphoric head.

This edition incorporates several new features and new or expanded coverage of many important current topics—for example:

▲ Expanded coverage of the direct-instruction/constructivism issue, summarized on the inside front cover

▲ Suggestions for Internet-based activities at the end of each chapter and additional Web-related suggestions summarized on the inside back cover

▲ More than 100 additions to the glossary and 450 additions to the bibliography (most published within the last three years)

▲ More detailed treatment of multicultural education, formative and summative evaluation, legal issues in testing, teacher burnout, morality, educating the talented and gifted, children with special needs, and many other topics

A Guide to the Tenth Edition

Here are some of the features that are designed to make this edition of the Bear the most effective teaching/learning tool it can be—and you, the best teacher you can be.

To help you organize your study, at the beginning of every chapter . . .

Outlines tell you at a glance where the chapter is going.

Chapter Previews serve as advance organizers by highlighting the most important concepts in the chapter.

Focus Questions phrase the chapter's objectives in the form of questions that direct your attention and focus your study.

Vignettes lead you into the chapter with a brief, sometimes humorous, always relevant story.

Throughout the text . . .

Boxed Inserts present high-interest enrichment material.

Figures and Illustrations summarize important findings and clarify main points.

Ppc footnotes—comments from reviewers and other readers (*pre-*publication *c*ritics)—provide different insights—and sometimes humor.

Cases describing actual classroom interactions are used to illustrate practical applications of psychology for teaching.

Every chapter includes *Concept Summarizing Tables* that organize and simplify important ideas.

At the end of each chapter, *Main Points* summaries provide a comprehensive review of the principal ideas. These can be an excellent tool for study and review.

Applied Questions rephrase each of the focus questions found at the beginning of the chapter, transforming them into actual problems, exercises, and activities closely related to your preparation for teaching.

Internet Activities present questions and topics to be researched using InfoTrac or other Web-based resources.

Study Terms list all of the important terms in the chapter. Each of these is defined in the running glossary at the bottom of the page where the term first appears and is found again in the alphabetical glossary at the end of the book. These can be useful as a quick check of your mastery of chapter content.

Suggested Readings provide quick leads about up-to-date sources of additional information and can be useful for further study and research, or for term papers.

A *Chart* on the inside front cover of the book summarizes the constructivism/direct-instruction issue.

Internet Sources on the inside back cover of the book introduce InfoTrac College Edition; they also present a selection of other World Wide Web addresses that provide free information and resources useful for teachers and for teachers-in-training.

Thank-You to . . .

I'm not sure where to start any more. After ten editions, there are simply too many of you to name, including:

▲ All of the researchers, theorists, and street philosophers whose ideas are acknowledged in these pages

▲ All of the above whose ideas sneaked in unrecognized

▲ Assorted scoundrels who continue to motivate me (Do you really *want* to be like them? asks my grandmother. No, she answers for me, ever accomplished in the twisted methods of reverse psychology, making of them reverse models.)

▲ Richard L. Greenberg, old friend, editor for the first Bears

- Roger Peterson, Bob Podstepny, Marshall Aronson, Joan Garbutt, Stephanie Surfus, Ken King, Suzanna Brabant, and Sabra Horne, editors for the middle Bears
- Dianne Lindsay, editor for this most recent Bear
- Tony Hall and Jeff Littlejohn, cartoonists and very funny people
- Trudy Brown, production editor
- Jan deProsse, copyeditor
- Hespenheide Design, designer
- Reviewers of the first nine editions whose positive influence continues still: Jo Alexander, Auburn University, Montgomery; Pauline Applefield, University of North Carolina, Wilmington; J. D. Ayers, University of Victoria; Steven Banks, Marshall University; Ted Bayer, State University of New York, Albany; Harold D. Beard, Central Missouri State University; Sylven S. Beck, George Washington University; Karen K. Block, University of Pittsburgh; Gloria Bonner, Middle Tennessee State University; Laura Bursuk, York College, City University of New York; William Cerbin, University of Wisconsin, Lacrosse; Frank H. Chou, University of Kansas; Steven L. Christopherson, University of Texas, San Antonio; Michal Clark, California State University, Bakersfield; Richard Clark, State University of New York, Albany (Professor Emeritus); Henry P. Cole, University of Kentucky; Donald Cunningham, Indiana University; Alan M. Dahms, Metropolitan State College of Denver; Myron Dembo, University of Southern California; William B. Dragoin, Georgia Southwestern State University; James Dunn, Cornell University; Juan N. Franco, New Mexico State University; A. J. H. Gaite, University of Oregon; Gordon Greenwood, University of Florida; Janice C. Hayes, Middle Tennessee State University; Elmer Haymon, Jr., University of Alaska; Peggy F. Harris, Tennessee State University; Robert L. Hohn, University of Kansas; Yolanda Jaini, Heritage College; Leonard Kise, Northern Illinois University; Gerald Larson, Kent State University; Kathryn Linden, Purdue University (Professor Emerita); Sharon McNeely, Northeastern Illinois University; William L. Merrill, Central Michigan University; Janet Moursund, University of Oregon; Barry C. Munro, University of British Columbia; Wayne A. Nelson, Southern Illinois University, Edwardsville; Harry Osser, Queens University, Kingston, Ontario (Professor Emeritus); Diane Papalia, University of Wisconsin, Madison; Ann Pratt, Capital University, Columbus; P. J. Porter, University of Northern Iowa; Dan Rea, University of Wisconsin, Whitewater; Robert S. Ristow, Western Illinois University; Steven M. Ross, University of Memphis; Avis J. Ruthven, Mississippi State University; Dick T. Sampson, Eastern Washington University; Jay Samuels, University of Minnesota; Thomas F. Sawyer, North Central College; Mari Scott, Central State University; Thomassine Sellers, San Francisco State University; Mark Seng, University of Texas, Austin; Thomas Sherman, Virginia Polytechnic State University; Paul Shore, Moorhead State University; Douglas Stanwyck, Georgia State University; Hazel Stapleton, East Carolina University; John Starkey, Northern Illinois University; Sandra Stein, Rider University; Hershel Thornberg, University of Arizona; Ignatius J. Toner, University of North Carolina, Charlotte; Harold L. Wilson, Central Missouri State University; Sharon Wilson, University of Cincinnati; Joan R. Yanuzzi, Indiana University of Pennsylvania; Ronald Zellner, University of Northern Colorado; Henry Zurhellen, University of Memphis
- Reviewers of this edition for your time, patience, and wisdom I am truly grateful: Sylven Beck, George Washington University; Shelia Greenlee, Christopher Newport University; Judith Hassel, Ohio Wesleyan University; Karen Kletzing, Aurora University; Fred Kreamelmeyer, Grace College; Patricia O'Grady, St. Leo College; Charles Stanley, Jr., Florida A&M University; David Tanner, California State University, Fresno; Atilano Valencia, California State University, Fresno; German Velasco, California State University, Northridge; Charles Weiner, Henderson State University; Leslie Zorko, University of Wyoming
- Marie, Laurier, Claire, Rémi, Elizabeth, Liam, and Zachary, who make it all worth a great deal more than my while.

Guy R. Lefrançois

"Begin at the
beginning," the
King said, gravely,
"and go on till you
come to the end;
then stop."

Lewis Carroll, *Alice in
Wonderland*

The Beginning

Psychology for Teaching

There is only one chapter in Part One of this text—only one beginning. And when we get to the end, we stop.

The beginning says as clearly and simply as it can what educational psychology is; the remaining 12 chapters are the content of educational psychology—of *psychology for teaching*. These 12 chapters are organized into parts according to their major emphases. Part Two looks at human development, describing how children change through the school years. Part Three provides explanations of how we learn and applies these explanations to teaching. Part Four explores diversity in the classroom, looking at individual differences in social, intellectual, and physical development and functioning, as well as ethnic variability. And Part Five looks at topics important to effective instruction: motivation, classroom management, and assessment.

And somewhere the subtitle of this book becomes more significant.

Thousands . . .
Kiss the book's outside
who ne'er look within.

William Cowper, *Expostulation*

Psychology for Teaching

PREVIEW

Each chapter in this text opens with a preview followed by a list of focus questions. Previews organize and summarize important concepts and increase the meaningfulness of the material to be learned—sometimes by stimulating recall of important previous learning, sometimes by providing new information, and sometimes by clarifying relationships. This first chapter is a preview for the remainder of the text. Among other things, it points out that there are some important reasons for taking this course other than the fact that it might be compulsory.

Focus questions serve as objectives for the chapter that follows. They indicate some of the things you will know and understand more clearly when you have finished the chapter. And at the end of each chapter, the chapter-opening focus questions are translated into more practical review questions and assignments.

FOCUS QUESTIONS

▲ How are psychology and education related?

▲ What are theories, laws, principles, and beliefs? How are they related?

▲ What are some different models of teaching and of teachers?

▲ What are the basic elements of a useful model of teaching?

▲ What are some of the characteristics shared by expert teachers?

▲ What do bears have to do with educational psychology?

My teaching career began with John George Scott. He and I started school on the same day up in the wilds of northern Saskatchewan—a one-room school in Pascal where my father was the teacher. John George was a Cree First Nations who, at that time, spoke neither English nor French.

The first thing my dad did that morning is underline, in both French and English, some of the rules of the school like where's the cloakroom for boys and the one for girls and don't go into the wrong one and how many fingers to raise for a call of nature depending on the nature of the call. He didn't mention the strap right away, which surprised me because I figured that was a pretty big part of school. Instead, he started to pass out spellers, which is when John George turned, stared at the door for a second or two, and then, as if he'd just made up his mind, pulled himself out of his desk and lurched outside. "He's bolted," I thought, half wishing I had enough courage to do the same.

But John George hadn't bolted at all. He had simply felt the call of nature. So, what the hey, this being his usual custom, he had gotten out of his desk, trotted to the far corner of the school yard, squatted, and was now attending to that call. Watching through the windows, some of us laughed so hard we had to fight a call of nature of our own.

My father, a resourceful and thoroughly capable teacher, had rushed outside immediately. We could see him in the corner of the yard trying to explain to John George, using very interesting body language, that the little building in the other corner was equipped to handle problems of the kind John George had already solved. But some gestures are not universally understood by frightened six-year-old boys whose pants have settled around their ankles.

So my dad came back inside the school and made me a teacher. This, in retrospect, colored a big part of my life. "Show him where it is and what it's for," he said.

I took John George with me and showed him. And now that I think of it, at that moment, too, I noticed a bear ambling across the pasture just beyond the school yard. He wasn't a very old bear—but that was a long time ago.[1]

▯ PSYCHOLOGY FOR TEACHING

Showing people things *is* an important part of teaching. In fact, in Spanish the word *enseñar,* means both to teach and to show. Good teachers show students, or help them discover for themselves, all sorts of things like what ideas are and how they can be used and the meanings of numbers and how to operate machines and on and on.

However, teaching is often more complex than it might appear from straightforward tasks such as showing people about outhouses—my successful assignment with John George notwithstanding. And although this text, *Psychology for Teaching,* might not have been very useful to me that day—hey, I could scarcely read—it would

---

[1] **PPC Comment:** It might be useful for students to know whether this is a true story. (A PPC is a pre-publication critic—one of several dozen people [mostly educational psychologists, but also one cantankerous grandmother] who read the manuscript prior to its publication.)

Author: Yes, this is a true story.

have come in handy many years later when, as a beginning teacher, I tried teaching other less natural things to people whose need to learn was not quite so insistent. You see, contrary to what I had hoped, teaching skills are not hereditary; we can't count on our genes to endow us with teaching ability, or with what is called the "craft knowledge" of teaching—the knowledge that expert teachers seem to have. Fortunately, though, we now have a large body of information to help novice teachers become more expert. This information can contribute dramatically to the effectiveness of teachers and of schools. This textbook is your introduction to that information. Its goal is to make you a better teacher. As its title indicates, it presents a *psychology for teaching*.

▛ TEACHING AND YOUR BELIEFS

Teaching involves a highly complex sequence of ongoing actions. It can involve as many as a thousand or more teacher–student interactions in a single day. Each of these interactions requires a decision: what to do, what to say, how to react, where to go next.

Much of what the teacher is required to do in the classroom is immediate: There is often little time for careful reflection. Hence, many of the teacher's actions are based on habit and on preestablished beliefs. In fact, everything a teacher does in the classroom reflects personal beliefs. This does not mean, of course, that all of a teacher's behaviors are carefully premeditated. When a teacher's responses have to be immediate, as is often the case, there is little time to plan and deliberate. But even our most impulsive and habitual actions reveal our underlying convictions and implicit theories—in other words, our beliefs. For this reason, suggests Smith (1997),[2] getting teachers to change is often a very difficult undertaking. We don't easily discard old beliefs and adopt new ones.

What Are Beliefs?

Beliefs are personal convictions. Unlike knowledge, which tends to be impersonal and impartial, a **belief**[3] often has strong emotional components. Thus, beliefs are reflected in attitudes, prejudices, judgments, and opinions.

Experiences, both personal and secondhand, are closely involved in the development of our beliefs. Pajares (1992) notes that beliefs are often formed early in life and may be maintained even in the face of strong contradiction. Such beliefs act as a sort of filter through which people view the world and interpret information. Not surprisingly, as Lederhouse (1997) demonstrated, following observations of teachers with strong evangelical religious backgrounds employed in public school systems, when a teacher's beliefs run counter to school practice, tension and conflict can arise.

Beliefs result not only from personal experiences, but also from information acquired through education and other sources. For example, what we believe about the effects of smoking may reflect more of what we have read or heard than what we have experienced. Similarly, what we believe about human personality, or about human learning, may be based partly on our own experiences and partly on what we have learned from more formal educational experiences.

---

belief The acceptance of an idea as accurate or truthful. Beliefs are often highly personal and resistant to change.

---

[2] References in this text are cited in the style approved by the American Psychological Association. Thus, authors' names are followed by the year of publication. The alphabetical list of references at the end of this text gives all the information necessary for locating each source.

[3] Boldfaced terms are defined in the glossary at the end of the text and on the page where they first appear.

Last Weekend, Tommy and I . . .

THE SITUATION: Mr. Busenius' sixth-grade language class. The students are generally well behaved; most appear interested and attentive—except for Helena who, in Mr. Busenius' not-too-polite words, "is one #!!*# of a nightmare."

Today, students are asked to write two paragraphs describing the most interesting thing that happened to them over the weekend. Helena does not seem especially eager to write about her weekend. Instead, she finds a brush and begins to brush her hair.

But before she has completed her third stroke, Mr. Busenius has quietly reached her desk, taken the brush from her, and jabbed his calloused index finger twice, quite emphatically, on the blank sheet of paper on Helena's desk.

She bends to her task. "Last weekend," she writes, "Tommy and I, I don't know if I should write this, but I will, what we did is . . . ."

How Beliefs Affect Decisions

Beliefs guide our thinking and our actions. All teachers have beliefs about their work, their students, how learning occurs, and the subjects they teach. A teacher who believes students learn best by memorizing assigns memory work; one who is convinced students remember only what they understand takes more pains to explain and clarify. A teacher who believes students cheat when given the opportunity supervises her examinations closely; one who thinks students are basically honest prepares her lessons while students take their tests.

As an example, see the case "Last Weekend, Tommy and I . . . ." Note that Mr. Busenius believes, among other things, that:

1. Offenders must be made to stop immediately before misbehavior spreads.

2. It is better to reprimand silently and at close range without disrupting ongoing classroom activities.

Mr. Busenius might have selected other options. For example, he might simply have ignored Helena—if he believed that her behavior was designed to get attention and that it would, therefore, be less likely to be repeated if he ignored it. Or he might have used some form of punishment, such as detention, believing that Helena would subsequently behave herself to avoid punishment. Alternatively, he might have gone over to Roberta and praised her remarkable paragraphs just loudly enough to draw Helena's attention, believing that this might encourage Helena to build her own remarkable paragraphs. Also, he might have taken the time to explain how important it is to learn to express oneself, in the belief that this might motivate Helena to greater efforts. Or he might have explained to Helena that her hair brushing was distracting and upsetting the others, believing that her need for social approval would convince her to put her brush away.

Which of these behaviors is best? Is it always best? Which of these beliefs is most accurate and most useful?

This text is designed to help you answer these questions.

This Text and Your Beliefs

Beliefs about teaching and learning are already well established by the time teachers begin their training. And, as we have noted, teachers are resistant to change. For example, Yerrick, Parke, and Nugent (1997) looked at the effects of a summer institute intended to change teacher's beliefs about how they should teach and assess scientific knowledge. At the end of the institute, many of the teachers continued to maintain their original beliefs.

Still, beliefs are certainly changeable. For example, Agne, Greenwood, and Miller (1994) found marked differences between the belief systems of novice teachers and those of expert teachers (in this case, teachers who had been selected as Teacher of the Year). Among other things, the expert teachers tended to be more student oriented (more humanistic) in their approaches to classroom management; novices were often more rigid and stricter. This suggests that the beliefs of the expert teachers might have changed from the time they were novices—but it doesn't prove it because the expert teachers might well have had different belief systems in the first place.

Additional evidence that teachers' beliefs do change is provided by Rust (1994), who conducted an in-depth investigation of the beliefs and behaviors of two beginning teachers. Both these teachers developed new beliefs about teaching and learning during their first year— beliefs that were sometimes very different from those they thought they had learned in their teacher education programs.

Beliefs that are inaccurate or prejudiced can lead to teaching behaviors that are inappropriate and ineffective. One of the important aims of this text is to encourage you to examine your beliefs—especially those that have to do with learners and with teaching—and to discard or alter them if necessary. This text tries to do this in two related ways: *first,* by providing you with important information about learners of different ages and about the processes involved in learning, organizing, remembering, thinking, solving problems, and being creative; and *second,* by describing and illustrating practical strategies for facilitating the teaching/learning process.

As Alexander, Murphy, and Woods (1996) note, teachers have to be aware of the relatively stable and general characteristics of learners such as those that might be apparent, for example, in the processes that underlie thinking. They also need to be aware of changes in the world that have significant impacts on the lives of learners—changes such as those implicit in the explosion of information and how information is now transmitted. In the days of our distant forefathers, information was primarily transmitted orally, at first only in face-to-face contact, but later, at a greater distance using telephones and radios. In my father's age, much of the world's knowledge could be found printed in books and other publications, and written transmission of information had become dominant. Now various forms of hypermedia provide electronic storage and transmission of increasing amounts of our knowledge.

Today's expert teacher obviously needs to be aware of these changing aspects of the learner's world and of the more stable characteristics of learners. Thus, among the most useful of your beliefs as a teacher are those that relate to how students change, how they learn, what motivates, reinforces, and punishes them, and what is interesting and important to them. These topics fall within the realm of **psychology**. Hence this *psychology for teaching.*

PSYCHOLOGY

Psychology is the science that studies human **behavior** and thinking. It looks at how experience affects thought and action; it explores the roles of biology and heredity; it examines consciousness and dreams; it traces how people

---

psychology The science that examines human behavior (and that of other animals as well).

behavior The activity of an organism. Behavior can be either overt (visible) or covert (invisible or internal).

TABLE 1.1
What Psychologists Do

SUBFIELD*	MAJOR CONCERNS AND ACTIVITIES
Clinical	Diagnosing and treating emotional illnesses and disturbances, often in a hospital or clinical setting
Counseling and guidance	Evaluating and counseling clients with behavioral, emotional, and other problems not serious enough to require hospital or clinical treatment; also, assisting with important decisions (career, marriage, and so on)
Developmental	Studying changes that define growth, maturation, and learning from birth to death; applying findings in education programs
Educational	Researching learning, thinking, remembering, instructing, and related topics in educational settings; developing and applying learning programs for students
Industrial and personnel	Applying psychology in business and industry; developing and administering tests to evaluate aptitudes; conducting workshops and programs dealing with motivation, management, interpersonal relations, and related areas
Personality	Identifying and describing important, stable characteristics of individuals; developing classification schemes for personality characteristics and methods for identifying and assessing these characteristics
School	Identifying individual aptitudes and skills among learners in a school setting; developing and administering tests pertinent to school-related abilities
Experimental, comparative, and physiological	Exploring psychology as an experimental science; conducting research on comparisons among species; investigating physiological functioning as it relates to psychological functioning
Psychometrics	Testing and measuring psychological characteristics and making sense of resulting measures; developing tests and measurement devices
Social	Doing research and consulting on the relationship between individuals and groups

*Not all psychologists fall neatly into one of these categories. Many have interests and engage in activities that span several subfields.

develop from infants into adults; it investigates social influences. Basically, psychology tries to explain why people think, act, and feel as they do. It is a fascinating but highly complex discipline. As a result, although all psychologists are concerned with behavior in one way or another, many specialties and subdivisions have arisen within the field, each concentrating on specific aspects of the human experience. For example, developmental psychologists examine how behavior changes over time; clinical psychologists deal with behavioral and emotional problems; and educational psychologists are interested in the scientific study of behavior in educational settings. These are only three of the divisions in psychology; Table 1.1 labels and describes several other divisions and provides a clearer picture of psychology's scope.

Science and Psychology

Psychologists don't try to understand behavior by simply thinking about the various factors that might be involved in behaving. Rather, psychology as a **science** involves the application of scientific procedures and approaches in an attempt to understand human behavior.

Science is as much an attitude as a collection of methods. As an attitude, it insists on precision, consistency, and replicability. The methods resulting from this attitude consist of rules intended to eliminate subjectivity, bias, and the influence of random factors—in short, rules designed to maximize the extent to which we can have confidence in the conclusions of science. For most of the 20th century (psychology is approximately 100 years old), the attitudes and methods that have governed psychologists' search for a greater understanding of humans and their behavior have emphasized precision, replicability, and objectivity above all else.

Experiments Science's most important tool in its quest for knowledge and understanding is the **experiment,** a situation where the investigator systematically manipulates aspects of the environment to determine the effect of so doing on some important outcome. What is manipulated or controlled is called the **independent variable;** the effect of this manipulation is reflected in the **dependent variable.** Most experiments can easily be worded in terms of an "if-then" statement. The experimenter is saying, in effect, "if such and such, then such and such." The "if" part of the equation is the independent variable; the "then" part is the dependent variable.

As an example, consider the prediction (termed a **hypothesis**) that *rewarding learners will have a positive effect on subsequent learning.* Phrased as an if-then statement, this might be translated as "*if* learners are rewarded, *then* there will be an improvement in their subsequent learning."

To test this prediction, the experimenter must first define the abstract concepts involved in terms of behaviors or actions (operations) that can actually be observed and measured; these are called **operational definitions.** An operational definition of "rewarding learners," for example, might specify that learners will be given high grades, verbal praise, special privileges, and so on. In the same way, "subsequent learning" might be operationally defined in terms of learners' performance on a predetermined test. Thus, an experiment designed to examine the hypothesis *rewarding learners will have a positive effect on subsequent learning* might consist of an arrangement where some learners are paid for their grades and others not, all are subsequently exposed to a learning experience, and the performance of the rewarded group is compared to that of the unrewarded group. In this case, the *independent variable* (the "if" part of the if-then equation) is the monetary reward; the dependent variable (the "then" part) is the learner's subsequent performance.

Facts and Theories Science, as we have seen, is a collection of methods and attitudes that relate directly to how we discover and accumulate

---

science An approach and an attitude toward knowledge that emphasize objectivity, precision, and replicability.

experiment A deliberately controlled arrangement of circumstances under which a phenomenon is observed.

independent variable The variable that is manipulated in an experiment to determine whether doing so causes changes in the dependent variable: the "if" part of the if-then equation implicit in an experiment.

dependent variable The variable (measurement, outcome, behavior) that reflects the effects of manipulations of the independent variable(s) in an experiment. The "then" part of the if-then equation implicit in an experimental hypothesis.

---

hypothesis An educated guess that can be tested. A prediction, generally based on observation, intuition, or theory, which must then be verified experimentally. A hypothesis can usually be expressed as an if-then statement.

operational definition A concrete or behavioral definition of an abstract term. That is, a definition that permits an abstract concept to be observed and measured or evaluated.

facts. In this context, however, the word **fact** is perhaps too strong; it implies a degree of certainty and accuracy that is not always possible in psychology or education. In these areas, our facts are simply observations of events, behaviors, or relationships. Science insists that these observations be made under controlled conditions so that the same observations can be made by anyone—that is, so that they can be replicated.[4]

Facts (or observations), by themselves, would be of limited value to educators and psychologists if they were not organized, summarized, and simplified. That's where **theory** comes in. In a simple sense, a theory is a collection of related statements whose principal function is to summarize and explain observations. For example, when I observe that Roland Littlefork repeatedly refuses to join us for our annual fishing excursion, our regular poker games, our Christmas celebration, or our Halloween masquerade, I might develop a theory about his behavior. "I have a theory about Roland," I might say, and everybody would understand what I meant. "He doesn't like social gatherings," I might continue. That, in a nutshell, would be my theory. It summarizes and explains my observations admirably. It is a statement that might be described as a **naive theory** or, as Grippin and Peters (1984) label it, an

implicit theory. Naive or implicit theories differ from more formal theories in one important respect: Naive theories express personal convictions that need only be believed but not scientifically proved; formal theories must be tested. It isn't enough to simply assume that a psychological theory accounts for all the important observations and relationships; this must be demonstrably true.

Some theories are more useful than others. Some, for instance, don't reflect the facts very well. Let's say, for example, that Roland Littlefork plays poker regularly with George's group and that he also accepts other social invitations. If this were true, my theory about Roland's behavior would not fit all the facts.

That a good theory reflect all important facts is only one of its requirements. Thomas (1996) suggests several others: A theory is good if it (1) accurately reflects observations, (2) is expressed clearly, (3) is useful for predicting as well as explaining, (4) lends itself to practical applications, (5) is consistent rather than self-contradictory, and (6) is not based on numerous assumptions (unproven beliefs). A good theory should also be thought provoking and should provide satisfying explanations, says Thomas (1996). (See Table 1.2.)

The most useful theories are those that not only serve to explain observations but also to predict events. My naive theory about Roland Littlefork, for example, allows me to predict that he will refuse all social invitations, no matter who issues them. As we saw, however, in this case the prediction is inaccurate because the theory does not account for certain important facts (specifically, that he accepts other people's invitations). Presumably, a theory that fits the facts better would lead to more accurate predictions.

A theory, then, is a statement or, more often, a collection of related statements whose main function is to summarize, simplify, organize, and explain observations and to permit predic-

---

fact Something that observation leads us to believe is true or real. Ideally, the observations that determine our facts are sufficiently objective and repeatable to assure us that they accurately reflect how things actually are.

theory A body of information pertaining to a specific topic, a method of acquiring and dealing with information, or a set of explanations for related phenomena.

naive theory An expression used to describe psychological theories based on intuition and folk belief rather than on science. Also termed *implicit theory.*

---

[4] *PPC:* It might be useful to emphasize how important observations are to science.

Author: Yes. In the words of the bear's friend and mentor, Yogi Berra (the bear claims Yogi as his guru): "You can observe a lot by watching."

TABLE 1.2

Criteria of a good theory, applied to Grandma Francœur's fertilizer theory. This theory holds, in part, that horse manure stimulates potatoes and carrots, that chicken droppings invigorate cabbages, and that dried cow dung excites flowers.*

CRITERIA	GRANDMOTHER FRANCŒUR'S THEORY
Does it reflect the facts?	Yes, if carrots, potatoes, and other plants behave as expected under specified conditions.
Is it clear and understandable?	It is quite clear and understandable except to the very stupid, who are seldom asked to judge theories.
Is it useful for predicting as well as explaining?	Very. For example, the theory allows the gardener to predict in the spring what will happen in the fall, depending on the fertilizers used. And the predictions are clearly falsifiable. Thus, the theory can be tested directly.
Is it practically useful?	Clearly, yes, for those engaged in the growing of vegetables.
Is it internally consistent?	Unfortunately, no. The old lady has sometimes claimed that chicken droppings are better for potatoes than horse manure.
Is it based on many unverifiable assumptions?	No. The assumptions upon which it is based could be verified—or falsified.
Is it satisfying and thought-provoking? Does it have heuristic value?	Oh, yes!

*From *Theories of Human Learning: What the Old Man Said*, (4th ed.) by G. R. Lefrançois. Copyright © 2000 Wadsworth. Used by permission.

tions about events relating to this set of observations. Some of these statements may be described as laws, others as principles, and many as beliefs.

Laws, Principles, and Beliefs Laws are statements whose accuracy is generally beyond question. Physics, chemistry, astronomy, and other natural sciences have discovered numerous important laws ($E = mc^2$, for example). As we saw earlier, however, human behavior is rarely characterized by the regularity and unwavering predictability of laws.

Principles are statements that are probable rather than certain. Unlike laws, they are always open to a degree of doubt, to a certain level of probability (and improbability). Accordingly, most psychological statements about human behavior and experience take the form of principles rather than laws.

Beliefs are more private and personal than either principles or laws. Beliefs are our individual convictions, our personal attempts to explain observations. Beliefs are often based on personal experience but can also be based on the same sorts of scientific observations that give rise to more formal theories. One of the most important goals of *Psychology for Teaching* is to provide you with a more valid basis for forming and examining important personal beliefs. One important step in that direction is to look at the sorts of models that underlie your thinking.

law A statement that is accurate beyond reasonable doubt.

principle A statement relating to uniformity or predictability. Principles are far more open to doubt than laws but are more reliable than beliefs.

Models A **model** is like a pattern or a blueprint; it's a representation of how things are or of how they can or should be. We could also say that a model is an organized set of beliefs about something important.

Models can be very specific and concrete and are often included in, or derived from, theories. For example, there are models of atomic structures, models of the universe, and teaching models.

Models can also be very general. For example, they can represent all of our beliefs and assumptions about human nature. In this sense, each of us has implicit models that govern our view of the world and guide our beliefs and our behavior.

Psychological models are essentially metaphors. They don't say "humans are this or that" as much as "humans behave as though they were like this or like that." Accordingly, models, like theories, should not be judged in terms of their accuracy but rather in terms of their usefulness. A theory—or a model—is neither right nor wrong, say Wellman and Gelman (1992); it is simply more or less useful.

MODELS OF LEARNERS AND TEACHERS

There are different ways of describing teaching and learning—various models of the roles of learners and teachers. For example, Sfard (1998) describes two models (or metaphors) that explain what learning is and how it occurs: The first model views learning as being largely a process of *acquisition* by learners—a process of progressively accumulating information. The second views *participation* as the basis of learn-

ing. Teachers who subscribe to the **acquisition metaphor** typically view their role as one of helping students to accumulate information and concepts. Those who subscribe to the **participation metaphor** are more concerned with the processes of learning—that is, with the student's active participation in learning. Both metaphors, argues Sfard, are valid and useful, and both should guide the teacher's behavior.

Constructivism and Direct Instruction Models

These two metaphors lead directly to two very basic and important instructional models; we will refer to these often throughout this text. One is a highly teacher-centered model based on the acquisition metaphor. It says, in effect, that because learning is largely a matter of *acquiring* information, the teacher's principal role should be one of **direct instruction**. This view of learning and teaching sees the teacher as the principal source of information and assigns to the teacher the role of organizing and imparting information in the most effective way possible.

In contrast, the *participation* metaphor leads to the view that the learner should be an active participant in the teaching/learning process—that learners are, in fact, responsible for *discovering* and *constructing* information for themselves. Accordingly, **constructivist approaches** to instruction are highly student- rather than teacher-

---

model A representation, usually abstract, of some phenomenon or system. Alternatively, a pattern for behavior that can be copied by someone.

acquisition metaphor A model of teaching marked by a view of learning as being largely a process of *acquisition* and accumulation by learners.

participation metaphor A model of teaching characterized by the view that *participation* is the basis of learning. Teachers who subscribe to the participation metaphor are greatly concerned with the processes of learning.

direct instruction A phrase used to describe teacher-directed approaches to teaching—in contrast with more student-centered approaches such as reciprocal-teaching and co-operative learning (often included among *constructivist approaches*).

Two teaching methods

Models of the Teacher

Besides the teacher's basic beliefs about learning as a process of acquisition or participation, the role of the teacher, note Fenstermacher and Soltis (1992), often appears to reflect one of three basic models of teachers: the executive model, the therapist model, or the liberationist model.

The **executive model** sees the teacher as someone who has mastered the craft of teaching and who bears the main responsibility for arranging the teaching/learning situation so that learners acquire prescribed skills and information. This model emphasizes teaching techniques and materials preparation. It tends to favor direct instruction over the more student-centered constructivist approaches.

The **therapist model** views the teacher not as an executive but rather as a highly sympathetic individual whose primary responsibilities are the healthy and happy development of learners. Instead of focusing on methods and content, this model is highly student-centered. It favors constructivist approaches rather than direct instruction.

Finally, the **liberationist model** regards the teacher's role as one of freeing students' minds

centered. Discovery and cooperative approaches to teaching are good examples of constructivism.

Several writers in education have recently begun to insist that we are currently in the throes of a revolution in educational practice—specifically, a constructivist revolution. Others point out that in many ways this is not a revolution at all but simply a continuation—or perhaps a revival—of some century-old ideas first popularized through the writings of John Dewey. What is now labeled constructivism, says Evers (1998), was then called **progressive education.** In his words, "School reformers today are still trying to put into effect the turn-of-the-century progressive education ideas of John Dewey and others—often these days under the banner of 'discovery learning'" (p. 1). And then he adds that "these ideas were largely misguided a hundred years ago, and they are largely misguided now" (p. 1).

Clearly, not everyone agrees.[5]

---

constructivist approaches General label for instructional methods that are highly learner-centered and that reflect the belief that meaningful information is constructed by students rather than given to them. Often contrasted with *direct instruction*, constructivist approaches are reflected in discovery learning, cognitive apprenticeship, and humanistic approaches to teaching.

progressive education An educational reform movement closely associated with John Dewey and identified primarily by child- rather than teacher-centered instructional approaches. Constructivist approaches to instruction (such as discovery learning) are essentially examples of progressive education movements under new labels.

executive model A view of the teacher as a master teacher (executive) responsible for arranging the teaching/learning situation, delivering lessons, and teaching learners prescribed skills and information.

therapist model A primarily humanistic view of the teacher's role—namely, that of facilitating healthy growth and self-actualization.

liberationist model This model views the teacher's role as one of freeing students' minds by providing them with the tools and attitudes necessary for learning.

---

[5] **PPC:** Perhaps the bear should let his readers know whether there actually is a revolution. And which side is he on anyway?

Author: The bear would not so soon reveal his biases—if he had any. He doesn't. But later in this text, and especially in Chapter 6, there is much information about and discussion of these weighty matters. Also, the front inside cover of this book clarifies the issues.

TABLE 1.3
Models of Learning and Teaching

MODEL	PRINCIPAL BELIEFS	MOST LIKELY INSTRUCTIONAL APPROACH	POSSIBLE TEACHER BEHAVIOR
Acquisition Metaphor View of Learning	Learning consists of the progressive accumulation of information.	Direct instruction	Emphasis on preparing presentations and organizing information and concepts to maximize accumulation of facts and concepts.
Participation Metaphor View of Learning	Learning evolves from the student's active participation and involvement in lessons.	Constructivist approaches	Greater concern with the processes of learning. More of a facilitating than information-giving role. Greater emphasis on cooperative activities and individually motivated activities.
Executive Model of Teacher	Teacher's role is executive function of preparing best materials/lessons for learners (recipients)	Direct instruction	Teacher-prepared lessons/activities are main source of information.
Therapist Model of Teacher	Teacher's role is that of empathetic facilitator of student growth and self-development.	Constructivist approaches	Cooperative group activities designed to foster positive self-concepts.
Liberationist Model of Teacher	Teacher's function is to liberate students' minds, empowering them to learn on their own.	Constructivist approaches	Cognitive strategies programs and guided discovery experiences; students are encouraged to examine their own intellectual processes and to become aware of and develop intellectual strategies.

by providing them with the tools and attitudes necessary for learning. For example, one major focus of this model is on ensuring that students become aware of the strategies they can use to do important cognitive (intellectual) things like organizing, remembering, and solving problems—in other words, ensuring that they learn how to learn. This model, too, favors constructivist approaches.

In essence, your teaching model consists of your *beliefs* about what teachers are and should be. It includes your beliefs about teachers' roles and relationships relative to students as well as the roles and responsibilities of students.

Your teaching model is extremely important for determining the sorts of activities you select for your classroom and your relationship with your students. And, of course, it will affect your students' interactions with you as well as their own learning activities. Thus, if you see yourself as an executive, you are likely to prepare well-structured lectures and lessons designed to optimize learning in your students. In contrast, if your model of teaching is more that of a therapist, you will pay greater attention to the healthy development of your charges—to their happiness and the development of positive self-concepts. And if you see your teaching role as that of a *liberationist,* you will concentrate on encouraging your students to learn how to learn. (See Table 1.3.)

These models are simply ways of describing different emphases that teachers might have; they describe various views of the teacher's role. Clearly, however, most teachers don't subscribe to only one model to the exclusion of all others. Most engage in a variety of behaviors reflecting a mixture of beliefs.

A MODEL OF TEACHING

To simplify without unduly distorting reality, teaching can be described in terms of three stages, each characterized by different demands on the teacher: before teaching, during teaching, and after teaching (see Figure 1.1). And contrary to what we might immediately assume, the teaching stage is no more important than what occurs before or after.

Before Teaching

To be an effective, perhaps even exemplary, teacher, you must make some critical decisions before you even walk into your classroom and actually engage in the business of teaching. First, you must decide on both the long-range and short-term goals of the instructional process. To determine these goals, you need to answer some questions for yourself: What specific learning outcomes do you intend and expect? How do these tie in with the broad goals of the educational process in this subject? this grade? this school? this city or county? How do these goals fit in with your values and beliefs? How important are they?[6]

Once you have determined your instructional goals, you need to select a teaching strategy to attain these goals, and you must invent, make, or at least collect materials that are useful for teaching. What is required here is not only knowledge of the strategies themselves but also of the skills required to implement them effectively. And, perhaps most important, you must know whether students are ready for this specific teaching/learning experience. Student readiness involves a variety of factors, including essential prerequisite knowledge and skills and appropriate motivation. Clearly, students who are eager to learn are most likely to profit from instruction, and students who have already mastered prerequisite knowledge and skills are more likely to attain instructional objectives. These considerations highlight the importance of knowing how students learn and develop and what motivates them.

---

[6] **PPC:** The importance of goals needs to be emphasized.
Author: True. In the words of the bear's mentor, Yogi Berra, "You got to be careful if you don't know where you're going, because you might not get there." But Yogi is also reported to have said, "If you come to a fork in the road, take it." The bear thinks he was dead serious.

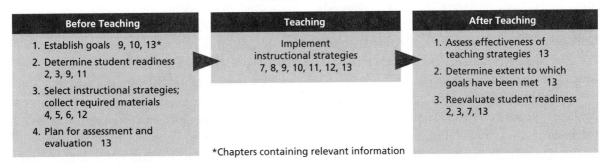

The Instructional Process

Before Teaching	Teaching	After Teaching
1. Establish goals 9, 10, 13*	Implement instructional strategies 7, 8, 9, 10, 11, 12, 13	1. Assess effectiveness of teaching strategies 13
2. Determine student readiness 2, 3, 9, 11		2. Determine extent to which goals have been met 13
3. Select instructional strategies; collect required materials 4, 5, 6, 12		3. Reevaluate student readiness 2, 3, 7, 13
4. Plan for assessment and evaluation 13		

*Chapters containing relevant information

FIGURE 1.1 A three-stage model of the teaching process

Another critical step in the preteaching phase is planning for assessment: How will you determine to what extent instructional goals have been met? By what procedures will you evaluate the instructional process itself and the changes that might occur among learners? How will the results of your evaluation procedures influence subsequent teaching decisions?

In summary, the preteaching phase involves at least four steps: setting appropriate goals, determining student readiness, selecting appropriate instructional strategies, and planning for assessment.

Teaching

The instructional process—commonly called teaching—involves implementing strategies designed to lead learners to attain certain goals. In general, these strategies involve communication, leadership, motivation, and control (discipline or management). As we saw earlier, the precise nature of your teaching strategies will be heavily influenced by your model of learners and learning—for example, whether you view learning as largely a matter of the acquisition and accumulation of information, or whether you see it mainly as a process where the student's participation is central. Whether you view the teacher's role as an executive, therapist, or liberationist will also directly affect how you teach.

Following a review of research on effective teaching, MacKay (1982) identifies 28 behaviors that most often characterize the teaching strategies of highly effective teachers. MacKay describes these as "suggested" or "recommended" behaviors, rather than the firm conclusions of scientific research. These behaviors are related to four aspects of the teaching process: classroom management and discipline; instructional organization, sequence, and presentation; verbal interaction (communication); and interpersonal interaction. The 28 behaviors are summarized in the box entitled "Recommended Behaviors for

Effective Teaching." In a year-long study involving 72 teachers of third- and sixth-grade mathematics and language arts, researchers found a positive relationship between student achievement and most of these 28 strategies.

After Teaching

The third phase of the teaching process involves assessing the outcomes of instruction in relation to the goals that you set in the preteaching phase. This process of evaluation reveals the effectiveness of your teaching; it might also say a great deal about the appropriateness of your instructional goals, the readiness of your students, the appropriateness of your teaching strategies, and even the relevance and appropriateness of your evaluation procedures.

BEAR MUSINGS

Recommended Behaviors for Effective Teaching

1. Teachers should use a system of rules dealing with personal and procedural matters.
2. Teachers should prevent misbehaviors from continuing.
3. Teachers should direct disciplinary action accurately.
4. Teachers should move around the room a lot (monitoring seat work).
5. Teachers should handle disruptive situations in a low-key manner (nonverbal messages, proximity, eye contact).
6. Teachers should ensure that assignments are interesting and worthwhile, especially when children work independently.
7. Teachers should use a system of rules that allows students to carry out learning tasks with a minimum of direction.
8. Teachers should optimize academic learning time. Students should be actively involved and productively engaged in learning tasks.
9. Teachers should use a standard signal to get students' attention.
10. Teachers should not begin speaking to the group until all students are paying attention.
11. Teachers should use a variety of instructional techniques, adapting instruction to meet learning needs.
12. Teachers should use a system of spot-checking assignments.
13. Teachers should relate mathematics (or other) games and independent activities to the concepts being taught.
14. Teachers should use techniques that provide for the gradual transition from concrete to more abstract activities.
15. Teachers should use an appropriate mixture of high- and low-order questions.
16. Teachers should be aware of what is going on in the classroom.
17. Teachers should be able to attend to more than one issue at a time.
18. Teachers should facilitate the smooth flow of the lesson or facilitate a smooth transition from one activity to another.
19. Teachers' behavior should maintain the pace of the lesson.
20. Teachers should be clear in their presentations to the class.
21. Teachers should be able to motivate students.
22. Teachers should provide evidence of caring, accepting, and valuing the students.
23. Teachers should respond accurately to both obvious and subtle meanings, feelings, and experiences of the students.
24. Teachers should direct questions to many different students.
25. Teachers should use techniques such as rephrasing, giving clues, or asking a new question to help students give improved responses when their answers are incorrect or only partially correct.
26. Teachers should use praise to reward outstanding work and to encourage students who are not always able to do outstanding work.
27. Teachers should use mild criticism on occasion to communicate their expectations to more able students.
28. Teachers should accept and integrate student-initiated interactions such as questions, comments, or other contributions.

Source: Adapted from research on effective teaching by A. MacKay, "Project Quest: Teaching Strategies and Pupil Achievement." Occasional Paper Series, Centre for Research in Teaching, Faculty of Education, University of Alberta, Edmonton, Alberta, 1982, pp. 42–44.

PSYCHOLOGY APPLIED TO TEACHING

Psychology's potential contribution to teaching becomes clear when viewed in terms of our simple, three-stage teaching model (preteaching, teaching, and postteaching activities). Psychology, after all, is most likely to provide us with answers to some of the most important questions implicit in the model—questions such as: How do people learn? How can we use what we know about learning and motivation to increase the effectiveness of our instructional procedures? What do we know about people that might be of value to teachers who face student misbehavior or want to avoid being

---

TABLE 1.4
13 Tasks with Which Teachers Want Help
(ranked from most important to least important)

1. Developing effective learners and a mastery of basic skills.

2. Guiding children to set up and achieve realistic goals.

3. Locating materials and in-service support for more effective teaching.

4. Establishing and maintaining discipline.

5. Identifying and understanding readiness factors that affect learning.

6. Motivating children to learn.

7. Designing assessment devices and interpreting the resulting data.

8. Supporting teaching and technological methods and materials.

9. Understanding the interpersonal factors that influence a child's educational goals.

10. Developing a greater understanding of human behavior.

11. Updating curriculum content areas and methodologies.

12. Improving multipurpose classroom grouping techniques.

13. Obtaining administrative assistance with instructional planning.

Source: From K. D. Moore and P. E. Hanley, "An Identification of Elementary Teacher Needs." American Educational Research Journal, 1982, pp. 19, 140. Copyright 1982, American Educational Research Association, Washington, D.C.

---

faced with such behavior? How can we motivate learners? and a thousand other related questions.

By answering these questions, psychology can make a tremendous contribution to teaching. In fact, when teachers are asked what kind of assistance they require to become more effective, the needs they express typically reflect these questions. For example, following a survey of 247 randomly selected elementary school teachers (22 male and 225 female), Moore and Hanley (1982) identified 13 specific tasks with which teachers felt they could use help (see Table 1.4). Mentioned most often was the need for assistance in helping students become better learners, especially with respect to acquiring basic skills. Other needs that these teachers expressed had to do with discipline, motivating learners, identifying and developing readiness for learning, and helping students establish realistic goals. Each of these needs falls within the scope of educational psychology.

This is not to suggest that educational psychology has now answered, clearly and simply, all of the teachers' most important questions.

Following a review of 93 separate investigations of teacher training, Wideen, Mayer-Smith, and Moon (1998) conclude that, in most cases, traditional programs of teacher education don't appear to have much effect on the student teachers' firmly held prior beliefs. In fact, as Kennedy (1997) points out, the connection between research in educational psychology and the actual business of teaching is not always very strong or clear. She argues that research needs to be more authoritative, relevant, and readily available to teachers. Similarly, Wideen et al. (1998) suggest that the most useful research on teaching is that which is most *ecological.* By ecological research, they mean inquiry that takes into consideration the actual teaching-learning context—that is, what beginning teachers (or teachers-in-training) already know and believe—and research that also considers the characteristics of students and school systems. Kennedy also suggests that the educational system must itself become more open and flexible so that when research clearly indicates that a specific change would be desirable, the system *can* change.

Educational Psychology

Educational psychology may be defined as the study of human behavior in educational settings. As Wittrock (1992) emphasizes, it involves not only the application of existing psychological knowledge to educational theory and practice, but also the development of new knowledge and procedures. Accordingly, educational psychology deals with learning processes, human development and motivation, social learning, human personality (especially characteristics such as intelligence and creativity), discipline and other aspects of classroom management, the measurement and evaluation of student development and learning, and other related issues. These broad topics, divided into five major units (13 chapters), are the substance of this text.

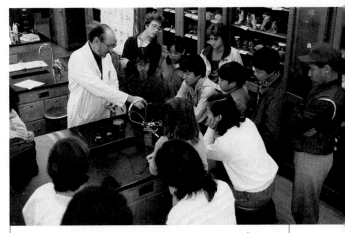

Educational psychology answers important questions about how people learn, what motivates them, and what instructional procedures are most effective for which students and for which teachers.

▛ TEACHING AS DECISION MAKING

In the simplest sense, to teach is to impart skills, knowledge, attitudes, and values. It involves bringing about, or at least facilitating, changes in learners. Teaching can be accomplished by telling and persuading, by showing and demonstrating, by guiding and directing learners' efforts, or by a combination of these actions. It might involve only the teacher's own resources, knowledge, and skills, or it might rely on professionally prepared materials (films or computer software, for example), resource people, or a combination of learners' own talents, skills, and information. It can occur in large or small groups, in competitive or cooperative arrangements, in formal or informal settings. . . .

It's clear that all teaching activities require decisions. As Pasch et al. (1995) explain, decisions made *before* teaching center around planning for teacher and student action; decisions made *during* teaching have to do with implementing action, observing its effects, and making ongoing modifications; and decisions made *after* teaching involve reflection, prediction, and modification. One of the goals of this textbook is to provide you with sound bases for making teaching decisions.

▛ TEACHING AS PROBLEM SOLVING

Another way of looking at teaching is to view it as an exercise in problem solving. According to this model, teaching involves the ongoing solution of a series of problems. Some problems such as those relating to specific course or lesson objectives are obvious. For example, if one of the goals of a lesson in mathematics is for students to learn division, then the problem that requires a solution is to arrange for student experiences that lead to the competency in question. Other

---

educational psychology A science concerned primarily with the study of human behavior in educational settings. Applies existing psychological knowledge to instructional problems and develops new knowledge and procedures.

related problems are not so obvious. These have to do with managing the classroom environment, monitoring ongoing activities, evaluating and assessing the interest and understanding of individual students, and so on.

TEACHING TO EMPOWER STUDENTS

From the teacher's point of view, then, teaching can be viewed as a decision-making and problem-solving activity—that is, as an ongoing process involving finding solutions to problems relating to communication, instruction, motivation, classroom management, evaluation, and so on, and making decisions that reflect these solutions.

Another way of looking at teaching is to view it in terms of its objectives, rather than its processes. The teacher must be concerned not only with the details of lesson organization and with the hundreds of routines and procedures that contribute to classroom management and effective learning, but also with the goals of the instructional process. What is it that schools ought to accomplish? What are the important objectives of education?

The answers to these questions are fundamental to the teaching/learning process. They determine the content of the school curriculum and also the goals of the instructional process. Educational goals can be very general (for example, to develop good citizens) or very specific (to teach children to add two-digit numbers).

Traditionally, says Sehr (1997), we have accepted as common sense that the main purpose of education is an economic one. Stated simply, we educate our children (and our youth and adults) so that they will find good jobs—so that they will become productive, independent, self-sufficient members of society. But perhaps this commonsense view is neither the most useful nor the most accurate. For our purposes, it might be far more useful to look at educational objectives in the broadest, most general terms possible: Viewed in this light, the main goal of education is to empower students.

Literally, to **empower** means to give power to—in short, to enable. At the most obvious level, education empowers students by enabling them to do things they could not otherwise do. Reading, writing, and arithmetic empower us as surely as do sight, hearing, and our other senses, because although our senses enable us to perceive the world, the three Rs empower us to deal with it at a very complex, sophisticated level. Without all sorts of school-related knowledge, we would be hard-pressed to function easily and effectively. We need to know a great deal to use banking machines and computers, understand instruction manuals and civic regulations, deter-

Teaching empowers learners not only by giving them important information and skills but also by fostering in them feelings of personal worth and confidence. Thus, a reading class can empower every bit as much as can a class in mathematics or in art.

empower To enable; to give power to. One of the most important goals of education is to empower students by providing them with both specific information and learning/thinking strategies and by helping them to develop the feelings of personal power that accompany the realization that one is competent and worthwhile.

mine how much we owe the grocer and the tax-man, read newspapers and books, and on and on. Empowering in this sense clearly has important economic benefits.

Knowledge of specific things like reading and writing is only one of the sources of empowerment that schools bestow. Schools also foster in students both the personal power that comes with social competence and the accompanying feelings of personal confidence—of being unique and worthwhile individuals.

Schools provide empowerment not only through the information they impart and the feelings of confidence and personal power they foster, but also through the learning strategies they develop in students. It is becoming increasingly clear that because so much information exists in our advanced technological societies, it is impossible for students to learn more than a fraction of it. And, given the rate at which information changes or becomes obsolete, it would probably be unwise for them to try. As a result, it is perhaps more important to learn how to learn and how to solve problems. Expanding students' ability to learn by providing them with strategies for acquiring, processing, and remembering information is one of the most important student-empowering functions of schools, notes Goldberg (1996). In fact, argue Husén and Tuijnman (1991), formal schooling actually increases people's measured intelligence. That's because the sorts of strategies we learn in school are what we use to think, to analyze, and to monitor and evaluate our intellectual activities. These strategies can be applied to all sorts of situations throughout our lives. It's hardly surprising that such strategies are a tremendous source of personal power—of empowerment.

When students are allowed to become *active* participants in their education, says Kohn (1993), the resulting sense of empowerment can have a tremendous positive effect on their achievement, their behavior, and their values—not to mention their sense of well-being. Similarly, Brunson and

Vogt (1996) argue that an empowering educational philosophy is typically reflected in more tolerant, more trusting, and better learners. It is perhaps a cliché that schools must do more than just teach subjects; it is far more important that they teach individual students.

☐ TEACHING AS A REFLECTIVE ACTIVITY

One relatively recent movement in education views teaching as a *reflective* activity. **Reflective teaching** implies a process where teachers systematically and actively think about (reflect upon) their teaching activities (Moallem, 1997). Although the widespread use of the expression *reflective teaching* is relatively new in education, the concept is many decades old. For example, it was defined by John Dewey in 1933 as "the active, persistent and careful consideration of any belief or supposed form of knowledge in light of the grounds that support it" (p. 9). Advocates of reflective teaching encourage teachers to consider the consequences of their actions, to examine the beliefs upon which they base their behaviors, and to take an active role in acquiring new information and in improving their teaching (Eby, 1998). In other words, reflective teaching is *proactive* teaching—proactive in the sense that teachers are asked to assume more responsibility for constructing curriculum, for evaluating their own performance, for setting school and class goals, and so on.

Advocates of reflective teaching also stress the value of storytelling (using narratives) as a means of reflecting on teaching (Parker, 1997). For example, teachers are sometimes encouraged to keep diaries in which they narrate stories of

---

reflective teaching A process where teachers systematically and actively think about (reflect on) their teaching activities; often makes use of personal narratives in an effort to clarify and improve teaching and learning.

specific teaching experiences, or to tell these stories to other teachers. They are encouraged, as well, to use **case studies** as an aid to reflection—that is, to examine and reflect upon the specific teaching experiences of other teachers (Gillespie, 1996). The object is for teachers to arrive at a clearer understanding of the beliefs that underlie their teaching behaviors, to re-examine these beliefs, and to evaluate teaching behaviors in the light of values and objectives as well as in the light of student responses. The use of this type of personal narrative is one form of what is described as **action research**—a nonexperimental, highly personal attempt to demystify some aspects of the act of teaching (Dinkelman, 1997). The ultimate objective of action research is to improve teaching and learning.

Reflective teaching strategies, although not yet very clearly defined, are sometimes described as strategies that lead students to discover and learn for themselves (Freiberg & Driscoll, 1992). Just as reflective teachers are encouraged to reflect upon what they do in the classroom and why, reflective teaching strategies insist that learners, too, should reflect on what they are learning; how they are progressing; and the strategies they have been using (or should be using) to remember, to organize, to solve problems and, most importantly, to assume personal responsibility for their learning. In fact, research indicates that one of the most important factors for effective teaching is helping students to feel personally responsible for their successes and failures (Kirby & Paradise, 1992).

Reflective teaching strategies are based on a philosophy that views the learner as an active discoverer rather than as a passive recipient of information—and sees the teacher as a facilitator of learning rather than as the source of all knowledge. Not surprisingly, then, among the strategies most often described as reflective teaching strategies are those that lead to student inquiry and guided discovery. As we saw earlier, these are among the most important characteristics of constructivist teaching strategies. These topics are discussed in Chapter 6.

TEACHING AS A CRAFT

There is a great deal more to teaching than simply reflecting on the processes involved. In fact, there are many specific skills and strategies that teachers can learn and use effectively in their teaching—and there are many very important strategies and procedures that students can learn and use in their learning. Specific teaching strategies make up what is sometimes referred to as **craft knowledge**—that is, knowledge related to the craft of teaching. Elements of this craft are discussed in many places throughout this text. The specific learning and thinking strategies that students become aware of are often called *metacognitive* skills. Metacognition refers to knowing about knowing, and this includes skills such as those involved in remembering, organizing information, studying, and so on. These skills are discussed in more detail in Chapters 5 and 6 and elsewhere in the text.

---

case study An investigation that involves specific actions, episodes, or individuals. Case studies generally involve one single participant or event or no more than a small number of individual cases.

action research A highly subjective approach to educational research typically involving single cases or episodes. A common tool in reflective teaching.

reflective teaching strategies A loosely defined collection of teaching strategies that involve teachers and students who are actively and deliberately thinking (reflecting) about events in the teaching/learning process.

---

craft knowledge Knowledge of the specifics of teaching. The science of teaching and a sort of practical wisdom that includes general information about teaching along with specific information about teaching particular subjects and lessons to students with identifiable characteristics.

Craft knowledge is a sort of practical wisdom, say Sykes and Bird (1992), that cannot always be clearly verbalized but that can be learned through practice or perhaps by studying and analyzing cases that illustrate teaching problems and principles. Craft knowledge includes general information as well as specific information about teaching particular subjects and lessons to students with identifiable characteristics. It can also include "fragmentary, superstitious, and often inaccurate opinions," says Leinhardt (1990, p. 18); that is, craft knowledge can be based on inaccurate and inappropriate beliefs.

Knowledge of the craft of teaching is often evident in the patterns and routines that are such an important part of the classroom. These routines involve two different sets of activities: those relating to classroom management and discipline and those having to do specifically with instructing—giving students information and guiding them in their acquisition of strategies for learning. Accordingly, acquiring these patterns and routines—that is, learning the *craft* of teaching—requires a wealth of information about learners and the process of learning. The purpose of this text is to provide you with that information. In fact, craft knowledge is one of the things that distinguishes expert teachers from nonexperts.

Expert versus Nonexpert Teachers

Expert teachers are especially adept at applying elements of the craft of teaching. This, note Sternberg and Horvath (1995), is one of the defining characteristics of teaching expertise.

---

expert teachers Teachers who, by virtue of experience, training, and other intangible skills, share characteristics that make them better, more effective teachers than novices. In Sternberg's prototypical model of teaching expertise, these characteristics relate to knowledge, efficiency of problem solving, and insight for solving educational problems.

There are others. The expert teacher is not simply someone who has been teaching a long time. In fact, there are many nonexperts who have years of experience and perhaps more than a few experts who have newly joined the ranks of teachers. Expert teachers are those who, by virtue of experience, training, and other more intangible skills, share several characteristics that make them better, more effective teachers. Sternberg and Horvath (1995) suggest that the best way of arriving at a model of teaching expertise is to look at the characteristics that most clearly distinguish excellent from less excellent teachers—that is, look at the characteristics that such teachers share. These characteristics can then be used to define the *ideal* or *prototypical* expert teacher.

Sternberg and Horvath's (1995) prototype model of teaching expertise identifies three areas in which experts share common characteristics: (1) knowledge, (2) efficiency in problem solving, and (3) insight with respect to solving educational problems.

Knowledge Not surprisingly, expert teachers tend to be more familiar with the subjects they teach than are nonexpert (novice) teachers. That is, they have greater *content knowledge*. And, to a large extent, this greater subject-matter proficiency allows expert teachers to see relationships and connections more easily (Tochon, 1993). This is one reason that expert teachers are better teachers.

Not only do expert teachers have more content knowledge, but they also have more *pedagogical knowledge*—that is, knowledge of teaching and learning principles. Thus, expert teachers are better able to organize and deal with subject matter issues and are also better classroom managers (Randhawa & Pavelich, 1997).

Efficiency As a result of relegating more teaching activity to well-practiced and highly effective routines, expert teachers are better able to monitor the flow of their lessons, to anticipate problems, to evaluate their teaching, and to modify their teaching activities. Sternberg and Horvath (1995), note that experts are more efficient than nonexperts. They do more in less time and sometimes with much less apparent effort. Thus, they are better problem solvers, perhaps because they have learned how to automatize certain activities. They are also better planners. Expert teachers have developed sequences of routines and strategies that they can apply almost unconsciously as they teach (Kagan, 1988).

Insight When novice teachers reflect on their teaching experiences, Manning and Payne (1996) report, they are often highly judgmental. That is, their reflections tend to be concerned mainly with self-evaluation rather than being directed toward improving their teaching. In contrast, the reflections of expert teachers have more to do with understanding and evaluating the teaching-learning process and improving it.

Sternberg and Horvath (1995) note that expert teachers appear to be more insightful than nonexperts. Although both groups apply knowledge and insight to the solution of problems, experts are more likely to arrive at creative or insightful solutions. With respect to classroom management problems, for example,

experts appear to be more sensitive to the possibility of restlessness and inattention even before these occur. Not only are these teachers skilled at recognizing potential problems, but they are also adept at applying unobtrusive solutions. Automatically—and without breaking the continuity of their ongoing activity—they can bring into play new patterns of interaction to shift the focus, draw students back into the flow of activity, and rechannel student attention.

Nonexpert teachers tend to view every classroom management and discipline issue as separate and to look for an isolated and immediate solution for each problem, notes Butcher (1993). In contrast, expert teachers tend to have a hierarchical conceptualization of classroom management issues. That is, they see direct relationships between student behavior and teacher actions. Not surprisingly, when Swanson, O'Connor, and Cooney (1990) compared 24 novice teachers with 24 expert teachers, they found that the experts had better ongoing plans for identifying, defining, and solving discipline problems. As a result, experts understand better than nonexperts do the implications of the many preventive and corrective management strategies they have at their disposal. Thus, their classroom management is more insightful. (Table 1.5 summarizes some of the characteristics of expert teachers.)

TABLE 1.5
Some Characteristics Shared by Expert Teachers

- ▲ Excel at teaching
- ▲ Possess high level of content knowledge
- ▲ Possess high level of pedagogical knowledge (knowledge of the craft of teaching)
- ▲ Perceive meaningful patterns and relationships in their teaching
- ▲ Are highly efficient in responding to students and making rapid teaching decisions
- ▲ Understand teaching problems at a deep level

- ▲ Devote considerable time to analyzing teaching problems
- ▲ Arrive at insightful solutions for pedagogical and management problems
- ▲ Have become skillful at monitoring and evaluating teaching behaviors
- ▲ Possess well-developed memories for ongoing teaching behaviors

Sources: Based in part on Chi, Glaser, and Farr (1988) and Sternberg and Horvath 1995).

The Art of Teaching

There is more to being an expert teacher than can be learned in one textbook—or even in a dozen texts. You need information about learners and learning, about human development, and about motivation and interests, and you also need to synthesize this information—to understand it, to integrate it with your values, your goals, your personality, and your preferences. Teachers each have their own styles of teaching. No teacher training program can, or should, make us all alike. Furthermore, as Clandinin and Connelly (1996) point out, what appears to be effective teaching in one school may not be very effective in another school where the context—or as these authors phrase it, the "knowledge landscape"—is different. One particular set of teaching methods might be highly effective in a highly traditional school whose goals are clearly defined as teaching every child to read, write, and do arithmetic and whose success is measured as much by the respect its children show their teachers and other adults as by the grades. But the same teaching methods in a more reform-oriented school, where success is reflected in the creativity and independence of its charges, might be deemed highly "nonexpert."

Partly because of this, teaching has often been described as both an art and a science. Every successful teaching performance, says Eisner (1982), can be analyzed not only in terms of the science involved in instruction and classroom management, but also in terms of the art involved in creating the environment—the context—in which learning occurs.

Sadly, the art of teaching does not lend itself to analysis as readily as does its science. The art of teaching has too much to do with the personalities of teachers and of learners, with the complexities of human interactions, with classroom ambience, and perhaps with magic and poetry. As a result, a textbook such as this is forced to deal with the science rather than with the art of teaching. Keeping in mind, however, that art isn't something that a teacher should resort to only when science fails; rather, art—that is, poetry, laughter, magic, emotion—can and should be a part of all classroom activity. Art can have a place in even the most apparently mundane lesson in an ordinary classroom on a Tuesday. That is one of the things that makes teaching so exciting.

TEACHING AS A CAREER

My father was a teacher for 41 years. Not all of those years were easy. For some of the first years he didn't always get paid, and when he did, it was never very much. And many years he had enormous classes—as many as 50 students in an isolated, one-room school, spanning the first through the eighth grades. Nor were the teaching tasks always simple and straightforward; often, his beginning students didn't even know English—only French or Cree.

But my father still says, as he always has, that he liked his work, that he was proud to be a teacher, that teaching children is something really major, really important. Maybe this was partly why he taught as well as he did. In the end, despite being situated in an economically depressed and very isolated area, his one-room school produced several dozen university graduates, including several who obtained master's degrees and at least two who earned doctorates.

Teaching is important. It's stimulating and exciting, and it can be highly rewarding. But it isn't overwhelmingly lucrative. (The average teacher's yearly salary in the United States in 1996 was $37,700; U.S. Bureau of the Census, 1997.) Nor is it exceedingly easy.

Some Problems and Challenges Facing Today's Teachers

Teaching in today's schools is often challenging and difficult. In fact, reports Chan (1998), as many as one-third of all teachers regard teaching as highly stressful. Possible effects of high stress include teacher apathy and alienation, cynicism, chronic absenteeism, and, occasionally, the decision to abandon a teaching career—symptoms sometimes collectively labeled **teacher burnout.** Equally significant, Guglielmi and Tatrow (1998) summarize extensive research which indicates that the stress that many teachers feel is often associated with poor physical health. They caution, however, that the direction of causality is not always very clear. Although the research has been quick to identify stress as an important cause of poor physical health, the conclusion rests on badly designed and often unreliable investigations. In some cases, they argue, poor health may itself be an additional source of stress.

But it is nevertheless clear that there are a wide variety of possible sources of stress for teachers. Consider, for example, the tremendous cultural and social diversity exemplified in the case "Surviving High School." There are obvious problems associated with teaching students who represent such a vast range of motivation, abilities, time, and energy—problems that are compounded by shrinking educational budgets that lead to overcrowded schools and classrooms and overworked teachers. In such schools, there is often tension between the need for control and the need for learning. Social control, note Cohn and Kottkamp (1993), is a basic requirement for effective teaching. In their words, "Crowded classrooms present teachers with behavioral control problems so pressing that until they are solved, nothing else can be attempted" (p. 201).

Besides the challenges related to overcrowding and student diversity, dramatic increases in the amount of information available to today's teachers (and students), coupled with increas-

ingly sophisticated tools for handling that information (computers, for example), have made teaching far more demanding than it was in my father's time. Martin (1996) notes that education is really about transmitting our cultural wealth to the next generation. But, says she, there's too much to teach—we suffer from an overabundance problem: We can no longer teach everything. More and more, we have to equip learners to learn on their own. We must teach them that school is only the beginning of their learning careers.

Also potentially highly stressful are increasing demands for teacher accountability. These demands are sometimes reflected in the public's insistent call for hard evidence that teachers are effective—and the notion that perhaps teachers should be paid according to measures of their effectiveness.[7]

Add to these possible sources of stress the challenge of changes in legislation requiring that children with special needs, and sometimes very complex ones, be the responsibility of teachers in ordinary classrooms (a policy labeled **mainstreaming** or *inclusive education,* discussed in Chapter 9).

Not surprisingly, beginning teachers typically experience more problems than experienced teachers. There are four reasons for this, says Valli (1992): *First,* beginning teachers have a strong tendency to imitate teachers they had as students. The result is that they fail to develop

---

teacher burnout A general label for a condition marked by a teacher's profound negative reaction to teaching. One possible effect of high stress. Sometimes evidenced by cynicism, unhappiness, chronic absenteeism, and perhaps a decision to change careers.

---

mainstreaming The practice of placing students in need of special services in regular classrooms rather than segregating them. Also termed *inclusion* or *inclusive education.*

---

[7] *PPC:* One of my pet peeves is that evidence of teacher competence is so often based on how well students do at the end of the year on systemwide tests or some other standardized measure. This never takes into account how much diversity exists in different classrooms.

Author: Nor does it reflect many other subtle changes in students that aren't so easily measured—just one reason teacher accountability is a difficult and controversial area, as is merit pay tied to measures of teacher competence.

Surviving High School

THE SITUATION: Reporter Marina Jimenez spent one week in a local high school as an undercover student (Jimenez, 1992). She reports:

At 2,300 students, the school is the largest in western Canada, serving people from a tremendous range of backgrounds and offering a huge variety of programs. Some students are primarily in academic programs, taking such core courses as English, social studies, and the sciences. Others study skin and nail care, learn to drive cars, or earn full course credits for grilling hamburgers in the school cafeteria. Of the students who graduated from the school last year, 34 percent earned diplomas or certificates that did not qualify them for admission to university. Many work 25 or more hours a week in shops, garages, or fast-food outlets. Some of these still manage to do well in academic programs; others come to school primarily for its social opportunities.

Many of these students go to bars and clubs, not only on weekends but during the week, and often don't get home until 3 or 4 in the morning. Attendance is low in many classes.

Not surprisingly, some students sleep through class, and 72 students in this school live on their own, many because of serious problems at home.

There is racial tension in this school. Last year there were racially motivated brawls. And this year a police officer has been assigned to the school on a permanent basis.

---

effective, personal approaches to teaching based on well-informed beliefs. *Second,* starting teachers tend to be isolated from other teachers; hence, they have little emotional support during difficult times and little opportunity for tuition and guidance from more experienced and more expert teachers. *Third,* novice teachers often find it difficult to transfer what they have learned in teacher education programs to the solution of actual problems in the classroom. As a result, much of what has been learned may be put aside as irrelevant theory. *Finally,* many new teachers become overly concerned with discovering or applying the correct teaching technique. Consequently, they fail to develop more spontaneous and creative—and often more effective— approaches.

The Rewards of Teaching

"As far as the money is concerned, no, I wouldn't teach. I wouldn't choose it again," says Karen, a teacher, when she is asked: "If you could choose all over again, would you choose to be a teacher?" (Cohn & Kottkamp, 1993). But my friend Nora, who has now been teaching for almost 30 years, retorts, "I think the pay's just real fine. It's one of those few things where the men don't get paid a cent more than us."

There are obviously other rewards of teaching, not the least of which are the intrinsic rewards—feelings of satisfaction, of accomplishment, of being and doing something worthwhile, of making a difference. Then, there are extrinsic rewards—such as the prestige and respect accorded the profession and sometimes the political and social influence associated with teaching. Also, as Kottkamp, Provenzo, and Cohn (1986) point out, there are various ancillary rewards—rewards that are byproducts of the teaching profession but aren't related directly to teaching itself. For example, many view the typical school schedule, with its long summer vacation, as an important reward. Similarly, many people desire a common five-day work week, with each day being six or seven hours long, and the security that has traditionally been associated with a tenured (permanent) teaching contract—in terms of continued employment, stable income and an eventual pension.

Career Stability and Change

Many teacher candidates never finish their teacher preparation, report Marso and Pigge (1997) following an investigation of 551 prospective teachers. Others fail to become certified even after completing their studies. And a relatively large proportion of beginning teachers either do not obtain starting positions or abandon their careers after a few years. For example, Murnane, Singer, & Willett (1988) report that half of all young male teachers leave the teaching profession within 12 years of first starting teaching; about one-fourth of these male teachers later resume teaching. Not surprisingly, given that many interrupt their careers for childbearing and -rearing, half of all beginning female teachers are no longer teaching within six years. However, almost one-third of these female teachers subsequently return to teaching. Thus, although many beginning teachers abandon or switch their careers, the majority make lifelong careers out of teaching.

Many—perhaps most—love what they do.

⌐ CULTURAL AND GLOBAL DIVERSITY

Half a century ago, the principal nations of the world gathered in Paris to formulate the Universal Declaration of Human Rights, a document designed to protect the fundamental rights of every human being. Article 26 of the resulting declaration (30 articles make up the entire document) stipulates that (1) everyone has the right to an education, that it shall be *free and compulsory* at least at the elementary level, and that more advanced professional and technical edu-

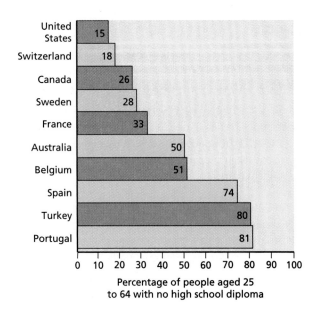

FIGURE 1.2 Percentage of people ages 25–64 who do not have a high school diploma, by country. Based on U.S. Bureau of the Census, 1997, p. 836.

cation shall be available to all equally on the basis of merit; (2) education shall be directed toward the full development of the human personality, toward the strengthening of respect for human rights, toward respect for fundamental freedoms, and toward tolerance, understanding, and friendship among all groups; and (3) parents have the right to choose the kind of education their children shall receive.

Those of us reared in areas where school *is* universal, compulsory, and free tend to become blasé about its role and its effects on society: We lose sight of the effects of schooling. Perhaps it would be good to remind ourselves occasionally that conditions are not the same everywhere else as they are here. The contrast might highlight some of the differences that teaching and learning can make. (See Figure 1.2 for an indication of how variable schooling achievement is, even in relatively advanced countries.)

Global Disparity

Consider, for example, that infant mortality in the United States and in Canada is now less than nine per 1,000. In contrast, in many parts of the nonindustrialized world, more than 100 infants die per 1,000. In fact, the United Nations reports that more than 13 million of the world's children under the age of five die each year from preventable causes, the vast majority of them in developing countries (Grant, 1993). Almost eight million die from pneumonia, diarrheal dehydration, or vaccine-preventable diseases such as measles, tetanus, and whooping cough; another five million or so die from starvation. That's more than 35,000 children under five dying every day somewhere in the world!

What does this have to do with education? A great deal. Research makes it clear that exposure to schooling in the Third World is significantly correlated with a much higher probability of infant survival, as well as a reduction in birthrate. For example, mothers can be taught that simple hygiene can prevent diarrhea, and they can be schooled in the inexpensive oral rehydration therapies that could save many lives.

It is clear that lack of schooling, illiteracy, poverty, and high infant mortality go hand in hand. Sadly, in most developing countries, especially in Africa, fewer than half of all children attend school (Tsang, 1988). For those who do attend school, the quality of education is extremely low, and the relative cost is very high; dropout rates are also very high. And although school enrollments in Third World countries have increased approximately fivefold since 1950, lack of funds is seriously curtailing the growth of schooling and is having a significant negative impact on the quality of education (Grant, 1993).

It is easy for us to imagine the impact of a high-quality, universal educational system in some remote Indian or African village; it is not so easy to see its impact closer to home. It might be a valuable exercise to imagine the eventual effect on our society were we to abandon universal schooling and instead turn our children out into the streets. (For an indication of the economic impact of schooling in North America, see Figure 1.3.)

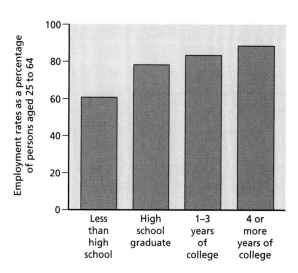

FIGURE 1.3   Increasing employment as a function of educational attainment: Based on U.S. Bureau of the Census, 1997, p.399.

Being a Student

When we consider the impact of schooling, notes Pallas (1993), we tend to look at the *effect* of what is taught and learned in schools. This is not surprising, because the content of school learning does have a tremendous impact on what we are subsequently inclined—not to mention *able*—to do: Unemployment rates are about twice as high for high school dropouts than for high school graduates (22.5% compared with 12.1%; U.S. Bureau of the Census, 1997).

But, says Pallas (1993), the impact of schooling involves much more than the subjects schools teach and the employment opportunities they open up. Schooling is a social activity. *Being* a student is an enormously important social role, closely tied to a variety of transitions that take place throughout the course of life. For example, the transitions from dependent preschooler to increasingly independent schoolchild, or from adolescent to adult, are often linked to the individual's status as a student. In societies characterized by prolonged compulsory schooling, much of the socialization of the individual that might once have been shaped by family and other social institutions now occurs in school.

Cultural Diversity

There are enormous variations in the effects of schooling for different individuals, even within a single society. In North America, for example, educational opportunities and experiences can be profoundly affected by social class, ethnicity, language, background, gender, and the special challenges and needs experienced by many individuals. For example, minority students are far more likely than majority students to fail or drop out of high school; they are also less likely to enroll in postsecondary educational institutions and significantly more likely to drop out if they do. In 1996 83% of white Americans had completed at least four years of high school, whereas 74% of blacks and 53% of Hispanics had done likewise. Similarly, 24% of whites, but only 14% of blacks and 9% of Hispanics had completed four or more years of college (U.S. Bureau of the Census, 1997).

Diversity in classrooms is evident not only in the variety of ethnic and social groups they house, but also in the presence of increasing numbers of children with special needs. The educational experiences of these children—their relationships with teachers and other students and other aspects of their student lives—might be vastly different from those of the majority of students.

Kantor and Lowe (1995) point out that, in North America, educational policy has been driven by the belief that education can eliminate poverty, expand employment and economic opportunities for minority groups, and help those with special needs meet their challenges. Given the enormous diversity in many North American schools, this belief in the effectiveness of education, coupled with the conviction—indeed, the legal mandate—that all students are entitled to the best education possible, presents interesting and difficult challenges for teachers.

But Perez (1994) notes that teachers should view diversity as an opportunity rather than as a problem. Classrooms characterized by the greatest variety—not only in terms of student abilities and needs, but also in terms of cultural/ethnic and social backgrounds—provide the greatest opportunities for exposing all students to diversity. One of the effects may be greater social understanding and tolerance—and ultimately perhaps less strife, hatred, bigotry, and other things that the bear does not much like.[8]

---

[8] **PPC:** Why doesn't the author expand on this? Why doesn't the bear tell us more about injustice and intolerance and what teachers can do about them?
Author: The bear never wanted to be a preacher—just a teacher.

MAIN POINTS

1. Teaching skills are not hereditary; psychology can contribute significantly to their development. Information about how students develop and learn, what motivates them, and how they think and remember can help shape our beliefs. Beliefs (personal convictions based on knowledge and experience) underlie our teaching decisions.

2. Psychology is the study of human behavior and thinking. Its principal means of discovery and of knowing is science. Science insists on precision, consistency, objectivity, and replicability. Its most important tool is the experiment. The principle function of theories is to summarize and explain related observations, to guide research, and to make predictions and practical applications. Laws

are statements whose accuracy is beyond question; principles are statements that are probable rather than certain; and beliefs are private, personal convictions.

3. Models are representations of the way things are (or should be) and are often implied by our theories and beliefs rather than explicitly stated. The acquisition metaphor views learning as the progressive accumulation of information. It supports a teacher-centered, direct instruction approach. The participation metaphor emphasizes student involvement; it leads to a more student-centered, constructivist approach to teaching. Models of the teacher include the executive model (teacher as master of the craft of teaching who organizes and conducts the classroom to maximize learning), the therapist model (teacher as sympathetic individual concerned with wholesome development of learner), and the liberationist model (teacher as facilitator of learning, responsible for freeing students' minds).

4. A simple teaching model describes the teaching process in terms of activities that occur before teaching (establishing goals, determining student readiness, selecting instructional strategies and collecting necessary materials, and planning for assessment and evaluation), activities that occur during teaching (implementation of teaching strategies), and activities that occur after teaching (assessing effectiveness of teaching strategies, determining the extent to which goals have been met, and re-evaluating student readiness).

5. Teaching can be viewed as an ongoing sequence of problem solving and decision making. Part of the craft knowledge of expert teachers involves developing sequences of routines and strategies that allow them to solve or avert many classroom problems almost automatically.

6. Teaching empowers students (makes them capable) by giving them important information and skills, by fostering in them the feelings of personal power that come with social competence and self-esteem, and by helping them to develop the learning/thinking strategies that are essential for learning how to learn.

7. Advocates of teaching as a reflective activity encourage teachers to reflect about their teaching in the light of their goals and beliefs. Teachers are encouraged to become proactive—to take an active role in acquiring information, designing curriculum, and improving their effectiveness. Reflective teaching stresses the importance of storytelling (narratives) as a means of reflecting and encourages the use of *action research* and *case studies.*

8. Teaching is a craft because it involves the application of relevant psychological knowledge to educational theory and practice. Expert teachers share a variety of characteristics that distinguish them from nonexperts: knowledge (content as well as procedural knowledge); efficiency (ability to do more in less time, have automatized routines, and to be better problem solvers); and insight (finding more creative solutions for pedagogical and management problems).

9. The craft of teaching requires a wealth of information about students, teaching, and learning, as well as some measure of art.

10. Teaching is not as lucrative as playing professional baseball or arranging to have wealthy parents. Teaching positions are sometimes scarce, and the demands and stresses of teaching can drive young teachers out of the profession. But many stay and love it.

11. Given that most of us live where schooling is compulsory, it is easy to lose sight of the impact of education on our lives. Conditions in Third World countries underscore the relationship between lack of schooling and poverty, high infant mortality, and other forms of misery. Cultural diversity in North American classrooms can be viewed as a source of opportunities rather than problems.

Applied Questions

▲ Why is it important for teachers to study educational psychology?
▲ Define laws, principles, beliefs, and theories.
▲ Differentiate between direct instruction and constructivist approaches to teaching.
▲ What is meant by the assertions that teaching is a problem-solving activity? that teaching involves empowering students? that teaching is a reflective activity? that teaching is a craft?
▲ Outline the basic elements of a useful teaching model.
▲ List some of the characteristics that differentiate expert from nonexpert teachers.

Internet Activity

Use InfoTrac College Edition or other World Wide Web sources to research the following topic: Write up your findings. (See the inside back cover of this text for suggestions about where to begin.)

Teaching as a career.
Sample search terms: teaching career

Study Terms

acquisition metaphor **12**
action research **22**
behavior **7**
belief **5**
case study **22**
constructivist approaches **13**
craft knowledge **22**
dependent variable **9**
direct instruction **12**
educational psychology **19**
empower **20**
executive model **13**
experiment **9**
expert teachers **23**
fact **10**
hypothesis **9**
independent variable **9**

law **11**
liberationist model **13**
mainstreaming **26**
model **12**
naive theory **10**
operational definition **9**
participation metaphor **12**
principle **11**
progressive education **13**
psychology **7**
reflective teaching **21**
reflective teaching strategies **22**
science **9**
teacher burnout **26**
theory **10**
therapist model **13**

Suggested Readings

Education has always had critics, many of whom insist that schools aren't as good as they used to be. Others, borrowing the famous Will Rogers phrase, argue that they never *were* as good as they used to be (see Maehr & Maehr, 1996). The following book is a collection of presentations whose principal theme is that education is in need of a major overhaul. Whether you agree or not, this can serve as a useful starting point for reflecting about your own beliefs and teaching practices.

Evers, W. M. (Ed.) (1998). *What's gone wrong in America's classrooms.* Stanford, CA.: Hoover Institution Press, Stanford University.

Although there have been many changes in the teaching profession in recent years, there is also considerable stability in the roles and expectations associated with teaching. The following book looks at stability and change from the teacher's point of view and presents an insightful look at the requirements, challenges, and rewards of teaching.

Cohn, M. M., & Kottkamp, R. B. (1993). *Teachers: The missing voice in education.* New York: State University of New York.

The authors of the first of the following two books explain that decisions about what to do in the classroom require teachers to understand the *context* in which learning occurs, the *content* of what will be taught, and, perhaps most importantly, a great deal about the learners themselves; this is a highly practical guide to various strategies and procedures for classroom use. The second book is a collection of detailed cases describing actual classroom situations. These can be especially useful for reflecting upon and discussing the various decision-making issues that teachers face.

Freiberg, H. J., & Driscoll, A. (1996). *Universal teaching strategies* (2nd ed.). Boston: Allyn & Bacon.
Greenwood, G. E., & Fillmer, H. T. (1999). *Educational psychology cases for teacher decision-making.* Upper Saddle River, NJ: Merrill.

A detailed analysis of teaching as a contemporary career, with attention to the goals, functions, and philosophies of schools, is presented in:

Ryan, K., & Cooper, J. M. (1998). *Those who can, teach* (8th ed.). Boston: Houghton Mifflin.

Bears are rather large, bobtailed mammals. They walk on the soles of their feet; eat flesh, roots, and other vegetable matter; and have five toes on each foot (Cameron, 1956).

PART TWO

It's all that the young can do for the old, to shock them and keep them up to date.

George Bernard Shaw,
Fanny's First Play

Development and Teaching

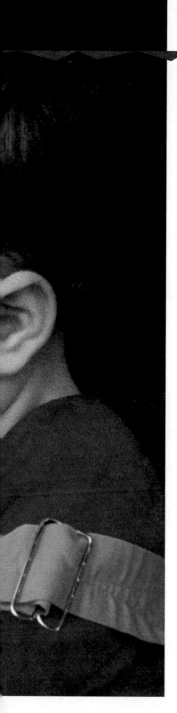

Good teachers cannot afford to be shocked too often by the behaviors of the young. If they are to teach them effectively, they must know what to expect of them. Teachers should not be surprised at a 6-year-old's occasional bewilderment in the face of the unfamiliar, nor should they be taken aback by the sometimes startling but often impractical logic of the adolescent. Much of growing up means becoming familiar with things, and much of schooling involves learning how to use the mind well.

The two chapters in Part Two trace the development of children through the school years. We look at the forces that shape human development and examine the educational implications of our knowledge of how children develop.

The childhood
shews the man,
As morning shews
the day.

John Milton, *Paradise Lost*

An Overview of Development

PREVIEW

To teach children effectively, it's useful to know what to expect of them. We don't expect our 6-year-olds to understand Boolean logic. Nor do we expect our teenagers to become excited at the prospect of being allowed to play on the swings if they color their drawing of mommy nicely, staying inside the lines. But what *can* 6-year-olds understand? And what *does* excite teenagers? In this chapter we present the beginnings of answers for questions such as these by summarizing some important findings in the study of child development. Keep in mind, however, that our discussion is necessarily limited to that mythical but convenient invention, the "average child." Your children are not likely to be average; they will need to be understood as individuals. Nevertheless, knowledge of the average can prove valuable for understanding the individual.

FOCUS QUESTIONS

▲ What is a cohort? Why are cohorts important in studying human development?

▲ How are development, growth, learning, and maturation related?

▲ What major principles characterize human development with respect to genetics and environment? differential growth rates? the importance of the timing of environmental influences? the sequence of development? the stages of development? sex (and other) differences?

▲ What is morality? How does it develop?

▲ How do children learn language?

That year, I dreamed often of bears. "Bears," John George's grandmother whispered to me, "have power. They have power to kill. And power to heal, too." When John George asked me, I couldn't remember whether she used the Cree word muskwa, *which means black bear, or the word* okistu'towân, *which means grizzly.*

One night I dreamed a huge bear reared on his hind legs in front of me down by the creek where I had gone to see could I snare a sucker. The bear's breath made me gag and I thought I might throw up, but I couldn't move. And when I did wake up I found that I had thrown up and my mother said, "Poor thing, he's got the grippe again," refusing to believe that the smell of a dream bear could have made me sick. I was anxious for morning so I could tell John George's grandmother about the dream.

But the next day, my father dragged me off to my first fair, and sitting in the big tent smelling the sawdust and cotton candy and elephant dung, I watched the "freaks" and forgot all about the dream. A guy strutted onto the stage, threw back his head, and swallowed a sword about as long as my leg. Then they brought out a woman and stuffed her into a box and sawed her in half, which almost made me throw up again except there was no blood. When they opened the box, the two halves of her were glued back. After that

came a midget who stuffed flaming balls into his mouth and spit out fire—which would have been a neat trick for Father Paradis to use in his Sunday sermons.

As soon as I got home, I ran to tell John George about the fair, but I forgot to tell his grandmother about my dream.

▣ CONCEPTS IN HUMAN DEVELOPMENT

I am still fascinated by fairs, freaks, and fools.[1] When the fair came to our town one summer, I quickly offered to take my youngest, who was then 7 years old. He was not overly enthusiastic, Saturday being cartoon day. Besides, he didn't yet know how wonderful fairs are.

So we went to the fair. And, in the words of the old song, all the wonderful things were there.

But my son didn't see them! When we stood in front of the sideshow tent, listening to a man with a voice like a bullhorn urging us to come in and see the two-headed calf, the woman with the skin of an elephant, the largest man in the whole world, and the one-handed midget concert pianist, my son didn't even look skeptical. He just looked bored. But I dragged him in anyway.

Later that night, when we talked about the fair, I learned that my son had seen neither the calf with the two heads nor the woman with the skin of an elephant. All he had seen was an unfortunate one-headed calf with a hint of a second head where its right ear should have been and a pathetic woman with a revolting skin disease. Nor had he seen a giant with a great rum-

---

[1] **PPC:** I don't think you should make fun of those less fortunate. One of them might be offended.

Author: I mean fools in the sense of clowns. I use the term because of the alliteration. Besides, few of the other kinds of fools would actually read a book like this. Also, even though the bear is not a choir boy, he would not be so bold as to use this kind of language when describing a contemporary scene. This is history; this event occurred in the olden days when it was not yet politically incorrect to notice freaks and fools and call them just that.

bling voice. Instead, he had watched an unhappy, grotesquely obese man walk painfully across a barren stage, making plaintive breathing noises as he moved. And he had not heard heartrending sonatas played by the one-handed midget; all he had heard was a handful of sad notes played on a tinny miniature piano.

I had always thought there was magic at the fair—perhaps because the world in which I was raised had fewer wonders. My son's world is far less naive than mine was. Television and computers, among other things, have seen to that. And, at least partly because of our dramatically different **contexts,** my son and I have developed into people who respond very differently to the same things.

Developmental psychology tries to understand and explain how people develop and change and how they come to respond differently—or similarly—to the same things. Among other things, it looks at how contexts influence the changes that occur between conception and death and how contexts interact with genes to influence and determine these changes. It provides teachers with descriptions of human characteristics at different ages and explanations of the processes that account for developmental changes. Thus, developmental psychology describes what it's like to be a 7-year-old, how 7-year-olds are different from 14-year-olds, how 7-year-olds got to be as they are, and how and why they will continue to change. This information is important to teachers, who must always be concerned with students' interests, capabilities, and readiness to learn.

Cohort and Context

One factor that's especially important to developmental psychologists is the place and time in which an individual is born and raised. My son and I are clearly a case in point. We are of different worlds—of different contexts. As developmental psychologists would say, we are of different cohorts.

A **cohort** is a group of individuals who were all born within the same period of time—say, the 1940s or the 1970s. A cohort is initially of a fixed size and composition; it cannot grow in size after the time period that defines it has elapsed. In fact, it becomes smaller with the passage of time as members die. Other predictable changes also occur in most cohorts. For example, the proportion of males to females changes because males tend to die sooner than females throughout the world. Thus, although there are 105 males born for every 100 females, the numbers of each still alive by early adulthood are approximately equal. But by age 85, only 44 males are still alive for every 100 females (U.S. Bureau of the Census, 1997). These predictable changes have implications for understanding the lives of men and women.

From developmental psychology's point of view, the most important thing about a cohort is that its members have had a similar sequence of historical influences in their lives, particularly if their geographic, social, and other circumstances are also similar. The identities that we develop, notes Frable (1997), are very much a product of our gender, our ethnic background, our social class—in other words, of our social and historical cohorts.

When interpreting the conclusions of developmental psychology, we need to keep in mind that many of these conclusions are based on research conducted with a small number of cohorts—often only one. These conclusions might not be valid for other cohorts. In our

---

context Refers to all of the developmentally important characteristics of the environment in which development occurs—for example, culture, cohort influences, the family, historical events, and educational experiences.

cohort A group of individuals born within the same specified period of time. For example, the cohort of the 1950s includes those born between January 1, 1950, and December 31, 1959, inclusive.

increasingly multicultural societies, differences among individuals are magnified, and the need for teachers to take these differences into account becomes more important.

This chapter gives an overview of some important general findings about human development. The next chapter deals more specifically with cognitive and social development.

Definitions in Development

Development is a process of change and adaptation. It involves growth, maturation, and learning.

Growth refers to physical changes such as increases in height and weight. These changes are quantitative rather than qualitative; that is, they are changes in quantity or amount rather than transformations that result in different qualities.

Maturation, a somewhat less precise term than growth, describes changes that are relatively independent of the environment. Maturational changes are closely related to the influences of heredity. In most areas of development, however, there is a very close interaction between heredity and environment. For example, learning to walk depends on the maturation of certain muscle groups and on increasing control over movements (maturational developments), and the opportunity to practice the various skills involved (the effects of experience, of learning). Maturation is clearly illustrated by the changes occurring in early adolescence that lead to sexual maturity (**puberty**)—changes col-

lectively labeled **pubescence**. Although the onset seems to be affected by environmental conditions (**menarche**—the onset of menstruation—occurred progressively earlier between 1850 and 1970, apparently because of nutritional factors; see Frisch & Revelle, 1970), the changes of pubescence are largely genetically programmed.

Learning is defined in terms of actual or potential changes in behavior as a result of experience. Thus, all relatively permanent changes in behavior are examples of learning unless they are the result of maturation or of external factors, the effects of which are unrelated to environment (such as the temporary effects of drugs or fatigue). (See Table 2.1.)

⌐ PRINCIPLES OF HUMAN DEVELOPMENT

The following sections summarize some of the most important and useful information in developmental psychology. This summary takes the form of eight statements described as *principles of development*. These do not constitute an exhaustive summary of developmental psychology; rather, these principles have been selected mainly for their relevance to the teaching/learning process.

Nature and Nurture Interact

It is clear that development is influenced by both heredity (**nature**) and environment (**nurture** or

---

development The growth, maturational, and learning processes occurring from birth to maturity.

growth The quantitative, physical aspects of development.

maturation The process of normal physical and psychological development. Maturation is defined as occurring independently of particular experiences.

puberty Sexual maturity.

pubescence Changes of adolescence leading to sexual maturity.

---

menarche A girl's first menstrual period, an event that transpires during pubescence.

learning Changes in behavior due to experience; does not include changes due to motivation, fatigue, or drugs.

nature Genetic influences; heredity.

nurture The effects of experience, as opposed to the effects of heredity (nature).

TABLE 2.1
Human Development: Definitions

Psychology	The science that studies human behavior and thought.
Developmental Psychology	Division of psychology concerned with changes that occur over time and with the processes and influences that account for these changes.
Development includes:	
Growth	Physical changes such as increases in height and weight
Maturation	Naturally unfolding changes, relatively independent of experience (for example, *pubescence*—the changes of adolescence that lead to sexual maturity)
Learning	Relatively permanent changes in behavior or in potential for behavior that result from experience

experience). We know, for example, that our genes are responsible for many of our physical characteristics, such as hair and eye color, facial features, and to some extent height and weight. We know too, that experience affects not only what we learn (to speak Spanish rather than English, for example), but that it can also affect physical growth. Thus, although some physical characteristics (for instance, hair and eye color) appear to be entirely under the control of our genes, other characteristics (for instance, height and weight) clearly are also influenced by environmental factors (such as what and how much we eat).

Efforts to separate the effects of genes and the environment have led to a long-standing controversy in psychology: the **nature-nurture controversy.** In effect, this controversy pits two camps against each other: On the one hand are those who believe that experience (nurture) is the most significant influence in determining important human characteristics such as intelligence; in the other camp are those who think

genes (nature) are most important. Questions relating to the effects of nature and nurture on intelligence are examined in some detail in Chapter 8.

We should say at the outset that science does not clearly support either camp—in fact, the clearest thinking regarding this controversy readily admits that neither genes nor the environment produce anything by themselves. The current emphasis in genetic research, notes Lerner (1993), is on finding out how genes and contexts work together to bring about human development.

Twin Studies In spite of the recognition that both heredity and environment are centrally involved in human development, much research has been done in an attempt to sort out and clarify their relative contributions. Unfortunately, however, it is extremely difficult to determine how qualities such as intelligence and creativity are influenced by heredity and the extent to which they can be modified by the environment.

Many studies that have attempted to clarify this question focused on identical twins because, as Gould (1981) notes, they are "the only really adequate natural experiment for separating genetic from environmental effects in humans"

---

nature-nurture controversy A long-standing argument over whether genetics (nature) or environment (nurture) is more responsible for determining human development.

(p. 234). This is because **identical twins** (termed **monozygotic**) are genetically identical, a condition that is not true for any other pair of humans, including **fraternal twins** (**dizygotic**). Therefore, if intelligence is genetically determined, identical twins should have almost identical intelligence test scores (not exactly identical because we cannot measure intelligence completely accurately). But if intelligence is largely a function of the environment, fraternal twins and other **siblings** should resemble each other about as closely as identical twins—and far more

closely than identical twins who are brought up in separate homes.

Figure 2.1 presents a summary of studies of the relationship between intelligence and genes. What does this figure reveal? First, note that the **correlation** coefficient (a measure of relationship that ranges from −1 to +1) for intelligence test scores is lowest for those who are least alike genetically (unrelated persons) and becomes progressively higher as the degree of genetic similarity increases. Thus, the median (midpoint) correlation for identical twins is above .80, which is a very high correlation. The conclusion: Intelligence is clearly influenced by heredity.

But note as well that the correlations are higher when the environments are more similar. Thus, the intelligence test scores of identical twins reared together are more alike than those of twins reared apart (correlations of .85 and .67, respectively). Also, fraternal twins, who are no more alike genetically than are other pairs of sib-

---

identical twins Twins whose genetic origin is one egg. Such twins are genetically identical.

monozygotic Twins resulting from the division of a single fertilized egg. This process results in identical twins.

fraternal twins Twins whose genetic origins are two different eggs. Such twins are as genetically dissimilar as nontwin siblings.

dizygotic Resulting from two separate eggs and forming fraternal (nonidentical) twins.

siblings Offspring whose parents are the same. In other words, brothers and sisters.

---

correlation A statistical relationship between variables.

No. of Correlations	34	3	3	8	41	69	2	32	4	2	4	5	6	8	8	16
No. of Pairings	4,672	65	410	982	5,546	26,473	203	8,433	814	200	1,176	345	369	758	1,397	3,817
Median Correlation	.85	.67	.73	.475	.58	.45	.24	.385	.22	.35	.145	.29	.31	.19	.18	.365

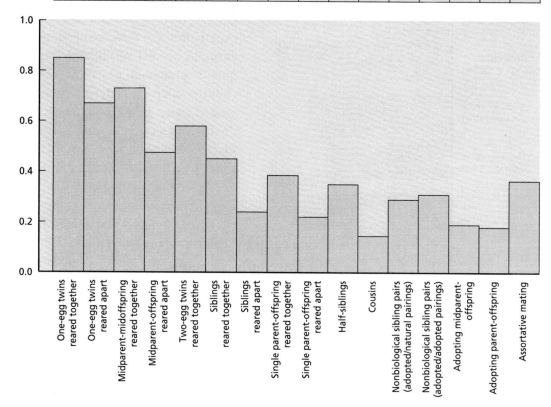

FIGURE 2.1 Median correlation coefficients for intelligence test scores from a large number of studies: The high correlation for identical twins shows the strong genetic basis of measured intelligence. The greater correlation for siblings or twins reared together compared with those reared apart supports the view that environmental forces are also important for determining similarity of intelligence test scores. (From T. J. Bouchard and M. McGue [1981]. Familial studies of intelligence: A review, *Science, 212,* 1055–1059. © 1981 by the AAAS. Used by permission.)

lings, nevertheless manifest higher correlations for measured intelligence—presumably because their environments are more alike than are those of most siblings. After all, fraternal twins are exactly the same age and are often exposed to the same experiences at about the same time.

Studies of Adopted Children Studies of adopted children also provide a rich source of information for disentangling the interactions of heredity and environment. When it's possible to obtain information about adopted children—about their biological and adoptive parents and about other natural children their parents might have had—we can make comparisons among individuals who have common environments or common genes, or both. For example, adopted children and their adoptive parents are not biologically related but share a common environment. On the other hand, adopted children and their biological mothers have common genes but separate environments. And the natural children of adoptive parents share both genes and environment.

As Figure 2.2 shows, the highest correlations for intelligence test scores are for those who share both genes and environment; the lowest are for

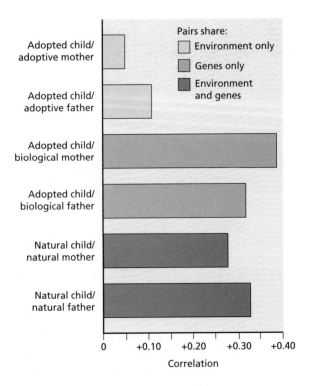

FIGURE 2.2 Correlations for general cognitive ability from a 20-year longitudinal study of adopted and natural children. Source: Plomin, R., Fulker, D. W., Corley, R., & DeFries, J.C. (1997). Nature, nurture, and cognitive development from 1 to 16 years: A parent-offspring study. *Psychological Science, 8*, 442–447.

those who share environments but are not biologically related—clear evidence of the importance of genes in determining measured intelligence. Note, for example, that the correlation between adopted children and their biological mothers is *higher* than that between adopted children and adoptive mothers, a finding that has been corroborated in a variety of adoption studies (for example, DeFries, Plomin, & Fulker, 1994). That is, on average, adopted children's measured intelligence is significantly more like that of their biological parents than that of their adoptive parents. Plomin et al. (1997) note, after a study that followed 490 children over a 20-year period, that this appears to become increasingly true as children age. In their investigation, correlations of the older children with their biological parents were higher than correlations for these same children when they were younger.

A Conclusion Studies of twins and of adopted children both lend strong support to the notion that genes are extremely powerful forces in shaping human development. But we should not forget that there is also considerable evidence that experiences also exert tremendous influence. For example, studies of children exposed to high-quality preschool programs reveal that these children often do better on measures of intelligence (Zigler, 1994). And in a study of 128 children, Molfese, DiLalla, and Bunce (1997) found that the single best predictor of measured intelligence was the environment in the home.

As we stated at the beginning of this section, development is influenced by both heredity and environment, forces that interact in complex ways to determine what you and I become. From a teacher's point of view, the effectiveness of experience is the most important factor. Although we can do relatively little about heredity at this point, much of the environment—most especially, of the classroom environment—still remains under our control. (See Chapter 8 for further discussion of the roles of heredity and environment relative to intelligence.)

Growth Occurs at Varying Rates

Over time, development occurs at different rates for the various parts of an organism. This does not mean that the left foot grows rapidly for a short while, then the right foot, and then one arm. What it means is that various parts of the body and some aspects of personality and intellectual and perceptual ability might grow at different average rates, experience different growth spurts, and reach their maximum development at different times. For example, Bloom (1964) reports that by the age of $2^1/_2$, humans have reached half of their future maximum height. In fact, if a male infant grew at the same rate during years 2 through 6 as he does during the first year of life, he would enter his seventh year weighing close to 4 tons and measuring some 18 feet in height!

Bloom also suggests that half of a male's tendency to be aggressive toward others is established by age 3 and that much of our intellectual potential has already been developed by age 6, a fact that may be partly related to how and when the brain grows.[2]

Investigations of brain development reveal several interesting and important facts. First, most of the *neurons* (nerve cells) that make up the human brain are formed during the prenatal period, although some additional neurons may form during the first few months after birth (DeLong, 1993). At birth, the infant's brain weighs approximately one-fourth of what it will weigh at its maximum, which is reached at about age 25. Most of the increase in brain weight between birth and adulthood seems to be caused by the growth of *axons* and *dendrites* (the elongated portions of the nerve cell that permit neural transmission) and by *myelination* (the growth of a protective covering around the axon) and not by the growth of new cells.

Second, brain growth also seems to be subject to varying rates. The brain does not grow at a uniform rate between conception and birth nor between birth and adulthood. Instead, it appears to grow in spurts. These growth spurts are reflected by increases in cranial (head) circumference. Examinations of head measurements suggest that there is a dramatic spurt in brain growth during the later stages of fetal development. This time of rapid brain development appears to be a critical period during which the effects of maternal malnutrition can be especially severe (Crawford et al., 1993). In fact, Crawford and colleagues note that the most vulnerable period for neural development is the prenatal period. Not surprisingly, maternal nutrition is closely related to the birthweight of newborns, as well as to the circumference of their heads. In the majority of the world's underdeveloped nations, where malnutrition is most prevalent, scientists have observed smaller than average head circumferences among children. Bellamy (1997) reports that almost half of all children in the least developed countries of the world are moderately or severely underweight; half of these suffer from permanently stunted growth.

Another phenomenon related to the principle of varying growth rates is that of **lateralization.** Lateralization refers to the fact that the two halves (hemispheres) of the brain do not exactly duplicate each other's functions. In newborns, the hemispheres do not seem to be highly specialized, but in early infancy the **principle of opposite control** becomes evident (Leask & Crow, 1997). This principle is manifested in the observation that the right hemisphere is typically involved in sensations and movements of the left side of the body, and vice versa. Hemisphere asymmetry is also evident in the fact that about 90 percent of all people are right-handed; only 10 percent are left-handed (Halpern & Coren, 1990). This seems to have been true of our ancestral cave dwellers as well, a conclusion deduced from the observation that about 90 percent of all primitive hand tracings are of the left hand (hence, presumably drawn by the right hand) (Springer & Deutsch, 1989).[3]

---

lateralization A term that refers to the division of functions and capabilities between the two hemispheres of the brain.

principle of opposite control Describes the tendency for sensations and movements on either side of the body to be controlled by the opposite cerebral hemisphere.

---

[3] ***PPC:*** That is a clever deduction, worthy of Sherlock Holmes.

Author: Thank you, says the bear offhandedly. And then he refers again to his mentor, Yogi Berra, whose understanding of handedness was perhaps less clear. "Right-handers go over there," he is reported to have said, "and left-handers go over there. The rest of you, come with me."

Maybe his confusion stems from his desire to be both left and right handed. "I'd give my right arm to be ambidextrous," he declared.

---

[2] Statements such as these are hypothetical approximations at best and refer to variation rather than to absolute amount. The important point is simply that major personality and intellectual characteristics appear to be strongly influenced (and perhaps partly determined) by early experiences.

Additional evidence of hemisphere special-ization includes the observation that in most individuals (95 percent of right-handed people and 70 percent of left-handed) the left hemi-sphere is somewhat more involved in language production functions (Bradshaw, 1989). How-ever, this does not mean that the right hemi-sphere is not involved in language. In fact, when the left hemisphere suffers damage early in life, the right hemisphere frequently takes over lan-guage functions with little apparent subsequent difficulty. When damage is suffered later, how-ever, recovery may not occur at all or may be more limited (Bradshaw, 1989).

Findings such as these have led some to speculate that in the majority of people the right hemisphere is more concerned with emotions and with the spatial and the temporal (for example, art and music) and that the left hemi-sphere is concerned more with logic, math, sci-ence, and language. Thus, individuals who are logical are sometimes described as "left-brain oriented"; those who are more intuitive and artistic, as "right brained." Some, such as Sonnier (1991), for example, believe that *hemi-sphericity*—that is, a predominance of one hemisphere over the other—may be one of the important contributors to individual differ-ences. Several researchers and theorists point out that our current educational practices emphasize left-brain functions, as reflected in our preoccupation with verbal learning, mathe-matics, science, and logic (see, for example, Sonnier & Sonnier, 1995; Sonnier & Sonnier, 1992). Our schools neglect right-brain func-tions, they claim. Hence, we should change our educational fare and philosophy to educate both halves of our students' brains. The phrase **holis-tic education** has been coined to represent this point of view. One advocate of holistic educa-tion describes it as a radically new approach that is person-centered, ecological, global, and spiri-tual (Miller, 1990).

Unfortunately, investigating the dual func-tion of the brain has proved difficult, and much of what passes for information is speculation rather than fact (Bruer, 1997). Following a review of the evidence that links creativity with the right hemisphere, Hines (1991), for example, concludes that there is little such evidence and that the topic is characterized by naive, uncriti-cal, and pseudoscientific beliefs. Similarly, Brown and Kosslyn (1993) emphasize that the brain does not function in terms of simple dichotomies. That is, it is simplistic and mislead-ing to insist that the left hemisphere is logical and analytical whereas the right hemisphere is "artistic." They suggest that the dichotomy is more a matter of degree—that the right and left hemispheres might be *relatively* better for some tasks than for others, but that there is consider-able overlap in their functions. However, this does not lessen the importance of holistic educa-tion's emphasis on some of the often-neglected aspects of education—specifically, those con-cerned with the more affective and artistic aspects of the human experience.[4]

---

holistic education A comprehensive term for educational approaches that attempt to remedy what is seen as the fail-ure of traditional education to educate the whole brain. Advocates of holistic education believe that the right hemi-sphere—speculatively linked with art, music, and emotion— is neglected by curricula that stress reason, logic, language, science, and mathematics.

---

[4] **PPC:** This whole business has become pretty controversial in our dis-trict. They brought some lady in to do a workshop on right- and left-brain functions, and she convinced a lot of teachers they should do some pretty wild things with how they place student desks, how they use different colors, and on and on. Does the bear have any further thoughts on this?

Author: Yes, two things. First, he's curious about what was involved in the "on and on" part of your workshop recommendations; second, he wants to underline that what is most important about the so-called holistic education movement is its emphasis on worthwhile areas of development that might otherwise be neglected. But to say that the bear is a creative and intuitive thinker because he is right brained—or to say that he is a right-brained individual because he is creative and intuitive—is really not saying anything at all. Labels name and categorize; they don't explain.

Timing of Environmental Influences Is Important

The observation that growth and development occur at different times and at different rates for various human features leads directly to a third, important developmental principle described by Bloom (1964, p. vii): Variations in environment have the greatest quantitative effect on a characteristic at its period of most rapid change and the least effect on the characteristic at its period of least rapid change. This principle can be clearly illustrated with respect to physical growth: 24-year-old Rudolph, who was malnourished through much of his childhood and who is now 5 feet tall, is not likely to grow an additional foot as a result of a sudden change in his diet. In contrast, the eventual height of 24-week-old Christianne is clearly more susceptible to the effects of dietary changes.

This principle also holds true for intellectual development. As we saw earlier, for example, brain growth is highly vulnerable to malnutrition during growth spurts, especially during prenatal and early postnatal development (Yoshioka et al., 1995). Similarly, there is evidence that cognitive development may be more sensitive to environmental influences earlier rather than later in life. For example, Lee (1951) examined intelligence test scores of three groups of African Americans living in Philadelphia. One group included individuals who had been born in the South; the other two were comprised of individuals who had moved to Philadelphia either before first grade or during fourth grade. The greatest increases in intelligence test scores were for children who had moved from impoverished backgrounds to better school environments before first grade. In addition, the greatest changes occurred during the first few years. Not surprisingly, those born and raised in Philadelphia scored higher than the other two groups at all grades (see Figure 2.3).

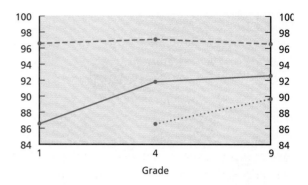

FIGURE 2.3 Changes in intelligence test scores on measures obtained in first, fourth, and ninth grades for African American students born and raised in Philadelphia (dashed line), those born in the South who moved to Philadelphia in the first grade (solid line), and those who did not move to Philadelphia until the fourth grade (dotted line). Adapted from E. S. Lee, *American Sociological Review*, 1951, p. 231. Copyright 1951 by the American Sociological Association. Used by permission of the author.

Additional evidence suggesting that the timing of environmental influences can be very important is found in language acquisition: Infants and young preschoolers can easily learn two or more languages simultaneously and well, whereas adults experience more difficulty and less success.

Educational Implications Environmental influences may be most influential during periods of rapid growth. This has important educational implications. It suggests, for example, that educators need to know about periods of greatest and least rapid change, and they need to arrange for relevant experiences to occur during these periods. This line of thinking is illustrated in preschool programs such as Project Head Start, in which disadvantaged children are given experiences designed to allow them to catch up with more advantaged children.

Timing of environmental influences may also be critically important for interventions designed to minimize a variety of school-related problems. For example, Srebnik and Elias (1993) suggest that one fruitful approach toward reducing school dropout rates might be to not only try

Certain environments appear to be more conducive than others are to optimal intellectual, social, and physical development. But it would be a mistake to assume that people from less-advantaged backgrounds are always at a disadvantage or that those from the richest backgrounds will always fare better.

to make school more attractive and meaningful to students, but also to do so *before* problems become apparent. Similarly, Kendall-Tackett and Eckenrode (1996) argue that the timing of interventions is critically important in programs designed to prevent and reduce the negative effects of child abuse and neglect on school performance.

Sequential Development

Human development is, in many ways, an orderly and predictable process. In fetal development, the heart appears and begins to function before the limbs reach their final form; the lips and gums form before the nasal passages do; the tail regresses before the permanent tooth buds form, and so on.

In motor development, children can lift their chins from a prone position before they can raise their chests, they can sit before they can stand, they can stand before they can crawl, they can crawl before they can walk, and they can walk before they can climb mountains.

The same principle seems to apply in intellectual development, although the sequences are less obvious and the stages less distinct. Piaget's

theory (see Chapter 3) is based on the assumption that human development is characterized by a distinct sequence of stages. For example, his investigations of children's play reveals two distinct developmental sequences: One deals with the child's actual behavior in game situations; the other reflects the child's ability to explain rules verbally. Until about age 3, says Piaget, children don't understand the concept of rules, and they play as though there were none.

During the second stage, lasting until age 5 or so, children have begun to imitate aspects of the ways that adults and older children use rules in their games. But the rules young children use in their play are idiosyncratic (highly individualistic) and constantly changing. They make rules up as they go along. But if they are asked about rules, they describe them as external and unchangeable.

In the third stage (until age 11 or 12), children realize that rules are human inventions that can be changed by humans. But their play behavior is again a contradiction of their verbalized beliefs: Now they follow the rules rigidly, seldom changing them.

In the fourth stage (beyond age 11 or 12) children's play behavior finally reflects their understanding of the function of rules. Now, although

TABLE 2.2
Piaget's Description of Children's
Verbalized Understanding and Use of Rules

APPROXIMATE AGE	VERBALIZED UNDERSTANDING OF RULES	PLAY BEHAVIOR
Before 3	No understanding of rules	Don't play according to any rules
3 to 5 or so	Believe rules come from God (or some other authority) and cannot be changed	Break and change rules constantly
5 to 11 or 12	Understand social nature of rules; know that they can be changed	Don't change rules; adhere to them rigidly
After 11 or 12	Complete understanding of rules	Change rules by mutual consent

they play according to rules, they occasionally change them by mutual consent. (See Table 2.2.)

The understanding of rules is only one small aspect of child development that follows an orderly and predictable sequence. Piaget's investigations suggest that notions of reality, logical reasoning, understanding of time and space, and a wealth of important cognitive and perceptual events are also sequential and predictable.

The observation that much of human development follows an orderly and predictable sequence is especially valuable for teachers, who need to be concerned with their students' readiness. Teachers need to know when specific skills and abilities develop if they are to present children with tasks that are not impossible for them but are challenging enough to be interesting and to promote growth. As we demonstrate in the next chapter, it is also extremely important to understand the factors that enhance—or retard—development.

Development Can Be Described in Stages

Many developmental theories are stage theories; that is, they describe important developmental events in terms of stages. Often the stages are age-based. Stage theories reflect the belief that, although development is a relatively smooth and continuous process, distinct and important stage-like changes nevertheless occur.

Stages are a little like hooks upon which we can hang our facts; they simplify our understanding, help our organization, and facilitate recall. They have been used extensively by theorists such as Sigmund Freud, Erik Erikson, and Jean Piaget. Like theories, stages are invented by theorists to clarify and organize their observations. They are best evaluated in terms of their usefulness rather than their accuracy.

Given that stages are inventions, it is not surprising that the stages described by different theorists are usually different; they are expressions of different points of view, and they often describe different features of child development.

Age-based stage theories are especially useful for teachers who need to have at least a general idea of the characteristics and capabilities of average (and not-so-average) children at each age (or grade). Stage theories provide teachers with this kind of information. Many also provide suggestions for strategies that might facilitate the transition from one stage to the next. We consider these matters again in the next chapter.

Correlation versus Compensation

Correlation, not compensation, is the rule in development—although one popular stereotype contradicts this principle. This stereotype assumes that those who are gifted in one area must not be nearly as well endowed in others. The stereotype informs us that the egghead is a blundering social idiot, unattractive and frail, weak-sighted, and completely useless at any kind of task requiring even the smallest degree of dexterity. The same stereotype insists that an athlete may be stunningly attractive but is also remarkably stupid, spells with difficulty, cannot write a check without an accountant to correct it, reads only simple comic books, and laughs uproariously at unfunny events.

Not so. In fact, as we see in Chapter 8, a person who excels in one realm is more likely to excel in others. Less optimistically, it's also true that people who are below average in one area tend to be below average in other areas as well. Although there are clearly many exceptions to this principle, it nevertheless serves as a useful guide for understanding the overall development of children.

BIZARRO   By DAN PIRARO

Bizarro © *Chronicle Features*. Distributed by Universal Press Syndicate. Reprinted with permission. All rights reserved.

There are Predictable Differences between the Sexes

There are systematic, predictable differences in the development of boys and girls. From birth until early adolescence, boys are both taller and heavier than girls. But by about age 11, girls' average weight surpasses that of boys, and by age $11\frac{1}{2}$, the average girl is taller than the average boy. At about age 14, boys catch up and surpass girls—and remain taller and heavier for the rest of their lives (on average).

The temporary height and weight advantage that girls have over boys in early adolescence reflects the fact that girls mature sexually (reach puberty) earlier than boys. On average, girls undergo the dramatic growth spurt of early adolescence, one of the first of the changes of pubescence (changes that lead to sexual maturity), about two years earlier than boys. These changes are accompanied by important hormonal changes that are evident not only in physical developments but also in changing interests and awakening sexuality.

At about age 12, the average adolescent girl has her first menstrual period—termed menarche and usually taken as a signal of puberty; the average boy reaches puberty at about age 14. But individuals are not average; they are unique. For some girls, the changes of pubescence can begin as young as age 7—or quite a bit later.

Evidence suggests that early or late maturation can be a disadvantage when it puts an adolescent dramatically out of step with peers, especially if the changes (or lack of change) are seen as undesirable (Petersen, 1988). (See the case entitled "I Just Want to Be Average.") Early maturation is generally more positive for boys than girls, perhaps because the precocious boy's greater social maturity is seen as something to be admired and because male sexuality is still more acceptable than female sexuality. By the same token, boys who mature significantly later than

I Just Want to Be Average

When Sandra was in fourth grade, she often spent hours in front of her mirror trying on different bulky sweaters and loose-fitting shirts, trying to make herself look normal. That's all she wanted. Just to look normal. But no! She was only 9, and she already had to let out her breath to fasten her bra—which was, in fact, her mother's bra.

But she refused to get her own, a bigger one, because it seemed to her that maybe if she could hold "them" in tight in her mother's little bra, they wouldn't be so noticeable. She was, after all, only in fourth grade, and it didn't seem right that she should already have such big ones, almost like an infirmity, when all her friends were still nice and flat.

average are sometimes more restless, more attention-seeking, less confident, and less well-adjusted than those who mature early (Crockett & Petersen, 1987).

Besides the predictable sex differences in the average age of maturation, there are other gender differences in interests and abilities. However, unlike maturational timetables, which are largely controlled genetically, differences in interests and abilities—where they exist—are often a function of varying experiences and expectations. Gender differences are discussed in Chapter 3.

Each Human Is Unique

Each of us is different from every other. Except for those who have an identical twin, each of us inherits different genetic blueprints. Each of us is also profoundly influenced by a unique and personal environment. No matter how unique each of us is, though, we can still make valid generalizations about human behavior and development. But—and this is extremely important—these generalizations apply to children as a group and not to any individual child. There is no normal, average child; the average child is a myth invented by grandmothers and investigated by psychologists.

The preceding developmental principles constitute an overview and summary of some educationally relevant statements about developmental processes. They do not suggest highly specific instructional implications, but they can nevertheless provide teachers with general concepts that might be useful for understanding students better.

On average, the adolescent growth spurt occurs two years earlier for girls than for boys. But within sexes, it can also occur at widely different ages, as evident in the different physical sizes of these sixth graders. Age of sexual maturation can have important implications for the well-being and happiness of adolescents.

Of course, there is far more to human development than can be summarized in eight principles. From the teacher's point of view, cognitive (intellectual) development is absolutely central to the teaching/learning process; it is discussed in Chapter 3. Two other important topics for teachers are moral development and language development. We turn to these next.

MORAL DEVELOPMENT

Morality has to do with human interactions that give rise to questions of ethics, of values, of trust, of rights. There are four steps involved in behaving morally, argue Carroll and Rest (1982): First is the need to recognize the moral problem. Second, the person must make a judgment about what ought to be done, about what is right or wrong. Third is the need to decide what to do. Finally, a plan of action must be put into effect.

Note that Carroll and Rest's view of morality is clearly based on the individual's *cognition* (understanding) of a situation. In this view, behaving morally (or immorally) is largely a matter of decision making and also involves acting on decisions. In other words, morality is not simply a matter of *innate* goodness or badness as some sort of deep-seated personality trait. In the view of many theorists (Piaget and Kohlberg, for example), morality develops even as do language and intellect.

Piaget's Two-Stage View

Many decades ago, Piaget (1932) questioned children to find out what they knew about rules and laws, right and wrong, good and evil. He found that very young children do not behave according to abstract concepts of right and wrong but instead respond in terms of the immediate personal consequences of their behavior. In effect, the morality of young children is governed by the principles of pain and pleasure. Young children consider to be good those behaviors that have pleasant consequences (or at least do not have unpleasant consequences); bad behaviors are those that have unpleasant consequences. Piaget's label for this initial stage of moral development is **heteronomy**. During this stage, the child responds primarily to outside authority, which is the main source of rewards and punishments. The morality of heteronomy is a morality of punishment and obedience.

This initial stage is followed by the appearance of more personal and independent moral judgments. Stilwell et al. (1998) point out that, as children develop, they gradually begin to associate moral behavior with volition (will). As a result, they become less obedience-oriented in their judgments of what is good or evil, but rather more *autonomous*—hence, Piaget's label: **autonomy**. As autonomy replaces heteronomy, behavior is guided more and more by internalized principles and ideals.

Kohlberg's Morality of Justice and Reason

Some three decades after Piaget's pioneering studies, Kohlberg (1964) began to study moral beliefs and behaviors using stories involving moral dilemmas. He would tell these stories to

---

morality The ethical aspect of human behavior. Morality is intimately bound to the development of an awareness of acceptable and unacceptable behaviors. It is therefore linked to what is often called *conscience*.

heteronomy Piaget's label for the first stage of moral development, marked by reliance on outside authority.

autonomy Piaget's label for the second stage of moral development, characterized by a reliance on internal standards of right and wrong as guides for action and for judging the morality of an action.

TABLE 2.3
Kohlberg's Levels of Morality

Kohlberg identified levels of moral judgment in children by describing to them situations involving a moral dilemma. One example is the story of Heinz, whose wife is dying. One special drug, discovered by a local druggist, might save her, but the druggist is selling it at an exorbitant price. So Heinz, after failing to borrow the money he needs, pleads with the druggist to sell the drug cheaper or let him pay later. But the druggist refuses. Should Heinz steal the drug for his wife? Why? (Kohlberg, 1969, p. 379)

Level I: **Preconventional**	**Stage 1:** Punishment and Obedience Orientation	"If he steals the drug, he might go to jail." (punishment)
	Stage 2: Naive Instrumental Hedonism	"He can steal the drug and save his wife, and he'll be with her when he gets out of jail." (act motivated by its hedonistic consequences for the actor)
Level II: **Conventional**	**Stage 3:** "Good Boy, Nice Girl" Morality	"People will understand if you steal the drug to save your wife, but they'll think you're cruel and a coward if you don't." (reactions of others and the effects of the act on social relationships become important)
	Stage 4: Law-and-Order Orientation	"It is the husband's duty to save his wife even if he feels guilty afterward for stealing the drug." (institutions, law, duty, honor, and guilt motivate behavior)
Level III: **Postconventional**	**Stage 5:** Morality of Social Contract	"The husband has a right to the drug even if he can't pay now. If the druggist won't charge it, the government should look after it." (democratic laws guarantee individual rights; contracts are mutually beneficial)
	Stage 6: Universal Ethical Principles*	"Although it is legally wrong to steal, the husband would be morally wrong not to steal to save his wife. A life is more precious than financial gain." (conscience is individual; laws are socially useful but not sacrosanct)

Source: Based on Kohlberg (1971, 1980).

*None of Kohlberg's subjects ever reached Stage 6. However, it is still described as a "potential" stage. Kohlberg suggests that moral martyrs like Jesus or Martin Luther King, Jr., exemplify this stage.

---

his study participants (or have them read them) and then ask them how they would behave under similar circumstances and why. The subjects' responses suggested to Kohlberg that there are three sequential levels of moral orientation, each of which can be divided into two stages (see Table 2.3). In general, these stages are similar to Piaget's description of a progression from heteronomy (control by others) to autonomy (self-control). Each of the levels and stages is described briefly here.

Level I: Preconventional At the **preconventional level,** children respond mainly in terms of the **hedonistic** (pain-pleasure) consequences of their behaviors and the power of those who have authority over them. Thus in Stage 1 (punishment

preconventional The first of Kohlberg's three stages of moral development, based on hedonistic or obedience-oriented judgments.

hedonistic Relating to the pain–pleasure principle—the tendency to seek pleasure and avoid pain.

Calvin and Hobbes

by Bill Watterson

Calvin and Hobbes © Watterson, Dist. by Universal Press Syndicate. Reprinted with permission. All rights reserved.

and obedience orientation), the child believes that obedience is good in and of itself. Evaluation of the morality of an action is totally divorced from its more objective consequences but instead rests solely on its consequences to the actor. Behavior for which one is punished is bad; that for which one is rewarded must necessarily be good.

In Stage 2 (naive instrumental hedonism), there is the beginning of reciprocity ("Do for me and I will do for you"). The reciprocity characteristic of this stage is strikingly practical. Children will do something good for others only if they expect it to result in someone's doing something good for them in return. Their moral orientation remains largely hedonistic (pain and pleasure oriented).

Level II: Conventional Conventional morality is a morality of conformity: Good behaviors are those that maintain the established social order. This level reflects the increasing importance of peers and of social relations and is expressed in two stages. In the first (Stage 3: "good boy, nice girl" morality), children judge their actions largely in terms of their role in establishing and maintain-ing good relations with authority and with peers. Approval is all-important and is assumed to be the result of "being nice." And in the next stage (law and order), morality is characterized by blind obedience. What is legal is, by definition, good. The good person is the one who is aware of the rules and obeys them unquestioningly.

Level III: Postconventional At the highest level of moral reasoning, the **postconventional,** the individual makes a deliberate effort to clarify moral rules and principles and to arrive at self-defined notions of good and evil. In Stage 5 (morality of social contract), for example, there is still an element of conformity to laws and legal systems, but the important difference is that legal systems are interpreted as good to the extent that they guarantee and protect individual rights. Individuals can now evaluate laws in terms of social order and individual justice and are capable of reinterpreting and changing them.

The sixth and final stage of moral development (universal ethical principles) is characterized by individually chosen ethical principles that serve as major unifying guides to behavior.

---

conventional Kohlberg's second level of morality, reflecting a desire to establish and maintain good relations with others (law and order; obedience).

postconventional Kohlberg's third level of morality, reflecting an understanding of social contract and more individualistic principles of morality.

These individual moral principles are highly abstract rather than concrete. They are not illustrated in rules like the Ten Commandments but are implicit in deep-seated convictions that guide behavior—for example, beliefs in justice or equality.

Appraisals of Kohlberg's Model Kohlberg's research has had a tremendous influence on our understanding of morality and has generated an enormous amount of research; much of it has not been very kind to Kohlberg's conclusions and to his theorizing.

Some researchers suggest that his view of morality is too limited, that morality should not be restricted to questions of justice and rational decision making. According to Walker et al. (1995), for example, when you ask people to describe *actual* moral dilemmas they have faced and to explain how they behaved and why, a rather different picture emerges. You quickly discover, they say, that adult moral decisions are highly sensitive to real, practical considerations ("Will I lose my job?" "Will she still like me?" and so on). Furthermore, moral decisions tend to reflect cultural background as well as religion or faith. For example, in cultures such as the Chinese, marked by **filial piety**—characterized by unquestioned respect for parents and a strikingly high level of obedience—moral judgments are quite different from those typical of North American cultures. In fact, when presented with Kohlberg-type dilemmas, even adult Chinese subjects typically responded at a stage 1 level, punishment and obedience orientation (Walker et al., 1995).

Other researchers suggest that the stories Kohlberg used are too abstract and too verbal,

especially for young children. There are too many details in the stories, too much to keep in mind and remember when trying to resolve complex situations. As a result, there is considerable evidence that Kohlberg might have underestimated children's level of moral reasoning (Buzzelli, 1992).

Gilligan's Research: Female Morality

Not only are Kohlberg's moral dilemmas not very meaningful, says Gilligan (1982), but his subjects were all males. Hence, the picture his model presents might be misleading not only for males, but even more so for females.

Gilligan attempted to examine morality in women by presenting meaningful moral dilemmas. She interviewed a sample of pregnant women struggling with a decision about abortion. All 29 women in the sample had been referred by a counseling clinic for pregnant women; 21 of these women subsequently had an abortion, four carried their babies to term, one miscarried, and three remained undecided throughout the duration of the study. Gilligan found that it is not so much the decision itself (to have or not to have the baby) that reflects a person's level of moral development as that person's reasons for the decision.

Gilligan identified three stages in the women's moral development. In the first stage, the woman is moved by selfish concerns ("This is what I need . . . what I want . . . what is important for my physical/psychological survival"). In the second stage, there is a transition from selfishness to greater responsibility toward others. This change is reflected in reasoning that is based not on simple, selfish survival but on a more objective morality (notions of what is right and wrong; specifically, a growing realization that caring for others rather than just for oneself is a form of "goodness"). The third stage reflects what Gilligan labels a "morality of nonviolence" toward self and others: The woman will now

---

filial piety A fundamental virtue in many oriental cultures. In effect, it says that people should always, under all circumstances, and at all ages, display the highest devotion and complete obedience to their parents, and that the welfare of parents always comes first. (My kids are occidental.)

accept sole responsibility for her decision, and she bases this decision on the greatest good to herself and others. The best moral decision at this level is the one that does the least harm to the greatest number of those for whom the woman is responsible.

In summary, Gilligan describes adult female moral development in terms of three stages, beginning with a selfish orientation, progressing through a period of increasing recognition of responsibility to others, and culminating at a level at which moral decisions reflect a desire to treat the self and others equally—that is, to do the greatest good (or the least harm) for the greatest number. At each of these three levels, what women respond to most when initially considering their moral dilemmas are the emotional and social implications of their decision for the self and, subsequently, the implications for others as well. In contrast with Kohlberg's description of a male moral progression that moves from initial hedonistic selfishness toward a greater recognition of social and legal rights, Gilligan describes a female progression from selfishness toward greater recognition of responsibility to self and others.

Phrased another way, one important difference between male and female morality (as described by Kohlberg and Gilligan) is that moral progression in males tends toward the recognition and use of "universal ethical principles"; in contrast, women respond more to considerations of fairness and equality for the self and others. As Petrie and Willis (1998) phrase it, women's morality is a morality of "*caring*" rather than of "*abstract justice.*"

Additional corroboration of these sex differences is implicit in various studies demonstrating that girls frequently reach Kohlberg's third stage, morality of good relations, earlier than boys and remain at that level long after boys have gone on to the fourth stage, morality of law and order (Eisenberg et al., 1991). One plausible explanation for this phenomenon is that girls are more responsive to social relationships, more concerned with empathy and compassion, and more in touch with real life and less concerned with the hypothetical. In contrast, boys are more concerned with law and order, social justice, and the abstract as opposed to the personally meaningful dimensions of morality.

Educational Implications of Moral Development

Knowing how children develop morally can be valuable for teachers in several ways. First, knowing how and why children judge things to be morally right or wrong relates directly to the types of rationalizations a teacher might use when trying to convince students to "behave" and not to "misbehave." There is evidence, for example, that rationalizations that stress the object—"the toy might break"—are more effective for younger children than more abstract rationalizations—"you should not play with toys that belong to other children" (see Chapter 11). By the same token, the types of rationalizations that might be given to adolescents would be quite different from those offered to younger children. Also, the most meaningful rationalizations for girls might stress social relationships, empathy, and responsibility; the most meaningful rationalizations for boys might stress legal rights and social order.

Knowledge of moral development would also be useful for actually teaching morality—an important undertaking, because there appears to be a close relationship between level of moral development and actual behavior (Kohlberg & Candee, 1984). Teaching morality in the schools sometimes takes the form of **values education:** a direct attempt to teach students good values, or **values clarification programs,** which do not so much attempt to teach specific values as to encourage students to examine their own sets of values. These programs are discussed in more detail in Chapter 7.

Teachers, says Giroux (1992), have played three different types of roles in the moral development of their students. The teacher as master is an advocate of good behavior and strong conscience. This role emphasizes teaching values and principles. The teacher as facilitator tries to help students develop and understand their own values, sometimes using discussion or other approaches such as values clarification programs. This role views the student rather than the teacher as the source of values. The teacher as mentor is a guide and a friend, an enlightened leader, a source of vision and wisdom. In the role of mentor the teacher is an example rather than a tutor.

Each role underlines the importance of the teacher's own personal morality.

LANGUAGE DEVELOPMENT

All of the major achievements of human culture—law, literature, science, art, architecture—depend on **language,** notes MacWhinney (1998). Language is a uniquely human phenomenon, the crowning manifestation of an intellectual ability that is unparalleled among animal species. Without language, says Deacon (1997), we could not *imagine,* could not *invent,* could not make up worlds. "We live in a world that no other species has access to," he writes. "We inhabit a world full of abstractions, impossibilities, and paradoxes.

We alone brood about what didn't happen, and spend a large part of each day musing about the way things could have been" (p. 22).

Our ability to communicate through language separates us from other beasts because language makes it possible for us to communicate with one another at levels of abstraction beyond the imaginations and capacities of these other beasts. Language also separates us from wild and domestic beasts in at least two other related ways: It provides us with a means for storing our knowledge and wisdom, and it allows us to transform that knowledge. More than this, language is what makes possible the universality of meanings and the sharing of human experience. And because language is the chief medium of instruction in the schools, its importance can hardly be overestimated.

Language and Communication

Language is not synonymous with **communication.** Animals communicate, but they don't have language. A dog who gets its master's attention, walks to its dish and barks, looks its master in the eye, and then begins to growl is not using language but is nevertheless communicating very effectively. Even wild animals communicate. Pronghorn antelope convey alarm by bristling their rump patches, white-tailed deer by flagging their long tails. Pheasants threaten rivals by crowing, elk by bugling, and moose by grunting. Much of this communication, notes Hebb (1966), is purely reflexive. The behavior of the dog is an example of *purposive* communication, but it is still not language.

To communicate is to transmit a message; it requires a sender and a receiver. To communicate

---

values education Instructional programs and strategies designed to teach specific values (notions of right and wrong), thereby promoting good behavior and developing good "character."

values clarification program A program designed to encourage learners to examine their personal beliefs about right and wrong, with a view to improving and clarifying their awareness of their own morality.

language The use of arbitrary sounds in the transmission of messages from one individual or organism to another. Language should not be confused with communication.

---

communication The transmission of a message from one organism to another. Communication does not necessarily involve language because some nonhuman animals can communicate, usually through reflexive behaviors.

through language is to make use of arbitrary sounds or symbols in a purposeful manner to convey meaning. Further, the use of language involves sounds or other signs that can be combined or transformed to produce different meanings. A parrot, for example, can mimic a word or even a phrase and can be taught to make the sequential noises of a phrase so that its utterance will appear to be purposive. A parrot that says "you bore me" after a guest has been talking incessantly for two hours may appear to be using language in a purposeful manner, but the parrot is not using the phrase with the intention of communicating meaning and cannot deliberately transform the phrase to change its meaning. That would demonstrate the use of language as opposed to simple imitation.

The Elements of Language

There are four basic components of language, the linguists inform us: phonology, semantics, syntax, and pragmatics.

Phonology refers to the **phonemes,** or sounds, of a language. A phoneme is the simplest unit of language and is nothing more complex than a single sound such as that represented by a consonant or vowel. There are 45 phonemes in the English language. Some languages have more; others, fewer.

Combinations of phonemes form **morphemes,** which are a language's units of meaning or **semantics.** Morphemes can be whole words or they can be made up of sounds such as -*ing* or -*ed*—word endings that affect the meanings of words.

Organizing words into meaningful sentence units requires a knowledge of **syntax,** or grammar—the set of rules governing the combinations of words that will be meaningful and correct for the speakers of that language.

As children practice and master sounds (phonemes), meanings (semantics), and grammatical rules (syntax), they must also learn a large number of unspoken rules and conventions governing conversation. In other words, they must learn the **pragmatics** of language. An implicit knowledge of pragmatics is what tells children when and how they should speak. It includes uncounted rules and practices governing manners of expression, intonation, accents, and all the other subtle variations that give different meanings to the same morphemes and that might vary appreciably from one context to another. For example, parents use shorter sentences, speak in higher-pitched voices, and use more concrete names and fewer abstractions when speaking with young children than with other adults; this is a function of their knowledge of pragmatics.

Phonology, semantics, syntax, and pragmatics are the elements of language. Most of us acquired these elements of our native language in an amazingly effortless, effective, and efficient way without really being conscious of what we were doing.

Two Explanations of Language Development

Some researchers view language as a sort of special gift given only to humans and not other animals and believe that the acquisition of language

---

phonology The structure of speech sounds of a language.

phoneme The simplest unit of language, consisting of a single sound, such as a vowel.

morpheme A combination of phonemes that make up the meaningful units of a language.

semantics The meanings of the words of a language.

syntax The arrangement of words to form sentences.

pragmatics The implicit language rules that govern practical things such as when to speak and how to take turns in conversation.

cannot be explained without reference to things extraordinary and mysterious. Such explanations have been described as **hopeful monsters** by Deacon (1997). The best known of the *hopeful monster* theories of language development is that of linguist Noam Chomsky (1972). Chomsky argues that because children learn language, and especially grammar, so rapidly, and because they make so few of the errors that one might expect them to make if they had to learn each rule and each exception individually, they must be born with a powerful biological predisposition to learn language. This predisposition, Chomsky speculates, takes the form of neurological prewiring in the brain, a sort of brain organ whose wiring corresponds to language and to grammar. He labels this neurological prewiring the **language acquisition device (LAD)**.

Chomsky's theory is an example of what MacWhinney (1998) labels **nativism**. Nativism refers to explanations that assume that at least some aspects of language learning depend on a pre-existing module or organ in the brain. Nativism is a *hopeful monster* type of explanation.

A second explanation views language learning as the end result of a learning process that is highly dependent on interaction with other speakers. This explanation sees language as something that *emerges* gradually and is labeled **emergentism** by MacWhinney (1998). A well-known explanation that illustrates emergentism is based on what we know about the effects of reinforcement on behavior (described in Chapter 4). This explanation maintains that an infant, while babbling, emits wordlike sounds that tend to be reinforced by adults. Also, parents or siblings may repeat the infant's vocalizations, thus serving as models. Eventually, through reinforcement, children learn to imitate the speech of those around them. Were it not for this imitation and reinforcement, the frequency and variety of speech sounds would probably decrease. This is borne out by the observation that at the age of 6 months deaf children make sounds much like those made by hearing children, but by the age of 9 months, they have typically stopped babbling (Eilers & Oller, 1988).

Learning the First Language

Researchers who have studied the origins of language have been particularly interested in infants' first sounds and gestures and the interactions of infants and their caregivers. It seems clear that the ability to use and understand words develops through a complex series of such interactions, which Bruner (1983) labels the language acquisition support system (LASS). Among other things, this system involves learning how to make eye contact, how to direct attention through eye movements, and how to emphasize and communicate meaning through facial and other bodily gestures.

For convenience and simplicity, language learning can be divided into a series of stages. Wood (1981) describes six stages, summarized in Table 2.4. The first of these, the prespeech stage,

---

hopeful monsters Deacon's label for explanations that resort to what is sometimes termed *Deus ex machina*—a "God in a machine." Such explanations rely on an assumed but unseen and unprovable entity, organ, or feature to explain what cannot easily be explained otherwise.

language acquisition device (LAD) Chomsky's label to describe the neurological something in our brains that corresponds to grammar and that is intended to explain how we can learn, understand, and use language.

nativism An explanation for language learning, such as Chomsky's, that assumes that language learning depends on a pre-existing neurological organ or pattern in the brain corresponding to a universal language grammar. Nativism is a *hopeful monster* type of explanation.

---

emergentism An explanation that views language learning as the result of a gradual learning process involving social interaction, where understanding of grammar gradually emerges, rather than being prewired.

TABLE 2.4
Stages of Grammatical Development in Children

STAGE OF DEVELOPMENT	NATURE OF DEVELOPMENT	SAMPLE UTTERANCES
1. Prespeech (before age 1)	Crying, cooing, babbling	Waaah, Dadadada
2. Sentencelike word or holophrase (by 12 months)	The word is combined with nonverbal cues (gestures and inflections).	Mommy (meaning: "Would you please come here, Mother?")
3. Two-word sentences (by 18 months)	Modifiers are joined to topic words to form declarative, interrogative, negative, and imperative structures.	Pretty baby (declarative) Where Daddy? (question) No play. (negative) More milk! (imperative)
4. Multiple-word sentences (by 2 to 2$\frac{1}{2}$ years)	Sentence includes a subject and a predicate. Grammatical morphemes are used to change meanings (-*ing* or -*ed*, for example).	She's a pretty baby. (declarative) Where Daddy is? (question) I no can play. (negative) I want more milk! (imperative) I running. I runned.
5. More complex grammatical changes and word categories (between 2$\frac{1}{2}$ and 4 years)	Elements are added, embedded, and permuted within sentences. Word classes (nouns, verbs, and prepositions) are subdivided. Clauses are put together.	Read it, my book. (conjunction) Where is Daddy? (embedding) I can't play. (permutation) I would like some milk. (use of *some* with mass noun) Take me to the store. (use of preposition of place)
6. Adultlike structures (after 4 years)	Complex structural distinctions are made, as with *ask-tell* and *promise*.	Ask what time it is. He promised to help her.

Source: Based in part on B. S. Wood, *Children and Communication: Verbal and Nonverbal Language Development* (2nd ed.), 1981, p. 142. Reprinted by permission of Prentice-Hall, Inc., Englewood Cliffs, New Jersey.

spans most of the first year of life. It is marked by the appearance of the infant's intention to communicate (evident in gestures and grunts well before words first appear) and in the eventual discovery that things and actions have their own names (Masur, 1993).

Achievements of the Prespeech Stage The infant must learn at least five things to progress from the prespeech to the speech stage: turn-taking, the use of gestures, sound discrimination, sound production, and words.

Turn-Taking Turn-taking is basic to adult conversation. If we are to converse with someone, we have to know when it's our turn to listen and when we should speak. Amazingly, infants seem to begin to learn turn-taking very early in life. Elias and Broerse (1996) report that even 3-month-old infants often take turns when interacting with their caregivers. When the mother does something, for example, the infant is quiet and attentive, but when the mother stops, the infant coos or squirms.

Gestures Evidence of the infants' intention to communicate, notes Masur (1993), is clear in the repertoire of gestures and signals that are clearly meaningful for mothers and infants. Among the most common of early gestures is the gaze. Another is pointing, which becomes progressively more refined as the infant learns when pointing is most appropriate and most useful (Franco & Butterworth, 1996).

Sound Discrimination Understanding and speaking a language depend on being able to discriminate among sounds and also being able to produce intended sounds.

Moffitt (1971) reports that infants appear to be able to discriminate sounds at a very early age. In one study, for example, he monitored the heart rates of infants 5 and 6 months old while they listened to taped recordings of two highly similar sounds: "bah" and "gah." That these infants could tell the difference between these sounds was evident in changes in their heart rates whenever the sounds changed.

There is also considerable evidence that pre-verbal infants can discriminate among complex and highly similar sounds and that they can also detect word and sentence structures. McDonald (1997) reports, for example, that young infants prefer speech patterns that are interrupted between clauses. Similarly, they prefer continuous sequences of words that are interrupted *between* rather than *within* words. McDonald suggests that young infants use this sort of phonological information (information about sounds) to figure out the structure of the language they are learning.

Sound Production The first sounds that infants make are cries—cries of pain, of hunger, of pleasure. All cries express emotions.

By the age of 3 months, infants begin to *coo*. Cooing is a more controlled form of sound which tends to be highly melodic. And by the age of 6 months, the highly controlled and repetitive but meaningless sounds that define **babbling** appear. It was long thought that infants produce all of the sounds of all of the world's languages in their babbling. Not so, says MacWhinney (1998). In fact, many sounds are *never* made by infants whose languages don't require them.

By the age of 10 months, most hearing infants babble systematically and clearly; those who are deaf typically never reach this stage (Deal & Haas, 1996). Even babbling is highly dependent on hearing.

Achievements of the Speech Stages The second stage in Wood's (1981) description of language development, the first of five speech (as opposed to *pre*speech) stages, begins with the appearance of **holophrases,** or sentencelike words. This usually occurs by the age of 12 months. Holophrases are so called because, in the beginning, many of the infant's newly discovered words contain a great variety of meanings—meanings that an adult could not easily express in less than an entire sentence. For example, the holophrase "up," uttered in an unmistakably imperious tone by 1-year-old Elizabeth, means very clearly, "Pick me up right now and tell me a story or else I may yell and think of some forbidden thing to do."

Two-word sentences (the third stage), made up primarily of modifiers joined to nouns or pronouns, appear by the age of 18 months. At this stage, speech is still highly telegraphic; that is, complex meanings are squeezed into simple, and sometimes grammatically incorrect, two-word utterances. For example, the sentence "Mummy gone" may mean something as complex as "my dear mother is currently on a business trip in Chicago." During this third stage, there is ordinarily a tremendous spurt in the acquisition of vocabulary. The learning of the first 100 or so words, notes MacWhinney (1998), can take several months, but subsequently, vocabulary growth leaps forward.

The fourth stage, use of multiple-word sentences, is reached between ages 2 and $2^{1}/_{2}$. Sentences may now be five words long or longer.

---

babbling The relatively meaningless, highly repetitive sounds that young infants make in the early stages of language learning.

holophrase A sentencelike word uttered by young children early in the course of learning a language. A holophrase is a single word that the child uses to convey as much meaning as an adult would convey with a much longer phrase.

Although they continue to be telegraphic, they make use of more grammatical variations to express different meanings, and they typically include appropriate subjects and predicates.

Between ages $2^1/2$ and 4, children learn to use progressively more complex grammatical structures (the fifth stage), culminating in adult-like structures in the late preschool years.

Although ages are assigned to each of these stages, these are simply approximations based on the average performance of large groups. Here, as in all areas of human development, it is normal for some to display a behavior earlier and others later. An average is not an expression of normality in the sense that those who deviate from it are abnormal; it is simply a mathematical indication of a point around which observations are distributed.

Language and Intelligence

The most verbally strong children, note Smedler and Torestad (1996), tend to achieve at the highest levels. In fact, they often achieve better than might be predicted solely on the basis of their measured intelligence. There is also a very high correlation between verbal ability and measured intelligence (Beitchman et al., 1996). That is, those with high measured intelligence also tend to be the most advanced and the most accomplished verbally—and vice versa.

The close relationship between intelligence and language may be partly due to the fact that most measures of intelligence are highly verbal. These usually require children not only to understand verbal directions but also to make oral or written responses to questions. In addition, many tests measure the extent and sophistication of vocabulary directly.

That verbal ability should be given such an important role in measures of intelligence is hardly surprising. One of our defining attributes as human beings is, after all, language. Language is what makes us *homo sapiens*—the *wise human*. Of the thousands of species with brains, notes Deacon (1997), we are the only one that has ever wondered about its place in the world because we are the only one that is able to. The symbols of our languages allow us to *imagine*. They allow us to create and wonder about realities that don't exist—imaginary realities.

Even very young children—children who are just learning their first language—create imaginative realities, Emde, Kubicek, and Oppenheim (1997) inform us. They make use of what is familiar, of what they remember, to create and try out new possibilities. Yet even toddlers are seldom confused about the difference between the real and the make-believe. They know the difference between the concrete, the touchable, and the tasteable (which are built of plastic, rubber, wood, or metal) and the imaginary, which is built only of words.

Such is the power of language that there is nothing you can imagine that language cannot build.

MAIN POINTS

1. A cohort is a group of individuals who were born during the same time period and who are therefore subject to the same historical influences. Sociohistorical influences define context.

2. Development can be viewed as comprised of all changes attributable to maturation (natural unfolding), growth (physical changes), and learning (the effects of experience).

3. Studies of twins and of adopted children indicate that both genetics (nature) and

context (nurture or environment) are centrally involved in determining the outcome of development.

4. Development takes place at different rates for different features of the organism. For example, the brain seems to grow in spurts, with a major spurt occurring just before and just after birth (during which nutrition is critical).

5. Environmental changes are most effective during the period of fastest growth and least effective during slowest growth. In practice, this principle favors early intervention, particularly with respect to such things as language development.

6. Development follows an orderly sequence, although the age at which various events occur can vary considerably from one child to another.

7. Development can be described in terms of arbitrary stages. Stages are useful inventions for organizing our observations about children.

8. Correlation, not compensation, is the rule in development.

9. There are systematic, predictable differences in the development of boys and girls. But in spite of the generality of our developmental principles, individuals vary considerably.

10. Moral development in boys seems to proceed from a preconventional level (hedonistic and obedience-oriented) to a conventional level (conformity; desire to maintain good relationships). The postconventional level (individual principles of conduct) is seldom, if ever, reached by anyone. Moral development in girls may be more tied to social responsibility, empathy, and social relationships than to law and social order.

11. Knowledge of moral development might help teachers select the most effective rationalizations for different children. Also, it might be possible to foster moral growth through systematic educational programs.

12. The ability to use language for purposive communication is one of the traits that most clearly separates us from other animals. The elements of language are phonology (speech sounds), semantics (meanings of sounds), syntax (rules for sentence formation), and pragmatics (implicit rules governing conversation).

13. Nativist explanations of early language acquisition speculate that the human brain must contain some prewired (*native*) neurological model or organ corresponding to a universal language grammar (also termed a *hopeful monster theory*). Emergent explanations speak of the gradual emergence of language as a function of interaction with other speakers.

14. The early development of language is facilitated by a complex network of caregiver–infant interaction. In the prespeech stage (first year of life), the infant learns turn-taking, the use of gestures, sound discrimination, sound production, and finally, the first word.

15. Wood's six stages of language development are prespeech (before age 1; cooing and babbling), sentencelike words, or holophrases (by age 1), two-word sentences (by 18 months), multiple-word sentences containing subject and predicate (ages 2 to $2^1/_2$), more complex sentences and grammatical changes (by age 4), and adultlike structures (from age 4 onward).

16. Language and intelligence are highly correlated. Language is what makes us wise.

Applied Questions

▲ How might age and grade cohorts be from very different cultural contexts?

▲ Give an example of each: development, growth, learning, and maturation.

▲ Explain the educational relevance of at least one developmental principle relating to genetics and environment, differential growth rates for different aspects of development, why timing of experiences can be important, how development follows an orderly sequence, and gender differences.

▲ In what ways are preconventional, conventional, and postconventional moral reasoning evident in the classroom? Provide examples of each type of reasoning.

▲ Observe and do a brief diary description of a toddler's language development.

Internet Activity

Use InfoTrac College Edition or other World Wide Web sources to research the following statement: Write up your findings. (See the inside back cover of this text for suggestions about where to begin.)

Nature and nurture interact in determining human characteristics.

Sample search terms: nature and nurture

Study Terms

autonomy 52
babbling 61
cohort 39
communication 57
context 39
conventional 54
correlation 42
development 40
dizygotic 42
emergentism 59
filial piety 55
fraternal twins 42
growth 40
hedonistic 53
heteronomy 52
holistic education 46
holophrase 61
hopeful monsters 59
identical twins 42
language 57
language acquisition device (LAD) 59
lateralization 45
learning 40

maturation 40
menarche 40
monozygotic 42
morality 52
morpheme 58
nativism 59
nature 40
nature-nurture controversy 41
nurture 40
phoneme 58
phonology 58
postconventional 54
pragmatics 58
preconventional 53
principle of opposite control 45
puberty 40
pubescence 40
semantics 58
siblings 42
syntax 58
values clarification program 57
values education 57

Suggested Readings

For elaboration on and greater clarification of the developmental principles outlined in this chapter, you might consult the following textbooks:

Lefrançois, G. R. (1995). *Of children: An introduction to child development* (8th ed.). Belmont, CA: Wadsworth.

———. (1999). *The lifespan* (5th ed.). Belmont, CA: Wadsworth.

Plomin describes his little book as an exploration of the hyphen in nature-nurture. It is a clearly written look at the evidence we have concerning the relationship between heredity and environment. Among other things, it explores the thesis that genes and environment are not entirely independent of each other but that, in particular, genes affect the environment:

Plomin, R. (1994). *Genetics and experience: The interplay between nature and nurture.* Thousand Oaks, CA: Sage.

Deacon's book is a fascinating, intelligent, and somewhat revolutionary account of the coevolution of brains and our ability to symbolize.

Deacon, T. W. (1997). *The symbolic species: The co-evolution of language and the brain.* New York: W. W. Norton.

According to folklore, many years ago in Switzerland, bears were worshipped because the faithful believed that humans were descended not from Adam and Eve, but from the bear (Engel, 1976).

The parent who could see his boy as he really is would shake his head and say: "Willie is no good: I'll sell him."

Stephen Leacock, *The Lot of the Schoolmaster*

Cognitive and Social Development

CHAPTER 3

PREVIEW

Of the theories that have been used to explain human development, those that look at the growth of mind are among the most important for teachers. In this chapter we describe two of these theories—Piaget's and Vygotsky's—and consider their educational implications. We look as well at the development and significance of gender roles and at Erikson's description of personality change through childhood.

FOCUS QUESTIONS

▲ What are gender roles and gender typing?

▲ How real and pervasive are sex differences?

▲ What is psychosocial development?

▲ How does Piaget describe human development?

▲ What are the main characteristics of sensori-motor development? preoperational development? concrete operations? formal operations?

What is Vygotsky's cultural/cognitive theory?

When an infant was about to be born among the Mundugumor of New Guinea, the parents would adorn themselves with their most prized clothing and jewelry. The father would wear a skirt of brilliant parrot feathers, and he would hang plumes and beetle shells around his neck; the mother would decorate herself with bracelets of wild orchids, and she would perhaps wear a necklace of smoothly polished dog teeth. Through her nostrils she would run the long white leg bone of a wild guinea fowl. If others in the village looked at the parents in admiration, this would bode well for the child.

The Mundugumor considered this business of dressing well for a birth extremely important. But they also knew that other matters that they could not so easily control are even more important. For example, the Mundugumor knew without any doubt that only infants who are born with their umbilical cords wrapped around their necks have any chance of becoming great artists. And among the Mundugumor, to be a great artist is a lucky and wonderful thing. Amazingly, the Mundugumor were right: Infants not born with their umbilical cords coiled around their necks simply did not become great artists—to absolutely no one's surprise.

My various siblings and I were born at home in the woods of Northern Saskatchewan—in a house

perhaps a little more sturdy than a New Guinea hut. And although the medical training or knowledge of the midwife and the grandmother who assisted our various births was perhaps no more advanced than that of the Mundugumor, in the end that probably made little difference. My parents were more likely to absentmindedly crush beetles and kick them aside than to collect their carapaces and make necklaces of them, but this may not have mattered all that much either. And that my mother was not fond of wearing bones in her nostrils or dogtooth ornaments may have been as much of a relief for my father as it surely was for our old dog, happily chewing said bones with said teeth.

When we were born, my siblings and I, our parents were not particularly concerned with the positions of our umbilical cords—unless, of course, the cord was wrapped dangerously tightly around the baby's scrawny neck. You see, my parents knew without any doubt whatsoever that the position of our umbilical cords at birth had absolutely nothing to do with whether or not we would become great artists. Besides, where I was born and raised, becoming a great artist was not a common ambition.

Still, my parents were very much like the Mundugumor in their attempts to foretell our futures at birth. No, they didn't look at the locations of our umbilical cords. Instead, they looked for an appendage between our legs. Why? Because, based on the presence or absence of this appendage, my parents could predict with stunning accuracy a great many of our eventual characteristics.

GENDER ROLES

My parents knew, for example, that those of us with this appendage would be fast and strong and tough and just a little aggressive (it's not a bad thing in this dog-eat-dog world, you know). And those without, well, they'd be gentler and more emotional and not nearly so aggressive, and they'd want to help out in the house, but no way would they be interested in chopping wood or hunting and fishing or becoming great scientists.

My parents were heir to a vast body of beliefs dealing with the most likely characteristics associated with gender. These characteristics define **gender roles** (also called sex roles). There are masculine roles and feminine roles. These roles are defined in terms of the behaviors, personality characteristics, and attitudes that a culture finds appropriate for each sex. Learning behaviors according to one's gender is called **gender typing** (or sex typing).

Development of Gender Roles

As for all aspects of human development, there are two main influences on the development of gender roles: genetics and environment.

The impact of the environment is summarized in what is termed **gender schema theory**. According to this theory, the child begins with no understanding of the nature of gender—no notion of what is called **basic gender identity**. But notions of gender identity begin to develop

very early in life. In fact, claim Serbin, Powlishta, and Gulko (1993), one of the first social dimensions that children notice is sex. And even within the first year of life, they begin to develop what researchers label **gender schemas**—notions about what male and female mean and what the characteristics of each are (or should be) (Bem, 1981, 1989). Children can correctly label people as "man" or "woman," "boy" or "girl" almost as soon as they can talk, and they can also predict the sorts of activities in which each is most likely to engage.

Witt (1997) points out that parents exert an enormously important influence on the development of gender role in their children. Children internalize many of the subtle messages parents send out regarding gender and, especially, regarding what is expected and appropriate for boys and girls. Thus do children begin to develop **stereotypes** of masculinity and femininity. Stereotypes are highly culture-specific notions about how males and females should think, act, and feel (Levy, 1993).

Once children have begun to develop gender schemas, these act as powerful constraints on their behavior. Bussey and Bandura (1992) found that even at the age of 2 children have already begun to approve of sex-typed behavior and to disapprove of cross-sex behavior. As a result, notions of gender act as very important guides for children's behavior. Because boys aren't supposed to cry, Robert bites his lip and tries hard to hold back his tears; because girls aren't supposed to like playing with boys' things, Elizabeth tries to ignore her brother's gleaming red fire truck.

In rare cases, some children experience significant difficulty in developing a clear and

---

gender roles Attitudes, personality characteristics, behavior, and other qualities associated with being male or female. Gender roles define masculinity and femininity. Also termed *sex roles*.

gender typing Learning behavior appropriate to the sex of the individual. The term refers specifically to the acquisition of masculine behavior by a boy and feminine behavior by a girl.

gender schema theory A cognitive gender typing theory that recognizes the usefulness of elements of both cognitive explanations (the child's growing understanding of the nature and meaning of gender) and social learning explanations (the influence of models and reinforcements) to account for the shaping of gender roles.

basic gender identity The individual's implicit understanding of the fundamental characteristics of masculinity and femininity.

---

gender schemas Notions about the characteristics associated with being male or female.

stereotype A strong, relatively unexamined belief typically generalized to a class of superficially similar situations or individuals.

strong notion of their own sexual identity. Some find themselves highly uncomfortable with their biological sex. This problem, labeled **gender identity disorder**, is sometimes apparent in situations where boys feel themselves to be girls—or desperately wish they were (Soutter, 1996). More rarely, it can also be seen in situations where girls are highly uncomfortable with their gender and sense themselves to be male rather than female (Fridell et al., 1996).

As we noted, biology also contributes to the development of gender roles. Quite apart from the obvious fact that biology, after all, determines whether we are male or female, there are strong indications that some male–female personality differences may have biological roots (Maccoby & Jacklin, 1980; Jacklin, 1989). This is most obvious in the greater aggressiveness of males relative to females. Evidence that at least some of the males' greater aggressiveness is biological is found in the observation that males tend to be more aggressive not only in most human societies, but also among most nonhuman animal species. Male aggressiveness may be linked to the presence of male hormones. In fact, when females are given testosterone injections, they too tend to become more aggressive.

But even with respect to the greater aggressiveness of males, the influence of social roles and expectations cannot be ignored. In North American societies, for example, most occupations and many sports requiring **aggression** have traditionally been restricted to males; those requiring nonaggressive, more nurturant behavior have typically been considered appropriate for females. As a result, society provides children with clear models. Children see them everywhere: at home, on television, on the playground, and, of course, at school. The message is unmistakable that certain behaviors, occupations, interests, and attitudes clearly are highly probable and appropriate for a given gender and others, just as clearly, are not. And portrayals of sexual stereotypes and gender roles on television have not changed significantly in 40 years, report Olson and Douglas (1997).

Gender Role Stereotypes and Preferences

When young North American children are asked which personality characteristics are masculine and which are feminine, they generally agree on the characteristics for each gender. And when they are asked about boys' and girls' toys and preferences, they again show marked agreement. Interestingly, however, both boys and girls are far more likely to think that girls might like boys' toys and activities than the opposite. When Henshaw, Kelly, and Gratton (1992) questioned groups of 8- and 9-year-old boys and girls, they found that only 7 percent of the children thought "John" might like girls' toys; in contrast, half agreed that "Sally" might like boys' toys.

In this study, there were many indications that masculine roles are more constraining than feminine roles. Although it is often acceptable for girls to show masculine interests and to engage in masculine activities, it is far less acceptable for boys to be feminine. "Girls in trousers are acceptable in a way that boys in dresses will probably never be," note Henshaw and colleagues (1992, p. 230). Or, as one of the boys in this study put it, "Skipping's for girls—I wouldn't skip and my friends wouldn't skip" (p. 234). Interestingly, even highly nontraditional, female teachers (described by the researchers as "feminist") appear to be far more tolerant of cross-gender role aspirations and behaviors among girls than among boys (Cahill & Adams, 1997).

---

gender identity disorder A label for the relatively rare condition where individuals don't feel comfortable with their anatomical sex—where they feel themselves to *be* the other sex and have strong preferences for that alternative.

aggression In human beings, a much-studied characteristic that is generally defined as the conscious and willful inflicting of pain on others.

North American gender stereotypes have traditionally reflected strong agreement about the appropriateness and likelihood of certain behaviors for girls and boys. But there are growing indications of change.

Parents, too, agree on proper behavior for boys and girls. In general, they feel that boys should be more aggressive, more boisterous, more adventurous, and less emotional and that girls should be more passive, more tender, more emotional, and less boisterous (Holland, Magoon, & Spokane, 1981).

Although boys might be more constrained by their roles, both boys and girls generally agree that the masculine role is the preferable role, as is shown dramatically in the "sex-change" study conducted by Tavris and Baumgartner (1983). The study is simple and straightforward: Boys and girls were asked, "If you woke up tomorrow and discovered that you were a girl (boy), how would your life be different?" "Terrible," the boys answered. "That would be a catastrophe." "A disaster." "I would immediately commit suicide." "I would be very depressed." But the girls responded very differently: "Great," they said. "Now I can do what I want." "Now I can play sports." "Now I can be happy."

When, Intons-Peterson (1988) replicated this study five years later, using the same sex-change question, she reported no major changes

and no surprises. Boys still responded negatively to the thought of becoming female. They saw girls as more passive, weaker, more restricted in their activities, more emotional, and burdened by menstruation. And although most girls were content with their gender, the majority nevertheless responded to the sex-change question by describing what they saw as the highly positive aspects of being male. They viewed males as more active, less concerned with their appearance, more aggressive, more athletic, and better able to travel and develop a career.

One Example of Gender Inequity In recent decades, strong opposition has developed against the basic inequities of gender roles and the stereotypes that they foster and against the injustices of traditionally male-dominated societies. And much progress has been made in reducing gender inequities, although much remains to be done. For example, although the number of women working outside the home has increased significantly—in the United States, 61 percent of all women above age 16 in 1995, compared with 38 percent in 1960 (U.S. Bureau of the Census, 1997)—jobs held by women are still not on a par with jobs held by men in terms of status, prestige, or income. In Canada, the average income for women is approximately 62 percent the average for men (Statistics Canada, 1996); in the United States, it's about 66 percent (U.S. Bureau of the Census, 1996). In 1994, women with a bachelor's degree or more could expect to earn about as much as men with one or two years of college—and less than two-thirds as much as men who also had college degrees (see Figure 3.1).

Gender Differences

Parents, children, and society in general assume that there are important differences between males and females and that these differences should be reflected in their attitudes, interests,

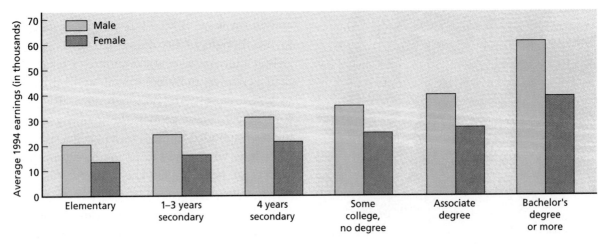

FIGURE 3.1 U.S. male and female earnings by educational attainment in 1997 (based on U.S. Bureau of the Census, 1996, p. 474)

and behaviors—in other words, in their different *gender roles.* Most of us can even agree on the nature of these differences with little difficulty. But just because our naïve psychologies agree does not mean that they are always correct.

Following an early review of research on gender differences, Maccoby and Jacklin (1974) suggested four areas in which gender differences are significant: (1) verbal ability, particularly in the early grades, favoring females; (2) mathematical ability, favoring males; (3) spatial-visual ability (evident in geographic orientation, for example), favoring males; and (4) aggression (lower among females).

But many of these differences no longer seem as clear at the turn of the century as they did in 1974. In fact, gender differences among adolescents, especially in academic areas, have declined dramatically in recent decades (Slate et al., 1998). There is mounting evidence that when early experiences are similar many of these male–female differences are nonexistent. Furthermore, even when differences are found, they tend to be modest and far from universal. Still, to the extent that there might be predictable differences in school-related areas such as verbal ability and science and mathematical achievement, these differences can be important for teachers. Knowledge that there are

no consistent gender differences might be even more important.

Verbal Ability Differences in verbal ability, which were once thought to favor girls (especially in the early elementary grades), are no longer readily apparent. For example, Rosen (1995) found no significant differences between boys and girls on measures of verbal ability. Similarly, Robinson and associates (1996) found no gender differences in verbal measures among groups of preschoolers.

Mathematics and Science There is evidence, however, that boys do better than girls on measures of mathematical skills, beginning very early in elementary school (Robinson et al., 1966; Fennema et al., 1998). The same appears to be true for sciences such as physics and chemistry. And for both mathematics and science, gender differences often appear to increase at adolescence (Burkam, Lee, & Smerdon, 1997).

Males are also more variable than females on most tests (Bielinski & Davison, 1998; Hedges & Friedman, 1993). That is, more males are at the highest and at the lowest levels.

The reasons for these gender differences are not entirely clear. There is some evidence, for example, that girls tend to use more concrete strategies when solving problems. Boys' use of more abstract approaches might help them perform better, especially with more advanced problems (Sowder, 1998). Also, gender differences in mathematics and science achievement are closely related to culturally determined interests and motivation. For example, Jovanovic and King (1998) report that, even in performance-based science classrooms where the emphasis is on active participation, girls participate significantly less than boys do. And, not surprisingly, girls' personal estimates of their abilities in science tend to decrease with the passage of time.

Hyde and Jaffee (1998) suggest that teachers' stereotypes about the different abilities and interests of boys and girls may well lead teachers to treat them differently and to expect different levels of performance from them. Interestingly, several studies conducted in Hawaii in schools marked by a more egalitarian view of males and females report results that are directly opposed to those most often reported in North America. In those studies, girls typically perform better than boys on standardized mathematics tests (Brandon, Newton, & Hammond, 1987).

The Implications of Gender Roles for Teaching

Knowledge of gender roles and gender stereotypes are clearly important for teachers—keeping in mind that many apparent gender differences are trivial (or even nonexistent) and others are quite unjust.

As a teacher, you need to know what interests individual students, what they're good at, and what they like to do. But although teachers need to treat all children equally and fairly, this doesn't mean that all children need to be treated in exactly the same manner. If girls are less interested than boys are in violent contact sports, it would be more than a little foolish to insist that they don shoulder pads and participate in the

school's football games. And if girls' interest in the opposite sex manifests itself earlier and sometimes expresses itself in different ways, that too needs to be taken into consideration. However, teachers sometimes desperately need to be aware of and to work to eliminate the many flagrant and subtle instances of sex bias that still permeate our attitudes, our books, our schools, and our society.

See the case "And for Noon Detention, Here Is the List . . ." for examples of gender inequities that persist in today's schools. These inequities are found in three areas, note Sadker, Sadker, and Klein (1991):

1. There is still sexism in school administration. At Wes Horman School, the principal and vice principal are both male; the majority of teachers are female. In the United States in 1988, fewer than one-third of elementary school principals and 11 percent of high school principals were female (and about 4 percent of superintendents (Jones & Montenegro, 1988). Yet most teachers are female. And in recent years, female graduate students in education have outnumbered male graduate students (National Center for Education Statistics, 1989).

2. There is inequity in the treatment of students. When Tom and Teddy called out, Ms. Fenna responded to them directly. But when Rosa echoed Tom, Ms. Fenna reprimanded her: "In this class, we raise our hand," said she.

   Is this unusual? No. At virtually all educational levels, teachers interact more with male students than with female students (Sadker & Sadker, 1986). On average, boys receive more instructional time and attention from their teachers. They also receive more praise and more encouragement. And, like the detainees at Wes Horman School, they are also more often the subject of reprimands and punishment.

3. Sexual stereotypes are still found in books, in the curriculum, in classroom examples, and

And for Noon Detention, Here Is the List . . .

THE TIME: EARLY MORNING AT WES HORMAN SCHOOL

THE PLACE: MS. FENNA'S FIFTH-GRADE CLASS

Morning messages are just ending on the intercom. "And," says Mr. Sawchuk, school principal, "for noon detention in Mr. Klein's office, the list is Ronald West, Frank Twolips, Eddie Mio, and Eddie Nyberg . . . and I hope there won't be any more by noon."

Ms. Fenna: You heard that, Ronald?

Ronald nods.

"Also," continues Mr. Sawchuk, "grade sixers who aren't going on the field trip: The boys will spend the day in Mr. Klein's phys ed classes, and the girls will go to the art room. . . . That's all."

Ms. Fenna: Now, class, I want you to open your math workbooks to page 34, which we started yesterday, and finish the assignment on that page before we go on.

Tom Larsen: I finished mine. What can I do now?

Ms. Fenna: I'll come check it in a minute.

Rosa Donner: Me too.

Ms. Fenna: In this class, we raise our hand, Rosa.

Teddy Langevin: Can we read our Tom Sawyers if we're finished?

Ms. Fenna: How many are finished with page 34?

---

elsewhere. At Wes Horman school, boys who need looking after because they did not go on a field trip are sent to gym classes; girls are sent to the art room. And for those who have finished their arithmetic, the reading assignment is *Tom Sawyer*. Although "male hero" books are no longer as pervasive in schools as they once were, boys are often portrayed as more dominant and girls as more helpless (Sadker, Sadker, & Klein, 1991).

It isn't sufficient simply to know that schools reflect much of the racism, the sexism, and other prejudices of our society. Teachers (and principals) need to be on guard constantly, lest they unconsciously propagate the same old stereotypes and inequities. In the United States, gender equity is mandated by laws that prohibit discrimination by sex in any federally funded educational program. But this doesn't mean, as Klein and Ortman (1994) point out, that all inequities have been wiped out. There is still much to be done.

PERSONALITY DEVELOPMENT: ERIK ERIKSON

Gender is one very important aspect of our **personality**. But personality is much more than our notions of being male or female together with related attitudes and interests. It includes all of the abilities, predispositions, habits, and other qualities that make each of us different from every other person.

Precisely how personality develops—for example, the extent to which personality characteristics are innate or result from our experiences—is not entirely certain. But one highly useful theory of personality development for teachers is that of Erik Erikson.

Much of Erikson's theory was inspired by Sigmund Freud. Unlike Freud, however, Erikson

---

personality The set of characteristics that we typically manifest in our interactions with others. It includes all the abilities, predispositions, habits, and other qualities that make each of us different.

downplays the importance of sexuality and sexual conflicts in human development. Instead, he emphasizes the importance of the child's social environment. The result is a theory of **psychosocial** rather than **psychosexual** development. The major emphasis in Erikson's theory is on the development of a healthy self-concept, or **identity**, to use his term.

Psychosocial Stages

One of Erikson's most important contributions to the study of human development, argues Eagle (1997), is that he extended development beyond childhood. Development, says Erikson, doesn't end with childhood but spans the entire course of life. It can be described in terms of eight stages. The first five stages span infancy, childhood, and adolescence; the last three describe adulthood. Each stage involves a conflict, brought about mainly by a person's need to adapt to the social environment. And because the demands of a given environment tend to be much the same for all individuals within that culture, we tend to go through the same stages at about the same ages—hence the notion of stages.

Trust versus Mistrust For example, for infants to adapt to an initially complex and largely bewil-

dering world, they have to develop a sense in this world—although they are initially mistrustful because the world is strange and unfamiliar. Hence, the basic psychosocial conflict is *trust versus mistrust*. Resolving the conflict results in a sense of competence and enables infants to continue to develop and grow. The most important person in a child's life during this first stage, says Erikson, is the mother or another primary caregiver. That is because successful resolution of the conflict between trust and mistrust depends largely on the infant's relationship with this caregiver and on the gradual realization that the world is predictable, safe, and loving. According to Erikson, if the world is unpredictable and the caregiver is rejecting, the infant may grow up to be mistrustful and anxious.

Autonomy versus Shame and Doubt Initially, infants don't deliberately act upon the world; instead, they *react* to it. Sucking, for example, is something that happens when stimulation is appropriate; it isn't something that the infant deliberately decides to do. But during the second year of life, children gradually begin to realize that they are the authors of their own actions. As a result, they begin to develop a sense of autonomy. Now, it's important for parents to encourage their attempts to explore and to provide opportunities for independence. Overprotectiveness can lead to doubt and uncertainty in dealing with the world.

Initiative versus Guilt By the age of 4 or 5, children have begun to develop a sense of autonomy—a sense that they are separate individuals. Now they must discover who they are. This discovery, Erikson (1959) explains, comes about largely as a result of children identifying with their parents. Erikson, true to his Freudian orientation, assumed that children seek to discover who they are—and, in fact, become what they will be—largely by trying to be like their parents.

---

psychosocial Pertaining to events or behaviors that relate to the social aspects of development. Erikson's theory is psychosocial; it deals with the resolution of social crises and the development of social competencies (independence or identity, for example).

psychosexual A term used to describe psychological phenomena based on sexuality. Freud's theories are psychosexual because they attribute development to sexually based forces and motives.

identity In Erikson's theory, a term closely related to self. Identity refers to the individual's self-definition, a sort of personal sense of who and what one is. To achieve identity is to arrive at a clear notion of who one is. One of the important tasks of adolescence is to select and develop a strong sense of identity.

During this stage of development, children's worlds expand dramatically, not only in a physical sense, but also through their use of language. With their increasing ability to explore and know the world, children need to develop a sense of initiative with respect to their own behaviors. They are autonomous as well as responsible for initiating behavior. The central process involved in resolving the initiative versus guilt conflict is one of identification, so the parents and the family continue to be the most important influences in children's development—although preschool teachers may now begin to assume an increasingly important role. Parents and teachers should encourage the young child's sense of initiative and nurture a sense of responsibility, claims Erikson.

Industry versus Inferiority The fourth developmental phase spans the elementary school years. Keeping in mind that each of Erikson's stages reflects the principal social/cultural demands in the child's life, this stage is naturally marked by children's increasing need to interact with and be accepted by peers. It now becomes vital that children receive assurance that their selves, their identities, are significant, worthwhile. During this stage, children often take advantage of opportunities to learn things that they think are important in their culture. It is as though, by so doing, they hope that they will become someone important. And successful resolution of this stage's conflict depends largely on how significant agencies—especially schools and teachers—respond to children's efforts. Recognition and praise are crucial for developing a positive self-concept. If children's work is continually demeaned, seldom praised, and rarely rewarded, the outcome may well be a lasting sense of inferiority.

Identity versus Identity Diffusion Adolescence brings with it an extremely critical, and sometimes very difficult, task: that of developing a strong sense of identity. The crisis implicit in this stage concerns a conflict between a strong sense of self and a vague, uncertain **self-concept**.

The formation of an identity, notes Erikson (1959), involves arriving at a notion not so much of who one is but rather of who one can be. The source of conflict is the almost overwhelming number of possibilities open to children. The conflict is made worse by the variety of models and the opposing values evident in society. In the absence of clear commitment to values, and perhaps to vocational goals as well, adolescents are in a state of **identity diffusion**. Later in adolescence, children may experiment with a variety of identities. In this sense, Erikson explains, adolescence serves as a sort of "moratorium"—a period during which adolescents can try out different roles without a final commitment. The crisis of adolescence is simply the conflict between the need to find an identity and the difficulties involved in doing so. And resolution of the crisis is implicit in the achievement of a relatively mature identity—which is not something that all adolescents manage to achieve by the time they are out of their teens.

Erikson's description of adolescent identity formation has been clarified by Marcia (1966, 1993). There are essentially four distinct types of identity status, explains Marcia, each distinguishable in terms of the absence or presence of crises and commitments: *identity diffusion; foreclosure; moratorium;* and *identity achieved.*

Adolescents in a state of identity diffusion are characterized by a total lack of commitment and by the absence of any real crisis. These are

---

self-concept The concept that an individual has of him- or herself. Notions of the self are often closely allied with individuals' beliefs about how others perceive them.

identity diffusion An expression for a stage in early adolescence. During this stage the adolescent has a vague and changing sense of identity with no firm vocational commitment and an ambiguous belief system.

individuals whose political, social, and religious beliefs are either ambiguous or nonexistent and who have no vocational aspirations. Identity diffusion is characteristic of early adolescence. Older adolescents (and adults) marked by identity diffusion are recognizable as full-time "fun-seekers" says Marcia, or as immature and disturbed individuals characterized by high anxiety and low self-confidence (Marcia, 1980).

Foreclosure describes a strong commitment to an identity without having gone through a crisis. Foreclosure is often characteristic of individuals reared in close-knit religious communities where there is no need to make vocational, political, or religious choices. The most striking characteristic of *foreclosure* individuals is obedience and high adherence to authoritarian values.

Erikson describes adolescence as a developmental period that provides adolescents with an opportunity to experiment with various roles and to toy with vague, changing commitments while struggling with the problems of developing a strong sense of identity. In this sense, adolescence is a **moratorium**. Moratorium individuals are those who are not yet committed (to occupational, political, or religious roles, for example) and who are going through crises of varying severity.

Identity-achieved adolescents are those who have experienced a crisis and made a choice (commitment). Note, however, that identity develops independently in different areas. For example, an adolescent who is married and has a

child has achieved a relatively high level of identity with respect to social relationships, but the same adolescent might still be in a stage of identity diffusion or moratorium with respect to career development.

Adolescents who have achieved a sense of identity, notes Marcia (1980), are more independent, better able to cope with stress, and marked by higher self-esteem.

However, as for all of Erikson's stages, solutions for the crises and conflicts of adolescence are seldom static and completely permanent. Throughout life, explains Cavell (1996), we continue to achieve our identities and to build on them. And the outcome is partly a result of what we have been given (by nature) and partly a result of what we, ourselves, have been able to build as we struggle to achieve social competence and meaningfulness. (See Table 3.1 for a summary of Marcia's descriptions of identity status.)

Stages of Adulthood Erikson describes three additional psychosocial conflicts that occur during adulthood and old age. Each of these reflects the most common social realities in North American cultures. And each requires new competencies and adjustments.

The first of the adult stages, *intimacy and solidarity versus isolation*, reflects most adults' need for intimate relationships with others (as opposed to being isolated). Such relationships are especially important for those who seek marital and parental roles. For others, developmental tasks might be quite different.

The second adult stage, *generativity versus self-absorption*, describes individuals' need to take on social, work-related, and community responsibilities that will be beneficial to others (generative). The basic conflict here is between a tendency to remain preoccupied with the self (as are adolescents, for example) and cultural demands that individuals contribute to society in various ways.

---

foreclosure Marcia's term for the adoption of a ready-made identity.

moratorium Erikson's term for the social function of the hiatus between childhood and adulthood. In Marcia's description, moratorium individuals are those who have not yet made a commitment and who are in a state of crisis (conflict) as they examine and experiment with various identities.

identity achieved Marcia's term for individuals who have experienced a crisis and made a commitment, thus achieving a sense of identity.

TABLE 3.1
Marcia's Descriptions of Identity Status in Terms of Crisis and Commitment*

STATUS	COMMITMENT	CRISIS	CHARACTERISTICS
Identity Diffusion	None	None	Ambiguous belief systems; no vocational commitment
Foreclosure	Strong	None	Commitment predetermined by political, social, or religious affiliation
Moratorium	None	Yes	Period of exploration of alternatives
Identity Achieved	Yes	Finished	Crisis finished; commitment made; higher independence and self-esteem; clearer sense of self

*A crisis is defined as a period of active and conscious decision making during which various alternatives are examined and evaluated. Commitment is acceptance of a combination of political, social, religious, or vocational alternatives. The level of crisis and commitment can be different in each of these areas.

The final adult stage in the human lifespan, *integrity versus despair*, has to do with facing the inevitability of our own death and realizing that life has meaning—that we should not despair even though the end of life is imminent. (Erikson's stages are summarized in Table 3.2.)

The Relevance of Erikson's Theory for Teachers

Erikson's theory, notes Douvan (1997), has had a profound influence on psychoanalysis, on psychology, and yes, on how we view children and adolescents. This theory is especially important for teachers because of the insights it provides concerning normal, healthy development. It also emphasizes the role of teachers and parents in helping children to develop the competencies that underlie the successful resolution of developmental conflicts.

According to Erikson, although developmental progress involves resolving major conflicts by acquiring new competencies, the resolution is never quite complete. That is, aspects of each of the central conflicts that describe one developmental stage may be present throughout life. As Baltes and Silverberg (1994) note, for example, the conflict between the need to be autonomous and the urge to remain dependent continues after infancy. In the same way, the need to trust and the opposing tendency to mistrust also continues throughout life.

To the extent that each of Erikson's stages reflects some truth about human nature, perhaps about our most basic tendencies and conflicts, it can help teachers to better understand children. And just as parents are the most important source of influence in the lives of infants, so too are teachers a fundamental source of influence in the lives of schoolchildren. Erikson's theory emphasizes the importance of the child's self-concept. As we have noted, teachers can do a great deal to enhance self-concept. They can also do a great deal to facilitate the adolescent's occasional struggles with issues of identity.

COGNITIVE DEVELOPMENT

Cognition, says my dictionary, is "the art or faculty of knowing." Hence, cognitive theorists are concerned with how we obtain, process, and use information. *Cognitive development* refers to the

---

cognition To cognize is to know. Hence, cognition deals with knowing, understanding, problem solving, and related intellectual processes.

TABLE 3.2
Erikson's Eight Psychosocial Stages

ERIKSON'S PSYCHOSOCIAL STAGES	FREUD'S CORRESPONDING PSYCHOSEXUAL STAGES	PRINCIPAL DEVELOPMENTAL TASK	IMPORTANT INFLUENCES FOR POSITIVE DEVELOPMENTAL OUTCOME
Trust vs. mistrust	Oral (0–18 months)	Developing sufficient trust in the world to explore it	Mother; warm, loving interaction
Autonomy vs. shame and doubt	Anal (18 months– 2 or 3 years)	Developing feeling of control over behavior; realizing that intentions can be acted out	Supportive parents; imitation
Initiative vs. guilt	Phallic (2 or 3–6 years)	Developing a sense of self through identification with parents and a sense of responsibility for own actions	Supportive parents; identification
Industry vs. inferiority	Latency (6–11 years)	Developing a sense of self-worth through interaction with peers	Schools, teachers; learning and education; encouragement
Identity vs. identity diffusion	Genital (11 years and older)	Developing a strong sense of identity—of ego (self); selecting among various potential selves	Peers and role models; social pressure
Intimacy vs. isolation	Genital (young adulthood)	Developing close relationships with others; achieving the intimacy required for marriage	Spouse, colleagues, partners, society
Generativity vs. self-absorption	Genital (adulthood)	Assuming responsible adult roles in the community; contributing; being worthwhile	Spouse, children, friends, colleagues, community
Integrity vs. despair	Genital (older adulthood)	Facing death; overcoming potential despair; coming to terms with the meaningfulness of life	Friends, relatives, children, spouse, community and religious support

Source: Derived from *Identity and the Life Cycle* by Erik H. Erikson, used by permission of W. W. Norton & Company, Inc. Copyright © 1980 by W. W. Norton & Company, Inc. Copyright © 1959 by International Universities Press, Inc.

stages and processes involved in the child's intellectual development.

In the remainder of this chapter, we look at cognitive development, paying particular attention to the theory of the Swiss psychologist Jean Piaget—a theory that is easily the most influential child development theory of the 20th century. Piaget's approach examines how a child's interaction with the environment leads to cognitive development. In this chapter we also look at Lev Vygotsky's theory, which is mainly concerned with how culture and language affect development.

PIAGET'S MOST BASIC IDEAS

Piaget's theory presents a complicated and fascinating view of human development that he refined over a career that spanned seven decades (he died at age 84 in 1982). During this career, he produced, by one count, 52 books and 478 articles (five more articles and another five books were published after his death)—a total of more than 26,000 pages (Smith, 1993). All of this writing was in French, and many of the books and articles were coauthored by Barbel Inhelder, his closest associate and collaborator. Much of Piaget's work, although far from all of it, has been translated. But, complains Jurczak (1997), translators often imposed their own views on Piaget's sometimes obscure writings, frequently leaving out or changing his metaphors and, in the process, blurring links among important ideas.

Perhaps the most basic of all of Piaget's ideas, notes von Glasersfeld (1997), is this: *Human development is a process of adaptation. And the highest form of human adaptation is cognition (or knowing).*

This view owes a great deal to the fact that Piaget's early training was in biology rather than psychology. As a result, he approached the study of children as would a biologist, asking the two fundamental questions of the evolutionary biologist:

1. Which characteristics of the organisms under study enabled them to adapt to their environments?

2. What is the simplest, most accurate, and most useful way to classify living organisms?

Translated to a study of children, these questions become:

1. What are the characteristics of children that enable them to adapt to their environment?

2. What is the simplest, most accurate, and most useful way to classify or order child development?

Piaget's answers to these questions form the basis of his theory. Many of these answers result from the application of a special technique for studying children developed by Piaget: the

méthode clinique. This is an interview approach in which the experimenter has a relatively clear idea of the questions to ask and of how to phrase them. However, using this approach, the investigator occasionally allows the child's answers to determine the next series of questions. Hence, the technique provides for the possibility that the child will give unexpected answers and that further questioning will lead to new discoveries about thinking.

Piaget's answers to the two questions of biology (What permits adaptation and how can development be classified?) are complex and detailed but can be simplified, as follows:

Assimilation and Accommodation Permit Adaptation

"Babies are very competent," says Bower (1989). "They are set to use whatever information we give them" (p. ix). Even the newborn is a remarkable little sensing machine. Almost from birth, it can detect sounds, odors, sights, tastes, and touches; it can respond by squirming and wriggling, by crying, by flinging its limbs about and grasping things, and by sucking.

Characteristics of the Newborn But can it think? Does it have a store of little ideas? Of budding concepts? We can't answer these questions easily; the **neonate** (newborn) doesn't communicate well enough to tell us. But Piaget tells us that the child probably does not have ideas or concepts—does not think—in the sense that we ordinarily define these terms. The newborn does not have a store of memories or hopes and dreams—does

---

méthode clinique Piaget's experimental method involving an interview technique where questions are determined largely by the subject's responses. The flexibility of this method distinguishes it from ordinary interview techniques.

neonate A newborn infant. The neonatal period terminates when an infant regains birth weight (about two weeks after birth).

not have a fund of information about which, and with which, to think.

But what this little sensing machine does have are the characteristics necessary for acquiring information. Flavell (1985) describes these characteristics somewhat like this: *First*, in order for the human system to acquire as much information as quickly as it does, it must be predisposed to process an extraordinary amount of information, even when there is no tangible reward (such as food) for doing so; that is, the system must be primarily intrinsically (internally) motivated—it must derive satisfaction from its own functioning and from the gradual acquisition of information.

Second, the human information processing system must be preset to focus on the most informative—and therefore the most cognitively useful—aspects of the environment. Accordingly, the system must respond most strongly to novelty, surprise, and incongruity. It should search out the unexpected, because there the greatest amount of new information can be found. Similarly, it should be pretuned to attend to speech sounds and to make the hundreds of subtle distinctions that are so important for learning a language.

The human newborn that Jean Piaget describes is exactly such a system. It continually seeks out and responds to stimulation, and by so doing it gradually builds up a repertoire of behaviors and capabilities. The system is initially limited to simple reflexive behaviors, such as sucking and grasping. Rapidly, however, these behaviors become more complex, more coordinated, and eventually purposeful. The process by which this occurs is **adaptation**. And, to answer the question posed just before the beginning of this section, adaptation is made possible through the twin processes of **assimilation** and **accommodation**.

Assimilation and Accommodation Assimilation involves making a response that has already been acquired; to accommodate is to change a response. Or, phrased another way, to assimilate is to respond in terms of pre-existing information using previously learned behaviors. This often involves ignoring some aspects of the situation to make the response fit. In contrast, to accommodate is to change a behavior in response to a given situation. As a result, explains Piaget, assimilation involves little change in the child's cognitive system because old learning and old behaviors are being used and practiced. But accommodation involves changes in the mental system because old behaviors and old learning are now being modified.

As an illustration, imagine an infant lying idly in her crib, not doing anything in particular. Now she waves her little hands haphazardly in the air, and one of them comes in contact with a pacifier that is fastened to her shirt by means of a safety pin and a length of purple ribbon. Her hand closes immediately around the familiar object, raises it into the air, and brings it unerringly to her mouth, which has already opened in anticipation and which closes greedily around the rubber end of the pacifier. Suck! Suck! Suck!

In Piaget's terms, there are **schemata** (singular: *schema*) involved here—mental representations of the infant's knowledge of pacifiers,

---

adaptation Changes in an organism in response to the environment. Such changes are assumed to facilitate interaction with that environment. Adaptation plays a central role in Piaget's theory.

assimilation The act of incorporating objects or aspects of objects into previously learned activities. To assimilate is, in a sense, to ingest or to use something that was previously learned.

accommodation Modification of an activity or ability in the face of environmental demands. In Piaget's description of development, assimilation and accommodation are the means individuals use to interact with and adapt to their world.

schemata (*sing.*: schema) The label used by Piaget to describe a unit in cognitive structure. A schema is, in one sense, an activity together with whatever structural connotations that activity has. In another sense, a schema may be thought of as an idea or a concept.

including information concerning their suitability as objects to be grasped, to be transported toward the mouth, and to be sucked. The pacifier is being *assimilated* to these schemata; it is being understood and dealt with in terms of previous learning.

Imagine, now, that a generous grandmother replaces the infant's familiar old pacifier with a brand new one—one of those with the patented Easy Suck bulb on one end and an Easy Grab plastic knob on the other. The infant swings her tiny arms around again until one pudgy little hand accidentally strikes the new object. Her hand closes on it at once; that's what hands are for. And again, her mouth begins to open; that's one of the important ways of exploring the world. Besides, in the very beginning, what can't be sucked on isn't all that valuable.

But the Easy Grab knob is too large, the little girl's grip is inadequate, and the new pacifier squirts away.

"Here, sweetie," grandmother purrs, shoving the object back into the child's hand. Now the infant's grip is rounder, more secure; subtle changes have occurred in the positioning of the fingers and in the pressure of the palm. In Piaget's terms, she has begun to *accommodate* to the characteristics of this new object. She has *adapted*. As a result, the mental system—the arrangement of schemata—has changed in subtle ways.

Assimilation and accommodation are the processes that make adaptation possible throughout life. However, these are not separate and independent processes. All activity, Piaget maintains, involves both assimilation and accommodation. We cannot begin to make changes in schemata (to accommodate) without first having some basis for responding—that is, relevant previous learning to which we can assimilate new situations. Thus, all accommodation requires assimilation. All instances of assimilation also involve some degree of change to

schemata, no matter how familiar the situation or how well learned the response—even if the change is no more significant than that the response will be a tiny fraction better learned and more readily available in the future. As Flavell (1985) phrases it, assimilation and accommodation are simply two sides of the same cognitive coin; both always occur together.

Equilibration One of the governing principles of mental activity, explains Piaget, is a tendency to maintain a balance between assimilation and accommodation. (He labels the process of maintaining this balance **equilibration**.) At one extreme, if the infant always assimilated stimulation to previous learning and responses, there would be no new learning. Everything would simply be sucked or looked at or grasped in the same way as always—a state of disequilibrium that would lead to little cognitive change (hence, little learning). On the other hand, if everything were always accommodated to, behavior would be in a constant state of flux, forever changing—again an extreme state of disequilibrium resulting in little new learning.

As a further illustration, using a school-related example, if Matthew always calculates area by multiplying two dimensions of a figure, he can be said to be assimilating all area problems to what he has already learned about the area of squares and rectangles. This state of disequilibrium will lead to an incorrect answer every time an area problem involves a different geometric figure (such as a circle or a triangle), and it will also result in little new learning about calculating area. However, if Matthew insists on using a different method of calculating area each

---

equilibration A Piagetian term for the process by which we maintain a balance between assimilation (using old learning) and accommodation (changing behavior, learning new things). Equilibration is essential for adaptation and cognitive growth.

time he is faced with a new problem, he will be accommodating (modifying responses) excessively and inappropriately. Again, this state of disequilibrium will lead to few correct answers and not much new learning.

Factors that Shape Development The tendency toward equilibration, says Piaget (1961), is one of the four great forces that shape a child's development, accounting for the *construction* of knowledge. The second is *maturation*, a biologically based process closely related to the gradual unfolding of potential. According to Piaget's system, maturation does not actually determine development but simply makes certain kinds of learning possible and even probable. Thus, physical maturation allows infants to learn to control tongue, lip, and mouth movements, enabling them to learn to speak. But without the right experiences, of course, physical maturation alone would not result in a child who speaks. Hence, the need for *active experience*, another of the four factors that shape development. Through active interaction with the real world, claims Piaget, the child develops important notions about objects and their properties. Similarly, through *social interaction*—that is, interaction with other people—children elaborate their ideas about things, about others, and about the self. The importance that Piaget

assigned to social interaction has largely been underestimated, claims DeVries (1997). (See Table 3.3.)

Human Development Consists of Stages

The answer to the second of Piaget's questions (What is the simplest, most accurate, and most useful way to classify or order child development?) is found in Piaget's description of the series of stages through which children progress as they develop. Each of these stages is characterized by certain kinds of behaviors and certain ways of thinking and solving problems. Piaget's descriptions of these ways of solving problems, of behaving, and of thinking can be valuable for helping teachers to understand their students. This is essentially a description of how cognitive structure develops and changes.

CONSTRUCTION OF THE INTELLECT: PIAGET'S THEORY

One of the main purposes of theories of intellectual development (also called cognitive theories) is to describe both how we process perceptual (sensory) information to derive meaning from it

---

TABLE 3.3
Piaget's Four Factors that Shape Development

The development of progressively more advanced ways of representing the world and of interacting with it (that is, the construction of knowledge) depends on:

EQUILIBRATION	The tendency to balance assimilation (responding in terms of previous learning) and accommodation (changing behavior in response to the environment)
MATURATION	Genetic forces that do not determine behavior but are related to its sequential unfolding
ACTIVE EXPERIENCE	Interaction with real objects and events allows individual to discover things and to invent (construct) mental representations of the world
SOCIAL INTERACTION	Interaction with people leads to the elaboration of ideas about things, people, and self

and how we organize the resulting meanings into long-term memory. In effect, the organization of our long-term memories defines what is meant by **cognitive structure**.

Piaget is a cognitive theorist. His principal interests have to do with the origins of cognitive structure—specifically, with its development from birth to adulthood. For Piaget, as for other cognitive theorists, cognitive structure can be thought of as the contents of the intellect—that is, those properties of the intellect that underlie knowledge and behavior. These properties are inferred rather than real. A cognitive structure can neither be isolated and looked at nor described in concrete terms. It is, after all, only a metaphor.

In newborns, cognitive structure consists of **reflexes**—the simple, unlearned behaviors (like sucking or grasping) of which the neonate is capable. Piaget labels each reflex a "schema." Schemata become more firmly established as children assimilate objects to them, and they change as children accommodate to objects. A schema is usually named for the activity it represents. For example, there is a sucking schema, a looking schema, a reaching schema, a grasping schema, even a crying schema. Structure in later stages of development, usually after age 7 or 8, is defined less in terms of overt acts than in terms of mental activity. By this age, says Piaget, children have succeeded in *internalizing* activities. By this he meant that they can now represent activities mentally—they can *think* them (and think *about* them as well).

In a sense, then, thought consists of internalized actions that are subject to certain rules of logic. These internalized actions and the rules to which they conform define the term **operation**. In its simplest sense, an operation is a logical thought process. In Piaget's system, operations, or mental activities, are an outgrowth of real activities with concrete objects.

Piaget's description of the stages of development is really a description of changes in cognitive structure that occur at certain ages. The details of these developmental changes are discussed next (see Table 3.4).

Sensorimotor Intelligence: Birth to 2 Years

During the first two years of life, Piaget explains, infants understand the world only in terms of the actions they perform and the sensations that result—hence, his label **sensorimotor intelligence**. It seemed to Piaget that, until the child develops a way to represent the world mentally, intelligent activity must be confined mainly to sensorimotor functions.

The Object Concept   The child's world at birth is a world of the here and now, says Piaget. Objects exist when they can be seen, heard, touched, tasted, or smelled; when they are removed from the infant's immediate sensory experience, they cease to be. One of the child's major achievements during the sensorimotor stage is the

---

cognitive structure The organized totality of an individual's knowledge. Also termed *mental structure.*

reflex A simple, unlearned stimulus–response link such as salivating in response to food in one's mouth or blinking in response to air blowing in one's eye. For Piaget, behavioral reflexes such as looking, reaching, grasping, and sucking are especially important for early intellectual development.

operation In Piaget's system, a term that remains relatively nebulous but essentially refers to a thought process. An operation is an action that has been internalized in the sense that it can be "thought" and is reversible in the sense that it can be "unthought."

sensorimotor intelligence The first stage of development in Piaget's classification. It lasts from birth to about age 2 and is so called because children understand their world during this period primarily in terms of their activities in it and sensations of it.

TABLE 3.4
Piaget's Stages of Cognitive Development

STAGE	APPROXIMATE AGE	SOME MAJOR CHARACTERISTICS
SENSORIMOTOR	0–2 years	Motoric intelligence; world of the here and now; no language, no thought in early stages; no notion of objective reality
PREOPERATIONAL	2–7 years	Egocentric thought
PRECONCEPTUAL	2–4 years	Reason dominated by perception
INTUITIVE	4–7 years	Intuitive rather than logical solutions; inability to conserve
CONCRETE OPERATIONS	7–11 or 12 years	Ability to conserve; logic of classes and relations; understanding the concept of number; thinking bound to concrete; development of reversibility in thought
FORMAL OPERATIONS	11 or 12–14 or 15 years	Complete generality of thought; propositional thinking; ability to deal with the hypothetical; development of strong idealism

acquisition of what Piaget calls the **object concept**—the notion that objects have a permanence and identity of their own and that they continue to exist even when they aren't being immediately sensed.

To investigate infants' understanding of the permanence of objects, Piaget (1954) devised a simple experiment: An attractive object is shown to an infant and then hidden. At the earliest level, children will not even look for the object, evidence that they believe it doesn't exist when they can no longer see or touch it. Older children will begin to search for the object if they have watched it being hidden. Not until around age 1 will children usually search for an object that they have not just seen.

The processes by which infants discover that the world is real and permanent depend on experiencing and interacting with real objects and events. Nor is this a trivial achievement. Our understanding of the world and our reasoning about it absolutely depend on our belief that

things are real and permanent and that they continue to exist even when we're not looking at them or touching them. It also depends on our belief that the physical world is subject to certain laws that allow us to predict the effects of different events. We are not born with this understanding, says Piaget; we develop it later.

Imitation One of the most important means by which young infants begin to develop understanding and to learn revolves around the process of **imitation** or what Piaget calls *internal representation*. Imitation is closely involved in the early acquisition of language, among other things.

Early in the sensorimotor period, there is no language but there is the beginning of symbolization—that is, the beginning of the internal representation of objects and events. This, says Piaget, is what makes thinking possible. In fact, as we saw, Piaget describes thought as the internalization of activity. Thinking begins when

---

object concept Piaget's expression for the child's understanding that the world is composed of objects that continue to exist apart from his or her perception of them.

imitation Copying behavior. To imitate a person's behavior is simply to use that person's behavior as a pattern. Piaget also terms this *internal representation*. Bandura and Walters describe three different effects of imitation.

children can represent to themselves (in a sense, imitate) a real activity. The first step in this process of internalization involves activities relating to objects or events that are in the children's immediate presence. At a later stage, that of **deferred imitation**, children can imitate in the absence of the object or event. This internal imitation is a symbolic representation of aspects of the environment. It is also the beginning of language, because words will eventually come to replace—that is, *represent*—more concrete actions or images.

Imitation in infancy makes at least three different kinds of learning possible, claim Hay, Stimson, and Castle (1991): (1) Children learn about *places* by imitating the movements of other people and following them around; (2) by copying the behaviors of peers and adults, children learn *familiar social behaviors* such as sharing toys; and (3) they learn *new social behaviors*, such as those involved in speaking a language, by observing them in others.

Accomplishments of the Sensorimotor Period
Among the important accomplishments of the sensorimotor period is the establishment of early internal representations of the world—the acquisition of internally controlled schemata. In other words, by age 2, children have made the transition from a purely perceptual and motor representation of the world to a more symbolic representation. They have begun to distinguish between perceiving and thinking.

A second major accomplishment is the development of a concept of objective reality. Much of children's development can be viewed in terms of how they organize and represent information about the world. As long as chil-

dren don't know that the world continues to exist by itself, they are not likely to have a very stable representation of it. Thus, the development of a notion of object constancy is absolutely essential for children's further cognitive development.

A third accomplishment of this period is the development of some recognition of cause and effect. This is an essential prerequisite for intention because intentional behavior is engaged in deliberately for its effect. Piaget sees intention as being inseparably linked with intelligence; for him, intelligent activity is activity that is, in fact, intentional.

Although these accomplishments describe children at the end of the period of sensorimotor intelligence, they are not the general characteristics of that period. Those are implicit in the label given to this stage: "sensorimotor." In general, the first two years of life are characterized by a motor representation of the world. The next stage progresses from the sensory and motor realm to the conceptual.

The Preoperational Period: 2 to 7 Years

The preoperational period is so called because, according to Piaget, children do not acquire operational (logical) thinking until around age 7. Until then, their fumbling attempts at logic abound with contradictions and errors.

The period of **preoperational thinking** is often described in terms of two substages: the period of preconceptual thought and the period of intuitive thought.

---

deferred imitation The ability to imitate people or events in their absence. Deferred imitation is assumed to be crucial in the development of language abilities.

preoperational thinking The second of Piaget's four major stages, lasting from around age 2 to age 7 or 8. It consists of two substages: intuitive thinking and preconceptual thinking.

Preconceptual Thought: 2 to 4 Years The period of **preconceptual thinking** is preconceptual not in the sense that children don't use concepts but because the concepts they use are incomplete and sometimes illogical.

Preconcepts Piaget illustrates this point by describing his young son's reaction to a snail they had seen while out walking one morning. The boy's reaction, paraphrased, went something like this:

"Papa! Cher Papa! Mon cher Papa!" (Swiss children love their papas.) "Papa! Papa! Papa!" he repeated. "Voici un escargot."

To which Piaget probably replied, "Mon fils, mon fils, mon cher fils! Oui, mon fils, c'est un escargot!" All of which is interesting, but not especially remarkable. However, a short while later they came across another snail, whereupon the boy again turned to his father and said, "Papa! Cher Papa! Mon cher Papa! Mon Papa! Voici encore l'escargot! Regardez! Regardez!"[1]

This, Piaget says, is an example of preconceptual thinking. The child does not yet understand that similar objects define classes (all snails are snails) but are not identical (snail A is not snail B). In the same way, a child who is shown four different Santa Clauses in four different stores, all on the same day, and who still thinks there is only one Santa Claus, is illustrating preconceptual thinking. She evidently knows something about the concept "Santa Claus," because she can recognize one, but she doesn't know that objects with similar characteristics can all belong to the same class, yet each have an identity of its own. Thus a young child who sees another child with a toy identical to one that he has at home can hardly be blamed for insisting that he be given back his toy.

Transduction Another feature of thinking in the preconceptual stage is that the preschooler often uses what is called **transductive reasoning**. *Inductive reasoning* proceeds from particular instances to a generalization (these 20,000 horses have manes; therefore, all horses have manes); *deductive reasoning* begins with the generalization and proceeds toward the particulars (all horses have manes; therefore, this new racehorse should have a mane). In contrast, transductive reasoning goes from particular instances to other particular instances. It is not a logical reasoning process, but it does occasionally lead to the correct answer. Consider, for example, the following transductive process:

A gives milk.

B gives milk.

Therefore, B is an A.

If A is a cow, and B is also a cow, then B is an A. However, if A is a cow but B is a goat, B is not an A. Surprising as it might seem, sound, young children do appear to reason in this way, as is evident when a child calls a dog "kitty" or a stranger "Daddy."

Animism Piaget (1960) illustrates another way in which the thinking of the preschooler is *preoperational* (or prelogical) when he relates a conversation he had with a young child as they walked. "Does the sun move?" asked Piaget (p. 215). "Yes," the child answered, going on to explain that the sun, like the moon, went wherever he went, that it stopped when he

---

preconceptual thinking The first substage in the period of preoperational thought, beginning around age 2 and lasting until age 4, so called because the child has not yet developed the ability to classify.

---

[1]***PPC:*** Should this be translated?

Author: But of course!

"Dad! Dear Dad! My dear Dad! Dad! Dad! Dad! Here is a snail. My son, my son, my dear son! Yes, my son, it is a snail. Dad! Dear Dad! My dear Dad! My Dad! Here is the snail again! Look! Look!"

---

transductive reasoning The type of reasoning that proceeds from particular to particular rather than from particular to general or from general to particular. One example of transductive reasoning is the following: Cows give milk. Goats give milk. Therefore goats are cows.

stopped, turned when he turned, moved fast when he ran, and that it must surely be alive.

The belief that inanimate things are alive illustrates **animism**. Animistic thinking grants a different magic to the thinking of the 2-year-old, a magic that sees life in all things that move or otherwise act as though they were alive. But even among preschoolers, animism has its limits. Bullock (1985) suggests to a 4-year-old that if the moon or the sun are alive because they move, then surely a car, which clearly moves, must also be alive. But the child is not so easily fooled. How can this thing of metal and rubber and plastic be alive? In fact, says Bullock, animistic thinking is relatively common among very young preschoolers, but it is rare among 4- and 5-year-olds. And even among the very young, animism is often limited to things like the sun, the moon, clouds, the wind, and other things about which even we adults are not always entirely certain; it seldom applies to rocks and trees and pitchers of cold water.

Intuitive Thought: 4 to 7 Years After age 4, children's thinking becomes somewhat more logical, although it is still largely dominated by **perception** rather than by reason. Thinking at this stage is characterized by egocentricity, improper classification, and intuition—hence, it is **intuitive thinking**.

The Egocentric Thought of Preschoolers As an example of **egocentrism**, Piaget describes the solutions given by children for this simple problem: Two dolls are placed side by side on a string.

One is a girl doll, the other a boy. A screen is placed between the child and the experimenter, who are facing each other. The experimenter holds one end of the string in each hand so that the dolls are hidden behind the screen. The child is asked to predict which doll will come out first if the string is moved toward the right. Whether the child is correct or not, the boy doll is moved out and hidden again. The question is repeated; again the boy doll will come out on the same side. This time, or perhaps next time, but almost certainly before many more trials, the child will predict that the other doll will come out. Why? "Because it's her turn. It isn't fair." The child interprets the problem only from a personal point of view, from an egocentric view.

Perception Dominated Preschooler's Thinking Michael, a 2-year-old, is asked to take a bead and place it in one of two containers. As he does so, a researcher places a bead in another container. They repeat this procedure until one of the containers is about half full. To confuse Michael, the researcher has put her beads in a low, flat dish whereas the Michael's container is tall and narrow. The researcher now asks, "Who has more beads? Or do we both have the same number?" "I have more," says Michael, "because they're higher." Or he might just as easily have said, "You have more 'cause they're bigger around." In either case, his answers reflect his reliance on the appearance of the containers. This reliance on perception, even when it conflicts with logic, is one of the major differences between children and adults.

Classification Problems Another striking characteristic of children's thinking during the intuitive period relates to the problems they experience with classification: 5-year-old Sandra is shown a collection of wooden beads; ten are brown and five are yellow. She acknowledges that

---

animism Attributing lifelike qualities to inanimate objects—as young children are wont to do.

perception The translation of physical energies into neurological impulses—that is, stimuli into sensations—that can be interpreted by the individual.

intuitive thinking One of the substages of Piaget's preoperational thought, beginning around age 4 and lasting until age 7 or 8, marked by the child's ability to solve many problems intuitively and also by the child's inability to respond correctly in the face of misleading perceptual features of problems.

egocentrism A way of functioning characterized by an inability to assume the point of view of others. A child's early thinking is largely egocentric.

Aren't Dinosaurs Real?

The Place: Marie's second-grade classroom

The Setting: A dinosaur expert from the Provincial Museum is visiting the class. He has brought with him what looks like a large stuffed tyrannosaurus.

Expert: Dinosaurs are extinct. Does anyone know what that means?

Roseanne: Means there's no more.

Billy: Means they stink bad. (burst of laughter)

Ronald: Means they're all gone and all dead and there's no more, and . . . and I don't know.

Expert: That's right. It means there's no more. They're all gone. They're extinct.

Roseanne (very seriously, pointing to the stuffed tyrannosaurus): Is that a real dinosaur?

---

all the beads are wooden, but when asked whether there are more, fewer, or the same number of brown beads as wooden beads, she says there are more. Piaget's explanation for this apparent contradiction of common sense is simply that asking children to consider the subclass (brown-colored beads in this case) destroys the larger class for them (all brown and yellow beads). In other words, children at this level understand that classes can contain many different but similar members (they would not make the preconceptual "escargot" error), but they do not yet understand that classes can be "nested," one inside the other, in hierarchies (as the class of brown beads is nested within that of wooden beads, each being separate but related).

Reliance on Intuition among Preschoolers Children's problem solving in this period is largely intuitive rather than logical. Whenever possible, mental images rather than rules or principles are used to arrive at answers, as is strikingly illustrated by Piaget's rotated-bead problem: Three different-colored beads are placed on a wire, and the wire is then inserted into a tube so that 4-year-old Linda can no longer see the beads. She knows, however, that the red one is on the left, the yellow in the middle, and the blue on the right. She is then asked what the order of the beads will be if the tube is rotated through a half turn, a full turn, one-and-a-half turns, two turns, and so on. Linda, like most young, preoperational children, is thoroughly confused by the question. Older children will solve it correctly as long as they can imagine the actual rotations—but they will not apply any rule to the solution of the problem (odd versus even number of turns, for example).

The thinking of 6- and 7-year-olds, says Piaget, is more magical than ours. It does not draw as fine a line between reality and imagination; the logic that governs it is less compelling and more easily swayed.

The dinosaur case (see "Aren't Dinosaurs Real?") shows how magical thinking operates. Dinosaurs are completely extinct, yet there remains the chilling possibility that there might still be a real one somewhere, maybe even in this classroom, today. When, later that day, the teacher asked this same class, apropos of something entirely different, "How many of you have ever seen a real dinosaur?" fully one-third of those little second-grade hands shot instantly in the air.

A Summary of Preconceptual Thinking In summary, the thought processes of the intuitive period are not always entirely logical. Often, they are egocentric and dominated by perception. Children have not yet acquired the ability to classify or apply formal rules of logic for problem solving. And one final significant difference between thought at this period and during the subsequent period of concrete operations is that preconceptual children have not yet acquired the ability to conserve.

Some of the general characteristics of preoperational thought are well illustrated by an experiment in which Fabricius and Wellman (1993) asked 4- to 6-year-olds to judge the distances covered by different routes going to the same destination. Some of the routes were direct, some were indirect, and some were segmented by different objects. Strikingly, many of the participants insisted that the indirect and segmented routes were shorter than the most direct routes. Why? Perhaps, suggest Fabricius and Wellman, because the children could only focus on one aspect of the route at a time, and were misled by appearances, as Piaget had suggested. And perhaps, too, because they had difficulty representing and comparing the routes mentally, thus making it very difficult for them to solve the problem intuitively.

One of the great advances of preoperational thinking over the sensorimotor period is that children begin to apply logic for solving problems, explains Smith (1993). But their attempts to use logic do not ensure that they will always answer correctly. In fact, the incomplete logic that preschoolers often use sometimes dooms them to

error. Consider, for example, the following simple problem: A child is shown a drawing of a jar partly filled with liquid, with the horizontal water level clearly shown, and is then asked to draw what the water level would look like in a tilted jar. When a 3- or 4-year-old is presented with this problem, the typical response, say Thomas and Lohaus (1993), is "a scribbling or the like" (p. 9). But when 5- to 7-year-olds are given the same problem, they immediately apply a clever but inappropriate logic, as is shown in part A of Figure 3.2. Kuhn (1984) points out that the children have never seen anything like this drawing; hence, the response does not reflect actual experience with the real world. But what it does reflect is an understanding that water level is ordinarily parallel to the bottom of its container, and a logical application of that understanding. (See Figure 3.3 for a summary of preoperational thought.)

> Readers who are not already familiar with Piaget should stop at this point.
>
> If you have available an electroencephalograph (EEG), a cardiograph, a thermometer, and a pupillometer (or any other graph or meter), these should be connected and read at once. Alpha waves, together with decelerated heart rate, abnormal temperature, and reduced pupil size, are symptoms of imminent **jargon shock**. This condition in its advanced stages can be extremely detrimental to concentration and learning. Several hours of sleep or another amusement can bring about a significant improvement.
>
> If you don't have any of this sophisticated electronic gadgetry readily available, you can substitute a hand mirror. Hold the mirror up to your face, and look at your eyes. If they are closed, you are probably in the terminal stage of jargon shock.

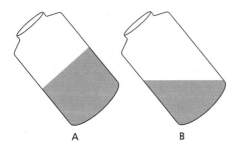

FIGURE 3.2 When young children are asked to draw the fluid level in a tilted jar, they typically draw the figure shown in A rather than B—not because they have ever seen anything like A in the real world, but because the logic they use in their attempts to make meaning out of their experiences is not always appropriate.

jargon shock See glossary entry on page 547.

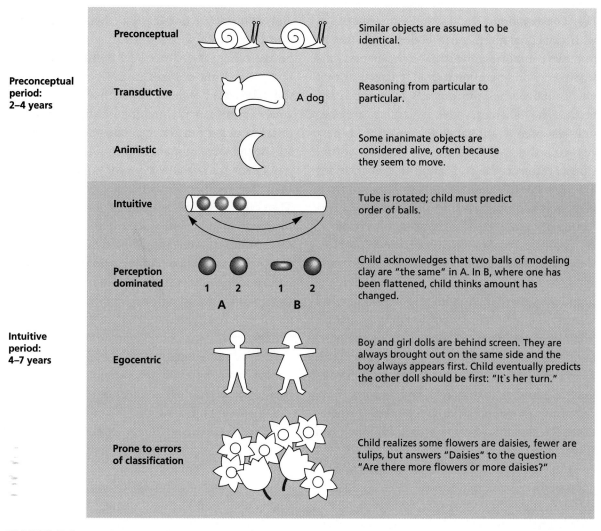

FIGURE 3.3 Some characteristics of preoperational thought

Concrete Operations: 7 to 11 or 12 Years

An operation is a mental activity—a thought, in other words—that is subject to certain rules of logic. Before the stage of concrete operations, children are described as preoperational not because they are incapable of thinking but because of the limitations on their thinking. As we saw, these limitations are related to their reliance on perception and intuition and their egocentric tendencies.

With the advent of **concrete operations**, children make a fundamentally important transition from a prelogical form of thought to thinking characterized by rules of logic. The operations—or thought processes—of this stage apply to real, concrete objects and events. The period of concrete operations is distinguished most clearly from the preoperational period by the appearance of one group of capabilities: the ability to conserve.

---

concrete operations The third of Piaget's four major stages, lasting from age 7 or 8 to approximately age 11 or 12, and characterized largely by the child's ability to deal with concrete problems and objects or objects and problems that are easily imagined.

The Conservations Recall the experiment in which an equal number of wooden beads are put into two containers of very different shapes, thus leading the preoperational child to conclude that one container has more beads than the other because it's taller or wider. This illustrates not only the preoperational child's reliance on perception, but also lack of conservation. **Conservation** is the realization that quantity or amount doesn't change unless something is taken away from or added to an object or a collection of objects, despite changes in appearance.

A correct response to a conservation problem is evidence that children are using one or more rules of logic that now govern and limit their thinking. Among these rules are **reversibility** and **identity**. The rule of reversibility specifies that for every operation (internalized action or thought) there is an inverse operation that cancels it out. The rule of identity states that for every operation there is another that leaves it unchanged. Both rules can easily be illustrated with number operations. For example, the operation of addition can be reversed (and nullified) by subtraction ($2 + 4 = 6$; $6 - 4 = 2$). The identity operator for addition is zero (that is, $2 + 0 + 0 + 0 = 2$); for multiplication it is 1 ($2 \times 1 \times 1 \times 1 = 2$).

The importance of these rules for children at the concrete operations level of thinking is evident in conservation problems. The child who has placed one bead in a tall container for every bead placed by the experimenter in a flat container—

and who now maintains that there is the same number in each despite their appearances—may be reasoning as follows: (1) If the beads were taken out of the containers and placed again on the table, they would be as they were before (reversibility); or (2) nothing has been added to or taken away from either container, so there must still be the same number in each (identity).

There are as many types of conservation as there are measurable characteristics of objects. Thus, there is conservation of number, length, distance, area, volume, continuous substance, discontinuous substance, liquid substance, and so on. None of these conservations is achieved before the period of concrete operations; even then, some (volume, for example) will not be acquired until quite late in that period. Several experimental procedures for conservation are described in Figure 3.4, together with the approximate ages of attainment. The experiments are interesting and easily replicated, and the results are often striking.

One of the intriguing things about conservation is that preoperational children can be made to contradict themselves many times without ever changing their minds. After the experiment on conservation of liquid quantity, for example, the experimenter can pour the water back into the original containers and repeat the question. The subject now acknowledges that they contain the same amount of water, but as soon as the water is again poured into the tall and flat containers, that decision may be reversed.

Besides conservation, children acquire three other abilities as they come into the stage of concrete operations: the abilities to classify, to seriate, and to deal with numbers.

Classification To classify is to group objects according to their similarities and differences. The **classification** process involves incorporating subclasses into more general classes, while maintaining the identity of the subclasses. This process leads to the formation of what Piaget calls

---

conservation A Piagetian term for the realization that certain quantitative attributes of objects remain unchanged unless something is added to or taken away from them. Such characteristics of objects as mass, number, area, and volume are capable of being conserved.

reversibility A logical property manifested in the ability to reverse or undo activity in either an empirical or a conceptual sense. An idea is said to be reversible when a child realizes the logical consequences of an opposite action.

identity A logical rule that specifies that certain activities leave objects or situations unchanged.

1. Conservation of substance (6–7 years)

A

The experimenter presents two identical modeling clay balls. The subject admits that they have equal amounts of clay.

B

One of the balls is deformed. The subject is asked whether thay still contain equal amounts.

2. Conservation of length (6–7 years)

A

Two sticks are aligned in front of the subject. The subject admits their equality.

B

One of the sticks is moved to the right. The subject is asked whether they are still the same length.

3. Conservation of number (6–7 years)

A

Two rows of counters are placed in one-to-one correspondence. Subject admits their equality.

B

One of the rows is elongated (or contracted). Subject is asked whether each row still contains the same number.

4. Conservation of liquids (6–7 years)

A

Two beakers are filled to the same level with water. The subject sees that they are equal.

B

The liquid of one container is poured into a tall tube (or a flat dish). The subject is asked whether each still contains the same amount.

5. Conservation of area (9–10 years)

A

The subject and the experimenter each have identical sheets of cardboard. Wooden blocks are placed on these in identical positions. The subject agrees that each cardboard has the same amount of space remaining.

B

The experimenter scatters the blocks on one of the cardboards. The subject is asked whether each cardboard still has the same amount of space remaining.

FIGURE 3.4 Some simple tests for conservation, with approximate ages of attainment

hierarchies of classes (Piaget, 1954); an example is given in Figure 3.5. Preoperational children's incomplete understanding of classes was illustrated in the experiment involving the ten brown and five yellow wooden beads. Recall that at that stage children thought there were more brown than wooden beads, even while acknowledging that all the beads were wooden. Children in the concrete operations stage no longer make this error.

---

classification The act of grouping items in terms of common properties. Classification involves abstracting the properties of objects or events and making judgments concerning their similarities or differences from other objects or events.

hierarchies of classes Arrangements of concepts or classes in terms of their inclusiveness. At the top of the hierarchy is the concept (class) that is most inclusive (for example, writing instruments); below this highly inclusive concept are those included in it (for example, pens, typewriters, pencils).

Seriating Understanding **seriation**—that is, understanding how to order objects in terms of an attribute—is essential for understanding number. One experiment that Piaget conducted to investigate the understanding of seriation involves presenting children with a series of different-size dolls. The problem is simply to arrange these dolls in order, a task that preoperational children find very difficult. Typically, they compare only two dolls at a time and fail to make an inference that is almost essential for the solution of the problem: If A is greater than B, and B is greater than C, A must also be greater than C. Preoperational children don't hesitate to put C before A if they have just been comparing B and C (see Figure 3.6).

seriation The ordering of objects in terms of one or more properties. To seriate is to place in order.

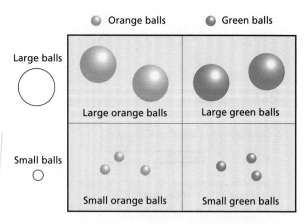

FIGURE 3.5 The use of multiplication to answer the question "If there are orange balls and green balls, and some are large whereas others are small, how different kinds of balls are there?" illustrates the classification abilities of children during the period of concrete operations.

Numbers Understanding numbers depends on classification and seriation. A number involves classes in the sense that it represents a collection of objects (cardinal property of numbers); it

.6 A test of children's understanding of seriation: The ele-
ries are presented in random order, and children are asked to
sequence by height. The top row was arranged by a 3½-
year-old, ...bottom, by an 8-year-old.

Children's understanding of number and of classes, says Piaget, grows out of actual experiences they have with real objects. School experiences, too, are real-life experiences.

involves seriation because it is ordered in relation to larger and smaller numbers (ordinal property of numbers). And because children don't develop a complete understanding of classification and seriation until the period of concrete operations, Piaget suggests that their understanding of number would also develop at about the same time. However, as we will show shortly, we know that many preschoolers have a very advanced *intuitive* knowledge of numbers—a knowledge that allows many of them to count, to add, and to subtract unerringly in real-life situations (like when they're buying candy). As Piaget suggests, adding and subtracting skills grow out of children's experiences with combining and separating real objects (Voss, Wiley, & Carretero, 1995).

To summarize, children at the stage of concrete operations can apply rules of logic to classes, to relations (series), and to numbers. Their thinking has also become relatively decen-

tered; it is no longer so egocentric or bound by perception. However, these children are still incapable of applying rules of logic to objects or events that are not concrete. In other words, they deal only with what is real or what they are capable of imagining. Their ready answer to the question "what if Johnny West had a short nose?" is "Johnny West does not have a short nose!"

Formal Operations: 11 or 12 to 14 or 15 Years

The final stage in the development of thought structures is labeled **formal operations**—formal because children can now deal with completely hypothetical subject matter, and their thinking may involve a formal set of rules of logic.

One example of the difference between the thinking of children at the formal operations level and at the concrete level is provided by an item from Binet's reasoning test (the forerunner to the well-known Stanford-Binet test). The item deals with abstract relations: Edith is fairer than Susan; Edith is darker than Lilly. Who is the darkest of the three? This problem is difficult not because it involves seriation (seriation has already been mastered in the stage of concrete operations) but because of the abstract nature of the characteristics to be ordered. If Edith, Susan, and Lilly were all standing in front of a 10-year-old subject, the subject could easily say, "Oh! Edith is fairer than Susan, and she is darker than Lilly—and Susan is the darkest." However, when the problem is not concrete but verbal, it requires thinking that is more formal (abstract).

In a second experiment that illustrates one distinction between formal and concrete

---

formal operations The last of Piaget's four major stages. It begins around age 11 or 12 and lasts until age 14 or 15. This stage is characterized by the child's increasing ability to use logical thought processes.

thinking, participants are presented with four test tubes. Certain combinations of the tubes, when combined with the contents of a fifth tube, will yield a yellow liquid. The object is to discover which combination(s) yields the yellow liquid.

When presented with this problem, typical 10-year-olds might begin by combining two of the liquids, then perhaps two more, and so on—continuing, almost haphazardly, to try to guess what the correct combination might be. And if, by chance, they stumble across one of the two possible correct solutions, they will have no way of knowing whether there might be another. Because their approach is unsystematic, it will seldom exhaust all possibilities.

In contrast, bright 14-year-olds might well approach the problem systematically, combining all tubes by twos, then threes, then finally all four, thus testing every possible combination (as shown in Figure 3.7).

What this problem demonstrates most clearly is: (1) the concrete nature of younger children's thinking—every combination is an actual hypothesis translated into an immediate real test, an actual behavior; and (2) the hypothetical and deductive capacities of older children's thinking. Thus, children in the formal operations stage begin by imagining all the possible solutions and then trying them out. The logic involved is described by Piaget as a form of "combinatorial thinking." This is a far more powerful logic than the concrete thinking of younger children. Among other things, it allows children to begin to understand abstract concepts such as proportion and heat, and it allows them to deal with the hypothetical world rather than merely what is immediately real. As a result, one important feature of formal operations thinking is an increasing concern with the ideal. Once children are able to reason from the hypothetical to the real or from the actual to the hypothetical, they can

conceive of worlds and societies that, hypothetically, have no ills.

Beyond Formal Operations

For a long time, developmental psychologists believed that the main intellectual changes of human development take place between birth and the end of adolescence. This model held that after adolescence there is a long period of relatively little change, a sort of plateau, that is eventually followed by a gradual decline in old age.

Piaget's description of intellectual development reflects this long-prevalent model. Thus, he describes intellectual growth in terms of changes reflected in identifiable stages. The last of these stages, formal operations, is a stage descriptive of adolescents; beyond that—nothing.

But what of adults? Is adulthood merely a plateau followed by inevitable decline? Are no more positive changes possible?

The simple answer is no; there is good evidence that important positive changes often come in adulthood. In fact, even formal operations thinking is not characteristic of all adolescents or even of all adults. Some people's thinking remains at a concrete stage throughout life; for others, thinking never even progresses beyond the intuitions of the preconceptual level.

But the truly adult thinker, Basseches (1984) informs us, does not think like the schoolchild or the adolescent. Cognitive development, Basseches insists, continues after adolescence. But instead of becoming more logical—more unwaveringly rational—thinking becomes more relative, more attuned to conflict, and more sensitive to moral, ethical, social, and political realities. It is a form of thinking that Basseches terms **dialectical thinking**. Dialectical thinking struggles to create meaning and order by resolving conflict. The dialectical thinker is always aware of other possibilities and recognizes that no solution is necessarily absolute and final.

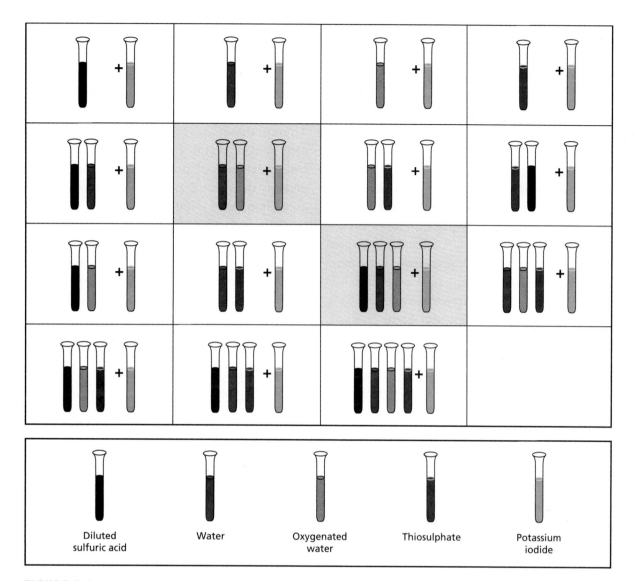

FIGURE 3.7 All possible combinations of the four test tubes to which the fifth can be added: The experiment requires the subject to discover the combination(s) that yields a yellow liquid when potassium iodide is added. The correct solutions have a light gray background.

Labouvie-Vief (1980) agrees. Formal logic, she informs us, might be entirely appropriate for some of the problems that children face, especially in school. But it might be inadequate and perhaps even largely irrelevant for many of the problems that adults face. The most logical solution may well be entirely inappropriate, even wrong. Mature reasoning requires "concrete pragmatics"; that is, it must take into account what will work and what is acceptable—what is, in other words, pragmatic (Labouvie-Vief, 1986). The thinking of the truly wise person is not simply bound by logic—which is not to say

---

dialectical thinking Thinking that recognizes, accepts, and attempts to resolve conflicts. Dialectical thinking is thought to be more characteristic of adults than of children or adolescents.

that it is illogical. Instead, it is sensitive to a wide range of possibilities; it considers implications; it factors in social and moral realities.

In summary, Basseches, Labouvie-Vief, and others concerned with the intellectual growth of adults claim that Piaget's model is inadequate for describing adult thought processes. According to these theorists, adult cognitive growth can take the form of learning new ways to resolve a wide range of personal problems that could involve relationships, artistic activities, business transactions, religion—indeed, all of life. They argue that adult thinking is more sensitive to and tolerant of ambiguity and contradictions and that it is more likely to bring into play a variety of factors (for example, morality, social and political implications, economic considerations, and so on) besides simple logic.

An Assessment of Piaget's Theory

Piaget's stature in developmental psychology and his influence on research and theorizing are unequaled. His theories have had an important influence on educational practice as well, (White & Cahan, 1997). Still, he has critics. Among the standard criticism is that he did not use sufficiently large samples, sophisticated analyses, or adequate controls. One way of examining at the validity of this criticism is to look at whether replications support his findings.

Of the many hundreds (or thousands) of studies that have attempted to replicate Piaget's findings, a majority agree that the sequence of intellectual stages is much as Piaget described. However, many of these studies suggest that Piaget has drastically underestimated the cognitive achievements of preschoolers; others indicate that he has overestimated the formal operations capabilities of adolescents (and even of adults).

Achievements of Preschoolers Current research suggests that it is inappropriate and misleading to refer to the preschooler's mind as "preconceptual," "preoperational," or "prelogical" (see, for example, Flavell, 1985; Campbell, 1993). This research indicates that significant cognitive achievements of this period were either underemphasized or simply overlooked by Piaget. Among these are monumental advances in preschoolers' abilities to represent symbolically and to discover relationships among ideas. And perhaps the most dramatic illustration of children's impressive abilities with respect to discovering and working with relationships is their understanding of numbers. It's clear that children's knowledge of concepts like big and small, or few and many, as well as their understanding of the effects of adding or subtracting, are often highly developed by the time they start school. What they appear to have, explains Aubrey (1993), is an intuitive knowledge of mathematics very similar to the *street mathematics* that unschooled street vendors might develop. Street mathematics is the type of knowledge required for calculating, say, the price of two or more things given the price of one. It allows the street vendor or the street urchin (or the preschooler) to buy or sell and to make change. And, in some instances, very sophisticated intuitive knowledge of number operations is required. Nunes, Carraher, and Schliemann (1993) reviewed Brazilian studies of the mathematical knowledge of street vendors and found that it is not the same as the more formal kind of mathematics knowledge that is learned and required in school.

Gelman (1982) and colleagues (Gelman, Meck, & Merkin, 1986) describe two kinds of knowledge about numbers that appear during the preschool period. First are *number abstraction skills*. These give the child an understanding of number, or quantity—of how many things there are in a collection of, for example, baby mice in one's pockets. A number of principles underlie number abstraction skills. These include the one-on-one principle (if you're going to count mice, you must assign one, and only one, number to every mouse that is to be counted); the stable order principle (the correct order for counting is one, two, three, four . . . and not one, three, four, two . . .); the cardinal order principle (the last number assigned is the one that indicates the quantity of the collection); the abstraction principle (absolutely anything and everything can be counted); and the order irrelevance principle (the order in which the mice are counted is irrelevant to the final outcome of the counting operation).

These five number abstraction principles address how to count, what to count, and what it means to count. Children as young as 2 or 3 often behave as though they understand these principles clearly, even though they might still make mistakes (often systematic errors) in their counting.

The second kind of knowledge about numbers that appears during the preschool period relates to *numerical reasoning principles*. This is the knowledge that permits the child to reason about or predict the outcome of simple numerical operations such as adding to or taking from.

Number abstraction and numerical reasoning are important and complex cognitive activities. They serve as dramatic illustrations of the cognitive achievements of the preschooler, in sharp contrast to Piaget's description of the intuitive, egocentric, perception-dominated, prelogical, preoperational child.

The Limits of Formal Operations Some criticism of Piaget's stage of formal operations has been based on the observation that many people still aren't capable of formal operations thinking during adolescence or even beyond (Papalia, 1972; Rubin et al., 1973). Piaget (1972) has conceded that this stage may be less general than he had originally thought.

Piaget is sometimes also criticized for using difficult, unclear, and often unnecessary terms and concepts in describing formal operations, and for making errors in his use of models of logic to describe adolescent thought (Ennis, 1976, 1978).

The Importance of Criticisms When evaluating the importance of these criticisms, keep in mind that Piaget's theory, like other theories, is simply a metaphor. Specifically, Piaget's theory is a philosophical/biological metaphor intended to explain intellectual adaptation through the growth of intellectual capabilities and functions. Some of the criticism of Piaget's theory stem from a misunderstanding of the basic metaphor and intentions of the theory and from too narrow an application of its principles, argue Lourenco and Machado (1996). In the final analysis, it may not be fundamentally important to the basic metaphor that some of the observations upon which it is based are inaccurate or that there are errors of logic, interpretation, or emphases in its description. The explanatory strength and practical usefulness of the theory may be far more important.

EDUCATIONAL IMPLICATIONS OF PIAGET'S THEORY

Piaget's cognitive theory is monumental in child development and has had (and continues to have) a profound impact on educational practices. Its most useful instructional applications relate to three topics: constructivist instructional theory, the acceleration of development, and the derivation of specific principles for teaching.

Constructivist Instructional Theory

Theories such as Piaget's emphasize that learning is far more than a simple process of moving items of information from *out there* (perhaps in a teacher's head or in a computer) into the child. The view that the role of teachers is to organize and impart ready-made and digestible information, and that the role of students is to ingest this information, was once quite prevalent. In fact, this view still underlies much of what many teachers do. As we saw in Chapter 1, this view is evident in **direct instruction**.

A second view, reflecting Piaget's theory (as well as theories such as Bruner's, discussed in Chapter 6) emphasizes that meaningful learning and development result from a highly active process in which learners *construct* knowledge. This view, labeled **constructivism**, is apparent in discovery-oriented and cooperative approaches to teaching. One of its main tenets is that knowledge is not so much *given to* as *constructed by* learners. It reflects Piaget's belief that, through continued interaction with the social and physical world, children build up (*construct*) a representation and an understanding of the world and invent a set of rules that permit them to deal with it.

Constructivism does not imply that teachers need do nothing to facilitate learning—that the learner should assume complete responsibility for acquiring and organizing information. But it does imply that teachers need to be keenly aware of the learner's capabilities, of what the learner already knows, of what is likely to be meaningful and interesting. In the constructivist classroom, notes Johnson (1996), the role of the teacher is to promote the child's view.

Robert Gagné (1985) describes an instructional model based on the notion that learning is hierarchical and that higher order skills and concepts depend on subordinate capabilities. Hence, instruction based on this model always begins by analyzing what is to be learned and arranging content into a hierarchy of tasks—a process called **task analysis**. Case (1975) suggests that Gagné's instructional theory can be combined with Piaget's developmental theory to suggest how teachers can help learners *construct* knowledge. Specifically, Piaget's theory can be used to assess the learner's developmental level and cognitive capabilities. Careful task analysis can reveal why certain tasks are too difficult—for example, for preoperational children—and might also suggest how tasks can be structured to be more compatible with the students' developmental level.

The Acceleration of Development

Piaget was not concerned specifically with the possibility of changing what appears to be the natural course of development, but his theory at least suggests that certain carefully structured experiences might be useful for speeding up development. Not surprisingly, many researchers have looked at ways to accelerate the appearance of developmentally important concepts—such as conservation, for example. But the results have generally been mixed, with many researchers failing to bring about any significant change. What should be one of the easiest teaching tasks possible—simply convincing a 5-year-old that a given amount of modeling clay does not change unless something is added to or taken away from it—is actually next to impossible. And although several systematic training procedures have succeeded in accelerating the appearance of conservation behavior in young children, no evidence has yet been provided that this has a generally beneficial effect on other aspects of intellectual functioning (see, for example, Campbell & Ramey, 1990; Perry, Pasnak, & Holt, 1992). As Nagy and Griffiths (1982) conclude, "attempts to prescribe instructional strategies that accelerate intellectual development have borne little fruit" (p. 513). It is unclear, though,

---

direct instruction A phrase used to describe teacher-directed approaches to teaching—in contrast with more student-centered approaches such as reciprocal teaching and cooperative learning (often included among *constructivist approaches*).

constructivism A general term for student-centered approaches to teaching such as discovery-oriented approaches, reciprocal learning, or cooperative instruction—so called because of their assumption that learners should build (construct) knowledge for themselves.

---

task analysis The process of analyzing what is to be learned in terms of a sequential series of related tasks. Task analysis provides the teacher with information about important skills and knowledge that might be prerequisite for what is to be taught.

whether the general failure of these attempts is because intellectual development cannot easily be accelerated or because we simply don't understand enough about the nature of intellectual development to devise more effective strategies.

Instructional Principles

Development, insists Piaget (1961), does not just occur all by itself, completely independently of children's surroundings and activities. To the contrary, as we saw, it depends on four important factors: equilibration, maturation, active experience, and social interaction. These four factors are the cornerstones of Piaget's system. They also suggest important instructional implications. Some of these implications are summarized here. They are not intended as recipes for classroom practice but rather as guiding principles for developing your own teaching style. Clearly, each of these general implications is basic to a *constructivist* classroom—that is, a classroom where the emphasis is on the learner's point of view and on learners' discovering and organizing their own knowledge.

Providing Opportunities for Physical and Mental Activity Activity, says Piaget, is fundamental to building concepts and understanding the world. For example, children's ability to deal with classes, relations, and numbers results from the activities of combining, separating, and setting up correspondences among real objects during the preoperational stage. Internalized mental activities—Piaget's phrase for concepts or thinking—are *constructed from* these actual physical activities. It follows, then, that teachers should provide children with many opportunities to engage in meaningful activities with real objects, as well as opportunities for mental activity (thinking).

As an illustration, consider the case entitled "The B Store." In many ways, this little classroom store mirrors real life, thus giving the learning of mathematics a degree of realism, practicality, and meaningfulness not often found in cold numbers on workbook pages. Not only does it provide for actual activity in meaningful circumstances, but it also gives the teacher a simple way of administering or withholding reinforcement. And it permits teaching an extremely wide range of mathematical concepts besides simple addition and subtraction. For example, multiplication concepts can be introduced easily by doubling (or tripling) all prices; division might involve selling a fraction of something and then calculating what the price of the fraction should be, and so on.

Providing Optimal Difficulty Cognitive growth, says Piaget, arises from a tendency toward *equilibration*—that is, maintaining a balance between assimilation and accommodation. Recall that assimilation and accommodation are children's two ways of interacting with the world; all activity involves both. Assimilation occurs when children can react to new objects or events largely in terms of previous learning; accommodation involves modification or change. Assimilation requires that a situation be somewhat familiar; accommodation will take place only if the situation is also somewhat different.

If schools are to encourage equilibration, an optimal discrepancy between new material and old learning is required. Learners need to be provided with experiences that are familiar enough that they can understand them (assimilate them); they also need to be challenged so that they will be forced to accommodate. The result, ideally, will be the construction of new understanding (accommodation) on the back of old learning (assimilation).

Providing learners with an optimal level of difficulty presupposes that teachers know their level of functioning, their interests, and their capabilities—hence the fundamental importance of understanding how children think.

Understanding How Children Think Although it has always been recognized that there are some important differences between children and

The B Store

THE PLACE: MISS MOSKAL'S THIRD-GRADE CLASSROOM

The Mathematics Learning Center: In the corner of the room, the children have set up a small store. Items for sale vary from week to week. These items are sometimes made by the students, donated by parents, or purchased with school funds. Among the various items for sale this week are some tiny potted plants that Miss Moskal has started from seeds. Also, there are "privilege" cards. Some of these cards allow children to erase the blackboards; others provide access to special books; still others allow their purchaser to be captain of one of the play teams, leader of one of the cooperative learning teams, storekeeper for a day, bank teller, or payroll clerk. Price tags, attached to each item, are printed in bold, colorful numbers.

In this class, each student receives a basic weekly "salary," with the possibility of bonuses for various behaviors—and sometimes fines as well. The payroll clerk is responsible for keeping track of everybody's salary, adding in bonuses and subtracting fines, and writing "paycheques." Student auditors are charged with verifying the pay clerk's calculations. Cheques are "cashed" at a bank adjoining the store or are sometimes used at the store when making large purchases (like lunch with Miss Moskal). During specified periods, sales clerks sell items from the store, taking responsibility for making change.

Students were responsible for naming the store. The name was Sandra's idea.

"Let's call it the B store," she said.

"Why?"

"Because that's a little better than a C store."

---

adults, Piaget, more than anyone, has demonstrated precisely what some of these differences are. When a child says that there is more water in a tall container than in a short, flat one, she truly believes what she is saying. When a row of disks is made shorter than a corresponding row, and the child changes his mind and says that now there are fewer disks in that row, he is not really contradicting himself because he sees no error and therefore no contradiction. When a second-grade student becomes completely confused by a verbal seriation problem—for example, "Frank Twolips has a shorter nose than Johnny West, and Johnny West has a longer nose than John George. Who has the longest nose?"—she is not being stupid.

These and other discoveries about the world of young children should help teachers both to communicate more effectively with children and to understand and be sensitive to the limitations of their thinking. Teachers need to know, for example, that concepts of proportion cannot easily be taught to 7-year-olds, nor can conserva-

tion of volume be taught to 5-year-olds. Besides, certain concepts such as those involved in conservation seem to be acquired naturally, without tuition; children are much less likely to learn to read without instruction.

Providing Social Interaction One of the chief factors in making thought more objective, claims Piaget, is social interaction. The egocentric point of view of the young child is essentially one that does not recognize the views of others. Children become aware of the ideas and opinions of peers and adults largely through social interaction. Piaget contends that the socialization of thought, the development of moral rules and game rules, and even the development of logical thought processes are highly dependent on verbal interaction. One implication for teaching is that instructional methods should provide for learner–learner as well as teacher–learner interaction. As DeVries (1997) notes, "The obvious general educational implication of Piaget's social theory is to value a socially interactive classroom and foster social exchanges of a cooperative type in order to promote operational development" (p. 14).

Assessing Students' Readiness Detailed accounts of Piaget's experimental procedures and findings provide the classroom teacher with many informal and easily applied suggestions for assessing students' thought processes. It is not particularly difficult or time-consuming, for example, to ascertain whether a child has acquired conservation of numbers or the ability to seriate. Both abilities are important for early instruction in mathematics.

Several researchers have attempted to develop scales to assess Piagetian concepts in children (for example, Pinard & Laurendeau, 1964; Goldschmid & Bentler, 1968; Uzgiris & Hunt, 1975). Unfortunately, none of these scales has been widely used or standardized. Still, a general knowledge of Piaget's theory and some of the related research can do much to improve teacher knowledge of students' cognitive processes. Consequently, such knowledge can also do much to suggest more optimal ways of teaching.

⌐ VYGOTSKY'S CULTURAL/ COGNITIVE THEORY

The emphasis in Piaget's theory, notes Bruner (1997a), is on the development of the logical systems that underlie the child's construction of meaning. In contrast, the emphasis in Lev Vygotsky's theory is on the centrality of culture and of social influences in human development. As Kitchener (1996) points out, Piaget sees development as a sort of unfolding guided by internal tendencies; Vygotsky sees development as the result of the child's interaction with other people. Hence the central contrast between the two positions is that one sees the main forces that impel development as being *within* the individual (Piaget's theory); the other attributes a

primary role to *external* social forces (Vygotsky's theory) (Cole & Wertsch, 1996). Vygotsky apparently spent a considerable amount of time attacking and criticizing Piaget and trying to get Piaget to engage in dialogue with him (Van der Veer, 1996). Piaget never responded.

Vygotsky's Main Ideas

A quick look at current writings in education and psychology might make one think that Lev Vygotsky is a contemporary theorist. Almost all major psychology textbooks have at least one or two references to him, but many of his major works have only recently been translated into English (for example Vygotsky, 1992, 1993; Vygotsky & Luria, 1993). In fact, one book that might be important for teachers has not yet been translated from the Russian (Vygotsky, 1991; see Davydov, 1995).

But Vygotsky is not contemporary in a literal sense; he has been dead for more than half a century (he died of tuberculosis in 1934 at the age of 38). And although Vygotsky was already a major intellectual force in the Soviet Union by the time he was 28, his work was not well known outside that country until much later. In fact, because Vygotsky worked in the field that was labeled **pedology** in the former Soviet Union, for several decades after his death it was forbidden to reprint or even to discuss his work. Soviet authorities had determined that pedology, a science of child development that used Western tests for assessing development and diagnosing developmental disorders, was a "bourgeois pseudoscience" and, in effect, they wiped out the

---

pedology A Soviet discipline of child development, very popular in the Soviet Union in the 1930s, that used Western tests for psychoassessment. Vygotsky and Luria were pedologists. In the mid-1930s, the Soviet government decreed that pedology was a "bourgeois pseudoscience" and ordered that it no longer be written about, researched, or even discussed, thus wiping out all pedology centers and putting all pedologists out of work.

discipline, closing down all pedology centers and repressing all related research and publications. Imagine what Vygotsky's contributions and stature might have been had his work not been repressed—and had he lived as long as Piaget.

Vygotsky has been described as "the Mozart of Psychology," its child genius, notes Davydov (1995). By age 28, he had assimilated all of the major theories and findings of the psychology of the day, and he had begun to map out a new theory with ideas that still seem fresh even today. Unfortunately, however, many of these ideas are complex and not entirely clear. As Nicolopoulou (1993) phrases it, "Despite the fact that his writings are full of intuitions and illuminations, they are often sketchy and at times incomplete" (p. 7).

Three underlying themes unify Vygotsky's complex and far-reaching theory. The first theme is the importance of culture; the second has to do with the central role of language; the third relates to the developing child's relationship with the environment. We look at each of these briefly.

The Importance of Culture Human development, says Vygotsky, is fundamentally different from that of other animals. Why? Because humans use tools and symbols and, as a result, create **cultures**. And cultures are powerful things; they have a life of their own. They grow and change, and they exert tremendously powerful influences on each of us. Cultures specify what the end product of successful development is. They determine what we have to learn, the sorts of competencies we need to develop. As Tappan (1997) puts it, cultures necessarily shape human mental functioning. Hence, during different historical periods, psychological development might be very different—just as it might be very different from one culture to another. We are not only culture-producing, notes Bronfenbrenner (1989), but also culture-produced, giving voice to one of the most fundamental contemporary themes underlying the study and understanding of human development. Amazingly, more than six decades ago Vygotsky had already adopted this theme as the very basis of his theory.

The importance of culture in Vygotsky's explanations of human development is highly evident in the distinction he makes between what he calls *elementary mental functions* and *higher mental functions*. Elementary functions are our natural, and therefore unlearned, capacities, evident in such behaviors as the newborn's ability to attend to the mother's voice, to remember smells, to gurgle, and to cry. In the course of development, these elementary capacities are gradually transformed into higher mental functions such as problem solving and thinking, largely through the influence of culture. Culture, after all, makes language possible, and social processes bring about the learning of language (referred to as signs). Language, or signs, ultimately make thought possible. Thus, during the preverbal stage of development, infants' intelligence is a purely practical, purely natural capacity that is closely comparable to that of apes.[2]

The Role of Language Language makes thought possible and regulates behavior, explains Vygotsky. Language, which is the basis of human culture, is also the basis of consciousness, and consciousness was one of Vygotsky's central concerns. Without language, we would be limited to elementary mental functions—animalistic activ-

---

[2]*PPC:* How about the bear? What is his intelligence like?

Author: He is possessed of a great wisdom, tempered by a savage cunning. He is an accomplished dialectical thinker, both pragmatic and poetic. And sometimes he plays at being stupid, thinking that to be one of the sources of his mentor Yogi Berra's wit. "Would you like your pizza cut into 4 or 8 slices?" the waitress asked Yogi. "Four," he reportedly answered, "I don't think I can eat 8 pieces today."

---

culture The pattern of socially acceptable behaviors that characterizes a people or a social group. It includes all the attitudes and beliefs that the group holds about what it considers important.

ities such as sensing and perceiving. But with language, we can interact socially. And with social interaction comes what Vygotsky describes as "upbringing[3] and teaching," which is essential for development.

Vygotsky (1962) describes three stages in the development of the functions of speech: social, egocentric, and inner speech.

Social speech (or external speech) emerges first. Its function is largely to control the behavior of others (as in "I want juice!") or to express simple and sometimes poorly understood concepts.

Egocentric speech predominates from ages 3 to 7. It serves as a bridge between the primitive and highly public social speech of the first stage and the more sophisticated and highly private inner speech of the third stage. During this stage, children often talk to themselves in an apparent attempt to guide their own behavior. For example, they might speak about what they are doing as they do it. Unlike older children, however, they are likely to say things out loud (externalize) rather than silently, as though they believe that if language is to direct behavior, it must be spoken.

Inner speech is silent self-talk. It is characteristic of older children as well as adults. It is what William James (1890) called the "stream of consciousness." Our self-talk—our inner speech—is

what tells us that we are alive and conscious. It permits us to direct our thinking and our behavior. More than this, it makes all higher mental functioning possible (see Table 3.5).

The Concept of a Zone of Proximal Growth Higher mental functioning involves activities such as thinking, perceiving, organizing, and remembering. These functions originate in social activity and are inseparably linked with language, which is also a social phenomenon. In a very real sense, these higher mental functions define intelligence.

Vygotsky had a strong interest in maximizing intellectual development. He was far less interested in measuring past accomplishments or in assessing current levels of functioning than in arriving at some notion of potential for future development. Every child, he maintained, has a sphere or a zone of current capabilities—in Vygotsky's words, a **zone of proximal growth**, a sort of potential for developing (Belmont, 1989). Take, for example, two 5-year-olds who can both, under normal circumstances, answer questions that other average 5-year-olds can also answer. Their mental ages might be said to correspond to their chronological ages, and their intelligence would be described as average. But if, when prompted, one of these children could successfully answer questions corresponding to a mental age of 7 but the other could not, it would then be accurate to say that the first child's zone of

---

social speech In Vygotsky's theorizing, the most primitive stage of language development, evident before age 3. During this stage the child expresses simple thoughts and emotions out loud. The function of social speech is to control the behavior of others.

egocentric speech Vygotsky's intermediate stage of language development, common between ages 3 and 7; during this stage children often talk to themselves in an apparent effort to control their own behavior.

---

[3] Davydov (1995) explains that the translation of the Russian word *vospitateli* as "upbringing" is inexact—that the term *nurture* might be closer but less comfortable. He notes, as well, that the Russian expression that we translate to mean " teaching" would be better translated as "teaching/learning," showing how close these two processes are in the minds of Russian educators and theorists.

---

inner speech Vygotsky's final stage in the development of speech, attained at around age 7, and characterized by silent "self-talk," the stream-of-consciousness flow of verbalizations that give direction and substance to our thinking and behavior. Inner speech is involved in all higher mental functioning.

zone of proximal growth Vygotsky's phrase for the individual's current potential for further intellectual development. Conventional measures of intelligence assess current intellectual development rather than the potential for future development. Vygotsky believed that the zone of proximal growth (future potential) might be assessed by the use of further questioning and hints and prompts while administering a conventional intelligence test.

TABLE 3.5 Vygotsky's Stages and Functions of Language	
STAGE	FUNCTION
SOCIAL (external) (to age 3)	Controls the behavior of others; expresses simple thoughts and emotions
EGOCENTRIC (3 to 7)	Bridge between external and inner speech; serves to control own behavior but spoken out loud
INNER (7 onward)	Self-talk; makes possible the direction of thinking and behavior; involved in all higher mental functioning

proximal growth is greater than the other's (that is, it spans a wider range of higher functions).

Davydov (1995) explains what is meant by zone of proximal growth as follows: "What the child is initially able to do only together with adults and peers, and then can do independently, lies exactly in the zone of proximal psychological development" (p. 18). Later, when we look more closely at the educational implications of Vygotsky's theory, we will see that the task of educators, parents, and others charged with the "upbringing/teaching" of children is to arrange for children to engage in activities that lie within this zone—activities that, by definition, are neither too difficult nor too simple and that therefore lead to continued growth. In Davydov's (1995) words, "Teaching must lead development forward and not lag behind" (p. 18).

EDUCATIONAL IMPLICATIONS OF VYGOTSKY'S THEORY

Russian education is currently in a state of reform, claims Davydov (1995), and much of this reform is based on the ideas of Lev Vygotsky. Many of his ideas also have important applications for education in other parts of the world. Davydov summarizes five of these ideas as they apply to education (p. 13):

1. Education, which includes teaching/learning and upbringing (nurturing), is intended to develop children's personalities.

Vygotsky's theory suggests that the most useful educational experiences lie within the child's zone of proximal growth—specifically, activities that at first the child can understand and accomplish only with the help of adults or more competent peers but that the child can later accomplish alone. Effective tutoring, as illustrated here, reflects this principle.

2. Because the development of personality is linked with the development of creative potential, one of the important tasks of schools is to provide opportunities for the development of this creative potential.

3. Teaching/learning and upbringing require actual *activity* on the part of students; hence, students must be true participants in the teaching/learning process.

4. Teachers should be guides and directors of student activity without forcing their will on students. Hence, teaching should be a *collaborative* process.

5. The most effective teaching methods are those that take into consideration individual differences among learners. Thus, the best teaching methods cannot be uniform in a class.

Many of these ideas, which are based on Vygotsky's decades-old theory, reflect recent theories and beliefs almost exactly. In fact, most of these ideas are discussed in some detail in various parts of this text. For example, Vygotsky's belief that teaching/learning (and upbringing) are intended to develop personality is reflected in the humanistic insistence on the importance of self-development discussed in Chapter 7; his attention to the development of creative potential is reflected in detailed sections on intelligence and creativity in Chapters 8 and 9; his view that learning requires active involvement finds expression in Piaget's theory and in many other theories of learning; his belief that learning should be collaborative is reflected in the recent proliferation of cooperative approaches to learning discussed in Chapter 7; and his admonition that the best teaching methods must be sensitive to individual differences is at the center of the multicultural and inclusive education movements.

Scaffolding

One of the most important educational implications that can be derived from Vygotsky's theory is **scaffolding**. Essentially, scaffolding is defined as the many different methods teachers use to provide support for students as they learn— much as a scaffold might be used by a pair of energetic farmhands building an especially tall, multilevel doghouse.[4] To elaborate the analogy, in the early stages of the construction, the scaffold has to be very close to the ground and very sturdy, because there is nothing else to stand on or even to lean against. As the construction progresses, the scaffold must also rise or it would soon become useless. But now the farmhands can hang onto the wall studs of the new construction; they can sometimes even stand on the first rafters of the lower levels. Eventually, the doghouse will have been built, and they will no longer need any scaffolding at all. In fact, if they want to, they'll be able to walk on the very highest roof.

Learning, too, requires scaffolding, claims Vygotsky. In the early stages, scaffolding—that is, guidance and support—is often essential. For example, a preschooler who knows nothing about the significance of the letters of the alphabet can hardly be expected to discover or accurately invent the various sounds they represent. By telling, demonstrating, pointing, correcting, the teacher/upbringer *builds scaffolds* for the child. And as the child begins to learn, the nature of the scaffolding required changes. Often there is less need for scaffolding as the learner begins to build on previous learning by gradually learning how to learn.

Scaffolding, note Hogan and Pressley (1997), is a metaphor that translates into a model of learning through gradual increments as a result of an interactive process. In essence, it implies a process of collaboration between a teacher and student learners—ideally, between a single

---

scaffolding Vygotsky's concept to describe the various types of support that teachers/upbringers need to provide for children to be able to learn. Scaffolding often takes the form of directions, suggestions, and other forms of verbal assistance and is most effective if it involves tasks within the child's zone of proximal growth.

---

[4] ***PPC:*** Why a doghouse? Wouldn't the bear have preferred a . . . what? . . . a bearhouse?

Author: It's just an analogy to explain a metaphor. They didn't actually build a doghouse at all. Besides, the bear is a wild and poetic creature whose soul cringes at the thought of being domesticated— like a dog—and made to sleep in a house, for crying out loud!

learner and a teacher in a one-on-one tutoring relationship. There are a tremendous variety of specific types of scaffolding—in other words, support—that teachers and parents can build for children. These include:

- Demonstrating how to do things
- Explaining procedures
- Providing written or actual models
- Systematically developing all the prerequisite skills required for more demanding tasks
- Asking questions that lead to certain important realizations
- Correcting on-task errors
- Identifying and correcting misconceptions
- Motivating students
- Providing clear and realistic objectives

Scaffolding and the Zone of Proximal Growth
"Hey," you say, "so what's new? Seems to me that most of what good teachers do involves what you're calling *scaffolding*." Yes, but what is new is the relationship between Vygotsky's concept of scaffolding and his notion of the zone of proximal growth. Recall that the zone of proximal growth is defined in terms of tasks of which learners are capable *with the help of adults or peers*. In other words, the zone of proximal growth describes tasks that require support (that is, scaffolding). The implication for teachers (and other *upbringers*) is very clear: Scaffolding requires that teachers arrange for children to engage in activities that lie within this zone. Specifically, to the extent that the environment requires that children perform at a level slightly in advance of their current developmental level, progress will be enhanced. Vygotsky suggests that the level at which instructions and questions are phrased is extremely important. These, he argues, should be sufficiently ahead of the student's developmental level that they present a genuine intellectual challenge—but they must not be so far ahead of the child's current biological maturation and developmental level that they present too great a challenge (Valsiner, 1987).

Vygotsky's social/cognitive developmental theory underscores the role of culture (and its most important invention, language) for the development of higher mental functions. Without culture, he argues, our intelligence would be comparable to that of apes—hence, the fundamental role of education is cultural transmission.

We knew that. But perhaps we were not entirely aware of the theoretical underpinnings of this belief.

Do bears have a culture?

MAIN POINTS

1. Gender roles are learned patterns of culturally approved masculine and feminine behaviors; they are a combined function of genetic, family-based, and cultural forces. Traditional gender roles, which are changing slowly, reflect males as being more aggressive, more boisterous, and more adventurous than females. Both boys and girls tend to prefer male roles to female ones.

2. Sex differences are sometimes evident in the greater aggressiveness of males. There is also a declining tendency for males to score slightly higher on tests of mathematics and science. Generally, sex differences in abilities are too trivial and too inconsistent to be important to teachers. But teachers must remain sensitive to the interests of boys and girls and to the many instances of sexual bias that still permeate our society.

3. Erik Erikson's theory of personality development describes a series of psychosocial stages, each involving a major conflict, the resolution of which leads to greater social competence: trust versus mistrust, autonomy versus shame and doubt, initiative versus guilt, industry versus inferiority, identity versus identity diffusion, intimacy versus isolation, generativity versus self-absorption, and integrity versus despair. Marcia elaborates Erikson's notion of identity development by describing four types of identity status: identity diffusion (no crisis, no commitment); foreclosure (no crisis, early foreclosure); moratorium (crisis pending commitment); and identity achieved (commitment post crisis).

4. Piaget's theory stems partly from his biological orientation and focuses on cognitive (intellectual) development as it results from equilibration—the tendency to balance using previous responses (assimilation) with modifying behavior (accommodation)—maturation, active experience, and social interaction. This theory describes the characteristics of human behavior that permit adaptation, and it classifies important intellectual events in terms of sequential developmental stages.

5. Achievements of the sensorimotor period (birth to 2 years) are the learning of language, the acquisition of the object concept, the development of internally controlled representational schemes, and the recognition of cause-and-effect relationships.

6. The preoperational stage (preconceptual period,ages 2 to 4, and intuitive period, 4 to 7) is marked by thinking that is intuitive, dominated by perception, and egocentric.

7. The stage of concrete operations (ages 7 to 11 or 12) is marked by the appearance of thought processes that are subject to some logical rules, labeled *operations*. Operations are evident in concepts of conservation (the realization that certain qualities of objects are invariant unless something is added or subtracted) and in new skills relating to classifying, ordering, and dealing with numbers.

8. During the formal operations stage (ages 11 or 12 to 14 or 15), the child becomes free from concrete objects and events and can deal with the hypothetical. Researchers such as Basseches (dialectical thinking) and Labouvie-Vief (pragmatic reasoning) argue that, although formal operations are appropriate for problems requiring nothing but logic, mature adult reasoning is more sensitive to and tolerant of ambiguity and contradiction and is more likely to consider the practical, social, ethical, and personal implications of decisions.

9. Replications of many of Piaget's experiments have tended to confirm the general sequence of stages up to formal operations, although Piaget sometimes underestimated children's capacities and the ages of some developmental accomplishments.

10. Piaget's theory suggests that learning and development are a highly interactive process in which learners *construct* knowledge. Constructivistic approaches to teaching emphasize the learner's responsibility for creating and discovering. Important instructional principles that follow include the need to provide opportunities for student activity, to recognize that there is an optimal level of difficulty for new learning, and to be aware of the characteristics and limits of children's abilities.

11. Vygotsky's social/cognitive theory stresses the importance of culture and of its principal invention and main tool, language. Culture,

and especially language, removes us from apelike, elementary mental functions and makes possible the higher mental functions involved in thinking, reasoning, remembering, and so on. Children progress through three stages in developing language functions: social (external) speech, predominant before age 3 or 4, used largely to control others or to express simple concepts; egocentric speech (ages 3 to 7 or so), which is self-talk that is spoken out loud and has a role in controlling and directing the child's own behavior; and inner speech, marked by unspoken verbalizations that control thought and behavior.

12. Vygotsky's zone of proximal growth is the child's potential for development and is defined in terms of what the child can do with the help of adults and competent peers. His theory presents a strong argument for language-related activities in schools, for instruction at the upper edge of the student's zone of proximal growth, and for *scaffolding*, an interactive process wherein teachers provide various forms of support for students as they learn.

Applied Questions

▲ Read Margaret Mead's *Growing Up in New Guinea* or *Sex and Temperament in Three Primitive Societies*. Can you find similar examples of gender typing in your world?

▲ Debate the proposition that gender differences are more fanciful than real.

▲ What are the main characteristics of each of Erikson's stages of psychosocial development?

▲ Describe Piaget's answers for the primary biological questions he asked: How do children adapt? How can development be classified?

▲ What are the most important features of children's behavior at each of Piaget's developmental stages?

▲ Give an example of what is meant by the zone of proximal growth. What are the educational implications of this concept?

Internet Activity

Use InfoTrac College Edition or other World Wide Web sources to research the following topic: Write up your findings. (See the inside back cover of this text for suggestions about where to begin.)

Scaffolding
Sample search terms: scaffolding and teaching

Study Terms

accommodation **81**
adaptation **81**
aggression **70**
animism **88**
assimilation **81**
basic gender identity **69**
classification **93**

cognition **78**
cognitive structure **84**
concrete operations **91**
conservation **92**
constructivism **100**
culture **104**
deferred imitation **86**

dialectical thinking **97**
direct instruction **100**
egocentric speech **105**
egocentrism **88**
equilibration **82**
foreclosure **77**
formal operations **95**

Suggested Readings

Theorists such as Erikson, Piaget, and Vygotsky were prolific and sometimes difficult writers. It is generally easier and perhaps more valuable to begin with secondary sources for information about their theories. The following are useful starting points:

Miller, P. H. (1993). *Theories of developmental psychology* (3rd ed.). New York: Freeman.

Thomas, R. M. (1996). *Comparing theories of child development* (4th ed.). Belmont, CA: Wadsworth.

Wadsworth, B. J. (1996). *Piaget's theory of cognitive and affective development: Foundations of constructivism.* New York: Longman.

The following is of particular value in understanding the logical thought processes of children in the concrete operations and formal operations stages:

Inhelder, B., & Piaget, J. (1958). *The growth of logical thinking from childhood to adolescence.* New York: Basic Books.

A comprehensive collection of articles that deal with many important aspects of gender and its implications:

Beall, A. E., & Sternberg, R. J. (Eds.). (1993). *The psychology of gender.* New York: Guilford.

The first of the following two books includes articles that present a high-level discussion of the theories of both Piaget and Vygotsky, with an emphasis on their similarities and differences. The first part, which deals with educational interventions based on these theories, is especially valuable for teachers. The second book is an in-depth look at Vygotsky's work and his contributions to understanding humans as language processors:

Smith, L., Dockrell, J., & Tomlinson, P. (1997). *Piaget, Vygotsky and beyond: Future issues for developmental psychology and education.* New York: Routledge.

Frawley, W. (1997). *Vygotsky and cognitive science: Language and the unification of the social and computational mind.* Cambridge, MA: Harvard University Press.

For clarification and elaboration of what is meant by scaffolding and how it can be applied in the classroom, see the following collection of articles:

Hogan, K., & Pressley, M. (Eds.). (1997). *Scaffolding student learning: Instructional approaches and issues.* Albany, NY: State University of New York.

Delayed implantation is one of the common features of brown bears and polar bears, badgers, mink, and some other animals. The fertilized egg does not become implanted in the uterine wall shortly after conception but may remain dormant for weeks and sometimes even months. Although delayed implantation clearly has survival value, ensuring that the young will be born at the optimal time of the year, the mechanisms that delay embryonic development and later serve to trigger it are not understood (Matthews, 1969).

We know that you
are mad with much
learning.
Petronius, *Satyricon*

Learning and
Teaching

Learning is what the educational process is mostly all about—although it does not ordinarily make us mad. The four chapters in Part Three deal with learning and thinking and especially with the instructional implications of what we know about these topics. The first chapter presents a behavioristic look at learning, and the next two chapters look more closely at thinking, problem solving, decision making, and remembering. The last chapter presents an antidote to the accusation that our sciences tend to mechanize and dehumanize: It presents some humanistic approaches to teaching.

A little learning is a
dangerous thing
Drink deep or taste
not the Pierian spring

Alexander Pope, *Essay on Criticism*

Behaviorism and Social Learning Theory

PREVIEW

For teachers, one of the most important questions about learning is: Which conditions lead most effectively to desirable changes in behavior? In other words, how can what we know about learning be applied to instruction? But before we can begin to answer this question, we must look at psychology's explanations of learning. In this chapter we present two kinds of explanations: the behavioristic (which examines how behavior is controlled by its consequences) and the social cognitive (which also takes into consideration our ability to think and anticipate).

FOCUS QUESTIONS

▲ What is learning?

▲ Why are theories like those of Pavlov, Watson, Thorndike, and Skinner labeled "behaviorism"?

▲ What are classical and operant conditioning?

▲ What is the difference between negative reinforcement and punishment?

▲ Why might schedules of reinforcement be important in the classroom?

▲ What are the processes and effects of learning through imitation?

My mother says I used to really like milk, that I once drank it just like everybody else. I don't remember that. I feel like I've never much liked milk. I know for sure that I don't like it now. I never drink it, and for a long time, I didn't even like to see it in my cereal, although now I can at least stand that.

I still remember the last time I drank a whole glass of milk. We were living up in Pascal in northern Saskatchewan. They hadn't yet bothered to string electrical lines up there; it was very much out of the way and (in their opinion at least) there was nobody of any consequence in that wilderness. So we had no refrigeration in the summer—and way too much of it in the winter.

We used to get our milk from Delisle's farm. I'd trudge over there in the morning, down the dusty road, and pick up a couple of quarts of still-warm milk, leaving a dime and a nickel in their place.

So when we drank milk, it was usually at about room temperature. And by evening, it had often begun to sour. I'd always try to find some excuse not to drink it.

The last time I drank a whole glass of milk, my father said, "Guy, you're not going to leave the table until you drink all your milk." In the end I did, holding my breath and gulping it down as fast as I could because I knew if I stopped I'd never be able to start again.

And when I finished, I immediately threw up.

LEARNING

That was the last time I drank a whole glass of milk. A few weeks after that, my father again insisted that I not set such a bad example for the younger ones and drink my glass of milk. He was convinced that my little stomach upset was long gone, that it had by now become just an excuse.

I managed only a couple of swallows before I threw up again.

I was apparently the victim—or the beneficiary—of what psychologists call **one-shot taste aversion learning** (see Lefrançois, 2000). It's a type of learning easily illustrated with animals like rats. When rats are given something to eat and then exposed to a single dose of radiation, which makes them ill, they subsequently refuse to eat the food that they ate just before the radiation. This is a special kind of learning that can be extremely important for survival. If we, and other animals, didn't easily learn to avoid things that make us ill, many of us wouldn't be here today: Too many of our ancestors would have poisoned themselves.

A Definition of Learning

The learning of taste aversions is a biologically based phenomenon, of little direct importance to the business of teaching. However, more general forms of learning are absolutely central to the educational enterprise.

Learning, you see, is the acquisition of information and knowledge, of skills and habits, and of attitudes and beliefs. It always involves a change in one of these areas—a change that is

---

one-shot taste aversion learning A powerful disinclination toward eating or drinking certain substances, acquired after a single pairing of the substance with subsequent nausea or illness. Taste aversions are easily learned, are highly resistant to extinction, and demonstrate biological predispositions.

learning Changes in behavior due to experience; does not include changes due to motivation, fatigue, or drugs.

Learning, psychology informs us, is the acquisition of information and knowledge, of skills and habits, and of attitudes and beliefs. It always involves a change in one of these areas—a change that is brought about by the learner's experiences. Take tying shoelaces, for example. This complex skill requires knowledge about how laces can be twisted and looped and pulled, hours of practice and experience, and maybe just a little luck as well.

Potential Changes in Behavior

Evidence of learning is found not only in *actual* but also in *potential* changes in behavior, because not all changes involved in learning are obvious and observable. For example, in the case entitled "The Talking Marks," there are some immediately apparent changes in the students' actual behavior—as, for example, when Tyler makes a pair of "talking marks" and places them appropriately, a behavior of which he was earlier incapable. There may also be other important changes that are not apparent but are still a fundamental part of learning.

Disposition For example, there may be an unfortunate change (a reduction) in Jenna's eagerness to participate in class activities following Ms. Swann's refusal to allow her to do so and also the loud scolding she received for the *may I–can I* grammatical error. This change is also an example of learning, but in this case it involves changes in the learner's **disposition**—that is, in the person's inclination to do or not to do something, rather than immediately observable changes in actual behavior. Changes in disposition have to do with motivation—a topic discussed in detail in Chapter 10. Motivational changes cannot always be observed but are no less real or important.

brought about by the learner's experiences. Accordingly, psychologists define learning as *all relatively permanent changes in potential for behavior that result from experience but are not due to fatigue, maturation, drugs, injury, or disease.* (See Figure 4.1.)

Experience	Learning	Change in Behavior
Contact with, participation in, and exposure to external or internal events to which the organism is sensitive	All relatively permanent changes in potential for behavior that result from experience but are not due to fatigue, maturation, drugs, injury, or disease	Actual or potentially observable changes, following experience, that provide evidence that learning has occurred

FIGURE 4.1 Evidence of learning is found in actual or potential changes in behavior as a result of experience. But learning is, itself, an invisible, internal neurological process. From *Theories of Human Learning: What the Old Man Said* by G. R. Lefrançois. Copyright © 2000 Wadsworth. Used by permission.

disposition An inclination or tendency to do (or not to do) something; an aspect of motivation.

The Talking Marks

THE PLACE: LYNN SWANN'S SECOND-GRADE CLASS

THE SITUATION: A PUNCTUATION LESSON ON QUO-TATION MARKS

Ms. Swann: And what we have to do is put the talking marks around the words that come right out of Mr. Brown's mouth (demonstrating with a cartoon character who has just said, "Here's my dog").
Tyler: Can I do it, Ms. Swann? Can I?

Ms. Swann: *May* I, Tyler. It's *may* I. Yes you *may* and we'll see if you *can*. (Ms. Swann erases the quotation marks. Tyler takes the green pen and makes a pair of recognizable opening and closing quotation marks. The children have already practiced making these "talking marks.")
Ms. Swann: Very good, Tyler. I see that you *can* do it.
Jenna: Can I do it too? Can I?
Ms. Swann: Weren't you paying any attention at all, Jenna? It's *may*! *May*, not *can*. No, you may not do it right now. We have to move along because it's going to be lunch time soon. (And the lesson continues . . .)

Capability Learning involves not only changes in disposition but also changes in **capability**—that is, changes in the skills or knowledge required to do something. Like changes in disposition, changes in capability are not always observed directly. For instance, in Ms. Swann's class, many other students will probably also learn to make quotation marks and to place them "around the words that come right out of Mr. Brown's mouth." But, like Jenna, most will not be given an opportunity to demonstrate this learning immediately. To determine whether students' dispositions or capabilities have changed following instruction, teachers need to give them an opportunity to engage in the relevant behavior. The inference that dispositions or capabilities have changed—in other words, that learning has occurred—will always be based on **performance**.

Performance Performance refers to actual behavior. If instruction affects learners so that their behavior (their performance) after instruction is observably different from that before instruction, we can conclude that learning has occurred. As we saw, however, learning often involves changes in both capabilities and dispositions that will not be evident in performance until learners are placed in a situation requiring the relevant performance.

Psychologists sometimes distinguish among three kinds of learning based upon the type of performance involved. Thus, learning that involves muscular coordination and physical skills (**motor learning**) appears to be different from learning involving emotions (**affective learning**) or that involving information or ideas (**cognitive learning**). These three distinctions are based on fairly obvious differences among the responses involved.

---

capability A capacity to do something. To be capable is to have the necessary knowledge and skills.

performance Actual behavior. The inference that learning has occurred is typically based on observed changes in performance.

motor learning Learning that involves muscular coordination and physical skills. Such common activities as walking and driving a car involve motor learning.

affective learning Changes in attitudes or emotions (affect) as a function of experience.

cognitive learning Learning concerned primarily with acquiring information, developing strategies for processing information, decision-making processes, and logical thought processes.

◻ THREE APPROACHES TO HUMAN LEARNING

Learning, as we saw, is defined as changes in potential for behavior as a function of experience. Not surprisingly, therefore, one of the first scientific approaches to understanding learning looks at actual behavior. This approach, labeled **behaviorism**, begins by trying to explain simple behaviors—observable and predictable responses. Accordingly, it is mainly concerned with conditions (called **stimuli**) that affect organisms and that may lead to behavior and with simple behaviors themselves (**responses**). Behavior-oriented (or behavioristic) researchers try to discover the rules that govern the formation of relationships between stimuli and responses (the rules of **conditioning**). For this reason, these theories are often referred to as **stimulus–response (S–R) theories** or **behavioristic theories**.

In contrast to behaviorism, a second approach, termed **cognitivism**, looks at the more intellectual or mental aspects of learning. Cognitive approaches deal mainly with questions relating to cognition, or knowing. Cognitive theorists are concerned with how we develop our fund of knowledge and how we eventually arrive at notions of ourselves as learners and rememberers and problem solvers. Children's gradual development of an awareness of themselves as knowers, their growing awareness of the strategies they can use to acquire and process information, and their ability to direct their efforts and to evaluate their cognitive activities are aspects of **metacognition**. Phrased another way, cognition refers to knowing; *metacognition* refers to knowing *about* knowing. Cognition-oriented researchers attempt to understand the nature of information: how it is acquired and organized by learners; how it can be recalled, modified, applied, and analyzed; and how the learner understands, evaluates, and controls the activities involved in cognition. Piaget, whose theory is described in Chapter 3, is a good example of a cognitive theorist.

A third approach to understanding human behavior is **humanism**. Humanistic psychologists are more concerned with human individuality and uniqueness than with discovering general rules to explain human responses. They focus more on emotional development than on information processing or stimuli and responses.[1]

---

behaviorism A general term for theories of learning primarily concerned with the observable components of behavior (stimuli and responses).

stimulus (*pl.* stimuli) Any change in the physical environment capable of exciting a sense organ.

response Any organic, muscular, glandular, or psychic process that results from stimulation.

conditioning A type of learning describable in terms of changing relationships between stimuli, between responses, or between both stimuli and responses.

stimulus–response (S–R) theory A learning theory with primary emphasis on stimuli and responses and the relationships between them. Such theories are also termed *behavioristic theories*.

cognitivism Theories of learning primarily concerned with such topics as perception, problem solving, information processing, and understanding.

metacognition Knowledge about knowing. As we grow and learn, we develop notions of ourselves as learners. Accordingly, we develop strategies to recognize our limitations and allow us to monitor our progress and take advantage of our efforts.

humanism A philosophical and psychological orientation primarily concerned with our humanity—that is, with our worth as individuals and those processes that are considered to make us more human.

---

[1] *PPC:* I think maybe the bear should point out to students that the section they've just finished reading is a very important summary of the next four chapters. It's a wonderful organizer, and maybe everyone should read it at least twice before continuing. And then come back to it later and it will all make a lot of sense.

Author: Okay. The section you've just finished reading *is* a summary of the next four chapters. And, yes, you probably should read it again. The jargon may seem imposing, but the concepts are really pretty straightforward. And it will all be absolutely clear when you come back and read it again after you've finished this section.

In this chapter we deal with some of the behaviorists' explanations of learning and their implications for teaching. Chapters 5 and 6 look at cognitive explanations. Chapter 7 discusses humanism (see Table 4.1).

PAVLOV'S CLASSICAL CONDITIONING

Some simple forms of learning require little information processing or understanding. They depend, instead, on the formation of *associations* which are often unconscious. A general label for this type of learning is **associative learning** (Wasserman & Miller, 1997).

---

associative learning A simple type of learning where one event comes to be associated with another because of past experience. Both classical and operant conditioning are forms of associative learning.

As an example of associative learning, see the case entitled "Of Pig Grunting and Flinching." We can probably assume that, before Robert began telling lies and being punished, he would not have flinched to hear Mrs. Grundy squeal. That he subsequently did so is an example of a simple, unconscious, and sometimes very powerful type of associative learning called **classical conditioning**. The qualifier *classical* is used simply to differentiate this specific form of learning from other forms of learning loosely referred to as *conditioning* in ordinary speech.

---

classical conditioning Also called "learning-through-stimulus substitution" because it involves the repeated pairing of two stimuli. Eventually a previously neutral (conditioned) stimulus comes to elicit the same response (conditioned response) that was previously elicited by the first stimulus (unconditioned stimulus). This was the type of conditioning first described by Pavlov.

TABLE 4.1
Three Approaches to Learning

APPROACH	MAJOR FOCUS	KEY VARIABLES/ CONCEPTS	REPRESENTATIVE THEORISTS	PRINCIPAL USEFULNESS FOR TEACHERS
Behaviorism	Behavior	Stimuli Responses Reinforcement Punishment Behavior modification Associative learning	Pavlov Watson Thorndike Skinner Bandura	Explains learning of skills and attitudes Emphasizes reinforcement
Cognitivism	Knowing	Decision making Understanding Cognitive structure Perception Information processes Memory	Ausubel Bruner Piaget	Explains development of understanding (meaning) Emphasizes importance of meaningfulness and organization
Humanism	The person	Self-concept Self-actualization Self-worth	Maslow & Rogers	Focuses on affective development Emphasizes adjustment and well-being

Of Pig Grunting and Flinching

THE TIME: 1848

THE PLACE: Mrs. Evelyn Grundy's classroom in Raleigh, North Carolina

THE SITUATION: 6-year-old Robert has been Misbehaving to Girls and Telling Lyes

In this Raleigh school system in 1848, the prescribed punishment for Misbehaving to Girls and Telling Lyes totals 17 lashes.* But because two separate infractions were involved, Mrs. Grundy deems it wise and judicious to double the punishment to 34 lashes. She administers the lashes herself. And every time she raises the cane to strike Robert, the effort makes her squeal hoarsely, a little like a pig grunting. By the tenth lash, Robert has begun to flinch just before the cane hits. He cries out quite loudly when it lands.

Later that day, when Mrs. Grundy is passing out the spellers, her back turned to Edward, his ruler-propelled spitball catches her just behind the left ear. She squeals loudly. And Robert flinches.

———
* **PPC:** The punishment sounds a little extreme. Readers will think you're making this up. Are you?
Author: Nope. See Table 4.4 if you don't believe me.

Ivan Pavlov, the Russian physiologist whose name will probably be associated forever with classical conditioning, stumbled upon his most famous observation almost by accident. At the time, his investigations dealt mainly with digestion in dogs. In fact, in 1904 he was awarded a Nobel prize in medicine and physiology for his work on digestion—strong evidence, claims Smith (1995), of Pavlov's remarkable experimental and inferential skills.

What Pavlov noticed in the course of his work on digestion was that the dogs in his laboratory began to salivate when they were about to be fed, even before they could see or smell the food. Strangely, they seemed to be salivating at the mere sight of their keeper or even when they simply heard his footsteps.

This simple observation led Pavlov to conduct a series of well-known experiments; he would ring a bell or sound a buzzer—neither of which ordinarily leads to salivation—and then immediately present the dogs with food, a stimulus that does lead to salivation. Pavlov soon found that if the procedure were repeated often enough, the bell or buzzer alone began to elicit salivation.

In Pavlov's experiments, the bell is referred to as a **conditioned stimulus** (CS); the food is an **unconditioned stimulus** (US); salivation in response to the food is an **unconditioned response** (UR), whereas salivation in response to the bell or buzzer is a **conditioned response** (CR).

The Mrs. Grundy/Robert case is a simple illustration of classical conditioning (as shown

---

conditioned stimulus (CS) A stimulus that initially does not elicit any response or that elicits a global, orienting response but that, as a function of being paired with an unconditioned stimulus and its response, acquires the capability of eliciting that same response. For example, a stimulus that is always present at the time of a fear reaction may become a conditioned stimulus for fear.

unconditioned response (UR) A response that is elicited by an unconditioned stimulus.

unconditioned stimulus (US) A stimulus that elicits a response before learning. All stimuli that are capable of eliciting reflexive behaviors are examples of unconditioned stimuli. For example, food is an unconditioned stimulus for the response of salivation.

conditioned response (CR) A response elicited by a conditioned stimulus. In some obvious ways, a conditioned response resembles, but is not identical to, its corresponding unconditioned response.

in Figure 4.2). In this example, the sound of the grunt serves as a conditioned stimulus. The fear reaction (flinch) is the initial unconditioned response; the pain of the cane serves as an unconditioned stimulus.

In general terms, a stimulus or situation that readily leads to a response can be paired with a **neutral stimulus** (one that does not lead to a response) to bring about classical conditioning. This learning is typically unconscious—that is, learners do not respond to the conditioned stimulus because they become aware of the relationship between it and an unconditioned stimulus. In fact, classical conditioning can occur even for responses over which the subject ordinarily has no control. For example, the application of a cold or hot pack directly to the skin can bring about constriction or dilation of blood vessels. If these stimuli are paired with a neutral stimulus such as a tone, the tone by itself will eventually lead to vascular constriction or dilation.

WATSON'S ENVIRONMENTALISM

According to J. B. Watson (1913, 1916), who was greatly influenced by the work of Pavlov, people are born with a limited number of reflexes. Learning, explained Watson, is just a matter of classical conditioning involving these reflexes. Hence, differences among people are entirely a function of their experiences. (This point of view, referred to as **environmentalism**, is discussed in more detail in Chapter 7.)

---

neutral stimulus A stimulus that does not initially lead reliably to a predictable response. For example, neutral stimuli are not associated with emotional responses until learning has occurred; at this point they are referred to as conditioned (rather than neutral) stimuli.

environmentalism The belief that whatever a child becomes is determined by experience (the environment) rather than by genetic makeup.

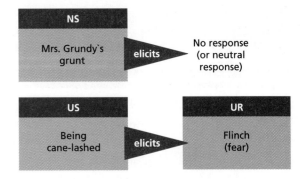

Before Conditioning

An unconditioned stimulus elicits an unconditioned fear response.

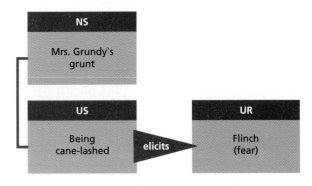

Conditioning Process

A neutral stimulus is repeatedly paired with the US.

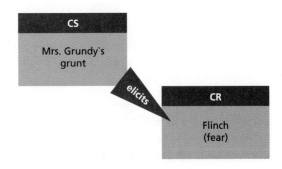

After Conditioning

The previously neutral stimulus becomes a conditioned stimulus eliciting the conditioned response of fear.

FIGURE 4.2 Classical conditioning: An initially neutral stimulus (NS) is paired with an unconditioned, fear-producing stimulus (US) so that the subject is eventually *conditioned* to fear the previously neutral stimulus. Fear is now a conditioned response (CR) to a conditioned stimulus (CS).

Watson's view was extremely influential in the early development of psychology in the United States. His insistence on precision, rigor, and objectivity was very much in line with the scientific spirit of the times—as was his rejection of popular but difficult to define (and measure) terms such as *mind*, *feeling*, and *sensation*. The belief that what we become is a function of our experiences also presents a just and egalitarian view of humans. If what we become is truly a function of the experiences to which we are subjected, we are in fact born equal. Watson declared that any child can become a doctor or a judge. In fact, however, things are not quite that simple: Not everybody can become a doctor or a judge (see Chapter 7).

Educational Implications of Pavlov's and Watson's Behaviorism

Classical conditioning, especially of emotional reactions, occurs in all schools, virtually at all times, regardless of any other kind of learning going on at the same time. And it is largely through these unconscious processes that students come to dislike schools, subjects, teachers, and related stimuli—or to like them.

To illustrate, a school subject, assuming that it is new to the student, is a neutral stimulus that evokes little emotional response in the beginning. But the teacher, the classroom, or another distinctive stimulus in the student's immediate environment that is repeatedly associated with the subject can serve as an unconditioned stimulus. This unconditioned stimulus might be associated with pleasant responses (a comfortable desk, a friendly teacher) or with more negative reactions (a cold, hard desk; a cold, hard teacher with a grating voice and squeaking chalk). Following successive pairings of the subject (mathematics) with this distinctive unconditioned stimulus (teacher's unpleasant voice, and so on), the emotions (attitudes) associated with the unconditioned stimulus may become classically conditioned to the subject. Mathematics will now be associated with the negative responses previously linked with the unconditioned stimulus (see Figure 4.3). Phrased

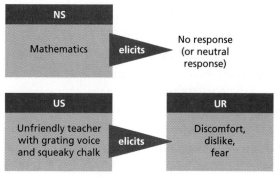

Before Conditioning

Mathematics elicits no strong emotional response; the unconditional stimulus elicits negative reactions.

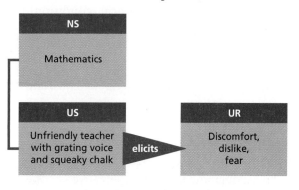

Conditioning Process

Mathematics is paired repeatedly with the unconditioned stimulus (teacher).

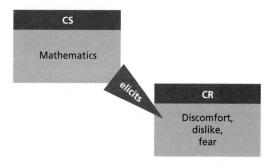

After Conditioning

Mathematics has become a conditioned stimulus associated with negative reactions.

FIGURE 4.3 Classical conditioning of math phobia

another way, students learn attitudes toward subjects, learning, and school largely as a function of classical conditioning. Thus, it is entirely possible to teach students mathematics and at the same time teach them to dislike mathematics. Learning mathematics is likely to involve cognitive processes (and perhaps some form of conditioning as well, particularly if repetitive skills are involved), whereas learning to dislike mathematics can involve mainly classical conditioning.

Behaviorist theories such as these lead to teacher-centered, **direct instruction** approaches to teaching—as opposed to more student-centered, **constructivist approaches**. That is, these theories emphasize the teacher's role in organizing the learning situation and imparting information—rather than the student's role in discovering and understanding.

The clearest and most important instructional implications of classical conditioning include the following:

▲ Teachers need to do whatever they can to maximize the frequency, distinctiveness, and potency of pleasant unconditioned stimuli in their classrooms.

▲ Teachers should try to minimize the unpleasant aspects of being a student, thus reducing the number and potency of negative unconditioned stimuli in their classrooms.

▲ Teachers must know what is being paired with what in their classrooms.

---

direct instruction A phrase used to describe teacher-directed approaches to teaching—in contrast with more student-centered approaches such as reciprocal teaching and cooperative learning (often included among *constructivist approaches*).

constructivist approaches General label for instructional methods that are highly learner-centered and that reflect the belief that meaningful information is constructed by students rather than given to them. Often contrasted with *direct instruction*, constructivist approaches are reflected in discovery learning, cognitive apprenticeship, and humanistic approaches to teaching.

The old adage that learning should be fun is more than a schoolchild's frivolous plea; it follows directly from classical conditioning theory. A teacher who makes students smile and laugh while she has them repeat the 6-times table, because of the variety of stimuli and responses being paired, may succeed in teaching students (1) to smile and laugh, a worthwhile undertaking in its own right; (2) to associate stimuli such as 6 × 7 with responses such as "42," a valuable piece of information; and (3) to like arithmetic—and the teacher, the school, the smell of chalk, the feel of a book's pages, and on and on.

What does a teacher who makes students suffer grimly through their multiplication tables teach?

THORNDIKE'S CONNECTIONISM

People are always trying to show how intelligent their pet animals are, claimed psychologist Edward L. Thorndike (1898). If a dog gets lost and then finds its way home, newspapers run stories about how smart dogs are. Stories about the hundreds of dogs who go out for an evening stroll and stupidly get lost, never to find their way home again, are much less interesting and seldom get published—except in the lost-and-found column.

Trial-and-Error Learning

But are animals really intelligent? asked Thorndike. He reasoned that anecdotes make very poor scientific evidence. And so he devised a series of tasks that, in a sense, serve as crude measures of animal intelligence. The most famous of these are the so-called *puzzle boxes*; the most common one is illustrated in Figure 4.4. It's designed so that a cat locked in the box can get out only if it does three things: pull a string to release one lock, step on a lever to release a second, and flip a latch upright so that the door will open. To make

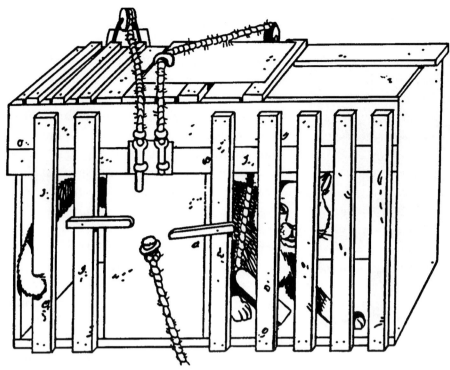

FIGURE 4.4 Thorndike's puzzle box: To escape from the box, the cat had to pull a string to release one of the door locks, step on the lever to release the second, and then flick one of the door latches down. From E.L. Thorndike, "Animal intelligence: An Experimental Study of the Associative Processes in Animals." *Psychological Review Monograph Supplement*, 1898, 2(8).

sure that the cat will be highly motivated to get out, Thorndike typically placed a juicy morsel, like a dead fish, just far enough away that the cat couldn't quite reach it through the bars.

So what does a hungry cat do in this situation? It uses up all of its ready-made solutions like trying to squeeze between the bars, scratching and clawing at the door, and meowing for help. And when none of these strategies work, it doesn't sit back and contemplate the situation, trying to figure out a solution. No, says Thorndike. What the cat does instead is continue to try out dozens of different actions until, by chance, it stumbles upon the right combination of actions and escapes from the puzzle box. Remarkably, however, the next time the cat is placed in the same situation, it escapes quicker—and even quicker the third time, and the next. As Figure 4.5 shows, one typical Thorndikean cat

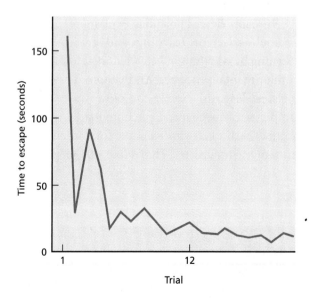

FIGURE 4.5 The behavior of one cat in Thorndike's puzzle box: The cat took almost three minutes to escape the first time but almost always less than one minute after the first successful escape. From E.L. Thorndike, "Animal Intelligence: An Experimental Study of the Associative Processes in Animals." *Psychological Review Monograph Supplement*, 1898, 2(8).

"That is the correct answer, Billy, but I'm afraid you don't win anything for it."
Drawing by Lorenz; © 1986 The New Yorker Magazine, Inc.

The essence of Thorndike's explanation of human learning can then be summarized as follows: In a given situation, a person makes a variety of responses until a response leads to a solution (or, in Thorndike's words, "a satisfying state of affairs"). That response is then learned or, again to use Thorndike's words, "stamped in." Thus, learning involves the "stamping in" of connections between stimuli and responses: Hence the theory is labeled **connectionism**.

Contiguity or Reinforcement

There are two competing explanations for the formation of associations between stimuli, between responses, or between stimuli and responses. The one favored by Watson and Pavlov is the **contiguity** explanation. It maintains that the simultaneous occurrence of events is sufficient to bring about associative learning. Thus, it is sufficient to pair the buzzer and the food x number of times (that is, to present them in contiguity) for learning to occur.

A second option is the **reinforcement** explanation. This explanation, introduced by Thorndike and popularized by B. F. Skinner, is labeled a reinforcement approach. It maintains that the consequences of a response lead to it being learned (or not learned).

took almost three minutes to escape the first time—which is really not very long at all. But after that, it typically took far less than one minute.

It seems clear, Thorndike explained, that this is **trial-and-error learning** and certainly not learning by what might be called **insight** or other similar mental processes. And people, Thorndike insisted, learn in exactly the same way: "These simple semi-mechanical phenomena . . . which animal learning discloses are the fundamentals of human learning also" (Thorndike, 1913b, p. 16).

---

trial-and-error learning A Thorndikean explanation for learning based on the idea that when placed in a problem situation, an individual will emit a variety of responses but will eventually learn the correct one as a result of reinforcement. Trial-and-error explanations for learning are sometimes contrasted with insight explanations.

insight The perception of relationships among elements of a problem situation. A problem-solving method that contrasts strongly with trial and error.

---

connectionism A theory that explains learning as the formation of bonds (connections) between stimuli and responses. The term is attributed to Thorndike.

contiguity The occurrence of things both simultaneously and in the same space. Contiguity is frequently used to explain the occurrence of classical conditioning. The simultaneity of the unconditioned and conditioned stimulus is assumed to be sufficient to explain the formation of the link between the two.

reinforcement The effect of a reinforcer; specifically, to increase the probability that a response will occur.

Thorndike's Laws of Learning

Much of Thorndike's theory deals specifically with the conditions that lead to the stamping in or stamping out of "bonds," (his word for connections or associations). Details of these conditions are expressed in a series of laws of learning; most of these were derived directly from experiments with animals. Later in Thorndike's career (after 1930), he made major changes to several of the most important of these laws. These laws form the basis of his theory of human learning.

The Law of Effect Probably the most important of Thorndike's laws is the **law of effect**. It maintains that *responses occurring just prior to a satisfying state of affairs are more likely to be repeated.* The converse is also true, although less important, claimed Thorndike: *Responses occurring just prior to an annoying state of affairs are more likely not to be repeated.* Thus, what Thorndike called *satisfiers* and *annoyers* are critical to learning.

"Hold on!", staunch behaviorists might object at this point. Terms like *satisfying* and *annoying* are simply too subjective to be acceptable to behaviorists. Not so, responded Thorndike, because *satisfying* and *annoying* can be defined completely objectively. A satisfying state of affairs is one that the animal (or person) tries to maintain, or at least does nothing to avoid. And an annoying state of affairs is one that the animal (or person) either tries to change, or does nothing to maintain (Thorndike, 1913a). These definitions have nothing to do with the organism's *feelings,* but only with *behavior.*

After 1930, Thorndike (1931) modified the law of effect in an important way. He had previously believed that annoying states of affairs lead

to connections being stamped out (forgotten). But further experimentation led him to the view that *satisfiers* lead to learning, whereas *annoyers* do not lead to forgetting but simply lead the learner to do something else.

The Law of Readiness Thorndike's **law of readiness** recognizes that certain responses are more or less likely than others to be learned (stamped in), depending on the learner's readiness. Such factors as maturation and previous learning are clearly involved in determining whether learning is easy, difficult, or impossible. This important law provides the basis for Thorndike's definitions of **reward** and **punishment**. Specifically, the learner's readiness determines whether a state of affairs is pleasant or not. Thorndike maintained that a pleasant state of affairs—a reward—results when a person is ready to do something and is allowed to do it. By the same token, not being allowed to do something when one is ready, or being forced to do something when one is not ready, results in an annoying state of affairs—punishment.

The Law of Exercise, Repealed The **law of exercise** expresses Thorndike's initially strong belief that

---

law of effect A Thorndikean law of learning that states that the effect of a response leads to its being learned (stamped in) or not learned (stamped out).

---

law of readiness A Thorndikean law of learning that takes into account that certain types of learning are difficult or impossible unless the learner is ready. In this context, readiness refers to maturational level, previous learning, motivational factors, and other characteristics of the individual that relate to learning.

reward An object, stimulus, event, or outcome that is perceived as being pleasant and that can therefore be reinforcing.

punishment Involves either the presentation of an unpleasant stimulus or the withdrawal of a pleasant stimulus, as a consequence of behavior. Punishment should not be confused with negative reinforcement.

law of exercise A Thorndikean law of learning that states that bonds (connections) become more strengthened the more often they are repeated (exercised). Thorndike rejected this law later in his career.

bonds become more strengthened each time they are repeated (or exercised). This conviction had a tremendous influence on education in North America throughout several decades of the 20th century because it lent scientific credibility to the belief that practice and repetition were among the most important of all instructional techniques. Ironically, however, Thorndike rejected this law of learning most emphatically after 1930. He had determined through experimentation—with human subjects this time—that repetition alone does not cause learning. In his words, "The repetition of a situation may change a man as little as the repetition of a message over a wire changes the wire" (Thorndike, 1931, p. 14).

Subsidiary Laws Several subsidiary laws also form an important part of Thorndike's theory. These can be summarized briefly as follows:

- ▲ The **law of multiple responses** is based on Thorndike's observation that individuals faced with a difficult problem for which they have no ready solution will engage in a variety of responses until one response produces a satisfying effect. In other words, it is through trial and error that problems are solved. As a result of this law, Thorndike's theory came to be known as the theory of trial-and-error learning.
- ▲ The **law of set or attitude** recognizes that learning is partly a function of predetermined attitudes or tendencies to react in given ways (a tendency to react is defined as a set). Attitudes are strongly influenced by culture. For example, in some cultures, people are more likely to react aggressively than in others—and thus more likely to be reinforced for and to learn aggressive responses.
- ▲ The **law of prepotency of elements** suggests that organisms typically react to the most significant (or *prepotent*) elements of a situation. Thus, the cat in the puzzle box doesn't spend much time scratching at the ceiling but is more likely to try different responses with the lever and the string, both of which are more salient (striking) features of the situation.
- ▲ The **law of response by analogy** points out that when we are placed in a new situation we tend to react in ways that would be appropriate in similar (analogous) situations. That is, we transfer responses from one situation to another, an ability that is extremely important to our adaptation. For example, because of transfer (or, in Thorndike's terms, *response by analogy*), we are able to apply laws of addition and subtraction when we buy new items in stores where we have never shopped before.

Instructional Applications of Thorndike's Theory

Much of Thorndike's research and writing was directed specifically toward applying his findings to education; therefore, his theories are rich with instructional implications. As is true of all behavioristic positions, these instructional

---

law of multiple responses One of Thorndike's laws based on his observation that learning involves the emission of a variety of responses (multiple responses) until one (presumably an appropriate one) is reinforced. Because of this law Thorndike's theory is often called a theory of trial-and-error learning.

law of set or attitude A Thorndikean law of learning that recognizes that we are often predisposed to respond in certain ways as a result of our experiences and previously learned attitudes. This subsidiary law acknowledges the influence of culture and experience in determining our attitudes and, therefore, our most likely responses in a given situation.

law of prepotency of elements A Thorndikean law of learning that states that people tend to respond to the most striking (prepotent) of the various elements that make up a stimulus situation.

law of response by analogy A Thorndikean law to explain transfer. An analogy is typically an explanation, comparison, or illustration based on similarity. In Thorndike's system, response by analogy refers to responses that occur because of similarities between two situations.

implications are more relevant to a model of *direct instruction* than to more *constructivist* approaches such as discovery learning or cooperative approaches.

Rewarding Correct Trials Perhaps most important are the implications of his belief that learning results from correct trials being rewarded (leading to a satisfying state of affairs). It follows that teachers and schools need to provide opportunities for students to emit a variety of responses and that correct responses need to be rewarded. This theory also stresses that rewards and punishments must be tailored to the situation and to the child and that, among other things, the child's readiness should be taken into consideration.

Establishing Attitudes Many of the instructional implications of Thorndike's theory are found in his subsidiary laws. The law of set or attitude, for example, recognizes that people often respond to novel situations in terms of the sets, or attitudes, that they bring with them. Teachers often exercise considerable influence in determining student attitudes. For example, they can encourage students to develop attitudes that place a high value on creativity. Subsequently, students will be more likely to prize creative behavior and perhaps even to respond creatively.

This law also implies that cultural background and immediate environment not only affect how a person responds but also determine what will be viewed as satisfying or annoying. For example, the student's environment may determine that academic success will be satisfying—or that popularity will be more satisfying than academic success.

Readiness It seems obvious that a learner who is ready for a specific type of learning is far more likely to profit from such learning experiences than another who is not ready. The question is: Precisely what is involved in being ready?

Readiness can depend on physical maturation, on the development of intellectual skills, on the acquisition of important background information, and perhaps on motivation. Hence, to assess and to enhance readiness, teachers need a knowledge of children's emotional and intellectual development—topics that we covered in Chapters 2 and 3. They also need to know something about how students learn and about their motivation, topics covered in the chapters that make up Part Three of this text and in Chapter 10 as well.

Attracting Attention The law of prepotency of elements recognizes that people respond to the most significant or the most striking aspects of a stimulus situation and not necessarily to the entire situation. Obviously, students should not and probably cannot respond to all the sights and sounds that surround them at any given moment. Hence, teachers must be careful to stress (make prepotent) important aspects of the learning situation (for example, by underlining or boldfacing, through the use of color, through the use of voice and gestures, through repetition, and so on).

Generalizing Generalization (sometimes referred to as **transfer** or *response by analogy*) is one of the important goals of education. Generalization occurs whenever a previously learned response is transferred to a new situation—or when a new stimulus is reacted to as though it were familiar. When Tammy uses a multiplication rule she

---

generalization The transference of a response from one stimulus to a similar stimulus (stimulus generalization) or the transference of a similar response for another response in the face of a single stimulus (response generalization). A child who responds with fear in a new situation that resembles an old, fear-producing situation is showing evidence of stimulus generalization. Also termed *transfer*.

transfer A general term for the application of old learning to a new situation. Also termed *generalization*.

learned in school to determine how many packs of bubble gum two quarters will buy, she is generalizing. Thorndike believed that the transference of a response to a new stimulus is a function of the similarity between the two stimuli—hence the law of response by analogy.

Thorndike suggested that teachers can facilitate transfer by pointing out a variety of situations where a single response (or rule) is applicable. He also emphasized the importance of pointing out connections among ideas. These connections, Thorndike insisted, are the basis of knowledge.

SKINNER'S OPERANT CONDITIONING

By definition, behaviorists are concerned with behavior. They define learning in terms of changes in behavior and look to the environment for explanations of these changes. Their theories are associative; they deal with connections or associations that are formed among stimuli and responses. And, as we have seen, these theories make use of one or both of two principal classes of explanations for learning: those based on *contiguity* (simultaneity of stimulus and response events) and those based on the *effects of behavior* (reinforcement and punishment). Pavlov and Watson are contiguity theorists; Thorndike is a reinforcement theorist. And so is B. F. Skinner, one of the most influential psychologists of the 20th century and the originator and chief spokesperson for the theory of **operant conditioning.**

operant conditioning A type of learning that involves an increase in the probability that a response will occur as a function of reinforcement. Most of Skinner's experimental work investigates the principles of operant conditioning.

Respondents and Operants

Skinner was among the first to make a distinction between two types of behaviors—a distinction that Rehfeldt and Hayes (1998) say many psychologists still consider valid and important. On the one hand, many responses can be brought about by a stimulus and can become conditioned to other stimuli in the manner described by Pavlov and Watson. Skinner referred to these responses as **elicited responses,** and he labeled the behavior **respondent** because it occurs in response to a stimulus.

But Skinner claimed that there is a second, much larger and more important class of behaviors. It consists of behaviors that are not elicited by any known stimuli but are simply **emitted responses.** These are labeled **operants** because, in a sense, they are operations performed by the organism. Another way of making this distinction is to say that in the case of respondent behavior, the organism is *reacting to* the environment, whereas in the case of operant behavior, the organism *acts upon* the environment. Another way of distinguishing between respondents and operants is to note that respondents appear largely involuntary, whereas operants are more voluntary (Skinner would not have used these terms, however; he believed them to involve unnecessary speculation). (See Table 4.2.)

elicited response A response brought about by a stimulus. This expression is synonymous with the term *respondent.*

respondent A term used by Skinner in contrast to the term *operant.* A respondent is a response elicited by a known, specific stimulus. Unconditioned responses are examples of respondents.

emitted response A response not elicited by a stimulus but simply emitted by the organism. An emitted response is, in fact, an operant.

operant Skinner's term for a response not elicited by any known or obvious stimulus. Most significant human behaviors appear to be operants (for example, writing a letter or going for a walk).

TABLE 4.2
Classical and Operant Conditioning

CLASSICAL (PAVLOVIAN)	OPERANT (SKINNERIAN)
Deals with respondents, which are elicited by stimuli and appear involuntary	Deals with operants, which are emitted as instrumental acts
Reactions to the environment	Actions upon the environment
Type S conditioning (S for stimuli)	Type R conditioning (R for reinforcement)

The distinction between respondent and operant behavior can be clarified further by examining some simple behaviors. Sneezing, blinking, being angry, afraid, or excited—these are all respondents. What they have in common is that they are largely automatic, involuntary, and almost inevitable responses to specific situations. In other words, they are responses that can be reliably elicited by specific stimuli. Such responses can be classically conditioned.

In contrast, driving a car, writing a letter, singing, reading a book, and kissing a baby are generally operants. Their common characteristics are that they are deliberate and intentional. They occur not as inevitable responses to specific stimulation but as personally controlled actions (rather than reactions). And they are subject to the laws of operant conditioning.

Operant conditioning is somewhat different from Thorndike's conception of learning and his law of effect, because it does not involve obvious stimuli. Thorndike believed that the effect of reinforcement is to strengthen the bond that exists between the stimulus and the response, whereas Skinner declared that the stimulus is usually unknown and, in any case, it is irrelevant to learning: The link is formed between response and reinforcement rather than between stimulus and response. Essentially, all that happens in operant learning is that when an emitted response is reinforced, the probability increases that it will be repeated.

What Is Operant Conditioning?

The clearest illustration of operant conditioning involves a typical Skinnerian experiment. In this experiment, a rat is placed in a **Skinner box**, a small, controlled environment (see Figure 4.6). The Skinner box is constructed to make certain

---

Skinner box Various experimental environments used by Skinner in his investigations of operant conditioning. The typical Skinner box is a cagelike structure equipped with a lever and a food tray attached to a food mechanism. It allows the investigator to study operants (for example, bar pressing) and the relationship between an operant and reinforcement.

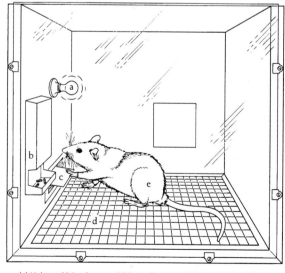

(a) Light   b) Food tray   (c) Bar or lever   (d) Electric grid   (e) Rat

FIGURE 4.6 A Skinner box: from G. R. Lefrançois, *Theories of Human Learning: Kro's Report.* (3rd ed.) Copyright © 1995 Wadsworth. Used by permission.

responses highly probable and to make it possible for the experimenter to measure these responses and to punish or reward them. For our typical experiment, the box contains a lever, a light, an electric grid on the floor, and a food tray, all arranged so that when the rat depresses the lever, the light goes on and a food pellet is released into the tray. Under these circumstances, most rats will quickly learn to depress the lever, and they will continue to do so for long periods of time even if they do not receive a food pellet each time they work the lever. Similarly, rats can quickly be trained to avoid the lever if depressing it activates a mild electric current in the floor grid. However, rats will also learn to depress the lever if doing so turns off the current which is otherwise constant.

Most of the basic elements of Skinner's theory are evident in this situation. The rat's action of depressing the lever is an operant—an almost random behavior that is simply emitted rather than being elicited by a specific stimulus. The food pellets serve as reinforcement. Their presentation as a result of the rat's depressing the lever increases the probability that whenever the rat finds itself in this situation, it will saunter over to the lever and depress it.

In general terms, operant conditioning increases the probability that a response will occur again. This increase is a result of reinforcement (more about this shortly). Furthermore, Skinner's model of operant conditioning states that the reward, together with whatever **discriminated stimuli** (S^D)[2] were present at the time of reinforcement, are stimuli that, after learning, may bring about the operant. For example, the rat's view (and smell) of

the inside of the Skinner box may eventually serve as stimuli for lever-pressing behavior. But, cautions Skinner, these are not stimuli in the sense that a puff of air in the eye is a stimulus that elicits a blink. Rather, these discriminated stimuli serve simply as signals that a certain behavior may lead to reinforcement. (See Figure 4.7 for a model of operant learning in the classroom and Figure 4.9 for additional classroom examples.)

Before Conditioning

Stimulus Context: Classroom

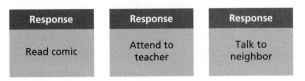

Various responses are emitted
in a certain stimulus context.

Conditioning Process

Stimulus Context: Classroom

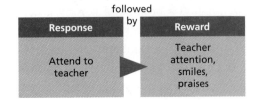

One response is systematically reinforced.

After Conditioning

Stimulus Context: Classroom

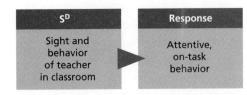

The reinforced response becomes more frequent.
Stimuli accompanying the reward (discriminated
stimuli, or S^D) acquire control over the response.

---

discriminated stimulus (S^D) A stimulus that is perceived by the organism. In operant conditioning, the discriminated stimulus elicits the response.

---

[2] Also called discriminative stimuli; refers to those aspects of a situation (stimuli) that differentiate it from other situations.

FIGURE 4.7 Operant conditioning in the classroom: In operant conditioning, unlike classical conditioning, the original response is emitted rather than elicited by a stimulus. In this example, a variety of off-task and on-task behaviors are emitted. Reinforcement leads to the more frequent occurrence of on-task behaviors.

Reinforcement

The causes of behavior, Skinner insisted, are *outside* the organism; they have to do with the consequences of actions. Thus, his science of behavior seeks to discover and describe the laws that govern interactions between the organism and the environment (Skinner, 1969). To do this, he relies on what he describes as the **experimental analysis of behavior.**

Recall that experiments involve two kinds of variables: independent variables (factors that can be directly manipulated experimentally, like reinforcement) and dependent variables (those that are affected by manipulations of the independent variables, like the rate of response). The main independent variables in Skinner's system are the *type of reinforcement* and the *reinforcement schedule* (how reinforcement is presented). The main dependent variables are the rate at which responses occur, the length of time required for learning, and the length of time that the behavior persists after reinforcement stops (see Table 4.3). We look at each of these variables in the following sections.

Reinforcement Defined Skinner made an important distinction between two related terms: **reinforcer** and *reinforcement.* A reinforcer is, in Skinnerian terms, a stimulus; reinforcement is the *effect* of this stimulus. For example, candy can be a reinforcer because it can be reinforcing and because it is a stimulus. A piece of candy, however, is not a reinforcement, although its

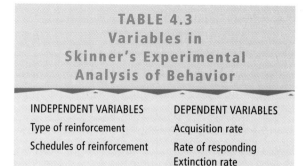

TABLE 4.3 Variables in Skinner's Experimental Analysis of Behavior	
INDEPENDENT VARIABLES	DEPENDENT VARIABLES
Type of reinforcement	Acquisition rate
Schedules of reinforcement	Rate of responding
	Extinction rate

effect on a person can be an example of reinforcement.

The most widely accepted definition of a reinforcer is that it is *any stimulus that increases the probability that a response will occur.* This definition makes it clear that the effect of a stimulus determines whether it will be reinforcing. Thus, the only objective proof that a stimulus is a reinforcer resides in the increased intensity, frequency, or duration of a presumably reinforced response. This means that a given situation (stimulus) can be highly reinforcing for one person but not at all reinforcing for another. First-grade students may react with renewed interest and effort when they are presented with little gold stars in recognition of their work. College students whose professor offered them little stars might think, with some justification, that the professor was a bit strange.

Reinforcers can be primary or generalized. A **primary reinforcer** is a stimulus that is naturally reinforcing—that is, that the organism does not have to learn is reinforcing. Primary reinforcers are ordinarily related to an unlearned need or drive: food, drink, or sex. Stimuli that satisfy

---

experimental analysis of behavior A phrase typically associated with Skinner's system. The term reflects his emphasis on the objective analysis of the variables involved in behavior—specifically, what the organism does, the circumstances under which the action occurs, and the consequences of the action (whether behavior occurs again under similar circumstances).

reinforcer A stimulus that causes reinforcement.

---

primary reinforcer A stimulus that is reinforcing in the absence of any learning. Such stimuli as food and drink are primary reinforcers because, presumably, an organism does not need to learn that these are pleasant.

these drives tend to be highly reinforcing for most organisms. They are referred to as *positive stimuli*.

A **generalized reinforcer** is a previously neutral stimulus that, through repeated pairings with other reinforcers in various situations, has become generally reinforcing for many behaviors. Prestige, money, and success are examples of extremely powerful generalized reinforcers.

Reinforcers can be either positive or negative. A **positive reinforcer** is a stimulus that increases the probability of a response occurring when it is added to a situation. A **negative reinforcer** has the same effect as a result of being removed from the situation. Negative reinforcers tend to be *aversive* stimuli (such as an electric shock or detention). Their effect, when removed or discontinued, is an increase in behavior. Positive reinforcers tend to be *pleasant* stimuli.

In the Skinner box example, food pellets are pleasant stimuli that serve as positive reinforcement—as does the light. However, if a mild current were turned on in the electric grid that runs through the floor of the box, and if this current were turned off only when the rat depressed the lever, turning off the current would be an example of an aversive stimulus serving as a negative reinforcer.

Reinforcement and Punishment in the Classroom

In summary, there are two types of reinforcement: One involves presenting a pleasant stimulus (positive reinforcement; *reward*); the other involves removing an aversive stimulus (negative reinforcement; **relief**). Similarly, there are two types of punishment, each the converse of one type of reinforcement. On one hand is the punishment that occurs when a pleasant stimulus is removed (**penalty**; often termed *removal* punishment); on the other hand is the more familiar situation when an aversive stimulus is presented (castigation; sometimes called *presentation* punishment).

Keep in mind that both positive and aversive stimuli can be used for either reinforcement or punishment. As Figure 4.8 illustrates, this

---

relief A common expression for negative reinforcement—the type of reinforcement that results when an unpleasant stimulus is removed as a consequence of behavior.

penalty The type of punishment that involves losing or giving up something pleasant.

---

generalized reinforcer A stimulus that is not reinforcing before being paired with a primary reinforcer. Generalized reinforcers are present so often at the time of reinforcement that they come to be reinforcing for a wide variety of unrelated activities. Stimuli such as social prestige, praise, and money are generalized reinforcers for human behavior.

positive reinforcer A stimulus that, when added to a situation, increases the probability that a response will recur. This usually takes the form of a pleasant stimulus (reward).

negative reinforcer A stimulus that has the effect of increasing the probability of occurrence of the response that precedes it. Negative reinforcement ordinarily takes the form of an unpleasant or noxious stimulus that is removed as a result of a specific response.

Teacher reinforcements

	Behavior Strengthened	**Behavior Weakened**
Added to a situation after a response	Positive reinforcement (reward) [Louella is given a jelly bean for being good]	Presentation punishment (Type I: castigation) [Louella has her nose tweaked for being bad]
Taken away from a situation after a response	Negative reinforcement (relief) [Louella's nose is released because she says "I'm sorry."]	Removal punishment (Type II: penalty) [Louella has her jelly bean taken away for being bad]

FIGURE 4.8 Reinforcement and punishment

depends on whether stimuli are added to or taken away from the situation following a behavior. *Also keep in mind that whether a stimulus is reinforcing or not depends entirely on its effect on behavior.*

Figure 4.8 summarizes the four possibilities implicit in adding or removing pleasant or aversive stimuli; the sections that follow illustrate each of these in the classroom.

Positive Reinforcement (Reward) Examples of positive reinforcement in the classroom are so numerous and so obvious as to make citing any one appear platitudinous. Whenever a teacher smiles at students, says something pleasant to them, commends them for their work, assigns high grades, selects someone for a special project, or tells a mother how clever her child is, the teacher is using positive reinforcement. (See Chapter 11 for a more detailed discussion of various kinds of classroom reinforcement.)

Negative Reinforcement (Relief) Implicit or explicit threats of punishment, failure, detention, ridicule, parental anger, humiliation, and sundry other unpleasant eventualities make up the bulk of the modern, well-equipped teacher's arsenal of aversive stimuli that can be used either as negative reinforcers or as one kind of punishment. When these threats follow unruly, undisci-

plined, or otherwise unacceptable behaviors, they illustrate presentation punishment, or *castigation* (the presentation of an unpleasant stimulus following undesirable behavior). When the threat of any of these possibilities is removed following acceptable behavior, this provides an example of negative reinforcement (the removal of an unpleasant stimulus following desirable behavior, termed *relief*). Negative and sometimes maladaptive behaviors, such as the tendency to escape or avoid situations, often result from the overly zealous administration of negative reinforcement.

Presentation Punishment (Castigation) The type of punishment that results from the presentation of an aversive stimulus, usually used in an attempt to eliminate undesirable behavior, is sometimes labeled **presentation punishment**. One classic example is the use of the lash in one North Carolina school in the year 1848 (see Table 4.4 and Mrs. Grundy's case, earlier in this chapter)—a practice that is no longer widely accepted.

---

presentation punishment A label for the kind of punishment that results from presenting an aversive stimulus (such as a frozen boot) following a behavior. So called because it involves presenting an aversive stimulus. Also called Type I punishment.

TABLE 4.4
Excerpt from a List of Punishments in a North Carolina School, 1848

NO.	RULES OF SCHOOL	LASHES
1	Boys and Girls Playing Together	4
3	Fighting	5
7	Playing at Cards at School	4
8	Climbing for Every Foot over Three Feet up a Tree	1
9	Telling Lyes	7
11	Nick Naming Each Other	4
16	For Misbehaving to Girls	10
19	For Drinking Spirituous Liquors at School	8
22	For Wearing Long Finger Nails	2
27	Girls Going to Boys' Play Places	2
33	Wrestling at School	4
41	For Throwing Anything Harder than Your Trab Ball	4
42	For Every Word You Miss in Your Heart Lesson Without Good Excuse	1
47	For Going about the Barn or Doing Any Mischief about the Place	7

Source: From C. L. Coon. (1915). *North Carolina schools and academies*. Raleigh, N.C.: Edwards and Broughton.

Removal Punishment (Penalty) Punishment that involves the removal of a positive stimulus following a behavior (penalty) is sometimes labeled **removal punishment** (because, in contrast with *presentation punishment*, it involves removing a stimulus). The fairly common practice of detaining students after regular class hours, insofar as it removes the apparently positive privilege of going home, is an example of this type of punishment. (See Figure 4.9 for classroom examples of operant conditioning.)

The Power of Reinforcement and Punishment

The simple fact that reinforcement often leads to changes in behavior that define learning can eas-

ily be demonstrated in the behavior of both animals and people. That punishment has an equal, if opposite, effect is not nearly so obvious. As Thorndike conceded in 1931, pleasure is much more potent in stamping in responses than pain is in stamping them out.

The Case Against Punishment Leaving out ethical or humanitarian considerations, there are several other reasons that the use of punishment is not an entirely satisfactory means of behavior control:

▲ Punishment does not ordinarily illustrate or emphasize desirable behavior but simply draws attention to undesirable responses, so it is not very useful in a learning situation.
▲ Punishment is often accompanied by highly undesirable emotional side effects that can be associated with the punisher rather than with the punished behavior.

---

removal punishment A label for the kind of punishment that results from removing a pleasant stimulus (such as permission to watch television) following a behavior (penalty). Also called Type II punishment because it involves removing a stimulus.

Stimulus Context: Classroom

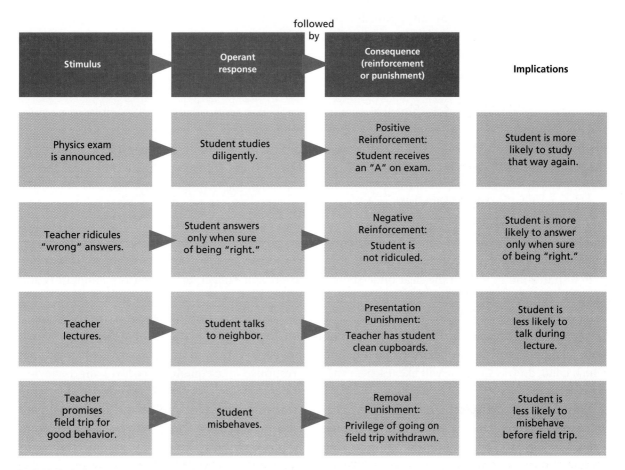

followed by

Stimulus	Operant response	Consequence (reinforcement or punishment)	Implications
Physics exam is announced.	Student studies diligently.	Positive Reinforcement: Student receives an "A" on exam.	Student is more likely to study that way again.
Teacher ridicules "wrong" answers.	Student answers only when sure of being "right."	Negative Reinforcement: Student is not ridiculed.	Student is more likely to answer only when sure of being "right."
Teacher lectures.	Student talks to neighbor.	Presentation Punishment: Teacher has student clean cupboards.	Student is less likely to talk during lecture.
Teacher promises field trip for good behavior.	Student misbehaves.	Removal Punishment: Privilege of going on field trip withdrawn.	Student is less likely to misbehave before field trip.

FIGURE 4.9   Classroom examples of operant conditioning: The first two examples (positive and negative reinforcement, respectively) lead to an *increase* in the likelihood of the response. The last two examples (both forms of punishment) lead to a *decrease* in the likelihood of the response. Teachers may also inadvertently reinforce maladaptive behaviors (second example).

▲ Punishment does not always lead to the elimination of a response but sometimes only to its suppression. That is, a behavior is seldom forgotten as a result of punishment, although it may be avoided—sometimes only temporarily.

▲ Punishment simply does not often work. Sears, Maccoby, and Lewin (1957) report that parents who punish their children severely for being aggressive are more likely than other parents to have aggressive children. And mothers who are unduly punitive when attempting to toilet train their children are more likely to have children who wet their beds.

All of this might indeed constitute valuable advice, whether it be interpreted by sages or by fools.[3]

---

[3] *PPC:* Perhaps Lefrançois should point out that the use of punishment is sometimes highly effective and highly appropriate. Or was it punishment that beat the choirboy out of the bear?

Author: I do this in Chapter 12. And the bear always had more dog meat than choirboy in him; punishment had nothing to do with it.

Aversive Controls It should be stressed again that negative reinforcement and punishment describe two very different situations. The two are often confused because each can involve aversive stimuli. But both are defined in terms of their *effects* on behavior—and these effects are very different. Specifically, punishment results in a reduction in behavior, whereas negative reinforcement, like positive reinforcement, increases the probability that a response will occur. Thus, a child can be encouraged to speak politely to teachers by being smiled at for saying "please" and "thank you" (positive reinforcement). Another child can be beaten with a cane (or threatened therewith) when pleases and thank-yous are forgotten (punishment)—with the clear understanding that the cane will be put away only when behavior conforms to the teacher's standards of politeness (negative reinforcement). In the end, both children may be wonderfully polite. But which child, do you suppose, will like teachers and schools more?

Strange as it might seem, the use of negative reinforcement as a means of control is highly prevalent in today's schools, homes, and churches, as is the use of punishment. These methods of **aversive control** (in contrast to **positive control**) are evident in the issuance of low grades and verbal rebukes, threats of punishment, detention, and the unpleasant fates that await transgressors in most major religions. These methods are evident as well in our legal and judicial systems, which are extraordinarily punitive rather than rewarding. Material rewards for being good are seldom obvious, but criminality is clearly punished. In fact, the reward for being good frequently takes the form of *not* being punished. That, in a nutshell, is negative reinforcement.

It is difficult to determine which is more important in our daily lives—positive or negative reinforcement. Nor is it always easy to separate the two in practice; daily life is considerably more tolerant of ambiguity than is psychological theory. Consider, for example, that I work to obtain the "good" things in life: food, prestige, power, and a soft, wet kiss. It seems obvious that I am controlled by positive reinforcement. Or is it true, as my grandmother suggested, that I am really working to prevent hunger, to escape from anonymity and helplessness, and to avoid loneliness?

This issue cannot be easily resolved, but I am much more likely to be a happy person if positive rather than aversive contingencies (response consequences) control my behavior. Indeed, what is called **avoidance learning** (learning to avoid unpleasant situations) and **escape learning** (learning to escape from unpleasant situations) are among the most important consequences of aversive control. A child who performs well in school because of parental and teacher rewards probably likes school; another who performs well to escape parental wrath and school punishments will probably have quite different emotional reactions to school, may avoid further noncompulsory schooling, and might even consider escaping from the situation.

---

aversive control The control of human behavior, usually through the presentation of noxious (unpleasant) stimuli, in contrast to techniques of positive control, which generally use positive reinforcement.

positive control Control of human behavior, usually through the presentation of pleasant stimuli. This is in contrast to techniques of aversive control, which generally use negative reinforcement.

avoidance learning A conditioning phenomenon usually involving aversive (unpleasant) stimulation. The organism learns to avoid situations associated with specific unpleasant circumstances.

escape learning A conditioning phenomenon whereby the organism learns the means of escaping from a situation, usually following the presentation of aversive (unpleasant) stimulation.

Aversive control of behavior can have one additional, highly undesirable effect. Ulrich and Azrin (1962) placed two rats in a situation where they had to turn a wheel to avoid an electric shock; the rodents fell, tooth and nail, upon each other. Although each understood (in a primitive way, to be sure) that the source of their pain was the wheel and not the other rat, they insisted on behaving in a most unfriendly fashion.

The most dedicated proponents of applied behavioral techniques and principles strongly advocate the use of positive rather than aversive control methods. This was especially true of B. F. Skinner.

Types of Reinforcement Schedules

Recall that the independent variables Skinner was most interested in investigating were *type of reinforcement* and *reinforcement schedule* (how reinforcement is presented). He looked at how these affect characteristics of behavior such as how rapidly learning occurs, the rate of responding, and how long behavior persists in the absence of reinforcement (summarized in Table 4.3).

One of Skinner's important early conclusions is that even a very small reward will lead to effective learning and will maintain behavior over a long period. It is also clear that too much reward (satiation) may lead to a cessation of behavior. Several guidelines for the use of reinforcement are presented in Chapter 11. However, these should be interpreted cautiously.

The relationship between behavior and how reinforcement is administered (referred to as the **schedule of reinforcement**) has been investi-

gated extensively. Schedules invariably involve **continuous reinforcement**, where every correct response (termed a *trial*) is reinforced, or **intermittent reinforcement** (also called partial reinforcement), where only some of the correct responses are reinforced—or some combination of both continuous and intermittent reinforcement.

Intermittent schedules of reinforcement might involve reinforcing a certain proportion of trials (a **ratio schedule**), or else the schedule might be based on the passage of time (an **interval schedule**). A ratio schedule might, for example, reinforce one out of five correct responses; an interval schedule might reinforce one correct response for every 15-second lapse. In either case, there are two more options: Reinforcement can be given in a predetermined fashion (**fixed schedule**) or in a more haphazard manner (**random** or **variable schedule**). Or, to really confuse things in proper psychological fashion, different schedules might be used sequentially in what is termed a **combined schedule**.

---

schedule of reinforcement The time and frequency of presentation of reinforcement to organisms.

continuous reinforcement A reinforcement schedule in which every correct response is followed by a reinforcer.

intermittent reinforcement A schedule of reinforcement that does not present a reinforcer for all correct responses. Also termed *partial reinforcement*.

ratio schedule An intermittent schedule of reinforcement that is based on a proportion of correct responses.

interval schedule An intermittent schedule of reinforcement based on the passage of time.

fixed schedule A type of intermittent schedule of reinforcement. The reinforcement occurs at fixed intervals of time (an interval schedule) or after a specified number of trials (a ratio schedule).

random schedule A type of intermittent schedule of reinforcement which can be of either the interval or the ratio variety and is characterized by the presentation of rewards at random intervals or on random trials. Although both fixed and random schedules can be based on the same intervals or on ratios, one can predict when reward will occur under a fixed schedule, whereas it is impossible to do so under a random schedule. Also termed *variable schedule*.

combined schedule A combination of various types of schedules of reinforcement.

There are no more choices, fortunately ... except maybe one more. This is called a **superstitious schedule**. A superstitious schedule provides regular reinforcement no matter what the learner is doing. In fact, it's a fixed interval schedule without the provision that there must be a correct response before reinforcement occurs. Skinner (1948) left six pigeons overnight on a superstitious schedule (they received reinforcement at regular intervals no matter what they did). He found that by morning one bird had learned to turn clockwise just before each reinforcement, another pointed its head toward the corner, and

several had learned to sway back and forth. Skinner suggests that we too learn superstitious behaviors as a result of reinforcement that occurs independently of what we do. For example, some of us frown when we're thinking or chew our hair or scratch our heads. Do we do these things because they actually help us think? Or do we do them because we happened to be doing them when we were reinforced (perhaps by having a good idea) in the past?

The section about schedules of reinforcement may, at first glance, appear somewhat confusing. If so, read it again slowly and consult Figure 4.10. It is really quite simple. Experimenters have two choices: If they choose A, they have no more choices, but if they choose B, they have two new options. Each of these, in turn, offers two further options. And finally, the last four options can be combined, or else the experimenter can throw in a superstitious schedule.

---

superstitious schedule A fixed-interval schedule of reinforcement. The reward is not given after every correct response but rather after the passage of a specified period of time. This schedule is called superstitious because it leads to the learning of behaviors that are only accidentally related to the reinforcement.

A. Continuous

Every correct response is reinforced.

B. Intermittent (Partial)

	Ratio	Interval	Superstitious (variation of fixed interval)	Combined
Fixed	For example, every fifth correct response is reinforced.	For example, the first correct response is rewarded after a 15-second time lapse.	For example, reinforcement occurs after every 30-second time lapse, no matter what the organism is doing.	(This gets complicated.)
Random (variable)	For example, an average of one out of every five correct responses is rewarded at random.	For example, reinforcement follows a correct response an average of once every 15 seconds, but at unpredictable times.		

FIGURE 4.10 Schedules of reinforcement: Each type of reinforcement tends to generate its own characteristic pattern of response.

Effects of Various Schedules

Recall that much of Skinner's work was directed toward discovering the relationship between various schedules of reinforcement and three measures of learning: **rate of learning**, **response rate**, and **extinction rate**. Some of these results have important implications for teaching.

The Effects of Schedules on Rate of Learning In the early stages of learning, it appears that continuous reinforcement is most effective. When learning simple responses such as pressing a lever, the rat might become confused and would almost certainly learn much more slowly if only some of its initial correct responses were reinforced. In terms of classroom practice, this means that initial learning, particularly for very young children, requires far more reinforcement than does later learning (Lee & Belfiore, 1997).

The Effects of Schedules on Rate of Extinction Interestingly, although continuous reinforcement often leads to more rapid learning, it does not usually result in longer **retention** of what is learned. In fact, the rate of **extinction** for behavior that has been continuously reinforced is considerably faster than for behavior that has been reinforced intermittently. Extinction means the cessation of a response after a behavior is no longer reinforced. The extinction rate is simply the time that elapses between the beginning of the unreinforced period and the cessation of behavior.

The use of extinction in schools is widespread and highly effective. Sometimes it involves nothing more complicated than the withdrawal of attention (presumably a positive reinforcer) in the case of unruly, attention-seeking behavior. Often, however, extinction requires that the teacher take active steps to withhold reinforcement or to prevent it from occurring. Several illustrations are provided in Chapter 11.

In general, therefore, the best schedule would appear to consist initially of continuous reinforcement, followed later by intermittent reinforcement. Among the intermittent schedules, a random ratio arrangement ordinarily results in the slowest rate of extinction.

The Effects of Schedules on Rate of Responding Among animal subjects, the rate of responding is clearly a function of the schedule used. Pigeons and rats, for example, often behave as though they had developed expectations about reward. A pigeon that has been taught to peck a disk and is reinforced for the first peck after a lapse of 15 seconds (fixed interval) often stops pecking immediately after being reinforced and starts again just before the end of the 15-second interval. If, on the other hand, the pigeon is reinforced on a random ratio basis, its response rate will be uniformly high and constant, often as high as 2,000 or more pecks per hour. (See Figure 4.11.)

The Effects of Schedules on Humans So! One can reinforce the behavior of rats and pigeons in a variety of clever ways and note a number of consistent effects that this will have on their ridiculously simple behaviors. From this, many graduate dissertations and great quantities of

---

rate of learning A measure of the amount of time required to learn a correct response or, alternatively, a measure of the number of trials required before the correct response occurs.

response rate The number of responses emitted by an organism in a given period of time. Response rates for operant behaviors appear to be largely a function of the schedules of reinforcement used.

extinction rate The lapse of time between the cessation of a response and the withdrawal of reinforcement.

retention A term often used as a synonym for *memory*.

extinction The cessation of a response as a function of the withdrawal of reinforcement.

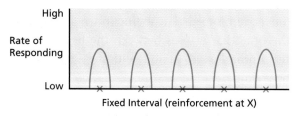

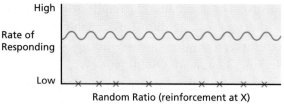

FIGURE 4.11 Idealized graphs showing pigeon pecking with two reinforcement schedules

published research can be derived for the erudition of the scholars and the amazement of the people.

But what of human beings? How are they affected by schedules of reinforcement?

Kollins, Newland, & Critchfield (1997) reviewed 25 studies that had looked at this question. Many, they report, had concluded that humans are less sensitive than nonhumans to the scheduling of their reinforcers. But closer inspection of these 25 studies suggests that this conclusion is invalid. These authors argue that, in fact, humans seem to respond to schedules of reinforcement much as animals do. In the early stages of learning, we perform better under continuous schedules, but our responses are more durable and more predictable if we are later reinforced intermittently. For example, the attention-seeking behaviors of young children are so highly persistent precisely because their behaviors are reinforced intermittently, suggest Bandura and Walters (1963).

There are many examples of the effects of schedules on people's behaviors. The fisherman who goes to the same stream time after time although he rarely (but occasionally) catches fish is demonstrating the persistence that results

from an intermittent schedule of reinforcement. The small-town student, who was at the top of her classes for eight years but now finds herself being outdone in the fierce competition of a new school, ceases to study; she is demonstrating the rapid extinction that follows continuous reinforcement.

Knowing how schedules of reinforcement affect people's behaviors can be useful in a variety of practical situations—as the wife who occasionally but not too frequently praises her husband's appearance or his cooking will attest. He may continue to cook and to look good despite long sequences without reinforcement.

Shaping Through Operant Conditioning

It is relatively simple to train a rat to press a lever, a pigeon to peck a disk, or a 2-year-old to pronounce "Wazoo." Why? Because these are some of the things that rats, pigeons, and children do. But as Guthrie (1935) observes, "We can not teach cows to retrieve a stick because this is one of the things that cows do not do" (1935, p. 45).

Yet, it might well be possible to train a cow to retrieve a stick. The psychologist charged with that task could stand there, leaning on the fence, day after day, watching for the behavior in question to appear. And when the cow finally decided in her cowlike way to pick up the stick, it would be a simple matter (theoretically, to be sure) to reinforce her—say, with a nice new bale of timothy hay—thus increasing the probability that the behavior would occur again. Unfortunately, both the psychologist and the cow would likely die of old age before the desired operant appeared.

Another, much better way of teaching animals complex behaviors using operant conditioning is called **shaping**. Shaping involves reinforcing the animal for every behavior that brings it slightly closer to the desired behavior. For example, if the objective is to teach the cow to pick up a stick, the experimenter might initially reinforce the cow every time it turned toward the stick. Later, once the cow had learned to turn reliably and predictably toward the stick, it would no longer be reinforced until it moved slightly closer to it. And if the reinforcements were accompanied by a distinctive stimulus such as the sound of a cowbell (a discriminated stimulus), eventually the cow might walk directly to the stick every time it heard the bell. And, following the systematic reinforcement of behaviors successively closer to the desired operant, in the end the cow might have learned to pick up and retrieve the stick, placing it in the psychologist's hand. Which would surely have amazed and confounded my grandmother!

For obvious reasons, shaping is also called the **differential reinforcement of successive approximations**. It is one of the most common techniques used in training performing animals. In fact, Lukas, Marr, and Maple (1998) suggest that taking students to the zoo and letting them observe and work with animal trainers might be one of the best ways of teaching them about operant conditioning. But does shaping have any relevance to the lives of humans?

Shaping and People Yes, a great deal of human behavior is shaped through reinforcement. For example, as previously reinforcing activities become habitual and less rewarding, they tend to be modified. A motorcyclist may initially derive considerable reinforcement from the sensation of turning a sharp corner at high speed, but in time the sensation diminishes and the excitement decreases. And as the reinforcement begins to decrease, speed increases, imperceptibly but progressively. The motorcyclist's behavior has gradually been shaped as a consequence of its outcomes.

Many examples of shaping can be found in the classroom. For example, Lee and Belfiore (1997) describe many systematic reinforcement programs designed to improve school performance. But many instances of shaping are not deliberate. For example, peer approval or disapproval, sometimes communicated in subtle, nonverbal ways, can dramatically shape a student's behavior. The classroom clown would probably not continue to be a clown if no one paid any attention to her. Indeed, she might never have been shaped into a clown had her audience not reinforced her in the first place.

Generalization and Discrimination

It isn't possible for schools and teachers to expose their students to all the situations where the behaviors they learn will be appropriate. Nor is it possible to give them experience with all situations in which a specific learned behavior

---

shaping A technique whereby animals and people are taught to perform complex behaviors that were not previously in their repertoires. The technique involves reinforcing responses that become increasingly closer approximations of the desired behavior. Also termed *the method of successive approximations* or *the method of differential reinforcement of successive approximations.*

differential reinforcement of successive approximations The procedure of reinforcing only some responses and not others. Differential reinforcement is used to shape complex behaviors.

will *not* be appropriate. Yet one of the most important tasks of schools is to prepare their charges to respond appropriately in new situations. And reassuringly often, children do respond appropriately when faced with completely new situations. Also, they often discriminate between situations where a particular behavior is appropriate and others where it isn't. The first process, that of *transferring* a response from one situation to another similar situation, is labeled *generalization.* **Discrimination** involves refraining from making the response in question because of a difference between this situation and other situations for which the response was clearly more appropriate.

As an example, many children learn very early in life that they will receive their mother's attention if they cry. And they soon learn to generalize this behavior from specific situations where they have obtained their mother's attention to new situations where they desire her attention. And often, a wise mother can bring about discrimination learning simply by not paying attention to her child in those situations in which she doesn't want to be disturbed. While she is on the phone, she might completely ignore her child's crying; soon the child will learn to discriminate between situations in which attention-seeking behavior is not reinforced and other situations in which it is more likely to be reinforced.

Educational Implications of Operant Principles

The principles of operant learning are extremely relevant for teaching. As Sparzo (1992) points out, Skinner made major contributions with his analysis of the role of behavior's consequences and also

in the areas of understanding verbal behavior, programmed instruction, and social behavior.

A classroom is in many ways like a gigantic Skinner box. It is engineered so that certain responses are more probable than others. For example, it is easier to sit at a desk than to lie on one, and it is easier to remain awake when sitting than when lying down. And at the front of a million classrooms stand those who are among the most powerful dispensers of childhood reinforcement—teachers. They smile or frown; they say "cool" or "that stinks"; they give high grades or low grades; occasionally they grant special favors; at other times they withhold or cancel privileges. By means of their use of reinforcement and punishment, sometimes deliberate and planned and sometimes quite unconscious, teachers shape the behavior of their students.

Drawing an analogy between a classroom, a teacher, and a student on the one hand and a Skinner box, a psychologist, and a rat on the other is somewhat unappealing and perhaps a little frightening (shades of Orwell's *1984*). Yet, this analogy is relevant and potentially useful. As illustrated in Table 4.5, classroom teachers can often profit immensely from the discoveries of experimental psychologists. (Also see Chapter 11 for a detailed discussion of the systematic use of rewards and punishments in the classroom and a description of the various kinds of reinforcers available to teachers.)

One of the first direct applications of Skinner's theory to teaching involved using operant conditioning techniques in the systematic delivery of information by means of written programs (Deutsch, 1992). These programs were a form of programmed instruction—a topic discussed in some detail in Chapter 12.

Another application of the theory to **instruction** has taken the form of a strong

---

discrimination Processes involved in learning that certain responses are appropriate in specific situations but inappropriate in other, similar situations. Generalization is an opposite process.

---

instruction The arrangement of external events in a learning situation to facilitate learning, retention, and transfer.

emphasis on methods of *positive* control (positive reinforcement, for example) rather than *aversive* control (negative reinforcement and punishment). In an article entitled "Why Teachers Fail," Skinner (1965) claimed that efforts to improve education seldom involve attempts to improve teaching as such and that therefore teachers continue to teach as they themselves were taught. Unfortunately, chief among their methods are the techniques of aversive control. Skinner is a strong advocate of positive reinforcement together with "attractive and attention-compelling" approaches to teaching. He also presents numerous suggestions for the development of a **technology of teaching** in a book by that title (Skinner, 1968). Interestingly, ten years later another behaviorist, Fred Keller (1978, p. 53), was to assert: "Never before in the history of mankind have we known so much about the learning process and the conditions under which an individual human being can be efficiently and happily trained." Many believe that the effectiveness of behavioristic principles for teaching is unequaled by any other approach.

The specific and systematic application of operant conditioning principles to education requires that teachers become behavior analysts—that they dedicate themselves both to identifying and establishing environments that will lead to desirable behaviors and providing reinforcement contingencies that will serve to maintain these behaviors. The success of such an approach has been demonstrated experimentally numerous times, perhaps most dramatically with mentally retarded, autistic, and other learning-disadvantaged children. A collective

label for the application of these principles in education and in therapy is **behavior modification**. Specific behavior modification techniques are discussed in Chapter 11. (See Table 4.5 for a summary of classroom applications of operant conditioning principles.)

A SUMMARY OF BEHAVIORISTIC CONTRIBUTIONS TO INSTRUCTION

"To satisfy the practical demands of education, theories of learning must be 'stood on their heads' so as to yield theories of teaching" (Gage, 1964, p. 269). Presumably, the same results would be obtained if students were asked to stand on their heads while the theories remained upright. Unfortunately, however, even as extreme a measure as standing these behavioristic theories on their heads would be unlikely to yield theories of teaching. On the other hand, they need be tilted only very slightly to produce a variety of principles of practical value—many of which are mentioned and illustrated earlier in this chapter. Most of these principles are highly teacher-centered. That is, they emphasize the role of the teacher in organizing and transmitting information and in controlling important aspects of the learning situation. As such, these principles are highly compatible with a model of direct instruction rather than with the more student-centered, constructivist approaches. The most important of these principles can be summarized as follows:

▲ Reinforcement is critically important in determining learning and behavior. This belief forms the cornerstone of both the Skinnerian and Thorndikean systems.
▲ Punishment is not very effective for eliminating undesirable behavior (Thorndike, 1932).
▲ Interest in work and in improvement is conducive to learning (Thorndike, 1935).

---

technology of teaching A Skinnerian phrase for the systematic application of the principles of behaviorism (especially of operant conditioning) to classroom practice.

behavior modification Changes in the behavior of an individual; also refers to psychological theory and research concerned with the application of psychological principles in attempts to change behavior.

TABLE 4.5
Some Operant Conditioning Concepts Applied to Instruction

CONCEPT	EXPLANATION/EFFECT	ILLUSTRATION	PROBABLE CONSEQUENCES
Positive Reinforcement (reward)	Probability of behavior increases following the presentation of a consequence usually perceived as positive.	Ellen writes an original poem, reads it in class, and receives high praise.	An increase in the likelihood that Ellen will write more poems and read them in class.
Negative Reinforcement (relief)	Probability of a behavior increases following the removal of a consequence usually perceived as aversive.	Leonard is terribly afraid of making a fool of himself when he presents his science experiment to the class; he stays home on the day of the science fair; his fear disappears.	An increase in the likelihood that Leonard will subsequently try to avoid stressful situations.
Negative Punishment (castigation)	Probability of a behavior decreases following a consequence usually perceived as aversive.	Leonard's father reprimands him severely for staying home from school.	Leonard may be more likely to go to school in the future, even when faced with fearsome tasks.
Positive Punishment (penalty)	Probability of a behavior decreases when it leads to the removal of a stimulus ordinarily perceived as positive.	Sammy bullies the smaller children on the playground; as a consequence, his teacher slashes his playtime in half for a week.	Sammy is less likely to bully the playground children again.
Shaping	A complex behavior is brought about or modified through reinforcement of successively closer approximations.	Early in her Spanish class, Sylvia is praised for saying "hey meee, nah me emportay," and other similar phrases, no matter how poor her pronunciation is. But later in the class, she receives praise only for phrases that no longer contain her most elementary errors. Finally, there is praise only for correctly pronounced phrases.	Sylvia's pronunciation improves dramatically throughout the course.
Generalization	Responses learned in one situation are transferred to another similar situation.	A second-grade teacher sets up a "store" in her multicultural ESL class where children can use play money to buy various objects.	Juan, who is newly learning English, can subsequently shop in his neighborhood store with far more confidence, applying addition and subtraction rules learned and practiced in school.

TABLE 4.5 (continued)
Some Operant Conditioning Concepts Applied to Instruction

CONCEPT	EXPLANATION/EFFECT	ILLUSTRATION	PROBABLE CONSEQUENCES
Discrimination	Responses learned in one situation are judged inappropriate in another similar but not identical situation.	In early September, all the children yell and shout at each other on the playground during recess; many first-grade children continue to do so when they go back into their classrooms after the buzzer sounds; teachers use various combinations of reinforcement and punishment to suppress some of the noise.	By October most of the first-grade children have learned to discriminate more readily between situations where loud noise is appropriate and situations where it is less appropriate.
Extinction	Responses that are not reinforced become less frequent.	Cheryl delights in making her classmates laugh, usually by contorting her face or making rude noises with her palms and her armpits, often disrupting the flow of classroom activities; she pays no attention to the teacher's requests that she stop these behaviors and appears unfazed by the various punishments devised by the teacher and principal. In the end, the teacher asks the students to ignore Cheryl as much as they possibly can; they comply.	Cheryl's acting out becomes more and more infrequent, finally disappearing altogether.[4]

▲ The significance of the subject matter and the attitude of the learner are important variables in school (Thorndike, 1935).
▲ Repetition without reinforcement does not improve learning (Thorndike, 1931).

---

[4] **PPC:** I think the author should point out that this is just theory. I know it doesn't always work in practice.

Author: This is theory, but not *just* theory. It's theory that leads to application, much of which does work remarkably well—as shown in Chapter 12.

Another Point of View

There are many others, however, who are quick to point out that behaviorism is not a universal cure for all our educational ills. Even if we agree that behavioristic principles should be applied whenever possible, we would soon discover that in countless instances they cannot be applied very effectively at all. As Walker (1979) points out, teachers seldom control the most powerful reinforcers that affect student behavior—for example, peer acceptance and praise, parental approval, and so on. This means that teachers are often relegated to using what are, at least for some students, relatively weaker reinforcers—teacher approval and grades.

A second problem is that one of the central tasks of teaching is often to bring about a desired response rather than simply to increase its frequency or to prevent it from being extinguished. This is quite unlike the Skinner box situation, where the major problem has been to control and maintain a specific response through the manipulation of reinforcement; eliciting the response is often a minor problem.

A third problem is that although operant principles can be used to control maladaptive behavior, its application sometimes has serious limitations. Palardy (1991) points out that behavior modification techniques applied to behavior problems ignore the causes of misbehavior, place insufficient emphasis on prevention, and often lack long-term benefits. However, he also notes that these techniques are effective and that all teachers should be familiar with them; they simply are not sufficient by themselves. (We will discuss specific behavior modification techniques in Chapter 11.)

There are indeed problems in applying behavioristic principles, and these principles are not easy solutions for all teaching problems. But this should not blind us to their potential. Some of that potential is discussed in greater detail in Chapters 11 and 12.

BEYOND FREEDOM: A PHILOSOPHICAL DISCUSSION

If our most significant human behaviors are controlled by reinforcement or the lack thereof, it follows that we are controlled by our environments and that the freedom that we are so proud of is merely an illusion. If I awaken in the morning and decide to brush my teeth, am I really free to make the choice? Can I either brush or not brush according to the whim of the moment? Or am I bound by the dictates of past reinforcement (and/or punishment), real or imagined? In Skinner's book on freedom and dignity, he asserts that the autonomous person is a myth. "Autonomous man," he explains, "is a device used to explain what we cannot explain in any other way. He has been constructed from our ignorance, and as our understanding increases, the very stuff of which he is composed vanishes" (Skinner, 1971, p. 200). We are controlled by our environment, says Skinner, but he reassures us that this is an environment of which we are almost totally in control—or at least an environment that is almost wholly of our own making. But there is a fundamental difference between the two: An environment over which we have control implies that we are free, because we can change the reinforcement contingencies of that environment. An environment of our own making, but over which we have no immediate control, implies that we are *not* free. Maybe as a species we control our own destiny, but as individuals we do not control our own actions.

Skinner discusses at length the possibility of applying a science of human behavior for the benefit of humanity, an undertaking that implies a high degree of control over human behavior (Skinner, 1953, 1961). This aspect of his work has met with the greatest resistance and has led some to speculate that Skinnerian behaviorism can as easily be made a weapon as a tool. The question is an ethical and moral one. The science exists, imperfect and incomplete as it is. And it is sometimes used deliberately and systematically. Skinner (1961) describes, for example, how advertising uses emotional reinforcement by presenting alluring women in commercials and how motivational control is achieved by creating generalized reinforcers—as when a car becomes a powerful reinforcer by being equated with sex. He describes a society that controls through positive reinforcement in the form of wages, bribes, or tips—or one that controls through drugs, such as "fear reducers" for soldiers and steroids or cocaine for athletes.

But all of this began happening before Skinner, and as he notes, "no theory changes what it is a theory about; man remains what he has always been" (1971, p. 215).

Nevertheless, this description of the human condition has come under severe attack from a wide variety of critics—as Skinner predicted it would. In essence, he has questioned the control exercised by the "autonomous" person and has demonstrated the control exercised by the environment, in his attempt to create a science of behavior. The approach itself brings into question the worth and dignity of people. "These are sweeping changes," Skinner said, "and those who are committed to traditional theories and practices naturally resist them" (1971, p. 21).

The dispute is essentially between humanistic psychologists (those more concerned with humanity, ideals, values, and emotions; see Chapter 7) and experiment-oriented psychologists (those more concerned with developing a rigorous science of behavior). But the two positions are not really incompatible: "Man is much more than a dog," Skinner tells us, "but like a dog he is within range of scientific analysis" (1971, p. 21).

BANDURA'S SOCIAL COGNITIVE THEORY

One of the characteristics that makes humans more than dogs, the cognitive psychologists suggest, is that they *understand* something of the consequences of their behaviors. That is, they can anticipate and reason and decide to act or not to act. Behaviorists such as Skinner did not

deal with mentalistic concepts such as these, but this does not mean that behaviorists denied that these events take place. What it means, instead, is that they believed that it was unnecessary and wasteful to include such poorly defined, imprecise, and often unobservable activities in a science of human learning and behavior. However, some psychologists, such as Albert Bandura (1977; Bandura & Walters, 1963), have attempted to recognize and understand these mentalistic activities while still remaining faithful to the behaviorists' emphasis on observable events. Thus, Bandura makes extensive use of the concepts of operant conditioning in a theory that examines some of the more cognitive aspects of social learning and behavior. Conceptually, the theory serves as an important transition between behavioristic and cognitive approaches and is often labeled a **social cognitive theory**.

Social Learning

In psychology, the phrase **social learning** is often used without precise definition, as though everybody intuitively knows exactly what it means and all of us agree about that meaning.

Not so. In fact, the term is used in two ways: For some writers, it means all learning that occurs as a result of, or involves, social interaction (Salomon & Perkins, 1998). Others use the term to signify the type of learning involved in finding out what sorts of behaviors society accepts and expects and those that are unacceptable. This

social cognitive theory A label for Bandura's theory. It attempts to explain human social learning through imitation, using principles of operant conditioning while recognizing the importance of intellectual activities, such as imagining and anticipating. Hence, the theory serves as a transition between purely behavioristic and more cognitive approaches.

social learning The acquisition of patterns of behavior that conform to social expectations—learning what is acceptable and what is unacceptable in a given culture.

difference in meanings is essentially a distinction between process and product. In other words, *social learning* might refer to how learning occurs (that is, through social interaction) or else to what is learned (the product: acceptable behaviors).

Socially Accepted Behaviors: The Product Socially acceptable behavior varies from culture to culture and even from group to group within a single culture. For example, it is socially acceptable for students in some Asian countries to bow to their teachers and to offer them gifts. In most Western countries, a student who habitually bows to teachers and offers them gifts might embarrass both himself and his teacher.

Similarly, socially acceptable behavior is often a function of age and sex. Young children are not expected to address teachers and other adults by their first names; they are expected to learn and obey an assortment of unwritten rules of respect and of social distance. In much the same way, some behaviors are socially expected—hence, culturally appropriate—for males but not for females and vice versa.

Probably one of the most important tasks of the home in the early years of a child's life (and later, of the school) is to foster the development of appropriate behaviors—a process called **socialization**. This process involves transmitting the culture of a society to children and teaching them behaviors appropriate for their sex and social circumstances—or, in a more ideal world, teaching them that the appropriateness of behaviors does not depend on sex or on social circumstances.

Learning Social Behaviors: The Process One of the most important questions from a teacher's point of view is: how does the child learn socially acceptable behaviors? Bandura's answer is that social learning occurs largely through *imitation*, a process that is also called **observational learning**. Learning through imitation, or observational learning, involves acquiring new responses or modifying old ones as a result of seeing a model do something. According to Bandura (1969), the processes involved in imitation are "one of the fundamental means by which new modes of behavior are acquired and existing patterns are modified" (p. 118).

Fads and expressions sweep through countries largely through the processes of social learning and imitation: Overnight (almost), men begin to wear their hair long or short; short skirts are in, then out, then in; everyone is saying "yeah" or "outasight"; things are "cool" or "neat" and people are "beautiful."[5]

But these are trivial matters in the grand scheme of more cosmic events—although how to dress and what to say are by no means trivial in our more private, less cosmic, worlds. Social learning theory explains much more than just our fads and expressions.

Overview of Bandura's Social Cognitive Theory

Much of our learning, says Bandura, results from imitation. And the best way to understand how

---

observational learning A term used synonymously with the expression "learning through imitation."

---

[5] **PPC:** Your faddish words are now a bit outdated. How about "totally" or "vertical" or "deep" or one of the other snowboarder expressions to add to the list?

Author: This is no longer a real young bear. But he is pretty dialed in, and fer sure he gets stoked on a bluebird day and he can rip a bong and shred with the best of them, and he knows not to eat the yellow snow (which some of them don't). In truth, the bear has almost stopped trying to keep up with fads. He says every time he learns new slang which he thinks is, like, real rad, even k-rad, the next day he finds out it's all outdated, which he finds pretty distressing.

---

socialization The complex process of learning both those behaviors that are appropriate within a given culture and those that are less appropriate. The primary agents of socialization are home, school, and peer groups.

learning through imitation works is by reference to operant conditioning. Bandura's theory of observational learning can be summarized as follows:

- Much human learning is a function of observing and imitating the behaviors of others or of **symbolic models** such as fictional characters in books or television programs. Using Skinner's terms, imitative behaviors can be considered operants.
- When imitative behaviors result in positive contingencies or in the removal or prevention of aversive contingencies, they become more probable (Masia & Chase, 1997).

Besides being based on operant conditioning principles, and perhaps even more important, Bandura's theory recognizes the fundamental importance of our ability to symbolize, to imagine, to ferret out cause-and-effect relationships, and to anticipate the outcomes of our behaviors. The environment clearly affects our behavior, Bandura informs us; there is little doubt that we engage in many behaviors because of the reinforcing consequences of so doing. But reinforcement does not control us blindly; its effects depend largely on our awareness of the relationship between our behavior and its outcomes. As Grusec (1992) points out, the main emphasis of Bandura's theory is on the informational capacities that guide an individual's behavior. Reinforcement does not lead to or affect behavior directly, notes Bruner (1985), because reinforcement occurs after the behavior (sometimes considerably after). Rather, the individual's *anticipation* of the consequences immediately affects learning and behaving.

Our ability to symbolize and to anticipate is reflected not only in our ability to imagine the consequences of our behavior and therefore govern ourselves accordingly, but is also reflected in our habit of deliberately arranging our environments to try to control the consequences of our actions. As Bandura (1977) phrases it, "By arranging environmental inducements, generating cognitive supports, and producing consequences for their own actions, people are able to exercise some measure of control over their own behavior." Accordingly, one of Bandura's labels for his theory is **reciprocal determinism**.

The Processes of Observational Learning

Although reinforcement is important for learning through imitation, Bandura (1977) makes it clear that the effects of models are largely a result of what he calls their "informative function." In other words, from observing models, we learn *cognitively* how to do certain things and also what the consequences of our actions are likely to be.

According to Bandura (1977), four distinct processes are involved in observational learning: attentional processes, retention processes, motor reproduction processes, and motivational processes (see Figure 4.12).

Attentional Processes Clearly, we are not likely to learn much from models unless we closely observe the significant features of the behaviors we want to learn. Many of the behaviors in which our models engage have no value for us; therefore, we pay little attention to them and do

symbolic model A model other than a real-life person. Any pattern for behavior may be termed a symbolic model if it is not a person. For example, books, television, and written instructions can provide symbolic models.

reciprocal determinism Bandura's label for the recognition that even though environments affect individuals in important ways, individuals also affect environments by selecting and shaping them. Thus, the influence (determinism) is two-way (reciprocal).

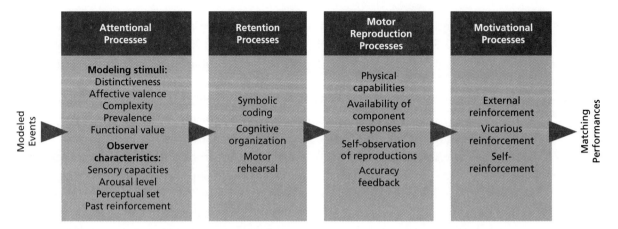

FIGURE 4.12 Component processes governing observational learning in social learning theory. From A. Bandura, *Social Learning Theory*, © 1977, p. 23. Reprinted by permission of Prentice-Hall, Inc., Englewood Cliffs, New Jersey.

not learn them. For example, when I lived with my grandmother as a young adolescent, I was passionately interested in trapping and snaring wild things for food and money. And when I had the opportunity to go out into the woods with George Ahenikue, I watched his every move like a hawk—how he walked, how he looked around, how and where he stopped, how he fashioned his sets, and how he arranged his snares. These behaviors had high value for me. It also helped, as Brewer and Wann (1998) point out, that George Ahenikue was such a renowned trapper. In their terms, his expertise gave him *power* as a model. Teachers who have the greatest power (from knowledge, as a result of their reputations, or because they are sports stars or other sorts of local heroes) often serve as the most influential models.

But when I, as a novice trapper, caught a rabbit who stupidly blundered into my snare, I paid little attention to how my grandmother disjointed, sautéed, and stewed the beast; I just sat at the table and licked my chops in anticipation. The culinary preparation of the rabbit held no interest for me, although I relished the final result.

Not until many years later, when I had a rabbit to prepare in my own kitchen, did I realize how little I had learned from my grandmother about the mysteries of the kitchen. Although I had watched her prepare dozens of rabbits, the behavior had not been sufficiently valuable for me to pay proper attention.

So I called my grandmother and I asked her about the stewing of snowshoe hares and jackrabbits, and she explained. Her explanation was every bit as much a model as her behavior might have been years earlier (had I been paying attention), but it now became a symbolic rather than a real-life model.

Besides the affective and functional value of the behavior being modeled, a variety of other factors affect attentional processes. As we saw, these include the *power* of the model. They also include the distinctiveness, complexity, and prevalence of the stimuli. The characteristics of the learner are important as well, including arousal (motivation), perceptual set (readiness to observe), and history of previous reinforcement.

Retention Processes Just as we must pay attention if we are to learn, so too must we remember what we have observed. Because the effects of imitation are usually delayed rather than immediate, we need some way of symbolizing, understanding, and organizing our observations.

According to Bandura (1977), observational learning involves two types of representation systems: visual (his term is *imaginal*) and verbal. For example, to learn a complex motor skill, it is sometimes useful to observe a model closely and store a visual sequence of the behavior. It is then possible to mentally rehearse the desired behavior. Bandura (1977) cites research indicating that mentally rehearsing a complex motor sequence (as in high jumping, diving, or gymnastics, for example) can significantly improve performance. He suggests that the best way to learn from a model is to organize and rehearse the observed behavior cognitively and then act it out.

Motor Reproduction Processes Acting out a modeled behavior involves transforming actions that are symbolically represented (mentally visualized or imagined) into actual physical movements. Being able to do so successfully, of course, depends on essential physical capabilities: Clearly, some of us will never be able to jump very high no matter how many models we observe.[6] Accurate motor reproduction of an observed behavior also depends on the individual's ability both to monitor attempted reproductions and to use motor feedback to make corrections. Imitations of motor behavior are seldom perfect the first time—they have to be refined. A coach might repeatedly demonstrate how a batter should stand, how she should hold the bat, how she should distribute and shift her weight, and what her eyes and toes should do. But in the end, a truly good batter will have

refined and perfected her batting through a long succession of trials (motor reproductions). These, however, are not trial-and-error reproductions blindly repeated until the right one is accidentally found. Rather, they are carefully modeled trials that are evaluated and slowly modified as a function of feedback, involving, among other things, how often contact is made with the ball, how far the ball goes when it's hit, and whether the coach smiles or frowns while watching the batter.

Motivational Processes Much of what people observe and could learn is never manifested in their behavior. George Ahenikue, for example, was an important model for me with respect to trapping snowshoe hares; he knew a dozen clever little tricks for ensnaring them. I emulated as many of these tricks as I could and still remember the most important of them. But he also knew a fantastic trick for blowing his nose. I have little doubt that I learned it; I remember it very clearly. But I don't do it. Ever. Phrased another way, I have acquired the behavior but do not perform it.

The distinction between acquisition and performance is important in social learning theory because, as we have noted, much of what is observed and presumably acquired is never performed. Whether the modeled behavior will ever be performed is a function of reinforcement or, perhaps more precisely, of anticipated reinforcement.

In summary, observational learning begins with a modeled event (perhaps a real-life model doing something, a symbolic model, or a combination of these) and culminates in some sort of matching performance from the observer. Four processes intervene between the presentation of the model and the appearance of the modeled behavior. First, the observer must pay attention; second, the observer must represent the observed behavior cognitively, store it, and perhaps

---

[6] *PPC:* This might have been what Yogi Berra, the bear's guru, meant when he said, "If you can't imitate him, don't copy him."
  Author: Could be.

rehearse it; third, if the observer has the required capabilities, he or she reproduces and refines the observed behavior; and fourth, given appropriate motivational conditions (defined primarily in terms of anticipated reinforcement), the observer performs the learned behavior.

The Prevalence of Imitation

Copying the behavior of others is a widespread phenomenon. For example, it's very evident among certain birds such as black-capped chickadees who learn some aspects of their songs by hearing other birds sing (Hughes, Nowicki, and Lohr, 1998). Learning by imitation can even be demonstrated among pigeons who readily learn to peck at a disk or depress a lever as a function of watching other trained birds doing so (Kaiser, Zentall, & Galef, 1997).

Imitation is also obvious among nontechnological societies such as the Canadian Ojibwa. Until the turn of the 20th century, the Ojibwa depended almost exclusively upon trapping, hunting, and fishing for their living. In Ojibwa tribes, young boys followed their fathers around trap lines as soon as they were physically able. For the first few years, they simply observed. Later, they would fashion their own weapons and traps and set their own snares as they had seen their fathers do. Whatever they bagged would be brought back to the father's lodge. If a boy had a sister, she would learn how to prepare hides, meat, and fish, how to make clothing, how to erect shelters, and how to do the many other things she had seen her mother doing. When she was old enough, she would take care of her brother's catch, prepare his meals, and make his clothing.

In more technological societies such as ours, it is usually impossible to provide our children with miniature working replicas of the tools used by their parents—nor is it often possible for children to observe their parents at work. Still, knowledge of observational learning can be of

tremendous practical value for teachers. We may not learn from our parents to set traps or prepare furs, but we learn many other things from them—and from the wealth of other models that surround us.

Models The term *model* can refer to an actual person whose behavior serves as a stimulus for an observer's response, or as is more often the case in our society, it can refer to a symbolic model. As we have seen, symbolic models include such things as oral or written instructions, pictures, mental images, cartoon or film characters, religious figures, and—not least important—the content of and characters in books and television. For some children, symbolic models may be as important as real-life models. This is not to deny that peers, siblings, and parents also serve as models or that teachers and other well-behaved people are often held up as **exemplary models**. ("Why don't you behave like Dr. Lefrançois? See how nicely he sits in church with his eyes closed. He's praying for us, dear man.")[7]

Sources of Reinforcement in Imitation

There are two possible sources of reinforcement for imitative behaviors: *direct* and *vicarious*.

Direct reinforcement occurs when the consequences of the behavior lead to reinforcement. For example, direct reinforcement is apparent when parents praise an infant for repeating a word correctly, or a toddler for rolling a ball back to mother. It is also apparent when the imitative

---

exemplary model A good example. A teacher, for example.

direct reinforcement The type of reinforcement that affects the individual in question directly rather than vicariously.

---

[7] *PPC:* I trust you are careful not to snore . . . .
Author: How cynical.

behavior is effective in attaining a goal—such as a bottle of milk in response to the request for milk. Even though a child may learn to say "milk" partly as a function of imitation and partly as a function of her model's reinforcing her, she is not likely to go on saying "milk" unless someone occasionally gives her milk when she says the word.

In contrast with direct reinforcement, **vicarious reinforcement** involves deriving a kind of secondhand—hence, *vicarious*—reinforcement from observing someone else behave in a certain way. It is as though the observer assumes that the model does something because he or she derives reinforcement from that behavior. Therefore, using the observer's logic, anyone else engaged in the same behavior would receive the same reinforcement.

Interestingly, vicarious reinforcement can lead an observer to engage in ineffective behavior over a prolonged period of time. The behavior is maintained despite an apparent lack of direct reinforcement, which is evidence that some sort of vicarious reinforcement is involved. In fact, studies have shown that the administration of reward or punishment to a model has an effect on the behavior of observers similar to that of the direct administration of the reward or punishment. One such study (Bandura, 1962) involved exposing three groups of children to three different models. All the models behaved aggressively toward an inflated plastic doll. The first model was rewarded for doing so, the second was punished, and the third received neither positive nor negative consequences. Subsequently, the model-rewarded group behaved significantly more aggressively than the model-punished group. The effect of reward and punishment on the models was transferred vicariously to the subjects.

The Effects of Imitation

An examination of the responses involved in observational learning suggests that there are three categories of imitative behavior. Bandura (Bandura & Walters, 1963) describes these as the effects of imitation: the modeling effect, the inhibitory-disinhibitory effect, and the eliciting effect.

The **modeling effect** involves the acquisition of new responses. The **inhibitory-disinhibitory effect** involves the **inhibition** or **disinhibition** of deviant responses, usually as a result of seeing a model punished or rewarded for the behavior. The **eliciting effect** involves behavior that is neither novel for the observer nor deviant; it is manifested when the observer engages in behavior related (but not identical) to that of the model. Because of the importance of these effects in teaching, each of them will be illustrated and explained in detail (see Table 4.6).

The Modeling Effect The modeling effect involves the acquisition of a new behavior as a result of seeing a model emit that behavior. This effect is

---

vicarious reinforcement Reinforcement that results from observing someone else being reinforced. With imitative behavior, observers frequently act as though they are being reinforced when they are really not being reinforced; rather, they are aware, or simply assume, that the model is being reinforced.

modeling effect A type of imitative behavior that involves learning a novel response.

inhibitory-disinhibitory effect The type of imitative behavior that results either in the suppression (inhibition) or appearance (disinhibition) of previously acquired deviant behavior.

inhibition With imitative learning, the suppression of a previously acquired behavior. This sometimes occurs when a learner observes a model being punished for the behavior.

disinhibition The appearance of a suppressed behavior.

eliciting effect Imitative behavior where the observer does not copy the model's responses but simply behaves in a related manner.

TABLE 4.6
Three Effects of Imitation

LABEL	DEFINITION	ILLUSTRATION
Modeling Effect	Acquiring new behavior as a result of observing a model	After watching a television program, Kristina begins to use the word *not* in the sense of "no," as in, "Is she smart? Not."
Inhibitory-Disinhibitory Effect	Ceasing or starting some deviant behavior as a result of seeing a model punished or rewarded for similar behavior	Ralph burns all his cigarette papers and flushes his grass down the toilet after his brother is caught and punished by their parents.
Eliciting Effect	Engaging in behavior related to that of a model	Robin starts piano lessons after her cousin plays a trumpet solo at the family reunion.

well illustrated in the acquisition of aggressive behaviors, which have been extensively studied in laboratory situations, usually with nursery school children (see, for example, Huesmann, 1997). The typical experiment involves exposing the subjects to a real-life model, cartoon, or filmed model doing something aggressive to a large inflated plastic doll—like punching it, striking it with a hammer, kicking it, or sitting on it. Control groups are exposed to the same model sitting quietly with the doll. The results of experiments such as this almost invariably illustrate the modeling effect. That is, when left alone with the dolls, children exposed to aggressive models are more aggressive than children in the control groups; furthermore, their aggressive responses are usually precisely imitative. That is, if the model punched the doll, that is what subjects are most likely to do; if the model kicked the doll instead, then that, too, is what observers do.

Studies such as this have been widely used to support the belief that much aggression is learned through imitation and that television, because of its predominantly violent content, is highly influential in fostering aggressive behavior. Others point out that these studies involve laboratory situations that are somewhat unrealistic and that aggression directed at an inanimate object is a far cry from aggression against real people in real life. Ethical considerations, however, prevent the use of babies instead of dolls in these experiments. It is therefore difficult to illustrate the acquisition of meaningful aggressive responses experimentally. Still, general summaries of the television research suggest that watching TV violence does increase the violence of viewers (Rosenkoetter, Huston, & Wright, 1990; Cohen, 1993/94).

Many other behaviors are also transmitted through imitation and are examples of modeling. The initial learning of socially appropriate behavior in primitive cultures such as that of the Ojibwa provides one illustration; learning a language is another. This is especially obvious with adults learning to speak a foreign language by imitating a teacher or an audiotape.

The Inhibitory-Disinhibitory Effect The inhibitory effect is the suppression of deviant behavior in an observer, usually as a result of seeing a model punished for engaging in the same behavior. The disinhibitory effect is the opposite; it occurs when an observer engages in previously learned deviant behavior, usually as a result of seeing a model rewarded (or at least not punished) for the same behavior. The inhibitory-disinhibitory effect of imitation is especially important for teachers when dealing with deviant behavior.

Children who are shown films of models kicking and punching inflated plastic dolls often imitate these aggressive behaviors later. But it isn't clear that these findings can be generalized to more realistic settings—or that the findings say very much about the effects of television violence.

As experimental evidence of disinhibition, Bandura and Walters (1963) cite studies where viewing films leads to a disinhibition of aggression in children. In many of these studies, the aggressive responses are not novel but are previously learned behaviors that the children had suppressed. Typically, the number of aggressive responses manifested by members of experimental groups is significantly higher than the number engaged in by children in the control groups.

In one study, Bandura (1962) looked at the effects on observers of punishing or rewarding the model. Not surprisingly, punishing a model inhibited similar behavior in observers; rewarding the model had an opposite, disinhibiting effect. But perhaps even more striking is that, when observers were offered rewards for behaving aggressively, all differences between the groups were wiped out! Now those who had been exposed to models who were punished for being aggressive nevertheless behaved as aggressively as those whose models had been rewarded for being aggressive. This observation is especially important for explaining why punishing those who misbehave often fails to discourage other transgressors. One of the reasons for punishing criminals is to *inhibit* criminal behaviors in other potential imitators. Unfortunately, it follows from the Bandura experiment that as long as imitators have their own incentives for criminal behavior, the model may just as well be rewarded as punished, as far as deterrence is concerned.

A series of sobering experiments illustrates that socially unacceptable behavior in adults can be disinhibited through the use of models (Walters, Llewellyn, & Acker, 1962; Walters & Llewellyn, 1963). These studies, modeled after the famous obedience studies by Milgram (1963), illustrate that college students and other adults will willingly administer to other students what they believe are extremely dangerous, high-voltage electrical shocks—and that they will do so simply because they have been told to by an experimenter. Furthermore, prior exposure to violent film scenes dramatically increases the intensity of the punishment they are willing to administer.

The results of these studies have been used to explain various wartime atrocities perpetrated by apparently normal people who claimed they were simply obeying a powerful authority. These findings may also be important for interpreting and predicting the possible effects of television violence.

The Eliciting Effect The eliciting effect occurs when imitation leads to responses that don't precisely match but are simply related to those of the model. For example, a man might serve as a model of generosity if he works hard for civic organizations, church activities, and school functions. Several of his neighbors might be moved by his example to be generous in different ways: One might give money to local charities, a second might donate a prize for a church raffle, a third might give freely of advice. None of these observers imitates the model's behavior precisely, but each of them emits a related response that involves being generous.

Another illustration of the eliciting effect is found in the **herd behaviors** that are sometimes

apparent in crowds at sporting events. One person's applause might elicit cheering and accolades from the entire crowd; another person's booing and hissing might elicit related behaviors from others. Similarly, when people begin to rise for the national anthem, the same behavior can be elicited in a great many people who are not immediately aware of why they are standing. In each of these illustrations of the eliciting effect, no new behavior is involved (as is the case in the modeling effect), and the behavior in question is not deviant (as it is in the inhibitory-disinhibitory effect).

INSTRUCTIONAL IMPLICATIONS OF SOCIAL COGNITIVE THEORY

The greatest advantage of learning by imitation over other forms of learning is that it provides a complete behavioral sequence for the learner. There is no need for successive approximations, for trial and error, or for association by contiguity. Nobody would put a person behind the wheel of a car and allow the person to learn to drive by trial and error alone. One might, on the other hand, teach driving to someone by presenting one or more models: exposure to a person driving, a driving manual, and a series of oral instructions. In this, as in many other types of learning, it would be foolhardy to permit people to learn only by doing.

Analysis of the processes involved in social learning suggests several considerations that might be important for teaching. For example, many of the factors associated with attentional processes (such as distinctiveness of stimuli, the learner's arousal level, and history of past reinforcement) are at least partly under the teacher's control. Similarly, teachers can provide direction and opportunity for the activities involved in retention and in reproduction. And because the effects of reinforcement depend on our awareness of the connection between our behavior

---

herd behavior A type of imitative behavior involving large groups of individuals.

and its consequences, teachers can also exercise considerable influence on motivational processes. The deliberate use of social learning theory for changing and controlling behavior (sometimes included under the general term **behavior management**, or behavior modification) presents yet another important educational implication, considered in Chapter 11.

More recently, Bandura's social cognitive theory has taken a new twist, one that is even more clearly cognitive (Bandura, 1986; Evans, 1989). This involves what is termed **self-referent thought**—that is, thought that involves our own mental processes and, perhaps most important for teachers, our estimates of our personal effec-

tiveness, or what is labeled self-efficacy. "Efficacy beliefs," says Bandura (1993), "influence how people feel, think, motivate themselves, and behave" (p. 118). Hence, how we feel about our own personal competence is extremely important. That aspect of Bandura's theory is discussed in Chapter 10, which deals with human motivation.

---

behavior management The systematic application of psychological principles in attempts to change behavior. See *behavior modification*.

self-referent thought A thought that pertains to the self. Self-referent thought concerns our own mental processes (for example, thoughts that evaluate our abilities or monitor our progress in solving problems).

MAIN POINTS

1. Learning includes all relatively permanent changes in potential for behavior that result from experience but that are not simply due to fatigue, maturation, drugs, injury, or disease. Changes in disposition or capability are not always manifested in performance.

2. Behavioristic theories of learning are concerned with stimulus–response events and with the effects of repetition, contiguity, and reinforcement. Cognitive theories address problems relating to the organization of memory, information processing, problem solving, and metacognition (knowing about knowing). Humanistic approaches are more concerned with human worth and individuality.

3. Behaviorism deals with *associative learning*—a largely unconscious process by which associations form between stimuli, responses, and response consequences. Classical conditioning (Pavlov and Watson) is a type of associative learning involving the repeated pairing of a previously neutral stimulus (conditioned

stimulus, or CS) with an effective stimulus (unconditioned stimulus, or US) so that the CS eventually brings about a response (conditioned response, or CR) similar to that brought about by the unconditioned stimulus.

4. Classical conditioning is sometimes useful for explaining the learning of emotional responses. Thus, it is important for teachers to know what is being paired with what in schools and to maximize situations associated with positive emotions while minimizing those associated with negative feelings.

5. Thorndike's theory assigns an important role to reinforcement in bringing about learning (the law of effect). In the absence of previous learning, behavior will take the form of trial and error with attempted responses affected by set, by identical elements in stimulus situations, by classical conditioning, or by prepotent elements. Thorndike's theory suggests that teachers should teach for transfer

(generalization) by stressing connections among ideas, and it emphasizes the importance of students' readiness and of reinforcement, while recognizing the limited effectiveness of punishment.

6. Respondents result from a known stimulus (respondents are *reactions to*); operants are simply emitted (operants are *actions upon*). The model of operant conditioning maintains that when an operant is reinforced, the probability of its recurrence increases. A reinforcer is any stimulus that increases the probability that a response will occur. It can do so by being added to a situation (positive reinforcement, reward) or by being removed (negative reinforcement, relief).

7. Negative reinforcement is not punishment. The effect of punishment is to decrease, not increase, the probability that a response will occur. Punishment occurs when a pleasant stimulus is removed (penalty, removal punishment, type II punishment) or an aversive one is introduced following behavior (castigation, presentation punishment, type I punishment). Aversive control involves the use of negative reinforcement (often in the form of removal of threats) and of punishment. The emotional consequences of positive control are usually more desirable.

8. Reinforcement can be continuous (every correct response) or intermittent (variable). Intermittent reinforcement can be based on the number of responses (ratio) or the passage of time (interval) and can occur in a random or fixed manner (that is, it can be continuous, random ratio, random interval, fixed ratio, or fixed interval). In general, continuous schedules lead to faster learning, whereas intermittent schedules result in longer extinction periods.

9. Shaping, the differential reinforcement of successive approximations, can be used to teach animals novel behaviors or to subtly alter human behavior. To generalize is to respond to similarities (make the same response in similar situations); to discriminate is to respond to differences (distinguish among situations where identical responses are inappropriate).

10. Some people believe that behavioristic principles can provide us with a technology of teaching that is more effective than any other approach. These people lament the apparent reluctance of many educators to apply this technology. Others emphasize that the effectiveness of behavioristic approaches is limited, that teachers often control only the weaker reinforcers, and that many problems of instructing (organizing, sequencing, explaining, illustrating) cannot easily make use of behavioristic principles.

11. It is possible that we are not free, that we are controlled by our environment, and that we have only the illusion of freedom.

12. Bandura's social cognitive theory assumes that imitation (observational learning) is a central process in determining behavior. Social learning through imitation reflects the effects of reinforcement, the observer's awareness of the connections between behavior and outcomes, and the observer's ability to symbolize. Learning through imitation requires paying attention, remembering, reproducing, and being motivated to do so.

13. The term *model* refers to a person who serves as an example for another or to more symbolic models. Sources of reinforcement in observational learning include direct reinforcement (either by the model or as a consequence of behavior) and vicarious reinforcement (when the punishment or reward an observer believes a model has received affects the observer's behavior).

14. The three effects of imitation are the modeling effect (the learning of novel responses); the inhibitory-disinhibitory effect (deviant behavior is disinhibited or suppressed, usually as a function of response consequences to the models); and the eliciting effect (the emission of responses that are related to those made by the model but that are neither novel nor deviant). These three effects of imitation have important instructional implications.

Applied Questions

▲ Can you give school-based examples of changes that define learning?

▲ List several key terms most closely related to the theories of Pavlov, Watson, Thorndike, Skinner, and Bandura.

▲ Can you think of classroom-related examples of classical and operant conditioning?

▲ Illustrate the difference between negative reinforcement and punishment, using examples from a hypothetical instructional sequence.

▲ Explain why schedules of reinforcement might be important in the classroom.

▲ What is one example of how one of the effects of imitation might be applied in the classroom?

Internet Activity

Use InfoTrac College Edition or other World Wide Web sources to research the following topic: Write up your findings. (See the inside back cover of this text for suggestions about where to begin.)

The nature and effectiveness of current school punishments

Sample search terms: Punishment and (Schools or teaching or classrooms)

Study Terms

affective learning **118**
associative learning **120**
aversive control **138**
avoidance learning **138**
behavior management **159**
behavior modification **145**
behaviorism **119**
capability **118**
classical conditioning **120**
cognitive learning **118**
cognitivism **119**
combined schedule **139**
conditioned response (CR) **121**
conditioned stimulus (CS) **121**
conditioning **119**
connectionism **126**

constructivist approaches **124**
contiguity **126**
continuous reinforcement **139**
differential reinforcement of successive
    approximations **143**
direct instruction **124**
direct reinforcement **154**
discriminated stimulus (S^D) **132**
discrimination **144**
disinhibition **155**
disposition **117**
elicited response **130**
eliciting effect **155**
emitted response **130**
environmentalism **122**
escape learning **138**

Suggested Readings

Among the many attempts to apply learning theories to educational practice, the following three sources have been selected as the most representative and the most practical. Skinner's book is a collection of his papers on teaching; Lefrançois provides a simple explanation of early theories of learning; and Joyce, Weil, and Showers present a useful look at instructional models based on a variety of psychological theories:

Skinner, B. F. (1968). *The technology of teaching.* New York: Appleton-Century-Crofts.

Lefrançois, G. R. (2000). *Theories of human learning: What the Old Man said* (4th ed.). Belmont, CA: Wadsworth.

Joyce, B., Weil, M., & Showers, B. (1996). *Models of teaching* (5th ed.). Boston: Allyn & Bacon.

Skinner provides a highly readable and important behavioristic estimation of the human condition:

Skinner, B. F. (1971). *Beyond freedom and dignity.* New York: Knopf.

The social development theory of Bandura and Walters is presented in the following:

Bandura, A. (1977). *Social learning theory.* Morristown, NJ: General Learning.

Bandura, A., & Walters, R. (1963). *Social learning and personality development.* New York: Holt, Rinehart & Winston.

Hall and Kelson (1959) list exactly 130 subspecies and types of bears, ranging alphabetically from **Ursus absarokus**, found in 1914 at the head of the Little Bighorn River in Montana, to **Ursus yesoensis**.

The Right Honorable gentleman is indebted to his memory for his jests and to his imagination for his facts.

Richard Brinsley Sheridan, speech in reply to Mr. Dundas

Thinking and Remembering

CHAPTER 5

PREVIEW

Conditioning theories explain how associations are formed among stimuli, responses, and the consequences of behavior. Accordingly, these theories are useful for explaining many relatively simple behaviors—and perhaps some complex behaviors as well. But how well do they explain the processes by which you and I can recognize, or at least contemplate, the role of, say, metaphoric bears, in the grand scheme of things?

FOCUS QUESTIONS

▲ What is meant by cognitivism?

▲ What is the most basic current information processing model?

▲ What are the types and characteristics of long-term memory?

▲ What are some common theories of forgetting?

▲ How can memory be improved?

▲ What is meant by metacognition?

▲ How can students be taught to think?

"It hides in clothes closets and under beds," said my cousin, Claude. "Really dark places. It'll get you when you sleep mostly."

"What . . . ?"

"It'll bite your neck and suck your blood. Or it'll just take you away somewhere."

"You can't scare me," said my older brother, Maurice. "I heard that story before. Papooses aren't real."

But that night when we lay in the darkness beneath the old green comforter, while everybody else was sleeping, a sudden creaking of the house's ancient frame jolted Maurice bolt upright.

"Did you hear that?" he whispered hoarsely.

"Yeah."

"It might be a papoose."

"Nah," I answered bravely, but I couldn't still the beating of my heart.

"Go check the clothes closet."

"No, you go."

"You go first."

In the end, more because I was younger rather than braver, I checked the black recesses of the corner clothes closet, sticking my hand in behind the shirts like Maurice insisted. Then I got down and peered under the bed.

From that night on, we took turns, Maurice and I, looking into each of the four corners of the room, then the closet, finally under the bed. Only then could we sleep.

⌐ COGNITIVISM

I usually sleep better now. You see, we're grown up, Maurice and I. We've become totally familiar with our closets; we know there's nothing under our beds.

But, as I discovered again last week, things can still go bump in the night: I was spending the night alone in the little wilderness cabin not far from where I live when something startled me from my sleep in the small hours of a cold and moonless night. I jerked upright, my heart racing. I could see nothing in the gloom inside the cabin. I strained to hear what had awakened me.

Then I heard it again, more of a moan than a cry. Although I must have known almost at once that it was nothing but a great horned owl, for a moment my heart lurched and a jumble of emotions and images threatened to overwhelm me. I had just finished reading *Bendécime Ultima*, by Rudolfo Anaya, a book in which an old lady's *lechuza* (an owl) has strange and frightening powers. And only the week before, I had read stories of *La Llorona* and *El Silbón*.[1] And for one desperate moment, straining my eyes to see through the murky darkness of my little cabin, I saw again the papoose I thought I had left behind forever.

It's very difficult to understand mental processes such as these using the language and explanations of behaviorism. That's because, as we saw in Chapter 4, behaviorism emphasizes the study of actual behaviors and their consequences. In a behavioristic analysis of learning, the primary emphasis is on the *external* conditions that affect behavior and not on *internal*

---

[1] These are stories like that of the papoose, often told to young children to frighten them into being good. "Come la sopa o te va a llevar La Llorona." ("Eat your soup or the Llorona [the lady who is doomed to cry eternally because she has drowned her children] will come and get you.") Or "Cállete o te va a secuestrar El Silbón." ("Be quiet or the Silbón [the ghost you can hear whistling in the darkness—and the farther away the whistle, the more dangerous] will kidnap you.")

conditions like imagining and remembering and associating. Behaviorism cannot easily explain my unbidden imagining that the moaning of the owl might be the cries of the souls it has eaten, souls of the dead trapped forever in the owl's black gut.

Cognitivism versus Behaviorism

In contrast to behaviorism, **cognitivism** involves the study of mental events rather than actual behaviors. These mental events are concerned with acquiring, processing, storing, and retrieving information. Accordingly, the main emphasis in a cognitive analysis of learning is on the learner's **mental structure**, a **concept** that includes not only the learner's previous related knowledge but also the strategies that the learner might bring to bear on the current situation. In this view, the individual's pre-existing network of concepts, strategies, and understanding makes experience meaningful. Thus, because of images and ideas related to what I have recently heard and read, combined with leftover terrors from childhood, the cry of an owl might make my heart race. And for those of you who have not yet learned to fear, or perhaps even to respect, the *lechuza*, the same sound might make you smile as you snuggle beneath your dreams.

Because cognitivism deals with mental events rather than simply with observable behavior, it represents a dramatic departure from behaviorism, a departure that has led to considerable conflict and disagreement over the years. Amsel (1989), for example, uses a parliamentary metaphor to describe the confrontation between behaviorism and cognitivism: "I like to point out," says he, "that the S–R psychologists, who at one time formed the government, are now in the loyal opposition, the cognitivists being the new government" (p. 1). The rapidity and thoroughness with which the cognitivists appear to have become "the new government" has led many writers to refer to a *cognitive revolution* (for example, Bruner, 1992). This revolution, as we make clear in this and other chapters in this text, is having a profound effect on educational theory and practice.

Hunt (1989) asserts that cognitivism is a perspective rather than a discipline. It is a way of looking at things rather than a readily identifiable collection of findings. This way of looking at the world is characterized by basic underlying beliefs that are apparent in the metaphors of cognitivism.

The Metaphors of Cognitivism

Cognitivism abounds with metaphors, claims Bruner (1990b). That, of course, is because much of its subject matter cannot be described very precisely, cannot be pointed to or photographed, and, in short, must be inferred rather than actually seen—hence, our need for metaphors, which are simply a comparison. Metaphors don't say, "this is that"; instead, they say, "it is interesting, or amusing, or useful, to look at this as though it were *like* that." Thus, a metaphor cannot be judged by whether it is accurate but only in terms of whether it is useful—or interesting and amusing.

A Definition of Cognitivism Literally, to *cognize* is to know; hence, cognition is knowing. Cognitivism, the study of cognition, emphasizes the role of mental structure, or organization, in the processes of knowing. In other words, cognitivism deals with how mental representations are manipulated (Hunt, 1989). Cognitive psychology, as Hunt and Ellis (1999) put it, "is the

---

cognitivism Theories of learning primarily concerned with such topics as perception, problem solving, information processing, and understanding.

mental structure The organized totality of an individual's knowledge. Also called *cognitive structure*.

concept A collection of perceptual experiences or ideas that are related because they possess common properties.

scientific study of mental processes" (p. 4); behavioristic psychology is the study of *behavioral* events.

Not surprisingly, one major emphasis of cognitive approaches concerns how information is processed and stored. Note how dramatically this approach departs from the major emphasis of the behavioristic approach, which concentrates on behavior and its consequences.

A Computer Metaphor The dominant metaphor in cognitive psychology, note Massaro and Cowan (1993), is an **information processing (IP)** metaphor. This metaphor arose with the development of information processing machines, more commonly called computers. The metaphor is closely related to the branch of computer science concerned with **artificial intelligence (AI)**. This is the branch of computer science that attempts to

understand how brains are like computers and tries to simulate intelligent behavior using computers. It is also the branch of computer science that tries to make computers smarter, says Raphael (1976). One of the benefits of developing a truly smart computer is that doing so might clarify how our own information processing systems—our minds—work. Scientists concerned with this potential benefit typically use computers in one of two ways: to mimic the functioning of the human mind or to generate models of human functioning. In these models, the brain, with its neurons and their networks of interconnections, might be compared to the chips and storage and relay systems of computers. Or the mental processes involved in receiving, organizing, storing, and retrieving information might be compared to the programmed functions of the computer. In this case, the program rather than the computer itself serves as a model for human functioning. (See Figure 5.1.)

Other Metaphors The computer metaphor is very prevalent in the cognitive sciences. This metaphor says, in effect, "it is useful to look at human cognitive functioning as though it functioned like a computer."

---

information processing (IP) Relates to how information is modified (or processed), resulting in knowledge, perception, or behavior. It is the dominant model of the cognitive approaches and makes extensive use of computer metaphors.

artificial intelligence (AI) Describes models, procedures, devices, or mechanisms intended to simulate or duplicate some of the intelligent functions of human mental activity.

Function				Structure	
Human					
S	Cognitive acts (thinking, problem solving, creating, and other mental processes)	R	Senses	Nervous system (sometimes called *wetware*)	Response systems

Computer					
Input	Software (programmed operations)	Output	Sensors (keyboard)	Hardware (chips, relays, wiring)	Printers, screens

FIGURE 5.1 Analogies between computer and human structures and functions: Cognitive science's basic computer metaphor compares input to stimuli, output to responses, and the cognitive functioning of the nervous system to the computer's software-driven operations. From G.R. Lefrançois, *Theories of Human Learning: What the Old Man Said* (4th ed.) Copyright © 2000 Wadsworth. Used by permission.

Other approaches in the study of cognition invent different metaphors. Many of them look at cognitive functioning not in terms of something known, such as a computer, but in terms of something that is initially unknown and that requires its characteristics to be described. Some of these approaches use labels such as "knowledge base," "cognitive strategy," or "schema" for their metaphors. No one has seen a knowledge base, a cognitive strategy, or a schema; these are abstractions, inventions of cognitive theory. But each of these inventions can be described. And, once described, it is possible to say, "learners behave as though they have a knowledge base and cognitive strategies."

Our current model of cognitive functioning, as we have noted, is essentially an information processing model. This model looks at three things: First, it looks at what Chi and Glaser (1980) call the **knowledge base**—the storehouse of information, concepts, and associations that we build up as we develop from children into adults. Second, it looks at **cognitive strategies**—the processes by which information becomes part of the knowledge base, is retrieved from it, or is used. And third, it deals with the individual's awareness of the self as a knower and processor of information—with what is termed **metacognition**. We look at each of these aspects of cognitive functioning in this chapter. In Chapter 6 we examine the tremendous potential

contribution of the cognitive sciences to education, especially for developing ways to teach and improve cognitive strategies.

THE MODAL MODEL OF MEMORY

The most widely used model of information processing is essentially a model of human **memory** (our knowledge base, after all, is composed of all that we have in memory; and cognitive strategies are the means by which material either becomes part of the knowledge base, is retrieved from it, or is used). This model is based largely on the work of Atkinson and Shiffrin (1968) and is sometimes called the **modal model of memory** (Baddeley, 1997).

The *modal model of memory* makes an important distinction between two types of information storage: **short-term memory** (also called **working memory**) and **long-term memory**. In some versions of the model, such as that depicted in Figure 5.2, a third memory component is included: **short-term sensory storage** (sometimes called **sensory memory**).

memory The effects that experiences are assumed to have on the human mind. Refers to the storage of these effects. See also *retrieval*.

modal model of memory A widely used model of human memory that draws distinctions among sensory storage, short-term memory, and long-term memory. First developed by Atkinson and Schriffin.

short-term memory A type of memory wherein material is available for recall for only a matter of seconds. Short-term memory primarily involves rehearsal rather than more in-depth processing. It defines our immediate consciousness. Also termed *primary memory* or *working memory*.

long-term memory A type of memory whereby, with continued rehearsal and recoding of sensory information (processing in terms of meaning, for example), material will be available for recall over a long period of time.

short-term sensory storage The phrase refers to the simple sensory recognition of such stimuli as a sound, a taste, or a sight. Also termed *sensory memory*.

knowledge base The storehouse of concepts, information, associations, and procedures that we accumulate over time.

cognitive strategy A process involved in learning and remembering. Cognitive strategies include identifying problems, selecting approaches to their solution, monitoring progress in solving problems, and using feedback. Cognitive strategies are closely related to metacognition and metamemory.

metacognition Knowledge about knowing. As we grow and learn, we develop notions of ourselves as learners. Accordingly, we develop strategies to recognize our limitations and allow us to monitor our progress and take advantage of our efforts.

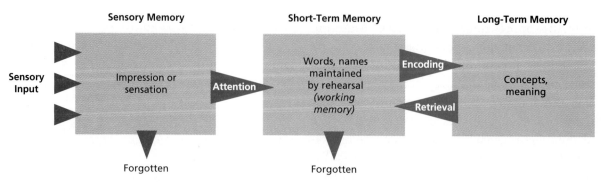

FIGURE 5.2 The three components of memory: The top row depicts three types of memory; the boxed items depict the content of the memory process. Sensory information first enters sensory memory (iconic or echoic memory). From there it can go into short-term memory (also called primary memory), where it is available as a name or word, for example, as long as it is rehearsed. Some of the material in short-term memory can then be coded for long-term storage, where it might take the form of meanings and concepts. Note that these three components of memory do not refer to three different locations in the brain or other parts of the nervous system, but to how we remember and to how we study memory.

Distinctions among the three types of storage are concerned mainly with the nature and extent of the **processing** that information undergoes. Processing refers to activities such as paying attention, organizing, analyzing, synthesizing, and rehearsing. Also, the three types of storage differ in their capacity and in the extent to which their contents are accessible. Bear in mind, however, that we are discussing a model—a metaphor. This is not intended to be a literal description of how things are actually stored in our brains. In other words, there isn't really a box or another type of container in our brains into which short-term memory items are placed, and another for long-term storage. In fact, this metaphor describes how psychologists choose to investigate and talk about memory far better than it does the physical and neurological characteristics of remembering.

This basic information processing model of cognitive psychology does two related things: First, it provides us with an overall model of human memory. Second, it addresses various learning-related questions that are critically important for teachers—questions concerning how information is organized and sorted, which teaching and learning methods can facilitate information processing, and how memory can be improved.

Sensory Memory

Our sensory systems (vision, hearing, taste, touch, smell) are sensitive to an overwhelmingly wide range of stimulation. Clearly, however, they respond only to a fraction of all available stimulation at any given time; the bulk of the information available in this stimulation is never actually processed—that is, it never actually becomes part of our cognitive structure. "Sensory memory" is the label used to describe the immediate, unconscious effects of stimulation.

Research indicates that much of the stimulation to which we aren't actually paying attention is nevertheless available for processing for perhaps a fraction of a second. If you are engaged in a conversation with someone in a crowded room, you might be totally unaware of what is

---

processing The intellectual or cognitive activities that occur as stimulus information is reacted to, analyzed, sorted, organized, and either stored in memory or forgotten.

being said in any other conversation. But if the topic in one of these other conversations turns to something that passionately interests you (for example, you hear your own name), you suddenly become aware of what you would not otherwise have heard. This occurrence is labeled the **cocktail party phenomenon** (Cherry, 1953). It describes a type of memory that is unconscious, fleeting, and very much like an echo—so much so, in fact, that Neisser (1976) labels it **echoic memory** (for auditory stimuli) or **iconic memory** (for visual stimuli).

Sensory memory is highly limited, both in terms of the length of time during which stimulus information is available for processing and in the absolute amount of information available—except, perhaps, in some rare cases, such as those described in the box entitled "Flashbulb Memories . . ." In other words, sensory memory is no more than the immediate sensory effect of a stimulus. If, without giving any prior instructions, I read you a list of numbers using a dry, professorial monotone and then ask you to repeat the numbers ten seconds later, you are not likely to remember many of the numbers. But if I interrupt my reading and ask immediately, "What was the last number I read?" you will, in all likelihood, respond correctly. In fact, each of the numbers is stored in sensory memory for a very short time, but if it is not attended to or processed within a fraction of a second, it will no longer be available (Alain & Woods, 1997).

---

cocktail party phenomenon An expression to describe sensory memory. The fleeting and unconscious availability for processing of stimuli to which the individual is not paying attention.

echoic memory Neisser's term for sensory memory involving auditory stimulation—the fleeting availability for processing of auditory stimuli to which the individual is not paying attention.

iconic memory Neisser's term for sensory memory involving visual stimulation—the fleeting availability for processing of visual stimuli to which the individual is not attending.

Short-Term Memory

Sensory memory precedes attention; it's simply the effect of a stimulus *before* you pay attention to it. When you attend to a stimulus (in other words, become conscious of it), it passes into short-term memory. Short-term memory consists of what is in our immediate consciousness at any given time. As Calfee (1981) notes, it is a sort of scratch pad for thinking. For this reason, short-term memory is often called *working memory*. The label describes the function of this level of memory rather than simply its duration.

One of the important characteristics of short-term memory is that it is highly limited in capacity. Following various memory experiments, Miller (1956) concluded that its average capacity is about seven separate items (plus or minus two); that is, our immediate conscious awareness is limited to this capacity, and as additional items of information come in, they push out some that are already there.

Short-term memory lasts a matter of seconds (not minutes, hours, or days) and appears to be highly dependent on rehearsal. That is, for items to be maintained in short-term storage, they must be repeated (consciously thought about). In the absence of repetition, they quickly fade—usually before 20 seconds have elapsed.

The apparent limitations of short-term memory are not nearly as serious as they might seem at first. Although we cannot easily attend to more than seven discrete items at one time, a process called **chunking** dramatically increases the capacity of short-term memory. In effect, a chunk is simply a group of related items of information. Thus, a single letter can be one of the seven items held in short-term memory, or it

---

chunking A memory process whereby related items are grouped together into more easily remembered chunks (for example, a prefix and four digits for a phone number rather than seven unrelated numbers).

might be chunked with other letters to form a single word—which can, in turn, be one of seven items in short-term memory. To illustrate this phenomenon, Miller (1956) uses the analogy of a change purse that can hold only seven coins. If the purse holds seven pennies, its capacity is only seven cents. But if it holds seven quarters, seven 50-cent pieces, or even seven gold coins, its capacity increases dramatically.

In summary, short-term memory is the ongoing availability of a small number of items, or chunks, of information in conscious awareness. Without continued rehearsal, these items are generally lost from memory within 20 seconds. The great usefulness of short-term memory is that it enables us to keep information in mind long enough to make sense of sequences of words and directions, to solve problems, and to make decisions.

Some Educational Implications of Short-Term Memory The most common way to measure short-term memory is to ask subjects to repeat a sequence of unrelated single-digit numbers they have just heard, a task that is used in many intelligence tests. Under these circumstances, adults and adolescents typically remember six or seven items (sometimes nine or more). In contrast, 6-year-olds are not likely to remember more than two or three items (Gathercole, 1998).

These differences can be very important for teachers. As Case (1991) suggests, perhaps certain problems are difficult or impossible for younger learners because they simply cannot keep in mind enough relevant information at one time—as might be true, for example, if a young child were asked to add several numbers at once. Not surprisingly, for example, John (1998) found that measures of short-term memory can be used to predict reading readiness in young children (ages 6–7). It appears that children who experience the most difficulty with keeping several items of information in mind at once—that is, children whose short-term mem-

ory is least developed—also experience the most difficulty in learning to read.

Teachers have two courses of action in such cases. If many of the young child's cognitive limitations result from a limited short-term memory capacity, teachers can either wait for appropriate changes in memory before progressing to more demanding tasks. Or they can take steps to improve the child's memory.

In practice, teachers most often resort to the first alternative; they simply wait for the child to mature. Recently, however, growing evidence suggests that it might be possible to teach certain aspects of cognitive strategies—such as rehearsal—that are important for short-term memory (more about this later).

Long-Term Memory

Long-term memory includes all of our relatively stable information about the world—what we

Recollections that make up our long-term memories are highly stable and not easily disrupted. In one week, these people are not likely to remember what they had for dinner tonight, but they are highly unlikely to forget the names of any of the people whose photographs they now recognize. The objective of schools is to teach for long-term memory.

know but is not in our immediate consciousness. In fact, one important distinction between short-term and long-term memory is that short-term memory is an active, ongoing, conscious process, whereas long-term memory is a more passive, unconscious process. Accordingly, short-term memory is easily disrupted by external events—as we demonstrate every time we lose our train of thought because of a distraction. In contrast, long-term memory cannot easily be disrupted. If you know the capital of Finland today, you are likely to know it tomorrow, next month, and even next year.

As we noted earlier, we transfer information from sensory storage to short-term storage through the process of attending, and we maintain information in short-term memory largely through rehearsal. But the transference of material from short-term to long-term memory involves more than simple rehearsal: It involves **encoding**, a process whereby meaning is derived from experience. To encode information is to transform or abstract it—to represent it in another form.

Encoding clearly involves information processing, an event that can occur at different levels. Craik and Lockhart (1972; Cermak & Craik, 1979), originators of the **levels of processing** model, suggest that memory reflects the level to which information is processed. Information that is not processed leaves only a momentary sensory impression (sensory memory), information that is merely attended to and rehearsed is

available for seconds (short-term memory), and information that is processed to a greater degree is stored in long-term memory. But not all material in long-term memory is processed to the same level. If, for example, subjects are asked to learn and remember a word, they can process it at a highly superficial level, paying attention only to its physical appearance. At a somewhat deeper level, they might pay attention to the word's pronunciation. And at the deepest level, they would take into account the word's meaning—a process called *semantic encoding*. (Table 5.1 summarizes the characteristics of all three levels of memory.)

The Constructive Nature of Long-Term Memory

Our long-term memories are seldom exact reproductions of our experiences. In fact, memories change considerably over time, often in predictable ways. As Loftus (1979) notes, they tend to be *generative* rather than purely reproductive. As an illustration, she asked subjects to view a film in which a sports car was involved in an accident. Later, she asked questions about the accident. For example, some subjects were asked, "How fast was the sports car going when it passed the barn while traveling along the country road?" Other subjects were asked instead, "How fast was the sports car going while traveling along the country road?" When subjects were later asked whether they had seen the barn, 17 percent of those who had earlier been asked the first question claimed to remember seeing one; fewer than 3 percent of the others actually remembered a barn. In fact, there was no barn in the film. In Schacter, Norman, and Koutstaal's (1998) words, long-term memory is **constructive memory**. Essentially, this means that much of

---

encoding A process whereby we derive meaning from the environment. To encode is to represent in another form. At a mental level, encoding involves the process of abstracting—representing something as a concept or a meaning.

levels of processing An information-processing theory, attributed to Craik and Lockhart, maintaining that memory is a function of the level of information processing. At the lowest level, a stimulus is simply recognized as a physical event (and is available momentarily in short-term sensory memory); at a much deeper level, a stimulus is interpreted in terms of its meaning (and is available in long-term memory).

constructive memory An alternate label for long-term memory, meant to emphasize the extent to which remembering involves reconstructing experiences. With the passage of time, we tend to remember less and less accurately.

Flashbulb Memories and Eidetic Images

Most of us are subject to what Brown and Kulik (1982) were the first to label **flashbulb memories**—unusually vivid and detailed recollections of the precise occasion on which we first heard about something highly important, emotional, or dramatic. Flashbulb memories, explains Cohen (1996), are extraordinarily clear recollections of what we were doing at the time, how we found out, what we felt, and what happened next. In the United States, the death of President Kennedy is easily the most highly researched source of flashbulb memories. In Great Britain, recent flashbulb memory research has focused on Margaret Thatcher's resignation and on the 1989 Hillsborough football disaster in which 96 people died (Wright, Gaskell, & O'Muircheartaigh, 1998). The death of Princess Diana would also be associated with flashbulb memories.

Flashbulb memories are relatively common, but **eidetic images**—also called "photographic memory"—are not. When we remember something, we sometimes say, "I can picture it in my mind," although most often, psychologists inform us, what we see in our minds isn't a clear picture at all. Instead, it's an imperfect representation that we have constructed from many memories, subject to all the distortions and inaccuracies to which memory is prone. Only rare individuals can actually see accurate mental images—that is, *eidetic* images. Such individuals, when shown the painting reproduced here for a few brief moments, might answer absolutely correctly when the picture is concealed and they are asked questions such as: "How many oranges are there in the tree?" "How many stripes are there in the flute player's

The Dream by Henri Rousseau, 1910. Oil on canvas, 6′ 8^1/$_2$″ x 9′ 9^1/$_2$″. The Museum of Modern Art, New York. Gift of Nelson A. Rockefeller. Reprinted by permission.

Table from *The Mind of the Mnemonist: A Little Book about a Vast Memory*, by A. R. Luria, translated from the Russian by Lynn Solotaroff. Copyright 1968 by Basic Books, Inc., Publishers. Reprinted by permission of Michael Cole and Jonathan Cape, Ltd.

skirt?" "How many flowers can you see?" Investigations indicate that recall based on eidetic imagery is very much like looking at the actual picture. Gifted individuals continue to "see" the picture after it has been removed and can actually count the oranges they had not previously counted. There is evidence, too, that some degree of eidetic imagery is common among young school-age children, but that it is far less common after adolescence (Ahsen, 1977a, b). But, contrary to popular opinion, eidetic imagery is not usually an advantage in school because it rarely involves any transference to long-term memory. In fact, eidetic images are seldom available for recall even one hour later.

Although eidetic images typically fade within minutes, there are some recorded cases of remarkable, eidetic-like memories that are not subject to the ravages of time. Among these, Luria's (1968) description of a young Russian known to us only as S is per-

haps the best known. S went to Luria, a psychologist, because he was bewildered and confused. His mind was such a jumble of sights, sounds, and colors that he had difficulty following ordinary conversations. S's problem, quite simply, was an absolutely remarkable memory. On one occasion, Luria presented S with the array of numbers shown here. After S spent 3 minutes examining the table, he was able to reproduce the numbers flawlessly in 40 seconds. Within 50 seconds, he read off each of the four-digit numbers forming the first 12 horizontal rows, as well as the two-digit number in the last row. But it is even more remarkable that, even after several months had elapsed, during which time the table was never again presented, S could reproduce it flawlessly (although he took somewhat longer to "reimagine" the array).

But memories such as S's are exceptionally rare. Most of the memories with which teachers come in contact are much more ordinary.

TABLE 5.1
Three Levels of Memory

	SENSORY	SHORT-TERM	LONG-TERM
ALTERNATE LABELS	Echoic or iconic	Primary or working	Secondary
DURATION	Less than 1 second	Less than 20 seconds	Indefinite
STABILITY	Fleeting	Easily disrupted	Not easily disrupted
CAPACITY	Limited	Limited (7 ± 2 items)	Unlimited
GENERAL CHARACTERISTICS	Momentary, unconscious impression	Working memory; immediate consciousness; active, maintained by rehearsal	Knowledge base; associationistic; passive; the result of encoding

what we remember is modified by intervening events and dulled by the passage of time. In the end, perhaps fewer than half of us will be able to identify the thief; even fewer will remember the color of his hair or eyes. And some of us will remember things that we have never even experienced.

One characteristic of long-term memory that might explain its constructive nature is that our memories appear to be scattered in many parts of our brains. Studies using **positron emission tomography** or **magnetic resonance imaging** (imaging techniques that can reveal location and patterns of neural activity in the brain) indicate that there isn't just one single memory trace for each item that we remember (Gabrieli, 1998). As a result, long-term remembering is a process of retrieving *from different brain locations* isolated features of the experience we are recalling and putting them together in a

sort of pattern-completion process (McClelland, McNaughton, & O'Reilly, 1995). Several problems can, and often *do*, result, note Schacter, Norman, and Koutstaal (1998). Often, only a fragment of the experience can be retrieved, because elements of the experience do not seem to be sufficiently "bound" together. As a result, people are unable to remember various details about an experience. Or they retrieve details of *different* experiences but now assume that these all belong to the same event. Or perhaps they remember an experience as though it were theirs (an episode in their own lives) when it actually isn't. Thus, we sometimes make poor witnesses without ever intending to lie.

Influences on Long-Term Memory Not all of our long-term memories are subject to distortions and inventions. As we saw, for example, highly significant emotional experiences sometimes give rise to long-lasting and remarkably detailed **flashbulb memories**. Similarly, our memories

---

positron emission tomography Also referred to as a *PET scan*. A medical diagnostic technique and research tool that can be used to provide computer-enhanced images of body structures and of neurological functioning. A powerful tool for brain and memory research.

magnetic resonance imaging Popularly referred to as MRI, a powerful medical diagnostic tool that makes use of computer-enhanced images of magnetic fields in the body to reveal details about physical and neurological structure and functioning. Highly useful for brain and memory research.

---

flashbulb memories Unusually vivid and relatively permanent recollections of the details surrounding first hearing some emotionally significant news.

eidetic image A particularly vivid type of visual image in memory. In many ways, it is as though the individual were actually able to look at what is being remembered—hence the synonym *photographic memory*.

for odors appear to be remarkably stable and long lasting (Annett, 1996). Goldman and Seamon (1992) bottled 14 odors, half of them associated with childhood (for example, bubble soap, crayon shavings, Play-Doh, fingerpaints) and the other half more closely linked with adulthood (chocolate, popcorn, soap shavings, cigarette tobacco). Adults correctly identified about 90% of recent odors and more than three-quarters of sometimes very distant odors.

Many of our recollections of real-life, day-to-day events are also remarkably accurate. For example, when Wynn and Logie (1998) questioned 63 adults about incidental but actual events in their lives, they found very little change in people's recollections of these events over time. Most of these adults continued to remember with a high degree of accuracy which seemed independent of the passage of time.

Several factors appear to be directly related to how clearly and how long we are likely to remember things. For example, highly arousing (emotionally important events) are far more likely to be remembered (Cahill & McGaugh, 1998). In fact, the most dramatic of these may lead to *flashbulb memories*.

Long-term memory is also influenced by understanding. With our highly *constructive* memories, we tend to remember the *gist* of what happened (or of what we heard or read) rather than all its details. That is, we tend to remember meanings, central ideas. When you hear a story and then repeat it, you first recollect its general "drift"—perhaps its punch line and its setting. And when you tell the story, you don't so much *repeat* it as *regenerate* it on the basis of your understanding of the story.

Long-term memory also appears to be influenced by certain drugs and other substances. For example, Tiplady and associates (1998) gave their subjects (15 individuals, ages 20 to 27) ethanol (the kind of alcohol found in beer and wine, for example) or temazepam (a relatively common anti-anxiety or tranquilizing

drug). Both of these drugs had very marked negative effects on long-term memory. Interestingly, increased oxygen intake appears to have a measurably positive effect on long-term memory, although increased glucose intake does not (Winder & Borrill, 1998).

Types of Long-Term Memory

When a meddling philospher asked a centipede how it managed to walk with its many legs, the poor thing was totally bewildered. You see, it had never really thought about the problem; it just darn well knew how. Sadly, after it had been asked the question, it began to try to understand the process, tried to figure out which leg went where, when, which next, and on and on, until, finally, completely perplexed and befuddled, it had wrapped its hundred legs in the world's biggest headache of a knot.[2]

Declarative and Nondeclarative Long-Term Memory

Much of our knowledge, too, is like the centipede's knowing how to walk. It isn't information that we know consciously and can put into clear, understandable words and instructions. Instead, it's knowledge that we have in our muscles or maybe in some unconscious part of our nervous systems. It includes information relating to things like riding a bicycle, hitting long

---

nondeclarative memory Refers to unconscious, nonverbalizable effects of experience such as might be manifested in acquired motor skills or classical conditioning. Also termed *implicit* or *procedural memory*.

---

[2] **PPC:** This doesn't sound like a good example for humans. We're far from having as many legs as a centipede. Or does the bear often trip over his four?

Author: The bear, old as he might be, walks with the sprightly step of those much younger. The point, however, is not how many legs we have or how elegantly we walk. Rather, it has to do with the fact that there are things that we know—hence, *remember*—that we cannot readily put into words. Read on.

drives in golf, or even our thoughtless responses to things that frighten or excite us. These kinds of memories are labeled **nondeclarative memory** (or **implicit memory**) simply because they can't be put into words.

But we also have many stable memories that we *can* put into words—memories having to do with our names, our addresses, the meanings of words, the colors of our cars, and on and on. These memories make up what is termed **declarative memory** (also called **explicit memory**). The principal difference between declarative and nondeclarative memory is that declarative memory is *conscious* memory for facts and events; nondeclarative memory is *unconscious* memory. The discovery that these are two distinct types of memory is one of the important recent achievements of the cognitive sciences, says Eichenbaum (1997).

Semantic versus Episodic Memory Declarative memory consists of at least two distinct types of memories, explains Tulving (1991). Abstract, general knowledge about the world, such as what children learn in school, for example, makes up what is called **semantic memory**. Each of us also has a large store of very personal recollections about the things we have done and thought, the experiences we have had, and so on. This autobiographical knowledge consists of all of the episodes of our lives and defines what is meant by **episodic memory**.

To summarize, there are two different kinds of long-term memories: those that are implicit, unconscious, and not easily verbalized (nondeclarative) and those that are explicit, conscious, and can be put into words (declarative). Declarative memories might be abstract and general (semantic) or more personal and autobiographical (episodic). Figure 5.3 summarizes these distinctions.

PROCESSES IN LONG-TERM MEMORY

The functioning of the information processing system (memory model) that we have been describing has a simple goal: to make sense of significant sensation and to organize and store for recall that which is potentially either important, interesting, or useful while ignoring or discarding more trivial matters. To achieve this goal, the system uses a variety of processes. As we saw, much sensory data that is not attended to (not processed) does not go beyond immediate sensory memory. Paying attention is one of the important activities, or processes, of our information processing system. By this means, information is transferred from sensory to short-term storage. Three other basic processes are involved in remembering: rehearsal, elaboration, and organization.

Rehearsal

Rehearsal involves repeating. The simplest rehearsal strategy is to state the material ("five, five, five, one, two, one, two") over and over again until it seems unlikely that it will escape from memory. Rehearsal serves not only to maintain information in short-term memory but also to transfer material from short- to

---

declarative memory Explicit, conscious long-term memory, in contrast with implicit (or nondeclarative) memory. Declarative memory can be either semantic or episodic. Also termed *explicit memory*.

semantic memory A type of declarative (conscious, long-term) memory consisting of stable knowledge about the world, principles, rules, and procedures and other verbalizable aspects of knowledge, including language.

episodic memory A type of declarative, autobiographical (conscious, long-term) memory consisting of knowledge about personal experiences, tied to specific times and places.

---

rehearsal A memory process involving repetition, important for maintaining information in short-term memory and transferring it to long-term memory.

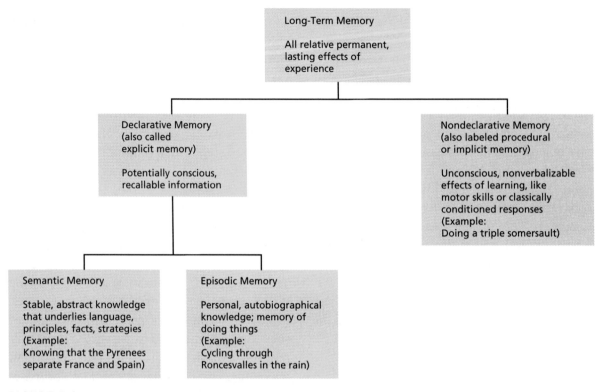

FIGURE 5.3 Types of long-term memory: Memories that are implicit, unconscious, and not easily verbalized are nondeclarative. Memories that are explicit, conscious, and can be put into words are declarative. Declarative memories can be either abstract and general (semantic memories) or personal and autobiographical (episodic memories).

long-term storage. Most children younger than age five do not rehearse spontaneously and cannot easily be taught to do so (Wellman, 1990).

Elaboration

Elaboration is a cognitive process whereby material is extended or added to (elaborated) to make it more memorable. One way of elaborating material is to associate mental images with items to be remembered. Higbee (1977) suggests that, because our memories are highly visual (photographs are more easily remembered than

paragraphs of text), the use of mental images is an important aspect of most mnemonic systems (systems for remembering). Some of these systems are described later in this chapter.

Sometimes, elaboration involves forming associations between new material and material that is already well known. Research suggests that elaborations that relate to meaning are highly memorable. For example, when Bradshaw and Anderson (1982) asked subjects to recall sentences such as "the fat man read the sign," those who had elaborated the sentence to something like "the fat man read the sign warning of thin ice" performed significantly better than those who had not elaborated. Children younger than age 12 do not deliberately elaborate to improve recall (Justice, 1985).

---

elaboration A long-term memory process involving changing or adding to material, or making associations to make remembering easier.

A map might reveal where we are, where we want to go, and how we can get there. But each of these revelations is totally dependent on the individual's ability to retrieve from memory all sorts of complex information about maps, space, movement, and direction. Even knowing that we know how to read a map is no small accomplishment.

Organization

Organization refers to grouping and relating material. Assume, for example, that you need to memorize the following list: man, dog, green, cayenne, woman, cat, child, canary, jalapeño. Some of you will immediately notice that the list can be easily organized into three groups of related items (pets, persons, and peppers) and will use this organization to help remember the items—which, again, is not something younger children will spontaneously do.

The organizational strategies that are so important to long-term memory can be either

---

organization A memory strategy involving grouping and relating material to maintain it in long-term memory.

extremely complex or quite simple. What most of these have in common, however, is that they are based on our recognition of similarities and differences. Humans (and perhaps other animals as well) seem to have a tendency to see similarities and differences (and other relations) and to generalize from them. Put another way, we seem to be information processing organisms whose function is to make sense of all the data that surround us. One of the important methods we use for making sense of the world is to extract common elements from various experiences, thereby compiling concepts or ideas that we can remember.

Besides this apparently natural tendency to look for relationships, there is evidence that many of our organizations of related concepts or ideas result from the application of learned strategies. More than this, as we become aware of various strategies that we can use to make sense of the world (and to learn and remember), we also become aware of ourselves as organisms capable of learning and remembering. We learn things, and we learn about learning. In other words, we develop *metacognitive* skills, (more about these later in this chapter).

EDUCATIONAL APPLICATIONS: TEACHING FOR RETRIEVAL

There is a common belief, note Semb and Ellis (1994), that students begin to forget much of what they have learned very soon after they have written their examinations. And, in fact, research on long-term memory seems to indicate that most of what is forgotten is lost very soon after it is learned and that, by the same token, things that we succeed in remembering days or weeks later may well continue to be available even years afterward. To the extent that this is true, it presents an important challenge for teachers. After all, one of the important functions of schools is

Boring with the Cost of Borrowing

THE PLACE: Medicine Hat High School

THE TIME: 3:00 p.m. Friday

THE SETTING: The beginning of Orville Radcliffe's class, Life and Career Skills 10, taught to a tenth-grade class of low achievers—administratively labeled an "opportunity class"

THE LESSON: Personal banking

There is much noise and shuffling, much talking and rest-lessness. Little attentiveness. Mr. Radcliffe glances at his lesson notes. He reads the main heads:

- ▲ The purposes of banks
- ▲ Alternatives
- ▲ Fluctuating interest rates
- ▲ The cost of borrowing . . .

"Borrrrrrring!" Mr. Radcliffe acknowledges to himself. He clears his throat.

"Ahem," says he, by way of getting their attention. It doesn't work.

"Today we're going to talk about personal banking," he mumbles uncertainly. Soon, he knows, he will have lost them all until the bell rescues him.

But that's the lesson he prepared, and so he forges onward: "Take out your notebooks 'cause you should make notes, 'cause there'll be questions about this on the exam, especially about the effects of interest rates and all that . . ."

How he wishes he had prepared a different lesson. . . .

to impart skills and knowledge that will be available to learners not specifically for examinations but rather for the rest of their lives. In short, the function of schools is to teach for long-term memory.

Fortunately, the belief that there is little long-term retention of material learned in school does not appear to be entirely true, claim Semb and Ellis (1994). They point out that the studies upon which this conclusion is based are mainly laboratory studies rather than school-based studies. In laboratory studies, the material to be learned is usually presented and learned in a single session. In contrast, schools typically provide learners with a tremendous number and variety of opportunities in which to learn, and schools make use of a far greater assortment of presentation modes (like films, lectures, CDs, demonstrations, books, and computer-based multi-media). Hence, when Semb and Ellis analyzed 62 studies that looked specifically at long-term retention of school-taught material, it isn't surprising that they found evidence of considerable long-term retention. Perhaps even more important for teachers, they also found clear evidence that long-term retention reflects how well students learn in the first place, a factor that is partly dependent on how they were taught and partly on the individual students' abilities.

The challenge for teachers is to find ways to improve learning—and, consequently, long-term retention. Consider, for example, the preceding case, "Boring with the Cost of Borrowing." Here is a lesson that has little chance of being absorbed, especially with this particular class on a Friday afternoon. But the lesson in the corresponding case, "I've Won the Bejiggered Lottery!"[3] might work wonderfully well—and might be remembered. Why? It begins with material that is striking, it presents a situation that is meaningful, it provides opportunities for relating items of information and for emphasiz-

CASES FROM THE CLASSROOM

I've Won the Bejiggered Lottery!

THE PLACE: Medicine Hat High School

THE TIME: 3:00 p.m. Friday

THE SETTING: The beginning of Orville Radcliffe's class, Life and Career Skills 10, taught to a tenth-grade class of low achievers—administratively labeled an "opportunity class"

THE LESSON: Personal banking

Orville struts to the front of the class, opens his briefcase flat on his desk so none of the students can see its contents—and then exclaims, "Now that's more like it!" And then he takes great stacks of money from the briefcase and begins to pile them on his desk (well, maybe not exactly money, but great stacks of newspaper cut just so, bound with rubber bands, with real bills on top).

"We don't get paid this much in a lifetime of teaching," says he. "But I've won the bejiggered lottery!"

And together, Mr. Radcliffe and his class examine the various banking alternatives available to a lottery winner, the implications of each, and on and on. . . .

ing concepts (perhaps with stacks of money), and it uses visual (and memorable) teaching aids. And it won't be difficult to find opportunities for rehearsal and repetition. This is one lesson students might remember.

Why We Forget

If teachers wish to teach for long-term retention, it might be useful to know why students forget. Knowing why forgetting occurs might suggest a variety of methods to impede the process.

As we saw earlier, memories appear to be distributed in different parts of the brain, which partly explains why much of what we remember is often at least partly reconstructed and not always entirely accurate (Schacter, Norman, & Koutstaal, 1998).

There are several possible explanations of what is involved in **forgetting**; each of these might have important instructional implications.

Fading **Fading theory** holds that material not brought to mind frequently enough (not used) tends to fade from memory. I know at this moment that we now have an accumulation of 15 centimeters of snow. Unless I review this information again or have it brought to mind by someone or something, I probably won't remember it next week—and certainly not next year. It will have faded.

Many psychologists don't consider fading theory (also called *decay theory*) very useful or informative. They argue that time, by itself, does not cause forgetting any more than it causes

---

[3] *PPC:* (Note to the Editor) I don't know what your policy is, but the bear borders on profanity. I don't really know exactly what *bejiggered* means, but I don't like the sound of it, and I think some of my younger students might be . . . well, "shocked" is probably too strong, but certainly, "taken aback."

Author: Bejiggered is an ancient Mayan word that means, literally, "hit on the nose by a long stick thrown by a left-handed beggar with one eye looking the other way." Hence, to be truly *bejiggered* is a rare thing. As, of course, is winning the lottery. The bear is not the least bit profane! Most of the time.

---

forgetting The cessation of a response as a function of the passage of time, not to be confused with extinction.

fading theory The belief that the inability to recall long-term memories increases with the passage of time as memory traces fade. Also termed *decay theory*.

metal to rust or mountains to erode: Other events that occur during the passage of time account for these phenomena.

Distortion Memories that don't entirely fade are often distorted or confused with other memories. As Schacter, Norman, and Koutstaal (1998) explain, it's as though the various features of a single past experience were inadequately bound together in memory. As a result, when the person tries to recall the experience, only fragments of the episode are available, and it becomes impossible to remember how and when the fragments were acquired. For example, it's now difficult for me to remember any one specific sunset accurately. I have seen so many that, when I recall features of sunsets, I can't tell to which specific sunset they belong. Even the most striking of my sunsets have become distorted until, in my memory of sunsets, there isn't a single one that looks very different from any other. It's sad but true. My sunrises seem somehow less subject to **distortion** (probably because I haven't seen as many).

Repression There is some evidence that people may forget events that are particularly unpleasant. One explanation for **repression** is Freud's belief that unpleasant memories filter into the subconscious mind, where the individual is not aware of them even though they may continue to have a profound effect on the person's emotional life.

Retroactive and Proactive Inhibition A highly researched theory of forgetting, and one with direct relevance for teachers, states that interference from previous or subsequent learning is an important cause of forgetting. When previous learning interferes with current recall, **proactive inhibition** is said to occur; **retroactive inhibition** takes place when subsequent learning interferes with the recall of previous learning. Teachers often have difficulty remembering the names of new students, especially if they have been teaching for a long time and have known many students with similar names. They confuse old names with new but similar faces. Their old learning interferes with learning something new—hence, *proactive inhibition*.

By the same token, once teachers have learned the names of all their current students, they sometimes find it difficult to remember the names of students from years past. Now newer learning interferes with the recall of old information—hence, *retroactive inhibition*.

Fortunately for us, as Banaji and Crowder (1989) note, not all laboratory findings concerning memory can be generalized to real life. Thus, although interference appears to describe what happens in the laboratory when relatively meaningless lists of words or syllables are being learned, interference does not describe well what happens in real life. If so, the more we learned, the more susceptible we would be to the effects of interference. Yet evidence suggests that, although old and new learning occasionally conflict, most of us can spend a lifetime learning new things without becoming totally confused.

Retrieval Cue Failure Some psychologists maintain that forgetting can be explained by the inability to retrieve from memory, rather than by simple memory loss, distortion, suppression, or

---

distortion One explanation for memory loss. Describes a process where the features of an experience are insufficiently bound together so that the person recollecting the experience cannot easily tell what happened when.

repression A Freudian term for the process by which intensely negative or frightening experiences are lost from conscious memory.

---

proactive inhibition The interference of earlier learning with the retention of subsequent learning.

retroactive inhibition Interference with the retention of previously learned material by subsequently learned material.

interference. In other words, individuals don't appear to remember simply because of what is termed **retrieval cue failure**—the inability to recall an item of information from memory. As Schacter, Norman, and Koutstaal (1998) explain, the learner may simply not have stored enough information to permit the clear and easy recall of an experience. Lack of clear retrieval cues is most likely to exist when different experiences resemble each other closely. In such cases, individuals are likely to remember only the *gist* or the general idea rather than the details.

Educational Implications of Theories of Forgetting

Implicit in the theories of forgetting that we have just discussed are several conclusions about what we are most likely to remember and why. These have highly important implications for teaching.

Fading Theory **Fading theory**, for example, suggests that information may be forgotten because it has faded or decayed through disuse. If students forget information because of disuse, teachers can provide repetition and review to remind them of important items. In fact, one of the reasons that our long-term memory for school-learned items seems better than memory for material learned in laboratory situations, suggest Semb and Ellis (1994), is precisely because schools do provide students with a variety of opportunities to practice and rehearse what they have learned. But in the absence of rehearsal, even well-learned items may soon be forgotten. For example, Reffel (1998) reports that when he asked more than 200 college students to write down the names of the 50 states on a blank sheet of paper, the average number of

states recalled correctly was only 32. Not surprisingly, participants were more likely to remember states contiguous to those in which they lived—presumably because they had occasion to rehearse these names more often.

Distortion Some of the distortion that occurs in memory results from the fact that we seldom remember all the features of a single experience. Instead, we might remember one or two and are then forced to reconstruct the others. One way for teachers to help counter this distortion is to emphasize the most important and distinct (the most memorable) aspects of a situation. Features that are highly distinct will be more easily and more accurately remembered.

Repression **Repression theory** holds that memories of highly unpleasant (traumatic) events may be unconsciously repressed. Ideally, schools and teachers seldom provide students with experiences so horrendous that they end up being buried in an unconscious place.

Retroactive and Proactive Inhibition Among the most important suggestions for countering the effects of *interference* and increasing the ability to recall information are those involving teaching for **transfer** (also termed *generalization*). As we saw in Chapter 4, transfer (or "generalization") refers to the effects of old learning on new learning; transfer can be either positive or negative. Positive transfer occurs when previous learning facilitates new learning and is sometimes evident in learning a second language. For example, it is easier to learn Spanish if you already know French than if you know only English; the similarities between French and Spanish facilitate positive transfer. Negative transfer occurs when previous learning

---

retrieval cue failure Inability to remember due to the unavailability of appropriate cues—as opposed to forgetting due to changes in memory traces.

---

transfer A general term for the application of old learning to a new situation. Also termed *generalization*.

interferes with current learning; this is similar to proactive interference. Negative transfer occurs, for example, when I go to Bermuda, rent a motor scooter, and discover that people are driving on the left side of the street.

One way to teach for positive transfer while still eliminating negative transfer is to relate new material to old material, emphasizing similarities and differences. The similarities should facilitate positive transfer; knowledge of differences should minimize negative transfer.

Retrieval Cue Failure *Retrieval cue failure* is a general term for the inability to find ways of remembering material. The assumption is that the material has not actually been forgotten (in the sense that it might have decayed or been interfered with), but that the learner simply lacks the cues—the specific retrieval tools—that would permit remembering.

There is evidence that for declarative (semantic) information—the explicit, conscious sorts of learning with which schools are most concerned—certain types of retrieval cues are most effective. For example, Tulving (1989) reports that the most effective retrieval cues are those that closely match the type of recall in question. Thus, if students will be asked to remember the meanings of words, then cues that emphasize meanings are best. In contrast, if they are to remember the spellings of words, cues that draw attention to letters are most effective. There are also a variety of other specific retrieval cues and techniques that can be taught and that are potentially very valuable in schools. We look at some of these next. (See Table 5.2 for a summary of theories of forgetting and some of their educational implications.)

Aids for Remembering

Many specific memory aids, or **mnemonic devices**, make use of what we know about human remembering and forgetting.

Rhymes and Other Sayings Rhymes, patterns, acronyms, and acrostics are common mnemonic devices that provide very specific—and sometimes indispensable—retrieval cues. "Thirty days hath September . . ." is a simple rhyme to help us remember how many days hath November. Similarly, the year in which Columbus sailed the ocean blue is nicely recalled by its little rhyme.

Acronyms are letter cues that help to recall relatively complex material. *NATO, U.N.,* and *UNESCO* are well-known acronyms. *Roy G. Biv* is another acronym, made up of the first letters of the words for the ordered colors of the visible light spectrum. Acrostics are similar to acronyms, except that they are generally in sentence form; the first letter of each word represents an item of information to be remembered. Without the bizarre sentence "Men very easily make jugs serve useful nocturnal purposes," I would have considerable difficulty recalling the planets in order from the sun. "Every good boy does fine" is meaningful to beginning music students.

Chunking, that is, combining items of information in meaningful patterns, is also a useful mnemonic aid. Chunking is the reason that the number 555-1212 is considerably easier to remember than would be "five million, five hundred fifty-one thousand, two hundred twelve."

Several more complex mnemonic techniques are described in detail by Higbee (1977) and are briefly reviewed here. All have one element in common: They make extensive use of visual imagery. Recall that visual material appears to have a greater impact on memory and can be retrieved much more easily than most nonvisual material.

---

mnemonic device A systematic aid to remembering, like rhymes, acrostics, or visual imagery systems.

TABLE 5.2
Theories of Forgetting and Some Educational Applications

THEORY	EXPLANATION	POSSIBLE INSTRUCTIONAL COUNTERMEASURES
Fading	Memory traces decay from disuse.	Provide opportunities for repetition and rehearsal; teach in a variety of settings using different approaches.
Distortion	Memory is constructive; we often remember the gist and make up the rest; hence, what is recalled changes over time.	Emphasize the most important or salient features of what is to be learned.
Repression	Traumatic experiences are unconsciously buried and no longer consciously accessible.	Avoid traumatizing students.*
Interference	Old memories interfere with learning new material (proactive), or new learning interferes with recall of old learning (retroactive).	Teach for transfer; highlight similarities and differences.
Retrieval Cue Failure	Learner lacks cues to enable specific recall.	Point out relationships and associations that can serve as retrieval cues; teach specific retrieval cues; teach learners some of the memory aids described in this chapter.

PPC: Is the bear serious? Was he traumatized as a cub?

Author: Yes, of course the bear is serious. Always. After all, teachers aren't like horror films, meant to be memorable because they are frightening. And no, neither the bear, nor the author, were traumatized as youngsters—that is, neither of them remembers being traumatized. But . . . shoot, come to think of it, repression being what it is, there is no way of remembering such things!

The Link System The simplest of these mnemonic techniques is the **link system**. It requires that the subject visualize the item to be remembered and form a strong visual association (link) between it and other items to be remembered. This is easily illustrated with reference to a grocery list. (Once you have mastered this system, you need never keep a grocery list again.) Suppose your list contains the following items: bread, salt, ketchup, dog food, and bananas. Visualize the first item: a loaf of bread. Concentrate on the picture that comes to mind first because it is likely to come to mind again when you think of bread. It might be bizarre, or it might be a simple image of a loaf or

slice of bread. Now visualize the second item, salt, and form a visual link between the first image and the second. For example, you might see a slice of bread perched delicately on a large silver salt shaker. The salt shaker is dripping with ketchup being poured from a bottle held by a hungry dog with a banana in its ear. In most cases, you need not spend more than a few seconds with each image, nor should you rehearse the images while you are learning the list.

The link system works amazingly well, although it has disadvantages. One is that it is sometimes difficult to remember the first item on the list. In that case, it might also be impossible to remember any of the other items because they are linked to each other. This problem can be overcome by forming a visual association between the first item and a setting that is likely to remind you

---

link system A mnemonic system wherein items to be remembered are linked to one another using visual images.

of the item. You might, for example, see the loaf of bread reclining in a grocery cart.

A second disadvantage of the link system is that if you cannot recall one of the items, it is unlikely that you will recall any of the subsequent items.

The Loci System A variation of the link system, the **loci system**, overcomes this second disadvantage. In effect, using the loci system you simply form associations between items that you need to remember and familiar places that you can therefore visualize clearly. Rooms in a familiar house make good loci (locus is Latin for "place"). You can quite easily "place" a grocery list in the rooms of a house by simply forming strong visual images of the objects, one in each of the rooms. The advantage of this system is that if you cannot remember what you placed in the hallway, you can still go to the kitchen—or bathroom—to see what you placed there.

METACOGNITION

Young children don't learn these memory strategies as readily as do older children and adults, and they are far less able to organize material. More than this, they are less aware of the importance of doing so. One of the very important differences between young children and older learners is that the former are not yet reflective about themselves as knowers; they have not yet recognized the special skills that allow them to extract information, to organize, to learn, and of course, to remember. In other words, they know far less about knowing; they understand less about understanding (Flavell, 1985). Using the current jargon, they have not yet developed the skills of *metacognition* or **metamemory**.

"*You simply associate each number with a word, such as 'Table' and 3,476,029.*"
© 1996 Sidney Harris

Metacognition, notes Sternberg (1998a), should be considered an important and integral aspect of human abilities. Metacognition is our knowledge and beliefs about knowing. Similarly, metamemory involves knowing about remembering. Because knowing necessarily involves remembering, metacognition includes metamemory. As an example, your belief that you can learn and remember better by underlining important parts of this text illustrates metacognition.

It's useful to distinguish between two different aspects of metacognition: personal knowledge and beliefs about cognition itself and the individual's attempts to regulate or control cognitive activity (Schraw, 1998). Thus, your belief about the effectiveness of underlining represents the first aspect of metacognition: knowledge about cognition itself. Your estimation of the difficulty of a chapter or a passage and your decision about whether it would be best to make notes, to underline, or simply to read the material illustrates the second aspect of metacogni-

---

loci system A mnemonic system wherein items to be remembered are associated with visual images of specific places.

metamemory The knowledge we develop about our own memory processes—our knowledge about how to remember, rather than simply our memories.

tion: your attempt to control your cognitive activity.

The skills of metacognition allow us to monitor our progress when we try to understand and learn something. They provide us with ways of estimating the effects of our efforts, and they allow us to predict the likelihood of being able to remember the material later. Metacognitive knowledge tells us that there are ways to organize material to make it easier to learn and remember, that some rehearsal and review strategies are more effective for one kind of material than another, and that some forms of learning require the deliberate application of specific strategies whereas others do not.

The Development of Metacognition

As we noted earlier, metacognitive skills seem to be largely absent in very young children. This does not mean that they make no use of cognitive strategies; it simply means that they are not aware of them and do not apply them consciously. By the same token, they are far less able to monitor, evaluate, and direct their own learning, or to reflect on its effectiveness. In most instances, they do not realize that there are strategies that might make it easier to learn and remember. When Moynahan (1973) asked young children whether it would be easier to learn a categorized list of words or a randomly ordered list, children below the third-grade level chose either list with approximately equal frequency. In contrast, older children almost invariably chose the categorized list; they knew more about knowing.

Young children's poorer metacognitive skills are often apparent in their behaviors. For example, Borkowski, Milstead, and Hale (1988) note that young children often fail to use memory strategies even when questioning reveals they know that these strategies (for example, grouping items) would make it easier for them to remember. Similarly, they seldom question the

source of their information—or misinformation. Unlike we older adults, who pride ourselves on not being naïve and gullible, young children just as readily believe what another misinformed child says as something a parent or a teacher might say. As Mazzoni (1998) found, many of their apparent memory errors, and perhaps much of their suggestibility as witnesses, stems from their willingness to accept misinformation.

Specific strategies of metacognition can be taught to young children (Lawson, 1993; Mayo, 1993). But they also need to be taught when to use the strategy. Unfortunately, teachers do not often teach the strategies of cognition systematically. Instead, children are left to discover them on their own.

The Strategies of Cognition

Fortunately, we appear to have a natural tendency to extract generalities from experience, and to learn how to learn and remember. As we learn how to learn, we begin to see ourselves as players of what Flavell (1985) calls the *game of cognition*, and we become aware of an increasing number and variety of strategies that can make us better players of this game. The object of the game of cognition is not to beat someone else; winners of this game are those who are successful in making sense of information and who can recall and use it effectively.

Some people play the game of cognition very badly. They learn and remember with difficulty; much that they encounter is bewildering and frustrating. Others play the game extraordinarily well; they learn rapidly and with apparent ease, and their understanding is often startling. One difference between those who play the game of cognition well and those who do not play it as well may involve how clearly each understands the process of learning and remembering—in other words, it has to do with their awareness of and use of the strategies of cognition.

Cognitive Strategies Defined Among other things, the best players of the game of cognition are those who have learned the best strategies and know when to use them. Simply defined, **cognitive strategies** are the tools of intellectual activity. These strategies allow us to learn, to solve problems, to study, and to understand. However, strategies themselves have little to do with the content of what we learn. They are general, relatively abstract, "contentless" series of tactics or procedures (Gagné & Briggs, 1983). Mastery of the strategies of cognition allows learners to learn how to learn and to become lifelong learners (Linn & Muilenburg, 1996).

Historically, most of the teaching (and learning) of cognitive strategies has occurred incidentally, in the course of teaching other things. Recently, though, concerted attempts have been made to develop programs designed specifically to teach cognitive strategies. Several of these programs are reviewed later in this chapter.

Learning/Thinking Strategies in Education

The teaching/learning process has two broad classes of goals, note Weinstein and Mayer (1986): those related to the *products* of learning and those related to the *process* of learning. Goals that relate to the products of learning are the *what* of the instructional process—the information being taught. Goals that have to do with the process of learning are the *how* of learning—the skills and strategies that can be used to acquire and process content; that is, they involve learning to learn.

Cognitive psychology's most important current contribution to educational psychology is a renewed emphasis on the second of these major goals: learning to learn. This emphasis is currently evident in the attention being given to cognitive strategies or to what are often labeled **learning/thinking strategies**. The phrase "learning/thinking strategy" is preferred over "cognitive strategy" for two reasons: It is broader, including specific strategies such as rehearsing or elaborating as well as metacognition; and it emphasizes that the strategies and processes involved in learning to learn are the same processes that we use for what we ordinarily define as thinking. Phrased another way, learning/thinking strategies are the learner's information processing/thinking tools.

Classes of Learning/Thinking Strategies And what, you may ask, are these learning/thinking strategies? Recall from earlier in this chapter that our basic information processing model (the memory model) describes three main processes or activities involved in maintaining material in short-term memory and encoding and transferring it to long-term memory: rehearsal, elaboration, and organization. Weinstein and Mayer (1986) tell us that there are learning strategies for each of these processes. Some are basic; others are more complex. Accordingly, there are basic rehearsal strategies, complex rehearsal strategies, basic elaboration strategies, complex elaboration strategies, basic organizational strategies, and complex organizational strategies.[4] And, besides these six classes of learning strategies, there are comprehension-monitoring strategies, which are essentially identical to what we have described as metacognitive skills; and affective and motivational strategies, which direct our attention, maintain our interest, and

---

learning/thinking strategy A process involved in learning and thinking; another expression for "cognitive strategy," introduced to emphasize that the strategies involved in cognition (knowing) are also involved in learning and thinking.

---

[4] *PPC:* Terms such as cognitive strategies, metacognition, learning/thinking strategies, and metacognitive strategies are used in different ways in the literature. This can be very confusing. Maybe the bear could straighten things out, once and for all.

Author: Perhaps not once and for all, but for the time being, see the box entitled, "Sorting It All Out Cognitively."

TABLE 5.3
Categories of Learning/Thinking Strategies

TYPE OF STRATEGY	EXAMPLE
Basic Rehearsal Strategies	Simple repetition: "hablo, hablas, habla, hablamos, hablais, hablan"
Complex Rehearsal Strategies	Highlighting all the important points in a text
Basic Elaboration Strategies	Forming mental images or other associations such as "*m*en *v*ery *e*asily *m*ake *j*ugs *s*erve *u*seful *n*octurnal *p*urposes" (The first letter of each word stands for a planet in the solar system.)
Complex Elaboration Strategies	Forming analogies, paraphrasing, summarizing, relating
Basic Organizational Strategies	Grouping, classifying, ordering
Complex Organizational Strategies	Identifying main ideas; developing concept-summarizing tables such as this one
Comprehension-Monitoring Strategies	Self-questioning; reciting main points; setting goals and checking progress toward those goals
Affective and Motivational Strategies	Anticipating consequences of academic success (for example, a scholarship); deep breathing and other relaxation activities; positive thinking

Source: Based on C. E. Weinstein and R. E. Mayer, "The Teaching of Learning Strategies." In M. C. Wittrock (ed.), *Handbook of Research on Teaching* (3rd ed.). New York: Macmillan, 1986, 315–327.

help us to relax and control impediments to learning and thinking (such as test anxiety).

Table 5.3 summarizes these eight classes of learning/thinking strategies and gives a simple example of each.

Educational Applications: Teaching Learners How to Think

We saw in Chapter 4 that behavioristic approaches to learning lead to a number of instructional recommendations. Among other things, these approaches emphasize the importance of reinforcement and attempt to sort out the particular kinds and schedules of rewards and punishments that are most effective in the classroom. Later (in Chapter 11, for example) we will see that behaviorism has also led to specific techniques for behavior modification.

At first glance, the educational implications of the cognitive perspective seem quite different from those of behaviorism. After all, cognitivism is concerned much less with behavior, stimuli, rewards, and punishments than with thinking. It asks how children become thinkers and how we can make better, more critical, more creative thinkers of them.

The cognitive perspective suggests a two-pronged answer to these important questions. First, learners must develop an awareness of themselves as thinkers, learners, and information processors; second, they must develop and practice the approaches and strategies involved in critical, creative, and effective thinking and problem solving. In other words, the cognitive perspective argues that learners must develop metacognitive skills as well as appropriate cognitive strategies. These are the skills involved in learning to learn.

As we noted earlier, schools have traditionally devoted the bulk of their formal efforts to teaching specific curriculum content; the learning of cognitive strategies and the development of metacognitive awareness have been largely incidental—and sometimes accidental. But the best teachers, suggest Artzt and Armour-Thomas (1998) are those whose own metacognitive skills are most highly developed and are reflected in

BEAR MUSINGS

Sorting It All Out Cognitively

Following are some common, educationally relevant terms in the new cognitive sciences:

Metacognition Knowing about knowing; our knowledge and beliefs about our own cognitive processes and our attempt to play the game of cognition well—that is, so that we learn and remember well. Metacognitive knowledge is what permits us to select different approaches for learning and remembering; it allows us to monitor our cognitive activities and assess the likelihood of success; it suggests alternatives when necessary.

Cognitive Strategies The tools of cognitive behavior; goal-directed sequences of actions such as rehears-ing, organizing, or elaborating; what we actually do to learn and remember.

Learning/Thinking Strategies A global term that includes both metacognition and cognitive strategies. The entire range of activities involved in learning and thinking.

Summary Learning/thinking strategies include metacognitive and cognitive strategies. Metacognitive skills are executive (control) skills; cognitive skills are nonexecutive (applied) skills.

Illustration of the Relationships Between Metacognition and Cognition I decide to learn the meanings of common, educationally relevant terms in the new cognitive sciences (setting a goal that I suspect I am capable of achieving: a metacognitive experience). I begin to read this box (cognitive activity). I stop after two lines; I have a vague feeling that I have missed something (metacognitive experience). I read the lines again (cognitive activity). I sense that I am understanding (metacognition). I continue reading. I repeat each separate definition mentally once or twice (rehearsal, a cognitive strategy). Something tells me I am learning (metacognitive experience). I finish. I look at each term and silently repeat the definition (cognitive activity). I am satisfied that I understand and will remember until tomorrow's quiz (metacognition).

their classroom practice. And the best learners, argues Gourgey (1998), are those who are most skilled in clarifying their purpose, understanding the meanings of things, making inferences, finding relationships, and monitoring their own progress—in short, those who are most advanced in metacognitive skills. Or, to put it another way, the best learners are those who are most skilled at reflective assessment (White & Frederiksen, 1998; Watson, 1998). These are learners who reflect on their cognitive activities and who can assess their effectiveness and modify them as needed. These learners possess *strategic* as well as domain-specific (content) knowledge. Strategic knowledge deals with how to do things: how to solve problems, how to learn and memorize, how to understand, and perhaps most important, how to monitor, evaluate, and direct these activities as they occur. In other words, strategic knowledge is *metacognitive* knowledge.

An increasing number of researchers have recently developed programs designed specifically to develop cognitive skills in learners. Many of these programs are designed both to make students aware of the existence of cognitive strategies and to teach them to monitor and evaluate their use of these strategies. Such programs advocate a variety of approaches to teaching, including group learning (for example, cooperative learning), individual instruction (for example, teachers' questions designed to foster specific thinking skills), modeling procedures (for example, a cognitive strategy is verbalized as it is being executed), reflective learning (actively reflecting about the effectiveness and direction of learning activities), and various programs where learners are trained to use specific strategies. The main objective that these programs share is to develop in learners metacognitive knowledge—knowledge that allows children to learn how to learn.

Learning How to Learn: Changing Views

Learning how to learn in schools is not entirely new. What is new is our attitude toward what it is that makes learning difficult or easy. Traditionally, we have simply assumed that the most important factor in learning is inherited or natural intelligence—recognizing, of course, that motivation, persistence, and other similar factors are important as well. Recently, however, our conceptions of intelligence have changed dramatically. We have begun to accept the view that among the important components of intelligent activity are cognitive functions that are largely learned, not inherited (Sternberg, 1998b). Does it not follow that, if they are learned, they can also be taught?

The simple answer is yes. And there is increasing evidence that this learning need not occur only incidentally—or even accidentally—as a byproduct of school activities with purposes that are far removed from teaching students how to learn. A mushrooming new field of research involves looking for ways to teach students not only the cognitive skills of rehearsing, elaborating, and organizing but also the metacognitive skills involved in monitoring their own levels of comprehension and making other important decisions about their cognitive activities and their personal capabilities. Psychologists have been increasingly successful at discovering the rules, strategies, and objectives of this game of cognition that all of us are called upon to play. And, as a result, today's students may be far better players tomorrow than they would otherwise have been.

Researchers who have developed and investigated programs designed specifically to teach students how to learn and think have emphasized a variety of skills. Nickerson's (1988) review suggests that there have been at least seven identifiable emphases:

1. Basic operations such as classifying or generalizing

2. Domain-specific knowledge (for example, mathematical functions or history)

3. Knowledge about reasoning principles (for example, logic)

4. Knowledge about informal principles of thinking that might be used in problem solving

5. Metacognitive knowledge—that is, learners' beliefs about their own learning and their attempts to monitor and control their cognitive activities

6. Values such as fairness and objectivity

7. Personal beliefs (for example, about problems, the world, causes of things, and the role of luck and effort)

These various emphases have led to the development of a variety of programs to teach thinking skills. These programs typically take one of two forms: *stand-alone*, where cognitive skills are taught as a separate subject; and *embedded*, where cognitive skills are taught within the context of subject matter. A third approach described by Prawat (1991), *immersion*, places more emphasis on ideas than on skills and processes but is much like an embedded approach. Several illustrative programs are described in the sections that follow; there are a great many others. These are complex and highly developed programs that cannot be thoroughly explained in a few paragraphs so that they can then be used by a beginning teacher. Their implementation generally requires a more detailed study of the approaches and often involves in-service training and workshops. At the same time, however, these summaries suggest a number of specific teaching strategies that can be useful by themselves.

Feuerstein's Instrumental Enrichment For example, Feuerstein (1979) has developed a stand-alone program designed to develop a wide range of cognitive skills in learners. In effect, the program attempts to increase intelligence.

In practice, notes Feuerstein, intelligence is most often assessed by performance on tests that reveal how much a person has benefited from past experience. Such tests, he argues, represent a static (rather than a dynamic) view of intelligence: They reveal what the child has done rather than what the child can do in the future. They do not assess learning potential.

More useful measures of intelligence, Feuerstein argues, would do more than reflect what a child has done in the past; they would provide some estimate of capacity for benefiting from future experience. To this end, he has developed the **Learning Potential Assessment Device (LPAD)**, which focuses on intellectual functioning—on cognitive processes—rather than simply on whether a child can answer correctly within a given time limit. This test allows the examiner to actually teach the child, to offer hints and clues, and to direct and help. The test, described as a dynamic rather than a static measure, makes it possible both to identify strengths and to detect absent or deficient cognitive functions. In Feuerstein's (1980) terms, the test permits the construction of a "cognitive map" of the learner, which can serve as the basis for analyzing the cognitive functioning of what he calls "retarded performers" and as a blueprint for remediation.

Among Feuerstein's greatest contributions is the development of a complex and far-reaching series of activities and exercises designed to improve cognitive functioning. This program, **Feuerstein's Instrumental Enrichment (FIE)**, is based squarely on the assumption that motivates all the learning-to-learn research: a strong belief in cognitive modifiability.

The FIE program is a logical outgrowth of the LPAD and is largely content-free; that is, it attempts to teach cognitive functioning rather than academic content. To do so, it uses a series of progressively more abstract paper-and-pencil exercises designed to help students identify strategies used in thinking and to encourage them to become aware of their use of those strategies. In all, there are more than 500 pages of exercises—enough for a one-hour daily lesson over the course of several years.

The FIE program was initially developed for use with "retarded performers" (Feuerstein deliberately avoids the term *mental retardation*), but Feuerstein argues that its principles are applicable to a wide range of ages and subjects. Use of the FIE program requires that teachers be specially trained.

Initial evaluation of the FIE materials involved a longitudinal experiment in which performance-retarded adolescents exposed to the FIE program were compared with similar adolescents in a more conventional, content-oriented enrichment program. Results were highly positive (Feuerstein, 1980).

Subsequent researchers in several countries, including Canada, the United States, Venezuela, and Israel, have concluded that FIE has generally positive results. For example, a study involving 11 children diagnosed as having "communicative" disabilities provides evidence of considerable improvement following exposure to the enrichment program (Unruh & Dupree, 1998).

Learning Potential Assessment Device (LPAD) Feuerstein's measure of intelligence, developed to provide a dynamic rather than passive measure of intelligence—a measure of how the child can profit from experience rather than simply a measure of the effects of past experiences. Assessment procedures allow the examiner to coach, to provide hints and clues, to direct, and to help.

Feuerstein's Instrumental Enrichment (FIE) A detailed and comprehensive program designed to teach cognitive strategies and to make learners more aware of their own strategies.

Similarly, a study of 71 institutionalized learning-disabled adults found significant improvement in cognitive functioning after the program (Lifshitz, 1998).

One of the major contributions of the LPAD and of Instrumental Enrichment, notes Feuerstein (1994), is reflected in the view that intelligence is the propensity to change and to adapt—in contrast to the view that intelligence is a relatively fixed and largely inherited quality—hence, the emphasis on assessment procedures that require adaptation and attempt to facilitate it and the development of instructional methods specifically designed to enhance cognitive functioning and, by definition, intelligence.

SPELT Another large-scale cognitive program is Mulcahy and associates' **Strategies Program for Effective Learning/Thinking (SPELT)** (Mulcahy et al., 1986; Marfo et al., 1991). Described as a learning/thinking instructional program, SPELT is designed for use with all children—from learning disabled to gifted. It focuses on cognitive processes rather than content, and it is aimed at elementary and junior high school students. Unlike Feuerstein's Instrumental Enrichment program, SPELT is an embedded rather than a stand-alone program. Embedded programs can have the advantage of being more relevant to students and are more easily applied because they are part of the regular curriculum. Also, because they don't require a separate classroom period, they are less expensive and easier to schedule than stand-alone programs.

SPELT has three major characteristics: First, its overriding goal is to actively involve students in the learning process. It attempts to make students increasingly aware of their own cognitive processes and is geared toward discovery rather than reception learning.

Second, SPELT requires active teacher participation in identifying and discovering strategies and in devising methods for teaching them. Initially, teachers are presented with tested strategies and methods; after continuing in-service training, they are encouraged to develop their own.

Third, SPELT is designed to encourage students to recognize and generate their own cognitive strategies. That is, students are expected to become increasingly aware of their own intellectual processes and to become actively involved in developing and improving these processes. In short, students are encouraged to recognize and develop the tools they will use to play the game of cognition. The main objective of SPELT, says Mulcahy (1991), is to develop autonomous learners—learners who have truly learned how to learn, who are in control of their own "cognitive as well as affective resources and activities" (p. 385).

The learning/thinking strategies developed and emphasized in SPELT cover a vast range of skills and activities—for example, general problem solving, math and reading strategies, memory strategies, study skills, test-taking strategies, mood-setting strategies, and general metacognitive strategies such as comprehension monitoring. Special effort is also made to develop social problem-solving strategies.

Implementation of SPELT occurs in three overlapping phases. In the first phase, students are taught learning/thinking strategies by teachers trained in using and teaching these strategies. Instructional procedures in this phase are direct and teacher controlled. Their basic elements include motivating students, modeling the strategies, providing memorization and practice drills with feedback, and evaluating students' learning. The goal of this phase, as expressed by Peat, Mulcahy, and Darko-Yeboah (1989), is "metacognitive empowerment"—a condition that

---

Strategies Program for Effective Learning/Thinking (SPELT) A program designed to involve students in the learning process and to foster the development of cognitive strategies—an *embedded* program that is taught as an integral part of regular courses.

comes about as students become increasingly aware of the existence of cognitive strategies and of the contribution that systematic use of them can make to learning and problem solving.

The objectives of the second phase are to maintain the use of strategies learned in the first phase, to begin to evaluate the effectiveness of these strategies, and to modify and extend them to different content areas. The principal instructional method is no longer one of direct tuition but rather of facilitating the application of previously learned strategies to new situations (teaching for transfer). The instructional method is now Socratic rather than direct; that is, students are encouraged to extend and apply strategies through an interactive question-and-answer process. Among the teacher's guidelines for questioning are the following (with illustrations) (Mulcahy et al., 1990):

▲ *Start with what is known.* What strategy did you find useful when you read the material in the box? (Student response involves underlining material and reviewing it.)

▲ *Ask for more than one reason.* Why? . . . Can you think of any other reasons why underlining and reviewing are useful?

▲ *Ask students to describe steps in their reasoning processes.* What were you doing that made this strategy useful? What did you do next? What did you think as you tried to review?

▲ *Formulate general rules from specific cases.* Could you use underlining and reviewing for reading other things? With what sorts of material do you think it would help you?

▲ *Provide counterexamples when student overgeneralizes.* Do you think underlining and reviewing would be useful when you're watching a video?

▲ *Probe for differences among cases.* Underlining and reviewing is a useful strategy for some written material. How is it different from, say, highlighting and rehearsing a multiplication table?

▲ *Ask students to make predictions.* Do you think you understand the box better after underlining and reviewing it? Do you think you'll do better on the test?

In the third phase of the SPELT program, the learner is encouraged to generate new cognitive strategies and to monitor and evaluate them. The principal instructional method continues to be that of Socratic dialogue. In contrast with the first phase, learning at this level is largely controlled by the students rather than the teacher.

The SPELT program was evaluated during a three-year project involving some 900 gifted, average, and learning-disabled students in grades 4, 5, 7, and 8. Results were positive, especially for learning-disabled students and most notably at the fourth-grade level, where reading comprehension and comprehension-monitoring skills improved so much that many were no longer classified as disabled. Gifted students also benefited significantly. The use and awareness of cognitive strategies improved at all grade levels and for all groups. Parents, teachers, and administrators also responded favorably to the program. One year after termination of the experimental project, more than 85 percent of the teachers reported that they continued to use aspects of the program in their teaching (Mulcahy, 1991; Peat, Wilgosh, & Mulcahy, 1996).

Reciprocal Teaching Reciprocal **teaching** is an instructional technique developed by Palincsar and Brown (1984) and designed to teach students how to think and understand specifically with respect to what they read. In reciprocal teaching, students are taught four cognitive strategies for increasing reading comprehension: generating

---

reciprocal teaching An instructional technique that involves teaching four cognitive strategies for increasing reading comprehension: generating questions, summarizing, clarifying word meanings and confusing text, and predicting what will happen next.

questions, summarizing, attempting to clarify word meanings and confusing text, and predicting what will happen next. In the early stages, teachers use **direct instruction** to help students with each of these strategies, by modeling and illustrating them with various examples of written text (Brand-Gruwel, Aarnoutse, & Van Den Bos, 1998). As we saw, *direct instruction* is a general label for instructional approaches where the teacher serves as the principal source of information.

As students systematically practice these strategies, they assume increasing responsibility for helping each other with hints, feedback, additional modeling, and explanations—hence, the label *reciprocal* teaching. They are encouraged to ask questions, comment on each other's predictions, ask for clarification, and help to clear up misunderstandings. Gradually, teachers do less and less of the work as students do more. Eventually, the procedure becomes somewhat like a cooperative instructional approach as one student asks questions, a second answers, a third comments on the answer, another elaborates, and so on. However, reciprocal teaching does not involve work in groups, as do other cooperative approaches (see Chapter 9 for a description of cooperative teaching). Rather, it is a cognitive strategies instructional program, specifically designed for developing useful strategies for increasing reading comprehension.

Several studies have reported highly positive results following experimental applications of reciprocal teaching, both with normal children (for example, Tomesen & Aarnoutse, 1998) and with children who have reading disabilities (Aarnoutse, Brand-Gruwel, & Oduber, 1997; Speece, et al., 1997). Rosenshine and Meister (1994) reviewed 16 studies on reciprocal teach-

ing. They concluded, "When experimenter-developed comprehension tests were used, students in the reciprocal teaching treatment had scores that were significantly superior to those of the control group in 8 of 10 studies" (p. 505).[5]

Promoting Cognitive Skills in Your Classroom

Feuerstein's FIE, Mulcahy and associates' SPELT, and Palincsar and Brown's reciprocal teaching are only a few of many learning/thinking programs being developed, modified, and evaluated.[6] Two things seem clear at this point: *First*, our attempts to teach students how to think and how to learn are not always as deliberate and as focused as they might be; and *second*, systematic programs can significantly improve learning and thinking for a variety of individuals and in many different contexts.

The foregoing should not be taken to suggest that teachers who do not use systematic programs for teaching their students thinking/learning skills are failing to meet their responsibilities. As Marzano (1993) points out, many classroom teachers use a variety of strategies and techniques to promote cognitive skills, even if these

---

direct instruction A phrase used to describe teacher-directed approaches to teaching—in contrast with more student-centered approaches such as reciprocal teaching and cooperative learning (often included among *constructivist approaches*).

[5] *PPC:* One of my pet peeves is that outcome studies rarely bother asking how students *feel* about the programs—whether they like them or not.

Author: A reporter once asked Yogi Berra how he felt about school. "How did you like school when you were growing up, Yogi?" he asked. "Closed," answered Yogi. Maybe it's because of the possibility of this sort of answer that the question isn't often asked.

[6] *PPC:* I don't think the author provides enough information for teachers-in-training to actually be able to use any of these programs with their classes.

Author: True. In fact, using most of these approaches requires systematic training, often via workshops and other in-service programs. Knowing about them is nevertheless very important for teachers who otherwise would not likely make the effort to study them in more detail. There may be also a significant benefit in simply accepting that teaching students how to learn is an important function of schools and in knowing that there are systematic ways to accomplish this.

aren't always entirely systematic—strategies that include various kinds of questioning and a variety of exercises designed to encourage learners to analyze, match, encode, and otherwise become aware of and improve their information processing.

It would clearly be premature to suggest that teachers should now begin using this or that program for this or that purpose, although it is not at all premature to repeat the claim of many education critics that the schools have not always done much to teach thinking and learning skills. The contemporary cognitive sciences are based on the assumption that much more can be done. They have also begun to show us how.

MAIN POINTS

1. The main emphasis of cognitive psychology is on the mental events involved in knowing, acquiring information, solving problems, and remembering. Cognitive psychology looks at three things: knowledge base (the learner's storehouse of information), cognitive strategies (processes used in learning and thinking), and metacognition (awareness of the self as a knower and capacity to understand and monitor cognitive processes).

2. A useful model (metaphor) for human cognitive functioning describes the learner as a three-level information processing and storage system; these levels are labeled "sensory memory," "short-term memory," and "long-term memory." Sensory storage is the unconscious, momentary availability of sensory data for immediate processing, lasting only a fraction of a second.

3. Paying attention to sensory information processes it into short-term (working) memory, where it is maintained for perhaps as long as 20 seconds, providing it is rehearsed. Short-term memory capacity for normal adults is seven (plus or minus two) items, some of which might include chunks of related material.

4. Material is transferred from short-term to long-term memory through encoding (transforming or changing to abstract generalities and deriving meaning). Encoding involves three processes: rehearsal (repetition), elaboration (extending), and organization (relating, sorting). Long-term memory can be either declarative (conscious, explicit) or nondeclarative (implicit, unconscious). Declarative memory might be semantic (general knowledge that can be verbalized) or episodic (personal, autobiographical knowledge). Declarative memory is highly constructive and subject to distortions and misremembering.

5. Theories of forgetting maintain that information is forgotten because it is unused, distorted, repressed, or interfered with or because the individual has a poor retrieval system. These theories suggest that teachers should both emphasize distinct and important aspects of situations and also stress similarities and differences, to minimize interference and maximize transfer.

6. Mnemonic devices (memory aids) include rhymes, patterns, acrostics, and acronyms. More complex mnemonic techniques are the link system and the loci system. Each of these is based on the principle that visual imagery is an extremely powerful aid to memory. Useful strategies for teaching retrieval emphasize meaningfulness, organization, visual imagery, and rehearsal.

7. As we learn about things (facts, problem-solving techniques, and so on), we also learn about learning. Knowledge about our own cognitive processes is called metacognition. The skills of metacognition allow us to direct, monitor, evaluate, and modify our ongoing learning and thinking.

8. Cognitive (learning/thinking) strategies are the tools of cognitive behavior. They are the skills involved in organizing, remembering, elaborating, and monitoring intellectual activity. Cognitivism asks how children become thinkers and how we can make better, more critical, and more creative thinkers of them. Part of the answer is to make them aware of themselves as knowers and information processors (metacognitive skills) and to teach them specific cognitive strategies (for example, how to rehearse, organize, and monitor). There are a large number of specific approaches for doing so.

9. Feuerstein's Instrumental Enrichment (FIE) program is based on the Learning Potential Assessment Device (LPAD), which attempts to assess the "retarded performer's" highest potential for achievement. It consists of paper-and-pencil exercises to develop cognitive strategies. It was developed primarily for adolescents with performance deficits (below-average intelligence or normal intelligence with learning disabilities or cognitive deficiencies).

10. The Strategies Program for Effective Learning/Thinking (SPELT), developed by Mulcahy and associates, is an embedded program (designed for use within the context of ordinary curriculum) for elementary and junior high school students. It encourages teachers and students to identify and generate cognitive strategies in a variety of areas (general problem solving, social problem solving, math, reading, studying, test-taking, mood-setting, and general metacognitive strategies).

11. Palincsar and Brown's reciprocal teaching attempts to develop strategies to increase reading comprehension by asking students to eventually assume responsibility for helping one another.

Applied Questions

▲ What are some of the most important metaphors of cognitive theory?

▲ Compare and contrast sensory memory, short-term memory, and long-term memory using school-based examples.

▲ Can you outline an educational implication related to each of the characteristics of short-term and long-term memory?

▲ Describe one educational implication for each of the common theories of forgetting.

▲ Describe and illustrate a mnemonic system.

▲ What would you include in a basic program designed to teach students how to think?

Internet Activity

Use InfoTrac College Edition or other World Wide Web sources to research the following topic: Write up your findings. (See the inside back cover of this text for suggestions about where to begin.)

How to improve your memory
Sample search term: Mnemonics

Study Terms

Suggested Readings

The following book is a clear and detailed description of contemporary cognitive psychology and its implications for education:

Hunt, R. R., & Ellis, H. C. (1999) *Fundamentals of cognitive psychology.* New York: McGraw-Hill.

Cohen's book is a scholarly but highly readable and fascinating description of what research tells us about everyday memory—for example, memory for routes and maps, for grocery lists, for dramatic events, for crimes we have witnessed, for stories, for dreams, and so on. The Pillemer book gives an account of *vivid* memories and discusses why certain events are remembered so clearly:

Cohen, G. (1996). *Memory in the real world* (2nd ed.). East Sussex, UK: Psychology Press.

Pillemer, D. B. (1998). *Momentous events, vivid memories.* Cambridge, MA: Harvard University Press.

A very practical, classroom-oriented book that examines how teachers can help students become more thoughtful:

Barell, J. (1995). *Teaching for thoughtfulness: Classroom strategies to enhance intellectual development* (2nd ed.). New York: Longman.

A highly readable, informative, and practical discussion of memory and mnemonic aids:

Higbee, K. L. (1977). *Your memory: How it works and how to improve it.* Englewood Cliffs, NJ: Prentice-Hall.

The Eskimo people believe that the soul of a wounded bear tarries near the spot where it leaves its body. Many taboos and propitiatory ceremonies are observed with regard to the slaughtering of the carcass and the consumption of the flesh (Engel, 1976, p. 69).

If a little knowledge
is dangerous, where
is the man who has
so much as to be
out of danger?

Thomas Henry Huxley, *Science and Culture*

Cognitive Approaches to Teaching

PREVIEW

Decision making, problem solving, analyzing, synthesizing, evaluating, remembering—these are all cognitive (or intellectual)
activities. Understanding them is the goal of cognitive theories. And several of these theories are
especially important for education because they
provide clear and highly explicit instructional recommendations and models. In this chapter we
examine two such theories: Jerome Bruner's theory, which advocates discovery-oriented learning;
and David Ausubel's theory, which supports the
methods of direct instruction. The merits of each
are discussed.

FOCUS QUESTIONS

▲ What are some of the conditions that facilitate learning through discovery?

▲ What are some conditions that foster reception learning?

▲ What does constructivism mean? How does it relate to teaching?

▲ What does research say are the best ways of teaching?

On a nearly perfect day in May when I was in tenth grade, our teacher, Sister Marie-Reine, took us on a field trip. This was an exciting thing because none of us had ever been on a field trip before. Where we lived, there were no museums, no art galleries, no factories, no fire halls, no libraries, no theatres, no dentists' offices, no McDonald's—none of the usual places for teachers to take their students on field trips.

But Sister Marie-Reine was a modern teacher, a teacher with a reputation for reading "the literature," as the superintendent called it. She liked to try new approaches.

"It's all part of progressive education," she explained as she outlined her plan. We'd leave right after the morning bell, everybody packing a lunch, and we'd go up into the hills on the lease behind my Uncle Gerry's farm on the edge of the lake. The objective of the trip: "We'll learn something."

And so, when the sounds of the bell had scarcely died down the next day, away we went, laughing and singing and absolutely loving progressive education, as you can imagine, twenty-some 15-year-olds—except for Thomas Savard who was already 17 because he'd missed a few years early on—larking about on a May morning instead of sitting at hard school desks like everybody else in the world.

Back and forth, darting here and there, running, jumping, teasing the girls—me trying to get Celine Tremblay's attention but pretending I really wasn't—we scrambled down the paths made by Uncle Gerry's cows, knowing not to step

where we shouldn't, laughing, giggling, until—bong-a-bang!—we heard the clanging of the bell Sister Marie-Reine had had the foresight to throw into her bag. And we ran to gather before her on the edge of the slough so that we could listen to the lesson she would now tell us; such a small price to pay for a day in May almost taken from us, as so many were (and still are) but, at the last minute, given back.

Sister Marie-Reine stood on the edge of the slough; her shoes and the bottom of her long black habit were covered with mud. Streaks of perspiration had smeared her cheeks and the white band was plastered tightly across her forehead, but she grinned triumphantly as she stood there. "What is it? Who can tell me what it is?" she challenged as she raised a gnarled, snakelike yellowish-white length of vegetable material above her head like some primitive conqueror. What she held was about as thick as my arm, four or five feet long, and looked a little like a piece of bleached octopus tentacle.

Not a single one of us had any idea what it was, even though we knew the good sister had dragged it out of the slough. So we guessed this and that and the other thing until the good sister said, "No, that's enough guessing; you're not learning anything just guessing; use your brains." And right there on the spot she divided us into groups of four or five—and the sad thing was I didn't get to be in Celine's group, which for some reason, maybe just bad luck, I never did once the whole year. And then the sister said that the assignment is each of the groups has to find out what this is and write a paper on how they found out and present in to the class. She gave us three weeks to do it.

In the end, all the groups identified the piece of vegetation that Sister Marie-Reine had sucked out of the muddy slough: It was a chunk of cattail root. Louis Boutin's group found out because his father knew what it was as soon as he saw it. Augustin Bonneau's group found out because they put a piece of it in a little box and sent it to the University in Saskatoon, and somebody wrote *back and told them what it was and told them all about it. The rest of us found out from somebody in one of the other groups because it's hard to keep important secrets in small communities. And Augustin's little sister copied the letter from the university and gave it to Celine so that, when we made our presentations, every group said that there were at least eight species of cattails in the world (two of them in Canada) and that you could eat the root and weave baskets with the plants, and on and on. We all got good marks.*

DIRECT INSTRUCTION AND CONSTRUCTIVISM

I still remember a little about cattails and their roots and a little about progressive education. **Progressive education** was John Dewey's term for his brand of educational reform. He advocated highly child-centered, discovery-based approaches to education.

As we saw in Chapter 1, the label "progressive education" has given way to a new expression: **constructivist approaches**. Like progressive education, constructivism is based on a learner- rather than a teacher-oriented view of the teaching/learning process. It emphasizes the importance of learners' *constructing* their own information and knowledge. Constructivist views of the learner follow naturally from developmen-

tal theories such as those of Piaget and Vygotsky. These are often apparent in problem-based approaches to instruction and in discovery-oriented classrooms (Kamii & Warrington, 1997).

Recall that constructivist approaches are often contrasted with the methods of **direct instruction**, which are highly teacher-centered because they view the teacher as the primary source of information and knowledge. The attitudes and methods of direct instruction are highly compatible with behavioristic theories of learning, which tend to emphasize the importance of the teacher's role. After all, the teacher arranges the conditions under which learning occurs and controls many of the rewards and punishments contingent upon learning (or not learning).

In the following pages of this chapter, we see that constructivist approaches also follow closely from cognitive theories such as that of Jerome Bruner, which advocates a discovery-oriented approach to learning. David Ausubel's cognitive theory is more closely related to the methods of direct instruction—although in his theory there is also much of value for the constructivist classroom. And in the next chapter, we will learn that cooperative approaches are also highly important and useful examples of constructivism in the classroom.[1] (See Figure 6.1 for a

---

progressive education An educational reform movement closely associated with John Dewey and identified primarily by child- rather than teacher-centered instructional approaches. Constructivist approaches to instruction (such as discovery learning) are essentially examples of progressive education movements under new labels.

constructivist approaches General label for instructional methods that are highly learner-centered and that reflect the belief that meaningful information is constructed by students rather than given to them. Often contrasted with *direct instruction,* constructivist approaches are reflected in discovery learning, cognitive apprenticeship, and humanistic approaches to teaching.

---

direct instruction A phrase used to describe teacher-directed approaches to teaching—in contrast with more student-centered approaches such as reciprocal teaching and cooperative learning (often included among *constructivist approaches*).

---

[1] ***PPC:*** My students always ask: Which method is the best one? They'd like the bear to say this method is better, or that one. I know it's not that simple, and I know this issue is covered elsewhere, but could you maybe say something about that here?

Author: The bear, who is sometimes old and crotchety, grumbles that you should tell your students to read this chapter first, paying particular attention to the last sections. Also, they should look at the book's inside front cover, and especially at the bottom of the page which lists some of the recurring themes of this book and some of the bear's conclusions—the most important one is that this is not an either-or issue.

	Direct Teaching	**Constructivism**
Some descriptive terms	Teacher-centered Traditional Old Didactic Behavioristic	Learner-centered Progressive New Reflective Humanistic
Metaphors of learning	Acquisition	Participation
Some approaches to teaching	Lecturing, telling, showing, directing, guiding, explaining	Discovery learning, cooperative learning, cognitive apprenticeship, learning styles
Models of teacher	Teacher as executive Teacher as director	Teacher as therapist Teacher as liberator
Some associated theories	Behavioristic theories such as Skinner's; cognitive theories such as Ausubel's	Cognitive theories such as Piaget's and Bruner's; Dewey's ideas

FIGURE 6.1 Comparisons of direct instruction and constructivist approaches: Educational reform has typically advocated changes that correspond with what is now labeled *constructivism*. But the methods of *direct instruction* have continued to dominate in most schools. See the inside front cover for some relevant conclusions and themes that run through this book.

comparison of constructivist approaches and direct instruction.)

Some Common Beliefs of Cognitivism

Constructivist approaches to teaching are directly grounded in beliefs and assumptions that are common to many cognitive theories of learning and development (such as those of Piaget, Vygotsky, and Bruner). Among these common beliefs and assumptions are the following:

Current Learning Builds on Previous Learning As we saw in Chapter 5, cognitive approaches to human behavior stress the importance of the learner's previous knowledge and skills—what R. Gagné (1985) terms *previously acquired capabilities*. Unlike behaviorism, which tends to view all learners as initially equal—equally susceptible to the effects of the consequences of behavior—cognitivism emphasizes that we often derive different meanings from experience.

Learners come with different motives, background information, and characteristics (gender, ethnicity, intelligence, personality characteristics, and so on). As a result, as learners discover and construct meaning, they often learn different things.

Learning Involves Information Processing Cognitive theories assume that the learner is a *processor* and not simply a recipient of information. Accordingly, these theories attempt to analyze learning in terms of what is often labeled "cognitive structure." At a simple level, cognitive structure is the content of the mind. It includes concepts, relationships that the learner establishes among concepts, and strategies used for abstracting concepts and organizing them in long-term memory. This view of the learner as an information processor emphasizes the *active* rather than the *passive* nature of learning.

Meaning Depends on Relationships Cognitive theorists maintain that knowledge does not exist in a vacuum but that it depends on relationships. As E. D. Gagné (1985) phrases it: "All of a person's declarative knowledge can be conceptualized as a large network of interrelated propositions." In this context, **declarative knowledge** is the same as declarative memory. It consists of all the facts we have learned and all the experiences we have had and can still recall and put into words—or at least recall features of. In short, declarative knowledge involves knowing that something is the case. Declarative knowledge is contrasted with **procedural knowledge,** (also called *procedural memory*), which involves knowing how to do something (that is, knowing a procedure for doing something). Procedural knowledge, too, derives its meaning from interrelationships (Anderson, 1983).

The idea that knowledge consists of networks of relationships is not new. Recall from Chapter 5 that our contemporary models of long-term memory are invariably associationistic; that is, they are models of relationships. What is new, however, is the recent upsurge of interest in exploring this idea in an effort to understand how we learn and know things and how we think. Thinking, according to this approach, involves the manipulation of what is represented mentally. In other words, it involves forming and manipulating relationships among items of information (Hunt, 1989).

An Illustration: First, to simplify, why do we say that knowledge and understanding depend on interrelationships among items of information? What does this concept mean?

Consider the following passage:

If the balloons popped, the sound wouldn't be able to carry since everything would be too far away from the correct floor. A closed window would also prevent the sound from carrying, since most buildings tend to be well insulated. Since the whole operation depends on a steady flow of electricity, a break in the middle of the wire would also cause problems. Of course, the fellow could shout, but the human voice is not loud enough to carry that far. An additional problem is that a string could break on the instrument. Then there would be no accompaniment to the message. It is clear that the best situation would involve less distance. Then there would be fewer potential problems. With face to face contact, the least number of things could go wrong. (Bransford & Johnson, 1973, pp. 392–393)

If you find this passage confusing and unclear, don't despair; so does almost everyone else. It's a frustrating experience because the language is clear and simple, the sentences are short and straightforward, none of the concepts is very difficult—yet the whole thing makes no sense.

Turn now to Figure 6.2 and glance at the illustration.

Now the passage makes sense. Why? Simply because the illustration provides a framework for understanding it; it activates what a number of cognitive psychologists (like Piaget) refer to as a **schema** (plural, *schemas* or *schemata*).

Schemata are metaphors for cognitive structure and functioning. They are like clusters of related items of knowledge that define concepts. They are what we know about things. For example, schemata relevant to understanding the balloon passage include, among other things, our knowledge that balloons filled with lighter-than-air substances will rise, our recognition of the

---

declarative knowledge All the facts, information, and experiences that are part of what we know. Also termed *declarative memory.*

procedural knowledge Knowing how to do something; knowing procedures as well as facts (declarative knowledge). Also termed *procedural memory.*

schema (*pl:* schemata) The label used by Piaget to describe a unit in cognitive structure. A schema is, in one sense, an activity together with whatever structural connotations that activity has. In another sense, a schema may be thought of as an idea or a concept.

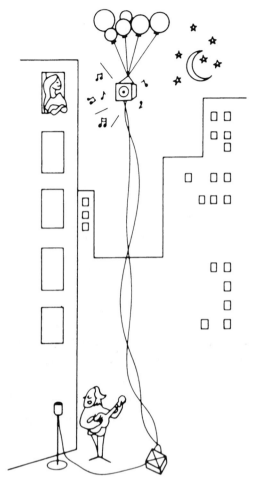

FIGURE 6.2. From J. D. Bransford and M. K. Johnson, "Consideration of Some Problems in Comprehension" (p. 394). In W. G. Chase (ed.), *Visual Information Processing.* Copyright 1973 by Academic Press. Reprinted by permission of Academic Press, New York, and J. D. Bransford.

musical equipment involved, and certain assumptions about the intentions and motives of the serenader and the serenadee. Each of these concepts is defined by one or more relationships (for example, the relationship between weight and falling or rising, the relationship between musical sounds and a guitar, and the presumed relationship between the individuals involved).

One aspect of schemata that is important for learning and remembering real-life things is called a **script**. Schank and Abelson (1977) describe a script as that part of cognitive struc-

ture that deals with routines and sequences. We all know countless routines and countless scripts. We know, for example, that a sensible way to dress is to put on undergarments, socks, shirts, pants, and shoes, more or less in that order. This is a verbal description of a common script. For dressing on a day like today in this somewhat harsh climate, I added a heavy coat and gloves to my script—in that order. Had I wanted to be creative this morning and altered my script—say, by reversing it—I might have found dressing considerably more difficult and time-consuming. And I would have had to wear my socks over my shoes and my shorts over my jeans, in which case I would probably not have been courageous or foolish enough to come to the university.

Scripts, like schemata, deal with relationships. A script is, in a sense, an expression of sequential relationships. Scripts and schemata are clearly useful. Nevertheless, they are only metaphors that need to be made more concrete for our purposes.

Teaching and Learning Should Stress Relationships and Strategies Cognitive approaches are concerned with how information is processed. Accordingly, these approaches look at how we derive information from the environment. They ask how we organize and interpret this information, teasing out relationships to abstract meaning from our experiences. They investigate how we organize and store meaning and how our thought processes make use of what we have stored.

From the educator's point of view, these concerns translate directly into a renewed emphasis on cognitive strategies and a recogni-

---

script A term describing our knowledge of what goes with what and in what sequence. Scripts are a part of cognitive structure that deals with the routine and the predictable.

TABLE 6.1
Beliefs and Assumptions of Cognitive Explanations of Learning

BELIEFS/ASSUMPTIONS	EXPLANATIONS/IMPLICATIONS
Current learning builds on previous learning.	Learners aren't equal to begin with; given their different backgrounds and motivation, they often construct different meanings from identical experiences.
Learning involves information processing.	This is an active process, highly dependent on what the learner already knows.
Meaning involves relationships.	Meaning derived (constructed) from experience reflects relationships between previous and new learning.
Teaching and learning should stress relationships and strategies.	The emphasis is on *meaningful* rather than *rote* learning; the objective is to help students learn how to learn, contrasted with simply acquiring isolated bits of information.

tion of the importance of relationships among items of information. Specifically, they suggest two things: first, the school's curriculum (and the teacher's presentation of that curriculum) needs to be organized to reveal and underline important relationships, and second, the school should pay systematic and deliberate attention to developing strategies involved in perceiving, interpreting, organizing, analyzing, evaluating, storing, and retrieving information. (See Table 6.1 for a summary of the characteristics of cognitive approaches to learning and teaching.)

Several cognitively based theories reflect these two educational applications especially well. Among these are the theories of Jerome Bruner and David Ausubel. In many important ways these theories are similar, although they use different terms to describe the units and processes of cognitive organization.[2] In one important respect, however, these theories are dramatically different from each other. Bruner advocates a constructivist approach to instruction in the form of **discovery learning**. He insists that learners should be guided toward organizing material for themselves, once they have been provided with opportunities to discover relationships. In contrast, Ausubel presents a strong

case for more direct instruction—for what he terms **reception learning** rather than discovery. He argues that in most cases the teacher should organize the material and present it to the student in relatively final form. In spite of this, as we see later, Ausubel's insistence on the

---

discovery learning The acquisition of new information or knowledge largely as a result of the learner's own efforts. Discovery learning is contrasted with expository or reception learning and is generally associated with Bruner, among others. It is an important instructional tool of the constructivist classroom.

reception learning A type of learning that involves primarily instruction or tuition rather than the learner's own efforts. Teaching for reception learning, often associated with Ausubel, usually takes the form of expository or didactic methods; that is, the teacher structures the material and presents it to learners in relatively final form rather than asking them to discover that form.

---

[2] **PPC:** Wouldn't the bear find life a lot easier if all cognitive theorists agreed to use the same clearly defined vocabulary, rather than so many insisting on inventing their own meanings or, perhaps worse, their own terms? Weren't *schema* and *schemata* and *script* and *cognitive structure* enough?

Author: Yes and no. No, those terms aren't enough, and yes, we need a variety of terms. Besides, the bear is an old bear; he's seen much jargon come and go. "The meaning is in the meaning, not in the jargon," he says. "Do you get my meaning?" he adds slyly.

importance of meaningfulness reflects an important feature of constructivist classrooms.

In the next two sections of this chapter we look at the theoretical bases for these apparently contradictory approaches to teaching and learning. And then we examine some really basic questions: Which approach is the right one? How should teachers teach?

BRUNER'S THEORY: DISCOVERY LEARNING

Cognitive psychology assumes that the learner is an active information processor. It asks how the learner derives information from the environment, how information is organized and interpreted, and how it is used. Jerome Bruner's theory provides one set of answers for these questions—and for many other questions as well.

Learning and perception, explains Bruner, are information processing activities that reflect our need to simplify and make sense of the environment (Bruner, Goodnow, & Austin, 1956; Bruner, 1973). Essentially, we simplify and make sense of the world by forming concepts (Bruner's term is **category**). We do so by abstracting common elements among events and experiences. From these abstractions, we derive implicit rules that allow us to categorize (conceptualize) the world. At the same time, we discover and invent a wealth of relationships among concepts. These relationships among concepts define what Bruner calls a **coding system**. Coding systems are simply metaphors for what is assumed to be a hierarchical arrangement of concepts of increasing (or decreasing) generality. Thus, our long-term memories—our relatively permanent store of knowledge, strategies, impressions, and so on—can be seen as a complex arrangement of categories (concepts) and coding systems. And all school subjects, as well as topics within these subjects, can also be seen as having a similar sort of structure. The structure of a subject, argues Bruner, reflects the most fundamental relationships and ideas in the field. Thus, to truly learn a subject and be able to think about it, learners need to develop their own coding systems—their own mental representations of these important ideas and relationships. And the best way of developing a coding system is to discover it rather than to have it presented in final form by a teacher. (See Figure 6.3 for a graphic illustration of a coding system.)[3]

Discovery Learning in Schools

As we saw in Chapter 3, Piaget's theory provides one way to describe cognitive development. As a function of interacting with the environment (through assimilation and accommodation), says Piaget, children gradually build up a store of knowledge. In a very real sense, it is as though learners *construct* knowledge—in contrast with a situation where the learners are given that knowledge by someone else (parents or teachers, for example).

Bruner's theory is based on the same belief, a belief that is fundamental to constructivist approaches to teaching. We make up our own versions of reality, says Bruner; we discover our own meanings (Bruner, 1990a). And the functions of schools, he insists emphatically, should

---

category A term used by Bruner to describe a grouping of related objects or events. In this sense, a category is both a concept and a percept. Bruner also defines it as a rule for classifying things as equal.

coding system A Brunerian concept; refers to a hierarchical arrangement of related categories.

---

[3] *PPC:* There's no getting around the fact that this chapter is heavy going. (I just put the kettle on for more coffee.) Can the bear make it simpler?

Author: Not without leaving out some really important stuff. Besides, it's not that hard, says the bear, quoting from his guru, Yogi Berra: Ninety percent of all this is half mental.

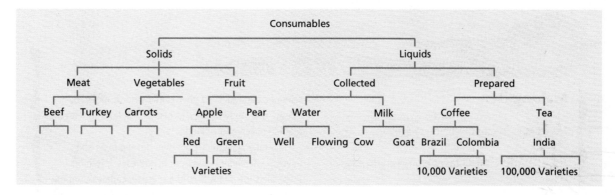

FIGURE 6.3 A coding system

be to provide conditions that will foster the discovery of relationships.

Discovery learning can be defined as the learning that takes place when students are not presented with subject matter in its final form but rather are required to organize it themselves. This requires learners to discover for themselves relationships that exist among items of information. In Bruner's theory, discovery is the formation of categories or, more often, the formation of coding systems, which are defined in terms of relationships (similarities and differences) that exist among objects and events.

The most important and most obvious characteristic of a discovery approach to teaching is that it requires far less teacher involvement and direction than most other methods. However, this does not imply that the teacher ceases to give any guidance once the initial problem has been presented. As Corno and Snow (1986) point out, teachers can offer a continuum of guidance (their phrase is "teacher mediation") by adapting their teaching to different students and different purposes. At one extreme, too little mediation or none at all can leave students without the means for discovery; at the other extreme, constant direction and guidance from the teacher may remove all opportunity for self-direction and discovery by the students.

The advantages of a discovery approach, claims Bruner, are that such learning facilitates

transfer and retention, increases problem-solving ability, and increases motivation (Bruner, 1961a). Following more recent research, advocates of the constructivist classroom and the discovery learning practices that are typically part of such a classroom claim much the same advantages as Bruner did more than 30 years ago. For example, Miles (1997) compared direct instruction preschool classrooms with discovery-based constructivist classrooms. She reports that constructivist classrooms are more effective in maintaining and increasing student interest, motivation, discussion, interaction, and learning.

Very often, discovery in the classroom takes the form of systematically following logical steps that guide the search for generalizable conclusions, as in scientific investigation. And one important part of the guidance that the teacher provides as "learning facilitator" revolves around the deliberate and systematic application of these steps. Summarized briefly, these involve:

- ▲ Formulating and clarifying a question or problem
- ▲ Collecting examples; making relevant observations
- ▲ Arriving at hypotheses (intelligent, observation-based guesses)
- ▲ Devising and conducting tests, experiments, and other observations to confirm or refute hypotheses

Making Dew

THE PLACE: Tremont Elementary School

THE SITUATION: Mr. Creasy's eighth-grade science class

THE TOPIC: The formation of dew

Mr. Creasy: So the question is: What causes dew?
Paul: I know. It's just rain.
Jackie: It's not. 'Cause there's dew when there's no rain.
Mr. Creasy: What's our method? How do we find out?
Chorus of answers: Scientific inquiry.

Patiently, then, Bob Creasy leads his class through what they have previously established as the steps of the scientific method. Next, they clarify what is meant by "dew," and students are charged with collecting relevant real-life observations and facts.

In a later class, they pool their observations and develop intelligent guesses, or hypotheses, based on these facts (dew falls from the sky, dew comes out of the air, dew comes out of objects themselves). Creasy guides the students toward making pertinent observations; he sometimes devises experiments to do so (dew forms on comparatively cool objects, there is dew on cloudless nights, dew forms even on objects that are completely dry initially).

Eventually, students begin to agree on a conclusion (the cooling of moist air by a relatively cool object "squeezes" out water droplets that collect on the object's surface). Students then devise various experiments to determine whether this conclusion is always correct.

▲ Applying, extending, generalizing, and "going beyond" the new information

The case entitled "Making Dew" provides one example of the application of this method of scientific inquiry in a discovery-oriented science unit. Keep in mind that, although the most obvious illustrations are often in science, these methods can also be used in a variety of other subjects.

Discovery as a Reflective Teaching Strategy

Recall from Chapter 1 that reflective teaching strategies are broadly defined as strategies that lead students to discover and learn for themselves (Freiberg & Driscoll, 1992). In general, these strategies require not only that teachers think about and analyze what is happening as they teach, but also that learners be encouraged to think about their own learning. Perhaps even more important, learners are encouraged to assume responsibility for their learning and thinking (Korthagen, 1993). Thus, reflective teaching mirrors a philosophy that emphasizes the active, discovery-oriented role of the learner and that views teaching as largely a process of facilitating learning and discovery rather than being the final source of all information. Viewed in this way, reflective teaching strategies are essentially *constructivist* strategies. Not surprisingly, the most important reflective teaching strategies are those that lead to student inquiry and guided discovery.

Conditions that Facilitate Discovery Learning

There are four sets of conditions, says Bruner (1961b), that can contribute to—or impede—

discovery learning: set, need state, mastery of specifics, and diversity of training. Teachers should know about each of these.

Set Set is a predisposition to react in certain ways. For example, a discovery-oriented person is one whose usual approach to a problem is to look for relationships among items of information. We might say that such a person is *set* to discover.

One way to affect set, says Bruner, is by issuing instructions. For example, a student can be encouraged to memorize subject matter as though it consisted of isolated bits of information by simply being told to do so—or by being tested only for knowledge of isolated items of information. This is what Marton and Saljo (1984) call the "surface approach" to teaching and learning. It focuses on memorizing facts, completing tasks, and passing tests.

As an alternative to "surface" teaching, students can be encouraged to look for relationships among items of information, either by being instructed to do so or by being told that they will be tested on their understanding of these relationships. This is Marton and Saljo's "deep approach." It focuses on relationships and on understanding, and it is fundamental to the constructivist classroom.

Need State Need state is the level of arousal, excitation, or alertness of the learner (see Chapter 10). Bruner suggests that a moderate level of arousal is more conducive to discovery learning than either an excessively high or low level. That is, students need to be alert rather than sleepy. They also need to be excited and interested rather than frightened or panicked.

Mastery of Specifics Mastery of specifics refers to the extent to which the learner has already mastered specific, relevant information. Discovery (which is really the formation of coding systems) is not accidental, insists Bruner; clearly, it is far more likely to occur when the individual is well prepared—and highly unlikely if the individual is not prepared. Herbert Gaudry, my childhood buddy who knew absolutely nothing about machinery, was not very likely to invent the round-bale hay baler. Similarly, a student who knows little of geography, history, and commerce is unlikely to discover that the locations of most major cities are not entirely accidental. As Bruner points out, the wider the range of information learners possess, the more likely they are to find relationships within that information.

Diversity of Training The fourth variable that is important in facilitating discovery learning is **diversity of training**. A learner who is exposed to information in a wide variety of circumstances, says Bruner, is more likely to develop coding systems to relate and organize that information. Partly for this reason, he recommends that the same subjects be taught to learners more than once—say, at different grade levels—but with differing amounts of detail and at different levels of abstraction depending on the changing interests, capabilities, and background knowledge of the learners.

---

set A predisposition to react to stimulation in a given manner.

need state Bruner's expression describing the arousal level of an organism.

mastery of specifics A Brunerian term for the learning of details. Mastery of relevant specifics is necessary for acquiring concepts and discovering relationships among them.

diversity of training Bruner's expression relating to his belief that exposure to information under a wide range of circumstances is conducive to discovering relationships among concepts.

Discovery-Oriented Methods for the Constructivist Classroom

Renewed interest in discovery approaches to education is most evident in constructivist approaches to teaching (for example, Brown, Collins, & Duguid, 1989). As we saw, these approaches are based on the assumption that students should build (construct) knowledge for themselves. Hence, constructivist approaches are basically discovery oriented.

Related to the constructivist approach is the **conceptual change movement**, which is also discovery oriented (Kelly, 1997). Conceptual change curricula present ideas that challenge the learner, contain problems and puzzles, and ultimately result in a reorganization of knowledge (hence, conceptual change). Research on conceptual change approaches to teaching indicate that these approaches are especially suitable for science (Bar et al., 1994) but that they can also be used with other subjects like social studies (Wade, 1994). They have been used with adult college students as well (Tillema & Knol, 1997).

Bruner advances some specific recommendations and observations that are especially important for the constructivist, discovery-oriented classroom. Among these are the following:

1. "... the curriculum of a subject should be determined by the most fundamental understanding that can be achieved of the underlying principles that give structure to that subject" Bruner advises (1961b, p. 31). After all, constructing meaning would be next to impossible without the knowledge of basic organizing principles. For example, a learner is unlikely to understand the relationship among aspen, birch, and alder without also knowing that they are all deciduous hardwoods. The principles that link these trees are related directly to characteristics that define their "treeness." Indeed, it is the "peopleness" of individuals, the "treeness" of trees, and the "birdness" of birds that allows the learners to react to them in similar ways and permits the learner to make inferences about specific people, trees, or birds—in Bruner's terms, this allows "going beyond the information given" (1957a). Bruner argues that unless the organization of the curriculum facilitates the formation of structure (coding systems), it will be learned with difficulty, it will not lend itself to transfer, and it will be poorly remembered.

2. "... any subject can be taught to any child in some honest form," Bruner informs educators (1961b, p. 52). Many have taken exception to this bold assertion, pointing out that certain concepts are simply too difficult for younger children. For example, proportion probably cannot be understood by a 4-year-old. Bruner's reply is that we should consider the possibility of teaching at least some aspects of any subject at any age level. Maybe some aspects of proportion *can* be taught to a 4-year-old. The important question is how to make teaching effective for very young children. Bruner's (1966) answer is that the form can be simplified and the mode of presentation geared to the simplest representational systems available. Because children progress from motor or sensory (**enactive**) representation to relatively concrete images

---

conceptual change movement Literally, cognitive changes such as might be evident in greater understanding, knowledge, and awareness. More specifically, this expression refers to instructional approaches designed to foster mental reorganization rather than simply to increase the number of facts learned.

enactive A term used by Bruner to describe young children's representations of their world. The term refers specifically to the belief that children represent the world in terms of their personal actions.

(**iconic**), and finally to abstract (**symbolic**) representation, it follows that the sequence in teaching should be the same. In other words, the best instructional sequence is to present a subject so that a child can first experience it, then react to a concrete presentation of it, and finally symbolize it. In support of this notion, Presno (1997) describes how computer instruction can be easily sequenced so that learners are first presented with demonstrations (enactive representation), followed by pictures and diagrams (iconic representation) and finally by verbal instructions (symbolic representation).

3. Bruner suggests that the most useful approach to organizing school topics is a **spiral curriculum** (Bruner, 1961b; 1966). A spiral curriculum is one that develops and redevelops topics at different grade levels. Spiral curricula are ideally suited to discovery. First, such a curriculum organizes subject matter according to principles, and it usually presents them systematically, from simplest to most complex. This progression parallels the development of coding systems. Second, a spiral curriculum involves the sort of repetition that is useful for constructing knowledge. To begin, learners are exposed to the most general, most inclusive idea and then to a series of specific simple instances of concepts. As they discover relationships among these concepts, they construct knowledge (coding systems) that is highly conducive to transfer, recall, and discovery.

As an example of a spiral curriculum, Schwill (1997) describes how computer science can be taught at each grade, from kindergarten through twelfth grade, by simply presenting fundamental ideas and principles at different levels of abstraction. Not only does this provide learners with a tremendous diversity of background knowledge, but it also allows them to remain up-to-date even in rapidly changing fields such as computing.

4. ". . . a student should be given some training in recognizing the plausibility of guesses," says Bruner (1961b, p. 64). Otherwise, students might be forever reluctant to guess, to risk error. In this connection, Bruner speaks of the usefulness of the *intuitive leap*—the educated guess that is more probable than a blind attempt but less certain than simply making inferences or predictions on the basis of what is known about similar instances. To discourage guessing, Bruner insists, is to stifle the process of discovery.

5. Bruner's recommendations for the discovery-oriented classroom also include an appeal that teachers use as many aids as possible in their teaching (audiovisual, concrete or symbolic models, and multimedia sources of information and inspiration). Aids of this sort provide students with direct or vicarious experiences and thus facilitate the formation of concepts.

---

iconic A term that refers to a developmental stage in children's representation of their world. The term is used by Bruner to describe an intermediate stage of development characterized by a representation of the world in terms of relatively concrete mental images.

symbolic The final stage in the development of children's representations of their world. The term is used by Bruner to describe the representation of the world in terms of arbitrary symbols. Symbolic representation includes representation in terms of language and also in terms of theoretical or hypothetical systems.

spiral curriculum Bruner's term for a curriculum that revisits the same topics repeatedly, often at different grade levels, at different levels of abstraction and generality, depending on the interests and background knowledge of the learners.

AUSUBEL'S THEORY: RECEPTION LEARNING

Not all educators agree that discovery is the best approach. Perhaps most outspoken among those who advocate a different approach is David

Ausubel (1963, 1977). Most people learn primarily through *reception learning* and not through discovery, claims Ausubel. That is, most of what students learn they receive in relatively final form rather than having to discover it for themselves. In the vast majority of school situations, he insists, discovery is ineffective and largely a waste of time. In this respect, the Ausubelian classroom is decidedly a classroom where direct instruction prevails. As we will see, however, much of Ausubel's cognitive theory supports some of the basic characteristics of the constructivist classroom. As Dowell (1997) argues, Ausubel's theory presents a useful balance between child-centered (constructivist) and teacher-centered (direct instruction) approaches to education.

Ausubel's Cognitive Theory

Ausubel's cognitive theory of learning is specifically intended to deal almost exclusively with what he calls "meaningful verbal learning." More important from the point of view of educational psychology, Ausubel's work is explicitly a search for the "laws of meaningful classroom learning."

Meaning According to Ausubel, an object has meaning when it elicits an image in the "content of consciousness" as a result of its relation to something already known. Similarly, a concept acquires meaning when it is related to an idea that is already present in the mind. In other words, for a stimulus or concept to have meaning, there must be something in the learner's cognitive structure (pre-existing ideas and knowledge) to which it can be related. For example, the word *car* has meaning for an individual only when it can be related to a mental representation of what cars are.

Meaningful Learning Meaningful learning, says Ausubel, requires the learner to have already learned associated concepts to which new material can be related—or, in Ausubel's terms, concepts that can "subsume" new learning. Learning therefore involves **subsumption**, of which there are two kinds. **Derivative subsumption** occurs when new material is so similar to what is already known that it could have been derived from it; **correlative subsumption** involves material that is sufficiently novel that it requires some change in existing cognitive structure. (See the box entitled "Zebras and Asses" for an illustration of these kinds of subsumption in the classroom.)

In Ausubel's model of learning (very much like in Bruner's), the construction of new knowledge is absolutely dependent on previous meaningful learning. As Novak (1993) points out, a high level of meaningful learning is indispensable both for cognitive development and for the construction of new learning. In this sense, in spite of Ausubel's insistence on the direct instructional approaches of reception learning, much of what he says about meaningful learning is basic to the constructivist view of classroom learning.

Cognitive Structure *Cognitive structure* consists of more or less organized and stable concepts (or ideas) in a learner's consciousness. Much like Bruner's, Ausubel's metaphor for cognitive

---

subsumption Ausubel's term for the integration of new material or information with existing information. This term implies a process whereby a new stimulus becomes part of what is already in cognitive structure.

derivative subsumption The type of subsumption (or learning) that takes place when new material can be directly derived from what is already known.

correlative subsumption The type of learning that takes place when new information requires an extension of what was previously known and therefore could not have been derived directly from it.

BEAR MUSINGS

Zebras and Asses

As part of a science lesson, a teacher wants to familiarize her students with some of the many breeds of cows. Her students already know what cows are; they also know colors. But they don't know that an Aberdeen Angus is a sleek-looking black cow. She tells them so. Is this likely to be meaningful learning? What type of subsumption is involved?

This teacher now wants to teach her class what a zebra is. She tells them what it is; she compares it with horses, donkeys, mules, and—being resourceful—asses; she then shows them a picture of a zebra. What type of subsumption is involved here?

Why would the simple statement that a zebra is a herbivorous, black-and-white African animal be almost meaningless for urban, North American children if they have never seen a zebra in a book or on television?[4]

A ZEBRA IS A HERBIVOROUS BLACK AND WHITE AFRICAN ANIMAL

---

[4] ***PPC:*** Hey, pretty well every North American child knows what a zebra is. And if they haven't seen one in the flesh, they've surely seen them in books or movies or on television. Can't the bear come up with another example?

Author: Well yes, the bear probably could. But for crying out loud, says he, it's only an example. Besides, he didn't want to get rid of the Tony Hall cartoon.

---

structure assumes that this organization is hierarchical, with the most inclusive concept at the apex and increasingly specific concepts toward the base. Therefore, argues Ausubel, instruction should proceed from the most general and inclusive idea toward details of specific instances. This is somewhat like Bruner's notion that teaching should follow a sort of spiral curriculum in which the big idea (the most general concept) is presented first and then systematically revisited, perhaps over a period of years, at increasingly more complex levels of abstraction. The fundamental difference between Bruner and Ausubel, with respect to their instructional theories, is that Ausubel argues that learners should be provided with organized information. Bruner, as we saw, maintains that students should be presented with specifics and allowed to discover their own

organization (coding systems). For a summary of Ausubel's theory, see Table 6.2.

Expository Teaching

If reception learning accounts for most of what students learn, then **expository teaching** is the instructional technique of choice. Expository teaching is a technique in which the teacher, who bears the major responsibility for finding and

---

expository teaching An instructional technique strongly advocated by Ausubel. The teacher bears the responsibility of organizing and presenting information in relatively final form. Expository teaching is associated with reception learning rather than discovery-oriented approaches and is essentially another label for direct instruction.

TABLE 6.2
Summary of Ausubel's Theory of Meaningful Verbal Learning

AUSUBEL'S JARGON	TRANSLATION
1. Subsumption can be derivative or correlative.	Learning (subsumption) involves either (a) relating new material to previously learned, highly similar material (derivative subsumption); or (b) extending previous knowledge to similar but new material (correlative subsumption).
2. Subsumption leads to a hierarchical arrangement of knowledge, from most general to most specific.	Learning is evident in new information and in changes in the learner's awareness of relationships among items of information.
3. Remembering is dissociative subsumption.	Remembering requires being able to separate new learning from old.
4. Forgetting involves zero dissociability, or obliterative subsumption.	Forgetting occurs when material can no longer be differentiated from what is already in the mind.

organizing information for learners, presents that information in relatively final form. Accordingly, the learner is not called upon to discover relationships but rather to learn them.

Expository teaching is, in effect, another label for direct instruction. It is, as Cienkus and Ornstein (1997) note, the teaching method that has dominated North American classrooms for at least the last two centuries. And it is still the most common approach to instruction in today's schools.

Ausubel argues that expository teaching can not only lead to a high level of understanding and generality but also that discovery approaches are extremely time-consuming without being demonstrably superior. In a review of the literature on discovery learning, Ausubel and Robinson (1969) conclude that research supporting such learning is virtually nonexistent. "Moreover," they state, "it appears that enthusiasts of discovery methods have been supporting each other by citing one another's opinions and assertions as evidence and by generalizing extravagantly from questionable findings" (p. 494).

Ausubel's emphasis on expository teaching and its outcome, reception learning, stems in part from the observation that most classroom learning seems to be of that type. Ausubel also believes that meaningful verbal learning, which his theory addresses, occurs mainly in the course of expository teaching. He argues that this type of learning is not passive and does not stifle creativity or encourage rote learning. Indeed, meaningful verbal learning is anything but rote, says Ausubel, because it involves relating new material to existing structure. In contrast, rote learning involves ingesting isolated bits of information.

Ausubel advances some general recommendations for the planning and presentation of subject matter in expository teaching. These take the form of a discussion of the most important variables involved in subsumption: advance organizers, discriminability, and meaningfulness.

Advance Organizers Advance organizers are complex sets of ideas or concepts given to the learner before the material to be learned is presented. Organizers are meant to provide cognitive structure to which the new learning can be anchored (subsumed). Another function of organizers is to increase recall (prevent loss of

---

advance organizer Introductory information given to learners to help them understand, learn, and remember new material.

what Ausubel calls **dissociability**—the ability to separate concepts from one another). (Ausubel's phrase for forgetting is **obliterative subsumption**) The use of advance organizers is advisable, then, under two circumstances: when students have no relevant information to which they can relate the new learning and when relevant subsuming information is already present but is not likely to be recognized as such by the learner (Ausubel & Robinson, 1969).

Grippin and Peters (1984) describe four characteristics of advance organizers: First, advance organizers are presented before the lesson. Second, they are designed to bring to mind prior knowledge that is relevant to the lesson (to activate related **subsumers**). Third, advance organizers are at a higher level of abstraction than the material presented later; that is, advance organizers are generic (highly general) concepts that include (subsume) more specific concepts. Finally, advance organizers make explicit the connection between prior knowledge and the lesson to be presented.

Ausubel describes two different types of organizers—one to be used when the material is completely new and the other when it is somewhat familiar. The first is labeled an **expository organizer** because it presents a description or exposition of relevant concepts. The second is called a **comparative organizer** because it is likely to make use of similarities and differences in new material and existing cognitive structure.

An expository organizer in a lesson on gold, for example, might describe the general, defining characteristics of metals before the lesson on the specific qualities of gold. The organizer is intended to provide concepts (subsumers) to which the new material can be related.

There are many examples of comparative organizers in this text. Many take the form of brief introductory sections that compare material about to be presented with material previously discussed. Some of the chapter previews are organizers of this kind. Recall that at the beginning of this chapter we associated Bruner with discovery learning and Ausubel with reception learning, before actually discussing their theories—another advance organizer. Of necessity, a textbook is primarily expository (although parts of it can lead to a type of guided discovery)—hence, the frequent use of organizers in most textbooks.

In the classroom, teachers sometimes unconsciously make use of something very much like advance organizers when they summarize earlier lessons before beginning a new presentation. However, these summaries often fail to make the connection between new and old learning sufficiently explicit nor are they abstract enough to qualify as advance organizers as Ausubel uses the expression. A summary is often simply a summary—an accounting of the subject matter that has been taught before. An advance organizer is more abstract; it draws a concept from previous learning, an idea that is general enough to subsume the new material to

---

dissociability A term used by Ausubel to indicate the ease with which material that is to be recalled can be separated (dissociated) from other related material that is also stored in memory.

obliterative subsumption Ausubel's term for forgetting. The incorporation of new material into pre-existing cognitive structure so that the new material eventually becomes indistinguishable—in other words, becomes obliterated (reaches zero dissociability, in Ausubel's terms).

subsumer The term used by Ausubel to describe a concept, an idea, or a combination of concepts or ideas that can serve to organize new information. Cognitive structure is therefore composed of subsumers.

expository organizer An idea or concept that serves as a description (exposition) of concepts that are relevant to new learning.

comparative organizer A concept or idea that serves to facilitate the learning of new material by making use of the similarities and differences between the new material and previous learning.

CASES FROM THE CLASSROOM

Why Turbo-Charged WZ 222As Cost So Much

THE PLACE: Carmel Mid-Valley School

THE SETTING: Introduction to Mr. Eddie Lemming's seventh-grade unit on gold and other precious metals

Mr. Lemming: So, can anyone tell me why turbo-charged WZ 222As are so expensive?

Bruce: Is it 'cause they cost more to make?

Mr. Lemming: Well, no, Bruce, not really. That'd be a good reason, though, if they did cost more.

Jack: 'Cause everybody wants one?

Sally: 'Cause there's not enough for everyone who wants one?

Mr. Lemming: Right. Right. You're both right.

Jack: It's like you said before, about workers and their pay. Too much demand . . .

Sally: And too little supply.

Mr. Lemming: Supply and demand. Keep that in mind. If nobody wants a thing, or if there's a lot of it, it won't cost very much. Like your textbook. Everybody wants it, so it costs an arm and a leg! Heh, heh. Supply and demand. Now, today we're going to talk about gold! Pretty exciting stuff, gold! And pretty expensive. Is that because of supply? demand? something else? Let's see what we can find out . . . .

be taught. (See, for example, the case entitled "Why Turbo-Charged WZ 222As Cost So Much.")

Notice that Eddie Lemming's lesson is preceded by a single, very abstract concept: the principle of supply and demand. Notice, too, that he promises to relate this concept to the question that constitutes the substance of today's lesson: Why is gold so expensive? The students have been reminded of a single, abstract, highly generic, stable concept upon which to anchor their new learning.

Research examining the effectiveness of advance organizers has often used organizers much like this one, sometimes presented in the form of a written paragraph, sometimes described by the teacher, sometimes elicited from students. Typically, the subsequent performance of a group of students that was given advance organizers is compared with that of a control group who had been given the lesson without advance organizers.

The results of much of this research are not entirely clear. Some researchers have found that advance organizers provide no measurable advantage (for example, McEneany, 1990); others report significant positive effects (for example, Thompson, 1997; Kiewra, 1997). White and Tisher (1986) note evidence suggesting that students who lack relevant prior knowledge are most likely to benefit from the use of advance organizers and that this may well explain the contradictions among studies. Teaching strategies such as these do not always lead to immediately measurable effects, so this should not be taken as clear evidence that the strategies are a waste of time. Many good things that teachers do are never measured—and perhaps they should not be.

Perhaps, just perhaps, the long-term effects of a single advance organizer might become apparent years later when the student, now an adult, correctly answers the $20 million question on a television game show. Or maybe the long-term effects will become evident when a bank-rupt speculator recollects that diamonds are not really very useful, that the demand for them is rather artificial, and that the supply is quite abundant after all.

Discriminability In Ausubel's theory, an important variable for determining the stability of what is learned is the ease with which a learner can discriminate new material from previous learning. Ausubel notes that information closely resembling previous knowledge (derivative subsumption) is quickly forgotten, whereas dissimilar material (correlative subsumption) tends to be retained longer. It follows from this that teaching techniques that highlight the differences between new material and old learning will lead to longer retention. But it is still necessary to relate the new to the old to facilitate subsumption (learning). Hence, comparing information in terms of similarities and differences should help both learning and retention. Also, the stability and clarity of the subsuming idea are directly related to the ease with which new material can be both incorporated into it and dissociated from it.

Making Learning Meaningful Ausubel's emphasis on reception learning as opposed to discovery learning is partly based on his belief that the most desirable kind of learning is meaningful, as opposed to **rote learning**[5]. This doesn't mean that discovery techniques don't lead to meaningful learning. However, Ausubel believes that exposi-tory approaches have some advantages, especially in terms of the efficient use of the learner's time and the meaningfulness of what is learned.

Learning is meaningful, says Ausubel, when there is a clear relationship between new material and existing cognitive structure (knowledge). Thus, meaning derives directly from associations that exist among ideas, events, or objects. However, no meaning will be derived unless the learner is aware of these associations. For example, students can quite easily learn—and quickly forget—to pronounce and spell words that don't relate to any of their existing ideas and are thus meaningless to them (see the box entitled "Meaningless Learning").

Meaning is not a property of the objects or concepts themselves. Objects or ideas are meaningful only in relation to the learner and in relation to other ideas in the learner's cognitive structure. Thus meaning is never taught directly but is instead *constructed* by the learner. And in this sense the most basic beliefs of Ausubel's theory underpin constructivist beliefs about teaching and learning.

DISCOVERY OR RECEPTION?

It is not especially difficult to reconcile the two apparently opposing views presented by Bruner and Ausubel; they are not nearly so different as their juxtaposition here might make them seem. In fact, in many ways they simply offer different emphases. Neither theory is necessarily superior to the other, and neither needs to be used to the exclusion of the other. Clearly, both have their uses. Even Ausubel suggests that discovery learning can be useful (Ausubel & Robinson, 1969); for example, it can be used with younger learners who do not yet have a large store of information to which new learning can be related. When this is the case, expository approaches are not always meaningful.

---

rote learning A mechanical type of memorization, with little or no attention to meaning.

---

[5] *PPC:* An example of rote learning that I often use with my classes is how children memorize prayers without understanding what the words mean. When I learned the Lord's Prayer, I learned, "Our Father Whart in heaven. . ." and for years I thought this guy in Heaven went by the strange name of Whart. And I couldn't figure out why anyone would want to hollow his name!

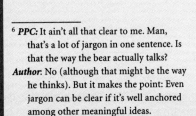

Meaningless Learning

"Learning involves the derivative or correlative subsumption of meaningful material to existing cognitive structure in such a way as to permit subsequent dissociability rather than obliterative subsumption."

This particular pearl of psychological wisdom is undoubtedly meaningful to you only because you know through previous learning what derivative and correlative subsumption are, what meaningful material is, and what type of beasts cognitive structure and obliterative subsumption are.[6] For anyone who did not already know these terms, the sentence would be meaningless.

It is remarkably easy for teachers to fall into the trap of asking students to learn material that is meaningless for them because they don't have the required background information. One widely cited example is the use of read-

ers oriented toward white, middle-class children for children from nonwhite, poor neighborhoods, or as was the case in the Arctic until recently, for Eskimo children. Eskimo children who had never seen a city, an automobile, a telephone, or an indoor toilet were asked to learn to read sentences similar to "John goes for a drive," "Fire fighters, police officers, and college professors are our friends." (Now, of course, many Eskimos have satellite dishes and access to hundreds of television

channels, so their cultural isolation has been much reduced.)

Do you remember learning that a demagogue is "an unprincipled politician who panders to the emotions and prejudices of the populace"? that the center of the earth is "in a stage of igneous fusion"? that the closest star is "several billion light-years away"? How meaningful was this information?

---

[6] **PPC:** It ain't all that clear to me. Man, that's a lot of jargon in one sentence. Is that the way the bear actually talks?

Author: No (although that might be the way he thinks). But it makes the point: Even jargon can be clear if it's well anchored among other meaningful ideas.

Discovery learning can also be used to test the meaningfulness of new learning. For example, learners might be asked to generate (that is, discover) instances in which some new learning might be applicable—for example, a new principle in arithmetic. In fact, Ausubel argues that discovery learning is essential for problem solving if students are to demonstrate that they understand what they have learned. Furthermore, says Ausubel, there are indications that students more readily apply to new situations information that they discover, as opposed to applying material that is presented to them in final form. Discovery approaches might also be more motivating than expository approaches, and self-learning might be more intrinsically satisfying.

Although Ausubel accepts the usefulness of the discovery approach in some instances, he remains a strong advocate of expository teaching. He argues that most learning is of the reception variety and that any alternative would be highly inefficient in terms of the time involved, the costs incurred, and the benefits to the learner. Relatively little school learning can be discovered by students, says Ausubel, not only because it would take too long but also because students are not always capable of discovering much that is significant. Even subjects that apparently lend themselves to discovery approaches can often be mastered as well and faster if the information is given to the learner in relatively final form. Ausubel believes that after the age of 11 or 12, learners possess enough background information to understand many new concepts clearly if they are explained simply. After this age, says Ausubel, asking a student to "discover" is largely a waste of time.

Comparisons of Instructional Approaches

Because several studies have attempted to compare discovery-oriented and reception-oriented approaches to teaching and learning, it should be possible to evaluate the two without relying solely on opinion, conjecture, or theoretical speculation. However, the research does not consistently support one approach over the other, and it is often confusing and contradictory. Why? Partly because studies often use different criteria for assessing the effectiveness of various approaches. For example, some studies look at the speed of learning, others are concerned with retention, some attempt to assess transfer, and still others look at affective or motivational changes in learners.

Another reason that the conclusions of teaching-outcome studies are sometimes contradictory is that it is often impossible to maintain consistency among the approaches used in different studies—or sometimes even within a single study. Students and classes are dramatically different from one another but so are teachers. A well-prepared expository lesson might be extremely effective when presented by Mr. Joneskowski, but Ms. Rudifesk might present the same lesson poorly. By the same token, one fifth-grade class might respond exceptionally well to a discovery lesson, whereas another might be totally confused by the same lesson presented by the same teacher.

Some Studies Studies that have attempted to evaluate the effectiveness of a single approach (rather than comparing two different approaches) have not led to clear conclusions either. For example, many studies have looked at the contribution of advance organizers to learning, retention, and transfer. Grippin and Peters (1984) point out that about half of these studies indicate that the use of organizers makes a significant difference; the other half find that learning is just as effective without the use of organizers. The most important conclusion from their survey, however, is that *good* organizers are effective more often than not.

The effectiveness of discovery approaches has also been extensively investigated. Here, too, there is often confusion and contradiction, resulting in part from inconsistent definition, inappropriate measurement, and uncontrolled (and often uncontrollable) differences among teachers and students. However, even strong advocates of other approaches generally concede that discovery approaches can be highly effective in a variety of circumstances, particularly when learners are given the right sort of guidance. For example, Hammer (1997) found that discovery approaches closely tied to student interests and needs are highly effective. And Miles (1997) reports that discovery-based constructivist

BEAR MUSINGS

Guided Discovery

Some school subjects lend themselves more readily to discovery-oriented techniques than do others. For example, some (though by no means all) scientific principles can be discovered by students in guided discovery situations that provide them with sufficient background information and the appropriate experimental equipment. Similarly, children on field trips can discover a variety of phenomena, although understanding and interpreting these phenomena (and even noticing them in the first place) often require considerable guidance.

The beginning teacher should not make the mistake of assuming that teaching through discovery implies letting students go out on their own with no more than the simple instruction to "discover." The processes of discovery must be taught—through experience and through more direct instructional procedures—and students must be given frequent guidance while in the process of discovering—hence the expression **guided discovery**. The guidance need not ruin the discovery or destroy its magic.

As an example of guided discovery learning, Bruner (1961a) describes how a class of elementary school children was led to discover important relationships between human settlements and geographic features. Among other things, they are asked where they would establish a settlement if they were exploring an area for the first time. Their reasons for settling in certain areas rather than others gradually lead them to "discover" that major settlements should be at the confluence of rivers and near natural harbors. Thus, their study of geography becomes an activity of discovering relationships between the environment and humans rather than simply memorizing maps and related data.

Can the principle governing the combustion engine be discovered by an eighth-grade class? Yes, it can. What would be the major features of a guided discovery lesson that you might design for this purpose?

---

approaches can significantly increase student motivation and involvement.

Some Conclusions What, then, should the teacher conclude? Should teachers use mostly discovery (constructivist) or mostly expository (direct instruction) approaches? The simple answer is that the question is not as simple as it sounds, nor are the choices as clear. A good teacher will, of course, use both. (See the box entitled "Guided Discovery").

Disturbing as this might be for those who prefer the uncomplicated comfort of a black or white position, it is quite often impossible to use only one instructional approach to the complete exclusion of others. Johnny, intensely motivated to discover the mating habits of that noble barnyard fowl, the turkey, runs to the local library and finds a learned exposition on turkeys. From this he learns a bewildering amount. Is this discovery learning? In contrast, Frank's teacher, a recent reception-learning convert, presents a brilliant essay on the mating habits of turkeys to his bench-bound students. During the course of this exposition, it occurs to Frank that turkeys have been unnecessarily and unjustly demeaned in recent times, as evidenced by the popular expression, "You turkey!" In the course of Frank's inspired musings, he discovers that turkeys might better be ranked along with eagles as birds worthy of our respect and admiration. Reception learning?

The confusion arising from these illustrations may be lessened by the realization that learning is what students do and teaching is what teachers do. A teacher who emphasizes discovery

---

guided discovery A reflective teaching technique. Students are given much of the responsibility for finding relationships and organizing knowledge, but teachers are careful to provide the necessary guidance to ensure that discovery and learning occur.

will try to arrange the teaching/learning situation so that students are encouraged to experiment, to think, to gather information, and, most important, to arrive at their own organization of that information. Teachers who emphasize expository teaching will be more concerned with organizing information so that it is immediately meaningful for students and therefore becomes a stable part of their existing cognitive structure. In the end, however, it is the student who learns. And, in spite of a teacher's emphases to the contrary, students may discover new information and new relationships for themselves or they may discover a structured exposition ready to be learned and assimilated as is.

With discovery-oriented instruction, students are given much of the responsibility for discovering concepts, principles, and relationships; with reception-oriented learning, teachers present the material in relatively final form, pointing out important relationships among new and old learning. Discovery learning, which is especially suitable in some science lessons, may have some advantages in terms of motivation of students and meaningfulness of the material learned. Reception learning, which lends itself well to large-group presentations, may offer advantages in terms of efficient and effective use of time.

⌐ SOME COGNITIVE INSTRUCTIONAL MODELS AND EMPHASES

The juxtaposition of apparently opposing points of view is sometimes a useful teaching device. It highlights differences and, if Ausubel is correct,

makes the points of view more memorable— more easily dissociated from each other.

But there is also a disadvantage to this approach: It exaggerates differences and masks similarities. It leaves the impression that the points of view are more different and the theorists more adamant in their beliefs than is actually the case.

This chapter is a case in point. Juxtaposing the theories of Bruner and Ausubel has underlined the differences between them—especially the discovery-versus-expository debate. At the same time, this approach has perhaps glossed over important points of agreement between them—especially the conviction of each that the key to successful cognitive processing is to be found in the learner's own organization of knowledge. Both positions are, after all, unwaveringly cognitive. Both present a view of the learner as an active, information processing organism for whom the environment is meaningful to the extent that new material can be related to existing cognitive structure. Furthermore, the descriptions that each theory provides of the formation of cognitive structure are similar, even though their language is different (categories and coding systems on the one hand, subsumers and subsumption on the other). And, as we have seen, in the final analysis discovery and reception learning are not totally incompatible approaches to teaching and learning. As described by Bruner and Ausubel, each is intended to lead to the acquisition of meaningful concepts, to maximize transfer, retention, and motivation, and to prevent school learning from becoming merely a passive exercise in rote learning.

Cognitive Apprenticeship

One important constructivist educational model that reflects many of the same cognitive emphases as the theories of Bruner and Ausubel is termed **cognitive apprenticeship** (Collins, Brown, & Newman, 1989). This model views the learner as an apprentice in much the same sense as novices who are apprenticed to experts to learn new trades and skills. In the cognitive sphere, the experts are parents, siblings, other peers, or adults, and most important, teachers. Within this model, the role of the teacher is less about filling the learner's mind with information, facts, figures, procedures, and so on than about presenting examples, inviting students to explore, and providing guidance and encouragement. This model suggests that teachers need to develop a variety of cognitive strategies so that their students are equipped to explore, organize, discover, and learn on their own.

Cognitive apprenticeship approaches are not restricted to adult teachers as experts and younger students of normal or above-average ability as apprentices. Evidence suggests that these approaches can be highly effective for special-needs learners (Rojewski & Schell, 1994), as well as for adult learners Cash et al., 1997). For example, Shabo, Guzdial, and Stasko (1997) found that cognitive apprenticeship can be highly effective in developing internet-related computer skills.

The Methods of Cognitive Apprenticeship Cognitive apprenticeship advocates the use of a number of specific techniques designed to clarify the role of the teacher (expert) and the learner (apprentice) (Farnham-Diggory, 1992). These include the following:

Modeling In its simplest sense, **modeling** involves having teachers show learners how something is done. The object, notes Farnham-Diggory (1992), is not so much for learners to simply copy the expert's performance, but rather to help learners to develop conceptual models of a task. Modeling is therefore as appropriate for cognitive as for motor tasks (this is, after all *cognitive* apprenticeship). But if an expert is to show a novice how to perform a cognitive task, it's

---

cognitive apprenticeship An instructional model wherein parents, siblings, other adults, and especially teachers serve as a combination of model, guide, tutor, mentor, and coach to foster intellectual growth among learners.

---

modeling Learning through observation (imitation).

Modeling is an instructional technique for showing learners how something is done. This is highly evident in physical education, for example, where learners can be easily shown actual examples of desired behaviors. It can also be an important part of learning how to perform cognitive tasks; it requires that teachers make cognitive procedures highly explicit and evident.

necessary for the steps and procedures involved in the task to be made explicit and evident— among other things, by describing how specific cognitive strategies, such as rehearsal or organization, are being used and using other forms of thinking out loud.

Coaching **Coaching** involves guiding specific aspects of the student's performance. Just as a cognitive apprenticeship approach uses modeling to demonstrate the performance of cognitive tasks, coaching, too, is aimed at guiding the learner's cognitive behavior. Teachers might use any of a variety of techniques designed to teach thinking (to develop cognitive and metacognitive strategies), which are discussed in Chapter 5.

Scaffolding Scaffolding involves providing support so that students can accomplish tasks that would otherwise be too difficult for them.

coaching A technique sometimes used in cognitive apprenticeship approaches to instruction. The learner's cognitive behavior is guided by an expert.

This concept is discussed in Chapter 3 in connection with Vygotsky's zone of proximal growth. Recall that scaffolding is defined in terms of the various types of support that teachers need to provide for children if they are to learn. Scaffolding often takes the form of directions, suggestions, and other forms of verbal assistance and is most effective when it involves tasks within the child's zone of proximal growth—that is, tasks that the child is initially incapable of performing but that can be accomplished with the support and guidance of others.

Wood, Bruner, and Ross (1976) describe six procedures or techniques that can be used in scaffolding. These are summarized and illustrated in Table 6.3.

Fading In a sense, **fading** is the complement of scaffolding. Scaffolding involves providing support and guidance so that learners can perform tasks within the zone of proximal growth (by definition, tasks that require the support and assistance of others). In contrast, fading involves removing supports as the learner becomes capable of performing a given task without assistance—in other words, as the task moves from Vygotsky's zone of proximal growth to within the sphere of the learner's acquired competence. Fading assures that students eventually assume responsibility for solving problems and for learning.

Articulation **Articulation** involves verbalizing ideas or putting them into words. As a cognitive apprenticeship technique, articulation encourages learners to put their conclusions, descriptions, and

fading A technique used in cognitive apprenticeship programs. It involves the gradual withdrawal of supports (scaffolds) for the learner as these become progressively less necessary.

articulation A cognitive apprenticeship technique. Learners are encouraged to put their conclusions, descriptions, and principles into words.

TABLE 6.3
Some Scaffolding Techniques

TECHNIQUE	DESCRIPTION	EXAMPLE
RECRUITMENT	Gaining the child's attention and focusing it on the requirements of the task	"Okay, what we want to do is calculate the area of this right-angle triangle when we know the length of all its sides. How many square inches (cm) does it contain?"
REDUCTION IN DEGREES OF FREEDOM	Reducing the tasks to manageable subtasks	"Remember how to find the area of a rectangle? Can you make this triangle into a rectangle?"
DIRECTION MAINTENANCE	Keeping the learner on track and motivated	"Why don't you draw out the triangle, make it into a rectangle, and measure each of the sides? Maybe try another triangle and see if it's the same."
MARKING CRITICAL FEATURES	Drawing attention to the most relevant aspects of the task	"How many identical right-angle triangles do you need to make a rectangle? Why don't you draw a triangle on the corner of this piece of paper and cut out three or four and make squares with them? Do you always need the same number of triangles?"
FRUSTRATION CONTROL	Easing frustration associated with difficulties the child might experience	"This is sometimes a hard problem even for eighth graders. You're doing really well."
DEMONSTRATION	Imitating the child's attempts but modifying them slightly so that they are more appropriate and can then be imitated in turn by the child	"Here, let me cut out two triangles exactly the same and, here, let me make a square? Now what's the area of this square? And . . . that's it . . . exactly half. And . . . right! That is the formula, you genius!"

Source: Based on Bruner, Wood, & Ross (1976).

the principles they have discovered, into words. Deliberate verbalization forces students to think more clearly about their cognitive processes, and it is frequently an important technique in programs designed to foster the development of cognitive strategies. One example of articulation is Mulcahy's (1991) use of the Socratic dialogue, a series of questions and answers designed specifically to lead learners to become aware of their own thought processes and cognitive strategies.

Reflection Closely related to articulation, **reflection** also requires that the learner think and ver-

balize the execution and results of cognitive tasks. But when reflecting, learners are encouraged to think more abstractly and perhaps to compare their cognitive activity with a conceptual model, or sometimes with an actual physical model.

Exploration **Exploration** is the final step in the cognitive apprenticeship instructional process—as in most instructional approaches. It involves generalizing about what has been learned or accomplished, and it is analogous to what behaviorists call transfer or generalization.

---

reflection In cognitive apprenticeship, a procedure where learners are asked to think about their cognitive activities and to compare them with those of others or with abstract models.

exploration A cognitive apprenticeship procedure that requires learners to apply or generalize what they have learned, to investigate and test the potential applications of their learning.

The Sequence in Cognitive Apprenticeship Three principles guide the sequencing of material in Collins, Brown, and Newman's (1989) model of cognitive apprenticeship. The *first* principle, **global before local**, refers to the belief that learners should be provided with an overall view of what is to be learned or performed before they begin to work on specifics. In practice, the global aspect of the instruction might take the form of a summary, an overview, a completed activity, a final rendition. In this sense, the global-before-local principle is similar to Ausubel's use of advance organizers.

Second, this model suggests that material should be presented in order of increasing complexity—that is, from simplest to most complex. This is very much in line with Bruner's notion that learners should begin with the simplest examples of concepts and proceed to more general, inclusive concepts.

Third, to increase transfer and meaningfulness of learning, the model suggests that knowledge and skills, once acquired, should be applied in an ever-increasing diversity of situations. Collins, Brown, and Newman (1989) state that much of what we learn from textbooks, lectures, and laboratories is never applied outside these situations, often because we don't know when or how to apply this knowledge. In this sense our knowledge is "inert" rather than active—hence, the importance of the exploration described earlier: the cognitive apprenticeship technique of applying and generalizing learning.

Cognitive Apprenticeship, Constructivism, and Reflective Teaching Earlier in this chapter we reviewed reflective teaching strategies and described their relationship to constructivistic

approaches. Reflective teaching strategies, we noted, are those designed to lead students to discover and learn for themselves, and they are designed as well to encourage students to think about their learning and thinking. More than this, they also require teachers to think about and analyze (reflect on) what is happening as they teach (Freiberg & Driscoll, 1992). Thus, reflective teaching is based on a philosophy that emphasizes the learner's active role in learning and views teaching as largely a process of facilitating learning and discovery. Hence, reflective teaching is essentially constructivistic.

Cognitive apprenticeship is based on exactly this philosophy: The learner is the apprentice; the teacher is a guide and mentor. The role of the teacher is essentially to serve as a master, an expert who shows the novice apprentice how various cognitive tasks can be accomplished. The expert also guides the apprentice's progression, selecting and arranging tasks, providing support (scaffolding) and then gently withdrawing it (fading) when it is no longer required.

An instructional model of cognitive apprenticeship, notes Roth (1993), can serve as a useful guide not only by structuring the instructor's activities (as well as those of the learner), but also by providing a metaphor for reflecting about teaching. This metaphor of "teacher as master guide" and "student as apprentice learner" lends itself especially well to teachers analyzing their instructional behaviors and evaluating the cognitive progress of their apprentices.

Empowerment: A Constructivist Emphasis

If you leave a door unlocked, says Wiske (1994), it is as though everyone has been given a key to it. The function of schools, she argues, is to unlock the doors to understanding. Hence, it is imperative that schools abandon the philosophy that considers intellectual riches as private property in the hands of masters who dole them out

---

global before local A phrase used to describe a sequencing principle in cognitive apprenticeship. Refers to the recommendation that learners should be given some notion of what the final performance, the final task, the final global rendition will be before being asked to work on the individual subtasks that make up the whole.

as they see fit. Instead, argues Wiske, schools need to view their purpose as one of sharing and collaborating with learners. According to this view, one of the most important goals of the constructivist classroom is to **empower** students. This goal, notes Mann (1994), should be the goal of all education—for gifted children as well as those less gifted. Empowering students, says Shannon (1994), is fundamental to the management of today's schools.

As we saw in Chapter 1, to empower is to enable, to give power. At a simple level, education empowers students by helping them to discover and build the skills and knowledge that enable them to do important things they could not otherwise do (for example, read newspapers, write love poems, or add up the money in their pocket or purse). At a deeper level, education empowers by contributing to the development of intellectual processes; that is, it empowers by teaching people how to think and how to learn. And finally, education empowers by developing in students the sort of power that comes from feelings of social, intellectual, and personal competence.

Misconceptions and Their Effects on Learning

Cognitive psychology's attention to how students learn and understand has led to some important discoveries about how they think. For example, many students (and many teachers as well) sometimes find it difficult to understand seemingly simple concepts and principles, simply because they have developed certain stubborn **misconceptions** that interfere with their learning. These are sometimes referred to as *alternative conceptions* or *children's science*, which are less negative expressions (Soloman, 1993).

There are numerous examples of common misconceptions. For example, more than three-quarters of fifth-grade students believe that eyes actually see objects—rather than responding to reflected light that travels in straight lines and bounces off various objects (Anderson & Smith, 1984). Similarly, elementary school children who readily state that the earth is round often have a conception that is different from the one that you or I might have of what a round earth means (Nussbaum, 1979). Some children see the earth as a flat round thing, something like a cookie, perhaps surrounded by water; others conceive of the earth as a huge globular object with the ground near the bottom of the globe, the sky at the top, and air in between. Others, report Vosniadou and Brewer (1992), see it as a flattened sphere or perhaps as a hollow sphere like a basketball. Many students have similar serious misconceptions about the flow of electrical currents (Sanger & Greenbowe, 1997); about decimals and fractions (Moloney & Stacey, 1997); about continents, oceans, and the earth's magnetic field (Marques & Thompson, 1997); about the atom (Peterson, 1997); and about a large variety of other scientific and social phenomena.

Many childish misconceptions are just that: childish misconceptions. With the increasing intellectual sophistication that comes with age and experience, many of them disappear—as, for example, does the Piaget 4-year-old's belief that you can increase the amount of gum in a wad by

---

empower To enable; to give power to. One of the most important goals of education is to empower students by providing them with both specific information and learning/thinking strategies and by helping them to develop the feelings of personal power that accompany the realization that one is competent and worthwhile.

---

misconception The result of conceiving wrongly, of misunderstanding. Misconceptions in fields such as science and mathematics are common among children (and sometimes adults as well), and often interfere with learning.

stretching it out real long, or the 2-year-old's *animistic* conclusion that the moon moves with her, or the adolescent's egocentric belief in the unshakeable power of logic. Knowledge of developmental theories such as those of Piaget and Vygotsky can do much to help the teacher understand learners' misconceptions, says Watson (1997). And knowledge of these theories can also be used to help teachers foster the development of more accurate concepts. For example, Liggitt-Fox (1997) describes how the use of advance organizers specifically designed to contrast new and old information can be highly effective for replacing misconceptions.

ANOTHER LOOK AT CONSTRUCTIVISM

There are many educators out there who claim that we are—or should be—in the throes of a revolution in education. The revolution goes by various labels; *constructivism* is perhaps the most common (though not necessarily the clearest). This revolution takes its cue from yet another revolution—one that theorists such as Bruner (1997a) refer to as the *cognitive* revolution. After all, cognitive theories such as those of Piaget and Vygotsky and Bruner underline the importance of *constructing* meaning. Truth and meaning are not something that can be *given* to a child, the cognitivists inform us; rather, they are discovered and created by the individual.

If there is a revolution, what side should you be on?

Most of today's new breed of educators seem to think they should be on the side of constructivism. It might seem backward and narrow and rigid to be on the other side. Constructivism, you see, is the "new" view. When contrasted with the "old", the new is always seen to be, well, *newer*. No one wants to have "old" beliefs.

Besides, constructivism is decidedly learner-centered, and that must surely be a good thing. It encourages the individual development of learners, and it recognizes their personal uniqueness as well as the uniqueness of the meanings they invent and build. Furthermore, constructivism emphasizes the *autonomy* and *self-directedness* of the learner, and it encourages their active involvement in the process of learning. And these, too, are all good things.

Still, the methods of constructivist classrooms (cooperative teaching, discovery-oriented classrooms, reflective teaching, cognitive apprenticeship, programs for the development of cognitive strategies) are far from universal. In fact, the methods of direct instruction (lecturing, explaining, outlining, assigning exercises) are still the most common instructional approaches in North American classrooms (Cienkus & Ornstein, 1997).

And perhaps they should be. Certainly, there are those, such as Evers (1998), who insist that the ideas of constructivist education are neither new (they are basically the same as those of the progressive education movement associated with John Dewey about a century ago) nor especially valuable. Others, such as Rhine (1998), point out that, although reform-minded teachers are often successful in providing rich environments for students to learn, they have been far less successful in creating *meaningful* activities for them. Projects and activities, Reed (1997–98) reminds us, are simply means to an end and not ends in themselves.

Those who would reform education in the direction of student-centered, activity-based, discovery-oriented, constructivist classrooms should bear in mind a few cautions: First, constructivism is basically a description of how children learn. That it is an instructional theory is a myth, declares Clements (1997); it's a philosophy of learning. As such, it doesn't provide teachers with clear instructional guidelines. In fact, it provides no evidence about how teaching should be carried out—although it sometimes leads to a second myth—namely, that learners should always be actively involved in reflecting upon and in constructing meaning. Evers (1998) points out that, although all learning (even rote memorization) is based on construction, this does not mean that the best way of teaching is always to try to have the student build, discover, and construct. Problem-centered and discovery approaches, claim Airasian and Walsh (1997), take more time than any of the direct instruction methods. Furthermore, these approaches are far more likely to lead to misconceptions—and far less likely to result in the replacement of mistaken notions with more accurate concepts.

MacIver, Reuman, and Main (1995) point out that the *raison d'être* of schools is to provide students with opportunities to learn.[7] "How best to learn something," notes Evers (1998), "is an empirical question" (p. 14). Empirical (real-life) questions can't easily be answered solely by reference to theories; they call for experimentation. The challenge for educators is to find the most effective means of providing students with opportunities to learn.

Effective Teaching

What is the most effective of all teaching methods? The one-on-one tutorial, claims Benjamin Bloom (1984), following an extensive review of the literature. In fact, an average student paired with a good **tutor**, says Bloom, can be expected to achieve at somewhere around the 98th percentile in a group of comparable students taught in a conventional classroom setting. In other words, in a tutorial situation, an average student will outperform 98 percent of the students in ordinary classrooms!

Other research generally corroborates Bloom's description of the effectiveness of tutoring—although not always quite as optimistically (for example, Shanahan, 1998; Fuchs et al., 1997). The potential for higher achievement is apparently there; only the method is lacking. Finding that method (or those methods) is the challenge. Hence, one of the most important current challenges for educational research is to discover or devise instructional procedures that are as effective with entire classes as one-on-one tutorials are with single students.

Educational literature abounds with research that has looked at the effectiveness of various instructional models and methods. This research spans a wide variety of age and grade levels and involves many subjects and instructional procedures. As a result, it is not easily described or summarized.

Still, Alexander and Judy (1988) claim that the research tells us many things; among these are two findings they describe as "undisputed facts." The first of these is that the more a learner knows about a specific subject (that is, the more domain-specific knowledge there is in the individual's cognitive structure), the better a learner will understand and remember. And their second finding is that learners who are most adept at monitoring and controlling their cognitive activities typically do better than learners who are less adept.

These two undisputed findings have profound implications for teachers' behavior. That those with the greatest amount of domain-specific prior learning (as opposed to more general information) are better learners highlights the importance of advance preparation for learning. It also emphasizes the cumulative and hierarchical nature of much of our learning, and it supports the contention that both lessons and curricula should present material so that new understanding builds on a firm base of knowledge

---

tutor A teacher involved in a one-on-one teaching situation. Tutors are frequently other students or else other teachers or experts.

---

[7] *PPC:* Unlike the bear, I think many students aren't multilingual. So maybe you should explain what this means.

Author: Perhaps they're not all multilingual. But they're bright as little sages. They need no explanation of such trivial matters.

and skills. It makes no difference whether we use the language of Bruner (numerous, varied instances of concepts presented so that the learner can discover coding systems that will permit going beyond the information given); or the language of Ausubel (learners need to be given—and reminded of—stable, relevant subsuming concepts so that cognitive structure can give meaning to new learning and new learning can be firmly anchored to that structure). In the final analysis, the instructional implications of each of these differently worded and somewhat jargon-laden statements are much the same: Understanding depends very much on what we already know. This isn't a particularly startling revelation, but it is a fundamentally important one.

The second of Alexander and Judy's (1988) "undisputed" facts—that learners who are best at monitoring and controlling their cognitive strategies perform better—also has clear instructional implications: Specifically, teachers must devote more time and energy to teaching the skills and strategies of thinking and learning; they must adopt methods and philosophies that reflect their fundamentally important role as guides and mentors and also the students' responsibility for their own learning. Approaches such as cognitive apprenticeship, various programs designed to teach cognitive and metacognitive strategies, inquiry-based instruction, reflective teaching, and the schools' recognition of their need to empower students are all logical outgrowths of this second undisputed finding.

Rosenshine and Stevens (1986) summarize a variety of experimental studies that have examined the effectiveness of theory-generated instructional programs in schools. These studies suggest that effective teaching is characterized by behaviors that can be taught and encouraged by teachers. Specifically, the most effective teachers, with respect to well-structured subjects, are those who:

▲ Start their lessons with a brief review of prerequisite learning
▲ Begin by stating the lesson's goals
▲ Present material in small steps, allowing students to practice between steps
▲ Give explicit and detailed instructions and explanations
▲ Allow all students to practice lessons actively
▲ Ask many questions to check students' understanding and obtain responses from all students
▲ Provide students with immediate guidance for initial practice
▲ Provide systematic feedback and correct students' errors as they occur
▲ Provide clear and explicit instructions for seat work and monitor students' performance as necessary

Rosenshine and Stevens caution that these teaching procedures do not apply to all students at all times. As noted, they are most applicable to well-structured content that can be presented in small steps and when the teacher can provide detailed and explicit instructions while allowing students to practice with immediate corrective feedback. But when the lesson deals with more abstract, less-structured content (such as morality and ethics, creative writing, or politics), different teaching approaches are necessary.

MAIN POINTS

1. Direct instruction describes teacher-centered instructional approaches such as lecturing, explaining, and assigning. Constructivist approaches, which are more learner-centered, try to provide opportunities for learners to construct their own meaning. They are based

on cognitive theories such as Piaget's and Bruner's and are reflected in discovery-oriented approaches, cognitive strategies programs, reflective teaching, and conceptual change programs.

2. Cognitive theories stress the importance of the individual learner's cognitive structure and look at how information is processed, organized, and recalled. Cognitive theories view knowledge as consisting of vast networks of relationships in which learning is built on previous knowledge and involves information processing. Declarative knowledge consists of all the facts we have learned (things that are or have been); procedural knowledge involves knowing how to do something. Schemata are metaphors for cognitive structure and functioning. Scripts are the aspects of schemata that deal with routines and sequences.

3. Cognitive psychology's main beliefs suggest that (a) the curriculum needs to be organized to reveal and emphasize relationships, and (b) schools should pay deliberate attention to developing strategies for organizing and using knowledge.

4. Bruner's cognitive theory describes learning and perception as information processing activities that involve the formation of concepts (categories) that result from abstracting commonalities among events and experiences. Hierarchical arrangements of related categories are referred to as coding systems. Coding systems are important for retention, discovery, and transfer.

5. Bruner's theory leads to constructivist approaches to teaching especially by its strong support of discovery approaches. Learning through discovery requires the learner to construct information by discovering the relationships that exist among concepts or principles. Discovery learning is affected by set (predisposition to learn in a given way), need state (degree of arousal), mastery of specifics (amount and detail of learning), and diversity of training (variety of conditions under which learning takes place).

6. Renewed interest in discovery approaches are found in constructivist approaches (based on the assumption that students construct knowledge), in the conceptual change movement (based on the recognition that teachers should be more concerned with the learners' concepts and cognitive strategies that lead to conceptual change than simply with factual information), and in reflective teaching strategies (designed to lead students to discover and learn for themselves).

7. Ausubel's theory attempts to explain meaningful verbal learning, especially in the classroom. He defines meaning as involving a relationship between new material and old material (cognitive structure). To learn is to subsume new material to existing cognitive structure. This can take the form of deriving material from pre-existing structure (derivative subsumption), or it can involve material that is an extension of what is already known (correlative subsumption). Loss of ability to recall (to dissociate new material from old) is obliterative subsumption.

8. Ausubel's most important instructional technique involves the use of advance organizers—highly generic concepts presented before the lesson, designed to bring to mind relevant prior knowledge and intended to clarify the relationships between new and old learning.

9. Discovery methods (basically constructivist) and expository teaching (direct instruction) are not mutually exclusive. Both are useful. Ausubel suggests that discovery can have advantages for teaching in the early grades, for testing meaningfulness and problem solving, for ensuring transferability, and for establishing intrinsic motivation. In the end, teaching is what teachers do, and learning is what students do. Discovery teaching does not always lead to discovery learning. And expository teaching might well lead to discovery learning.

10. Although Bruner and Ausubel present points of view that are opposite in many respects, both present a fundamentally cognitive view of the learner as an active, information processing organism whose efforts to derive meaning from the environment are closely related to the development of associated networks of concepts. Their recommendations for instruction are intended to lead to the acquisition of meaningful concepts, to maximize transfer, retention, and motivation, and to reduce passive rote learning.

11. The cognitive apprenticeship model suggests a relatively complex role for today's teacher—one that recognizes a wide diversity of desired learning outcomes (procedural as well as declarative knowledge, for example); a range of instructional approaches (including modeling, coaching, scaffolding, fading, articulation, and reflection); and some important sequencing principles (global before local, from simplest to most complex, and toward increasing diversity).

12. One important objective of education is to empower students by providing them with knowledge, skills, and confidence.

13. Occasionally, what students don't know or the inaccurate and misleading things they are convinced they do know (misconceptions) interfere with learning and understanding—hence the importance of advance organizers, questioning, and other approaches to ensure that all learners have the appropriate prerequisite knowledge and skills for new learning.

14. Constructivism is often associated with "new" ideas as opposed to the old, and with learner- as opposed to teacher-centered methods. The methods of constructivism (cooperative teaching, discovery-based approaches, cognitive apprenticeship) are far less common than the expository methods of direct instruction. Critics suggest that the problem-centered and discovery-oriented approaches of constructivism are often inefficient and ineffective.

15. Two findings from cognitive research have important implications for effective teaching: (a) The more background knowledge a learner has about a subject, the more effective the learning (domain-specific knowledge), and (b) learners who are most skilled at monitoring and controlling their use of cognitive strategies learn and solve problems (use strategic knowledge) most effectively.

16. The most effective teachers for well-structured material are those who (a) begin by reviewing (often using advance organizers), (b) state goals clearly at the beginning, and (c) present material in small, detailed, and explicit steps with both ample opportunity for practice and systematic feedback during the lesson and during seat work.

Applied Questions

▲ Design a guided discovery lesson.

▲ What would you include in an expository lesson making use of various kinds of advance organizers?

▲ Discuss the proposition that constructivism is a description of learning but not an instructional strategy.

▲ If you were to develop a mnemonic device for learning some behaviors and characteristics of the most effective teachers, what would you create?

Internet Activity

Use InfoTrac College Edition or other World Wide Web sources to research the following questions: Write up your findings. (See the inside back cover of this text for suggestions about where to begin.)

What is constructivism? direct instruction? Comment on how you are likely to use each in *your* classroom.

Sample search terms: constructivism *and* direct instruction

Study Terms

advance organizer 216
articulation 225
category 208
coaching 225
coding system 208
cognitive apprenticeship 224
comparative organizer 217
conceptual change movement 212
constructivist approaches 203
correlative subsumption 214
declarative knowledge 205
derivative subsumption 214
direct instruction 203
discovery learning 207
dissociability 217
diversity of training 211
empower 228
enactive 212
exploration 226
expository organizer 217
expository teaching 215
fading 225

global before local 227
guided discovery 222
iconic 213
mastery of specifics 211
misconception 228
modeling 224
need state 211
obliterative subsumption 217
procedural knowledge 205
progressive education 203
reception learning 207
reflection 226
rote learning 219
schema 205
script 206
set 211
spiral curriculum 213
subsumer 217
subsumption 214
symbolic 213
tutor 230

Suggested Readings

Original sources are among the best references for approaches to learning theory such as Bruner's and Ausubel's. The following references are clear presentations of their theories and educational recommendations:

Bruner, J. S. (1961). *The process of education.* Cambridge, MA: Harvard University Press.

Bruner, J. S. (1990). *Acts of meaning.* Cambridge, MA: Harvard University Press.

Bruner, J. S., Goodnow, J. J., & Austin, G. A. (1956). *A study of thinking.* New York: Wiley.

Ausubel, D. P. (1968). *Educational psychology: A cognitive view.* New York: Holt, Rinehart & Winston.

An excellent collection of articles dealing with the instructional implications of children's ideas about science:

Black, P. J., & Lucas, A. M. (eds.) (1993). *Children's informal ideas in science.* New York: Routledge.

Evers' collection is a brief and provocative look at current classrooms. Of particular relevance to this chapter is the first chapter in that book, which deals specifically with discovery learning. Discovery learning, claims Evers, represents the rebirth of the very old ideas of progressive education—ideas which were bad at the turn of the last century and which are still bad 100 years later:

Evers, W. M. (Ed.). (1998). *What's gone wrong in America's classrooms.* Stanford, CA: Hoover Institution Press, Stanford University.

The much feared grizzly bear (*Ursus horribilis*) weighs about 900 pounds at maturity. Many "experts" consider the grizzly to be a species of brown bear (*Ursus arctos*). The grizzly's enormous strength is attested to by one bear that moved an 850-pound trap one-quarter of a mile and then escaped (Soper, 1964).

There is surely a piece of divinity in us, something that was before the elements, and owes no homage unto the sun.

Sir Thomas Browne, *Religio Medici*

Humanistic Approaches to Teaching

CHAPTER 7

PREVIEW

Humanists object to what they see as the mechanistic and dehumanizing emphases of traditional approaches to psychology and education. They urge the adoption of new attitudes, concepts, and approaches in these fields. In this chapter we describe the fundamental characteristics of humanistic approaches to understanding people and to teaching. The most important point we make is that humanism, behaviorism, and cognitivism are compatible. Teachers can be and do all the good things that humanism implies and still use the knowledge offered by other approaches.

FOCUS QUESTIONS

▲ How is humanism different from other approaches?

▲ What are the principles of Carl Rogers' theory?

▲ What is humanistic education?

▲ What is an open classroom?

▲ What are the main strategies of cooperative learning?

When I came home at Christmas during my first year of college, I still believed that psychologists had devious and clever ways of peering into our minds and uncovering all sorts of dark things hidden there. That, after all, was why I had decided to study psychology. And, as a budding psychologist, I brought great armloads of explanations home to my grandmother, like chunks of firewood to stoke her fires and inflame her imagination. Because she wanted to know, I told her with stunning behavioristic clarity why pigs lie in their muddy wallows on hot summer days and why chickens crow in the morning and roost at night. I explained to her why cows always go into the same stall and why horses stand with their backs to a storm.

"Bah!" harrumphed my grandmother, refusing to see the magic in my explanations. "If I were a pig," she said, "I'd lie in the mud. And if I were a chicken I'd crow in the morning and roost at night."

"But . . ."

"And if I were a cow," she continued, keeping me from telling her that my explanations were still bang on . . . "if I were a cow, I'd be a wild cow. I'd never go into stalls!"

"But the point," I said (brilliantly, I thought), "is that you're not a pig, a chicken, or a cow. You're a person, and there are explanations for that too!" Quickly, I launched into a powerful behavioristic explanation of Frank's fear of cats and Louise's embarrassing attachment to her tattered scrap of a dirty-green baby blanket.

"But," countered my grandmother, "what about why Frank isn't scared of dogs, and he was bitten about eight times? And cats hardly ever bit him. And what about how Louise doesn't even like any other blankets or pillows? And why doesn't Lucy like her baby blanket?"

My grandmother, a practiced skeptic, could always ask questions more rapidly than I could answer them. And although I had enough of the beginnings of some answers to eventually convince her that Skinner, Freud, Piaget, and others each had important and useful things to say about Frank's fear of cats and Louise's love of a dirty rag, there was no way I could ever convince her that they, or I, knew more about Frank or Louise than she did.

As my grandmother so pointedly put it, "I personally know pigs that don't care to wallow in mud, chickens that never roost or crow, cows that park their arses wherever, and horses so contrary they'll face whichever way they bloody please."

HUMANISTIC PSYCHOLOGY

My grandmother was a humanist.[1]

Humanistic psychology is concerned with the uniqueness, the individuality, the humanity of each individual. It is an orientation that readily admits that some people smile when they wallow in mud, some turn up their noses but endure the embarrassment, and others find such behavior quite unacceptable. In more human

---

humanistic psychology A branch of psychology whose primary concern is with the development of the self and with the uniqueness of the individual. Sometimes referred to as *third-force* psychology; the other two forces are behaviorism and Freudian theory.

---

[1] **PPC:** Don't you think the language is a little strong, especially for a grandmother? After all, some students reading this have had pretty sheltered lives.

Author: She's one old lady who had a lot of dog meat in her: That's the way she talked if she felt like it. Students in shelters, please don't take offense. . . .

terms, humanism is based on the fundamental observation that, although we might resemble each other in many important ways, each of us is quite different from every other. Our uniqueness is our "self." And self is the most central concept in humanistic psychology.

Humanistic psychology has its roots in philosophy—especially in the existential philosophy of writers like Jean-Paul Sartre. (See Contat, 1974; Martin Buber, 1958, 1965; and Karl Jaspers, 1962, 1963.) These philosophers wondered about the nature and purpose of humanity and of human existence (hence the label **existentialism**). They were profoundly concerned about what it means to be human and how humanity grows and expresses itself in each individual.

Humanism versus Other Views in Psychology

These, too, are the concerns of humanistic psychology. This explains why humanists have not always been happy with the concerns and preoccupations of science. Science, humanists insist, tends to dehumanize people. It reduces them to averages and generalizations; it looks for what is common and predictable. And it ignores those things that are private and individual and uniquely human. In fact, it simply isn't equipped to deal with these things. Largely because of this there has historically been conflict between humanism and behavioristic or cognitive approaches. The conflict reflects orientations that are fundamentally different in terms of their most basic beliefs and attitudes toward human beings.

In a nutshell, what humanists object to is what they see as the technological orientation of approaches such as behaviorism. In its most extreme form, this technological orientation asserts that certain identifiable teaching processes, when used with such and such a type of student for such and such a kind of content, will predictably result in the attainment of specific, previously identified, and clearly intended objectives. Humanists object strongly to this process–product orientation. As Shulman (1986) observes, they see this as focusing too strongly on techniques that "should" be practiced by teachers and placing far too much emphasis on the measurable outcomes of the teaching/learning process, especially in terms of gains on standardized tests. Humanists are alarmed that the conclusions and recommendations of process–product research have often been used by school authorities as a basis for evaluating school systems, teachers, and teaching. Traditional emphases on teaching styles and teaching outcomes, notes Ornstein (1993a), ignore the humanistic aspects of teaching.

The Humanistic Teacher

The humanistic view emphasizes two things: the uniqueness of the pupil and the teacher's attitudes toward students. Hence, humanistic teachers are especially sensitive to diversity in their classrooms. As Bartolome (1994) notes, humanistic teaching is culturally sensitive. It respects and tries to enhance the history, culture, and different perspectives of individual students. Thus, the preparation of humanistic teachers must devote as much attention to teachers' beliefs and attitudes as is now given to subject matter and instructional strategies (Patterson & Purkey, 1993).

If teaching is both an art and a science—as we claimed in Chapter 1—humanists are on the side of art and behaviorists on the side of science. But before we rush forward to describe

---

existentialism A philosophical movement characterized by a preoccupation with existence. Existential philosophers often describe the human condition in terms such as *abandonment, loneliness, despair,* and *alienation.* These feelings are assumed to arise from our lack of certain knowledge about our origins and our eventual end. Hence the label *existentialism,* because the only knowable reality is existence.

what the humanists have to say about the art of teaching, notice that our use of terms in this section, and in much of this chapter, is almost shamefully loose and general. Real life is not so simple. Behaviorists are not often as technology-oriented as an exaggerated humanistic description of their views might suggest, nor are all process–product researchers behaviorists or cognitivists. In fact, later in this chapter we look at two important and quite specific instructional methods (one based on learning styles and the other on cooperative learning); each of these reflects much of the humanist's concern with the individual and with emotional growth but each is fundamentally concerned with both the processes and the products of instruction. The results of process–product research do not really suggest that teachers should ideally be quasi-robotic classroom mechanics who repair cognitive and behavioral deficits and impairments and produce wonderful little academic achievers.

Keep in mind that most educators do not fall neatly into either the humanist, the behaviorist, or the cognitive camp. Most are quite eclectic; they borrow from here and there.

So in this chapter we stretch the truth on two counts: We exaggerate the differences between humanism and other approaches—especially behaviorism—and we pretend that all that is not clearly humanistic is, by default, behavioristic. Exaggeration can be a useful pedagogical device—as long as you are not deceived.[2]

----

[2] **PPC:** This is an important point. Perhaps you should repeat it.

Author: Okay: Exaggeration can be a useful pedagogical device—as long as you are not deceived.

PPC: That's not what I meant. Can you make the point in a different way, to make it more memorable?

Author: Okay. Real life is seldom like the simple black-and-white pictures that we draw to depict our little theories and our precious ideological stances. We are still like children using crude wooden pencils. In our drawings we miss all the color, most of the nuances, and thousands of other poses that we could have drawn. We draw only frozen stick-men and stick-women, and then we pretend we have drawn something with a soul.

ROGERIAN HUMANISTIC THEORY

As an introduction to humanism, we look first at a summary of aspects of the writing of Carl Rogers that deal with personality and behavior; then we examine several approaches to education that reflect humanistic orientations. (Rogers is among the most influential theorists in this area; Abraham Maslow, another important humanist, is discussed in Chapter 11.)

Carl Rogers was first and foremost a psychotherapist. His main concern was with understanding human personality in order to understand how it might be changed, how happiness might be restored to saddened lives (Rogers, 1957). His theory emerged primarily as a reaction against other highly popular approaches to therapy such as Freudian theory and behaviorism. Rogers felt strongly that these approaches were far less respectful and humane than they should be, note Becvar and Becvar (1997).

Rogers' writings are not based so much on objective data as on his answers for questions about what individuals think of the world. How do they feel? How do they perceive their relationships to others? What conditions are required for them to change? Rogers' theory continues to have an enormous influence on psychotherapy and counseling. It also provides teachers with a different way of approaching and communicating with their students. In the words of Rogers' daughter, Natalie, ". . . he verified the notion that a safe, supportive environment allowed each person (including children) to journey down the path of self-discovery, self-esteem and self-directed learning" (Rogers & Freiberg, 1994, p. iii).

Main Terms in Rogerian Theory

Different terms are used to describe the various emphases of Rogerian theory. One label commonly used, **client-centered therapy** (also **person-centered therapy**), describes several aspects of the system. It indicates, first, that the theory is a therapeutic one; that is, it is designed to be useful to a counselor who deals with behavioral and emotional problems. Second, this label highlights the major difference between this and other approaches to **counseling**—namely, it indicates that the counseling procedures revolve around the individual. It proposes *client-centered* as opposed to **directive therapy**. The counselor's role in client-centered therapy is accordingly de-emphasized; the therapist, instead of giving advice or solving problems for clients, sets the stage so that the clients themselves define their own problems, react to them, and take steps toward their solution. (This process is actually much more complex than it may seem from the preceding statements; see Rogers, 1951, 1957.)

A second common term in Rogerian theory is **phenomenology**, a term that denotes concern with the world as it is perceived by an individual rather than as the world may actually be. Counselors and teachers can never truly know the individual's private, *phenomenological* world, notes Rogers. But to be truly effective, they must

try to understand it. Accordingly, empathy is an important characteristic of any humanistic educator (Bozarth, 1997).

A third Rogerian label is **humanism**. Humanism in literature, philosophy, and psychology has historically been concerned with human worth, with individuality, with humanity, and with the individual's right to determine personal actions. Accordingly, the development of human potential tends to be highly valued, while the attainment of material goals is de-emphasized. Thus, Rogers describes **self-actualization** as the end toward which all humans strive. His encouragement of client-centered therapy is also compatible with the humanists' emphasis on self-determination. In fact, the question of self-determination versus external control, together with a consideration of the ethical and practical problems of applying a science of behavior, was the subject of a well-known debate between Rogers and Skinner (1956).

The Behavior Control Debate: Rogers versus Skinner

The central issue in this debate concerns the application of behavior control techniques for personal control in social groups, for educational procedures, and for governments. Skinner expresses his concern that nonscientific procedures and ideas are muddying our thinking about human behavior. He argues strongly for openly applying the scientific, behavioristic techniques of positive control toward the

---

client-centered therapy A type of patient–counselor relationship. The counselor (therapist or psychiatrist) is not directive in the sense of telling clients how they should behave but rather attempts to allow patients to express themselves and discover their own ways of dealing with their own behavior. This therapeutic approach is generally contrasted with directive therapy. Also termed *person-centered therapy*.

counseling The act of giving advice.

directive therapy A type of counselor–client relationship in which the counselor takes the major responsibility for directing the client's behavior.

phenomenology An approach concerned primarily with how individuals view their own world. Its basic assumption is that each individual perceives and reacts to the world in a unique manner and that this phenomenological worldview is important for understanding the individual's behavior.

---

humanism A philosophical and psychological orientation primarily concerned with our humanity—that is, with our worth as individuals and those processes that are considered to make us more human.

self-actualization The process or act of becoming oneself, of developing one's potentialities, of achieving an awareness of one's identity; self-fulfillment. This term is central to humanistic psychology.

betterment of society—and, at the same time, abandoning many of the techniques of aversive control that are so widely used. (These topics were the basis of his 1948 novel, *Walden II*, an account of a fictitious society developed through the application of a behavioral technology.)

But, claims Rogers, Skinner underestimates the problem of power by making the false assumption that techniques of social control will be used in the best interests of society. Furthermore, Skinner fails to specify who will control society, who will be controlled, and what the goals for this behavioral technology should be. Rogers dismisses Skinner's claim that if behavioral scientists experiment with society, "eventually the practices which make for the greatest biological and psychological strength of the group will presumably survive" (Skinner, 1955, p. 549). Rogers argues instead that society's goals should be concerned primarily with the process of "becoming," achieving worth and dignity, being creative—in short, with the process of self-actualization.[3]

This debate resolves no issues; it simply exposes the fundamental conflict between those who favor human control (for our benefit) through the thoughtful application of a science of behavior and those who believe that science should not be used to change or control us but simply to enhance our capacity for self-control and self-determination.

---

[3] **PPC:** Students would probably like to know who, in the opinion of most contemporary researchers and educators, wins the debate. Could the bear provide some enlightenment? After all, this is no longer the ninth edition—what I call the "choir boy edition." Surely the bear is no longer afraid to risk his precious political correctness!

Author: As the next line notes, the debate resolves no issues. Besides, winning a debate doesn't prove the correctness of the winning side—although it might say something about the strength of its arguments and the persuasiveness of its defenders. And the bear's political correctness is not at issue here. The bear used to be politically correct, not because he lacked the courage of his convictions but simply because . . . well, he didn't want to offend anybody. Okay? Now he's back to his old self; he doesn't care anymore.

The Principles of Rogers' Theory

In Chapter 11 of *Client-Centered Therapy* (1951), Rogers presents an integrated account of his position in the form of 19 propositions (see also Rogers, 1992, a reprint of a 1957 article). Most of these ideas continue to this day to underlie Rogerian counseling practices and humanistic applications to education (Kirschenbaum, 1991). The most important of these ideas are summarized here (also see Table 7.1). Understanding these principles is important for understanding the rationale underlying the various approaches to humanistic education described later in this chapter.

Our Worlds Are Private, Phenomenological One of the most fundamental assertions of the phenomenologist is that every individual is the center of a continually changing world of personal experiences. This recognizes two features of human functioning that are particularly important for the teacher.

First, it implies that for any individual, the significant aspects of the environment are private.

Second, this principle suggests not only that the individual's phenomenological world is private but also that it can never be completely known by anyone else. Consider, for example, a child's simple complaint to his mother after waking up from a nightmare: "Mama, I'm scared." The fear that the child expresses is a real and significant aspect of his world, and his mother may draw on her own stored-up memories of past fears to imagine how her son feels. But she cannot really know his fear. The phenomenological world can never be fully shared.

The belief implicit in this first principle—specifically that meaning is private and cannot be fully shared—is absolutely central to **constructivistic approaches** to education.

Behavior Can Be Understood Only from the Individual's Perspective We react to the world as we experience and perceive it; that is our reality.

TABLE 7.1
The Major Characteristics of Human Personality According to Rogers (1951)

PRINCIPLE	CLARIFICATION
1. Our worlds are private; reality is phenomenological.	The significant aspects of reality are found in the world of private experience. Our realities are therefore completely individualistic. They can be intuited but not known by others.
2. Behavior can be understood only from the individual's point of view.	Our private experience determines our reality. Because behavior occurs within the context of personal realities, the best way to understand a person's behavior is by attempting to adopt his or her point of view; hence, humanism emphasizes the importance of open communication and empathy.
3. The goal of human existence is self-actualization.	Each of us has a basic tendency to strive toward becoming a complete, healthy, competent individual through a process characterized by self-government, self-regulation, and autonomy.
4. We construct our own selves.	We discover who we are on the basis of direct experiences and beliefs and values that we incorporate into our self-concepts from information provided by people who communicate to us what we are.
5. Behaviors are consistent with notions of self.	In general, we select behaviors that do not contradict who and what we think we are.

What we perceive and feel, labeled the **phenomenal field**, makes up our immediate consciousness. And because this field is defined in terms of the individual's private experience, reality is also private. Therefore, what is real for one individual is not necessarily real for another. A student who likes her teacher, no matter how unbearable that teacher appears to other students, has a likable teacher in her phenomenal field—and her behavior toward that teacher will reflect this reality. This is why it's important for a teacher to understand that students perceive their worlds in different ways. If teachers are to come close to

The world is understood only from the individual's point of view.

constructivist approaches General label for instructional methods that are highly learner-centered and that reflect the belief that meaningful information is constructed by students rather than given to them. Often contrasted with *direct instruction,* constructivist approaches are reflected in discovery learning, cognitive apprenticeship, and humanistic approaches to teaching.

phenomenal field The feelings, perceptions, and awareness that an individual has at any given moment.

understanding their students, they must try to adopt their points of view—as did Arnold Jackson (see the case entitled "Are You Sure It's *His* Problem?"). It is no accident that the teacher who seems to understand students best is often described as empathetic (able to intuit how

CASES FROM THE CLASSROOM

Are You Sure It's His Problem?

THE SITUATION: Arnold Jackson, who has been teaching for 13 years, reflecting on his first year of teaching:

I was only 22 and I had this grade 10 class, and, I'll admit, I was scared. What scared me most was I might have bad discipline, they wouldn't listen to me. So I watched real hard for misbehavior and rebellion because I was determined I'd wipe it out quick.

Well, there was this student, big guy named Randy, a bit older than all the others, and he wasn't doing very well. He'd already failed at least once but I think twice, and he could never answer any questions in class, and I just knew he was going to be trouble.

Which he was. Only maybe the second or third day of English class, and already he was slouched down in his seat, his legs sprawled way out into the aisle. So I straightened him out, just a quick, firm, verbal reprimand—which worked, but I had to do it twice more that class, and again the next day, until, finally, totally exasperated, I just walked down the aisle, put my foot under his outstretched leg, and flung it back under his desk.

At that moment, he looked at me like raw hate, and I knew I'd got me a bad enemy. And from there, it just seemed to get worse, day by day. Every time I looked at him in class, it's like he was doing something else, mostly not paying attention, deliberately not handing in his assignments on time, slouching his feet out in the aisle, and then drawing them back quickly as if he'd just thought of it.

Finally, I talked to Franklin Lohde, the vice principal who was pretty well in charge of discipline in the school. I explained to him how Randy'd been behaving. "He's got a real problem," I concluded. And I'll never forget what Franklin Lohde said:

"Are you sure it's his problem?" he said.

"What?"

"You sure it's his problem—that he's deliberately inattentive and defiant? Or is it maybe your problem?"

That one simple question turned me right around, turned my whole career around for sure. It made me think maybe I should ask, is this really Randy's problem? Is it possible there's a problem only because in my mind I think there is? Is it possible maybe this big kid slouches not because he doesn't have respect but just because he's so big in that desk? The more I thought about it, the more it made sense that maybe Randy didn't deliberately decide not to finish his work, but maybe he just couldn't.

I started to see him, and a lot of my other students, in a completely different way, almost like asking well, what would that feel like or be like if I was them?

others feel). In fact, empathy is one of the most important characteristics of successful Rogerian therapists (Parse, 1998).

The Goal of Human Existence Is Self-Actualization It is neither necessary nor useful to list a variety of needs or drives to account for human behavior, claims Rogers, (1951); we are driven by only one basic, overriding tendency—*self-actualization.*

One way of defining self-actualization is to say that it involves becoming whatever one can become through activities determined by oneself (Maslow, 1970). In other words, to become actualized is to become *actual* or *real*, to develop one's potentialities.

Self-actualization, Rogers explains, is a directional process in two senses: First, it tends toward maturation, increasing competence, survival, reproduction, and so on. These important, motivation-related objectives of human functioning are viewed as tendencies that characterize the overriding process of actualizing—of becoming.

Self-actualization is also directional because it moves toward increasing "self-government, self-regulation, and autonomy." It also moves away from "heteronymous control, or control by external forces" (Rogers, 1951, p. 488). This is one reason for the basic incompatibility between behavior control in a Skinnerian sense and the process of growth in the Rogerian sense.

In summary, Rogers believes that humans have an inner, directing need to develop themselves in the direction of healthy, competent, and creative functioning. This notion is absolutely basic to an understanding of the humanist's view of people as essentially good and forever striving toward a better state.

We Construct Our Own Selves As a result of interacting with the environment, and especially with other people, we develop notions of who and what we are. In other words, we begin to construct notions of "self." The self is a consistent pattern of beliefs we develop about "I" or "me."

Two important sources of information are related to the development of the self. The first is the child's *direct* experiences—experiences of being loved and wanted and feeling good as a result, experiences of being hurt and the consequent realization that the self does not like to be hurt, and experiences of gratification (for example, eating) together with the realization that gratification is pleasant. These direct experiences lead to the development of an awareness of self.

The child also experiences self-related events *indirectly*, often by being told things ("You're real smart, Guy. Good boy"). These experiences contribute too to the development of self-notions. Experiences like this lead to *positive* notions of self. But negative feedback (like poor grades or people snickering when you say something or saying things like "My, my, look at that kid's nose, will you!") can lead to *negative* self-concepts.

Sometimes an individual's direct and indirect experiences are contradictory and lead to conflicting notions of the self. Consider, for example,

"I've been a cow all my life, honey. Don't ask me to change now."

the student whose indirect experiences have led him to believe that he is academically gifted (his mother has often said to him, "You're academically gifted, son") but whose direct experience is that he constantly fails in school. The resolution of this conflict can take several forms. One, of course, involves accepting the direct evidence and concluding that he is not especially brilliant. Another alternative would be for him to accept the indirect information and distort his perception of direct experience. He might, for example, conclude that he is, indeed, quite brilliant but that his teachers don't like him. Or he might look for additional information to resolve the dilemma. Rogers suggests that the seeds for later maladaptive behavior are often found in the early failure to resolve the conflicting pictures of self that emerge from direct experience and what he calls **introjected values**.

Behaviors Are Usually Consistent with Self-Concepts Most ways of behaving that are adopted by the individual are consistent with the concept of self.

---

introjected values Rogers' phrase for values that do not result from direct experience but that are, in a sense, borrowed— sometimes from the reactions of others to the individual, sometimes from observations of how others appear to be, sometimes from the individual's unrealistic fantasies about the self.

One of the most important facts of the human condition, claim the humanists, is that the individual's world is private. How much can even a very sensitive teacher know of this Mexican American child's world?

Consider, for example, the man who thinks of himself as a gifted orator and who has been invited to address the local chapter of the Ear Realignment and Onion Society (EROS). This proposition predicts clearly that, in line with this person's image of self, he will accept the invitation. By the same token, a man who thinks of himself as inhibited and verbally inept would be likely to turn down such an invitation. In both these cases, and indeed in most instances of human behavior, the activity selected is compatible with the self-image.

Consider what happens, however, when the image of self is somewhat distorted—when, for example, the person who believes himself to be a gifted speaker has derived this notion not from direct experience—like the applause following past orations—but from the words of his wise and ancient grandmother: "You shpeak zo vell, Ludwig, you mus be a gud spichmakerrr." In line with his self-image, he accepts the invitation, but as the day approaches, he becomes afraid—not consciously but organically. This individual may suddenly find himself physically ill in a literal sense. How can a sick person be expected to address a large audience of ear realigners and onion lovers? And to refuse to do so when ill is quite congruent with this man's image of self-as-great-orator. In Rogers' words: "The behavior which is adopted is such that it satisfies the organic need, but it takes channels which are consistent with the concept of self" (1951, p. 588). This—the individual's attempt to satisfy a "real" need that is not consistent with the image of self—is assumed to be one of the primary sources of neurotic behavior in humans.

Evaluation of Rogerian Phenomenology

Many important aspects of Rogers' views of behavior seem intuitively correct. It appears obvious that each individual perceives the world in a manner not experienced by anyone else. It also seems obvious that, to understand others, it may be useful to adopt their points of view. However, some aspects of these propositions are not so obvious. In particular, the meanings of terms such as *self-actualization* are not always clear.

Rogers' approach is clearly highly subjective and not very scientific. That is, it is not based on rigorous, replicable research. Nevertheless, its merits for the progress of science may be considerable; even very speculative theorizing can sometimes generate fruitful ideas. This theory has had, and continues to have, tremendous impact on both counseling and teaching (Ryan, Hawkins, & Russell, 1992; Parse, 1998).

The important question now should be not whether this is a correct view of humanity but whether this is a useful way for teachers to look at students. It is.

HUMANISM IN THE CLASSROOM

When Agne, Greenwood, and Miller (1994) looked at differences between teachers who had been selected as Teacher of the Year and in-service teachers, they found that the Teachers of the Year were significantly more humanistic in the ways they interacted with their students. So, for those of you who aspire to be Teacher of the Year, being humanistic may be a good thing. The question is: What does it mean to be a humanistic teacher?

Humanists such as Rogers and Maslow, in line with their basic beliefs, present a strong plea for **student-centered teaching** (see also Combs, 1988, 1990). Student-centered teaching advocates a philosophy of teaching in which students are given a far more important role in curriculum decisions than has traditionally been the case. Such teaching advocates that teachers should be learning facilitators rather than didactic instructors and that, to be successful as learning facilitators, they must be trained to be sensitive, caring, genuine, and empathetic. Phrased another way, humanistic educators are more likely to espouse a constructivist classroom than a direct-instruction classroom.

Not surprisingly, humanistic approaches to education emphasize healthy social and personal development and also de-emphasize rigorous, performance-oriented, test-dominated approaches to subject matter. They strongly advocate providing students with experiences of success rather than failure; their orientation is toward discovery approaches (constructivist) rather than reception learning (direct instruction). The humanistic view of human functioning accepts individuals for who they are, respects their feelings and aspirations, and believes that every person has the right to self-determination. Such a view of students leads naturally to child-centered schools. And the basic premise in these

schools, claim Rogers and Freiberg (1994), is that "if we are genuine, caring, empathic and congruent as teachers, parents, or counselors, we will be fostering the growth and learning capacity of others" (p. iii).

But child-centered schools are not concerned solely with the emotional and personal development of the child—although it sometimes seems that way, partly because their emphasis is on affective growth and partly because this aspect of the humanistic movement has been exaggerated as a reaction against more rigorous approaches. Most humanistic programs, several of which are described next, are responsive to the important requirements of curricula. After all, even the most self-actualized individuals still need to know how to read, write, and name the major capitals of Europe. In fact, becoming self-actualized—that is, becoming all that one can and should be—may well depend on both knowledge of the three Rs and the wealth of cognitive and metacognitive strategies that our new cognitive instructional sciences use to build their teaching programs. Clearly, cognitive concerns can also be part of a thoughtful, humanistic approach to teaching. (See the box entitled "Behavior Control à la Rogers.")

Humanistic Movements in Education

The thinking exemplified in humanistic theory has become part of the so-called **third-force psychology;** the other two forces are behavioristic S–R theory and Freudian theory. In education, third-force psychology represents a movement pervaded by (1) a belief in the uniqueness and importance of the human individual and (2) a strong reaction against overly

---

student-centered teaching Rogers' expression for an approach to teaching based on a philosophy of self-discovered learning. The approach requires that the teacher genuinely care for students as individuals and that students be allowed to determine for themselves what is important in their lives.

---

third-force psychology A general expression for humanistic approaches to psychology such as those exemplified by the work of Carl Rogers and Abraham Maslow. The first two forces are psychoanalysis and behaviorism (S–R psychology).

Behavior Control à la Rogers

As an alternative to Skinner's behavioral technology, Rogers proposes the following five-point model for the control of human behavior (Rogers & Skinner, 1956, pp. 1063–1064):

1. It is possible for us to choose to value humanity as a self-actualizing process of becoming—and also to value creativity and the processes by which we acquire knowledge.

2. Science can help us to discover the conditions that lead to the development of these processes and can provide better ways of achieving this.

3. It is possible for individuals or groups to set conditions for growth without resorting to a great deal of external control or power. Current knowledge suggests that the only authority teachers require is the authority to establish certain qualities of interpersonal relationship.

4. Individuals exposed to these conditions become more responsible, make progress in self-actualization, and become more flexible and more creatively adaptive.

5. Choosing these humanistic values would lead to the beginnings of a social system in which values, knowledge, adaptive skills, and even the concept of science would be continually changing and growing. The emphasis would be upon the human being in the process of becoming.

mechanistic and allegedly dehumanizing approaches to understanding humans.

The humanistic movement in education is represented by a variety of alternative approaches to education that use labels such as "free schools," "open classrooms," "process education," and "community-centered education." The rationale for these methods is based on a genuine concern for the welfare of children—and a firm belief that humanistic approaches are better for their welfare, along with the conviction that current methods of schooling leave much to be desired. Thus, in Dennison's (1969) description of an alternative to traditional schooling, he speaks of the profound beneficial effects of that alternative on the lives of students. He also criticizes (very politely) the "military discipline, the schedules, the punishments and rewards, the standardization" of more conventional approaches (p. 9). His book, however, like many similar books, is not in itself a criticism of existing educational methods but rather an attempt to describe an approach that might be

better: "There is no need to add to the criticism of our public schools," Dennison informs us. "The critique is extensive and can hardly be improved upon" (p. 3).

The concerns and goals of humanistic education and those of more traditional schools are basically compatible. All schools are concerned with the current and future welfare of students; all recognize the worth and the rights of the individual; all pay lip service to such human and humane values as openness, honesty, selflessness, and altruism. But, as we will see shortly, the emphases of humanistic approaches are incompatible with the pressures of overcrowded classrooms, the regimentation and anonymity of bureaucractic educational systems, and the fierce competition for academic success. Rather, humanistic approaches strive for meaningful communication, the exploration of values, and the development of affect and of self. The challenge for the humanistic teacher is to remain true to these ideals in the context of a traditional classroom situation.

Common Emphases of Humanistic Education

Humanistic approaches to education are highly varied, but they share some common emphases. Perhaps the most evident of these is a greater attention to thinking and feeling than to the acquisition of knowledge. In this respect humanism is sometimes quite different from the more traditional approaches.

A second common emphasis of humanistic approaches is on the development of notions of self and individual identity. For example, Borton (1970) presents a highly humanistic, three-phase teaching model designed to identify students' concerns so that students can be *reached* as individuals, *touched* or motivated as human beings, and still *taught* in a systematic fashion compatible with traditional schools. (Labels for these three phases form the title of Borton's book, *Reach, Touch, and Teach.*) Similarly, Purkey and Novak (1996) are also concerned with the developing self-concepts of students. They draw a useful distinction between teacher behaviors that are "inviting" and those that are "disinviting." One of their major premises is that there are more students who are disinvited than disadvantaged. "A disinviting message," Purkey and Novak write, "informs its recipients that they are irresponsible, incapable, and worthless and that they cannot participate in activities of any significance" (p. 10). Disinvitation is often communicated to the child through a teacher's apparent indifference and failure to respond to students as people. A teacher *invites* students by communicating to them (in any of numerous ways) that they are valuable, able, and self-directed and by expecting behaviors and achievements that are compatible with their worth and their self-directedness—in short, by having and communicating highly positive feelings about students. Examples of disinvitations are presented in the box entitled "Disinvited Students."

Humanistic approaches' third major emphasis is on communication. Gordon's (1974)

BEAR MUSINGS

Disinvited Students

Purkey (1984) presents a strong argument for the encouragement of teacher behaviors that *invite* students to see themselves as valuable, responsible, worthwhile, and important people. It would be naive to assume that all teachers have attitudes toward students that lend themselves to inviting behaviors. Listed here is a sample of experiences that are clearly disinviting because they label students as irresponsible, incapable, or worthless—and sometimes all three (from Purkey and Novak, 1996, p. 16–17).

They put me in the dummy class, and it had SPECIAL EDUCATION painted right on the door.

One teacher told me I just wanted to cause trouble all the time.

She told the class we were discipline problems and were not to be trusted.

The teacher put me out in the hall for everyone to laugh at.

My teacher told me I was the worst kid she ever taught.

The teacher said to me in front of the whole class: "I really don't think you're that stupid!"

When the principal hit me with a paddle, he said it was the only language I understood.

She said I was worse than my brother, and I don't even have a brother.

My name is Bill Dill, but the teacher always called me "Dill Pickle" and laughed.

I transferred to a new school after it had started. When I appeared at the teacher's doorway, she said, "Oh, no, not another one!"

> ### TABLE 7.2
> ### Common Emphases of Humanistic Approaches to Education
>
> | EMPHASIS | PRACTICAL IMPLICATION |
> | --- | --- |
> | 1. Affect | School places much greater emphasis on feeling and thinking and less on the acquisition of information. |
> | 2. Self-concept | One of the most important educational goals is the development of positive self-concepts in children. |
> | 3. Communication | Teachers pay particular attention to the development of human relationships and honest interpersonal communication. |
> | 4. Personal values | Schools recognize the importance of personal values and try to facilitate the development of positive values. |

Teacher Effectiveness Training (TET) program illustrates this emphasis. It presents teachers with specific advice on methods of bringing about good teacher–student relationships, and it is based on the notion that teachers should be taught the principles and skills of "effective human relations, honest interpersonal communication, [and] constructive conflict resolution" (p. ix). Research indicates that teachers specifically trained in TET communication methods are better able to listen to students empathically (Percy, 1990). There is evidence as well that TET may contribute to children's moral development (J. M. Rich, 1993).

A final emphasis shared by most humanistic approaches is the recognition and development of personal values. Students are encouraged to know themselves and express themselves, to strive toward feelings of self-identity, and to realize their potential (see Table 7.2).

Common Humanistic Instructional Methods

The four common humanistic emphases—affect, self-development, communication, and values—lend themselves to certain instructional methods more readily than the more traditional emphases on mastery of academic content, good citizenship, and sportsmanship do. Thus, group process approaches, rooted in the **sensitivity group** and **encounter group** movements (sometimes referred to collectively as **growth groups**), are common instructional approaches in humanistic education. In groups, students can be encouraged to express their feelings more openly, to discover and clarify these feelings, to explore interpersonal relationships, and to articulate their personal value systems. Various communication games can enhance the genuineness and openness of interpersonal relationships. Role-playing games also offer a way to explore emotions and human relationships.

Perhaps the most important contribution that humanistic concerns can make to teachers' preparation is in the realm of attitudes rather than methods. Humanistic educators strive toward a true caring attitude, toward open and

---

Teacher Effectiveness Training (TET) Gordon's humanistic training program for teachers. It emphasizes good teacher–learner relationships, honest interpersonal communication, and conflict resolution.

growth group A general label for group process approaches to therapy and sometimes to instruction. These typically involve the use of techniques designed to foster communication, openness, self-discovery, sharing, conflict resolution, and so on, usually in small group settings. Also termed *sensitivity groups* or *encounter groups*.

effective communication, and toward genuineness, empathy, and warmth.

But these are vague terms, and vagueness is not what we need; we need examples and methods. Because no matter how appealing and convincing are the arguments for humanizing the teaching/learning process, if they leave us short of methods and strategies, we may ignore to them.

SPECIFIC HUMANISTIC PROGRAMS IN THE CLASSROOM

Schools and children don't always fit together very well. As a result, the experience of going to school is not a happy and effective one for all children. As Hess and Azuma (1991) note:

> Although learning is a natural process schools are not naturally conducive to learning. Children are compelled to attend; they have little choice in the content of a curriculum whose value may not be apparent; they must share the teacher's time and other resources with peers; classmates differ from one another in ability and experience, requiring many of them to deal with an instructional tempo not suited to their interest or preparation; and they are governed by a set of rules about personal acts such as talking, moving around, and attending to physical needs. In short, schools are not user-friendly (p. 2).

Various cultures react differently to the sometimes poor fit between students and schools. The Japanese culture, claim Hess and Azuma (1991), is most likely to require that students change to conform to the demands of the system. In contrast, North American cultures are more likely to try to make changes in the system to conform to the needs and wishes of students.

In spite of this, most classrooms in North America are what we might term *traditional*—that is, they are very much like the "user-unfriendly" school described by Hess and Azuma. We know what these classrooms are like; most of us have been through them. And most of us, given that we are here in this rarefied academic atmosphere—you there and me here—have not been treated too badly by this thing called traditional education.

But other choices exist and that is what this chapter is all about. In the sections that follow, we look at several alternatives to traditional education: *confluent education*, which attempts to integrate cognition and affect (emotion); *values education* and *values clarification*, which are concerned with the moral development of children; *open education*, which focuses on the affective development of students; and the *learning styles approaches*, as well as *cooperative learning*, both of which are driven by humanism's concerns for the individual, but both also retain more emphasis on academic and cognitive growth.

Confluent Education

Confluent education, a profoundly humanistic reaction *against* traditional education, describes an educational orientation that attempts to integrate (to achieve a flowing together, or *confluence* of) the affective and cognitive aspects of teaching and learning. But because traditional education is so clearly directed toward cognitive matters, confluent education has tended to emphasize the affective aspects of education.

Confluent education is best described in terms of its major emphases and attitudes, rather than in terms of any specific teaching methods. Among the most important of these attitudes are the following (Shapiro, 1998, pp. 11–13):

1. A process orientation: The "what" of learning (that is, the *outcomes* of learning) is seen as far

---

confluent education A highly humanistic approach to education that attempts to integrate the affective and cognitive aspects of learning and teaching; sometimes described as part of the *human potential movement.*

less important than the "how." Students are encouraged to think and talk about how they feel and about the processes by which they learn.

2. Emphasis on self-determination: Autonomy, self-direction, and self-evaluation replace teacher-directed learning and evaluation.

3. Affective bias: Feelings and personal experience are given preference over abstract, objective, impersonal approaches.

4. Encouragement of innovation: Confluent education tends to be antiauthoritarian. It is directed toward change.

5. Personal growth: The emphasis is on the development of each individual, rather than on the mastery of subject matter.

6. Individualism: Confluent education stresses the uniqueness and self-determination of each person.

Notice that each of these emphases is, in effect, a clear reflection of the most important of humanism's concerns. In a nutshell, humanism recognizes and encourages the fullest possible development of human potential. Not surprisingly, confluent education describes itself as an important methodology in the **human potential movement.**

Confluent education began with the writings of George Brown (see, for example, Brown, 1971), and eventually became an integral part of teacher training at several universities (for example, the University of California at Santa Barbara) (Shapiro, 1998). But, notes Shapiro

(1997), given traditional education's emphasis on cognitive matters, confluent education programs have typically been "marginal" programs operating in hostile environments. As a result, relatively few wide-scale confluent education programs are still in existence, although there are several smaller-scale programs. For example, Peloquin (1996) describes a confluent occupational therapy course where visual and literary arts are used to encourage students to examine their thoughts and feelings. Similarly, Shapiro (1995a,b,c) describes how confluent education programs can be used with postgraduate students in education.

Values Education and Values Clarification Programs

When teachers, both in training and in practice, were asked whether they thought values should be taught in schools, a convincing 95 percent of them said, unequivocally, "yes" (Zern, 1997). Yet the systematic teaching of values in schools remains a relatively rare and a highly controversial matter. Many remain convinced that homes (and churches) should impart values—and that schools should teach subject matter. Clearly, humanists—and many others who don't see themselves as humanists—don't agree.

But whether you deliberately teach values in your classes, you will, at the very least, reflect adherence to some fundamental beliefs about right and wrong. And about the most basic of these beliefs, most of us find little disagreement. As Kurtz (1997) phrases it, we agree on the "common moral decencies." These include virtues such as integrity, benevolence, fairness, and trustworthiness. Thus, when Zern (1997) asked teachers what values should be taught in schools, 75 percent or more agreed that responsibility, respect, honesty, caring, trustworthiness, and justice and fairness, should be among the values taught (see Figure 7.1).

---

human potential movement A label sometimes used to describe the combination of approaches in education, therapy, and other helping professions that stem from a humanistic orientation and reflect the conviction that the goal of each of these endeavors should be to foster the fullest development of each individual.

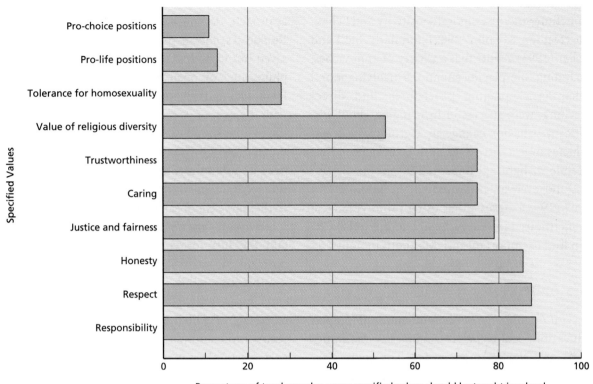

FIGURE 7.1 Percentage of 123 teachers and teachers-in-training who agree that the specified values should be taught in schools. Based on D. Zern (1997). The attitudes of present and future teachers about the teaching of values (in general) and of certain values (in particular). *Journal of Genetic Psychology, 158,* 505–507.

Values education refers to programs deliberately designed to teach values in schools. Such programs are common in many private schools (also termed charter schools) and are often part of religious education programs. **Values clarification programs** are designed not so much to impart values as to encourage students to actively reflect on what they think and believe about specific matters of morality and ethics. The intention is to have students examine their beliefs, assign some *value* to them, and act upon these values. Values education and clarification programs are often tied in with the development of morality, or of what is sometimes termed "character" (see, for example, Colby, James, & Hart, 1998). These programs are also often linked with the curriculum in environmental or health education and reflect attempts to impart ecological values (Fien, 1997).

Various techniques have been successfully used in schools to teach values and morality. For example, simply discussing moral dilemmas and evaluating the ethical implications of behavior

---

values education Instructional programs and strategies designed to teach specific values (notions of right and wrong), thereby promoting good behavior and developing good "character."

values clarification program A program designed to encourage learners to examine their personal beliefs about right and wrong, with a view to improving and clarifying their awareness of their own morality.

sometimes increases moral sensitivity and behavior (Damon & Colby, 1987). Similarly, Stoll and Beller (1993) report that a variety of approaches, including role-playing situations involving moral dilemmas, modeling procedures, and direct teaching, were successful in bringing about significant behavior change in a group of student athletes over a three-year period (evidenced by a decline in fighting, improved classroom behavior, and even an improvement in grades). And Hart (1998) suggests that using prototypes (real or fictitious models of highly moral behavior) can lead to important insights about morality.

The Open Classroom

Several decades ago, a phenomenon called **open education**, or the *open classroom*, became something of a North American fad. The open classroom differs from the traditional classroom in a variety of important ways. First, the principal goals of open education—specifically, individual growth, critical thinking, self-reliance, cooperation, and a commitment to lifelong learning—are not the kinds of goals that are ordinarily sought in traditional classrooms (Eshel & Klein, 1995). Second, in open education, the most important person is the student, not the teacher. And third, the open classroom does not typically adhere to the same curriculum-bound, age-locked, grade-locked system that typifies the traditional school but is far less formal.

The flavor of open education is perhaps best conveyed by Dennison's description of an open classroom. He describes an approach that emphasizes student-centered and intensive but relaxed teacher–pupil contact (made possible in his example by the extremely low teacher–pupil ratio). This approach de-emphasizes schedules—following Rousseau's notion that time is not meant to be saved but to be lost (Dennison, 1969, p. 13). The philosophy of open education, as expressed by Dennison, is that a school should be concerned with the lives of its children rather than with education in a narrow sense, that abolishing conventional classroom routines can lead to important insights about the roles of emotions and other features of the human condition, and that running an elementary school can be a very simple thing once it is removed from "the unworkable centralization and the lust for control that permeates every bureaucratic institution" (p. 9).

It is impossible, in this short section, to fully convey the atmosphere that permeates the type of school of which Dennison speaks. Indeed, it seems futile and perhaps misleading to describe such a school as one that has no administrators, no report cards, no competitive examinations, and extremely modest facilities; where every child is treated with "consideration and justice"; where the unfolding lives of the children are the primary concern. This is an accurate description of the school, but it is only a partial description. As Kohl (1969, p. 15) points out, it is difficult to say exactly what an open classroom is. Similarly, it is difficult to say what freedom is or to draw the line between chaos and student-determined order, between rebelliousness and the legitimate expression of individual rights, between wasting time and the productive use of time for activities outside the curriculum.

Open education is now rare in North America, although elements of it are found in some forms of **distance education**, where student

---

open education A student-centered alternative to traditional education that emphasizes personal growth, independence, and cooperation and is not committed to the curriculum-bound, pass–fail, age-locked, grade-locked system of the traditional school. Also termed *open classroom*.

distance education An educational delivery system that involves little or no face-to-face contact but wherein instructional material is presented at a distance, often using one or more of a combination of computers, electronic networking facilities, telephone conferencing, facsimile transmitters, radio, television, film, videocassette recordings, or other communication media.

interests are influential in determining course content, delivery, evaluation, and pacing (Norris & Pyke, 1992; Guri-Rozenblit, 1993). Interestingly, however, of the many studies that evaluated open education and compared it with more traditional approaches most found that open education was usually effective in reaching its most important goals. For example, students exposed to open classrooms have been found to be more independent (Eshel & Grosberger, 1993) and more creative (Houtz, 1990). However, these gains were usually at the expense of academic achievement as defined by more traditional measures. And, given a zeitgeist[4] that appears to emphasize academic achievement, open learning systems are not very popular at present (Rothenberg, 1989).

Learning Styles

When discussing traditional education, Dunn and Griggs claim: "The system works well for some, but not for others" (1988, p. 1). Why? Because, Dunn and Griggs explain, some students don't learn at all well in the morning but perform very well in the afternoon. Some work well in bright, noisy environments; others do their best work in quiet places with subdued lighting. Some excel with highly structured, teacher-directed instructional methods; others do far better in informal, unstructured environments. Some students need and want to be told what to do and when and how to do it; others perform best when working on their own initiative. In short, each student has a personal and unique **learning style**. Some of these styles are evident in clearly different preferences with respect to variables like approaches to studying, preferences for specific instructional methods, and personality characteristics (Sadler-Smith, 1997).

Unfortunately, traditional schools don't often take individual learning styles into account. As a result, they reward students whose personal styles happen to match that for which the traditional school was designed—and, by the same token, they unwittingly punish those whose rhythms are sounded on a different drum. Students whose biological rhythms make it difficult to concentrate in the morning must nevertheless come to school and sit through the same offerings as everyone else. Those who respond best to visual stimuli—or to tactile stimulation—are forced to listen just as much as those who are more responsive to auditory stimuli. Children with shorter attention spans are compelled to sit as long as those who are not so easily distracted.

This is not fair, argue Dunn, Dunn, and Perrin (1994); it is not an optimal learning situation. Schools, they insist, must take into account these fundamentally important differences in learning styles. But how?

Adapting Schools to Styles First, schools need to develop a profile of each student's learning style. Several instruments are available for this purpose. Among the most widely used is Renzulli and Smith's (1978) **Learning Styles Inventory (LSI)**. It is designed to help teachers customize their instructional procedures to match individual learners' attitudes toward such common instructional procedures as lectures, simulations,

---

learning style A unique and important learner variable manifested in differences in biological rhythms (morning versus evening people), perceptual strengths (visual versus auditory learners), sociological preference (whole-group versus small-group instruction), attention span (long or short), and a wealth of personality variables (dependence or independence, for example).

Learning Styles Inventory (LSI) An instrument used to assess student learning styles. Identifies individual students' preferences for different approaches to teaching and learning, and attempts to assess the relative effectiveness of different learning environments and approaches with specific students.

---

[4] **PPC:** Is the bear German? Why does he use such a big word? Maybe he should explain it.

Author: Okay. *Zeitgeist* means something like spirit of the times. As for the bear's ancestry—well, the less said the better.

TABLE 7.3
One Classification of Learners and Possible Instructional Strategies

TYPE OF LEARNER	CHARACTERISTICS	PREFERENCES	INSTRUCTIONAL APPROACHES
Activists	Impetuous; impulsive;open-minded; flexible	Variety; excitement; involvement; activity	Group processes; activity-based learning
Reflectors	Cautious; careful; deliberate; judicious	Evidence; time to think and reflect; opportunity to deliberate	Private study; reading assignments; self-paced learning
Theorists	Logical and rational; disciplined; inquisitive; objective	Rationality; coherence; careful explanation; models and theories	Computer-based instruction; conceptual models; scientific approaches
Pragmatists	Practical and down to earth; applied	Eager to try things out; new ideas and methods; practical solutions and applications	Supervised experience; hands-on experience; personal coaching

Source: Based on Reay (1994).

discussions, projects, games, drills, recitations, peer teaching, independent study, and programmed instruction.

Another approach, described by Reay (1994), classifies learners in terms of whether they are *activists*, *reflectors*, *theorists*, or *pragmatists*. Characteristics associated with each of these types of learners, and the best instructional approaches for each, are described in Table 7.3.

Identifying individual learning styles is only the beginning; dramatic changes are required in schools and in teachers' behavior if schools are to be truly responsive to students' individual differences. Dunn and Griggs (1988) visited ten schools where attention to learning styles had become the determining factor in educational offerings. Although there were many differences among these schools, they had several things in common. A description of these similarities is, in a sense, an idealized description of a humanistic school.

The Learning Styles–Driven School This idealized school gives learners an almost staggering assortment of options. It allows children to work alone on soft carpets or to work in groups at conference tables. It provides highly structured teacher-presented lessons, peer teaching, programmed instruction, computer-assisted instruction, and self-learning. It rotates presentation of core subjects so that they are offered at all times of the day, including early in the morning and late in the afternoon. It allows students to take examinations and work on projects at times that are compatible with their biological rhythms.

The idealized humanistic, learning styles–driven school is identifiable not only by its attention to differences among individual learners but also by its values and objectives. Far more than the traditional school, it stresses students' involvement at all stages of learning, and it emphasizes problem solving and creativity. It truly reflects a *constructivist* orientation.

Finally, this idealized school's most common instructional technique, especially for presenting new material, is a highly participatory, cooperative, small-group approach that is sometimes called **circles of knowledge**. This approach is described in the next section, which discusses cooperative learning.

This brief description of the translation of learning styles information into classroom practice cannot do justice to the complexity of the topic. There is no single, best program that we can describe simply and accurately; programs continue to change and develop. As we noted, most require profound changes in schools and teachers, and the changes required must be continual. They involve experimentation in and modification and clarification of programs, as well as refocusing of objectives and efforts, and on and on.

Evaluation of Learning Styles Approaches We can only tentatively evaluate the effectiveness of this approach. Dunn and Griggs (1988) report that in the ten learning styles–driven schools they visited, learners performed exceptionally well on a variety of measures of academic performance. Some had won national awards, and many had succeeded in passing subjects they had previously failed. And most said they liked—no, loved—school.

In general, notes Guild (1994), the research indicates that students of all learning styles can succeed academically. In fact, high and low achievers can't readily be discriminated on the basis of their learning styles (Burns, Johnson, & Gable, 1998). But most students tend to do better when they are allowed to use the strengths of their personal learning styles (for example,

Dunn & Stevenson, 1997). Students also do better when their learning styles are most similar to that of their teachers (Onwuegbuzie & Daley, 1998). Interestingly, the most common learning style of teachers is a *reflective* style (cautious, deliberate, judicious) (Lawrence & Veronica, 1997). Not surprisingly, then, the most successful students are often those who are most reflective. But the real lesson is simply that good teaching requires far more than one single instructional approach.

Unfortunately, as Rayner and Riding (1997) note, the current lists of learning styles, and the instruments used to measure them, are unorganized, lengthy, and include a large range of habits, personality characteristics, and abilities. For example, in a short booklet, Reiff (1992) describes several dozen learning styles that have been identified in the literature. And, more recently, Sternberg (1997b) suggests another classification scheme that includes three *functions*, four *forms*, and six *levels*, *scopes* or *leanings* of what he calls *thinking styles*. There is, as Rayner and Riding (1997) argue, a pressing need for integration.

Research has not yet established whether any of these classifications is more useful than another. Nor has it clearly shown which specific instructional approaches are best with which styles and under what circumstances this might be so. Learning styles, argue Thompson and Crutchlow (1993), are an important factor for teachers to consider, but they are only one factor, and their impact may well have been overrated in the enthusiasm that often accompanies new educational movements.

Perhaps when the bear is a very, very old bear, history will look back and say, "Hey, that learning styles stuff at the turn of the millennium was another one of those educational fads, like open schools and teaching machines and confluent education." Or maybe, just maybe, history's judgment will be: "Hey, just before the millennium—that's when it all started."

---

circles of knowledge A generic term sometimes used to describe a variety of small-group learning approaches. These approaches stress face-to-face interaction, peer help, and rewards for cooperative, group activities rather than for individual activity. Such approaches are highly cooperative rather than competitive or individualistic.

Cooperative Learning

According to Johnson and Johnson (1994), teachers have three basic choices: "In every classroom, no matter what the subject area," they write, "teachers may structure lessons so that students:

1. engage in a win–lose struggle to see who is best (competitive)

2. work independently on their own learning goals at their own pace and in their own space to achieve a preset criterion of excellence (individualistic)

3. work cooperatively in small groups, ensuring that all members master the assigned material (cooperative)" (p. 3).

These authors claim that, unfortunately, most students see schools as competitive because that is how grades are typically assigned. Not everyone can do well; to achieve at the highest level, students must compete with, and out-achieve, the others. And when schools are not competitive, they are most often individualistic; that is, students are urged to work toward the attainment of their own individual goals—without help, proudly, and independently! Only rarely are school experiences truly cooperative, where, according to Cohen (1994), students work "together in a group small enough that everyone can participate on a collective task that has been clearly assigned . . . [and where] students are expected to carry out their task without direct and immediate supervision of the teacher" (p. 3).

Another way of distinguishing among these three alternatives is in terms of rewards (Bossert, 1988). In a **cooperative learning** situation (also termed **collaborative learning**), the individual is rewarded in proportion to others in the group; in a **competitive learning** situation, individual rewards are inversely related to those others

receive; and in an **individualistic learning** situation, there is no relationship among individual rewards.

Occasionally, some schools present a few cooperative activities. Only rarely do schools and teachers make cooperative learning a fundamental part of their instruction. Schools that do, claim Schmuck and Schmuck (1997), are humanistic schools because cooperative learning is essentially a humanistic approach to education. It combines the cognitive and affective aspects of learning, and it emphasizes participation and active engagement, both of which are humanistic concerns. But perhaps more than other explicitly humanistic approaches, cooperative learning also stresses academic achievement and clearly defined curricular goals. In most schools that use cooperative learning methods, students do not have the unstructured freedom that they might be given in an open classroom, nor does the system cater to their personal strengths and preferences as it might in a school organized to respond to individual learning styles.

Why Cooperative Learning? Why is it important to learn to cooperate? Advocates of this approach present a variety of reasons. Among the most compelling is the nagging suspicion that it is our only hope for salvation—that if we

---

cooperative learning An instructional method where students work together in small groups so that each member of the group can participate in a clearly assigned, collective task. Also termed *collaborative learning.*

competitive learning One of the most common instructional approaches in North America. It involves students working against each other to see who is best. In competitive learning, student rewards are inversely related to the performance of others.

individualistic learning A common instructional approach where students work independently and at their own pace. Student rewards are independent of the performance of other students.

Humanistic classrooms are a highly student-centered alternative to more formal traditional approaches. They are often marked by low pupil-teacher ratios, a cooperative rather than a competitive orientation, and a more relaxed atmosphere.

do not learn to cooperate, we and our planet are doomed.

There are other reasons why we must learn to cooperate—if survival doesn't seem sufficiently important, or if our doom seems too distant, or if we simply prefer not to think about it. Cooperation, Bossert (1988) tells us, is the cornerstone of modern democracy. Nations cannot be governed without cooperation among leaders; cooperation is essential for political and economic survival.

At a more immediate level, teaching cooperation in the schools might do much to reduce students' dependence on teachers and to decrease divisiveness and prejudice among students. For example, the evidence from many different studies suggest very loudly that acceptance of—even respect for—those of other races and creeds, of lesser ability, or with a variety of handicaps can improve dramatically in cooperative learning situations (for example, Jacques, Wilton, & Townsend, 1998; Kamps et al., 1998; Iannaccone & Hwang, 1998).

Cooperative learning, Johnson and Johnson (1994) claim, may resolve two important crises: declining academic performance and pervasive feelings of alienation, isolation, purposelessness, and social unease among students. Hence, another reason for using cooperative learning is simply that it works. In Snow and Swanson's words, "The evidence clearly shows its effectiveness in achieving cognitive goals, but the methods also promote more positive attitudes toward school, improved student self-esteem, and improved relations among different types of students" (1992, p. 612).

Finally, students prefer cooperative approaches. When researchers asked students from three different cultures (Germany, Canada, and Iran) which approach to learning they most preferred, they chose cooperative learning (Huber et al., 1992).

What Is Cooperative Learning? When Antil and associates (1998) asked 85 teachers whether they used cooperative learning in their classrooms, an amazing 95 percent said "Yes, indeed!" And when this 95 percent were interviewed individually, each claimed to use cooperative learning approaches every single day.

But, claim Antil and associates, the vast majority of these teachers were not actually using cooperative learning approaches at all. As we see shortly, cooperative learning involves more than simply having students work together to achieve a common goal.

Many cooperative group activities have been developed and used in schools. They have a variety of names but are sometimes included under the generic labels "circles of knowledge" or "circles of learning":

Learning Together One of the most widely used cooperative instructional techniques is **learning together**, developed by Johnson and Johnson (see Johnson et al., 1984). In learning together, groups of four to six students are given a lesson or worksheet that they must learn or complete together. Members must help each other to ensure that everyone learns the lesson or completes the assignment. Members of each group are also encouraged to help other groups once they have completed the assignment. Praise is given for cooperating and finishing the assignment. In this approach, there is no competition among groups.

Learning together emphasizes four things. These are, in effect, the common characteristics of all true cooperative learning techniques: (1) face-to-face interaction (students are in groups of four to six); (2) positive interdependence (students work together to achieve a common goal); (3) individual accountability (students must later demonstrate that each has mastered and understands the material); and (4) interpersonal and small-group skills (students are taught how to work together and how to evaluate the functioning of their groups). These characteristics of cooperative learning are summarized in Table 7.4.

Where Antil and associates' (1998) teachers fell short of using true cooperative learning was with respect to individual accountability. Most of these teachers had developed their own "group" approaches, but few of them had worked out how to make each individual in the group *individually responsible* for achieving the group's goals. Research and theory clearly emphasize that two things are essential for cooperative learning to work: (1) the incentive to cooperate and (2) individual accountability. In most applications of cooperative learning, group recognition and interteam competition provide the incentive. And individual accountability exists to the extent that group or team performance depends on the performance of each individual in the group.

Student Teams–Achievement Divisions (STAD) Student teams–achievement divisions (STAD) is one of several forms of student "team learn-

---

learning together A cooperative instructional technique where groups of four to six students work together on a jointly assigned task using small-group interaction skills. In learning together, each member of the group is individually responsible for mastering the material.

student teams–achievement divisions (STAD) A cooperative instructional technique where students are assigned to heterogeneous groups of four to six (including high- and low-ability students and different ethnic groups) to work on certain tasks. Afterward, they are given quizzes (to be answered individually, without cooperation) and rewarded by *team* on the basis of the group's performance on the quizzes.

TABLE 7.4
Common Features of Cooperative Learning

▲ Cooperative learning requires face-to-face interaction among group members—usually four to six students.

▲ The relationship among group members can be described as one of positive interdependence; that is, members must cooperate in allocating resources, assigning roles, and dividing labor to achieve their goals.

▲ Cooperative learning assigns individual responsibility for sharing, cooperating, and learning. Various techniques are used to ensure that goals and rewards are contingent on the performance and contribution of *all* group members.

▲ Cooperative learning involves the use of interpersonal and small group skills, such as those involved in taking turns, facilitating, collaborating, and so on.

ing"; individual groups are teams that compete against one another (Slavin, 1995). In STAD, students are divided into heterogeneous teams of four to six students. Ideally, each team includes children of high and low abilities, of different ethnic backgrounds, and of both sexes. The instructional technique typically involves five steps:

1. *Presentation.* New material is typically presented to the class using conventional approaches like lectures, discussions, and videos.

2. *Teamwork.* Groups are given material to study and worksheets to complete. They can work on these individually, in pairs, or in larger groups. They are encouraged to help each other and to make sure that everybody understands and knows the material; the emphasis is on the performance of the team.

3. *Quizzes.* At the end of the study period, which typically lasts one week, students write quizzes based on that week's material—individually and without helping each other.

4. *Individual improvement scores.* Team scores are then calculated. And although recognition is given to teams that obtain the highest total scores, the winning teams are those whose indi-

viduals improved the most. In this way, low-achieving students can contribute as much to the team's total score as the more able students (and sometimes even more).

5. *Team recognition.* Teams are then rewarded, perhaps with certificates, tokens, prizes, and praise. Team scores may also be used as a factor for determining individual grades.

STAD produces dramatic changes in the classroom, claims Slavin: "[Students] begin to see learning activities as social instead of isolated, fun instead of boring, under their own control instead of the teacher's" (1983, p. 7). Also, he claims, they now help each other learn instead of resenting those who learn more easily or making fun of those who learn with more difficulty.

Teams–Games–Tournaments (TGT) Teams–games–tournaments (TGT) begin in exactly the same way as STAD, with the same teams, instructional sessions, and cooperative learning sequence. The difference is that at the end students engage in tournaments rather than take quizzes. In these

---

teams–games–tournaments (TGT) A cooperative instructional technique identical to student teams–achievement divisions (STAD) except that instead of being given quizzes at the end, students play tournaments of competitive games that center around content-relevant questions.

tournaments, team members are not assigned as a group but as individuals, to a table. Each table consists of three competitors of approximately equal ability (selected by instructors). Games occur simultaneously at all tables and involve drawing numbered cards, trying to answer questions corresponding to the numbers on the cards, and challenging incorrect answers. Players retain their cards when they answer (or challenge) correctly and lose them for incorrect challenges. At the end of the game (or period), points are assigned according to the number of cards in each player's possession, and total tournament points are computed for each team.

More complete rules for TGT can be found in Slavin (1995). Materials for STAD and TGT are available for a wide range of subjects in elementary and secondary schools from the Johns Hopkins Team Learning Project, Center for Social Organization School, Johns Hopkins University, 3505 North Charles St., Baltimore, MD 21218 (410-338-8249).

Jigsaw In **jigsaw**, developed by Aronson and colleagues (1978), the material to be learned is divided into separate units. Individual members of the group are then given separate, different, parts of the whole to learn, and they must teach what they have learned to other members of the group. No one member is given sufficient information to solve the problem at hand or complete the assignment in question, but when all the information is put together—voilà![5] The jigsaw is complete.

In a modification of the original jigsaw, labeled "jigsaw II," students are given the same narrative material to read rather than parts of the whole, a procedure that eliminates the need to prepare a lot of different material. Individual students are then assigned the responsibility for mastering various topics. They are encouraged to discuss these with members of other teams who have been assigned the same topics and then return to their own teams to teach their teammates what they have learned. Hence, the central feature of jigsaw is the interdependence of team members; performing well depends on how well individual members learn and teach their topics. As in STAD, teams are given quizzes and rewarded on the basis of team performance, taking into account individual improvement.

Group Investigation Group investigation, described by Sharan and Sharan (1992), is a cooperative technique that combines academic scholarship and inquiry with the principles of cooperation. Using this approach, students in a class select an area for study, typically a problem that lends itself to investigation. The subject area is then divided into subtopics, and the class divides itself into small groups of investigators on the basis of shared interest in a topic. Groups then formulate a plan for their investigation and assign responsibilities. Members can now work individually, in pairs, or as larger groups. Having completed their inquiry—perhaps over a period of some weeks—group members meet and share the fruits of their investigations. They decide, as well, how to present their integrated information to other members of the class. Finally, all groups

---

jigsaw A cooperative instructional technique. Individual members of groups are given the responsiblity for mastering different aspects of specific tasks and teaching them to other members of their group. The key feature of jigsaw is that successful performance depends on the various contributions of each member.

---

[5] *PPC:* Ha ha! A bilingual bear!
The bear: But of course!

---

group investigation A collaborative instructional technique where students identify topics and related sources of information, form groups on the basis of shared interests, assign responsibility for collecting material, gather and study relevant material alone and in groups, prepare group reports, and present these to the class.

meet for the final sharing of information. Throughout the process, teachers are involved in guiding students, helping them with both the academic skills required for successful inquiry and the social skills involved in group processes.

Implementing Cooperative Learning The techniques just described are only a few of many that have been developed and evaluated. For those interested in other approaches, the Suggested Readings section at the end of this chapter lists important sources of information.

Unlike the learning styles approach, cooperative learning does not require a major restructuring of the school day or a reordering of curriculum offerings. The learning styles approach attempts to cater to individual differences in learning styles and learning preferences, whereas cooperative group methods typically include all students simultaneously. In fact, one advantage of cooperative approaches is that they foster cooperation among students with varying strengths and weaknesses and perhaps those of different ethnic backgrounds, ages, and sexes.

Cooperative learning techniques are most often introduced as an adjunct to regular classroom offerings. In a typical situation, they might be used for 60 or 90 minutes per day. However, the most vocal advocates of this approach recommend that as much as 70 percent of class time involve cooperative activities, with 20 percent devoted to individualistic approaches and only 10 percent to competitive activities (Johnson & Johnson, 1994).

Although cooperative approaches normally make up only a small part of the total curriculum, their implementation usually requires careful preparation of materials. Depending on the specific approach used, the teacher will need to prepare worksheets, questions, resource materials, and so on, all carefully structured to foster cooperation while promoting learning.

Positive Evaluation of Cooperative Learning How well do these cooperative techniques work? One direct comparison of competitive and cooperative instructional approaches is provided by a meta-analysis of 46 studies (Qin, Johnson, & Johnson, 1995). Taken together, these studies indicate that members of cooperative teams typically outperform those in more competitive situations, regardless of whether achievement is measured in terms of verbal or nonverbal performance and whether the problems used to assess achievement are highly structured and clear or more poorly defined.

Many studies have corroborated these general findings. For example, Klingner, Vaughn, & Schumm (1998) found that fourth graders made greater gains in reading comprehension of social studies and in content knowledge when working in groups than when exposed to direct instruction. Interestingly, an analysis of student conversations during group activities revealed that 65 percent of the discourse related directly to the academic aspects of their activities, 25 percent dealt with procedures relating to their cooperative activities, and 8 percent involved interstudent feedback. An amazingly trivial 2 percent was off-task.

Stevens and Slavin (1995) also report markedly positive findings in an entire elementary school that switched to a cooperative instructional philosophy during the two-year span of the research—in marked contrast to the majority of studies which have typically been short term and involved only one or two teachers. In this school, cooperative learning approaches were used extensively in all academic subjects. Also, disabled students were mainstreamed throughout the school and were closely involved in cooperative learning. Teachers were encouraged to use collaborative approaches in their instructional planning as well—for example, peer coaching and direct collaboration with parents and the principal. After the second year

How Should I Teach?

The school system that hires you (and can also fire you) will almost certainly operate within a relatively well-defined set of regulations governing the conduct of teachers in classrooms—prescribed curricula, reporting and testing procedures, disciplinary actions, and so on. Yet, in the final analysis, you will deter-mine your own approach to teaching, and you will develop your own personal style of interacting with students.

No one is likely to force you to violate personal conviction. So if you firmly believe in the right of all children to be treated as human beings and to be allowed to develop so as to enhance their human qualities, you might be frustrated by the system (or by your interpretation of that system).

Many humanistic alternatives work even within the most traditional school contexts. If you want to know more about these, you would be well advised to explore some of the suggested readings at the end of this chapter.

of this program, both the academically handicapped and the nonhandicapped students achieved at significantly higher levels in reading vocabulary, reading comprehension, language expression, math computation, and math application. Furthermore, the gifted students also seemed to benefit significantly, outperforming their peers in noncooperative programs.

Vygotsky's (1978) theory suggests another reason that cooperative learning is effective and important. Learning, he claims, is highly dependent on social interaction. To a large extent, it depends on interactions with others who are better informed, and the results of learning are manifested in social interaction as well. Furthermore, learning—and all higher mental processes—depend on language. One of the great contributions of cooperative group learning is that it fosters the development and exercise of language skills.

Some Cautions: Cooperative Learning Doesn't Cure All Ills Cooperative learning, it seems, can be highly effective for imparting academic content and strategies and also seems to have beneficial effects on the social development and interpersonal relationships of students. Does this mean that all teachers and schools should now become mostly cooperative? Perhaps not. (See box entitled "How Should I Teach?")

Dividing classes into groups may not always be the most effective way to teach. In fact, on occasion, and for some students, it doesn't work. Nor is it appropriate for all subjects and all lessons, note Roy and Hoch (1994). It's possible for students to work *in* groups but not *as* groups. Students working in groups but not as groups can easily waste time talking about irrelevant matters or develop procedures wherein some group members dominate and others are ignored. As Blumenfeld and associates phrase it, "When practiced in an uninformed manner, it [cooperative learning] can stigmatize low achievers, exacerbate status differences, and create dysfunctional interactions among students" (1996, p. 37). What can happen, notes Bossert (1988), is that low-achieving students are sometimes embarrassed by their performance and ashamed that they lowered the group's score. As a result, they may become progressively more reluctant to participate in cooperative activities as their motivation and self-esteem deteriorate. The long-term effects of this situation might be lower achievement for these students—and perhaps lower achievement for their groups as well. However, the use of performance improvement as the basis for scores, as is done with STAD and TGT, can do much to counter this problem.

Bossert (1988) also cautions that those who advocate cooperative techniques as the dominant feature of classroom activity may be overlooking the possibility that cooperative learning is effective precisely because it presents a clear contrast to conventional classroom procedures (among other reasons). The shifts in attention and procedures required of students serve to increase concentration, to motivate students, and ultimately to enhance performance. But if all or even most classroom activity were cooperative, these shifts might not occur, and performance might not improve so dramatically—if at all.

Finally, Bossert (1988) argues that, even though it is important for children to learn to cooperate with one another, it is also important for them to learn competitive and individualistic skills.

It is worth noting, as well, that certain situations and subjects don't lend themselves particularly well to cooperative, group approaches. For example, expert contributions (sometimes in the form of guest speakers) may be far more efficient and effective as didactic presentations. Also, some students' individual preferences—in other words, their learning styles—favor individual or competitive rather than cooperative approaches.

SOME REACTIONS TO HUMANISTIC EDUCATION

To the extent that humanistic education represents concern for the individual lives and self-concepts of students and for the healthiest and happiest development of human potential, it is beyond reproach; all teachers must be humanistic.

However, humanistic education too often appears to deal with vague qualities and speculative conclusions. Advocates of approaches such as values clarification and open education have perhaps been too free with their use of imprecise terms and concepts such as *authentic, open, real, genuine, fully functioning,* and *meaningful.* How

do you distinguish between an authentic experience and one that is inauthentic? between a genuine teacher and an impostor? between a fully functioning student and one who is only three-quarters functioning? Although these terms are vague, they seem to represent good things and are therefore highly appealing. Unfortunately, the things they represent cannot be easily defined or measured, and as a consequence, the evidence upon which advocates of humanistic reforms base their arguments is not always convincing.

Perhaps the most telling criticism of general humanistic approaches to teaching is that most are highly dependent upon the personal qualities and skills of individual teachers. More conventional approaches to classroom practice are, in this respect, much more "teacher proof."

These criticisms are not entirely fair, however. They apply primarily to global approaches to humanistic education, such as those represented by "open" (or what have sometimes been called "free") schools. As we saw earlier, evidence from research suggests that although students who emerge from these schools appear to be more creative and more cooperative and have better self-concepts, these gains typically come at the expense of academic achievement. A large-scale evaluation in the United States found that these students performed more poorly than comparison groups on almost all achievement measures (Kennedy, 1978) (although few of these measures tap creative thinking skills, the ability to reason logically, or other important personality characteristics). It is not surprising that most of these schools have now closed. We should note, however, that various forms of nongraded schools (without age or grade placement or graded report cards) can have positive effects on student achievement (Gutiérrez & Slavin, 1992). But these schools are somewhat different from open schools because they typically present a structured curriculum in an ungraded, no-fail environment.

These criticisms of humanistic education—vagueness, too much attention to affective growth, and disregard of both standard curricula and cognitive development—are irrelevant with respect to two expressions of humanistic concerns detailed in this chapter: learning styles–oriented schools and cooperative learning. As we saw, both approaches can lead to superior academic achievement. Interestingly, among the important techniques of learning styles schools are the group methods that define cooperative learning.

One reason that various humanistic, student-centered approaches to instruction have been criticized, notes Waterhouse (1991), is that instructors have often been guilty of what he terms "technical mistakes" and incorrect assumptions about humanistic education. Chief among these are the belief that:

- students should immediately be granted complete autonomy
- the best instructional plans are always tailored for specific individuals (rather than for entire classes)
- student-centered instruction requires special material
- humanistic education should be highly permissive
- traditional instruction must be abandoned to make way for humanistic approaches

Keep in mind that humanism is not an educational technique, although it manifests itself most clearly in specific techniques. In effect, humanism is an educational philosophy characterized by the sorts of admirable attitudes toward students and toward educational goals that should be characteristic of all teachers. These attitudes, as mentioned earlier, are not subject to the same criticism that has been applied so generously to specific humanistic approaches to education. In the end, you may not need to copy the models or take the advice presented by the more visible humanistic educators. What *is* important is that you genuinely care about students as people.

CONSTRUCTIVISM, HUMANISM, AND THE BEST TEACHING PRACTICES

As we have pointed out several times, something of a revolution may be occurring in education. But because there are no guns and no bombs involved in this revolution—only a few sometimes half-hearted speeches, books, and occasional articles—we can't be certain that it's actually a revolution. In the end, it may turn out to have been only an attempted revolution by a minority of malcontents. History, as is her habit, will let us know later.

But if there is a revolution, it is marching toward what today's jargon labels *constructivist approaches* to education. These include a variety of learner-centered instructional techniques; among these are the humanistic approaches described in this chapter (as well as discovery learning, cognitive apprenticeship, and other approaches discussed elsewhere). Constructivist approaches are often contrasted with the more teacher-centered approaches that define *direct instruction.*

You, as a teacher, don't have to—and probably should not—adopt one or the other of these positions to the exclusion of the other as though they were religions and your salvation depended on making the right choice. Your salvation probably depends on other things. And what you need to do as a teacher is to use the combination of methods that is best suited for your purposes with your students.

But educational research does appear to be unified in many of its current recommendations, note Daniels and Bizar (1998); it might be wise to pay attention to some of these. What research

recommends, these authors explain, are classrooms that, among other things, are *more*

- ▲ student-centered
- ▲ experiential
- ▲ reflective
- ▲ authentic
- ▲ social
- ▲ collaborative
- ▲ democratic
- ▲ cognitive
- ▲ developmental
- ▲ challenging

This research also recommends that in schools there should be *less*

- ▲ whole-class direct instruction
- ▲ student inactivity (listening, receiving information)
- ▲ rewarding of silence in the classroom
- ▲ mindless worksheet activities
- ▲ textbook reading[6]
- ▲ rote memorization
- ▲ stress on competition and grades
- ▲ reliance on standardized tests (Daniels & Bizar, 1998, pp. 2–3)

The first list, things that we are told schools should be *more of*, describes many of the recommendations of constructivistic approaches—and humanistically oriented educators. And the second list describes much of what we associate with traditional education and direct instruction.

Perhaps it is a revolution after all.[7]

---

[6] **PPC:** Hey, wouldn't the bear say that it depends on the book.
Author: Absolutely.

[7] **PPC:** So if it is a revolution, will the bear take sides?
Author: The bear intends to be on the right side. Which he hopes will be the victorious side. Quoting from his great mentor, Yogi Berra, when he speaks of the revolution, he says, "I intend to be a big clog in their machine." Or he might just hibernate through the whole thing.

MAIN POINTS

1. Humanistic psychology is concerned with the uniqueness, worth, and dignity of the self. It presents an ideological conflict with the more mechanistic orientation of other approaches and objects to the schools' emphasis on academic achievement and its neglect of affective growth.

2. Carl Rogers' theory is phenomenological (the phenomenal world is the environment as it is perceived by one individual), humanistic (concerned with the individual, with self-actualization), and student centered. His position is opposed to Skinner's expressed concern with control through the application of the principles of operant learning. Rogers advocates student-centered schools.

3. Rogers believes that an individual's real world is private (phenomenological), the purpose of behavior is to achieve self-actualization (development of maximum potential), self-actualization is related to healthy and creative functioning, and the development of the "self" results from interactions with the world (direct experience) and from values about "me" that are borrowed from the actions of other people (indirect experience).

4. The major emphases of humanistic approaches are greater attention to thinking and feeling than to the acquisition of knowledge, the development of self, communication, the clarification of values, openness, honesty, and self-determination. Group process and cooperative approaches to education are most compatible with these emphases.

5. Confluent education describes an attempt to integrate the affective and the cognitive. It is process oriented, emphasizes self-determination, encourages innovation, and pays close attention to affect, personal growth, and individualism.

6. Values education refers to the direct teaching of values in schools. Values clarification relates to programs that encourage students to examine their beliefs and actions in light of their values and ultimately to act in accordance with them.

7. Open education is most concerned with the affective growth of students—with critical thinking, self-reliance, and commitment to learning. It is student centered rather than teacher centered, typically ungraded, and emphasizes personal growth rather than measurable academic achievement. Research suggests that graduates of open schools may be more creative and cooperative and have better self-concepts—but they usually have lower scores by traditional academic measures.

8. Learning styles are individual preferences and strengths as they relate to the best conditions for learning (for example, morning versus evening; visual, auditory, or kinesthetic; individual versus group; structured versus unstructured; and so on). Learning styles–driven schools attempt to match instructional methods, curriculum offerings, scheduling, and other aspects of instruction to each learner's personal style. Students in learning styles schools appear to do very well on standard academic measures.

9. Cooperative learning involves small-group techniques structured so that learners are rewarded for the group's results but are nevertheless individually accountable for learning and for helping other members of the group to learn. It is characterized by face-to-face interaction, positive interdependence,

individual responsibility, and the use of interpersonal and small-group skills.

10. Some techniques for cooperative learning include learning together (pure cooperation, common goal, no intergroup competition); student teams–achievement divisions (STAD) (groups are teams that compete against each other on the basis of performance improvement); teams–games–tournaments (TGT) (STADlike procedure but with three-member head-to-head competitions following learning); jigsaw (each group member given only part of the information; interaction with whole required to solve a problem or learn a lesson); and group investigation (whole class investigates single inquiry problem by dividing in groups for investigation and coming together to integrate and share).

11. Evidence suggests that cooperative learning techniques lead to superior academic achievement, high motivation, and the enhancement of social skills. These positive effects may be partly due to the greater curriculum structure required for cooperative learning and to the contrast these approaches present to the traditional classroom. They may also be due to the language and social skills that they foster. These techniques are most effective when two conditions are met: Students are given incentive to cooperate, and learners are individually accountable for their learning outcomes.

12. General humanistic approaches to education are often greatly dependent upon individual teachers' qualities and sometimes use vague and speculative terms. Humanism in education is less vulnerable to criticism as an attitude or philosophy than as a technique—and as an attitude it is perhaps more valuable to teachers. In this sense, all teachers should be humanistic.

13. There may be a revolution going on in education.

Applied Questions

▲ Compare and contrast the educational implications of humanism and behaviorism.
▲ Can you describe the principal beliefs and attitudes of a prototypical humanistic educator?
▲ List some characteristics that might differentiate an open classroom from a more conventional classroom.

▲ What is your preferred learning style? How would you outline the educational approach(es) most compatible with it?
▲ Could you prepare a lesson that incorporates one or more specific cooperative learning techniques.

Internet Activity

Use InfoTrac College Edition or other World Wide Web sources to research and summarize current attitudes and practices with respect to cooperative learning in the classroom. Write up your findings. (See the inside back cover of this text for suggestions about where to begin.) Sample search terms: cooperative learning

Study Terms

circles of knowledge 257

client-centered therapy 241

competitive learning 258

confluent education 251

constructivistic approaches 243

cooperative learning 258

counseling 241

directive therapy 241

distance education 254

existentialism 239

group investigation 262

growth group 250

human potential movement 252

humanism 241

humanistic psychology 238

individualistic learning 258

introjected values 245

jigsaw 262

learning style 255

Learning Styles Inventory (LSI) 255

learning together 260

open education 254

phenomenal field 243

phenomenology 241

self-actualization 241

student teams–achievement division (STAD) 260

student-centered teaching 247

Teacher Effectiveness Training (TET) 250

teams–games–tournament (TGT) 261

third-force psychology 247

values clarification program 253

values education 253

Suggested Readings

The first of the two following books is an important revision of Carl Rogers' classic book. It describes his theory and also describes classrooms that have placed his ideas into practice. It includes many vignettes and interviews with teachers and many useful suggestions for teaching and developing discipline. The second book is the completion of a collection of Rogers' own articles that he had begun to put together with Kirschenbaum and Henderson, but did not complete before he died in 1987:

Rogers, C. R., & Freiberg, H. J. (1994). *Freedom to learn* (4th ed.). New York: Merrill.

Rogers, C. R. (Edited by H. Kirschenbaum & V. L. Henderson). (1989). *The Carl Rogers reader*. Boston, MA: Houghton Mifflin.

For those interested in confluent education—the attempted integration of affect and cognition in the school—Shapiro's book is an excellent, historical account of this manifestation of the *human potential movement*:

Shapiro, S. B. (1998). *The place of confluent education in the human potential movement*. Lanham, MD: University Press of America.

The first of the following books is a provocative collection of articles on moral development, values education, and "character." The second presents a convincing argument for teaching what the author terms "humanistic virtues."

Colby, A., James, J. B., & Hart, D. (Eds.) (1998). *Competence and character through life*. Chicago, Ill: University of Chicago Press.

Kurtz, P. (1997). *The courage to become: The virtues of humanism*. Westport, Ct: Praeger/Greenwood.

The learning styles approach to education is well described in the following two books. The first is a detailed and highly practical description of the learning styles approach; the second is a brief booklet explaining a large variety of approaches for identifying student learning styles and suggesting ways for teachers to accommodate them.

Dunn, R., Dunn, K., & Perrin, J. (1994). *Teaching young children through their individual learning styles: Practical approaches for grades K–2.* Boston: Allyn & Bacon.

Reiff, J. C. (1992). Learning styles. Washington, D.C.: National Education Association.

The book by Johnson and Johnson is an excellent description of cooperative learning and of several schools that use this approach. Slavin's book describes specific approaches to cooperative learning, including sample exercises and classroom examples. The collection edited by Sharan contains many articles written by people who have developed and applied cooperative instructional approaches.

Johnson, D. W., & Johnson, R. T. (1994). *Learning together and alone: Cooperative, competitive, and individualistic learning* (4th ed.). Boston: Allyn & Bacon.

Slavin, R. E. (1995). *Cooperative learning: Theory, research, and practice* (2nd ed.). Boston: Allyn & Bacon.

Sharan, S. (ed.). (1994). *Handbook of cooperative learning methods.* Westport, Conn.: Greenwood Press.

The book by Daniels and Bizar is a clear and highly useful description of what are essentially constructivist classroom practices, most of which also reflect humanistic concerns:

Daniels, H., & Bizar, M. (1998). *Methods that matter: Six structures for best practice classrooms.* York, Maine: Stenhouse Publishers.

The Laplanders venerated the bear and called it the Dog of God. The Norwegians called it "the old man with the fur cloak" (Engel, 1976).

PART FOUR

We are all worms,
but I do believe I
am a glowworm.
Winston Churchill

Diversity and Teaching

We are all worms . . .

It's only a metaphor, not a literal description, I said in response to my grandmother's horror at my choice of this part-opening quotation. She professes to love all things great and small, but she doesn't much care for worms. Or rats.

The point is that even among worms, there is incredible diversity of shape, color, and size: segmented worms, rag worms, earthworms, sandworms, leeches, arrowworms, spoon worms, pinworms, jaw worms, beard worms. . . . There are even worms that glow like Sir Winston Churchill. Perhaps in the world of worms, these are special worms, exceptional worms.

The three chapters of Part Four look at human diversity—the shapes and sizes in which we come, not just in terms of intellect and personality, but also in terms of culture and background. Thus, in Chapter 8 we examine two of the most important characteristics that differentiate students from each other: creativity and intelligence. In Chapter 9 we suggest how teachers can enhance these qualities; we also examine other human characteristics that sometimes make us dramatically different from one another. And in Chapter 10 we look at multiculturalism and how instruction can be adapted and individualized for children from different backgrounds.

Since when was
genius found
respectable?

Elizabeth Barrett Browning,
Aurora Leigh

Intelligence and Creativity

PREVIEW

Intelligence and creativity, those nebulous and ill-defined characteristics, are among the most prized of our "possessions"—and perhaps among the most useful as well. In this chapter we examine the meanings of these terms, the forces that shape the qualities they represent, and some of the methods that have been devised to assess them. In this chapter we also look at the relationship between creativity and intelligence. Is it possible to be creative but stupid? to be intelligent but totally devoid of creative talent?

FOCUS QUESTIONS

▲ What is intelligence, as defined by Das, Sternberg, and Gardner?

▲ How are group and individual intelligence tests alike? different?

▲ What are the most common myths concerning intelligence?

▲ How are family and educational variables related to intelligence?

▲ What is creativity?

▲ What is the relationship between creativity and intelligence?

When I was in tenth grade, Sister Sainte Mélanie, our teacher, announced that someone would be sent from the Shell Lake School Unit office to give us an intelligence test. "You'll have to do very well on this test," she warned. "Or else."

"Or else what?" asked Barney, who never did well on any test. As my grandpa put it (wit rather than kindness was his main strength), "The only test Barney'll ever do good on is his urine test . . . but only if he stays up all night to study for it." (Maybe my grandpa's wit was not that much of a strength either.)

"Well," explained the good sister, "those who don't do well on this test, it means they got a poor IQ. And those that got a poor IQ are going to fail lots of things in life, they'll never get very far, maybe they'll just have to stay right here in Victoire and milk cows and fork hay for someone else until they die."

"And those that got good IQs," she continued, "they're the ones who'll get to go places and do things and make money and buy cows and be important. That's the way it is with IQ."

So for about a week we worried about this IQ test until finally the day came and the guy arrived with a box of tests and another one of pencils and he laid a pencil and a test, face down don't-you-dare-touch-it-until-I-give-you-the-signal, one on each desk and then, bang! he smashed his fist down on the stopclock to start it and yelled, "Go!"

and we turned our papers over and started to read questions and write answers like mad until, bang! he smashed down again on the clock and yelled "Stop!" which we did.

Then the guy placed the intelligence tests in a box, very carefully, and took them away with him. For a long time after that we wondered what our IQs were: Would he write us a letter and let us know? But he didn't do that. Instead, he stuffed all our IQs inside an envelope and brought them to school one day, and he and Sister Sainte Mélanie huddled over them, speaking in hushed whispers while we labored over our desk assignments. At recess they called Barney in and asked him what chores were his favorite. "I told them feeding the pigs," he explained to us, "and they said, 'With your IQ that kind of job would be just about perfect'."

Later they called in Priest, which is what we called Louis Boutin on account of how he was an altar boy and he'd been studying Latin since fourth grade. "What'd they tell you?" we asked Priest. "Told me I could be a brain doctor," he bragged, "or a science wizard."

Me, they never called me in so I never did find out for sure whether I had a high or a low IQ—because I never actually believed Horseface when he said he'd gotten into the school and copied out all the IQ numbers for everybody from where they were kept in Sister Sainte Mélanie's desk. But some of those who had big numbers thought he was telling the truth.

SOME VIEWS AND THEORIES OF INTELLIGENCE

Are big IQ numbers a blessing? Are small ones a curse that dooms us forever to do low and menial things and think base and shallow thoughts? What is this thing called IQ? What do IQ numbers mean anyway?

We in the Western world, notes Lund (1994), think that IQ is an extremely important concept. To a large extent, its importance represents an

CASES FROM THE CLASSROOM

Hiroki's About Average, Like Everybody Else

THE PLACE: Komatsudani Preschool, east side of Tokyo

THE SITUATION: Fukui-sensei, the preschool teacher, has been putting the children through their paces while a group of North American observers watches and takes notes. When the class ends for the day, the observers meet with Fukui-sensei.

Observer 1: That little boy, what's his name, the one with the yellow shirt, over on that side . . .
Fukui-sensei: That's Hiroki.

Observer 1: Yes, Hiroki. How intelligent he is. Compared to the others, I mean.
Observer 2: Yes, superintelligent . . .
Fukui-sensei: No, no. Hiroki's intelligence is about average, the same as everybody else's.
Observer 1: But he seems so gifted.
Observer 2: Yeah, he always finished his work before all the others. And then he sang those wonderful songs so well to entertain the others.
Fukui-sensei: But surely you don't think speed is the same thing as intelligence. And his entertaining the other children is a reflection not so much of intelligence as it is of his great need for attention.

Source: Based in part on Tobin, Wu, & Davidson, 1989, p. 24.

outgrowth of our preoccupation with the individual rather than with the group. IQ, we think, is a measure of one of the most important differences among individuals. One reason we consider IQ so important is that we naively believe it to be a mysterious quality of which each of us has only a fixed amount—no more. And we think, too, that those who have the most are the fortunate ones who will succeed at just about anything they try and those who have the least are doomed to sadness and failure.

As we see later in this chapter, these are just two of the myths that cloud our understanding of intelligence and measured IQ. Our belief in these myths explains our surprise that Priest did not become a brain surgeon or a scientist, that instead he became a drunk and panhandled for his living until a train finally ran over him. That Barney founded an oil company and is making tons of money also seems surprising—and says little for my grandfather's wisdom.

Is measured IQ of no consequence? Or is it sometimes simply measured badly? These are some of the questions we address in this chapter.

Western and Eastern Views

Not all cultures attach the same significance to intelligence. As an example, consider the case entitled "Hiroki's About Average, Like Everybody Else." Note how the teacher, Fukui-sensei, perceives and responds to individual talents—or, more precisely, how she fails to perceive individual differences. This culturally linked tendency might, in fact, be one of the most important differences between Japanese and North American schools.

In contrast, North American teachers and parents are alert and highly responsive to individual differences. In fact, most school jurisdictions allocate much of their resources to identifying individual strengths and weaknesses and responding to them. And of all the various measures of individual talent and capability, the one to which we attribute the greatest significance is clearly intelligence. Unfortunately, it is also one of the most global, the most poorly defined, and the most misunderstood of human characteristics.

Wagner and Sternberg (1984) suggest that there are basically three different views of intelligence. They label the first the "psychometric view." Historically, this has been the most common approach to understanding intelligence. **Psychometrics** refers to the measurement of psychological functions; hence, the psychometric view of intelligence is based on a measurement approach.

The second view is Piaget's. This perspective sees intelligence as an active process involving progressive adaptation through the interplay of assimilation and accommodation. The results of intelligent activity are manifested in cognitive structure. The principal characteristics of cognitive structure change with age; these changes are the essential features of Piaget's developmental theory.

The third view of intelligence is the information processing view. Like Piaget's approach, it is more qualitative than quantitative. That is, it seeks to describe the important characteristics of intelligence in terms of processes rather than to measure its products.

Some Definitions of Intelligence

There are a tremendous variety of definitions of intelligence. One of the earliest and most widely cited is Boring's (1923) who claimed that "intelligence is what the tests test" (p. 35). This definition is not entirely tongue-in-cheek. It is both an admission that intelligence is a difficult concept to define and an assertion that intelligence tests are useful if the scores they provide are related to success on tasks we believe require intelligence. Whatever these tests measure can then be called "intelligence," even if its exact nature is unknown. But, argues Gallagher

(1994), this definition is not especially productive or useful compared with more recent definitions that look more specifically at the actual processes involved in intelligent behavior.

A second important definition is Wechsler's (1958); he originated one of the better known and still widely used intelligence tests (the Wechsler tests). Intelligence, said Wechsler, is "the global and aggregate capacity of an individual to think rationally, to act purposefully, and to deal effectively with his [and, presumably, *her*] environment" (p. 7). This definition views intelligence as a matter of clear thinking, purposeful activity, and effective interaction with the environment. Wechsler also sees intelligence as a "global" capacity that underlies other abilities. This global capacity is often called "general intelligence" (commonly abbreviated *g*). This is an important contrast with other views that see intelligence not as a single underlying ability but instead as consisting of a variety of separate abilities or factors. Guilford and Gardner, whose work is reviewed later in this chapter, also suggest that it's useful to view intelligence as consisting of separate abilities.

Hebb (1966) offers a third definition, which refers to two different aspects of intelligence: "Intelligence A: The innate potential for cognitive development." . . . "Intelligence B: A general or average level of development of ability to perceive, to learn, to solve problems, to think, to adapt" (Hebb, 1966, p. 332). This definition makes an important distinction between intelligent behavior as it is currently manifested (on intelligence tests, for example) and the *potential* for further development. As Vygotsky (1986) points out, people are born with different potentials for development (Hebb's "Intelligence A"). However, conventional measures of intelligence

---

psychometrics Refers to the measurement of psychological functions and characteristics.

g The abbreviation for general intelligence—a basic intellectual capability sometimes assumed to underlie all manifestations of intelligence.

assess "Intelligence B"—current level of development—rather than Intelligence A. Inferences about potential are then based on measures of current performance. In contrast, Vygotsky's approach to measuring intelligence, as well as Feuerstein's (1980), gives test subjects hints and suggestions in an effort to arrive at a better estimate of potential performance. This approach to measuring intelligence is called **dynamic assessment** because it recognizes and attempts to assess the ability to change and learn (Kirschenbaum, 1998).

Another important view of intelligence is Cattell's (1971). He makes a distinction between two kinds of capabilities: those that seem to underlie much of our intelligent behavior and those that are essentially nonverbal and relatively unaffected by culture or experience—termed **fluid abilities**. Measures of general reasoning, memory, attention span, and analysis of figures reflect fluid abilities. And although these fluid abilities are less affected by culture and schooling, various programs designed to teach learning/thinking strategies can have a measurable effect on them. So, too, does general schooling, which is clearly associated with gains or losses in measured intelligence (Lohman, 1993). Interestingly, these abilities are also among the most likely to be negatively affected by age. It seems that as neurological functioning deteriorates, so too do fluid abilities (Boone, 1995).

In contrast with fluid abilities is a grouping of intellectual abilities which are primarily verbal and highly influenced by culture, experience, and education. These **crystallized abilities** are reflected in vocabulary tests, tests of general information, and arithmetic skills. Not surprisingly, performance on crystallized measures tends to increase with age, sometimes into very old age (Horn & Donaldson, 1980).

Sternberg (1997a) presents a simple and intuitively appealing definition of intelligence. Intelligence, he claims, consists of the mental abilities necessary for adapting to the environment and the abilities involved in selecting and shaping the environment to make adaptation possible. In this view, the processes that underlie intelligent behavior are common to all such behaviors. But manifestations of intelligence will be different depending on the context. Hiding one's scent by walking in a stream in a jungle permeated by people-eating beasts is clearly an intelligent, highly adaptive behavior. But if I were to try to walk in the Saskatchewan River on my way to work—to hide my scent, of course, I'd explain to the uniformed people who would soon appear—it's not likely that my behavior would be judged intelligent. Bizarre, perhaps, but far from intelligent. Especially now when it's below zero every day.

A Synthesis How, then, should we define intelligence? Is it what the tests test? a global and aggregate sort of thing? a two-sided thing involving potential as well as actual abilities? a different two-sided thing involving relatively pure capabilities and capabilities that are highly affected by experience? The capacity to adapt and to shape the environment? Or should we use a combination of all these definitions?

Way back in 1921, when experts were asked to define intelligence, their definitions typically

---

dynamic assessment Psychological assessment that attempts to measure the individual's ability to change (that is, to learn). May take the form of tests that gauge the extent to which testees profit from opportunities to learn new material.

fluid abilities Cattell's term for intellectual abilities that seem to underlie much of our intelligent behavior but are not highly affected by experience (for example, general reasoning, attention span, and memory for numbers). Fluid abilities are more likely to decline in old age.

---

crystallized abilities Cattell's term for intellectual abilities that are highly dependent on experience (verbal and numerical abilities, for example). These abilities do not appear to decline significantly with advancing age.

expressed the belief that intelligence is reflected in the ability to learn and to adapt to the environment. When another group of experts were asked the same question 65 years later, they responded in much the same way, except that many now added a third dimension to their definition: **metacognition** (the individual's awareness of and ability to monitor and control intellectual activity) (Sternberg & Kaufman, 1998).

In spite of this apparent agreement, the debate over whether intelligent behavior is undergirded by a basic general capacity (g) is still unresolved. Some theorists, such as Jensen (1998), argue that g is basic to all intelligent behavior and that, furthermore, it is strongly genetically based. As a result, claims Jensen, attempts to increase basic intelligence are largely a waste of time. The issue is highly controversial. Views such as Jensen's lead directly to the conclusion that differences in measured IQ that might be observed among various ethnic and racial groups reflect one group's superior genetic background—and, conversely, another's inferior inheritance.

Many psychologists and educators argue that we should abandon the search for this elusive, almost immeasurable thing called general intelligence (or g). "If I were a young psychologist," says Das (1992), "I wouldn't waste my life looking for g . . ." (p. 137). Trying to rank people on a single scale of merit like general intelligence fails to take into consideration the tremendous variation of interests, skills, and capabilities of different individuals, but it is also politically dangerous. It leads too easily to the conclusion that such and such a race is intellectually inferior, especially if we assume that intelligence is genetically determined—as do Jensen (1998) and Rushton (1988).[1]

Instead, says Das, we must look at three aspects of intelligence: the processes and components of intelligent behavior, the individual's

---

metacognition Knowledge about knowing. As we grow and learn, we develop notions of ourselves as learners. Accordingly, we develop strategies to recognize our limitations and allow us to monitor our progress and take advantage of our efforts.

---

[1] **PPC:** Perhaps the author should point out how controversial and inflammatory this issue is. I think the bear should be careful to divorce himself from statements such as those of Jensen and Rushton.

Author: This is a controversial and inflammatory issue, as illustrated later in this chapter (see, for example, the box entitled "Experience and Intelligence: a Debate"). Even a dog-meat rebel kind of a bear would never align himself on *that* side. No way.

competence in relation to the person's culture and age, and the possibility of improving competence through training and experience.

Das' PASS Theory of Intelligence

Das' description of the processes and components of intelligent behavior takes the form of an information processing theory of intelligence (Das, Naglieri, & Kirby, 1994; Das, Kar, & Parrila, 1996). Simplified, the theory recognizes three separate units involved in intellectual functioning. The *first*, basic to all mental processes, is simply attention and arousal. Without the proper level of arousal of the brain, and without attention, the individual would be largely unresponsive to the environment.

The *second* unit involved in intelligence, says Das, is actual cognitive processing—the processes by which the individual recognizes, organizes, interprets, or otherwise responds to stimulation. Cognitive processing involves two distinct types of processes: **Simultaneous processing** occurs when at least some of the elements of a situation can be responded to at the same time (are simultaneously "surveyable," in the authors' terms). As an example, a child's recognition of a geometric figure involves primarily simultaneous scanning because the recognition depends on interrelationships among the elements, and these interrelationships can be perceived immediately (or simultaneously). In contrast, **successive processing** involves the sequential processing of information. For example, solving a complex problem in mathematics may require successive processing if an ordered series of subordinate tasks must be sequentially accomplished to reach the final solution. Similarly, most motor tasks (such as writing or pitching a baseball, for example) involve successive processing.

The *third* unit in the Das model of intelligence is **planning**—processes by which the individual forms plans, puts them into effect, and evaluates their effectiveness. Planning corresponds to metacognitive strategies—the strategies that allow an individual to control cognitive activity, to monitor and evaluate it, and to modify it as necessary.

To summarize, the three units of intelligent functioning described by Das and associates (Das, Mishra, & Pool, 1995) are planning, attention, and successive and simultaneous processing: hence the acronym **PASS**. Not only does this model provide a useful cognitive processing view of intelligence, but there are also indications that it might be especially useful for suggesting ways of remedying cognitive deficits in some children with learning problems. In the **PREP program** (PASS remedial program) developed by Das and associates (Das, Mishra, & Pool, 1995), children are first assessed for deficits in simultaneous or successive processing using the Naglieri and Das (1997)

---

successive processing Cognitive processing where elements of a stimulus situation need to be responded to sequentially—as in solving some logical problems or executing motor tasks. This is an important element in the PASS model of intelligence.

planning In the Das model of intelligence, this is the intentional or conscious aspect; in other terms, metacognitive strategies.

PASS The Das model of intellectual functioning, based on a three-unit model of information processing: attending (involving arousal and paying attention); processing (successive or simultaneous processing); and planning (metacognitive components, that is, involved in monitoring and controlling cognitive activity).

PREP program A cognitive strategies training program based on the PASS model of intellectual functioning. It seeks to identify specific deficiencies and problems in cognitive processing and to remedy them by providing learners with tasks designed to develop processing skills.

---

simultaneous processing One of four major components of the PASS model of intelligence. Involves cognitive processing wherein important elements of the stimulus situation are reacted to simultaneously—as in perceptual recognition, for example.

One widely accepted Western view of intelligence maintains that intelligence is evident in the ability to adapt and to solve problems—sometimes very practical problems like: Where do these big round things go and in what order? When psychologists speak of intelligence they might also mean an innate, largely genetic capacity; some of the characteristics of this are evident in an individual's performance on an intelligence test.

cognitive assessment system. The children are then given a series of eight to ten tasks designed specifically to provide strategies to remedy deficits. These tasks typically involve procedures related to cognitive processes such as rehearsing, categorizing, predicting, and monitoring performance. In one study using PREP, a group of 51 children who had been experiencing reading problems showed significant improve-

ment following the training (Das, Mishra, & Pool, 1995).

Sternberg's Successful Intelligence

Instead of paying attention to traditional notions of intelligence, argues Sternberg (1996a; 1998b), we should focus on people who are successful in adapting to the world. These people are often successful not only because they learn well, but also because they are skilled at selecting and shaping their environments. What they have is **successful intelligence**—as opposed to measured IQ (or *psychometric intelligence*). In Sternberg's words, intelligence is the "purposive selection and shaping of and adaptation to real-world environments relevant to one's life" (1984a, p. 312). One important feature of this definition is that it emphasizes the individual's control over the environment. In effect, it says that intelligent individuals exercise control over their environments by changing and molding significant aspects of them and also by selecting them in the first place. Thus, it would be quite stupid for someone who is tone deaf to select a career in music or for someone who suffers from severe vertigo to buy a home high on a cliff.

Successful intelligence requires establishing a balance among selecting environments, shaping them, and adapting to them. It requires people to be able to assess their strengths and weakness. Those who are *successfully intelligent* capitalize on their strengths. They might also overcome or remedy weaknesses. Or, very often, they will simply select—or shape—the environment so that weaknesses are not called into play. A successfully intelligent worker who correctly knows that she has remarkable marketing skills

---

cognitive assessment system Naglieri and Das' test of intellectual functioning designed to identify cognitive deficits in challenged learners. It provides measures for each of the processes described by the PASS model of intellectual functioning.

successful intelligence Sternberg's view that intelligence involves a balance among selecting and shaping environments and adaptation to achieve personal goals and those of society.

selects an occupation that requires these skills, or perhaps *changes* aspects of her environment to maximize use of these skills.

A Triarchic Theory of Successful Intelligence
Successful intelligence, Sternberg (1996a) explains, requires *analytical* abilities. These are essential for sorting out and evaluating options, for monitoring failure and success, and for setting up strategies. Analytical abilities involve judging, evaluating, contrasting, comparing, analyzing.

Successful intelligence also requires *creative* abilities. These allow the individual to generate options, to generate ideas, and to try new ways of selecting and shaping the environment and of adapting to it. Creative abilities are evident in activities such as discovering, imagining, inventing, and supposing.

Finally, successful intelligence requires *practical* abilities. These allow people to carry out their options, to put into practice the behaviors and skills that are involved in selecting, shaping, and adapting to environments. Practical abilities, notes Sternberg (1995), often requires the use of **tacit knowledge**—knowledge that is implicit rather than explicit, that cannot easily be put into words. Recall from Chapter 5 that *nondeclarative memory* is another label used to refer to tacit memories.

These three components of successful intelligence make up what Sternberg labels the **triarchic theory of successful intelligence.** This theory has important implications for measuring intelligence. It suggests that conventional measures of intelligence might not be as useful as we had thought. As we see later in this chapter,

for example, intelligence tests seldom measure either creative or practical abilities. Thus, they might provide a very misleading picture of this thing called successful intelligence. (See Figure 8.1).

This triarchic view of intelligence also has important instructional implications. "Should we teach to strengths rather than weakness?" Sternberg asks. "No," he answers. "We should teach both to strengths and weaknesses" (1998b, p. 3). What teachers should do, he suggests, is teach for the development of analytical, creative, and practical skills, as well as for memory. He provides numerous examples of how this might be done. For example, in mathematics:

Memory: How much is 9×6?

Analytical: If $3x + 9 = 30$, what is *x*?

Creative: Write a test problem measuring understanding of factoring.

Practical: How might trigonometry be used in the construction of a bridge? (Sternberg, 1998b, p. 5)

One advantage of Sternberg's triarchic view of intelligence is that it highlights the importance

---

tacit knowledge Nondeclarative knowledge. Knowledge that cannot be easily or completely verbalized but that is implicit (such as how to ride a bicycle).

triarchic theory of successful intelligence Sternberg's model of successful intelligence as involving analytical, creative, and practical abilities.

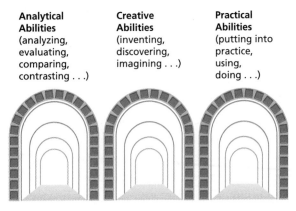

Successful Intelligence: a balance among selecting and shaping the environment and adapting to it to achieve social and personal goals

| **Analytical Abilities** (analyzing, evaluating, comparing, contrasting . . .) | **Creative Abilities** (inventing, discovering, imagining . . .) | **Practical Abilities** (putting into practice, using, doing . . .) |

FIGURE 8.1 The three arches of Sternberg's triarchic view of successful intelligence

of the individual's success in coping with the ordinary demands of life in the social and physical context; that is, this view removes intelligence from the realm of the abstract and theoretical and brings it to a concrete, more easily understood level. But this view also has several disadvantages: First, it is too inclusive. Because all adaptive behaviors are intelligent, almost all behaviors are potentially intelligent (even if they are perhaps somewhat stupid in one context, they may be adaptive in another context). Second, this model does not adequately describe the processes and structures that underlie intelligence; instead, it describes intelligence in terms of the characteristics and effects of behavior.

Gardner's Multiple Intelligences

Sternberg's model of successful intelligence and Das' PASS model are especially useful for teachers for one principal reason: They emphasize that intelligence is an activity—an information processing activity. In Sternberg's words, "abilities are a form of developing expertise" (1998c, p. 11). This view presents a sharp contrast to earlier views that tended to view intelligence as a mysterious quality or characteristic that some people were lucky enough to have a great deal of; other less fortunate people had to get by with much less. The cognitive processing view suggests that intelligence is a little like a box of tools that we use to play the game of cognition: We may not all have the same tools in our kits, but we can certainly improve how we use them, and we can learn a great deal from how others use their tools.

From a teacher's point of view, it's also important to recognize that intelligence involves different cognitive processes and that extreme competence and talent can be manifested in some but not necessarily all areas of human functioning. This underlines the need to encourage the development of competencies in areas

where an individual might be especially gifted and to provide support and assistance in other areas.

Gardner (1983) suggests that we have not one but seven (or perhaps even ten) largely unrelated kinds of intelligence. This **theory of multiple intelligences** describes competence in seven distinct areas—that is, it describes seven kinds of intelligence: logical-mathematical, linguistic, musical, spatial, bodily kinesthetic, interpersonal, and intrapersonal. As noted, Gardner has also begun to explore the possibility that we might have three additional types of intelligence: naturalist, spiritual, and existential, but he admits that the evidence for the existence of spiritual and existential intelligence is still sketchy (Gardner, 1998). (see Table 8.1).

Attempts to assess each of these seven (or more) capabilities encounter problems, note Gardner and Hatch (1989). First, most of our experience in measuring intelligence involves mathematical, linguistic, and logical tasks because in Western cultures, we assume that these sorts of tasks are most closely related to intelligent behavior. But the Gardner view of multiple intelligence requires the development of a range of new tasks to tap previously neglected competencies such as bodily kinesthetic, intrapersonal, interpersonal, naturalist, and perhaps spiritualist and existential.

Second, it now seems clear that intelligence cannot easily be separated from culture and background. As a result, assessing these multiple intelligences requires taking into consideration the extent to which social background influences a child's competence, interest, and even willingness in the testing situation: "The goal of detect-

---

theory of multiple intelligences Gardner's belief that human intelligence consists of seven distinct and largely unrelated areas of talent or capability: logical-mathematical, linguistic, musical, spatial, bodily kinesthetic, interpersonal, and intrapersonal.

TABLE 8.1
Gardner's Seven Intelligences

INTELLIGENCE	POSSIBLE OCCUPATION	CORE COMPONENTS
Logical-mathematical	Scientist Mathematician	Sensitivity to and capacity to discern logical or numerical patterns; ability to handle long chains of reasoning
Linguistic	Poet Journalist	Sensitivity to the sounds, rhythms, and meanings of words; sensitivity to the different functions of language
Musical	Composer Violinist	Abilities to produce and appreciate rhythm, pitch, and timbre; appreciation of the forms of musical expressiveness
Spatial	Navigator Sculptor	Capacities to perceive the visual-spatial world accurately and to manipulate the mental representations that result
Bodily kinesthetic	Dancer Athlete	Abilities to control one's body movements and to handle objects skillfully
Interpersonal	Therapist Salesperson	Capacities to discern and respond appropriately to the moods, temperaments, motivations, and desires of other people
Intrapersonal	Poet Writer	Access to one's own feelings and the ability to discriminate among them and draw upon them to guide behavior; knowledge of one's own strengths, weaknesses, desires, and intelligences
Naturalist	Biologist Evolutionary theorist	Ability to detect patterns and organization in nature
Spiritual	Preacher Monk	A concern with the spiritual, with origins, and with the afterlife
Existential	Philosopher Theologian	Interest in the purpose and meaning of existence

Note: The last three intelligences are recent additions; the last two are based on incomplete and uncertain evidence and are not yet clearly distinguishable.

Source: Based in part on Gardner & Hatch (1989). "Multiple Intelligences Go to School: Educational Implications of the Theory of Multiple Intelligences." *Educational Researcher*, 18(8): 4–10; and Gardner, H. (1998). Are there additional intelligences? The case for naturalist, spiritual, and existential intelligences, in J. Kane (Ed.), *Education, information, and transformation.* Englewood Cliffs, NJ: Prentice-Hall.

ing distinctive human strengths, and using them as a basis for engagement and learning may prove to be worthwhile . . ." conclude Gardner and Hatch, (1989, p. 9).

Gardner (1993) argues that schools need to pay far more attention to what and how they teach. And, in fact, the theory of multiple intelligences has led to the development of several school programs (see, for example, Krechevsky & Seidel, 1998). As Sternberg and Kaufman (1998) note, however, many of these programs are only loosely based on this theory, and the majority have not been properly evaluated. Theories such as this are really too broad to be easily applied in instructional practice, explains Klein (1997).

☐ MEASURING INTELLIGENCE

Current approaches to intelligence have two things in common: They stress processes more than products, and they recognize the diversity of skills and capabilities that compose intelligence. In spite of this, however, the *psychometric*, or measurement, approach to intelligence is still the most widely used. This is because of the close relationship between performance in schools (and elsewhere) and measures of intelligence. As a result, intelligence tests are mainly used for prediction. In a sense, an intelligence test is simply a prediction of whether an individual will do well on tasks that require intelligence. And, as we see later, tests like the Wechsler are very powerful predictors.

From an instructional point of view, intelligence is an important concept, both because it relates to school achievement and because it can sometimes require teachers to modify their instructional strategies. And from a practical point of view, teachers will most often obtain evidence of intelligence from the actual performance of their students and from more formal measures of intelligence.

The Concept of Correlation

Good teachers are sometimes remarkably good at estimating the IQs of their students with-out measuring them—and so are mothers, report Delgado-Hachey and Miller (1993). The **correlation** between teachers' estimates and actual measures is on the order of .55 (Follman, 1991). What does that mean?

Correlation is a frequently used term that is not always clearly understood. Two or more **variables** (properties that can vary) correlate if there is some correspondence between them. Size of shoe correlates with size of sock, income correlates with standard of living, size of house correlates with number of windows, and drunkenness correlates with alcohol consumption. These are all examples of **positive correlation**: As one variable increases, so does its correlate. The inverse relationship, labeled **negative correlation**,

means that as one variable increases, the other decreases. Correlations between number of wild animals and human populations, amount of pollutants in the water and fish populations, and sobriety and alcohol consumption are all generally negative.

The measure of correlation (called an *index* or *coefficient*) most often used ranges in value from −1.00 to +1.00. (The symbol used for a correlation coefficient is usually *r*.) Each extreme (plus or minus 1) indicates perfect correlation, whereas zero indicates complete lack of relatedness (see Figure 8.2). A correlation of .55, which Follman (1991) found between IQ scores and teachers' estimates of intelligence, means that there is a relatively high probability that if a teacher estimates a student's IQ as being high (or low), testing will reveal that it is indeed high (or low).

We should not make an inference of causality solely on the basis of correlation. Even though any two variables that vary together are, by definition, correlated, variation in one does not necessarily *cause* the other to vary. It's true, for example, that there is a high positive correlation between the number of liquor outlets in urban areas and the number of churches in those same areas. However, some people would prefer to think that one does not cause the other (see box entitled "Intelligence and Size of Brain").

The Meaning of IQ

A wide variety of intelligence tests are available; most yield a score referred to as the **intelligence quotient (IQ)**. The concept, invented by William Stern (1914), is quite simple. A child who can

---

correlation A statistical relationship between variables.

variable A property, measurement, or characteristic that is susceptible to variation. In psychological experimentation, qualities of human beings such as intelligence and creativity are considered variables.

positive correlation The type of relationship that exists between two variables so that high or low scores on one are associated with correspondingly high or low scores on the other.

negative correlation The type of relationship that exists between two variables when high values in one are associated with correspondingly low values in the other.

---

intelligence quotient (IQ) A simple way to describe intelligence by assigning it a number that represents the ratio of mental to chronological age, multiplied by 100. Average IQ is therefore 100 and is based on a comparison between an individual's performance and that of other comparable people.

Intelligence and Size of Brain

We somewhat arrogantly assume that of all the animals on earth, we are by far the most intelligent and the most inventive. Thus we have named ourselves *homo sapiens*, the wise one. As evidence of our wisdom, we point proudly to our increasing domination of nature, and we scoff at the perennial struggle for survival of those less gifted than we are.* So viewed, we appear to be the creature that has adapted best to the environment—and this, the ability to adapt, is a useful definition of intelligence.

Ironically, we, the self-designated wise ones, do not have the largest brain of all earthly species. In fact, the adult male brain weighs a mere 3¼ pounds, and the female brain weighs about 10 percent less—not even 3 pounds. This, compared with the 13-pound elephant brain or the brain of a whale, which in some cases weighs 19 pounds, is relatively unimpressive. However, there is a strong likelihood that the absolute weight of the brain is less related to intelligent behavior than is the ratio of brain to body weight, so we still retain the advantage. Our brain-to-body-weight ratio is approximately 1 to 50; that of the whale and elephant approaches 1 to 1,000. And among those few small monkeys that have even better brain-to-body-weight ratios than we have—as high as 1 to 18—the absolute size of the brain is so small that it probably can't do much more than handle simple physiological functioning.

But the dolphin, on the other hand, is not an inordinately small or large animal. In fact, it often weighs no more than an adult man. Yet its average brain weight is a full 33¾ pounds. This has led to a great deal of speculation and research on the dolphin's intelligence—research that has not yet succeeded in determining how intelligent the dolphin really is.

Although a fairly accurate ranking of species in terms of intelligence may be possible based on brain-to-body-weight ratios, such a crude indicator of intelligence does not appear to be of any real value in gauging the subtle but significant differences that exist between geniuses and less-gifted individuals within the human species. For this, instruments labeled "intelligence tests" are commonly used. These tests are generally unsuitable for nonhumans, however, and they are often suitable for only very specific groups within the human species.

*And we turn a blind eye to the dwindling supply of irreplaceable resources, our idiotic penchant for polluting the environment, our unreasoning failure to control our numbers, and the increasing risk of nuclear self-annihilation.

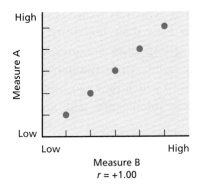

Measure A (vertical, Low to High) vs Measure B (horizontal, Low to High)
$r = +1.00$

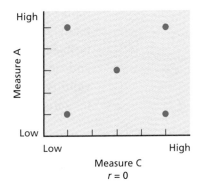

Measure A (vertical, Low to High) vs Measure C (horizontal, Low to High)
$r = 0$

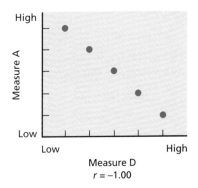

Measure A (vertical, Low to High) vs Measure D (horizontal, Low to High)
$r = -1.00$

FIGURE 8.2 Representations of correlation (r), indicating the extent to which two measures tend to vary together: The *direction* of the relationship (positive or negative) is shown by the *sign* of the correlation coefficient (plus or minus). The *strength* of the relationship is indicated by the *magnitude* of the correlation coefficient: The closer r is to ± 1, the stronger the observed relationship; the closer it is to 0, the weaker the relationship. In this example, scores on Measure A correlate perfectly with scores on Measures B and D and not at all with scores on Measure C.

reason and solve problems that, say, other average 4-year-olds can solve may be said to have a **mental age** of 4. Now if that child happens to be 4 years old (has a *chronological age* of 4), we can conclude that this is an average child. The ratio of this child's mental age (MA) to chronological age (CA) is 1. Multiply that by 100 and, voilà: an IQ of 100.

But if the child happens to be 5 years old and is only able to do what average 4-year-olds do, the IQ becomes $^{4}/_{5} \times 100 = 80$. And if the child is just 3 but is already reasoning at the level of a 4-year-old, the IQ would be $^{4}/_{3} \times 100 = 133$ (see Figure 8.3).

The average IQ of a randomly selected group of people on most tests is about 100. Approximately two-thirds of the population score between 85 and 115. About 11 percent score above 120, and 1.6 percent score above 140. Figure 8.4 depicts the distribution of measured intelligence in a normal population.

"If his IQ is based on guessing the right answers, perhaps we could assume he'll go through life being a remarkably successful guesser."
© 1996 Sidney Harris

IQ was originally defined as the ratio of mental age to chronological age multiplied by 100. (Multiplying by 100 gets rid of the decimal point and makes the average IQ exactly 100.)

That is, $IQ = \dfrac{MA}{CA} \times 100$

For example: If 10-year-old Len performs at the level of an average 8-year-old, his IQ is:

$\dfrac{8}{10} \times 100 = 80$

If 10-year-old Lena performs at the level of an average 12-year-old, her IQ is:

$\dfrac{12}{10} \times 100 = 120$

FIGURE 8.3 The original meaning of the IQ: In practice, now, mental age is seldom computed. Instead, tests come with tables of norms which are based on the average performance of large samples. These permit the tester to convert actual test scores directly into IQs.

---

mental age A measure or estimate of intellectual functioning expressed in terms of age. Thus an average 7-year-old has a mental age of seven.

Types of Intelligence Tests

There are two general types of intelligence tests: group and individual. The former are administered simultaneously to a group of test subjects; the latter require individual administration. Typically, **group tests** are either paper-and-pencil tests or else they are computer-administered (and often computer-scored as well). There are many more group tests than individual tests, probably because group tests are inexpensive and more widely used. Unfortunately, their **validity** (the extent to which they can be shown to actually measure intelligence and nothing

---

group test A type of test usually used to measure intelligence that may be given to large groups of subjects at one time. It is typically of the paper-and-pencil variety.

validity The extent to which a test measures what it intends to measure. For example, an intelligence test is valid to the extent that it measures intelligence and nothing else. Educational and psychological tests are limited by their frequently low validity.

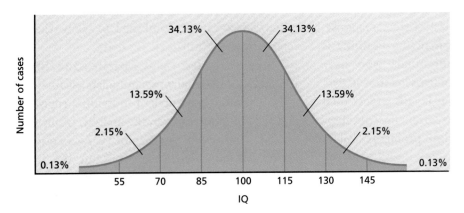

FIGURE 8.4 A normal curve depicting the theoretical distribution of IQ scores among humans. (Average score is 100; 68.26 percent of the population score between 85 and 115; only 2.28 percent score either above 130 or below 70.) The actual scores of a population may vary somewhat from this theoretical distribution.

else) and **reliability** (the accuracy with which they measure it) are often poor.[2] **Individual tests**, in contrast, are much more expensive in terms of equipment and administration time. The scores they yield are often more valid and more reliable, however. Hence, they can provide greater insight into intellectual processes. They are especially valuable for diagnosing specific learning problems in children. It is relatively rare, for example, to find school systems that base decisions to place students in special classrooms or programs simply on the basis of a group assessment. Typically, an individual assessment is required after initial screening with a group measure, partly to determine whether the test has been fair to the student.

Group tests can usually be administered and scored by any reasonably competent classroom teacher. However, with few exceptions the administration of individual tests requires a great deal of training and skill. Brief descriptions of some of the most commonly used individual and group tests are given here.

Individual Intelligence Tests

Individual intelligence tests, as we have seen, are administered to a single student at one time, usually by a trained examiner.

Peabody Picture Vocabulary Test–Revised (PPVT–R): This is among the most easily administered and easily scored individual intelligence tests. It is an untimed test, usually requiring 15 minutes or less per subject. It consists simply of having the subject point to the one picture out of four that represents a word that has been read by the examiner. There are two forms of the test (L and M), each consisting of 175 words (plates) arranged from easiest to most difficult. After six consecutive incorrect answers, the test is discontinued. An intelligence score can then be computed on the basis of the subject's

---

reliability The consistency with which a test measures whatever it measures. A perfectly reliable test should yield the same scores on different occasions (for the same individual), providing that what it measures has not changed. Most educational and psychological tests are severely limited in their reliability.

individual test A test, usually used to measure intelligence, that can be given to only one individual at a time.

---

[2] Validity and reliability of tests are discussed in more detail in Chapter 13.

age and the level of the last correct response. Because of this simple format, the Peabody is sometimes used with individuals who have severe communication problems or motor dysfunctions (Wagner, 1994). It is also widely used with children who are experiencing developmental delays such as reading problems (Facon & Facon-Bollengier, 1997).

Revised Stanford-Binet The Stanford-Binet test is among the best-known and most widely used individual measures of intelligence. A high degree of training and competence is required to administer it. It consists of a wide variety of tests graded in difficulty to correspond to various age levels. It yields a score that can be converted into an IQ. The most recent revision of the Stanford-Binet (4th edition, Thorndike, Hagen, & Sattler, 1985) yields scores in four separate areas: verbal reasoning, quantitative reasoning, abstract/visual reasoning, and short-term memory. It also provides a composite score that is described as a measure of "adaptive ability" and is generally interpreted as an IQ.

The Stanford-Binet is widely used to assess both children with normal abilities and those who have learning and developmental problems. It is also highly useful for identifying giftedness (Ellzey & Karnes, 1993) and can also be used as a preliminary screening test for children with autism (Carpentieri & Morgan, 1994). And, because of the wide age range it covers, it can be used with college students and older adults as well (Kaplan & Alfonso, 1997).

Wechsler Intelligence Scale for Children (3rd. ed.) (WISC-III) This individual test is similar to the Stanford-Binet, but it is somewhat easier to administer and is far more widely used. It also yields scores on a variety of specific tests (for example, vocabulary, block design, digit span, and comprehension) and two major "intelligence" scores—one verbal and one performance score. These can be combined to yield what is referred to as a "full-scale IQ score."

Because the test yields separate scores on its various subtests, many psychologists assume that these represent measures of individual cognitive abilities. In fact, however, the analysis of profiles on these individual tests is not very meaningful (Bray, Kehle, & Hintze, 1998). But the more global scores it yields have high predictive validity both for normal and for developmentally delayed children. Also, the test has been shown to have a very high reliability (consistency of scores from one testing to another) (Canivez & Watkins, 1998). And, besides the Wechsler scale for children, there are separate scales both for preschoolers and adults. Various subtests of the WISC-III are described in Table 8.2.

Group Intelligence Tests

Group tests of intelligence are usually paper-and-pencil or computer-administered tests that can be given to a large group at the same time. Here we briefly describe just a few examples of the hundreds of tests available.

Draw-a-Person Test This interesting measure of intelligence was first developed by Goodenough (1926) and was then called the *draw-a-man* test. It was later revised by Harris (1963) and Naglieri (1988), becoming the draw-a-*person* test to remove the sexist bias and to permit the drawing of female forms. Interestingly, research indicates that there is still a very strong male-gender bias in our interpretation of words like "human" or "person." As a result, explain Merritt and Kok (1997), for most children, there is little difference between hearing the instructions "draw a person" or "draw a man."

The Draw-a-Person test (DAP) is based on the assumption that children's drawings reflect their conceptual sophistication. The child is simply asked to draw the best person possible; no

TABLE 8.2
The Wechsler Intelligence Scale for
Children, (3rd. ed.) (WISC-III)

VERBAL SCALE	PERFORMANCE SCALE
1. *General information.* Questions relating to information most children have the opportunity to acquire (M)*	1. *Picture completion.* Child indicates what is missing in pictures (M)
2. *General comprehension.* Questions designed to assess child's understanding of why certain things are done as they are (M)	2. *Picture arrangement.* Child arranges series of pictures to tell a story (M)
3. *Arithmetic.* Oral arithmetic problems (M)	3. *Block design.* Child is required to copy exactly a design with colored blocks (M)
4. *Similarities.* Child indicates how certain things are alike (M)	4. *Object assembly.* Child assembles puzzles (M)
5. *Vocabulary.* Child gives meanings of words of increasing difficulty (M)	5. *Coding.* Child pairs symbols with digits following a key (M)
6. *Digit span.* Child repeats orally presented sequence of numbers in order and reversed (S)*	6. *Mazes.* Child traces the way out of mazes with pencil (S)
	7. *Symbol search.* Child performs symbol location task that measures mental processing speed and visual search skills (S)

*(M) mandatory, (S) supplementary

time limit is imposed (see Figure 8.5). Drawings are scored primarily on the basis of detail and accuracy, according to a well-defined set of criteria. Tables for converting raw scores to IQ scores are provided.

The test provides a fast and easy method of obtaining a general indication of cognitive development. It is also used clinically, sometimes to assess stress and emotional difficulties (for example, Rudenberg, Jansen, & Fridjhon, 1998; Riethmiller & Handler, 1997).

Cognitive Abilities Test (CogAT) This is a widely used, multilevel, paper-and-pencil test suitable for grades 3 through 13. It yields three scores—verbal, quantitative, and nonverbal—as well as a composite IQ score. The test includes tables for converting individual scores to percentile scores based on the performance of other children at the same grade level. (A percentile indicates the percentage of cases that fall at or below a given point. For example, a student who scores at the

(a) (b)

FIGURE 8.5 Two examples of the Goodenough-Harris Drawing Test: Both subjects were boys aged 10 ¾ years. The raw scores and IQ equivalents, respectively, for the drawings are (a) 41 and 110, (b) 4 and 54. The child who drew b also had a low Stanford-Binet IQ score. From the Goodenough-Harris Drawing Test. Copyright © 1963 by the Psychological Corporation. Reproduced by permission. All rights reserved.

75th percentile has performed as well or better than 75 percent of students in the same grade.) This test is widely used both for general assessment of students and in research (for example, Wallick, 1998; Langdon, Rosenblatt, & Mellanby, 1998).

Otis-Lennon School Ability Test The Otis-Lennon is designed to assess school-related ability. It consists of five levels of items suitable for grades 1 through 12. Items are intermingled (for example, vocabulary, reasoning, numerical, and other items are in random order) and are presented in order of increasing difficulty. The test yields a single standardized score labeled a "school ability index" (SAI).

The Otis-Lennon is a widely used test that has been shown to be useful, even with very young children, as an indicator of abilities related to performance in school. For example, Cadieux, Boudreault, & Laberge (1997) tested 261 kindergarten children and then monitored their performance for the next three years. They found that Otis-Lennon scores were significant predictors of how well the children would do and, specifically, how likely they were to be held back in a grade.

Myths Concerning Measured IQ

The measurement and meaning of IQ have long been controversial and uncertain. A recent book, *The Bell Curve* (Herrnstein & Murray, 1994), and reactions to it, serve as reminders of how potentially controversial the interpretation and use of IQ testing can be.

What *The Bell Curve* says, among other things, is that measured IQ is a clear and important predictor of success in a huge variety of endeavors (like school, parenting, business), that current IQ tests measure intelligence quite well and can therefore be used as selection devices, that IQ is highly inherited, and that there are

consequently some important racial differences in intelligence.

Many have been quick to disagree with some or all of these conclusions and especially with the social policy recommendations that follow from them (see, for example, Fischer et al., 1996). Most of these critics, note Sternberg and Kaufman (1998), have objected to the social policy recommendations that flow from the belief that IQ tests separate us not only on the basis of who is most likely to succeed, but also on the basis of race. This is not so, claim Fischer and associates (1996): "Research has shown that 'nature' determines neither the level of inequality in America nor which Americans in particular will be privileged or disprivileged; social conditions and national policies do" (p. xi).

But there *is* agreement with many of Herrnstein and Murray's less politically dangerous conclusions. For example, following an extensive review of the literature, Carroll (1997) suggests that most of *The Bell Curve's* conclusions appear to be supported by science. In particular, he emphasizes that IQ tests properly constructed and administered are not biased against social or ethnic groups. But, of course, not all are properly constructed or administered.

The controversy is still far from being resolved. But science has begun to clarify several myths that surround the interpretation and use of IQ testing. Teachers need to be aware of the most important of these:

Misconception #1 *IQ is a mysterious something, synonymous with intelligence, possessed in greater or lesser amounts by everyone.* This myth is evident in the question "What's your IQ?" or the expression "My IQ is. . . ." In fact, the numerical index of intelligence known as the IQ is simply a score obtained by an individual in a specific testing situation and on a specific "intelligence" test. And the intelligence tests on which estimates of IQ are based have less than perfect validity. That is, they tend to measure things other than intelligence itself, things such as the effects of past experience. Many also reflect (measure) the effects of other variables such as fatigue or motivation. Hence, IQ and intelligence are not synonymous although, as Mensh and Mensh (1991) note, the terms have been used synonymously "longer than almost anyone can remember" (p. 1).

Besides the imperfect validity of intelligence tests, they do not have perfect reliability (don't provide totally consistent measures). Measures of intelligence can vary considerably from one testing time to another for the same individual. This variation, technically known as the *error of measurement*, is such that any teacher looking at a specific intelligence quotient should reason: "This score of 130 means that this student probably has a measured IQ that ranges somewhere between 120 and 140." (See Chapter 13 for a more detailed discussion of reliability and validity.)

Misconception #2 *IQ is a constant. I have X, you have Y, and that's that.* Not so. Research increasingly points to the conclusion that measured IQ

is not fixed. In fact, Flynn (1987) examined data from 14 countries spanning 50 years and found that there have been massive gains in IQ in each of these countries during that half century—a phenomenon that has come to be known as the **Flynn effect**. The Flynn effect was recently illustrated in a wide-scale survey of military recruits and university applicants in Spain (Colom, Andres-Pueyo, & Juan-Espinosa, 1998). Each of the participants in this study was administered a variety of intelligence tests, and the results were compared with previously administered tests (16 and 28 years earlier). On most of the tests, there were significant increases over time.

From a teacher's point of view, it is important that schools are centrally involved in enhancing intellectual functioning. Schools do this not only by imparting the tools of cognitive functioning, but also by providing opportunities for interaction with other minds and with new technologies

---

Flynn effect A label used to denote that there are gains in measured IQ over generations.

Most intelligence tests are highly verbal and tend to measure abilities related to working with abstract ideas and symbols. Very few tap the communication and group interaction skills at play in situations such as the one depicted here. Yet these skills are a fundamental part of intelligent adaptation.

(such as computers or even calculators). Thus do schools increase measured intelligence.

Misconception #3 *Intelligence tests measure all the important things.* In fact, most intelligence tests measure relatively limited kinds of abilities—typically, the ability to work with abstract ideas and symbols. They seldom tap interpersonal skills, athletic ability, creativity, and a variety of other desirable human attributes. As Sternberg (1996b) notes, the skills that IQ tests measure don't often include important components of *practical* intelligence. For example, most measures of intelligence don't tell us anything about social intelligence, motivation, adaptive skills, or emotions.

Misconception #4 *Intelligence tests are impersonal, impartial, and fair.* Many intelligence tests are culturally biased; that is, they tend to favor children whose backgrounds are similar to that of the sample that was used as the norm for the test. In North America that sample has often consisted of white, middle-class children, which explains why many intelligence tests have long been unfair to a variety of minority groups. However, the most recent revisions of such tests as the Stanford-Binet and the Wechsler have expanded their standardization samples to include minority groups in a representative way. Accordingly, these tests are now fairer to minorities.

Several other tests—none of them widely used in practice, though some are used more extensively in research—attempt to minimize cultural bias. Such tests, sometimes labeled "culture-fair," or more accurately, "culture-reduced," are typically nonverbal. They attempt to tap intellectual functions through the use of problems involving pictures or abstract designs (for example, the Ravens Progressive Matrices Test).

Fact *IQ is related to success, both in school and in life.* This, however, might not mean that measured IQ is the most important predictor of future success. For example, Thorndike and Hagen (1977) and Cohen (1972) point out that although the correlation between intelligence test scores and school achievement is substantial, previous achievement correlates even more highly with future achievement than does IQ. Even Herrnstein and Murray (1994), who champion the importance of IQ, admit that much of the variation in measures of success can be accounted for by factors not measured by IQ tests.

But for predicting the likelihood of success or failure in school, IQ tests are clearly very powerful tools.

Use of Intelligence Tests in Schools

Although intelligence tests are still used in many school systems, they are no longer routinely administered to all students everywhere. This is partly because of a strong antitest movement among parents and others and partly because of a growing recognition of the potential weaknesses and abuses of testing. And, as we have seen, there have also been strong negative reactions to the social implications of Herrnstein and Murray's (1994) conclusion that IQ differentiates among those likely to succeed or fail, as well as among racial and ethnic groups, and that IQs should therefore be used as a screening device. Eysenck (1998) notes that many fear IQ tests may lead to increased gaps between social classes; he argues that the fear is totally unfounded.

Chief among the purposes for which intelligence tests are used are counseling, career guidance, class placement, and diagnosis for remedial or enrichment purposes. When IQ tests are skillfully administered and intelligently interpreted, they can doubtless be of considerable value for

"We realize you do better on your IQ tests than you do anything else, but you just cannot major in IQ."
© 1996 Sidney Harris.

any and all of these purposes. Much of their usefulness, though, depends on the extent to which they can successfully predict school achievement.

IQ and Achievement One assumption underlying the development and use of most intelligence tests is that intelligence is related to successful performance of school tasks. It is not surprising, therefore, that these tests correlate relatively highly with measures of school achievement. In fact, intelligence tests and achievement tests both measure much the same sorts of things—that is, both measure the effects of previous learning (achievement), and both typically are highly verbal. As Sternberg (1998a) notes, both achievement and ability are forms of *expertise* that are really not qualitatively different. The principal differences between intelligence tests and achievement tests are that IQ tests sample from a wider range of behaviors and (to some degree) emphasize the ability to apply knowledge and skills to new problems; in contrast, achievement tests tend to be limited to more specific areas of content expertise.

In view of the close relationship between what achievement and intelligence tests measure, it's not surprising that the correlation between the two ranges from .30 to .80 over a multitude of studies (Barrett & Depinet, 1991). Findings such as this justify using intelligence tests to select students for different programs. However, teachers and school administrators need to be very cautious when making placement decisions on the basis of IQ tests—especially if their decisions are more negative than positive. In the first place, although IQ scores tend to be relatively stable, an individual's test scores can fluctuate from one testing to another. Also, as we saw earlier, IQ tests don't measure all of the variables that might be important for success. Thus, IQ tests are probably the best tools we have for predicting how well groups of students are likely to do, but important school decisions should be based on much more than the results of one test or even a handful of IQ tests.

SOME INFLUENCES ON INTELLIGENCE

Intelligence doesn't just happen; it has a cause. And the causes of intelligence are also the causes of stupidity because one is the absence of the other.

As we saw in Chapter 2, intelligence, like most other human characteristics, results from the interplay of heredity and environment. Historically, there has been a great deal of controversy surrounding the importance of these factors. And much of this controversy has not yet been entirely resolved—as reactions to Herrnstein and Murray's *The Bell Curve* (1994) underline (see box entitled "Experience and Intelligence: A Debate"). Nevertheless, it's generally agreed that heredity versus environment is not the most important issue, especially for teachers. More important questions concern how individuals and environments interact during development, the processes that account for intellectual change, and how deficits can be remedied and gifts fostered (see Rose, 1995).

The Rubber-Band Hypothesis One of the better analogies used to describe the interaction of heredity and environment is Stern's (1956) rubber-band hypothesis. It compares our innate potential for intellectual development to a rubber band. Intelligence at any time is reflected by the length of the band. Obviously, a short piece (poorer genetic background) can be stretched; with a great deal of effort it can be stretched a long way. The forces that exert the pull on the band, or that fail to, are environmental. Hence, genetic and environmental forces interact so that less environmental stimulation may be required for average development if the genetic endowment is high. The reverse is also true. Thus, one

of the functions of schools is to stretch rubber bands (see Figure 8.6).

Birth Order, Family Size, and Spacing of Children

Following a study of 128 3- to 8-year-old children, Molfese, DiLalla, and Bunce (1997) conclude that home environment is the single most powerful predictor of intelligence at all of these ages. The important question is what specific qualities of family life are important. One answer suggests that family size, birth order, and the spacing of children may provide clues to these qualities.

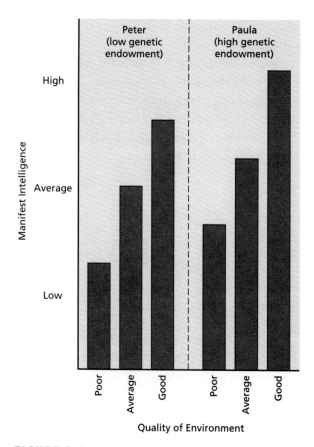

FIGURE 8.6 The Stern hypothesis: Individuals with different inherited potentials for intellectual development (genetic endowment) can manifest either below-average, average, or above-average intelligence as a function of environmental forces.

BEAR MUSINGS

Experience and Intelligence: A Debate

The most important question for an educator is whether a child's experiences can increase intelligence. A sample of the research relevant to this question, and to the general nature-nurture question, is summarized here in the form of an imaginary debate between John Watson (a champion of environmentalism) and Francis Galton (who believed that intelligence is entirely inherited). The debate is replete with glaring anachronisms.* To know all that Galton and Watson claim to know, they would both have to be older than 100.

Galton: My dear Watson, if you will simply open your mind to the problem, I can demonstrate for you beyond any doubt that heredity is the most powerful factor in development. As I said in 1869, "I have no patience with the hypothesis occasionally expressed, and often implied, especially in tales written to teach children to be good, that babies are born pretty much alike. . . ."

Watson: Give me a dozen healthy kids . . .

Galton: You've said that before. But just look at all the twins studies that have been done. As you know, identical twins are genetically exactly alike, but fraternal twins are as dissimilar as any two siblings.

*__PPC:__ "Replete with glaring anachronisms . . ." Even some of our brighter students won't know what this means. Isn't there a simpler way of saying this?
Author: Yes. I could have said: "Filled with instances that are out of temporal synchrony." Or "Filled with descriptions of events that did not or could not have happened when they are alleged to have happened." A watch on Robin Hood's arm would be an anachronism.

Watson: I know that.

Galton: Sorry, I didn't mean to talk down to you. Anyway, Burt's famous 1958 study shows that the IQ scores of identical twins, whether you raise 'em together or apart, are more highly correlated than the scores of fraternal twins. And I have no doubt that if we had more reliable measures of intelligence, the correlations would be even higher.

Watson: Whoa now! That is a highly prejudiced interpretation. If you look at the 1937 Newman, Freeman, and Holzinger study, you'll see just where environment comes in. Why do you suppose it is that the correlation for twins reared together is always higher than for twins reared apart? Ha! What do you say to that?

Galton: I say that studies involving the measurement of intelligence in people are highly suspect. Now, take rats, for example.

Watson: That's irrelevant!

Galton: It is not! Now you just hold on and listen here for a minute. In 1940, R. C. Tryon did a fascinating study, and it proves you wrong. Do you know it?

Watson: You mean Tryon's study?

Galton: Yes.

Watson: No.

Galton: I thought not. You don't read much, do you? You're just a popularizer. What Tryon did was take 142 rats and run them through a 17-unit maze 19 times. The brightest rat made, I forget . . . about 20 errors [author's note: actually, he made 14] and the dullest made 200 errors. [Again Galton is wrong. The dullest rat made 174 errors.] The brightest rats were then bred with each other, and the dull males were given dull females. That

usually happens to people, too. Heh! Heh! Well, after repeating the same procedure for only eight generations, a remarkable thing began to happen. The dullest rats in the bright group consistently made fewer errors than the brightest rats in the dull group. In other words, the brightest rats in the dull group were duller than the dullest rats in the bright group—or the dullest rats in the bright group were . . . you know. Imagine what we could do with people. John Humphrey Noyes would have done it if the American government hadn't outlawed polygamy. [Noyes set up a religious, communal, free-love group in Oneida, New York, in the late nineteenth century. He practiced selective breeding with the aim of producing a superhuman race but had to disband the group when polygamy was outlawed in the 1880s.]

Watson: So that's the kind of ridiculous evidence you base your eugenic movement on. [Eugenics is the term for the practice of selective breeding.] Let me tell you about a rat study, seeing as you're the one who brought it up. Hebb in 1947 and Krech, Rosenzweig, and Bennett—in 1960, '62, and '66—provide evidence that randomly selected rats can be significantly affected by environment. In the first case, Hebb showed in 1947 that rats raised as pets did better than laboratory rats on maze tests. Krech, Rosenzweig, and Bennett, in 1962, even changed the brain chemistry of rats by enriching their environments. And if you don't think that's enough evidence, consider Heyns' 1967 work in South Africa. He's been affecting the

(continued on next page)

Experience and Intelligence: A Debate (continued)

intelligence of babies by using vacuum cleaners.

Galton: Whoa, there, whoa up a little! Vacuum cleaners! You're going too far now.

Watson: That's what you think. It was reported in *Woman's Own* on February 4th, 1967.

Galton: You read *Woman's Own*?

Watson: My wife does. Anyway, what Heyns did was set up a decompression unit using a vacuum cleaner motor. He put this plastic bubblelike thing over the woman's abdomen and sucked the air out. It relieves all kinds of aches and pains and makes babies brighter, too.

Galton: It sounds like a gimmick to me. Jensen reviewed the research in 1998, and he concluded genes determine intelligence. And Scarr did the same thing in 1987 and she clearly concludes that the geneticists have won

the nature–nurture battle. And she re-emphasizes that conclusion in a 1992 article. And the monograph by Rowe in 1994—well, it provides pretty strong evidence that even families don't make that much difference—that genes are really the important thing.

Watson: Well, that's just one side of the debate. And if you look at Baumrind or Jackson's 1993 articles, you'll see the other side, which is not only the most accurate side, but also the most optimistic one. And the optimistic point of view is the one that teachers should have. It's my view. It's the view that says, you bet your sweet donkey, the family and the school and television and everything else that's important in the environment makes one whack of a difference. That's the optimistic view because you can do something about the environment, but you can't do a

dang thing about genetics. Changing the environment, that's what acceleration is and television for kids and books and programs for gifted kids . . .

Galton: Don't get carried away, Watson. Your point of view might be more optimistic, but it's less accurate. I'm a scientist, not a philosopher or a salesman.

The argument ends with Watson's wife calling him in to wash dishes.

But the debate continues, although most scientists now believe that both heredity and environment are important, that their relative influences cannot easily be separated. As Rose (1995) phrases it, "The questions are not whether genes matter, but, rather, how they matter and how genetic effects are modulated across lifespans of environmental interactions" (p. 627).

Birth Order More than a century ago, for example, Galton (1869) observed a much higher than expected number of firstborn children among the greatest scientists that Great Britain had produced. Since then, many studies have shown that firstborn and only children (who are necessarily also firstborn) speak more articulately and at a younger age than later-born children, score higher on measures of intellectual performance, have a higher need for achievement, perform better academically, are more likely to attend college and to achieve eminence, and of course, are more likely to become kings and queens (see, for example, Gaynor and Runco, 1992).

A closer examination of birth-order data suggests, however, that the contribution of birth order to such things as academic achievement or intelligence is negligible at best. Following a

massive investigation of 9,000 high school graduates and their brothers and sisters (more than 30,000 subjects), Hauser and Sewell (1985) found that birth order made absolutely no difference to measured intelligence or achievement. They did find, however, that size of "sibship" (number of brothers and sisters) has a negative effect on schooling. In other words, the larger the family, the more likely that academic achievement will be lower.

The Confluence Model What's important, says Zajonc (1975; Zajonc & Mullally, 1997), is not whether you're born first or last or how many children there are in the home but the intellectual climate of the home. For a variety of reasons, however, the intellectual climate of a home is strongly affected by how many children there are and by the spacing between them. Furthermore, it's possible to determine the influence of these variables by using what Zajonc and associates label the **confluence model**.

According to this model, each family member is assigned a value related to age: Parents are worth 30 points each; newborn infants, 0; and all other children, values that range from 0 to 30. The index of intellectual climate is then calculated by averaging values assigned to each individual in the family. For example, a firstborn child is born into an intellectual climate valued at 30 plus 30 (when there are two parents) plus 0 (for the infant), divided by 3 (this equals 20, for those whose calculators are not functioning). A child born later or born into a large family where there are many young children would be born into a family with a lower index of intellectual climate. The confluence model predicts, simply, that measured intelligence for large groups will be related to the intellectual climate index. And, in fact, there is some evidence that this is true. For example, Parker (1998) found that among a group of 828 academically talented youngsters, a preponderance were either first born or from very small families. It follows from the confluence model that these would be the children with the highest scores for home intellectual climate.

Do these observations support the notion that family size and birth order are important influences on intelligence? Perhaps not. Although the evidence seems clear that family size correlates inversely—and birth order, positively—with measured intelligence, these may not be important variables at all. In one of several large-scale and systematic investigations of this type, Page and Grandon (1979) found much the same correlations that Zajonc and Markus and others had previously reported. But they also found that when the variables of social class and race were included, correlations of these factors with manifested intelligence were even more significant than that of family size. Put more simply, in most studies that found a high correlation of family size, birth order, and intelligence, researchers did not consider that large families tend to be more common in lower social classes, in certain ethnic minorities, among rural rather than urban families, and among those who are less well educated. So perhaps the "intellectual climate" in large families is more a function of ethnic, social, and educational variables than of family size.

Spacing of Children Taken together, family size, birth order, and social class are important predictors of performance, achievement, measured intelligence, and even creativity. And the prediction becomes even more powerful if age intervals, or spacing of children, are factored into the equation. For example, Gaynor and Runco (1992) examined the correlation between the creative abilities of 116 children and the age intervals between these children and their closest sibling. They corroborated an often-reported finding: The larger the age interval between a child and the closest sibling, the greater the probability that this child will score high on measures of achievement and intelligence. As Wagner, Schubert, and Schubert (1985) conclude: "The findings on spacing effects are astonishingly consistent. Close spacing . . . seems deleterious to intelligence and achievement [and] to good relations between children and parents" (p. 196).

Where very small intervals exist between children, family size is typically greater—and the probability that the family will be characterized by social and economic variables associated with

---

confluence model Zajonc's term for the hypothesis that the intellectual climate of the home, determined principally in terms of the numbers and ages of family members, contributes in important ways to the development of children's intelligence. According to this model, children born into a relatively adult environment (firstborn and only children, for example) should, on average, have an intellectual advantage over those born in a less adult environment (later-born children, children in large families, children in single-parent homes).

developmental disadvantages is also higher. Hence, the influence of age intervals, like that of birth order and family size, is probably best explained in terms of the interaction of related variables (social and economic ones) and in terms of the sorts of family relationships and interactions that are most likely to result. A child whose siblings are either much older or much younger, Gaynor and Runco (1992) explain, is more likely than other children to be perceived by parents as special—and is also more likely to be born into a family with economic and social advantages.

A Conclusion The most reasonable conclusion at this point is that many variables are influential for determining intellectual development. Among the most important are genetic forces (we have relatively little control over these) and environmental variables such as formal schooling and interactions among children and their parents and siblings, as well as between children and technological aspects of society.

All of which is far from simple.

Finally, always keep in mind that the grand conclusions of social science are most often based on the average performance of large groups of individuals. Invariably, within these groups are many individuals whose behavior contradicts the conclusion at every turn. In other words, there are geniuses among families whose members number into the dozens and among all social and ethnic groups, and there are fools, dullards, and simpletons who are born first into tiny little advantaged families.[3]

⌐ CREATIVITY

While conversing with George Bernard Shaw, his biographer, Stephen Winsten, alluded to the proverbial hairsbreadth that separates genius

from madness: "The matter-of-fact man prefers to think of the creative man as defective, or at least akin to madness," he said. And Shaw replied, "Most of them are. I am probably the only sane exception" (1949, p. 103).

Although we no longer fear creative people as openly as we might once have, uneasiness and uncertainty remain. As Cross, Coleman, and Terhaar-Yonkers (1991) phrased it, **creativity** is still stigmatized in our society, and those who are exceptional are often subjected to tremendous pressure to conform—to behave like those who are more ordinary.

Are creative people nonconformists, eccentrics, radicals, and fools? Or are they just ordinary people? The answer is probably that there are some of both but that there is really no mystical or magical quality about creativity—although there is limited evidence that highly creative people are somewhat more prone to emotional disorders (Bowden, 1994; Richards, 1994). In general, however, creativity, like intelligence, is a quality of humans and of human behavior that everybody possesses to some degree. Just as low intelligence is stupidity, low creativity is ordinariness. There are few geniuses as identified by tests of intelligence; there are also few very highly creative people.

Some Definitions of Creativity

The central question in creativity research and speculation—what is creativity?—remains largely unanswered. There is no shortage of answers, but there is simply a lack of agreement about which answer is most useful.

As an example, here are three of many possible definitions:

---

[3] ***PPC:*** Is the bear a cynic? Does he mean this?
Author: Older bears are often cynical.

---

creativity Generally refers to the capacity of individuals to produce novel or original answers or products. The term *creative* is an adjective that can be used to describe people, products, or processes.

CASES FROM THE CLASSROOM

Different Colors of Creativity

THE NAME: Réné Choumard

THE PLACE: Pascal, Saskatchewan

For the past three years, Réné has been sitting on an inverted washtub on the porch of his seen-a-better-day shack, knitting himself purple mittens that have no thumbs and dreaming about what cows were really like when he was young. He talks to himself incessantly about everything he has ever seen or done.

THE NAME: Joseph Lalonde

THE PLACE: Pascal, Saskatchewan

Joseph is Réné's neighbor. He's the local wit. His humor is also local humor. His jokes are associations between extremely remote ideas—but they're not always funny.

"Here's one I just made up," he said to his wife this very morning. "Did you hear about the teacher who went to church to take his pills. Knelt on the pew, he did, and took his pills. You know why? Huhn? You figure it out yet? It's his pewpill—his pupil! Get it?"

THE NAME: Rollie Wozny

THE PLACE: Biomiracle Technologies

While carrying a cup of coffee, black, no sugar thanks, from the vending machine to his desk in the corner of the Biomiracle Technologies main laboratory, Rollie stumbles over a pile of discarded computer innards. He manages to hang onto the coffee cup but loses his grip on the test tube in his other hand, accidentally spilling a small amount of newly recombined DNA into a vat containing 1055.4 U.S. gallons (4,000 liters) of sweet cream. The cream immediately turns into four cows (a reversal phenomenon).

1. Creativity involves fluency, flexibility, and originality (Guilford, 1959).

2. Creativity is "the forming of associative elements into new combinations which either meet specified requirements or are in some ways useful. The more mutually remote the elements of the new combination, the more creative the process of solution" (Mednick, 1962, p. 221).

3. Creativity results in "a novel work that is accepted as tenable or useful or satisfying by a significant group of others at some point in time" (Stein, in Parnes & Harding, 1962, p. 86).

Consider the case entitled "Different Colors of Creativity." Each of the three individuals whose behavior is described—Réné Choumard, Joseph Lalonde, and Rollie Wozny—is creative by one definition but not by the others. Réné is creative according to Guilford: His behavior is original, and he shows remarkable verbal fluency and flexibility; however, he is not creative according to Mednick and Stein. Joseph, in contrast, meets Mednick's criteria for creativity—highly remote associations satisfying his own specifications. Perhaps he is even original, fluent, and flexible. But he doesn't produce anything "tenable or useful or satisfying." But Rollie Wozny, the scientist, does. Yet his behavior is not original, but simply clumsy. And he makes no remote associations whatsoever.

This discussion highlights the confusion that makes defining and assessing creativity so difficult. The problem can partly be resolved by accepting that creativity is a global term and that it does not necessarily represent only one event or quality. If we distinguish among the creative process, the creative product, and the creative person, many of the contradictions implicit in earlier formulations disappear. René is a creative person who doesn't produce anything; Joseph uses a creative process but also produces nothing creative;[4] the scientist is neither creative nor does he use a creative process, but he produces something valuable.

Although distinctions among the creative person, product, and process are useful, they solve only part of the problem because they are seldom reflected in current attempts to measure creativity (Cropley, 1996). The inference continues to be made, at least implicitly, that creative personalities and processes can be identified and assessed on the basis of products that are judged to be creative. (See Figure 8.7).

Identifying the Creative and Gifted

From an educational point of view, it's important to be able to define *creativity* and *giftedness* so that we can identify and select students for special programs. Accordingly, many school systems lump together various categories such as "creative," "talented," and "gifted" under a single label (such as "talented and gifted" or simply "gifted") and provide specific criteria for identifying students who belong to this group. The criterion most often used has been measured intelligence expressed in the form of an IQ, with a score of 140 being a common cutoff; that is, all those with IQ scores of 140 or more would have qualified as gifted. (Programs for the gifted are reviewed in the next chapter.)

Psychologists and educators have now realized that there are problems associated with defining creativity or giftedness solely (or even primarily) in terms of intelligence. In the first place, as shown in a later section, independent measures of creativity do not always correlate well with measured intelligence. For example, Tyler-Wood and Carri (1991) looked at the scores that a group of gifted children had obtained on four different measures of intelligence. They found that those who would have been identified as gifted varied widely depending on the test used. A second problem is that, given the rather unimpressive validity and reliability of our intelligence tests, using them to select students for special programs is often unfair. And third, defining giftedness solely on the basis of intelligence means overlooking other important characteristics that appear to be related to creative functioning. For example, Akande (1997) argues that creativity depends on the interaction of ability, high motivation, and perhaps a combination of other factors such as background knowledge, styles of thinking, and personality.

For these reasons, using high IQ as the sole index of giftedness would exclude many talented and gifted individuals. As we see in the next chapter, giftedness is now most often identified using a combination of criteria such as intelligence, creativity, achievement, and task commitment (Subhi, 1997). One of the results of using a combination of criteria such as these is that many students with IQs much lower than 140 are now included among the gifted.

Measuring Creativity

Ideally, schools try to identify the gifted as early as possible, not so that they can be labeled but to recognize and respond to their needs. Although there is considerable agreement about how to measure achievement, and perhaps even how to

---

[4] *PPC:* The bear's guru, Yogi Berra, is a good example of someone who came up with all sorts of creative sayings. One of my favorites is, "Nobody goes there any more . . . it's too crowded."

Author: One of the bear's favorite Yogi Berra sayings is, "I really didn't say everything I said"—which the bear thinks is true.

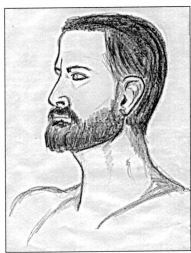

FIGURE 8.7 Which is the most creative of these six renditions of the same person, each drawn by a different artist? There is no easy answer; judgments of artistic creativity are a highly subjective matter. Not surprisingly, psychologists have been hard-pressed to reach agreement on what creativity involves and what it means. Part of the problem lies in the observation that creativity is evident not only in products (as illustrated in these six drawings, for example), but also in characteristic ways of doing things or processes, and also in a unique combination of personality characteristics. Drawings (clockwise from top left to bottom right) courtesy of David Mors, C. Stinson, Peter Sentkowski, David Rose, Tim Gallagher, and Andrew Ogus.

assess task commitment, measuring creativity has proven far more difficult.

One problem is that there isn't complete agreement about whether creativity is a general, underlying characteristic of gifted people, or whether it is more often specific to a single domain. For example Gardner (1997), as we saw earlier in this chapter, speaks of seven (or perhaps ten) largely unrelated kinds of intelligence; he believes that creativity (or giftedness) can occur in any one of these domains and be absent in all others. Wallach (1985) shares this view, arguing that it is possible to be highly gifted in one area of functioning but not in any other—as can be evident among musically or scientifically gifted people. This view underlies the use of **biographical inventories** to assess creativity. These inventories look at past production and behavior to predict future creativity.

The argument that creativity is largely domain specific is not shared by all researchers. Many believe that, although giftedness is often manifested in one domain rather than another, certain general underlying qualities allow a creative person to be described as generally creative. This assumption underlies the use of general tests of creativity.

Teacher Ratings of Creativity One of the simplest ways of identifying creative talent is to have teachers rate their students. However, Gallagher (1960) cites research indicating that teachers miss approximately 20 percent of their most highly creative students. As Shaklee (1992) points out, teachers don't often recognize giftedness in students who are not the high-achieving school or class leaders. Furthermore, says Shaklee, most schools confine children to a lock-step curriculum that is not likely to foster the development of giftedness or even to permit its recognition.

General Tests of Creativity General tests of creativity are designed specifically to assess qualities that are thought to be closely related to creative thought and behavior. Among the most common of these are **tests of divergent thinking**, first proposed by Guilford (1950) and developed by Torrance (1966, 1974: Torrance Tests of Creative Thinking). These tests are based on the assumption that creative ability comprises several separate factors, among which are **fluency**, **flexibility**, and **originality**. Tasks have been designed to encourage the production of a variety of responses, which can then be scored in terms of these and other factors. One such test is the Unusual Uses Test. Subjects are asked to think of as many uses as they can for an ordinary object, such as a brick or a nylon stocking. Responses are counted to arrive at an index of fluency. Flexibility is measured by counting the number of shifts among classes of response. For example, a brick might be used for building a house, a planter, a road, and so on. Each response scores for fluency but not for flexibility. A shift from this category of uses to one involving throwing the brick would illustrate flexibility. Originality is scored on the basis of the number of responses that are either statistically rare or judged unusual by the experimenter. A statistically rare response might be one that occurs in less than 5 percent of the responses. (See Table 8.3.)

Cognitive Style Measurements of Creativity Some tests of creativity try to assess the cognitive processes and thinking styles thought to be

---

biographical inventories Checklists or questionnaires designed to summarize the events and accomplishment of an individual's life.

test of divergent thinking A creativity test. These are usually open-ended, production tests designed to measure factors such as fluency, flexibility, and originality.

fluency A factor thought to be involved in creativity and evident in the production of a large number of responses or solutions in a problem situation.

flexibility A factor tapped by production measures of divergent thinking (creativity). It is evident in the ability or propensity to switch from one class of responses or solutions to another.

originality A measure of creativity evident in the production of novel (unexpected or statistically rare) responses or solutions in a problem situation.

TABLE 8.3
Sample Answers and Scoring Procedure
for One Item from a Creativity Test

Item How many uses can you think of for a nylon stocking?

Answers

☆ Wear on feet	✪✱☆ Make upholstery	✱☆ Tie up robbers
✪☆ Wear over face	✱☆ Hang flower pots	✪✱☆ Cover broken windowpanes
☆ Wear on hands when it's cold	☆ Hang mobiles	✪✱☆ Use as ballast in a dirigible
✱☆ Make rugs	✪✱☆ Make Christmas decorations	✱☆ Make a fishing net
☆ Make clothes	✱☆ Use as a sling	

Scoring

☆ Fluency: 14 (total number of different responses)

✱ Flexibility: 9 (number of shifts from one class to another)

✪ Originality: 5 (number of unusual responses—responses that occurred less than 5 percent of the time in the entire sample)

involved in creative behavior. Several researchers have developed questionnaires; among these the *Creativity Styles Questionnaire* is one of the better known (Kumar, Kemmler, & Holman, 1997). These questionnaires typically try to assess variables such as the extent to which participants value ideas, their attitudes toward originality, their approaches to solving problems, their persistence, perhaps their abilities and their cognitive strategies, and various aspects of their personalities (Martinsen, 1997).

Analysis of responses to style questionnaires indicates that the most creative individuals tend to value new ideas, hold fewer stereotypes about creativity, and are less likely to see themselves as too busy to think new ideas (Basadur & Hausdorf, 1996). Similarly, many appear to have a strong belief in unconscious processes, are less concerned about developing a final product, and use a greater variety of techniques in an effort to be creative than do those who are less creative (Kumar, Kemmler, & Holman, 1997).

The use of creative styles approaches for assessing creativity is still mainly restricted to research and to the development of theory where, notes Baer (1993–94), the validity of divergent thinking tests has been called into question. In practice, however, creativity tests are relatively seldom used in school settings where teachers and administrators need to identify the gifted and the talented. As we point out in the next chapter, gifted children are most often identified solely on the basis of academic achievement and measured intelligence—although the official criteria for giftedness typically include high aptitude in other areas such as creativity, leadership, psychomotor ability, and visual or performing arts.

CONNECTIONS BETWEEN CREATIVITY AND INTELLIGENCE

Unfortunately, if gifted students are selected primarily on the basis of measured intelligence and achievement with little regard for creativity and other important personality variables, the selection procedures may overlook some worthy candidates. Getzels and Jackson (1962), for example, found that creative students were not necessarily the most intelligent—although sometimes they achieved as well in school as those who *were* more intelligent. Interestingly, however, the highly creative students were not as well liked by the teachers. As Aranha (1997) notes, teachers have long suspected that highly creative children are more likely to be guilty of misbehavior in the classroom, although there is no clear evidence that this is actually the case.

Findings from the Getzels and Jackson study cannot easily be generalized. The average IQ in the school from which the subjects were chosen was an astounding 132. The average IQ for the groups described as "high creative, low IQ" was a more-than-respectable 127. With such a limited range in intelligence test scores, it is doubtful that any relationship between creativity and intelligence would be found, even if it existed. Besides, any findings from a study such as this might well apply only to especially intelligent children.

A related study (Wallach & Kogan, 1965) also identified four groups of students classified as either high or low in intelligence and creativ-

ity, respectively. The purpose of this study was to identify characteristics that might be different among the four groups. The results of this study are summarized in Figure 8.8. They indicate that highly creative but less intelligent students are most frustrated with school and that highly intelligent but less creative students are addicted to school and well liked by their teachers. Keep in mind, however, that these four groups represent extremes of measured intelligence and creativity. The vast majority of students are not extreme. Besides, these general descriptions of school adjustment and personality characteristics are just that—general descriptions. Even with groups as highly select as these, there are numerous individual exceptions.

Even though it's possible to find individuals who are highly creative or intelligent, but not both (as did Getzels and Jackson, or Wallach and Kogan), it seems clear that there is a close relationship between intelligence and creativity. Correlations between the two are typically positive and high (Maker, 1993). That is, those who are highly intelligent are also more likely to be

Measured Intelligence

	High	Low
High	High control over their own behavior; capable of adultlike and childlike behavior	High internal conflict, frustration with school, feelings of inadequacy; can perform well in stress-free environment
Low	Addicted to school, strive desperately for academic success; well liked by teachers	Somewhat bewildered by environment; defense mechanisms include intensive social or athletic activity; occasional maladjustment

Divergent Thinking (Creativity)

FIGURE 8.8 Characteristics of children identified as either high or low on measures of intelligence and of divergent thinking (creativity). Based on studies reported by Wallach and Kogan, 1965.

highly creative—and vice versa. As Eysenck (1998) phrases it, "What is obvious is that geniuses have a high degree of intelligence." Then he adds, "But not outrageously high" (p. 127).

It is also clear that intelligence tests by *themselves* are not a very good way of identifying creative children. The reason for this—as Fuchs-Beauchamp, Karnes, and Johnson (1993) found following a study of 496 children—is that, although measured intelligence correlates very highly with measured creativity for the general population of schoolchildren, this is not the case for those whose measured IQ is 120 or more. At that level of intelligence, other factors such as motivation, persistence, home background, personality traits, and the individual's patterns of intellectual strengths and weaknesses become more important. One important approach to identifying these patterns is represented by Guilford's model of intellectual functioning.

Guilford's Model of Intellect

It seems clear that talents and gifts can manifest themselves in a variety of different areas. So, too, can deficits. Yet many of our theories of intelligence, and our models of mental functioning, fail to take this into account.

One exception is J. P. Guilford's (1959, 1967) model of the intellect. This unusual representation is relevant both to intelligence and creativity. The model is organized around three main aspects of intellectual functioning: operations, products, and content. All abilities, says Guilford, involve a combination of these three aspects of functioning. Because there are 4 different kinds of content, 5 operations, and 6 types of products, there are at least 120 distinct human abilities (see Figure 8.9).

The Three Faces of Intellect Guilford's theory of intelligence is most easily understood by looking at the three aspects of intellectual functioning:

1. **Operations.** An operation is a major intellectual process. Operations include activities such as knowing, discovering, and being aware (cognition); retrieving from storage (memory); generating multiple responses (divergent thinking); arriving at a single, accepted solution (convergent thinking); and judging the appropriateness of information or decisions (evaluation).

The two operations that have stimulated the most research and interest are **convergent** and **divergent thinking**, which are the two operations most closely related to creativity and intelligence. Because convergent thinking involves producing a single, correct solution to a problem, it is a crucial factor in intelligence testing. Divergent thinking, which involves producing multiple solutions or hypotheses, is central to the creative process. In fact, the phrase "divergent thinking" is often used as a synonym for creative thinking.

2. **Content.** An operation is performed upon certain kinds of information. This information (or *content*) can be either figural, symbolic, semantic, or behavioral. Figural content is concrete information, such as images. Symbolic content is information in the form of arbitrary signs, such as numbers or codes. Semantic content is information in the form of word

---

operation As used by Guilford, a term that describes major kinds of intellectual activity, such as remembering, evaluating, and divergent and convergent thinking.

convergent thinking A term used by Guilford to describe the type of thinking that results in a single, correct solution for a problem. Most conventional tests of intelligence measure convergent rather than divergent thinking.

divergent thinking An expression used by Guilford to describe the type of thinking that results in the production of several solutions for one problem. Divergent thinking is assumed to be closely related to creative behavior, and the term is used interchangeably with the term *creativity*.

content A term used by Guilford to describe the content of a person's intellect. Intellectual activity (operations) involves content and results in products.

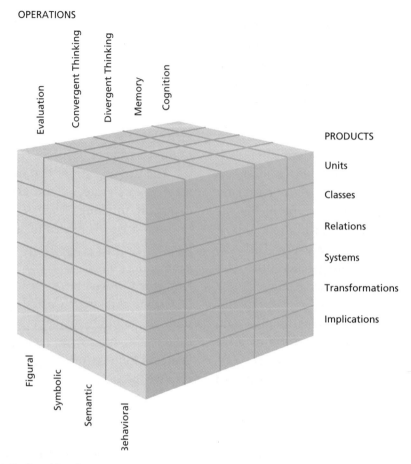

OPERATIONS

Evaluation
Convergent Thinking
Divergent Thinking
Memory
Cognition

PRODUCTS

Units
Classes
Relations
Systems
Transformations
Implications

Figural
Symbolic
Semantic
Behavioral

FIGURE 8.9 In Guilford's Model, intelligence comprises 120 separate abilities, each of which represents a combination of specific operation, content, and product. From J. P. Guilford, "Three Faces of Intellect," *American Psychologist*, Vol. 14, 1959, pp. 469–479. Copyright 1959 by the American Psychological Association and reproduced by permission.

meanings. And behavioral content is nonverbal information involved in human interaction—for example, emotion.

3. **Product**. Applying an operation to content yields a product—the form that information takes once it is processed. Products include single, segregated items of information (units); sets of items grouped by virtue of their common properties (classes); connections between items

of information (relations); organizations of information (systems); changes of information (transformations); and extrapolations or predictions from information (implications).

Guilford's model, like Gardner's theory of multiple intelligences, is based on the assumption that intelligence is not a single trait but a collection of separate abilities. This viewpoint resolves the apparent contradiction among some studies that have examined the relationship between creativity and intelligence. If intelligence is defined in terms of the entire structure and if creativity involves only some of the 120

---

product A term used by Guilford to describe the result of applying an operation to content. A product can take the form of a response.

abilities described in the model, there will likely be some correlation between the two. At the same time, the correlation may range from very low to very high according to the individual's pattern of abilities.

Instructional Implications of Guilford's Model
Guilford's model of the intellect has several important implications for the teaching/learning process. To begin with, the model draws attention to both the complexity of intellectual processes and the variety of forms in which these processes can be expressed. By so doing, it highlights the crucial role that instruction can play in intellectual development. For example, if teachers always require that students remember content as presented, only memory operations are being emphasized. And if only semantic content is involved, as is often the case, figural, symbolic, and behavioral content are being overlooked.

In short, consideration of this model makes it apparent that the intellectual development of students may well be shortchanged if only the traditional, highly limited operations, products, and content are taught. Although schools have traditionally fostered the development of a variety of abilities in children—providing repeated practice in psychomotor skills, mathematics, verbal skills, social skills, and so on—teachers have not always systematically attended to the development of all of the more complex abilities, such as those involved in creative thinking (divergent thinking), evaluating, and arriving at implications. Programs designed to foster learning/thinking strategies are attempts to correct this failure.

It is alarming that the school dropout rate for gifted adolescents is often higher than that of the general population (McMann & Oliver, 1988). There are a variety of possible reasons for this, including the frustration that can result when school programs do not permit adequate expression and development of special abilities.

In your school there may well be a Beethoven or a Mozart, a Shakespeare or a Neruda—or the next world chess champion—whose special talents remain dormant and unrecognized. That not all our inherent abilities become realized may have something to do with our schooling.

In addition, Kanchier (1988) suggests that the expectations that gifted adolescents have of themselves—and others have for them—may affect some of them negatively.

Perhaps we still know very little about teaching gifted and talented children. Although current educational practice and beliefs typically insist that identifying and teaching those who have disabilities requires special training, we remain strangely ambivalent about what should be done to identify and teach those who are highly gifted. As a result, in our schools there may be many Raphaels, da Vincis, Mozarts, and Einsteins unrecognized and undeveloped, disguised as ordinary people, totally unaware of their inherent abilities. Only in the right circumstances and with the right environmental demands will these talents become functional. Perhaps it would help if our schools demanded more evaluation, implication, and divergent thinking.

MAIN POINTS

1. There are three basic views of intelligence: psychometric (based on measurement concepts), Piagetian (based on child–environment interaction), and information processing (based on cognitive processes).

2. Intelligence is seen as an adaptive quality sometimes defined in terms of what intelligence tests measure, or in terms of an underlying general ability (*g*) that is merely potential or that might be manifested in behavior. Cattell describes fluid abilities (basic, nonverbal, and unaffected by experience) and crystallized abilities (primarily verbal, highly influenced by culture and education). Das describes an information processing theory of intelligence (PASS, involving *p*lanning, *a*ttention, and *s*imultaneous and *s*uccessive processing).

3. Sternberg's view of *successful intelligence* describes intelligence as a balance among selecting, changing, and adapting to real contexts. This view of intelligence is *triarchic* in that successful intelligence requires analytical abilities (judging, evaluating, analyzing), creative abilities (imagining, supposing, inventing), and practical abilities (acting, doing, putting into effect).

4. Gardner claims we have at least seven, probably eight, perhaps even 10, unrelated, multiple intelligences: logical-mathematical, linguistic, musical, spatial, bodily kinesthetic, interpersonal, and intrapersonal—and probably naturalist, and possibly spiritual and existential.

5. The main use of intelligence tests is for predicting. There is a relatively high correlation between IQ and achievement; a correlation coefficient is an index of relationship (covariance) but not of causation, between variables. Conventional measures of intelligence measure the extent to which the individual has directly profited from past learning experiences, and intelligence only by inference. These are less than perfectly valid (do not always measure only what they purport to measure) or reliable (do not always measure consistently). They do not typically tap several important qualities, such as interpersonal skills, creativity, and athletic ability, and many are biased against social and ethnic minorities.

6. Intelligence tests usually yield an IQ score ranging from perhaps 50 to 160 and averaging about 100 in an unselected population. They are ordinarily either group tests (i.e., Draw-a-Person test (DAP), Cognitive Abilities Test, Otis-Lennon School Ability Test) or individual tests (Peabody Picture Vocabulary Test–Revised, Revised Stanford-Binet, Wechsler Intelligence Scale for Children). Individual tests require trained testers, consume a great deal of time, and are consequently far more expensive, but they are more valid and reliable for important educational decisions.

7. The validity and reliability of intelligence tests, the extent to which intelligence is genetically determined, the possibility that there might be racial differences in intelligence, and the possibility that intelligence testing contributes to unfair educational practices and social stratification make this whole area controversial and politically dangerous. Common myths about the IQ are that it is fixed, constant, extremely important, and accurately measured by tests that are fair. Measured IQ does correlate highly with academic success.

8. Both creativity and intelligence appear to be a function of the interaction between heredity and environment. Family size and configuration also play a role, as do ethnic background and social class. None of these factors necessarily causes high or low intelligence, but they are related to other factors (such as educational opportunities, environmental enrichment, and social interaction) which contribute to intellectual development. The rubber-band hypothesis is an analogy that compares innate potential for learning to a rubber band: It can be stretched by a good environment, but it will shrivel in a poorer environment.

9. Creativity is defined in various, apparently contradictory ways. Much of the contradiction disappears when the creative product, process, and person are considered separately.

10. Creative, talented, and gifted individuals are often identified in terms of their performance on measures of intelligence and achievement. Teacher, self- , or peer ratings, or performance on creativity tests (production tests of creativity or cognitive style measurements) can also be used.

11. It is likely that relatively high intelligence is required for superior creative effort. Above a certain point, however, personality and social factors are probably more important than purely intellectual ones.

12. Guilford's model describes human intellectual functioning in terms of operations (major intellectual processes such as knowing and remembering) that are applied to content (cognitive information in the form of numbers, symbols, or words, for example) to yield a product (the result of processing information, describable as units, classes, relations, or implications). This model yields 120 separate abilities. Divergent and convergent thinking operations relate directly to creativity (divergent thinking) and intelligence (convergent thinking).

Applied Questions

- ▲ What are the educational implications of the views of intelligence advanced by Das, Sternberg, and Gardner?
- ▲ Explain why correlation does not prove causation.
- ▲ Debate the merits and educational implications of the belief that intelligence is modifiable.
- ▲ Using library resources, research the proposition that measured intelligence is related to family size, birth order, and spacing of children.
- ▲ How might lessons be modified to encourage creativity in students?
- ▲ Can you think of classroom examples of divergent and convergent thinking?

Internet Activity

Use InfoTrac College Edition or other World Wide Web sources to investigate current thinking about creativity and intelligence. Write up your findings. (See the inside back cover of this text for suggestions about where to begin.)

Sample search terms: Creativity and intelligence

312 Part Four Diversity and Teaching

Study Terms

biographical inventories **304**

cognitive assessment system **282**

confluence model **299**

content **307**

convergent thinking **307**

correlation **286**

creativity **300**

crystallized abilities **279**

divergent thinking **307**

dynamic assessment **279**

flexibility **304**

fluency **304**

fluid abilities **279**

Flynn effect **293**

g **278**

group test **288**

individual test **289**

intelligence quotient (IQ) **286**

mental age **288**

metacognition **280**

negative correlation **286**

operation **307**

originality **304**

PASS **281**

planning **281**

positive correlation **286**

PREP program **281**

product **308**

psychometrics **278**

reliability **289**

simultaneous processing **281**

successful intelligence **282**

successive processing **281**

tacit knowledge **283**

test of divergent thinking **304**

theory of multiple intelligences **284**

triarchic theory of successful intelligence **283**

validity **288**

variable **286**

Suggested Readings

The following two-volume encyclopedia contains more than 250 articles dealing with all aspects of intelligence and intellectual functioning, including most of the topics covered in this chapter:

Sternberg, R. J. (ed.) (1994). *Encyclopedia of human intelligence.* New York: Macmillan.

The pros and cons of intelligence testing, and some of the myths surrounding the meaning of IQ, are presented in the following three books. The first gave rise to enormous reaction; the second is an example of some of that reaction; the third is more of an introduction and summary to the entire field, written as much for the intelligent layperson as for the professional.

Herrnstein, R. J., & Murray, C. (1994). *The bell curve: Intelligence and class structure in American life.* New York: Free Press.

Fischer, C. S., Hout, M., Jankowski, M. S., Lucas, S. R., Swidler, A., & Voss, K. (1996). *Inequality by design: Cracking the bell curve myth.* Princeton, NJ: Princeton University Press.

Eysenck, H. J. (1998). *A new look at intelligence.* New Brunswick, NJ: Transaction.

The Steptoe book is a collection of often fascinating articles exploring some of the dimensions of exceptional giftedness by examining the lives of the world's greatest prodigies and creative geniuses. The Shaw and Runco book summarizes current thinking and research in creativity.

Steptoe, A. (Ed.) (1998). *Genius and the mind: Studies of creativity and temperament.* Oxford, Eng.: Oxford University Press.

Shaw, M. P., & Runco, M. A. (eds.) (1994). *Creativity and affect.* Norwood, N. J.: Ablex.

During hibernation, all the metabolic processes are slowed to an absolute minimum. The animal is exceedingly torpid and approaches death as closely as possible without actually dying. Bears do not truly hibernate, although they do "den-up" during severe weather (Matthews, 1969).

If you have built
     castles in the air,
     your work need
Not be lost; that is
     where they should
     be. Now put the
Foundations under them.

Henry David Thoreau

Learners with Special Needs

CHAPTER 9

PREVIEW

Today's schools are vastly different from my father's school—or my childhood school. And not just because of the appearance of new-fangled technologies like computers but maybe because today's average, ordinary classroom typically contains a sometimes bewildering diversity of students. For one thing, North American societies are becoming increasingly multicultural; for another, legislation now mandates that, wherever possible, exceptional children be educated in ordinary classrooms with more average students. As a result, the teacher's roles and responsibilities have become increasingly complex, as we see in this chapter.

FOCUS QUESTIONS

▲ How is giftedness defined for educational purposes?

▲ How do teacher's attitudes and styles affect creativity?

▲ What are the dimensions of exceptionality?

▲ What are the teacher's responsibilities with respect to intellectual exceptionality?

▲ What is ADHD?

"Suppose," my father said, "suppose you have a wild cow . . . no, make that a demented goose. . . ." Some of us chuckled a bit, squirming ahead in our seats to get closer and not miss anything. My father often began his lessons this way, especially when we were hot and sweaty and unsettled from recess. All he had to say was something like "suppose"—a rich word, pregnant with implications—and we would collectively hold our breath and listen for what was to come next. And when, in the same short sentence, he would wave in front of us an image like that of a wild cow or a demented goose, he had us—attention riveted, unwavering.

"A demented, cross-eyed goose," he continued. "A goose with a completely unnatural passion for Ford cars." Barney tittered suddenly, loudly, perhaps knowing or suspecting something about demented geese or unnatural passions of which the rest of us were not yet aware.

"Now suppose this loco goose is flying along at 30 miles an hour and he looks down and sees that he just happens to be over a nice Ford that's going in the same direction, only it's just going 20 miles an hour. Well, the goose is tempted to go right down and get closer to this Ford." Barney tittered once more.

"But," my father continued, "when the goose looks out in the distance with his crossed eyes, he sees another Ford. This other Ford is exactly 120 miles away and it's coming directly toward the first Ford at a steady speed of 40 miles an hour.

"Well, the mad goose can't resist, so it leaves the first Ford and flies straight toward the second one at 30 miles an hour. But when he gets to the second Ford, he remembers the first, changes his mind, and turns right around. Without slowing down a bit, he flies right back to the first Ford. Well, as I told you, this goose is a little strange, so when he gets back to the first Ford, he turns around again and flies right back to the second, always at 30 miles an hour and always without slowing down—back and forth and back and forth, honking madly and looking in both directions at once with his crossed eyes, until finally the two Fords run, kaboom! smack into each other.

"The question is," my dad announced into the expectant silence—and we knew that we had again been seduced into a math problem—"the question is, how far will that goose have flown before the two cars run into each other?"

Stan raised his hand at once: "I know the answer! Can I tell it?"

"Just write it down and hand it to me." We knew that Stan's answer would be correct, although I couldn't for the life of me see how he could have figured it out so fast. Most of the rest of us wrestled with the problem, writing numbers, dividing, multiplying, drawing lines, trying to figure out how many turns the goose would make, how much shorter each one would be. For his part, Barney drew exquisite replicas of two Ford cars, one in each of the bottom corners of a sheet of paper. Then he sketched a clearly delirious cross-eyed goose in one upper corner, drew a line from that corner to the other, curved the line down and back part of the way, curved it back again (but a shorter distance this time), and continued doing this, back and forth, until he had drawn what looked like a continuous series of diminishing esses down to the bottom center of the page. He then measured this line with a ruler and a string and announced, "374 miles—give or take a few." There was something about demented geese that Barney apparently didn't know.

THE TALENTED AND THE GIFTED

"That is an excellent goose!" my dad announced. He seemed truly proud, as if he were somehow responsible for Barney being able to draw and paint so well. "May I show it to the others, even if the goose didn't fly quite 374 miles?"[1] And even Barney was proud. One of my father's greatest gifts as a teacher was that he recognized gifts and talents in others and encouraged these attributes and thus made their owners feel proud.

Education doesn't always recognize talents and giftedness. Historically, with some notable exceptions, most school jurisdictions have not offered special programs for gifted children. And those that have were never quite certain which children to include in these programs. As Robinson and Clinkenbeard (1998) note, definitions of giftedness have long been a problem for educators and have ranged from extremely conservative (where, for example, only the top 1 percent of the population is included) to far more liberal definitions.

Defining Talent and Giftedness

Part of the problem is that our concept of giftedness is "fuzzy," says Adamson (1983). This concept might include any or a combination of superior academic achievement, high measured intelligence, exceptionally rapid learning, or evidence of a single extraordinary ability or talent. Unfortunately, however, a fuzzy concept of giftedness is of little value to teachers and school administrators who need to identify students for gifted programs.

Although the terms **talent** and **giftedness** are often used interchangeably, they mean different things. Giftedness refers to exceptional *general*

ability evident in superior performance and ability in a variety of areas. Talent is a narrower term; it refers to remarkable ability in a specific field like mathematics or music. The most precocious of the highly talented are sometimes referred to as **prodigies** (Feldman, 1993). Child prodigies have often been identified as those with extraordinary musical, artistic, or literary talent, such as Mozart (Steptoe, 1998) or John Stuart Mill (Howe, 1998).

Very often, of course, those who are gifted will also be talented. And because the distinctions between the two aren't very clear in practice, the phrase **talented and gifted** has become common in education. It includes all of those who require special educational services because of their exceptional abilities.

Public Law 91-230 The concept of giftedness was clarified somewhat in 1969, following the passage of U.S. Public Law 91-230. A section of this law (806) relates directly to the gifted and talented and includes the following definition:

> Gifted and talented children are those identified by professionally qualified persons who by virtue of outstanding abilities are capable of high performance. These are children who require differentiated educational programs and/or services beyond those normally provided by the regular school programs in order to realize their contribution to self and society.

---

talent Exceptional ability in a specific field such as music or literature.

giftedness Exceptional general ability.

prodigy An individual characterized by a distinct form of giftedness—marked by a highly focused talent or ability, such as musical or artistic talent, for example.

talented and gifted A phrase used to describe an advantageous combination of intelligence, creativity, and motivation that results in the potential for superior achievement in one or more fields.

---

[1] **PPC:** How far did the goose fly?
Author: I don't remember. But I could figure it out. Now, to reach the second Ford the first time . . .

The law goes on to state that capacity for high performance may be defined in terms of demonstrated achievement or potential for achievement in one or more of the following aptitudes and abilities:

- ▲ General intellectual ability
- ▲ Specific academic aptitude
- ▲ Creative or productive thinking
- ▲ Leadership ability
- ▲ Visual and performing arts
- ▲ Psychomotor ability

Interestingly, a 1978 modification of this legislation deletes the category "psychomotor ability" as a means of identifying gifted children. This was done not because children who are exceptional in this area are not considered gifted but simply because psychomotor giftedness is generally evident in superior athletic ability, an area that is well funded under other programs (Harrington, Harrington, & Karns, 1991).

Defining giftedness and establishing criteria for admission to this group is particularly important where special programs are available for gifted and talented children. The definition and criteria we use determine which children are eligible for special programs. By the same token, they determine which children are ineligible— that is, they implicitly label a large group of children "not gifted." Grossman (1995) notes important ethical and equity issues here, particularly in light of the serious problems with the procedures used to identify gifted children and those whose exceptionalities are less advantageous. Because of biases in identification procedures, non-European and poor children tend to be misrepresented in special education programs. They are overrepresented among programs for those with learning disabilities, emotional disorders, and related disabilities, and they are also underrepresented among the talented and the gifted.

Identifying Gifted Children

In practice, those who are talented and gifted are typically identified by their performance on group intelligence tests, through teachers' nominations, and perhaps through an individual intelligence test. Unfortunately, teachers' nominations of gifted students are heavily biased in favor of students who achieve exceptionally well in school subjects and who appear to be highly motivated to learn (Hany, 1997). This means that gifted underachievers are typically not identified as being gifted. When Rost and Hanses (1997) looked at teachers' ratings for 7,000 third-grade students, they found that more than two-thirds of the highly gifted underachievers had been overlooked.

The use of intelligence tests to select the gifted does not resolve all problems, given the ambiguity and confusion that often surround their use. As we saw in Chapter 8, what these tests measure isn't entirely clear. They tell us very little about some important things such as motivation, persistence, and other personality variables. And whatever they measure, they don't always measure very accurately.

In effect, then, what happens in practice with respect to identifying gifted children often does not reflect official definitions of giftedness. In the majority of cases, general intellectual ability and academic achievement are taken into consideration, but these are only two of the five criteria identified by the U.S. public law that defines giftedness. Although special talents and abilities in the other criteria (creative ability, leadership qualities, and talents in visual and performing arts) may affect teachers' nominations, they are seldom part of formal identification procedures.

Many researchers have attempted to develop assessment procedures and definitions of giftedness to reflect these concerns. For example, Renzulli, Reis, and Smith (1981) suggest that

from the teacher's point of view, giftedness can be recognized in terms of a combination of three things—either demonstrated or potential:

- High ability (might be evident in high achievement or high measured intelligence)
- High creativity (sometimes evident in production of novel ideas or in problem-solving ability)
- High commitment (manifested by a high level of persistence and task completion)

Renzulli's Scale for rating behavioral characteristics of superior students gives teachers a preliminary instrument for identifying gifted and talented students (Renzulli, 1986). Similarly, Subhi (1997) proposes a computerized identification procedure that includes achievement in addition to Renzulli's three factors of intelligence, creativity, and task commitment. Approaches such as these are essential if teachers and administrators are to fairly identify candidates for special programs. Teachers and schools should employ a variety of measures in their attempts to identify gifted children—and not use any single one of these measures as a means for excluding children from the program. That is,

even if a child functions at an average or below-average level with respect to one measure, other measures should also be considered before a final decision is made.

There are some remarkably gifted and talented individuals among the culturally different. Unfortunately, schools often overlook these people when selecting candidates for gifted and talented programs. This is partly because of biases in the selection procedures used and also because the culturally different are sometimes underachievers.

Some Characteristics of the Gifted By definition, the talented and gifted are marked by a significant advantage in intelligence, creativity, or motivation—or, most likely, all three. Many of them come from contexts—or cultures—where their gifts and talents are not only nurtured but are highly valued as well. As we see later in this chapter, given the right combination of ability and motivation, family and cultural background are probably the most important factors when determining gifted functioning and, specifically, eminence.

But are the gifted identifiably different from the more ordinary in other ways? Are they more likely to be geeks and eggheads and social misfits? The answer is a resounding no. In fact, following an extensive review of the research, Robinson and Clinkenbeard (1998) report that the gifted are likely to be at least as athletic, physically attractive, well-adjusted, insightful, and popular as those who are less gifted. In fact, if anything, on average the gifted tend to be somewhat superior in many of these areas.

Prevalence of Giftedness Estimates of the percentage of gifted and talented children vary considerably. Some researchers (Renzulli, 1986, for example) argue that as many as 20 percent of all children have the potential to be gifted. However, special programs are available for nowhere near this proportion of students. Heward and Orlansky (1992) report that gifted programs are provided for 3.6 percent of all students in 44 U.S. states.

Underrepresentation of Ethnic Minorities in Gifted Programs Ethnic minorities are vastly underrepresented in special programs for the gifted (Brown, 1997). Although in some cases their backgrounds might have impeded the development of the cognitive skills and motivation essential for performance at a high level, that is clearly not always the case. For example, Scott and associates (1996) gave a battery of cognitive tests to 400 kindergarten children in regular classrooms and to 31 children in a program for the gifted. The scores for the top eight students in the regular classrooms were higher than those of 81 percent of the gifted groups. And an astounding seven of these eight children were members of ethnic minority groups (Black or Hispanic).

Asian minorities, too, are vastly underrepresented among those selected for gifted programs, and research on these minorities is scarce (Plucker, 1996). One reason is that many of them, like so many of the culturally different, are underachievers (Wilgosh, 1991). Because they don't do as well as majority-group children in ordinary classroom programs, they are hardly likely to be viewed as potentially gifted. Besides, as Shaklee (1992) notes, because there are insufficient programs for gifted learners, educators tend to err on the side of *under-* rather than *over* identification of the gifted. What is needed, claims Maker (1996), are new programs, new identification procedures, and changes in beliefs and stereotypes.

Special Programs for the Gifted

Following the passage of PL 91-230 in 1969, which, among other things, attempted to define giftedness, a massive survey of programs for the gifted and talented was undertaken in the United States. The survey involved thousands of parents and educators and revealed several things. One was that the education of the gifted and talented was typically perceived as a very low-priority issue: Only 21 states had any legislation to provide facilities for the gifted, and in most cases this legislation represented intent rather than concrete action. Another revelation was that the programs that did exist did not generally reach the gifted and talented from ethnic and social minorities and that there were serious problems in identifying the gifted and talented (Marland, 1972).

A similar survey, conducted some six years after the passage of PL 91-230, found that all but eight states had some type of legislation concerning programs for the gifted and talented. And the National Research Center on the Gifted and Talented has been receiving nearly $10 million per year since 1990 to direct and coordinate research on the gifted and to establish gifted programs (Harrington, Harrington, & Karns, 1991). However, the majority of states (and Canadian provinces) still provide services to only a relatively small number of children in this category—a situation that can be attributed to lack of funding, lack of trained personnel, and lack of widely accepted procedures and criteria for identifying the gifted and talented. Sadly, an observation made by Terman (1925) more than six decades ago might still be true today: When comparing potential and achievement, we find that the most "retarded" group in our schools is the highly gifted. Torrance and Sisk (1997) agree: "It is time to devise concepts and procedures which will engage the gifted and non-gifted in such a way that all children may attain their highest potential" (p. vii).

Acceleration and Enrichment There are two broad approaches to educating the gifted: **acceleration** and **enrichment**. Each of these can occur in the regular classroom; each might also involve what is termed **ability grouping**.

These terms are essentially self-explanatory. Ability grouping implies segregating the gifted either in separate classes or sometimes even in special schools. As Torrance and Sisk (1997)

"But mom, I think acceleration is working. Billy's now flunking out twice as fast."

note, the current trend is to educate the gifted within regular classrooms rather than to separate them by ability.

Programs that accelerate simply move students more rapidly through the conventional curriculum, exposing them to the same material as other students. These programs attempt to compress or compact the regular curriculum into fewer lessons; these are sometimes referred to as compaction programs (Evans & King, 1994a,b). Programs that enrich provide gifted students with additional and varying school experiences in an attempt to deepen and broaden their knowledge and capabilities. Recall that both enrichment and acceleration can occur in the regular classroom, or both can involve ability grouping.

The enrichment approach is well illustrated by Renzulli's (1977) enrichment model, also called the **revolving door model** (Renzulli, Reis,

---

acceleration One approach used for the education of the gifted. Acceleration programs attempt to move students through the conventional curriculum more rapidly than normal.

enrichment An approach to the education of gifted children. Enrichment involves providing students with additional and different school experiences rather than simply moving them more rapidly through the conventional curriculum. Also termed the *revolving door model*.

ability grouping Grouping students on the basis of ability for instructional purposes.

---

revolving door model An enrichment program for gifted children advocated by Renzulli, available to the top 25 percent of students in a program (high ability, high creativity, high motivation) on an optional basis, so that students can opt in or out of the program (hence, the revolving door).

& Smith, 1981). This model advocates selecting gifted individuals on the basis of three characteristics: high academic ability, high creative potential, and high motivation. No rigorous cutoff scores are used; instead, all students whose achievement or apparent potential places them in the upper 25 percent of students in the school are designated as talented. Any of these students may then enter enrichment programs and drop out of them as they wish (hence, the revolving door). The programs vary according to the expressed interests of the students. When students identify a project and commit themselves to it, they are allowed to enter a resource room and work on the project. Under this model, enrichment programs tend to be schoolwide rather than restricted to specific classes or students (Renzulli & Reis, 1994).

The most common form of acceleration is simply grade-skipping. But, as Robinson and Clinkenbeard (1998) point out, grade-skipping is generally a response to a single student's achievement rather than a general, schoolwide program for gifted learners. Although this practice rewards the student for past accomplishments, it does little to modify the curriculum to make it more appropriate. Professional opinion on grade-skipping is quite negative, notes Heinbokel (1997), although she found little support for this negative view in her review of research that had examined the effects of grade-skipping in German elementary schools.

Stanley's (1976) **radical acceleration model**, initially developed primarily for students gifted in mathematics, is another example of acceleration. Radical acceleration attempts to compress the ordinary curriculum to enable gifted individuals to master a course of studies in only a fraction of the time ordinarily required. Subsequently, many of these accelerated youngsters are enrolled in university-sponsored courses for additional acceleration. For example, Noble and Smyth (1995) describe a radical acceleration program at the University of Washington where 14-year-olds are allowed to enroll in university courses. Robinson (1992) describes a similar program in China, and Gross (1992) outlines another in Australia. Their reports indicate that students often express boredom and frustration before acceleration, and higher levels of self-esteem, achievement, and better social relationships after acceleration (for example, see Gross, 1992).

The relative merits of acceleration and enrichment have long been debated among educators. One common argument against acceleration is that it might be harmful to move students much beyond their social and psychological levels of development, that they might eventually no longer "fit in" socially with their peers. Interestingly, a common argument *for* enrichment is precisely the argument used *against* acceleration; that is, educators simply assume that enrichment will not have the same social and psychological implications as acceleration would. After all, enrichment does not remove gifted children from their age and grade levels as does acceleration; it simply provides them with an opportunity to deepen and broaden their knowledge at each level.

In fact, however, enrichment and acceleration may not be that much different in practice. Slavin (1993a) suggests that most accelerated programs do not really involve acceleration at all, but are far more likely to be enrichment programs. And relatively recent studies that have looked at the effects of various combinations of enrichment and acceleration typically report that a balance between the two is most effective (for example, Kulik & Kulik, 1992; Keirouz, 1993).

---

radical acceleration model Stanley's acceleration program for gifted children, designed specifically for very high achievers in mathematics. Also termed a *compression* or *compaction program*, it attempts to compress the mathematics curriculum so that it can be covered in a fraction of the time that would ordinarily be required.

Mentoring and Tutoring An increasing number of programs for the gifted use mentors or tutors (Emerson-Stonnell & Carter, 1994); mentoring and tutoring are also used for students with learning disabilities (Fuchs et al., 1997).

A **mentor** is an individual who serves as a sort of intellectual and psychological guide. Mentoring implies a close relationship. The mentor may be a role model, consultant, advisor, source of wisdom—even a sort of protector. Hence, the term protégé is used to signify the one who is mentored (Jacobi, 1991). A **tutor**, on the other hand, is a teacher rather than a mentor, but unlike a regular classroom teacher, a tutor teaches only one student at a time (Raines, 1994).

Tutoring, says Bloom (1984), is clearly the most effective way to teach. His review of the research suggests that one-on-one tutoring will move the average learner from the middle of the pack (where, by definition, average learners are found) to about the 98th percentile. Tutoring also has beneficial effects on the tutors themselves—they develop more positive attitudes and gain understanding. And it has beneficial effects on children identified as being at risk of failure (Topping & Ehly, 1998).

Tutoring is often carried out by adults or older students. It can also be conducted by peers; in this case it may be called **peer-assisted learning (PAL)**. Peer-assisted learning involves children in school deliberately and systematically helping others. It may include any of a variety of activities sometimes described using labels such as peer modeling, peer tutoring, peer education, peer counseling, peer monitoring, and peer assessment.

Mentoring, which requires a more encompassing relationship between two individuals, has become more common in education in recent years and is especially useful for career development (Holland, 1994). For example, many school jurisdictions have instituted mentor programs wherein expert teachers are designated as mentors to assist the early development of novice teachers (Bainer & Didham, 1994). Similarly, mentoring programs are used at some universities, at both the graduate and the undergraduate level.

Individualized Educational Plans (IEPs) Another approach to the education of the gifted involves self-directed and independent study, often using learning/thinking strategies of the kind discussed in Chapter 5. Some self-directed study programs also use **individualized educational plans (IEPs)**, designed for students according to their individual needs and talents. IEPs are widely used for children with special needs, their use having been mandated in the United States by a 1975 law (PL 94-142). (IEPs are described and illustrated later in this chapter.) Torrance (1986) notes that IEPs are becoming more popular for use with gifted children; the plans usually involve a combination of approaches and materials such as self-directed study, mentoring, enrichment, perhaps acceleration, and programs for the development of learning/thinking strategies and motivation.

Special Schools Besides these approaches to the education of the gifted, some schools cater solely to these children, as do Saturday and summer

---

mentor An individual engaged in a one-on-one teaching/learning relationship where the teacher (mentor) serves as a fundamentally important model with respect to values, beliefs, philosophies, and attitudes, as well as a source of more specific information.

tutor A teacher involved in a one-on-one teaching situation. Tutors are frequently other students or else other teachers or experts.

peer-assisted learning (PAL) A form of tutoring in which the tutors are typically school peers rather than older students or adults.

individualized educational plans (IEPs) Individualized instructional programs tailored to a child's specific pattern of needs and abilities. IEPs may be used for gifted, learning-disabled, retarded, or average children. Also termed *individualized program plans* or *IPPs*.

programs and a variety of community or university enrichment programs. Their offerings can sometimes be included in IEPs designed for gifted children.

In spite of these special programs, many gifted and talented children—like many whose gifts and talents are below average—remain in regular classrooms and lack access to any formal "special" education. This does not mean, however, that teachers of regular classes can (or should) do nothing for them. In fact, as we discuss later in this chapter, legislation now makes it mandatory for many children who would otherwise receive special instruction to spend most of their time in regular classrooms. It has therefore become necessary for teachers in regular classrooms to learn about exceptionality and about what they can do for these children. Many suggestions included in this chapter are appropriate for both ordinary students and for those who are more extraordinary.

Suggestions for the Regular Classroom

"In the final analysis," write Harrington, Harrington, and Karns, "[we] must provide educational challenge for [our] bright people or else tomorrow we will be led by the mediocre, and on the day after, by the incompetent" (1991, p. 41).

Do schools do what they can (or should) for gifted and creative students? Perhaps not, if Ms. Bourgeois' class is any indication (see the case entitled "Your Dad's not the Teacher"). Schools have traditionally been geared toward developing students who are obedient, accepting of other people's ideas, popular, punctual, courteous, and respectful. And academic success is fostered by memorization and the ability to recognize and replicate accepted answers and procedures. Flexibility, risk taking, originality, inventiveness, and nonconformity are absent from these lists. Claire, like all other students in her class, was expected to learn a

simple odd-even rule and to repeat it when she was asked.

A *good* teacher would not have responded as Ms. Bourgeois did. Not only was she unwilling to consider the possibility that Claire's response might have merit—or at the very least, to ask Claire to explain her response—but she resorted to name calling. And even if Claire's response had been totally incorrect and inappropriate, it was nevertheless different, innovative, exploratory. As Matson (1991) notes, there is much to be said for rewarding *failure*—that is, for rewarding the brave and creative attempts of students even when they are incorrect.

Many highly gifted and talented students, note Torrance and Sisk (1997), achieve at levels far below what might be expected on the basis of their capabilities. Why? Because, these authors argue, they are simply not motivated to do well. Their lack of motivation may have any of a variety of sources. *First*, and perhaps most important, say Torrance and Sisk, is that learners cannot see any relationship between real life and what they are asked to learn. That is, they are provided with little or no opportunity to use their learning.

Second, many of the highly gifted lose their motivation following repeated exposure to evaluation systems that are shallow, meaningless, and totally inadequate. Sadly, many parents and teachers are far more interested in how students perform on tests than in what they learn and what they can accomplish as a result.

Third, teaching often presents gifted learners with tasks that are too ridiculously simple to maintain their interest. Conversely, in an attempt to avoid this problem, some programs for the gifted present concepts and activities that are too advanced, too abstract, too theoretical, or impractical.

Fourth, many school programs do not ask, or permit, gifted learners to use their most unique talents, nor do they provide them with an opportunity to learn according to their preferred learning styles.

CASES FROM THE CLASSROOM

Your Dad's not the Teacher

THE SETTING: Ms. Adèle Bourgeois' third grade arithmetic class. The class has been learning odd and even numbers.

Ms. Bourgeois: So who can tell me, you should all know this by now, which numbers between 1 and 10 can be divided by 2?

Thomas: All the even ones—2, 4, 6, 8, and 10!

Ms. Bourgeois: Very good, Thomas. That's exactly right.

Claire: That's not right.

Ms. Bourgeois (annoyed): What's that, Claire?

Claire: That's not right. I mean, not just the even numbers.

Ms. Bourgeois (quite angry): You always think you know better than the book, don't you?

Claire (more timidly, but sticking to her guns): But the odd ones too. My dad said . . .

Ms. Bourgeois: Your dad isn't the teacher, smarty pants. How d'you suppose you'd divide 5 by 2, hunh? Weren't you paying any attention at all when we talked about how all even numbers can be divided by 2?

Claire, red-faced, shrugs and whispers "2½" too softly for Ms. Bourgeois to hear.

The result of these shortcomings of schools, programs, evaluation systems, and parental and teacher expectations may well be a stifling of motivation and ambition and an appalling lack of achievement among those who could easily be society's very best achievers.

But teachers can do specific things to teach students different ways of thinking and perhaps foster giftedness and creative thinking. Among these are a variety of problem-solving techniques.

Brainstorming Brainstorming is among the most common group approaches for solving problems creatively. It has been used extensively, and successfully, in many school programs designed to foster creativity (for example, Paulus & Paulus, 1997; Herschel, 1994).

Developed by Alex Osborn (1957), **brainstorming** is a technique for producing a wide variety of solutions while deliberately suspend-

ing judgment about the appropriateness of any of them. This, the principle of deferred evaluation, is an important characteristic of brainstorming. It leads to the production of far more ideas than would be possible if evaluation were permitted. However, some research indicates that there is no particular advantage to producing tons of ideas and that perhaps more can be accomplished by emphasizing quality rather than quantity (Rowatt et al., 1997).

NOW CHILDREN——ANY CREATIVE IDEAS ON HOW TO MAKE TEACHER RICH....?

---

brainstorming A technique popularized by Osborn and used to produce creative solutions for problems. A brainstorming session usually involves a small group of people who are encouraged to produce a wide variety of ideas, which are later evaluated.

TABLE 9.1
Application of a Creative Brainstorming Checklist to the Question: How many suggestions can you make for different ways to manage a classroom?

CHECKLIST	EXPLANATION	SOME POSSIBILITIES SUGGESTED BY CHECKLIST
Adapt	Use ideas from other sources	Run class like a factory, a prison, or a playground.
Modify	Change	Change the composition of the class; change teaching methods; change approach to discipline problems.
Magnify	Make larger	Increase class size; increase number of teachers; increase number of assignments; increase magnitude of punishment or reinforcement.
Minify	Make smaller	Decrease class size; decrease number of assignments; reduce number of reprimands; reduce number of school days.
Put to other uses	Put to an unexpected use	Students are given the responsibility of entertaining the school at a social evening.
Substitute	Exchange	Replace teacher; replace entire class; exchange one or more members of the class with students from another class.
Rearrange	Reorganize, reorder, resort	Change physical aspects of class; change seating plan.
Reverse	Turn around; do the opposite	Turn desks to face the rear, the side, the front; have teacher face the opposite direction; exchange teacher–student roles.
Combine	Bring together; join	Combine one or more of previous suggestions; combine teaching/learning function with other function such as entertainment, problem solving, or discussion of noncurricular topics of interest.

In industry a brainstorming session may last for two or more hours and involve 5–12 people from a wide variety of backgrounds; brainstorming in a classroom is more likely to involve the entire class and last either all or only part of a class period. The leader (teacher) explains a few simple rules: Criticism of ideas is discouraged; modification of other ideas, or combinations of them, are encouraged; the emphasis is on producing many ideas; and all ideas are permitted, no matter how wild or unusual they might seem. The teacher then describes the problem to be solved, and the session begins.

During a brainstorming session, various specific aids to creativity are used. Most common are checklists for stimulating ideas. For example, Parnes (1967) provides a checklist of nine actions that could be applied to a variety of problems. As an illustration, Table 9.1 shows how each of these nine possibilities might be applied to a general problem in classroom management.

Conceptual Models A conceptual model (also termed a *concept map*) is a verbal or graphic presentation designed to assist the learner in developing a clear and useful mental representation of whatever is being studied. Such models, note Rafferty and Fleschner (1993), are especially useful in promoting meaningful learning and understanding. They are as Mayer (1989) phrases it, a

---

conceptual model A verbal or graphic representation of concepts and important relationships that exist among them. Designed to assist the learner in developing a clear and useful mental representation. Also termed a *concept map*.

special form of advance organizer such as those we discussed in connection with Ausubel's theory (see Chapter 6). Conceptual models used as advance organizers are typically developed by teachers. Gifted learners might also be encouraged to develop their own conceptual models (concept maps) as a way of organizing information and increasing understanding and retention.

Figure 9.1 is an example of a conceptual model that includes the most important elements required to understand how radar functions. Students who were allowed to examine this model for one minute before a short lecture on radar later recalled 57 percent more of the important concepts than did students who had been given the lecture without the model (Mayer, 1989). Perhaps more important, students who had examined the conceptual model were able to produce solutions that were 83 percent more accurate than the other group's for problems that required transferring what they had learned to new situations. In other words, these students were able to use creatively what they had learned, because they could now apply it to new situations.

Research with conceptual models suggests that they can be particularly effective in science (Roth & Bowen, 1993). "Better learning," argues Papert, "will not come from finding better ways for the teacher to *instruct*, but from giving the learner better opportunities to construct" (1993, p. 3). Making graphic representations with paper and pencil and inventing mental models are ways to construct. Constructionist emphasis in teaching and learning encourages learners to discover and build their own representations, their own models.

Other Factors Related to Gifted Achievement

Follow-up studies of children in Terman's longitudinal investigation of gifted children indicated that, in the end, many of these children were not outstanding achievers—although, on average, they tended to be better adjusted and more suc-

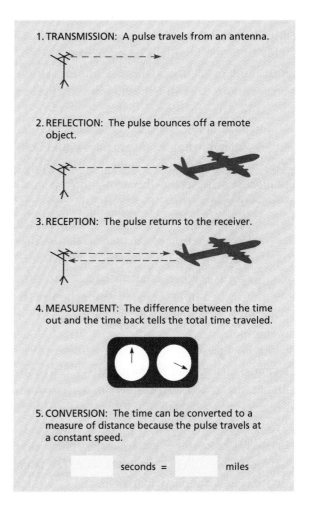

FIGURE 9.1 A conceptual model of how radar functions. Adapted from R. E. Mayer (1989), "Models for Understanding." *Review of Educational Research, 59,* 1, 43–64. Copyright 1989 by the American Educational Research Association. Reprinted by permission of the publisher.

cessful than comparable but nongifted individuals (see Fetterman, 1994). Some, however, were far more successful than others in terms of academic achievement, and also in terms of career and general happiness.

Family Context To find out why some children were more successful than others, Terman and Oden (1959) compared a group of the 100 most successful participants with a second group of the 100 least successful in this study. Their most important finding: The family backgrounds of the two groups were significantly different.

Subjects from the successful group were from highly educated families that encouraged exploration, independence, achievement, and ambition far more than did the families of the less successful participants.

Torrance (1993) reports remarkably similar conclusions following a 30-year follow-up investigation of gifted students (now adults). Among the highest achievers in this group, only a small number became truly, outstandingly eminent. These appeared to be individuals who had just the right combination of talents and personality characteristics and, perhaps most important, were also fortunate enough to have been born into the right family context and schooled in classroom climates that encouraged their development.

Classroom Climate and Teaching Styles **Classroom climate**, the general atmosphere of a classroom, also seems to be related to the encouragement of giftedness and creativity (Litterst & Eyo, 1993). However, phrases like "general atmosphere of a classroom" are uncomfortably vague, far from scientific, and not particularly useful.

Classroom climate can be described more specifically in terms of instructional approaches or **teaching style**. A teaching style is an identifiable and related group of teaching activities and routines. Thus, researchers speak of styles that reflect specific methods of instructing (for example, the lecturing style, the questioning style, the role-playing style). Or else they speak of styles that reflect the teacher's predominant relationship with students or the major roles that each assumes (for example, authoritarian versus democratic, teacher-centered versus learner-centered, traditional versus progressive).

Haddon and Lytton (1968) describe two types of schools, which they label "formal" and "informal." The formal schools are characterized by a teacher-centered, authoritarian approach to learning and teaching very much like what we have described as *direct instruction*. Teachers in these schools use a **formal teaching style**. Teachers whose styles are most formal teach each subject separately, emphasize individual rather than group work, assign class seating, restrict students' movements, emphasize assessment and achievement, and make extensive use of external motivators such as grades.

In contrast, informal schools tend to emphasize self-initiated learning and greater student participation. In other words, they are more student-centered (more constructivist). Teachers in these schools use an **informal teaching style**. Those whose styles are informal tend to integrate subjects, provide students with considerable freedom for determining their activities, typically allow students to select their own seating, do not emphasize tests and academic achievement, and tend to rely on internal sources of motivation like self-satisfaction.

There is some evidence that students in informal schools do better on measures of creative thinking than do students of comparable intelligence and socioeconomic status who attend formal schools (Haddon & Lytton, 1968; Clements, 1991).

---

classroom climate A vague expression that describes the general ambience of a classroom. Factors that contribute to classroom climate include the teacher's customary ways of interacting with students (teaching styles), physical features of the classroom, relationships and interactions among learners, and personal and decorative touches.

teaching style A customary way of teaching. Teaching styles are often described as either teacher-centered (also labeled *formal* or *direct instruction*) or learner-centered (*informal* or *constructivist*).

---

formal teaching style An approach to teaching that emphasizes competition, individual work, discipline, order, achievement, and external motivators.

informal teaching style A teaching approach that grants students a relatively high degree of freedom and autonomy and emphasizes individual growth and fulfillment rather than academic achievement and external rewards.

Some classes, like the one shown on the left, are highly formal: These emphasize order, individual work, discipline, and achievement. Others, like that on the right, are more informal: They grant students a higher level of autonomy and tend to emphasize personal growth rather than achievement and external rewards. To some extent, these teaching styles reflect the teacher's personality; they also reflect the influences of other factors such as teacher training programs, school goals and philosophy, and the wider influences of culture, politics, and religion. Neither approach is clearly superior for all purposes.

There is some evidence, too, to suggest that humanistic approaches to teaching are more likely to lead to creativity among students. Research reviewed in Chapter 7, for example, indicates that open education often leads to higher creativity scores, but it also often leads to lower scores on standardized achievement tests. Similarly, Turner and Denny (1969) found that warm, spontaneous, and caring teachers are more likely to encourage creative behavior in their students than are teachers characterized as highly organized and businesslike.

Teachers' Expectations and Students' Performance There are numerous examples of **self-fulfilling prophecies**—situations where what we expect to happen does happen. Often we assume that our expectations somehow affect outcomes. But surely, there are just as many situations where what we expect does *not* happen. Do the expectations of teachers have any effect on the behavior of their students?

Research Evidence The classic study of **teacher expectations** is Rosenthal and Jacobson's (1968a,b) "Oak School" experiment. Teachers in this school were told that they were participating in the validation of a new test designed to predict academic "blooming." They were also told that children, especially slow achievers, often show sudden intellectual spurts and that the new test could identify "spurters." But the tests that the Oak School children were given were actually only intelligence tests (the

---

self-fulfilling prophecy An expectation that is realized because it is expected to be. Teachers' expectations of students are sometimes self-fulfilling prophecies.

teacher expectations A phrase used to describe the often unconscious expectations that teachers have regarding the likely achievement and behavior of students. Teacher expectations often reflect biases related to variables such as gender, ethnicity, and social class.

Flanagan Tests of General Ability). These were administered in the spring; the following September, the teachers were given false information about the test results. They were casually given the names of students designated as spurters but actually chosen randomly to represent 20 percent of the student body. The only difference, then, between the spurters and other students (control groups) was that the teachers had reason to expect increased performance from the spurters.

Amazingly, report Rosenthal and Jacobson, their expectations were fulfilled. What is more surprising is that the increase affected not only academic achievement—which is to some degree under a teacher's control—but also intellectual ability as measured by the Flanagan tests. The most dramatic spurts were for first-grade students, probably those who had the greatest room for improvement. Indications are that intelligence is also more malleable at an earlier age (see Chapter 2).

The results of the Rosenthal and Jacobson study have since been questioned by some reviewers who claimed that there had been some misjudging, misrecording, and misrepresentation of the original data (see Rosenthal, 1987; Wineburg, 1987). Furthermore, many attempted replications have failed. But others have not.

Brophy and Good (1974) and Braun (1976) have since reviewed a wealth of teacher-expectation studies. Although few of these studies had results as dramatic as those first reported by Rosenthal and Jacobson, many reveal highly consistent patterns of expectations among teachers. For example, it seems that teachers often develop more positive expectations (with respect to academic achievement) for children who come from higher socioeconomic backgrounds, who are obedient and compliant, who are attractive, and who sit close to the teacher and speak clearly. And there is evidence, as well, that negative expectations are sometimes associated with ethnic minorities (Plewis, 1997), with lower employment levels of fathers (Childs & McKay, 1997), and with children identified as disruptive in the classroom (Winter, 1996). And Chandler (1994) found that many elementary school teachers' expectations for their students are clearly affected by gender. For example, many expect female students not to do as well in science and mathematics—and perhaps to do better in art.[2]

---

[2] **PPC:** So is the bear saying that some female students do less well in science and mathematics because that's what is expected of them? What does the bear really think about the power of expectations?

Author: Says the bear, expectations are really predictions. When you expect that something will happen, you are, in a real sense, predicting an outcome. And then he quotes again from his guru, Yogi Berra, who is alleged to have said, "Making predictions is a very uncertain thing. Especially about the future."

The Implications of Research on Expectations
Although the effects of teacher expectations are not always entirely evident, most researchers now accept that these can be an important influence on student achievement (Wang, Haertel, & Walberg, 1993). In many instances, notes Ozar (1994), negative expectations can adversely affect students' behavior or teachers' assessments. In one study, for example Babad (1985) reports a significant bias in teachers' grading of worksheets related to whether teachers believe the work to have been done by excellent or weak students.

Many studies have been designed to *change* teacher expectations. The goal is simply to raise expectations, especially for students for whom teachers might otherwise have unjustly low expectations (Babad, 1993). These studies often provide specific recommendations for equalizing teacher expectations and teaching practices and for making teachers more aware of their expectations. And although the results have not always been measurably positive, in general they support the belief that teacher expectations can be made to be more positive and can result in happier and more successful students. These studies also indicate that teacher expectations, like most of our beliefs, are not simple, easily changed ideas. As Weinstein, Madison, and Kuklinski (1995) note following a two-year in-school program designed to modify teacher expectations, teacher expectations go well beyond the teacher and the student. Attempts to change them need to take into consideration the context in which these expectations are embedded—for example, the wealth of long-established beliefs about race, sex, and gender that affect what teachers expect from their students. Researchers must also be aware of teachers' beliefs about the malleability of students, about the importance and meaning of characteristics like intelligence, and about the extent to which teachers can bring about significant change.

TEACHING THOSE WITH DISABILITIES

Most of the human population is what we consider normal or average—although each of us is different from every other person. But there are some who, in one or more ways, are different from the average. These are children who, from an educational, social, and sometimes medical point of view, can be described as having **special needs**.

Among them are those about whom we have been talking: those who are far more talented and gifted than the average. These include the academically talented, those who are endowed with superior motor skills or outstanding physical appearance, and those who are socially gifted. For these individuals, the label "exceptional" is appropriate.

There is also another dimension of **exceptionality**. It includes those less intelligent or less creative, those with physical and motor disabilities, and those with emotional and adjustment problems. You see, the term *exceptional* applies equally to those to whom nature and nurture have been noticeably generous and to those to whom they have been much less kind.

U.S. Public Law 94-142

Knowing how to identify exceptional children—and knowing, as well, how to administer the programs and resources available for them—has always been an essential part of the training of

special needs A phrase used to describe individuals whose social, physical, or emotional exceptionalities require special treatment and services for them to develop their potential.

exceptionality A term used to describe a significant deviation from the average in terms of physical, intellectual, or emotional behaviors, abilities, or skills. It is a two-dimensional concept because it can indicate either significant superiority or significant handicaps.

special education teachers. These are teachers whose express function is to provide educational services for children with special needs.

In recent years, however, the special needs of exceptional children have also become important to the regular classroom teacher—particularly since the passage of **Public Law 94-142** in 1975. This law was in part an attempt to correct the injustices that have sometimes existed in the treatment of exceptional children. The law was amended in 1990 by the **Individuals with Disabilities Education Act (IDEA)** and reauthorized by the U.S. Congress in 1995 (see Fuchs & Fuchs, 1995). The provisions of this law, and the related court interpretations, have been largely instrumental in revolutionizing how schools deal with exceptionality.

Among other things, the law provides four principal guarantees for children with special needs:

▲ Education in the "least restrictive environment"
▲ Free and appropriate educational services
▲ Fair, nondiscriminatory evaluation and due process of law
▲ An individualized educational plan (IEP)

We look at each of these provisions in the next four sections.

Inclusion: The Least Restrictive Environment PL 94-142's requirement that school jurisdictions pro-vide special services for qualified children in the "least restrictive environment" possible is reflected in what is termed **mainstreaming** or **inclusion** (*inclusive education*). The phrase "least restrictive environment" relates to a legal decision which specified that children with disabilities had a right to education in the "least restrictive environment." For practical purposes, in most instances this environment has been judged to be the regular classroom. This is why an increasing number of regular classroom teachers (as opposed to special education teachers) are called upon to teach exceptional children in regular classrooms or what are termed **inclusive classrooms**.

Inclusion resulted not only from the passage of PL 94-142, but was also influenced by at least two other related events in the field of special education. The first involves the recognition—sometimes by courts of law—that many who had been labeled "emotionally disturbed" or "mentally retarded" and who had therefore not previously been admitted into regular classrooms were indeed capable of learning and functioning effectively when given access to these classrooms. At the same time, a relatively new classification of learning difficulty was introduced: *learning disability*. This category generally includes individuals who do not have obvious disabilities (blindness, deafness, or profound mental retardation, for example) and have therefore been ineligible for special classes but have not functioned well in regular classrooms. (Learning disabilities are described in more detail later in this chapter.)

Thus, on the one hand, there is a recognition that some "special" children have been mislabeled and that, even if they have not been mislabeled,

---

special education teacher A teacher whose training and/or functions deal specifically with the education of exceptional children.

Public Law 94-142 A 1975 U.S. education act that guarantees special students a free and appropriate education, nondiscriminatory evaluation, due process, an individualized educational plan (IEP), and education in the least restrictive environment. Amended in 1990 by the Individuals with Disabilities Education Act (IDEA).

Individuals with Disabilities Education Act (IDEA) The act that updated Public Law 94-142.

---

mainstreaming The practice of placing students in need of special services in regular classrooms rather than segregating them. Also termed *inclusion* or *inclusive education*.

inclusive classroom A classroom that contains one or more children with special needs in addition to more average children.

Mainstreaming, or inclusive education, involves educating children with special needs in regular classrooms—as illustrated here by this blind pupil who is reading a braille book. There is some concern that full inclusion might lead to injustices as serious as those that could result from the routine segregation of all children with special needs.

they can benefit from regular classroom experiences. On the other hand, educators now recognize that some children in regular classrooms would greatly benefit from special attention.

Proponents of inclusion, note Gresham and MacMillan (1997), argue that it has at least three positive outcomes: increased peer acceptance and decreased rejection of students with disabilities by their peers; mutually beneficial social interactions between students with and without disabilities; and the learning of socially appropriate behaviors by students with disabilities as a result of modeling the behavior of the other students.

But subsequent research has not always confirmed the belief that all children with special needs would do better in regular classrooms. "To date," write Gresham and Macmillan (1997), "there is little solid empirical research supporting these presumed benefits in social and affective domains for students with mild disabilities"

(p. 379). One of the problems, explain Barnett and Monda-Amaya (1998), is that many teachers don't appear to be adequately prepared to implement instructional techniques more suited for the inclusive than the noninclusive classroom. As a result, many of the special education techniques that work well with children who have specific needs are seldom found in inclusive classrooms where most of the children do not have disabilities. Specifically, the techniques that work best with many exceptionalities are highly individual; in contrast, the main instructional methods in today's inclusive classroom are oriented toward the group rather than the individual (Fuchs & Fuchs, 1995).

Kauffman, Lloyd, and Riedel (1995) also agree that not all children with special needs should be included in regular classrooms. Such **full inclusion**, they note, denies some students a full and effective education. Students with more serious emotional and behavioral problems, for example, often do not fare well in regular classrooms where overtaxed and undertrained teachers cannot provide optimal services for them.

In spite of the widespread support that the inclusive classroom has recently enjoyed in North American education, some negative reaction has occasionally come from parents of students without disabilities who have feared that the education of their children might suffer—as well as from some parents of students with disabilities who also fear that their children might not receive the education that is best for them (Diamond & LeFurgy, 1994). Negative reaction has also come from student teachers—whose attitudes tend to become more positive during teacher training but more negative again after student teaching (Wilczenski, 1994). Similarly, some practicing teachers react negatively to

full inclusion The inclusion of all special needs children in regular classrooms regardless of the nature and severity of their handicaps.

inclusion, especially if they have not been trained specifically for inclusive education and receive inadequate support. For example, in a representative survey, more than half of 276 preschool teachers had children with disabilities in their classrooms, but more than 75 percent of them received no assistance from any special educators (McDonnell, Brownell, & Wolery, 1997). Finally, students without disabilities in inclusive classrooms may also react negatively to the presence of students with severe learning difficulties (Whitaker, 1994).

In spite of these difficulties, much of the recent research on inclusion indicates that the needs of special students can be met in regular classrooms. This is especially true of those with mild disabilities (Giangreco, 1997). Inclusive education nevertheless remains highly controversial, and the support for it is somewhat qualified (Audette & Algozzine, 1997). This is true at least partly because inclusion of special needs children in regular classrooms is expensive and difficult for school administrators, given legal requirements concerning unbiased and extensive testing and the need to consult parents, obtain their consent, and include them in educational planning teams. Integration also complicates the lives of teachers, not all of whom are well prepared, both in terms of personality characteristics and training, to deal intelligently and effectively with inclusive classrooms. The inclusive classroom requires changes in teacher education programs, with considerably more emphasis on identifying and providing programs for disabled and gifted children. Not surprisingly, when Pearman, Huang, and Mellblom (1997) surveyed 558 school administrators and teachers, they found that their primary concerns related to the lack of time for teaching all students well and the lack of proper training for managing students who present behavioral or learning challenges. (See the case entitled "Robert Goldberg, Bad Teacher.")

The controversy over inclusive education is not really about whether classrooms should or should not be inclusive. Rather, it concerns the *extent* to which they should be inclusive. And now there appears to be growing consensus that, just as the practice of segregating all special needs children led to serious injustices and poor educational practice, so too might full inclusion. As Huefner (1994) notes, school administrators need to avoid either extreme: the full inclusion model or blanket separation of all children with special needs. Decisions about the placement of a child, she argues, should be made individually and should honor the concept of least restrictive environment. For some children, that environment may be a segregated classroom; for others, it may be an inclusive classroom.

A Free and Appropriate Education Not only should decisions about services for children with special needs respect the principle of the least restrictive environment, but legislation mandates that these decisions should also conform to the principle that all children are entitled to education that is not only *free* but also *appropriate*. This might mean special materials, special instructional procedures, even a special curriculum. It might also mean only minor adjustments to the offerings of the regular classroom. Unfortunately, claim Audette and Algozzine (1997), there have been persistent problems in implementing this aspect of Public Law 94-142. Some of these problems relate to the referral and identification of students for placement; others have to do with confusing and contradictory laws, regulations, and policies that make inclusion costly rather than free.

Fair Evaluation and Due Process Part of the cost of inclusion has to do with fair evaluation and due process. The decision that a student has special needs is typically based on a variety of evaluation and assessment procedures; many of these are time-consuming and therefore expensive. Parents or teachers are usually first to notice that there might be a problem and to seek referral for further evaluation. PL 94-142

Robert Goldberg, Bad Teacher

A RECOLLECTION: by Blooma, a teacher-in-training

Mr. Goldberg was boring, dressed sloppily, and rarely talked to me. He spent more time with the smarter people and at many times I felt "left out." I recall an instance in the beginning of the school year when I sat in the front of the class with my best friend behind me. By the middle of the year he had moved the "smarter" people to the front and the "dumb" people to the back. You guessed it—I was classified as dumb and was separated from my friend, who was very smart. I was deeply hurt and I have never forgiven Mr. Goldberg.

mandates that an interdisciplinary assessment team be employed to determine whether comprehensive assessment is required. Assessment may involve various diagnostic and achievement tests; the stipulation is that these instruments will be as appropriate and as fair and unbiased as possible. That is, the tests must be given by people trained in their administration and interpretation, and they must also be selected to provide a complete and accurate assessment of the student's functioning. Thus, where there might be language problems, for example, tests should be given in the child's native language; if there are physical disabilities, special steps might be taken to enable the child to respond.

If the final determination is that the student requires special services, an individualized educational plan is prepared—often by the assessment team in consultation with the teacher and the parents.

Individualized Educational Plans (IEPs) Individualized educational plans (IEPs) (sometimes called individualized educational portfolios or individualized program plans—IPPs) are written programs, mandated by law for every child with disabilities. In inclusive classes, IEPs are often prepared by the classroom teacher and an education team made up of the principal, other specialists, parents, and sometimes students. As Snyder and Shapiro (1997) note, there can be important advantages in actively involving students in IEP conferences. IEPs are almost invariably implemented by the teacher, although sometimes with the assistance of one or more specialists. Hence, it is essential that all teachers know what is required in these plans, how to interpret them, and how to prepare them.

A number of steps typically occur before an IEP is prepared. First, someone—often a teacher, sometimes a parent—becomes aware that a student might require special services. Following this, if parents consent, the student may be referred for assessment, perhaps by school personnel, sometimes by outside agencies.

Public Law 94-142 stipulates that IEPs must contain the following:

- ▲ A description of the student's current performance and achievement
- ▲ A statement of annual goals, and short-range objectives
- ▲ A list of services and programs to be provided for the student
- ▲ The expected duration of the program, including specific dates
- ▲ Evaluation procedures that will be used to determine whether the program's goals are being met

An example of an IEP is provided in Figure 9.2.

STRATHCONA COUNTY BOARD OF EDUCATION

INDIVIDUALIZED EDUCATIONAL PLAN

NAME OF STUDENT Thea Murray   GRADE ECS   SCHOOL Wye   TEACHER C. Munoz

IEP TEAM MEMBERS

SIGNATURE	POSITION	SIGNATURE	POSITION
	Teacher		Special Needs Aide
	Assistant Principal		
	Counsellor		
	Speech Clinician		

PROGRAM GOALS (S)	INSTRUCTIONAL OBJECTIVES	STRATEGY/MATERIALS/ RESOURCES	DATE START	DATE END	EVALUATION CRITERIA	PLACEMENT/PERSON RESPONSIBLE
1. develop intelligibility	– to improve intelligibility	– through one-to-one assistance, provide Thea with the correct speech model – have Thea repeat the model speech – provide Thea with the opportunity to interact with her peers with appropriate levels of intelligibility	Oct. 3	June 28	– ongoing assessment notes will be kept on ongoing basis – periodic reassessment by L. Brent	– C. Munoz – E. Takata – H. Murphy – L. Brent * * L. Brent is responsible to train the assigned teacher aide to carry out the appropriate assistance program for goals 1–4.
2. develop correct production of /L/	– to improve production of /L/	– through one-to-one assistance, provide Thea with the correct speech model – have Thea repeat the model speech – encourage Thea to find words with 'L' in her environment – provide Thea with the opportunity to interact with her peers with appropriate /L/ usage	Oct. 3			

Handwritten annotations:
NB "r" "b" following as in library
much improved
check "got" — use of times at intended word — "forgot" is "forgot" — also syntax

FIGURE 9.2 Sample individualized educational plan (IEP). Reprinted by permission of Strathcona County School.

IEP – Page 2

STRATHCONA COUNTY BOARD OF EDUCATION
INDIVIDUALIZED EDUCATIONAL PLAN

NAME OF STUDENT ___Thea Murray___ GRADE ___ECS___ SCHOOL ___Wye___ TEACHER ___C. Munoz___

PROGRAM GOALS (S)	INSTRUCTIONAL OBJECTIVES	STRATEGY/MATERIALS/ RESOURCES	DATE START	DATE END	EVALUATION CRITERIA	PLACEMENT/PERSON RESPONSIBLE
3. develop receptive and expressive syntax	– to improve receptive and expressive syntax *i.e., "I don't got a turn."*	– through one-to-one assistance, provide Thea with the correct speech model – have Thea repeat the model speech – provide Thea with the opportunity to interact with her peers with appropriate receptive and expressive syntax	Oct. 3	June 28		
4. develop fine motor skills	– to improve fine motor skills *Second term effort observed— not improving giving now not where expected in ...*	– through one-to-one assistance, Thea will participate in a variety of fine motor skills including pasting, painting, drawing, manipulating, etc.	Oct. 3	June 28	– ongoing assessment – progress relative to expected performance	

FIGURE 9.2 (continued) Sample individualized educational plan (IEP). Reprinted by permission of Strathcona County School.

Even when exceptional children are part of inclusive classrooms, not all of them have their needs met only by their teachers and entirely in inclusive classrooms. Some may stay in a regular classroom, and the regular teacher may be assisted by an aide, an assistant teacher, or an itinerant specialist; others may be sent to a special resource room for part of each day or week; some may be in special classrooms part of the time and in a regular classroom for the remainder of the time; some may be in a segregated, special class full time. Still others may be in residential schools (the deaf or blind, for example) or in hospitals or other institutions.

Major Implications of PL 94-142 Besides the provision for education in the least restrictive environment, Public Law 94-142 brought about a number of other significant changes in the schools' treatment of exceptionality by stipulating that:

▲ Extensive effort be made to identify children with disabilities using procedures that are not racially or culturally biased.

▲ Parents have a right to be informed and to grant or withhold consent regarding assessment and educational plans for special needs children.

▲ School jurisdictions are compelled to provide special services for children who need them at no cost to parents or guardians.

▲ A written individualized educational plan (IEP) must be provided for every child with disabilities.

For obvious reasons, PL 94-142 is often described as the Bill of Rights for those with disabilities. But, as we have seen, even though the law has done a tremendous amount to reduce bias and unfair practices in the treatment of exceptional children, it has also presented some real difficulties of interpretation and implementation for educators. IEPs, for example, are difficult and time-consuming to

prepare and are therefore extremely costly, and they have not proved popular. Nor is it always easy or even possible to find tests for specific forms of exceptionality or to find tests in a child's native language. The law's most obvious practical manifestation—the inclusive classroom or mainstreaming—also remains controversial. (See Table 9.2 for a summary of PL 94-142.)

DEFINITION AND IDENTIFICATION OF EXCEPTIONALITY

Given the classroom teacher's role in identifying and providing services for children with special needs, it has become increasingly important for all teachers to be familiar with the various manifestations of exceptionality they are most likely to encounter.

Exceptionality, as we saw, has two dimensions: the exceptionally gifted and those with disabilities.[3] Exceptionalities are found in each of the three main areas of human functioning—the cognitive, the physical, and the social-emotional. In each area, abilities range continuously from some point just noticeably beyond the average to the furthest extremes in either direction. People at the extreme of the negative end include, for example, those with severe men-

---

[3] **PPC:** I note the bear is now using *disabled* where he used *handicapped* in an earlier edition. I know that *disabled* is more acceptable, but it too strikes me as more negative than necessary. Many of my special education colleagues now use the word *challenged*. Might that be better?

Author: In even earlier editions, other terms such as *deficient* were often used. And before the bear, words like *idiot*, *imbecile*, and *moron* were widely accepted psychological terms. Now these terms are carefully avoided. Terms such as these often have highly negative connotations and are quite uninformative. Maybe, as you suggest, *challenged* would be better. It's certainly more emotionally neutral. Unfortunately, it's also stunningly vague. But notice that the bear now seldom says "disabled children," but rather, "children with disabilities." The difference is subtle but important. This is not a bear with stupidity.

TABLE 9.2
Main Provisions of the Individuals with
Disabilities Education Act (IDEA or PL 94-142)

PROVISION	PRACTICAL IMPLICATIONS
Education in the least restrictive environment	Inclusive education (or mainstreaming) because the "least restrictive environment" is interpreted by the courts to mean the most normal environment that can meet the child's special needs
Free and appropriate educational services	Publicly funded special education programs provided without charge to all children with special needs
Fair, nondiscriminatory evaluation and due process of law	Students must be evaluated by experts using instruments that are free from bias and that take into consideration specific disabilities and problems the child might have (such as a different first language); parents have a right to be informed and to grant or withhold consent regarding assessment and educational plans for their children
Individualized educational plans (IEPs)	An individually designed educational plan for each child with special needs, developed by a team of teachers, administrators, specialists, and parents, and containing statements of goals, instructional programs, and assessment procedures together with specific time lines for each

tal disabilities, those with multiple physical disabilities (such as being blind, deaf, and quadriplegic), and those with serious emotional disorders (such as schizophrenia).

PL 94-142 provides an important official definition for the term *handicapped*: "Handicapped children means those evaluated as being mentally retarded, hard-of-hearing, deaf, speech impaired, visually handicapped, seriously emotionally disturbed, orthopedically impaired, other health impaired, deaf-blind, multihandicapped, or as having specific learning disabilities, who because of these impairments need special education and related services" (U.S. Office of Education, 1977, p. 42478).

The sections that follow examine exceptionality in all three areas—physical, cognitive (intellectual), and social (emotional)—with special emphasis on cognitive disabilities, which are often more relevant for the regular classroom teacher (see Figure 9.3). Teachers who major in special education would be expected to know much more than can be included in these few pages.

Physical Exceptionality

At one extreme among the physically exceptional are those endowed with superior capabilities that might be manifested in athletic skills and in other activities requiring motor coordination, strength, rhythm, and so on. At the other extreme are those with physical disabilities, sensory deficits, cerebral palsy, or a variety of diseases that might lead to problems in school. Among these, blindness and deafness may require special assistance beyond the capabilities and resources of the regular classroom teacher. On occasion, however, corrective devices (glasses and hearing aids) and special learning aids (large-print books, for example) can be used within the regular classroom in compliance with inclusive education regulations.

Social-Emotional Exceptionality

At the positive end of social-emotional exceptionality are children who are more socially adept, better adjusted, and more immune to the stresses and tensions of life than are ordinary

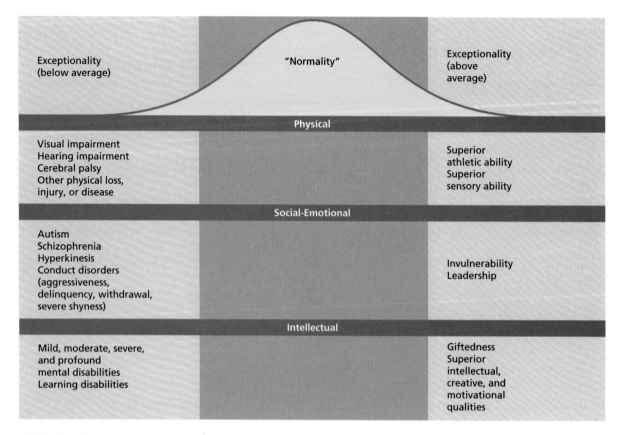

FIGURE 9.3 Dimensions of exceptionality

individuals. These exceptional individuals often go unrecognized and unheralded, although they might on occasion be envied.

At the other extreme are those variously described as "behavior-disordered," "emotionally disturbed," or "socially maladjusted." What these labels have in common is that each describes individuals who are troubled and often unhappy and who are also usually a source of difficulty for teachers, peers, parents, and others. The Individuals with Disabilities Education Act (IDEA) includes among the criteria for the **seriously emotionally disturbed (SED)** the inability to build or maintain satisfactory inter-

personal relations and inappropriate feelings or behaviors (see Gresham & MacMillan, 1997). More than 70 percent of students with behavioral disorders are very low achievers (Nelson & Pearson, 1991). Estimates of the prevalence of emotional disorders vary tremendously. Knitzer, Steinberg, and Fleisch (1990) suggest that between 3 and 5 percent of children are seriously emotionally disturbed. But only about 20 percent of these are identified and receive special services (Heward & Orlansky, 1992).

For the most severe manifestations of emotional disturbance (schizophrenia, for example), institutional care is generally required. In many cases, however, children who might be described as suffering from emotional disorders continue to function in regular classrooms. Of special interest to teachers is **attention deficit hyperactivity disorder (ADHD)**, an emotional disorder com-

---

seriously emotionally disturbed (SED) A general category of social/emotional exceptionality defined primarily in terms of inappropriate behavior and affect and the inability to establish normal social relationships.

monly called **hyperactivity**. ADHD is considered in more detail in a later section of this chapter.

Intellectual Exceptionality: Mental Retardation

On the one hand are the gifted and creative children that we discussed earlier in this chapter; on the other hand are children who have significant difficulty in learning some, if not all, of the things that others learn relatively easily. This dimension of exceptionality includes two important categories: those with mental disabilities (or with mental retardation) and those with learning disabilities.

Definition of Mental Retardation The most obvious feature of **mental retardation** is a depression in the ability to learn; a second important feature relates to problems with adaptation. These features are apparent in the widely accepted definition presented by the American Association on Mental Deficiency (AAMD), which reads as follows (AAMD, 1992, p. 5):

> Mental retardation refers to substantial limitations in present intellectual functioning. It is characterized by significantly subaverage intellectual functioning existing concurrently with related limitations in two or more of the following applicable adaptive skill areas: communication, self-care, home living, social skills, community use, self-direction, health and safety, functional academics, leisure, and work. Mental retardation manifests before age 18.

The meaning of this definition can be clarified by looking at each of its key components. First, "significantly subaverage intellectual functioning" is generally defined in terms of test scores on one or more of the well-known individual intelligence tests such as the Stanford-Binet or the Wechsler. An IQ score of 70 is the generally accepted, but arbitrary, cutoff between normality and retardation.

Second, "limitations in . . . adaptive skill areas" are apparent as significant maturational deficits, most evident in an inability to learn and failure to reach the levels of independence, social effectiveness, and social responsibility that would normally be expected of others of similar age and experience—such as a 4-year-old not yet able to talk. The 1992 AAMD definition's emphasis on adaptive skills and social support represents a very significant change from a traditional view of retardation as entirely, or at least primarily, an intellectual deficit to a recognition of the importance of adaptation and environmental support (Fredericks & Williams, 1998; Polloway, 1997). Various standardized inventories are available for assessing level of adaptive behavior, including one developed by the AAMD (see Stinnett, 1997).

Classifications of Mental Retardation Figure 9.4 presents some commonly used classification schemes for mental retardation. These labels are based primarily on performance on standard measures of intelligence, most commonly the Stanford-Binet. In practice, approximately 1 percent of the general population appears to have a mental disability when the level of adaptive behavior is also taken into account (Patton & Polloway, 1990).

Causes of Mental Retardation Psychologists and educators tend to classify mental retardation by level of retardation (as shown in Figure 9.4), although geneticists and psychiatric researchers (among others) tend to classify it by cause (Hodapp & Dykens, 1994). However, most of the

---

attention deficit hyperactivity disorder (ADHD) A disorder marked by excessive general activity for a child's age, attention problems, high impulsivity, and low frustration tolerance. Also termed *hyperactivity*.

hyperactivity A common term for attention deficit hyperactivity disorder.

mental retardation A significant general depression in the ability to learn, usually accompanied by deficits in adaptive behavior.

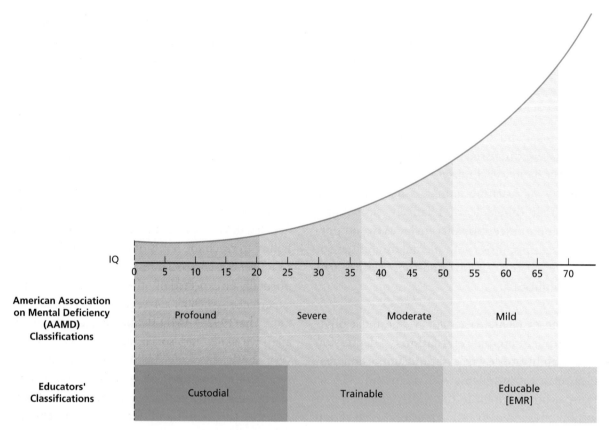

FIGURE 9.4 Two common classification schemes for mental disabilities: (These classifications are based entirely on measured IQ. In practice, adaptive skills would also be taken into account.) The AAMD classifications shown here are based on the Stanford-Binet or Cattell tests. The Wechsler scales have a different distribution and therefore different cutoff points: 55–69, mild; 40–54, moderate; 25–39, severe; below 25, profound.

time we don't actually know the specific cause of the retardation. In fact, the causes are so varied that classification by degree is far more common than classification by cause. Nevertheless, researchers often identify two groups of causes: those that are organic, whether pre- or postnatal; and the familial (Zigler & Hodapp, 1991). Organic causes of mental retardation include cerebral injury, chromosomal aberrations and defects such as Down's syndrome, and maternal infections at critical periods of fetal development. Familial causes include inadequate genetic endowment, growing up in an unstimulating environment, and a combination of environmental and genetic factors.

Characteristics of the Mentally Retarded The largest group of retarded children (about 75 percent) is marked by **mild retardation** (Hallahan & Kauffman, 1994). Relatively few of these children are identified as intellectually impaired before they have been in school for a period of time. Many are eventually capable of acceptable academic achievement in elementary school—at perhaps the sixth-grade level—and can adapt quite

---

mild retardation A classification of mental retardation identified by degree and usually defined in terms of an IQ range between 50 and about 70. Also termed *educable*, children with mild retardation are capable of adequate social adaptation and achievement at about the sixth-grade level.

well socially. The majority are usually main-streamed and can be described as **educable mentally retarded (EMR)**. Following a survey of the literature, Gresham and MacMillan (1997) report that mildly retarded children often have poorly developed social skills and are less likely to be selected as friends by their peers.

Severe retardation and **profound retardation** are generally associated with highly limited motor learning—virtually no communication skills in the case of profound retardation and only rudimentary skills for the severely retarded—and institutionalization throughout life. With profound retardation, institutional care is often of a custodial nature, involving feeding and clothing.

Moderate retardation is characteristic of about 20 percent of those classified as mentally retarded (Hallahan & Kauffman, 1994). These children learn to talk during the preschool period, and the majority also learn to walk, although their verbal and motor skills are generally noticeably inferior to those of other children. Many are educated in inclusive classrooms where, with the help of special programs and teachers, they may progress through the primary grades but not usually much further academically. Training in occupational skills is sometimes very helpful for these children.

In practice, many writers no longer include *moderate retardation* as a separate classification but speak instead of two groups with retardation: the mildly and the severely retarded (Winzer, 1997).

Intellectual Exceptionality: Learning Disabilities

Mental retardation usually affects all areas of cognitive functioning, whereas another type of intellectual impairment manifests itself in only a few areas of functioning—and frequently only in one. That is, there are children who, in the absence of any perceptible physical or emotional disturbance, nevertheless experience significant difficulty in learning specific skills. These children have sometimes been described as suffering from a learning dysfunction, hyperactivity, cerebral dysfunction, minimal brain damage, perceptual disability, dyslexia, or simply as being slow learners. Unfortunately, these terms are nonspecific, often confusing, and sometimes meaningless. Largely for this reason, the term **learning disability** was introduced. This term does not have the same negative connotations as do expressions like "cerebral dysfunction" or "slow learner," and its meaning can be expressed relatively clearly.

Defining Learning Disabilities The term *learning disability* is now used to describe a variety of conditions. Although Public Law 94-142 includes a definition of learning disabilities that serves as a guideline for the allocation of funds, the definition is open to several interpretations. As a result, many school jurisdictions have established their own criteria for identifying children with learning disabilities. Most

educable mentally retarded (EMR) A label for those who are mildly retarded—having approximately an IQ between 50 and 70.

severe retardation A level of mental retardation defined in terms of an IQ range between 20 and 40. Severely retarded people can learn to communicate and, with systematic training, to take care of simple hygiene.

profound retardation A degree of mental retardation defined in terms of a measured IQ below 20 or 25 and marked by limited motor development and a need for nursing care.

moderate retardation A degree of mental retardation defined in terms of an IQ range between 35 and 55. Those with moderate retardation can achieve at about the second-grade level and can profit from training in social and occupational skills.

learning disability A depression in the ability to learn specific things (for example, reading or arithmetic), where the learning difficulties are not related to mental retardation or emotional disturbance.

descriptions of learning disabilities emphasize four groups of characteristics:

1. There is a marked disparity between expected and actual behavior. This disparity is often apparent in general academic achievement that is significantly below what would be predicted on the basis of measured IQ.

2. The learning-disabled child displays an uneven pattern of academic achievement, doing quite well in some subjects but very poorly in others. Often, such a child is unable to do certain things that other children do very easily.

3. Learning disabilities are often evidenced by problems with one of the basic psychological processes involved in language or arithmetic. Hence, the disorder is apparent in disorders of listening, thinking, talking, reading, writing, spelling, or arithmetic.

4. Problems associated with learning disabilities are not the result of other problems relating to hearing, vision, or general mental retardation.

The clearest identifying characteristic of learning disabilities, according to government regulations, is a significant discrepancy between IQ and achievement, caused by problems in such basic psychological processes as remembering and perceiving. Children whose ability to learn is generally depressed or who suffer from environmental deprivation, emotional problems, or sensory defects are specifically excluded from the category of the learning disabled.

In practice, distinctions between mental retardation and learning disabilities are not always clear (Polloway et al., 1997). As a result, there can be considerable misdiagnosis in the field. For example, Shepard, Smith, and Vojir (1983) surveyed 800 children classified as learning disabled and found that many of them had characteristics that did not conform to the definitions found in government regulations. In fact, more than half this sample had emotional disorders, mild retardation, or specific language problems; they should not have been classified as learning disabled. Unfortunately, this misclassification may lead to the use of inappropriate treatment strategies with some of these children. It will almost certainly confound the results of research designed to investigate the incidence of learning disabilities and the effectiveness of various treatments.

Prevalence Children with learning disabilities make up the largest group of special needs students in North America. In fact, they compose almost 5 percent of the entire student body in U.S. public schools (U.S. Department of Education, 1991)—about two-thirds of all children with special needs. This may be because, as Lerner (1995) notes, the term is often applied to any student who is having problems in school and for whom no other label seems entirely appropriate. Perhaps this is partly why the number of postsecondary students with learning disabilities has increased dramatically in recent years (Raskins & Higgins, 1998).

Symptoms and Identification of Learning Disabilities
For the classroom teacher, first indications of learning disabilities are usually very tentative and uncertain. As we saw, the most obvious characteristic, and the one most likely to be noticed by teachers, is general academic retardation. Academic retardation by itself, however, does not define a learning disability—although it is often a result of a learning-disabled child's problems with reading, writing, and other aspects of the language arts.

A variety of other symptoms can also be associated with learning disabilities. These include inattentiveness, mood shifts, hyperactivity, and impulsiveness (see Table 9.3). Short-term memory problems are also common among those with learning disabilities (Swanson, 1993). Drug use may also be more common among these children, perhaps because

TABLE 9.3
Some Symptoms that May Be Associated with Learning Disabilities

- ▲ Inattentiveness (short attention span)
- ▲ Impulsiveness
- ▲ Hyperactivity
- ▲ Frequent shifts in mood
- ▲ Impaired visual memory (difficulty in recalling shapes or words)
- ▲ Motor problems (difficulty in running, hitting a ball, cutting, or writing)
- ▲ Disorders of speech and hearing
- ▲ Specific academic difficulties (reading, writing, spelling, arithmetic)

Source: Based on Clements (1966)

of their problems in school and subsequent adjustment problems (Karacostas & Fisher, 1993). For the same reason, adolescents with learning disabilities may be at a slightly higher risk of suicide (Huntington & Bender, 1993).

Various tests are available to help to identify the learning disabled. These are used to measure general intelligence and to examine the basic psychological processes involved in learning and remembering. It's also important to consider the possibility that other factors might be involved—such as visual problems, hearing deficit, physical or health handicap, low intelligence, or environmental disadvantages. In fact, there is evidence that between 14 and 65 percent of children with visual disabilities also have learning disabilities (Erin & Koenig, 1997). There is evidence, too, that some gifted children have learning disabilities; most are never identified (Brody & Mills, 1997).

Categories of Learning Disabilities The causes of specific learning disabilities remain largely unknown, although brain damage or another neurological impairment is suspected in many cases (Mercer, 1990). Various diseases and infections, malnutrition, and other environmental or genetic factors might also be involved. However, like mental retardation, learning disabilities are not classified by cause but by symptom, and learning disabilities are most often classified according to the specific area where the disability is most apparent. Thus, these disabilities are typically labeled according to whether they involve oral or written speech, comprehension or production of speech, or particular problems in spelling or arithmetic.

By far the most frequently diagnosed learning disabilities are those that involve language—especially reading. Thus, one common learning disability is **developmental reading disorder**—also called *dyslexia*, or *specific reading disability* (Stanovich, 1992). Its main feature is impairment in recognizing words and understanding what is read, in spite of normal or above normal intelligence and absence of problems such as deafness, blindness, or inadequate schooling. Developmental reading disorder is usually first noticed when a child has difficulty learning to read. It may later be evident in spelling difficulties or in a lag of several years in reading skills. Remedial teaching can sometimes be highly effective in overcoming some of the effects.

A second specific learning disability is **developmental arithmetic disorder** (American Psychiatric Association, 1994). Its principal feature is significant difficulty in developing arithmetic skills in the absence of other problems such as mental retardation. Consequently,

---

developmental reading disorder A learning disability manifested in reading problems of varying severity—sometimes evident in spelling difficulties. Also termed *dyslexia* or *specific reading disability*.

developmental arithmetic disorder A learning disability evident in specific problems in developing arithmetic skills in the absence of other problems such as mental retardation.

developmental arithmetic disorder is usually most apparent in computational problems (difficulties in adding, subtracting, multiplying, or dividing) or problems in processing visual or auditory information. As a result, children with arithmetic disabilities often have reading problems also (Semrud-Clikeman & Hynd, 1992).

Besides reading and arithmetic disorders, learning disabilities include what are called **process disorders**. These are defined as deficits in a basic psychological process such as perception (confusion of words that sound or look alike); memory (problems associated with remembering and generalizing what has been learned); and attention (a condition labeled "attention deficit disorder" associated with restlessness, hyperactivity, low tolerance of frustration, and distractibility). In practice, however, it is often difficult to separate a basic process disorder from a disorder that is manifested in a specific subject area.

Treatment In most instances, learning disabilities are treated in the regular classroom, often with the help and advice of learning disability specialists. These children are not typically different from other children in regular classrooms, except for the specific learning difficulty they experience. Most learning disabled children are well adjusted and well liked. When Juvonen and Bear (1992) compared the social adjustment of learning-disabled children with that of children without learning disabilities, they found no differences between the two in the proportion of each ranked as well liked or as rejected on sociometric scales.

---

process disorder A type of learning disability that involves a deficit in a basic psychological process such as perceiving, remembering, or paying attention. In practice, process disorders are difficult to separate from other specific learning disabilities such as developmental reading or arithmetic disorder.

Here, as in other areas of exceptionality, the onus of initial identification rests with the classroom teacher. In fact, the teacher's opinion may be relied on in place of more formal—and more expensive—testing. As Clarizio (1992) reports, the regular classroom teacher's opinion is often the most influential data with respect to determining whether a child has a learning disability. Unfortunately, the results of Clarizio's research indicate that relying solely on teachers' judgments would nearly double the number of students identified as learning disabled, resulting in a huge number of false identifications. Hence, there is a definite need for clear definition and strict adherence to accepted criteria when identifying all special needs children.

Attention Deficit Hyperactivity Disorder (ADHD)

Attention deficit hyperactivity disorder (ADHD), or hyperactivity, is a relatively common emotional exceptionality that is closely related to learning disabilities. In fact, many children who suffer from one of these conditions will also manifest symptoms of the other (Korkman & Pesonen, 1994).

Prevalence Estimates of ADHD vary enormously depending on the criteria used and also depending on whether diagnosis is based on teacher ratings, parent ratings, or both (Cohen, Riccio, & Gonzalez, 1994). One survey of 14,229 students in a school district identified 136 children with ADHD—slightly less than 1 percent (Reid et al., 1994). Another estimate suggests that as many as 5 million children in the United States are being medicated for ADHD or ADD (*attention deficit disorder* without hyperactivity) (Widener, 1998). Many believe that this condition is significantly overdiagnosed (Orford, 1998).

Symptoms and Diagnosis Overdiagnosis may well be a function of the most apparent features of

ADHD: excessive general activity for the child's age (often taking the form of incessant and haphazard climbing, crawling, or running); difficulty in sustaining attention and apparent forgetfulness; and impulsivity (tendency to react quickly, difficulty taking turns, low frustration tolerance).

A diagnosis of ADHD is often made inappropriately by parents and teachers who are confronted by these restless children who find it difficult to do the quiet things that adults sometimes demand—and who, consequently, often create discipline problems. But, as Kirby and Kirby (1994) note, the disruptive behavior of the ADHD child is not usually intentional. And if authorities were to rely primarily on the judgments of parents and teachers, far too many children would be classified as ADHD.

Strictly speaking, attention deficit hyperactivity disorder, as defined by the American Psychiatric Association (1994), must be apparent before the age of 7 to differentiate it from disorders that might arise as reactions to stressful events or illness. The disorder also requires the presence of the five criteria presented in Table 9.4.

There is now some doubt about whether it's useful or appropriate to specify that the symptoms of ADHD must be present by age 7. Not only is there considerable evidence of ADHD among adults, but there are indications that not all individuals with ADHD develop symptoms before age 7 (Barkley & Biederman, 1997; Applegate et al., 1997).

Causes The causes of ADHD are unclear, although the fact that between 80 and 90 percent more males than females are hyperactive suggests that it is at least partly genetic (Wolraich & Baumgaertel, 1997). Evidence also indicates that it sometimes results from a dysfunction of the central nervous system (Ward, 1994). As such, it may be partly a maturational problem. The activity level of hyperactive children is often similar to that of children of 4 or 5 years, and

many hyperactive children—though not all— also seem to outgrow their symptoms after adolescence (Henker & Whalen, 1989). As we have seen, however, the condition does exist among adults as well (Barkley & Biederman, 1998).

Other explanations for hyperactivity have sometimes implicated neurological impairment or brain damage and dietary or vitamin-linked causes. However, the evidence for either of these causes is weak (Erickson, 1992). There is some suggestion, too, that between 5 and 10 percent of hyperactive children react badly to certain food dyes and that these children might therefore be helped through dietary means (Ross, 1980).

Treatment The most common treatment for a child diagnosed as having an attention deficit disorder with hyperactivity involves the use of stimulant drugs such as dextroamphetamine (Dexedrine) and methylphenidate (Ritalin) (Heiligenstein & Anders, 1997). This might seem strange because stimulants ordinarily increase activity and ADHD children already suffer from excessive activity. However, these drugs appear to have what is termed a **paradoxical effect** on children. That is, they appear to sedate rather than stimulate. Some evidence suggests that these drugs are about twice as effective as behavior modification (primarily the use of rewards) for controlling problem behavior in many ADHD children, and for improving academic achievement (Pelham et al., 1993).

The use of stimulants to treat ADHD children is often associated with preventing continued achievement declines in school (Busch, 1993) and with increasing the manageability of the children in question, but it still remains a controversial treatment. These drugs can also have negative side effects such as weight loss,

---

paradoxical effect Literally, a surprising or contradictory effect. This phrase is used to describe the apparently sedating effect that some stimulants (such as Ritalin) have on children who suffer from excessive activity (hyperactivity).

TABLE 9.4
DSM-IV Diagnostic Criteria for Attention Deficit Hyperactivity Disorder

A. Symptoms from either group 1 or 2 must be present.

1. Six (or more) of the following symptoms of inattention have persisted for at least six months to a degree that is maladaptive and inconsistent with the developmental level:

   a. Often fails to give close attention to details or makes careless mistakes in schoolwork, work, or other activities

   b. Often has difficulty sustaining attention in tasks or play activities

   c. Often appears not to listen when spoken to directly

   d. Often fails to follow through on instructions and fails to finish schoolwork, chores, or duties in the workplace (not due to oppositional behavior or failure to understand instructions)

   e. Often has difficulty organizing tasks and activities

   f. Often avoids, dislikes, or is reluctant to engage in tasks that require sustained mental effort (such as schoolwork or homework)

   g. Often loses things necessary for tasks or activities (for example, toys, school assignments, pencils, books, or tools)

   h. Is often easily distracted by extraneous stimuli

   i. Is often forgetful in daily activities

2. Six (or more) of the following symptoms of hyperactivity-impulsivity have persisted for at least six months to a degree that is maladaptive and inconsistent with developmental level:

Hyperactivity

   a. Often fidgets with hands or feet or squirms in seat

   b. Often leaves seat in classroom or in other situations in which remaining seated is expected

   c. Often runs about or climbs excessively in situations in which it is inappropriate (In adolescents or adults, this can be limited to subjective feelings of restlessness.)

   d. Often has difficulty playing or engaging in leisure activities quietly

   e. Is often "on the go" or often acts as if "driven by a motor"

   f. Often talks excessively

Impulsivity

   g. Often blurts out answers before questions have been completed

   h. Often has difficulty awaiting turn

   i. Often interrupts or intrudes on others (for example, butts into conversations or games)

B. Some hyperactive–impulsive or inattentive symptoms that caused impairment were present before age 7.

C. Some impairment from the symptoms is present in two or more settings (for example, at school [or work] and at home).

D. There must be clear evidence of clinically significant impairment in social, academic, or occupational functioning.

E. The symptoms do not occur exclusively during the course of a pervasive developmental disorder, schizophrenia, or other psychotic disorder and are not better accounted for by another mental disorder (for example, mood disorder, anxiety disorder, dissociative disorder, or a personality disorder).

Source: *Diagnostic and Statistical Manual of Mental Disorders* (4th ed.) DSM-IV (pp. 83–85), 1994. Copyright © 1994 American Psychiatric Association. Reprinted with permission.

growth retardation, and mood changes. However, these negative effects are rare when the child has been properly diagnosed (Guffey, 1991).

Another form of treatment for children with attention deficit disorders involves the use of computer-based instrumentation that monitors the children's brain-wave activity and provides information about their brain functioning. Researchers have found that the brain activity of these children is measurably different from that of children without attention deficits (see, for example, Janzen et al., 1995). It appears that the children can be trained to alter their brain-wave activity so that it more closely resembles that of normal children. Training involves providing them with feedback—termed **biofeedback** or **neurofeedback**—about their brain activity while they are actually engaged in a task. The procedure, which is time-consuming and requires expensive instrumentation, is still experimental but initial results are positive (Lubar et al., 1995).

Identifying Exceptional Children in the Classroom

Mild mental retardation, learning disabilities, and emotional disturbances are seldom identified before the child goes to school. Several stages appear to be common in the identification of each of these manifestations of exceptionality.

Initially, these children begin school as ordinary students, but eventually the teacher realizes that the child has not progressed sufficiently to be promoted to the next grade. At this point, a child may be referred for further diagnosis—or, in other cases, will simply be promoted to the next grade (a "social promotion," reflecting the school's reluctance to separate the child from age peers).

Lynch and associates (1978) provide some suggestions to help teachers in the early stages of tentative diagnosis—when the important decision is whether professional assessment is warranted. *First*, teachers are urged to learn to observe carefully to identify children who seem difficult, hard to get along with, or slow. Having identified these children, teachers can then attempt to determine what might work with them and can try several different approaches. Frequently, it turns out that there is no problem.

Second, Lynch and colleagues suggest that teachers ask themselves key questions: Does the child learn so slowly, or is the child's adaptive behavior (ability to use language, to play with other children, and to be reasonably independent) so poor that the child cannot participate fully with the other children?

Third, and very important, teachers must be careful to distinguish between exceptionality and simple cultural differences. Very intelligent children whose dominant language and values are significantly different from those of the majority can sometimes appear less than normally bright.

Fourth, just as it is important to distinguish between the culturally different and those in need of special education, it is also important to recognize normal individual differences in temperament, motivation, interests, and so on. And teachers must always be aware of the possibility that difficulties between themselves and certain children might have to do with differences in personal style rather than with specific failings in the children.

Once teachers have determined that there is a real possibility of a problem requiring special attention, the next stage is to obtain professional help. Subsequent diagnosis—typically undertaken by professionals—usually involves assessments using prescribed instruments and consultation among members of an interdisciplinary team. Following diagnosis, remedial action will depend on the specific diagnosis,

---

biofeedback Information that we obtain about our biological functioning. In a specialized sense, biofeedback refers to information that subjects receive about the activity of their nervous system when they are connected to one of various sensors or instruments designed for that purpose.

neurofeedback Refers to information that subjects are given about the functioning of their nervous systems. Unlike biofeedback, which refers to feedback relating to all biological systems, neurofeedback relates specifically to information about brain functioning (EEG feedback).

Identifying Exceptionality

Some extremes of exceptionality are obvious and can easily be detected by parents and others not specifically trained in such things. However, most instances of exceptionality are not extreme, so their diagnosis and assessment are often difficult.

The final diagnosis and assessment of an exceptionality that requires special intervention are usually made by a professional team following extensive testing; however, initial identification of those in need of further evaluation is often made by parents or teachers. Hence, it is useful to know what to look for. But parents and others need to be extremely cautious in their tentative judgments of exceptionality, especially in cases when children (and sometimes adults) experience mild problems with subjects such as reading or arithmetic. It is extremely easy to misinterpret a common learning problem as evidence of a learning disability or mental retardation.

Some symptoms that parents and teachers might notice are listed here. Further assessment and evaluation, or referral, can usually be provided by school psychologists.

Cerebral Palsy

Diagnosis is made by a physician. Symptoms can include any, none, or most of the following and can range from very mild to very severe:

uneven gait
jerky movements
speech problems
rigidity
drooling
balance problems
uncontrolled fluttering movements
involuntary facial gestures
shaking movements
possible convulsions

Epilepsy

Diagnosis requires medical assessment. Observable symptoms are seizures. With *petit mal*, seizures are momentary lapses of attention lasting only seconds and can be accompanied by fluttering of the eyelids and suspension of activity. *Grand mal* seizures (also called fits, attacks, or convulsions) can involve sudden stiffening, falling, thrashing around, and moaning. Seizures may last only a few seconds and seldom last more than 5 minutes. Seizures that last longer require urgent medical attention.

Hearing Problems

frequent earaches
inattentiveness
speech problems
high volume on TV or radio

failure to respond
discharge from one or both ears
turns head to listen
speaks in abnormally loud voice

Vision Problems

rubbing of eyes
redness of eyes
headaches
difficulty seeing chalkboard
squinting
extreme sensitivity to light
holds material close to see

Schizophrenia

Requires psychiatric diagnosis. May be characterized by one or more of the following:

aloofness
refusal to cuddle
self-injurious behavior (head banging, for example)
lack of verbal communication
repetitive behaviors (twirling or rocking, for example)
abnormal attachments to objects
insensitivity to pain
poor balance
withdrawal
extreme distress when faced with change
high sensitivity to pain
poor coordination

especially for learning disabilities for which remedial prescriptions are based on as detailed a diagnosis as possible. As we have seen, most children diagnosed with mild mental retardation, an emotional disturbance, or a learning disability will continue to attend regular classes, although they may also be segregated for group or individual special services. For each of these chil-

dren, an IEP will need to be prepared and implemented. (See the box entitled "Identifying Exceptionality.")

Labels in Special Education

"Learning disabled," "educable mentally retarded," "attention deficit hyperactivity disor-

Attention Deficit Hyperactivity Disorder

Primarily a male disorder. At least some of the following characteristics have been present for at least 6 months and before the age of 7 and are more frequent and severe than in most other children of the same mental age:

often fidgets

difficulty remaining seated

easily distracted

difficulty awaiting turn

often blurts out answers

difficulty following instructions

difficulty sustaining attention

shifts often from one activity to another

difficulty playing quietly

talks excessively

often interrupts

often does not seem to listen

often loses things

often takes physical risks

Conduct and Personality Disorders

These disorders require psychological or psychiatric assessment. They span a wide range of behaviors and symptoms; these might include the following. (Only extreme and persistent manifestations of these behaviors would be considered disorders.)

high aggressiveness and hostility

extreme withdrawal and social isolation

severe shyness

lying

stealing

throwing temper tantrums

highly negative self-concept

Mental Disabilities: Moderate to Severe Retardation

Diagnosis and assessment require administration of individual intelligence tests by a trained psychologist. The most obvious feature is a deficient ability to learn, ranging from mild to severe, defined in terms of significantly subaverage performance on intelligence tests (IQ below 70) and deficits in adaptive behavior. Early symptoms of moderate to severe mental retardation include:

significant developmental lag in learning to crawl, walk, and talk

failure to learn developmental tasks such as eating, dressing, tying shoes

poor motor coordination

markedly inferior verbal skills

Mild Retardation

Ordinarily not detected before school age; once in school, the child may show the following symptoms:

significant difficulty in learning

problems with short-term memory

language deficits

motor problems

short attention span

Learning Disabilities

Identification and assessment are difficult even for trained professionals. Learning disabilities may be manifested in:

uneven pattern of academic achievement

academic retardation

learning problems that are not related to intelligence or environmental disadvantage

specific learning problems in language-related subjects or arithmetic

erratic spelling

frequent failure to recognize simple words

confusion of letters or numbers

persistent difficulty with simple arithmetic computations

inattentiveness, impulsivity, mood shifts

poor visual memory

---

der"—these and their common letter substitutes, (LD, EMR, and ADHD, respectively) are widely used labels in special education. But they are just that: labels. Labels do nothing more than name; they don't explain anything. To say that Eric has difficulty recognizing numbers because he is LD might mislead us into thinking we understand why Eric hesitates and struggles when he picks up the six of spades. But all the label "LD" tells us is that Eric's behavior manifests a combination of symptoms that we have agreed to label "LD." The label can be useful because it permits us to communicate with one another, and it gives us some basis for developing educational programs for children like Eric.

Still, labels do have disadvantages, and many argue against their use. Common arguments insist that labels are often unfair (given the social and cultural biases of intelligence tests), that they lead to lower expectations and thus present an additional disadvantage to those who are labeled, and that there is a remarkable lack of homogeneity among those who are given identical labels. There is also a growing tendency to treat disabled children as quantitatively rather than qualitatively different from normal children. The use of generally pejorative labels is clearly incompatible with this trend.

We have come some distance from labels that were once as widely accepted as those we use today—labels like "idiot," "moron," "imbecile," "cretin," "dolt," "nitwit," "nincompoop," "ignoramus," "dimwit," "booby," "simpleton," "halfwit," "dullard," "numskull."

MAIN POINTS

1. Talent refers to a remarkable ability in a specific field; giftedness is a more general characteristic. Prodigies display prodigious talent at an early age. Talented and gifted children are identified by professionals as being capable of high performance by virtue of outstanding capabilities that might be reflected in general intellectual ability, specific academic aptitude, creative or productive thinking, leadership, or artistic talent. In practice, these children are often nominated by teachers and identified on the basis of ability and achievement measures. The culturally different are often overlooked and are underrepresented among programs for the gifted.

2. Two main approaches to educating the talented and gifted are acceleration (students progress through the conventional curriculum at an accelerated pace—for example, Stanley's radical acceleration) and enrichment (students go beyond the conventional curriculum—that is, Renzulli's revolving door model). Other approaches include mentoring, IEPs, and special schools.

3. The irrelevance of school learning, inadequacy of evaluation systems, and lack of challenge in school can stifle the development of gifted learners. Brainstorming is a group approach for producing ideas and solving problems, using the principle of deferred evaluation. The use of conceptual models can also increase creative thinking and problem solving.

4. Family variables are very important for encouraging the qualities that lead to eminence, as is school climate; learner-centered informal schools (as opposed to those that are more formal) and warm, receptive teachers are more likely to encourage creativity. Similarly, formal teaching styles (structured, teacher-controlled, achievement-oriented, emphasizing individual work) may lead to higher academic achievement; informal styles (student-centered, integrative, intrinsically motivated—characteristic of open classrooms) are sometimes associated with higher creativity and motivation.

5. Teachers' expectations can serve as self-fulfilling prophecies and affect students' performance positively or negatively in accordance with these expectations. Expectations

are often higher for students from higher socioeconomic levels, for obedient children, for students with the most positive labels (for example, "learning disabled" rather than "mentally retarded"), and for those who sit front and center and speak clearly.

6. Besides mandating education in the "least restrictive environment" (inclusive education or mainstreaming), Public Law 94-142 and the Individuals with Disabilities Education Act (IDEA) establish the child's right to due process and nondiscriminatory evaluation, free and appropriate educational services, and an IEP for each child with special needs.

7. Inclusive education attempts to meet the needs of exceptional children in the regular classroom. For some children with special needs, full inclusion may be difficult and not entirely appropriate. IEPs must be prepared for all special needs children, following assessment and parental involvement and consent. These include statements of goals, duration of the program, and evaluation procedures.

8. Exceptionality describes significant deviation from the norm in cognitive, social-emotional, or physical functioning. It can be associated with either superior or deficient functioning.

9. Physical exceptionality may be manifested in exceptional athletic ability or extraordinary grace and elegance; at the other extreme, it may be apparent in sensory or motor impairments, physical disabilities, diseases, and so on.

10. Social-emotional exceptionality includes manifestations of emotional disturbance, behavioral disorders, and attention deficit hyperactivity disorder (ADHD), among others. All but the most severe forms of social-emotional exceptionality are ordinarily dealt with in the regular classroom.

11. Mental retardation is characterized by a marked depression in general ability to learn and by limited adaptation and can vary from mild to profound. Most mentally retarded children are mildly retarded and are thus capable of acceptable achievement in elementary school.

12. Learning disabilities are generally evident in a disparity between actual and expected achievement, with an uneven pattern of achievement often marked by one or more specific learning impairments (for example, developmental reading disorder or developmental arithmetic disorder).

13. Attention deficit hyperactivity disorder (ADHD) is a relatively common emotional disorder marked by excessive activity, attention problems, and impulsivity far in excess of what might be considered normal. ADHD is often treated with stimulant drugs (the paradoxical effect) and, more experimentally, with brain-activity feedback instrumentation (biofeedback).

14. Initial identification of exceptionality is often made by classroom teachers after the child has begun school. Mild retardation and learning disabilities are seldom diagnosed before this time.

15. Labels are useful in categorizing children and in providing for their special needs. But they simply name rather than explain and should not be pejorative.

Applied Questions

- ▲ Explain the most important elements of the legal definition of the talented and gifted.
- ▲ Write a personality and teaching-style profile of a hypothetical teacher whose approach is most likely to foster creativity.
- ▲ What are the two dimensions of physical, intellectual, and emotional exceptionality?

- ▲ Distinguish between mental retardation and learning disabilities.
- ▲ Describe the most important symptoms of attention deficit hyperactivity disorder (ADHD).

Internet Activity

Use InfoTrac College Edition or other World Wide Web sources to investigate the prevalence and treatment of ADHD: Write up your findings. (See the inside back-cover of this text for suggestions about where to begin.)

Sample search terms: Attention deficit hyperactivity disorder

Study Terms

ability grouping **321**
acceleration **321**
attention deficit hyperactivity disorder (ADHD) **341**
biofeedback **349**
brainstorming **325**
classroom climate **328**
conceptual model **326**
developmental arithmetic disorder **345**
developmental reading disorder **345**
educable mentally retarded (EMR) **343**
enrichment **321**
exceptionality **331**
formal teaching style **328**
full inclusion **333**
giftedness **317**
hyperactivity **341**
inclusive classroom **332**
individualized educational plans (IEPs) **323**
Individuals with Disabilities Education Act (IDEA) **332**
informal teaching style **328**
learning disability **343**
mainstreaming **332**
mental retardation **341**

mentor **323**
mild retardation **342**
moderate retardation **343**
neurofeedback **349**
paradoxical effect **347**
peer-assisted learning (PAL) **323**
prodigy **317**
process disorder **346**
profound retardation **343**
Public Law 94-142 **332**
radical acceleration model **322**
revolving door model **321**
self-fulfilling prophecy **329**
seriously emotionally disturbed (SED) **340**
severe retardation **343**
special education teacher **332**
special needs **331**
talent **317**
talented and gifted **317**
teacher expectations **329**
teaching style **328**
tutor **323**

Suggested Readings

The following references should be valuable for teachers concerned with the creative behavior of their students. The first has been translated into many different languages and continues to be popular. The second is a practical examination of talent and giftedness in the schools; it contains many suggestions for teachers of gifted and talented children in regular classrooms. And the third also presents practical strategies for a creative classroom.

Osborn, A. (1957). *Applied imagination.* New York: Scribner's.

Torrance, E. P., & Sisk, D. A. (1997). *Gifted and talented children in the regular classroom.* Buffalo, N.Y.: Creative Education Foundation Press.

Wilks, S. (1995). *Critical and creative thinking: Strategies for classroom inquiry.* Portsmouth, NH: Heinemann.

The following is a highly practical guide for teachers of exceptional children in the early childhood classroom. It deals with the characteristics of exceptional younger children and their identification and provides useful ideas for working with them.

Winzer, M. (1997). *Special education in early childhood: An inclusive approach.* Scarborough, Ontario.: Prentice-Hall.

The following two references are practical classroom guides for teachers in inclusive classrooms. The first outlines many specific strategies that teachers can use in various situations; the second presents a detailed look at some of the issues and problems in inclusion.

Polloway, E. A., & Patton, J. R. (1997). *Strategies for teaching learners with special needs.* Upper Saddle River, NJ: Prentice-Hall.

Coutinho, M. J., & Repp, A. C. (1999). *Inclusion: The integration of students with disabilities.* Belmont, Ca: Wadsworth/ITP.

In the summer, a bear's heart normally beats approximately 40 times per minute. In winter, when the bear is denned up, the heart rate may drop as low as ten beats per minute. Amazingly, extreme cold rouses the bear as readily as does warmth. Otherwise, many bears would freeze to death because it is necessary for the bear to awaken and warm up when the temperature drops too low (Matthews, 1969).

Any sufficiently
advanced technol-
ogy is indistinguish-
able from magic.
Arthur C. Clarke

Multicultural Education: Adapting Instruction for Learners

CHAPTER 10

PREVIEW

Although psychology is largely concerned with the individual, its theories deal mainly with groups that share similar characteristics. In psychology, as elsewhere, the individual is often the exception to which the rule—or the theory—does not apply. We know that we are shamelessly oversimplifying, but we find it convenient and useful to speak of learners as though all are pretty much the same. But, as underlined in Chapter 2, learners of varying ages and genders are very different. And, as illustrated in Chapters 8 and 9, we also know that there can be tremendous diversity in the skills, abilities, and interests of different individuals of the same age and gender. This tenth chapter looks at another source of diversity in the classroom: multiculturalism. And it describes a variety of ways to adapt the classroom to respond to this enormous diversity, including school language programs, programmed instruction, the use of computers in education, and specific teaching techniques founded on distinct theoretical principles.

FOCUS QUESTIONS

▲ What is multicultural education?
▲ What are some of the pros and cons of bilingual education?
▲ What are the characteristics of branching and linear programs?
▲ How might computers be used in education?
▲ What is mastery learning? Keller's PSI?

During the summer when I was six years old, I got a very bad pain in what I thought was my stomach. For several days I lay about the house feverish and plaintive while my mother and grandmother administered various home remedies. We lived in the wilds, pretty well at the end of the road, what seemed an enormous distance from the closest doctor or hospital, a distance that was never traversed except in cases of extreme emergency.

But, in the end, none of the home remedies seemed to work. So Mr. Delisle, who'd gone to Debden to buy a horse, sent back Réné Savard with his taxi, and he drove my dad and me all the way to the hospital in Prince Albert where Dr. Crooks yanked out my appendix and cured my stomach ache.

My father was there when I awoke. He explained what had happened, said he had to go back to teach school, and told me my mother would come back on the train next Monday and bring me home. I said "au revoir" to my papa. I hadn't started school yet and French was the only language I knew.

I soon wished I knew just a little English. Because before very long, I needed to go to the bathroom and I had no idea what to do. So when a nurse came in with a tray (containing liquids, of course, appendectomies being a serious matter in those days), I asked where the bécosse was; that was the word we used for outhouses. She smiled, apparently unaware of my desperation. It amused her that I spoke only French.

In the end, I humiliated myself—not only once, but several times—before eventually discovering the purpose of the strange-looking containers by my bedside.

By the time my mother came to get me, I had learned several English words. One of them, bedpan, *I've never forgotten. And I swore that when I got home, I'd get my dad to teach me a lot more of this English language.*

Which he did.

MULTICULTURALISM

Ours was not a mainstream culture so much as a combination of many cultures. In our home and among our relatives it was primarily a French culture. In other homes sparsely scattered throughout this wilderness, it was a more Anglo-Saxon or sometimes a Ukrainian culture. And only a half-mile from where we lived, among the homes of the Big River First Nations, it was a Cree culture.

And in the school, it was all of these cultures—a sort of *multiculture.*

Some Definitions

Multiculturalism has been a fact of life for many years in North America—which is to say that, for many years, North American societies have been composed of a multitude of different **cultures.**

To clarify, a culture is the totality of the customary ways of behaving, the beliefs, the attain-

---

multiculturalism Having to do with many cultures.

ments, the stories, the songs, the dances, of an identifiable group of people, or of a specified period of time. **Pluralistic societies** (or *multicultural societies*)—that is, societies such as those in the United States, Canada, Australia, and New Zealand that are made up of a large number of cultures—are often described by sociologists as having **macrocultures**. A macroculture is a sort of umbrella culture made up of the combination of many different cultures in what are termed **melting pot societies**. Within multicultural societies, there are typically also a large number of distinct **microcultures**—that is, identifiable groupings of people who share beliefs, values, and behaviors that are distinctly different from the mainstream ones.

In Canada, another expression is sometimes used to describe the multiple cultures that make up the nation, that of **distinct societies**. Rather than being viewed as a *melting pot* in which different cultures are ultimately assimilated to the dominant culture, two highly distinct ethnic groups, the French and the English, are each officially recognized in law and government. This situation has given rise to several issues; many of these involve political and emotional tensions. These are not our concern here.[1]

We often think of culture and **race** as though they were largely synonymous. But, strictly speaking, a race is a major biological subdivision of individuals who share a common genetic ancestry and who are often identified on the basis of physical characteristics. There is considerable controversy over the assignment of groups to races. This may be true partly because there has been a tremendous amount of intermingling of groups throughout the entire history of humanity. And this intermingling, note Aunapu and associates (1993), has accelerated so dramatically that North America alone has produced more hybrid families in the last two decades than were produced in the entire history of the world. As a result, there are many, often conflicting, classifications of human races. For most purposes, this concept is not only largely useless in any case, but it easily leads to **racism**, the belief that biologically distinct groups of humans have inherited different mental abilities and personality characteristics. In practice, racism often leads to the maltreatment of individuals from various minority groups.

As if these often vague terms were not enough, another one is frequently bandied about as though it meant both race and culture—which, in a sense, it does: **ethnic**. What *ethnic* signifies is membership in a racial, cultural, or language group where individuals share important things such as beliefs

---

culture Signifies the customs, beliefs, achievements, art, and literature that is particular to a distinct group of people.

pluralistic societies Societies composed of many different cultures.

macroculture The type of culture that results from the melding of aspects of a variety of different cultures over time.

melting pot societies Geographical or political entities composed of a variety of cultures that are gradually assimilated to the dominant culture. The end result is that individual cultures are no longer identifiable, and the dominant culture becomes a *macroculture*.

microculture Within a pluralistic society, identifiable minority groups who share a distinct culture different from that of the majority culture.

distinct society A metaphor used to describe the Canadian cultural scene where, theoretically, two distinct cultures coexist; neither has been assimilated to the other as would happen in a *melting pot society*.

---

race A biological term referring to an attempt to classify humans in groups distinguishable in terms of their genetic ancestry; often identifiable on the basis of physical, mental, or personality characteristics. The concept is unclear, contradictory, and not very useful.

racism The belief that identifiable groups of humans inherit different physical, mental, and personality characteristics.

ethnic Refers to the sharing of beliefs, values, history, or other characteristics, as might happen with distinct cultural or language groups.

---

[1] ***PPC:*** Isn't the bear French? Wouldn't he like to express his opinions on these matters?

Author: The bear is of many ethnic groups, about which he has endless wonderful things to say. But the issues that concern us here, he grumbles, are educational, not political.

and values, history, or other characteristics. This causes them to have a sense of shared identity, or belongingness. So when we speak of ethnic differences, we might be referring to language differences, cultural differences, or racial differences—or perhaps to all three.

Changing Dimensions of Multiculturalism

For many years, our cultural blinders in North America have been decidedly Eurocentric. That is, we have tended to think of North American society as primarily white, Anglo-Saxon, Protestant (**WASP**). That is understandable, given that the dominant majority throughout the early part of our history was white. And notions of our continent as a vast cultural melting pot seemed quite accurate. Our grandparents knew that no matter how many new spices and herbs you threw into the pot, so powerful was the main ingredient that all the flavors would be assimilated and what would come out in the end would still be highly predictable—and dominated by the main flavor: *white European.*

As recently as 1980, 78 percent of the school-age population (ages 5–15) in the United States was white; Hispanic children accounted for only 8 percent of school-age children. Now, in some states like California, the "minority" has become the "majority," reports Garcia (1993): 52 percent of students currently belong to "minority" categories. In fact, in 1995, more than one-fourth of California's total population was Hispanic (U.S. Bureau of the Census, 1997). Projections say that, by 2020, 50 percent of elementary school children in the United States will belong to nonwhite groups. At that time, Hispanics will make up about one-fourth of all elementary school children;

almost 20 percent will be African Americans. These changing demographics are partly due to lower birthrates and consequently smaller average family size among white families (3.18) than among blacks (3.62) and Hispanics (4.02) (U.S. Bureau of the Census, 1997). Immigration rates are also much higher for nonwhites (see Figure 10.1).

These projections are tremendously important for North American education because, if they are accurate, they will most likely be reflected in dramatic changes in the school. In 1980 the majority of U.S. schoolchildren spoke English—the dominant, standard, majority language—whereas by 2020, 70 percent of all beginning first-grade students will belong to a nonwhite group. What are the implications of these changes? Even today, more than 15 percent of all people in the U.S. speak a language other than English at home. And in more than half of these cases, that language is Spanish (U.S. Bureau of the Census, 1997).

Multicultural Education

The clearest implication of these changes is an increasing need for **multicultural education**—that is, education that reflects an understanding and appreciation of different cultures and that accommodates to the needs of children from different backgrounds.

Multicultural education is three things, explain Banks and Banks (1997): *First,* it's the idea that all children, regardless of their ethnic characteristics, should have an equal opportunity to learn and grow in school; *second,* it's a reform movement that is trying to change schools to make this idea a reality; and *third,* it's the ongoing, never-ending process of devising and implementing the changes that the reform movement requires.

WASP Acronym for "white Anglo-Saxon Protestant." Frequently used to describe the main characteristics of the group that has historically been the most common in North America.

multicultural education Educational procedures and curricula that are responsive to the various cultures and languages of students, with the goal of assuring that all children experience high-quality education.

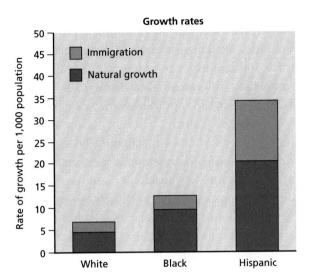

FIGURE 10.1 Rate of annual population growth from natural increase and immigration for three U.S. groups, 1996. Based on U.S. Bureau of the Census, 1997, p. 20.

Multicultural education is enormously challenging and also intensely controversial. This is clearly evident, for example, in the language issue that faces California. As we see later, in that state, there is a powerful movement to provide bilingual education for Hispanic students—and an equally powerful movement toward doing away with bilingual programs and throwing all children into the same "sink or swim" classrooms (Beltrame, 1998). Ironically, support *against* bilingual programs comes from two sources: parents of English-speaking students who fear the education of their children is being shortchanged as a result of too many resources being thrown into the education of cultural minorities, and parents of Hispanic students who fear their children aren't learning English fast enough or well enough in bilingual programs. The challenge, say Banks and Banks (1997), is to figure out how to treat all cultural minorities equitably without limiting the opportunities of other groups.

Besides these political (and highly emotional) issues, teachers face other difficult challenges. Lechner and Barry (1997) report that most teachers feel they know too little about var-

ious cultures to implement multicultural educational programs. They fear going counter to parents' values and perhaps offending them. When teachers are asked to prepare multicultural lesson plans reflecting African American, Hispanic, or Native American cultures, for example, they opt for "cute" materials and activities that they think will be safe and inoffensive.

But perhaps the greatest challenge teachers face relates directly to the most difficult task faced by newly-arrived learners from different backgrounds: developing the language skills required to permit normal learning and progress in school.

Why We Need Multicultural Education As we have seen, because of differing birth and immigration rates, the demographic characteristics of North American societies are changing rapidly; as a result, increasing numbers of students come to school with limited English-language proficiency. And it has repeatedly been shown that such students are at serious risk of failing in school (Jiménez, García, & Pearson, 1995). In 1995, for example, more than 45 percent of Hispanic youths 18 to 24 years old, compared with only 18 percent of whites, were high school dropouts (U.S. Bureau of the Census, 1997).

Brisk (1991) notes that the poor achievement of **English as a Second Language (ESL)** students in the United States was traditionally viewed as the students' problem—a problem for which schools need not accept any special responsibility. In some instances, the problem would rectify itself with exposure to traditional schooling, but in many cases students would simply fail. In fact, Edwards and Redfern (1992) also report significant, and often unrecognized, underperformance and failure among children from nondominant cultures in both Canada and England. These authors

---

English as a Second Language (ESL) An expression used to describe programs designed specifically for nonnative English speakers.

explain that although multiculturalism has long been a fact of life in these countries, through much of their history they have encouraged a sort of linguistic homogeneity. The clearest signs of this myth of homogeneity was found in schools where all instruction typically occurred in English and minority cultures and languages thus tended to remain largely invisible.

With the rapid demographic changes of the late 20th century, there has been increasing recognition and appreciation of the multicultural aspects of North American society. As a result, many school jurisdictions have begun to assume increasing responsibility for the growth and performance of all their students, now that an increasing number of them represent different cultures and languages.

The Goals of Multicultural Education

Multicultural education is a loosely defined concept that reflects the attempts of educators to take into consideration the cultural diversity of their classrooms and communities. And because it is very difficult to separate culture from language, in the majority of cases, multicultural education is also *multilingual*—that is, it involves instruction in more than one language.

Banks and Banks (1997) describe several important goals of multicultural education. One of its major goals, they note, is to reform educational systems so that all children are treated equally by the schools, regardless of their cultural and language background. A second related goal is to rid school systems of unequal treatment of boys and girls. Meeting these goals, note Banks and Banks, requires major changes not only in curriculum and teaching methods, but also in teachers' and administrators' attitudes.

Aspects of Multicultural Education

Multicultural education requires accommodating cultural diversity—which is not a simple matter. One problem is that many teachers have not been sufficiently exposed to different cultures and languages to appreciate the subtle but important differences that distinguish cultural groups. (See, for example, the case entitled "Adapting to Cultural Diversity.") As a result, note Pérez and Torres-Guzmán (1992), misconceptions about cultures and cultural groups often characterize teachers' and curriculum builders' approaches to multicultural education. Among these is the simplistic view that cultures are static and unchanging and easily described in terms of things like folk art, clothing, dances, and music. Perhaps even more misleading and simplistic is the assumption that minority cultures are highly homogeneous and that all individuals of a given culture are therefore pretty much the same. We have to keep reminding ourselves, argue Keogh, Gallimore, and Weisner (1997), that individual members of identifiable minority ethnic groups are as different from each other as are members of the more visible majority groups. Multicultural research, explain Baber, Garrett, and Holcomb-McCoy (1997), has been guilty of emphasizing differences *between groups* and has largely ignored differences *within* groups. Finally, our ethnocentrism leads us to the assumption that one culture—usually the dominant, majority culture to which most of you belong—is really better than the others and should be held up as a model for members of other cultures.

Ideally, say Banks and Banks (1997), multicultural education accomplishes several tasks. First, it integrates information and examples from a variety of different cultures, making all students, in a sense, *culture literate*. Second, it helps students understand how knowledge and beliefs are influenced by cultures (and by social class and language). Third and extremely important in an increasingly tribalistic world, it reduces racial prejudice through increasing understanding and, consequently, tolerance of other people and other belief systems. Fourth,

Adapting to Cultural Diversity

THE SITUATION: Eric Johnson, white Anglo-Saxon male, age 24, B.Ed., beginning teacher

Eric had always figured he'd be a good teacher: He'd gotten good marks, he liked kids, and he was well organized and hard working. So when they offered him one of the inner-city schools, one with a lot of immigrant children, he didn't even hesitate. He knew about multicultural education, about developing respect for other cultures, about molding his curriculum and his lessons to accommodate the richness of the cultures he would have in his class. He would welcome his fourth-grade minority-culture students with open arms; they would love it.

Or so he thought. But it didn't work that way at all. In fact, many of his immigrant students seemed lost and confused through much of that first school year. And not until much later did Eric begin to understand why. For example:

▲ The East Indian students were taken aback by the free-wheeling interchanges between the native-born students and the teacher; in their culture, teachers speak and students listen.

▲ The Japanese students were shocked at the possibility of disagreeing with the teacher—and even more shocked at the possibility of disobeying and scarcely being punished.

▲ The Vietnamese children felt humiliated by having their heads touched affectionately by the teacher.

▲ The Moslem girls were profoundly embarrassed by having to change into shorts for physical education.

▲ The boys from Afghanistan found it very difficult to take directions from the female principal.

Source: Based in part on Stewart (1993).

---

it reduces racial, social-class, and gender inequities. And fifth, it empowers all students so that even those from disadvantaged backgrounds or very different cultural groups can acquire information and skills and the confidence and sense of personal power necessary to succeed.

Second Language Programs

Multicultural education, because it usually deals with different cultures and languages, is typically also multilingual—or, more precisely, *bilingual*, because in many North American schools there is a clearly identifiable main second language. As a result, numerous bilingual or English as a Second Language (ESL) programs have been established. And although the main purpose of these programs, notes Brisk (1991), has been to prepare students to fit into the traditional, English-only school curriculum, this is no longer always the case. Brisk argues strongly that as stu-

dents become increasingly multilingual and multicultural, schools need to become more responsive to their needs. This does not mean preparing students to fit into a traditional English-only curriculum so much as developing a curriculum that truly integrates the diversity of students with different languages and cultural backgrounds. What schools should focus on, say Artiles and associates (1998), is becoming truly inclusive—that is, schools that are truly multicultural rather than those that simply admit students from diverse backgrounds and then try to make them all the same. But this, they note, requires changes in teacher education programs.

The Other Side of the Second Language Debate The multicultural education movement is one response to cultural diversity; there is another, notes Ogbu (1994). This is sometimes labeled the "core curriculum movement." It advocates that the most important offerings of schools are certain basic "core" subjects like arithmetic, reading, and writing—all offered in the dominant language. In North America, that language is English. And there are signs that English is rapidly becoming the dominant language in much of the world. There are a variety of reasons for this. One reason is that English has become the language of science, so there are very few top-level scientific laboratories in the world where scientists are unable to read and understand English. A second reason is that English is the language of computers, the dominant language of the Internet. And a third reason is that English is the language of business and commerce.

English is an enormously rich language, its defenders insist. As Parshall (1995) points out, it contains some 600,000 words (many, of course, borrowed from other languages). In contrast, German consists of perhaps one-third as many words, and French, only half as many as German. As a result, English boasts a wealth of synonyms and a depth and precision so great that in spite of it being a native tongue for fewer than 400 million of the more than 5 billion people on this planet, half of all the books published in the world are published in English—and some 80 percent of all computer text is in English. It is little wonder that Chinese parents in Hong Kong strongly favor the use of English as the medium of instruction in their schools (Tung, Lam, & Tsang, 1997). There are many pragmatic reasons for learning English.

In the United States, powerful, well-funded, and highly vocal groups of English-only advocates argue that English should be designated the official U.S. language, as it has been in at least 18 states (Padilla, 1991). Many members of these groups—English Only, English First, and U.S. English, to name three—are firmly opposed to the use of public resources for bilingual education.

The argument against multicultural education, notes Banks (1993b), is advanced not only by the *traditionalists* who want to maintain and defend the dominance of Western civilization, but also by various ethnic groups who believe that *their* culture (rather than multiple cultures) should be at the center of the curriculum.

Other groups, notably English Plus, advocate expanding bilingual programs for both adults and children. There is considerable tension surrounding this debate, notes Beltrame (1998). In fact, in the United States, bilingual education has been mandated by law following court decisions that found that putting all children in English-speaking classes, regardless of their language and cultural background, does not amount to treating all children equally. However, Los Angeles county later revised its bilingual policy, apparently because of declining English fluency (Daily Report Card, 1995). The emphasis is now more on English proficiency and on academic results. As a consequence, children who are not fluent in English are assigned to special classes for a much shorter period of time. In Canada, the right to instruction in both official languages (English and French) is guaranteed in some provinces but not in others. Most notably, Quebec's Bill 101 tends to entrench the use of only French in all public sectors in the province of Quebec (Padilla, 1991).

Language Immersion Programs

Research suggests that the best way to learn a second language is not to take occasional lessons, private instruction, expensive audio- or videotape courses, or concentrated study but to become immersed in the language. In essence, **language immersion** involves entering an environment where only the language that is to be learned is spoken. Immersion programs might be used for speakers of the dominant language who want to learn a second language (for

---

language immersion An approach to teaching a second language that involves placing the learner in an environment where only the second language is used.

example, English-speaking children in western Canada entering a French immersion program). These programs are also used to help children who speak a minority language to learn the dominant language (for example, Spanish-speaking children being placed in an English immersion program).

Stewart (1993) describes three different types of English immersion programs currently in use. Sheltered immersion is commonly used at the high school level and is designed for students who speak some English but who would profit from a higher level of proficiency. In a sheltered immersion class, students are taught subjects in English, but teachers attempt to keep the vocabulary and grammar at a level that can be understood by all students. In theory, when students have progressed sufficiently in their knowledge of English, they return to the regular program. But in practice, notes Valdés (1998), "many non-English-background students fail to learn English well enough to succeed in school" (p. 4).

Structured immersion typically begins in the first grade, although it may also begin later. It involves providing all instruction in the immersion language. And *pull-out immersion* is a program typically used when the school enrollment is too low for a structured immersion program. In such cases, students are pulled out of their regular classes for special instruction in the second language, which is very often given by teachers specifically trained in teaching English as a second language (ESL).

There is ample evidence to suggest that when immersion occurs early enough (soon after the first language is firmly established), children can painlessly learn a second language and perhaps even a third and a fourth.

French and Spanish immersion programs for English-speaking students are a mushrooming phenomenon in North America. Most of these are structured immersion programs that begin in preschool settings and continue through the elementary grades. In a typical pro-gram, teachers and teacher assistants speak only the immersion language in the first year; that is, the second language is not taught as a separate subject but is simply the language through which the regular curriculum is taught. In the second year, English is introduced for perhaps 10 percent of the school day. The percentage increases each year, until by sixth grade half the school day is conducted in English and half in the second language.

Research indicates that immersion programs of this kind can be extremely effective for teaching a second language (for example, see Ambert, 1991). Participants quickly reach high levels of proficiency in understanding and speaking the second language, as well as in reading and writing, although the majority do not reach as high a level of proficiency as native speakers. Perhaps only a small number will ever become what Diaz (1983) calls "balanced bilinguals" (individuals who are equally proficient in both languages). However, as Genesee (1985) points out, the language deficiencies of immersion students do not appear to interfere with their functional use of the second language. These students typically perform as well as students in conventional English programs in academic subjects such as mathematics, science, and social studies, and on measures of social and cognitive development. If the immersion program is conducted entirely in the second language and students have not yet received instruction in English language arts, of course they do not do as well on measures of English literacy. But Genesee (1985) reports that within one year of receiving English instruction, these students perform just as well as children in monolingual English programs. In fact, research summarized by Lindholm and Aclan (1991) indicates that bilingual proficiency relates positively to high academic achievement.

English as a Second Language programs for children whose native language is not English do not all meet with as high a degree of success. These programs, notes Valdés (1998), include the increasingly popular **dual-language immersion programs** where native English-speaking children and non-English-speaking children are immersed together. The theory is that this exposes the non-English-speaking students to a better quality of English than is often learned in schools where non-English-speaking students often tend to become isolated in their own groups. It also exposes the English-speaking students to another language environment. Unfortunately, the quality of instruction in the minority language is often inadequate, so the English-speaking students don't benefit as much as they otherwise might. Perhaps worse, minority-language students are often frustrated by their inability to understand and imitate the speech of the native speakers; even in these classes, they ultimately become isolated.

Not all minority-language students fare poorly in immersion programs. And when they do, it may be partly because of frustrations that these children sometimes experience in progressing through regular school subjects. Failure may also be related to the inadequate training of teachers and uncertainty about which approaches are most effective (Ochoa, Rivera, & Ford (1997).

Bilingual Programs

Language immersion programs teach a second language by immersing students in the language to be learned. However, many bilingual programs use other approaches. For example, Lam (1992) describes a variety of types of bilingual programs used in schools. These include programs designed primarily to establish English-language competency, programs intended to develop a high level of competency in a second language as well as in English, and various other programs for students with special needs.

Which Approach? There has been a staggering amount of research on the effects of different approaches to teaching a second language, says Cziko (1992). But the conclusions are neither clear nor simple. One of the problems, as Lam (1992) notes, is that some programs are exemplary and others are not; some students learn quickly, and others learn slowly. Also, sadly, some teachers are less competent than others. In fact, following a major evaluation of various approaches to bilingual education, Meyer and Feinberg (1992) conclude that it is unreasonable to expect any one method to be highly effective given "the unexceptional nature of the instruction" (p. 102). This evaluation, commissioned by the American National Research Council, compared three strategies for second-language learning: immersion programs, where teachers understand and speak both languages but use only the immersion language in school; early exit programs, where children who begin school with limited proficiency in English are placed in English classes as soon as possible; and late exit programs, which attempt to develop proficiency in English over time while maintaining a high level of proficiency in the native language. Among the conclusions was the observation that although these programs are theoretically distinct, in practice they are often indistinguishable.

Effects of a Second Language

Learning a second language is not always an entirely positive experience. Lambert (1975) coined the expression **subtractive bilingualism** to describe a situation in which learning a

---

dual-language immersion programs Immersion programs which include children who are native speakers of the dominant language and children who are learning the dominant language as a second language.

subtractive bilingualism A phrase used to describe a situation in which learning a second language has a generally negative effect, often evident in lower proficiency in both languages.

second language has a negative influence on the native language. **Additive bilingualism** describes the opposite situation. And **transitional bilingualism** describes a very common situation where the native language is completely replaced by the dominant language within a few generations.

Research indicates that the circumstances when learning a second language is most likely to be a negative experience involve minority-group children whose first language is a minority language. In such instances, the second language—the dominant, majority language—is extensively reinforced in the mass media and in society, whereas the minority language is not. Thus, learning the second language is a subtractive experience because, as children become more proficient in the dominant language, they become less functional and less fluent in the first (Pease-Alvarez & Hakuta, 1992). This may be the case, for example, with French-speaking children in Canada or Hispanics in the United States who learn English as a second language in school. Because television and other media (and perhaps most community transactions) use English, the first language receives little support and reinforcement outside the home—and perhaps not even in the home. As a result, the first language tends to be seen as less valuable and is used at a less advanced level (Landry, 1987). Moreover, speakers of the minority language in the home are often poor models of that language. Thus, the Spanish or French spoken at home might be more colloquial—less developed in terms of vocabulary, liberally sprinkled with English expressions, grammatically incorrect, and characterized by idiosyncratic pronunciation (Carey,

1987). And if the minority language is not part of children's schooling, they are unlikely to learn to read and write it. Ultimately, their first-language proficiency may be largely oral.

Learning a second language most often has a positive effect on children when the language learned is a minority language. This would be the case, for example, for English-speaking North American children enrolled in Spanish or French immersion programs. Growing evidence suggests that such programs are successful in developing a high level of proficiency in the second language and that they contribute to general academic achievement (Garcia, 1993). They frequently also strengthen the first language.

Of course, there are numerous exceptions to these simple generalizations; real life is rarely as simple as our interpretations of research might suggest. And if our demographic projections are accurate, these issues may become far more pressing by the year 2020.[2]

ADAPTING INSTRUCTION FOR DIVERSE LEARNERS

Ethnic differences between the various groups that make up the multicultural classroom are only one source of diversity with which teachers must contend; there are other sources of variation. And many of these are found *within* rather than simply *between* groups. We should not assume that members of distinct ethnic groups

---

additive bilingualism A phrase used to describe situations where learning a second language has a positive effect on the first language and on general psychological functioning.

transitional bilingualism This describes a situation in which a minority language is gradually replaced by the dominant language, essentially disappearing within a few generations.

---

[2] **PPC:** After all this stuff on language and language programs, it isn't entirely clear which side the bear is on. I'm sure my students will want to know.

Author: Even though the bear has more dog meat than choirboy in him, he is not foolish enough to take sides. It's partly the wisdom of advancing age, says he, quick to take offense at the suggestion that he has simply become chicken——with age. There was a time, he confesses, when, inflamed with the idealism of his bear-youth, he would have stepped over on the side of his convictions and made noises as loud as anyone's on the other side. "Maintenant, je ne dis rien," he says, with that sardonic twinkle in his eye. "Nada. En boca cerrada no entran moscas."

are homogeneous, warn Baber, Garrett, and Holcomb-McCoy (1997). Some students are bright, alert, inquisitive, and interested; others are less capable or less interested—or both. One single lesson, or even a course, does not necessarily fit all students equally well. Much of mass education is, well, for the masses; often, lessons are designed for all and sundry with little attention to individual differences. One fundamentally important question is: What can an ordinary classroom teacher do to implement what is termed **individualized instruction**?

One solution is for the teacher to spend time with each student individually, responding to the student's immediate needs and interests, explaining, probing, imparting strategies, and doing other things that good teachers do. Unfortunately, teacher–student ratios, the limited time available, and the demands of the curriculum make this a difficult and often impractical solution. As a result, teachers often resort to one or more educational strategies that take into consideration individual differences among learners. These strategies include ability grouping (or tracking), the learning styles approach discussed in Chapter 9, programmed instruction, computer-based or computer-assisted programs, and various specific individualized instructional programs such as Bloom's mastery learning and Keller's PSI. The details and merits of each of these strategies are the subject of the remaining pages of this chapter.

TRACKING

Tracking, or **ability grouping**, involves grouping students for instructional purposes. Ability grouping is the more specific term; it refers to

Although there is rarely enough time, money, or energy to implement completely individualized programs for all students, individualization on a more limited scale is possible in every classroom. Individualization of instruction does not mean that all students work individually at all times throughout the school day. But it does mean that, whenever possible, the teacher takes into consideration the needs, strengths, weaknesses, and wishes of individual students.

grouping on the basis of actual (or suspected) ability. Tracking is a more general term, referring to groupings that might be based on ability but that might also be based on interests, gender, vocational aspirations, social class, and so on. As the label implies, **within-class grouping** refers to groups or tracks that are formed within the reg-

---

tracking A general term for the formation of groups on the basis of any one or more of a variety of student characteristics such as ability, interests, social class, ethnic membership, language background, and vocational aspirations.

ability grouping Grouping students on the basis of ability for instructional purposes.

within-class grouping Ability groups or tracks that are formed and function within the regular classroom.

---

individualized instruction Instructional procedures that lend themselves to deliberate and systematic adaptation to the individual needs, interests, and abilities of students.

ular classroom; **between-class grouping** involves the formation of groups made up of students from separate classes.

Oakes and Guiton (1995) point out that tracking is generally based on one of three sets of criteria: race, social class, or apparent intelligence—low-income and minority students are significantly overrepresented among the low-ability groups.

As we have seen, tracking may also reflect job prospects and aspirations. This type of tracking is evident, for example, in the distinction between vocational (or technical) high schools and those that are more academic.

Finally, tracking decisions may reflect personal choice factors such as individual interests or parental pressure. Thus, parents may select certain programs for their children largely because of the aspirations and hopes they have for them. Or, in some cases, they may select schools on the basis of their reputations (or for social, cultural, or religious reasons).

Some Arguments for Tracking and Ability Grouping

Between-class grouping of students into high- and low-ability classes was once a relatively common way of attempting to match school offerings more closely to students' differences. When ability was used as the basis for tracking, the expectation was that the needs of students with lower abilities could be met more effectively if they received instruction in classrooms composed of individuals with similar abilities. As we see shortly, research has not been kind to this expectation, although there is evidence of small but positive benefits of within-class groupings for classroom instruction (Lou et al., 1997). Note, however, that these benefits were found for

within-class groupings and not for between-class groupings.

Educators have also argued that high-ability students would do better in an instructional environment designed specifically to cater to their needs and abilities. And research has been far more supportive of this expectation. For example, Rogers (1998) summarizes research which indicates that advanced students benefit from ability groupings far more than do low-ability students. Not surprisingly, McKerrow (1997) found that parents who are relatively advantaged (and whose children are therefore more likely to be in the more advanced groups) have far more positive attitudes toward tracking than do less advantaged parents.

These conclusions relate to what are termed **homogeneous groups**—that is, groups defined in terms of largely similar (hence *homogeneous*) characteristics of learners. Thus a homogeneous high-ability group consists of only high-ability individuals. **Heterogeneous groups**, in contrast, represent a range of abilities and backgrounds. As we saw in Chapter 7, heterogeneous groups are very common in cooperative learning groups. These are not the type of groups that educators or parents have in mind when they speak of tracking or ability grouping.

Some Arguments Against Tracking

The research is remarkably consistent in its negative evaluation of tracking. As Braddock and Slavin (1993) argue, at best, tracking is totally ineffective; at worst, it is harmful. In particular,

---

between-class grouping The assignment of learners to ability groups or tracks that function in separate classrooms.

homogeneous group An instructional group whose members are highly similar in terms of the criteria that define the group (for example, ability, race, gender, or vocational aspirations).

heterogeneous group An instructional group whose members represent a wide range of skills, abilities, interests, aspirations, and so on.

note Good and Marshall (1997), low-ability students benefit very little from tracking.

What are some of the problems associated with tracking? Weinstein (1996) lists four: *First*, groupings are typically based on tests whose ability to predict important adult accomplishments are extremely limited. Yet grouping decisions are often made on the basis of single-point differences between students!

Second, judgments of student ability are often based on the performance of an individual student relative to the performance of others within a group. Thus a student judged to be low ability in one group might be found to be of high ability in a different group.

Third, although research indicates that short-term rate of development is not highly predictive of later events, tracking decisions are often based on the performance of learners over a short period of time (for example, in the first weeks of the first grade). These decisions, insists Weinstein (1996), can be highly unfair.

Finally, there are relatively few places available in the highest-ability, or highest-status groups; this is at least as much a function of social and political policy than of the fact that there are few candidates worthy of membership in these groups.

That many student placements are inaccurate and unfair are not the only objections to tracking. George (1993), for example, argues that tracking tends to lock students in for extended periods of time regardless of their subsequent performance. Moreover, it stresses ability but minimizes the value of effort. And, as we noted earlier, racial, ethnic, and income differences among groups tend to be highlighted in school tracking decisions. In fact, note Friedkin and Thomas (1997), tracking systems within schools are perceived by students as a clear social status system. Tracking persists, argues McKerrow (1997), precisely because it protects the relative advantage of those with higher income and ability. Not only do advantaged children stand a much better chance of being selected for the high-status (high-ability) groups, but as Kubitschek and Hallinan (1998) found, the friendships these children develop will be selected primarily from within their school groups. Thus tracking fosters a class system which, ultimately, is unfair to those who are less advantaged.

Another objection to tracking is that, at least for low-ability students, it is not very effective. In fact, Burks (1994) cites evidence that ability grouping may actually have effects opposite to those intended. That is, ability grouping tends to be justified at least partly in terms of expected increases in the performance of low-ability students, following instruction ostensibly tailored more closely to their needs. But, says Burks, tracking often results in a magnification of the initial differences between low- and high-ability groups.

Detracking

As a result of considerations such as these, many groups have been highly outspoken in their attacks against tracking and in their calls for educational reform built around the concept of **detracking**—that is, removing the use of homogeneous groupings in schools.

But detracking schools is not a simple matter, for a variety of reasons. Perhaps the most important is that, as Weinstein (1996) points out, tracking absolutely permeates our educational system. It is implicit in a tremendous variety of decisions that educators make regarding matters such as a student's readiness for advancement to the next level, assignment to

---

detracking An educational reform movement based on the desire to rid educational systems of homogeneous grouping practices.

groups for reading or math, retention or promotion, admission to special programs such as those for the gifted or those with learning disabilities, and so on. Many of these decisions are based on misperceptions of ability, argues Oakes (1997), and many also unfairly reflect ethnic, cultural, or gender groupings.

Detracking is an important part of current educational reform in many jurisdictions (for example, George, Morgan, & Jenkins, 1997). There is evidence that this can lead to measurable educational improvement, especially for ethnic minority groups and low-ability learners (Cooper, 1996). Note again, however, that arguments against tracking apply primarily to *between-class grouping*. Within-class grouping, where groups of students are separated for specific learning experiences more closely suited to their needs but remain an integral part of the regular classroom, are not subject to the same objections. Nor is cooperative learning, which also makes use of grouping but typically uses *heterogeneous* rather than homogeneous groups.

Other approaches to individualizing instruction include the learning styles approach, mastery learning, peer tutoring, and computer-aided instruction.

☐ THE LEARNING STYLES APPROACH

The approach that perhaps goes furthest toward making the lesson fit the student is the **learning styles approach** discussed in Chapter 7 (see Dunn, Dunn, & Perrin, 1994). This approach recognizes that students learn in different ways—that each student has a unique **learning style**. Some students learn well in the morning; others awaken reluctantly and don't function well until later in the day.[3] Some excel with highly structured, teacher-directed, whole-class approaches; others perform much better with less-structured, self-initiated, individual approaches; still others achieve better in small-group, cooperative settings. Some students prefer to work in bright, well-lit surroundings with loud music; others require quiet, more subdued environments. Some learners have a marked preference for the visual or the auditory mode; some respond better than others to praise or criticism; some have longer attention spans than others . . . and on and on.

Advocates of learning styles approaches argue that to truly individualize instruction it is necessary to develop a profile of each learner. This profile should provide a detailed description of strengths and weaknesses, preferences and dislikes. Schools and classes can then be tailored to cater to each individual's style. As we saw in Chapter 7, in practice this approach requires a tremendous assortment of alternatives. Core school subjects must be presented at different times of the day; classes must be organized so that individuals can select among small-group, individual, or whole-class approaches; rewards must be restructured so that classes include individual, cooperative, and competitive situations; and instructional materials must be

---

learning styles approach An individualized instructional system that is designed specifically to cater to the learning style of each student.

learning style A unique and important learner variable manifested in differences in biological rhythms (morning versus evening people), perceptual strengths (visual versus auditory learners), sociological preference (whole-group versus small-group instruction), attention span (long or short), and a wealth of personality variables (dependence or independence, for example).

[3] *PPC:* We'd have a lazy bunch of students if we let them sleep all morning just because that's their learning style.
Author: The bear is not lazy, but he sleeps all winter. That's his lifestyle.

developed to appeal to visual, auditory, and kinesthetic sensory modes.

Learning Styles in the Regular Classroom

For many practical reasons, truly individualizing instruction as completely as suggested by a learning styles approach is often difficult or even impossible. Even if everyone concerned were convinced that this is the best of all possible instructional alternatives, in most instances there simply isn't enough time, money, or energy to implement all aspects of the program. But individualization on a more limited scale is possible in virtually every classroom. In fact, it is *essential*, especially in the now common **inclusive classroom** that can include any number of children with unique special needs. But even in a relatively homogeneous classroom, argues Bacdayan (1994), if instruction is not individualized to some extent, the result will be an inefficient and ineffective use of educational resources. The poorer students will struggle needlessly and perhaps unsuccessfully, and the better students will waste much of their time in a boring and unchallenging environment (Dunn & Stevenson, 1997).

Individualization of instruction does not mean that all students work individually at all times throughout the school day. Individualization means that instructional methods, class organization, evaluation procedures, and other components of the teaching/learning process are selected and modified in response to learners' characteristics, course and lesson goals, and practical constraints. In practice, this usually means that some students are exposed to differ-

---

inclusive classroom A classroom that contains one or more children with special needs in addition to more average children.

---

ent experiences at least some of the time; some of these experiences might well be individual, but many will occur in small groups. And even in classes where the teacher individualizes instruction, much can take place in whole-class situations (see the case entitled "Digging Up the Truth").

Among the instructional methods available to teachers are the teacher-centered approaches of direct instruction, which include methods such as lecturing, discussing, reciting, and questioning, and the more student-centered approaches of the constructivist classroom, which include methods such as facilitating guided discovery, using small or large group strategies, tutoring, peer teaching, and so on. Each of these has advantages for different purposes, but even the methods that research has identified as potentially "best" (for example, one-on-one tutoring) cannot, for practical reasons, be used exclusively. Even the methods represented by such global terms as *lecturing* and *discussing* are hardly ever used to the exclusion of all other methods by any teacher worth even slightly more than his or her salt. Thus, teachers do not typically lecture or discuss; they present lessons, an activity that involves talking, listening, questioning, demonstrating, using instructional materials, and sometimes standing on one's ear or nose. These activities might be directed toward an entire class of students (large or small), a single student, or a handful of students, or they might alternate among the various possibilities. And the activities might occur in connection with any of the specific techniques that have been developed to individualize, to systematize, to computerize, and to personalize instruction.

Several of these techniques, some derived directly from psychological theory and experimentation, are described in the remainder of this chapter: programmed instruction, computer-assisted instruction (CAI), mastery learning, and

Digging up the Truth

THE SITUATION: Edward Stewin, a good teacher, as recollected by Serge, teacher-in-training

Mr. Stewin, my grade 3 and 4 teacher, always made sure he knew what each student was most interested in, and he found ways of letting us work on these interesting

subjects, sometimes alone and sometimes in groups. For example, some of us were quite interested in native people, so he had us research a particular tribe and then build articles that they would have used. We then buried them in the schoolyard, and another team of students had to dig them up and assess their lifestyle. Then we got together and more or less taught the rest of the class about this tribe.

Keller's personalized system of instruction (PSI). Aspects of the methods and principles of each of these approaches might be profitably incorporated in the increasingly sophisticated arsenal of every contemporary teacher.

PROGRAMMED INSTRUCTION

The term **programmed instruction** can be used in a general sense to describe any organized **autoinstructional device**—that is, any device that presents information so that the learner can acquire it without the help of a teacher. In this sense, textbooks are a kind of programmed material, as are computers. A more specific definition of programmed instruction, however, limits it to material that is specifically designed to be autoinstructional and is arranged according to one of two patterns, linear or branching,

or a combination of the two. Skinner (1954) is usually associated with the **linear program**, whereas Crowder (1961, 1963) introduced the **branching program**.

Linear Programs

A linear program (also called a *Skinnerian program* after its originator) is one where all learners move through the same material in exactly the same sequence. Linear programs individualize instruction by permitting students to progress at their own rate.

Linear programs are based directly on an operant conditioning model. They present material that leads the student to emit a correct response, and then they reinforce the response. In effect, each response is an operant, and the knowledge that the response is correct is a

---

programmed instruction An instructional procedure that makes use of the systematic presentation of information in small steps (frames), in the form of a workbook or another device. Programs typically require learners to make responses and provide immediate knowledge of results.

autoinstructional device Any instructional device that is effective in the absence of a teacher. Common examples are workbooks and computers.

---

linear program The presentation of programmed material so that all learners progress through the same material in the same order. Linear programs typically make no provisions for individual differences in learning; however, the material is broken up into very small steps (frames).

branching program Programmed material that, in contrast to a linear program, presents a variety of alternative routes through the material. Such programs typically make use of larger frames than do linear programs, and they frequently use multiple choices. Also termed *Crowder programs*.

reinforcer. Accordingly, linear programs have the following characteristics to ensure that a student will almost always answer correctly:

▲ The material is broken down into small steps, referred to as **frames**, which are presented in logical sequence. Each frame consists of a minimal amount of information so that a student can remember this information from frame to frame.

▲ Students are required to make frequent responses—usually one in every frame and often as many as four or five in each frame. They are given **prompts** to ensure that they answer correctly.

▲ Linear programs provide immediate **knowledge of results**. Students know at once that they have answered correctly (or incorrectly). This knowledge is assumed to act as reinforcement. Because linear programs attempt, through the use of prompts and small frames, to ensure that the student makes few errors, most of the feedback is positive—positive feedback is more effective than negative feedback (knowledge that one is wrong).

To try your hand at a linear program, see the box entitled "Piagetian Jargon: A Linear Program" and follow the directions.

Branching Programs

Branching programs (sometimes called *Crowder programs* after their originator) present learners with much longer frames than linear programs

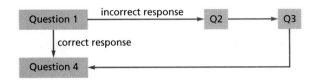

FIGURE 10.2   A branching program

do (sometimes an entire page at a time). And unlike linear programs, they require learners to select from among several alternative answers rather than making up their own. But the most striking difference between branching and linear programs is that with branching programs, not all students go through the program in exactly the same way. Students who give all responses correctly go through the shortest way possible. Students who make errors receive remedial instruction and further clarification. Typically, learners who answer incorrectly are sent to a **remedial frame** or sequence of frames and eventually return to the main branch. They then proceed from there (see Figure 10.2). One example of a branching program is presented in the box entitled "Bear Tracking: A Branching Program."[4]

The Usefulness of Programmed Instruction

Programmed instruction, as originally conceived and developed, is now mostly of historical interest. Searches of common educational and psychology databases indicate that very little research has been conducted on programmed instruction since its heyday as an educational fad in the early 1960s—although there is still a scattering of stud-

---

frame A unit of information presented in programmed instruction. A frame presents information and usually requires the student to make a response.

prompt A device used in programmed instruction to help to ensure that the student will answer correctly. These can take a variety of forms.

knowledge of results Knowledge about the correctness or incorrectness of a response. Knowledge of results is usually immediate in programmed instruction.

---

remedial frame A frame in a branching program to which students are referred when they make an incorrect response. The purpose of the remedial frame is to provide information required for a subsequent correct response.

[4] *PPC:* Does this program have anything to do with the subtitle of this book? Some of my students wondered last year.

Author: It's always a good sign when students wonder. Especially if they do so out loud and ask intelligent questions. One answer to this question is found in the Epilogue at the end of Chapter 13.

BEAR MUSINGS

Piagetian Jargon: A Linear Program

Directions: Fold a sheet of paper or use a strip of cardboard to cover the answers, which are given at the bottom of this feature. With the answers covered, read frame 1 and write your answer in the blank provided. Move the paper or cardboard down to check your answer before proceeding on to frame 2.

1. Jean Piaget has developed a theory that deals with human adaptation. It is a developmental theory of human _____.

2. As children learn to cope with their environment and to deal effectively with it, they can be said to be _____ to it.

3. Adaptation therefore involves interacting with the environment. The process of adaptation is one of organism–environment _____.

4. One of the central features of Piaget's developmental theory is that it attempts to explain _____ through interaction.

5. Interaction takes place through the interplay of two complementary processes: One involves reacting to the environment in terms of a previously learned response. This process is called assimilation. Assimilation involves a _____ learned response.

6. Whenever children use an object for an activity they have already learned, they are said to be assimilating that object to their

previous learning. For example, when Jennifer sucks a pacifier, she is _____ the pacifier to the activity of sucking.

7. Sam is given a paper doll. He looks at it curiously and then puts it in his mouth and eats it. He has _____ the doll to the activity of eating.

8. Assimilation is one of the two processes involved in interacting with or adapting to the environment. It is part of the process of

_____.

9. Adaptation involves two processes. The first is assimilation. The second is called accommodation. It occurs whenever a change in behavior results from interacting with the environment. Accommodation involves a _____ in behavior.

10. When children cannot assimilate a new object to activities that are already part of their repertoire, they must _____ to them.

11. Johnny West was presented with a very long pacifier on the occasion of his first birthday. Before that time he had been sucking a short "bulb" pacifier. The long pacifier matched his nose. He had to elongate his mouth considerably more than usual to suck this new pacifier. Johnny West had to _____ to the new pacifier.

12. If Johnny West had been given his old, short pacifier, he could more easily have _____ it to the activity of sucking.

13. . . .

Answers:

1. adaptation	5. previously	9. change or modification
2. adapting	6. assimilating	10. accomodate
3. interaction	7. assimilated	11. accomodate
4. adaptation	8. adaptation	12. assimilated

ies that examine it (for example, Munson & Crosbie, 1998; Strawitz, 1993). In the end, the legacy of this fad may be in the learning principles it revealed. Markle and Tiemann (1974; Markle, 1978) point out that these principles constitute the rudiments of an instructional theory that can be applied to either simple tasks of motor learning or to complex cognitive learning tasks. The

Bear Tracking: A Branching Program

Objectives: After you have read this program, you should be able to:

1. recognize a forest
2. recognize a bear's tracks
3. recognize a bear
4. run very rapidly in all directions

Note: Because only part of the program is presented here, only the first two objectives can be attained.

Directions: Read each frame very carefully; reread it if it appears confusing. Then select what you think best completes the statement presented, and follow the directions that correspond to that answer.

1. A forest is a collection of trees. It is a large collection of trees, just as a city is a large collection of people. A wood is a small collection of trees, just as a town is a small collection of people. A bush is a collection of small trees. What is a collection of small people? Never mind. Bears are often found in large collections of trees.
   If you were looking for a bear, you would go to:
   (a) a large collection of people
   (b) a forest
   (c) an ocean
   If you answered (a), go to frame 10.
   If you answered (b), go to frame 3.
   If you answered (c), go to frame 7.

2. Correct. Good. Now that you have found a forest, you must find some tracks. Remember, a bear's tracks look like this:

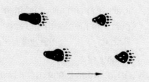

After you have found the tracks, follow them. Somewhere, a bear is standing in them. If you find these tracks:

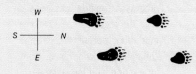

you should go
   (a) N
   (b) S
   (c) E or W
   If you said (a), go to frame 8.
   If you said (b), go to frame 12.
   If you said (c), go to frame 4.

3. You are correct. Bears are often found in forests. Occasionally, however, bears are also found elsewhere. You should keep this in mind. The best way to find a bear is to do two things: First, look for a forest; second, look for a bear's tracks. They look something like this:

The best way of finding a bear is to:
   (a) look for an ocean
   (b) look for its tracks
   (c) look for a forest
   If you answered (a), go to frame 7.
   If you answered (b), go to frame 9.
   If you answered (c), go to frame 2.

4. Your answer is incorrect, but it may not be unwise. If you are afraid of bears, you might even consider going south. Go to frame 12 to see what would happen if you went south.

5. It is obvious that you are afraid of bears. Your instructions are to go directly to your local university library (do not pass Go, do not collect $200, heh, heh). You are asked to read about counterconditioning, paying special attention to systematic desensitization. If you can afford to, you might consider hiring this textbook's author as a therapist. If you can't afford me, hire someone else.

6. Good! Good! You should do something else. But first you

three fundamental concepts of this programmed instruction theory are active responding, errorless learning, and immediate feedback.

Applying these principles to classroom practice involves presenting small units of information to maximize immediate comprehension and to minimize the number of errors students make while learning, thus providing for continual student involvement through active responding and also providing students

must return to the large collection of people. Having done that . . .

(Now go to frame 13.)

7. You are not paying attention. Go back to frame 1 and start again.

8. Good. You noticed the arrow. You may eventually see a bear.

If you answered (b), go to frame 5.

If you answered (c), go to frame 6.

9. That is incorrect. If you begin to look for a bear's tracks before finding a forest, you may never find either a track or a bear. Go back to frame 3.

but they are often found in large collections of trees (forests). You might waste a lot of time looking for bears in cities. Now go back and read frame 1 again.

11. Piety is an admirable quality in a student, but it is not the desired response here. You might seriously consider, at this point, whether you really want to track bears. If you are sure that you do, you are instructed to begin with frame 1.

12. Stop! You are going in the wrong direction. A bear faces toward the front of its tracks. This is an important point. Now you may go back to frame 2, but you might want to rest for a minute before continuing. You may do so, but you should probably begin at frame 1 when you are well again.

It is interesting, don't you think, that a bear always stands facing toward the front of its tracks, sniffing around? This makes it a lot easier to locate. After you have found the bear, you will have to make a decision:

Will you

(a) stop and pray?

(b) run home?

(c) do something else?

If you answered (a), go to frame 11.

10. That is incorrect. A large collection of people is a city. Bears are not usually found in cities,

13. The beginning of this program is included here simply as an illustration of a branching program. Frustrated would-be bear trackers are invited to consult their local library—or they can hire me as a guide (high-quality service at reasonable rates).

with immediate confirmation of correct responses. And although it is very time-consuming to structure lessons as logically as the programs require, such a sequence is conducive to learning.

COMPUTERS IN EDUCATION

Some principles of programmed instruction are also evident in another development that can contribute dramatically to individualizing instruction—the use of computers in schools. In fact, many computerized instructional programs are similar in format to the programmed texts that were briefly popular a handful of decades ago. And some researchers note a natural transition from traditional programmed instruction to computer-assisted instruction (Jonassen, 1993). The computer is an especially powerful interactive tool for presenting systematic instructional sequences like those that define programmed instruction.

The Computer Revolution

"The computer revolution is upon us!" we are told almost daily—and have been told for some time now. This is a big word: *revolution*. Small wonder that so many of us should ask what this computer revolution is, whether it actually is upon us, and whether it is good or bad.

The Third Wave Yes, the computer revolution *is* upon us, according to Alvin Toffler (1980), who earlier (1970) warned us that the coming of this revolution might send many of us into a state of shock. Toffler sees the computer revolution as the **third wave** in a series of monumental changes that have swept over humanity. The first wave, which occurred more than 10,000 years ago, was the agricultural revolution—a revolution that transformed our hunting and foraging ancestors into domesticators of animals and growers of food, changing the very essence of what it was like to be human in those times. The second wave, far more recent in our history, was the industrial revolution; its ultimate effects were to transform our workplaces, our homes, and our lives. Only history can ultimately tell us how profound will be the effect of the third

wave—the computer revolution that is sweeping over us now.

Part of this revolution is evident in what Tapscott (1997) has dubbed the **net-generation (N-Gen)**. The net-generation is the 88 million children in North America who are, in his words, the first generation ever to be "bathed in bits." These 88 million *N-Geners*, aged from birth to 20, now outnumber their parents—and, in some ways, they have surpassed them. There is no longer a generation gap, claims Tapscott; there is now a generation *lap* as the younger generation, fearless in the face of a technology that has surrounded them from birth, has lapped the parent generation in the ease with which they interact with computer technology.

Resistance to the Revolution But if there is a revolution, there must also be a status quo—which means there must be resistance to the revolution as well, inertia and humans being what they are. "Tomorrow," writes Wilson (1988), "we're going to need to do something entirely different. And that's frightening because people have to let go of who they think they are. A good caterpillar only wants to know how to be a better caterpillar. 'A butterfly?' she says. 'No way you're going to get me up in one of those things'" (p. 14).

Some teachers, and even some students, simply want to be good caterpillars. They are uneasy about computers, afraid of the changes that the revolution might require. But there are signs of change. Kristiansen (1992) studied teachers' attitudes toward computers in education over a 20-year period (1970 to 1990) and found marked increases in acceptance of, even enthusiasm for, computers in school—and a dramatic decline in fear. Yet even today, many college students suffer

---

third wave Toffler's expression for the computer revolution (the first two waves of monumental change are the agricultural and the industrial revolutions).

net-generation (N-Gen) A phrase coined by Tapscott to describe the current generation of children in North America; reflects their command of digital media and, especially, the World Wide Web.

from varying degrees of "technophobia"—they are apprehensive of the new computer technologies—and more of these students are female than male (Bernhard, 1992).

All this may well change, however, as today's net-generation grows. For them, the new technologies will not seem anything like a revolution.

Evidence of the Revolution Evidence of the computer revolution is all around us. Only thirty years ago, I wrote the first edition of this book using a 25-cent ballpoint pen and two dozen pads of yellow paper. Now I write to you on a computer linked to a laser printer—and linked as well to a university computing system, a network of library systems, an assortment of databases, a CD-ROM, and innumerable individuals throughout the world via *their* personal computers. Not that there were no computers in 1972. Quite the contrary, there were many of them, and surprising as it might seem, in many important ways they were not very different from today's computers in terms of their capabilities. But some important differences between first-generation computers and today's computers account for this revolution. Chief among those differences are the reduced size and price of today's desktop, or personal, computers, made possible by the microchip, a fingernail-sized wafer that contains all of the computer's processing units. New computer technologies have also succeeded in linking the world by means of that vast electronic web, the **Internet** (also called the *World Wide Web*). And these same technologies now make it possible to use computers to

Computers are rapidly becoming almost indispensable tools in the teaching/learning process. But not all estimates of their impact are entirely positive.

immerse people in simulated environments that seem so real they are labeled "virtual reality."

Now people (and schools) can own personal computers as easily as they can own television sets. In 1984, only approximately one of every four students had access to computers in school—and most of these students were in universities and colleges. In U.S. public schools, for example, there were an average of 63 students for every computer with a total of slightly more than a half-million computers. But by 1997, there were almost seven million computers in schools—one computer for every seven students. Internet access for schools was extremely unlikely in 1984, whereas now some 65 percent of all schools are linked to the World Wide Web (U.S. Bureau of the Census, 1997). (See Figure 10.3.)

Today's personal computer is also far easier to operate than its grandparents. It is, in the jargon of the trade, far more user friendly. Small

Internet The label for a worldwide, amorphous, changing web of computer linkages, mainly via telephone lines and satellites. The Internet uses the computing resources of many universities and industries and can be accessed by virtually anyone with a computer and a telephone, cable, or satellite link (modem). The Internet makes inexpensive electronic communication possible worldwide. Also termed *World Wide Web*.

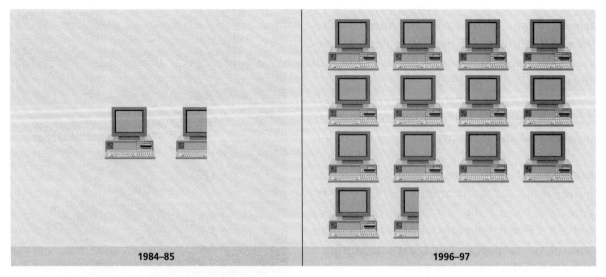

1984–85	**1996–97**

FIGURE 10.3 Computers per 100 students, 1984–85, 1996–97. U.S. Bureau of the Census, 1997, p. 171

wonder that personal computers have proliferated on the market. But what will their effect be on education?

The Potential Effects of Computers in Education

Computer enthusiasts and other optimists predict sweeping, somewhat radical, and highly beneficial effects from the widespread introduction of computer technologies into schools.

Positive Effects The effectiveness of computer technology for learning and instruction, explains Windschitl (1998), is closely related to the computer's ability to perform tasks that many of us now take for granted but that are truly amazing—tasks like sorting, changing numbers into charts and graphs, analyzing information, or when I instruct it to, reaching out electronically into a distant, almost mysterious place and providing me with virtually instant access to complete references and summaries for the dozens of articles that have been published *this very year* on the use of computers in schools. These func-

tions, argues Windschitl, can free students from tedious, low-level tasks (like walking through libraries, for example) and enable them to engage in higher-level activities.

Computers can make schools a part of large information exchange-and-retrieval systems where individual students will have virtually instant access to an almost unlimited quantity of high-quality information. Computers also enable students from all over the world, and from every imaginable ethnic grouping, to communicate with each other. There is no race, gender, or social class on a computer screen, or in a computer chat room. Perhaps one of the positive effects of the Internet will be to make possible the eventual appearance of the universal, multicultural classroom.

Pillay (1998) suggests that another positive effect of computers in education is that they can provide instruction more easily matched to individual learning styles. At the very least, they can be used to allow learners to progress at their own pace, much like programmed instruction.

Others predict that smaller, friendlier, more personal schools will again proliferate, once the resource disadvantages that sometimes characterize smaller schools disappear with the coming of the computer. Some of these enthusiasts insist that problems with reading, writing, and arithmetic will end as people master the new computer skills. Indeed, some even suggest that many of the ill effects of television will be replaced by the creative activities encouraged by computers and that family ties will be strengthened as more and more of the net-generation are able to work out of their homes, linked to their offices (if there still are such things) and to the world via spunglass fibers, gold filaments, infrared rays, satellite systems, or more mundane telephone lines.

Less Positive Possibilities   There is, of course, a less optimistic view of the likely long-term impact of computers. This view suggests that our basic computational skills may decline dramatically as computers take care of our computational needs, that reading skills are likely to suffer as children spend more time being amused by computers and their fantasy games and less time reading, and that violence may increase as a function of computer video games. Others believe that computers are unlikely to make knowledge and power more accessible to the masses but will instead have the opposite effect.

Parsons (1983), for example, argues that, according to our best historical evidence, computers are more likely to increase than to decrease the gap between the haves and the have-nots. Schools, notes Muffoletto (1994), must be especially careful to apply democratic principles of social justice when introducing computers in schools. At least in the first decades of computers in the school, poor and ethnic-minority students (and females) have clearly had less access to computers than wealthier, ethnic-majority students (and males) (Martinez, 1994).

North America believes in the power of technology, notes Mergendoller (1998). We believe that technology can solve all of our problems, even improve education and ultimately perhaps

make us happier. We have always tended to think that the most recent technology was about to revolutionize everything. When radio came along—then, motion pictures; next, television; eventually, programmed instruction and teaching machines—many educators were immediately convinced that this heralded enormous changes in the classroom and the end of schools as we knew them.

It didn't happen then and it isn't likely to happen now either, insist Grabe and Grabe: "Our confidence in technology," they write, "is justified only in classrooms led by dedicated and skillful teachers" (1998, p. xvii).

Computer enthusiasts are sometimes guilty of exaggerating and misrepresenting the benefits of computers in education, notes Parsons (1983). For example, he points out that these enthusiasts use the term *interaction* widely and inaccurately. Parsons sees interaction as a "meeting of minds," a sort of sharing of meaning (exemplified by conversation or reading a book). Typically, however, interaction with a computer is quite different: It primarily involves the giving of information. Furthermore, although computers are often described as expert systems of one kind or another, they do not resemble human experts in most fields (doctors, lawyers, professors, psychiatrists); computers are generally ill-equipped to provide us with advice—information, yes, but only occasionally advice.

In the final analysis, these opposing optimistic and pessimistic views of how computers are likely to affect our lives are no more than speculation based perhaps on reason and probability, but certainly based also on hope and fear. What will actually come to pass may not be affected a great deal by our often premature speculations. From a teacher's point of view, given the invasion of the computer in our lives and our schools, it is important to understand which uses of the computer will provide the greatest benefits to students.

Uses of Computers in Education

With educators' peculiar tendency toward jargon and acronyms, they have given us a whole series of computer-related expressions: CAI (computer-assisted instruction), CML (computer-managed learning), CBE (computer-based education), CAT (computer-assisted training), CBT (computer-based testing), CBT again (computer-based training), CMI (computer-managed instruction), CMT (computer-managed training), ITS (intelligent tutoring system), ICAI (intelligent computer-assisted instruction), and CAL (computer-assisted learning). Of these, **CAI** is perhaps the most general term.

Basically, there are three related things that students can do with computers; they can learn *about* them, they can learn *with* them, and they can use them simply as tools.

Computer Literacy Learning about computers is what computer literacy is all about. Just as learning something about cars is essential for most of us whose daily activities require us to drive, learning something about computers may well be essential for today's children who will most likely be required to do far more with computers than we are. If the effects of the computer revolution are anywhere near the magnitude of the agricultural and industrial revolutions, those who remain computer illiterates may be swept under and drowned by the third wave.

Or will tomorrow's computers, like today's computerized banking machines, be so simple that even nearly illiterate people will be able to operate them? Will they be dumbed down like fast-food cash registers with pictures of tiny hamburgers on their keys?[5]

CAI One of many acronyms related to the application of computer technology to education. Specifically, CAI refers to computer-assisted instruction, the use of computers for instructional rather than administrative purposes.

Making students computer literate may no longer need to be an important educational goal. If Tapscott (1997) is correct, the net-generation already know a lot more *about* computers than do their parents and many of their teachers. What we need now, say Lowther, Bassoppo-Moyo, and Morrison (1998), are programs that don't teach students *about* computers but teach them *with* computers. They argue for computer-*supported* rather than computer-*based* instruction.

Computers as Tools Computers should be viewed as another tool in the sophisticated teacher's assortment of tools and strategies, say Lowther, and associates (1998). Effective use of this tool requires that teachers (and learners as well) be technologically *competent* rather than simply computer literate. That is, they have to know how best to use the various capabilities of the computer to enhance student learning.

At a basic level, computers can be useful tools in the management of schools. They simplify routine clerical tasks such as registering students, storing data, solving scheduling problems, preparing and issuing report cards, and so on. And they are also tremendously useful computing and writing instruments for school administrators, staff, and teachers.

Computers can also be word processing and computing tools for students. In fact, notes Mergendoller (1998), the most common use of computers in elementary schools is mainly (sometimes entirely) for drill and practice exercises; the most common use in high schools is for word processing. And although some argue

---

[5] *PPC:* Or like highway signs that hardly ever have numbers or words on them anymore, just symbols and pictures.

Author: Ironically, for those of us who are literate, words might be far more precise and meaningful than symbols and pictures. Except for the bear's mentor, Yogi Berra, for whom words sometimes twisted themselves in bizarre ways. "You look nice and cool, Yogi," someone once said to him. "You don't look so hot yourself," he retorted.

that drill and practice is a wasteful use of such powerful technology, research indicates that computers are exceptionally good and highly effective at providing learners with these sorts of experiences (Consejero et al., 1998).

Computers are extremely important sources of information as well. Compact disc technology has not only increased the amount of information a **stand-alone computer** can store for the learner, but has also made retrieval almost instantaneous. In this sense, a computer can be very much like an encyclopedia. But information in a printed encyclopedia can only be accessed sequentially—specific related topics can be searched for separately and found in their scattered locations. In contrast, information on a compact disc can be accessed almost instantly—and all related information can be displayed (or printed out).

As sources of information, computers are not solely dependent on their own stored information but can be easily connected to any of a variety of **databases**. A database is a source of information typically organized in terms of one or more subject areas. While doing research for this book, for example, I repeatedly accessed education and psychology databases such as Psychinfo and ERIC. Doing so allowed me to quickly scan (and print out, if necessary) references and abstracts for many articles on related topics.[6]

When computers are connected to the World Wide Web, they provide students with an almost overwhelming assortment of sources of information (Fetterman, 1998). Unfortunately, the Web can also be a source of misinformation and a tremendous drain on student time. There can be an enormous opportunity cost involved in students' use of the Internet, claims Mergendoller: "Consider what is *not* learned during the days students roam the Internet for the right piece of information or collaborate with students in other lands around misunderstood, erroneous concepts" (1998, p. 44).

Computers can also be used as a source of advice about career decisions. Their great advantage in career guidance is that they can store a tremendous wealth of information concerning career opportunities and requirements that relate to the rapidly changing job market. They handle routine career-related questions quickly and efficiently, and they can be programmed to find relationships among a given student's achievement, aptitudes, and interests and the likelihood of success in various careers. Many career advice computer programs are now available and widely used in schools. Some of these provide information on thousands of careers, and most are designed to be used with the personal computers found most commonly in homes and schools.

Specific Computer Applications in Instruction

Although 65 percent of all U.S. public schools had access to the Internet in 1997, only 14 percent of classrooms did—with Internet access less than half as likely in schools with a high minority enrollment (U.S. Bureau of the Census, 1997).

---

stand-alone computer A computer system that is complete by itself because it includes a processing unit, a monitor, and an input device (keyboard)—in contrast with several computer terminals linked to a central computing system.

database A source of information accessible by computers. Common databases include library cataloguing systems or abstracts of current journal articles. Databases are often organized by topics. For example, PSYCHINFO is a vast database that contains summaries of an enormous number of articles published in journals relevant to psychology.

---

[6] *PPC:* Maybe the bear should draw attention to the Internet exercises at the end of each chapter in this book, which illustrate the usefulness of computers and the Web as sources of information.

Author: Okay. Also, see the inside back cover of this book for information about free access to useful World Wide Web sources, including databases such as ERIC and access to a powerful library resource and search tool, InfoTrac College Edition.

One of the problems, notes Mergendoller (1998), is that many of the computers still in schools are outdated (by computer standards) and cannot run much of the new software, including that required for Internet access. As we have seen, there are still many possible uses for computers in schools. And older computers are gradually being replaced by newer ones.

Computers for Drill and Practice Computers can be used for repetitive drill exercises (in mathematics or language learning, for example, or for learning things like keyboarding skills). When used for these purposes, computers are highly effective and can do a great deal to free the classroom teacher for other activities. And they can be used with even very young children (Carlson & White, 1998).

Simulations Happily, the computer's uses are not limited to drill and practice exercises but include computer simulations as well. **Computer simulations** mimic certain actions or phenomena. For example, programs are available that mimic the circulatory system, a chemical laboratory, or the in-flight responses of a Boeing 737. Simulations allow the learner to discover the results of specific responses without the risk and expense of actually performing them. Thus, when using a computer-controlled simulator, a pilot can learn that a particularly unlucky combination of aileron and rudder movements can cause a crash—and the pilot can learn this without actually destroying either a multimillion-dollar aircraft or human lives.

At a less dramatic level, a clever simulation of a chemical laboratory might allow students to discover the potentially disastrous effects of combining, chilling, heating, pressurizing, or eating different chemicals, without losing a school building or a human body in the process.

Virtual Reality Simulations Imagine that you are a student studying ancient Mayan civilizations. Today, you have chosen to explore a Mayan ruin. You climb the precipitous slope of the main pyramid's north face, skipping along the lower steps, then clawing your way up to where the ancient stones have crumbled. Finally, you stand on top. Deliberately, you look in each of the four directions. Now you take out your compass, turn it so that it points to 280 degrees, and search the jungle for signs of the opening into the sacrificial *cenote*. Finding it, you switch to "museum mode" and explore a database, complete with photographs, filled with information on Mayan sacrifices and related topics.

Is this possible? Almost, with the interactive videodisc environments used to produce computer simulations labeled **virtual reality** (**VR**). Such simulations typically involve one or more of the sensory systems, to heighten the sense of realism (Franchi, 1994).

In education, virtual reality describes a particular kind of computer–learner relationship (interface, in computer jargon) wherein the learner experiences aspects of an environment and makes choices or moves within that environment so that the experience seems virtually real. In a virtual reality system described by Ferrington and Loge (1992), individuals wear the computer's display systems on their heads, using something that looks like a helmet and goggles. This system presents the individual with three-dimensional visual and corresponding auditory displays and includes sensors that respond to the user's movements. If users look up, they might see the sky; to the

---

computer simulation Mimicking or modeling certain actions, procedures, or phenomena using computers. For example, computers might be used to simulate (copy the actions of) weather patterns or chemical reactions.

virtual reality (VR) A computer-based simulation that typically involves a number of sensory systems (such as bodily sensations, visual images, and auditory signals) in order to produce a sensation of realism.

left, another landscape; to the right, yet another. Furthermore, users make choices suggested by the display by manipulating an icon (termed a "puppet") that appears on the display. The puppet is controlled by a "dataglove" that is engineered so that finger and hand movements are translated directly into corresponding movements of the puppet. Thus, the user can open doors, grasp and move objects, and point in any direction to "move" in that direction.

Virtual reality systems are still largely experimental, but various interactive instructional/entertainment programs are available—including the Mayan program, called Palenque, just described (Wilson & Tally, 1990). Although Palenque doesn't use headset receivers or datagloves, it presents learners with individual point-of-view camera angles and permits a variety of places to be explored physically, or other modes such as "museum," which then permit still further choices such as entering different "rooms" within the museum (Kozma, 1991).

The simulations that VR systems might make possible are staggering to contemplate. Virtual reality simulations have been used in museums to make visitors feel as though they are part of some aspect of a display (Harvey et al., 1998). They have been used to study human responses to movement in space without requiring actual movement (Maguire et al., 1998). They have also been used for the treatment of conditions like **claustrophobia** (Botella et al, 1998), where patients' symptoms can be elicited without actually placing them in enclosed spaces. Virtual reality simulations are also widely used to train pilots. Fight simulators typically include changing kinesthetic and visual feedback made possible by manipulating the pilot's seat and controlling visual images and auditory stimulation.

Integrated Learning Systems Computer-based courses are widely available for a tremendous variety of topics and ages. Delivery systems might include a computing center and student terminals or else it might consist of one or more stand-alone units, each with its own computer and terminal. Typically, the learner interacts with the computer program by means of a monitor and a keyboard or another control device such as a mouse or joystick. This physical paraphernalia is collectively labeled **hardware**; the programs, which are really the brains of the computer—its information, instructions, and capabilities—are called **software**, or sometimes *courseware*.

The phrase **integrated learning system (ILS)** is used to refer to any of a variety of computer-based learning systems typically developed for mass marketing. The systems usually include hardware and software and can also involve links to external databases (Hativa & Becker, 1994). The ILS allows for various levels of objectives and activities and permits ongoing evaluation of students' performance. As a result, it also provides for diagnosis and automatically prescribes a series of courses for each student.

Research indicates that ILS systems can be highly effective for meeting measurable curriculum objectives (Mergendoller, 1998). However, they can be expensive, and not all teachers are prepared to implement such systems in the classroom. Their effectiveness is often a function of the teachers' knowledge and preparedness, the school context, characteristics of the students, and characteristics of the classrooms in which they are used (Hativa & Lesgold, 1996).

---

claustrophobia A disorder whose principal symptom is fear of enclosed or confined spaces.

hardware The physical components of a computer, including the monitor, controller, keyboard, chips, cards, circuits, drives, printer, and so on.

software Computer instructions; programs. Also termed *courseware*.

integrated learning system (ILS) A computer-based learning/instructional system that includes both hardware and software, often with links to external databases, and is designed to guide students through part or all of a curriculum.

Most ILS programs emphasize course content rather than the student's cognitive processes. Few approach the current ideal in the field of computer applications to education: intelligent systems.

Intelligent Tutor Systems (ITS) An **intelligent tutor system (ITS)** (also referred to as a *knowledge-based tutor*) is a program that takes into account the learner's strengths and weakness and modifies its offerings accordingly—very much as a good teacher does. The cornerstones of such systems, explains Gugerty (1996), are the procedures that the system uses to analyze the student. Intelligent tutor systems try to determine what a student knows (or needs to know) on the basis of the student's interactions with the system—that is, typically on the basis of the student's answers. The system then draws from its database the experiences and instructions that will be most effective for this student and the goals programmed into the system (Murray, 1998).

Intelligent tutor systems are best described in terms of five separate aspects or "modules" (Farnham-Diggory, 1992; Murray, 1998). The "expert module" is the source of knowledge—in computer jargon, a database. Like a good teacher, the ITS's database allows it to select from its expert knowledge information and activities that are appropriate for specific learners. Hence, it is a far more complex database than would be found in most integrated learning systems.

The "student module" is the computer's representation of what the student is like. It is the central feature of an intelligent tutoring system, says Weber (1996). This representation is derived from the student's responses but

must necessarily be based on certain preconceptions about learners that are built into the system. The system must also be designed so that it can obtain the information it needs to have about the learner. That is, just as a good tutor asks the learner to explain an answer, so too might an ITS—and it would then use this information to make qualitative judgments about the learner.

The "instructional module" consists of pedagogical, or teaching, rules built into the system. The rules might take forms such as: "If a student qualified as X gives response (explanation) A, then . . ."

The communication component consists of the interface, or link, between student and machine. It includes the ways that the learner interacts with the system (voice commands, a keyboard, a mouse, a joystick, a finger) and the ways that the system interacts with the learner (visual display, auditory signals).

ITS systems are still largely experimental. They are highly complex, very time-consuming to develop, very costly, and they require the resolution of numerous problems (Wu & Lee, 1998). One of the major problems, notes Farnham-Diggory (1992), is that computers do not process human language as we do; they cannot easily, in their own words, so to speak, explain the meaning of a prose passage—or comment sincerely on the learner's new shoes.

Logo Another fundamentally important use of the computer is evident in the learning of programming skills. As Papert (1987, 1993) has shown, these skills can be learned by very young children—children who, in his words, program computers rather than being programmed by them.

"If you've ever watched youngsters use Nintendo and other computer games," Soloman tells us, "you know there are powerful forces at work—concentration, commitment, and control.

---

intelligent tutor system (ITS) A computer-based learning system that takes into account the individual learner's strengths and weaknesses and modifies its presentations accordingly.

Schools need to harness that power . . ." (1992, p. 10). Teaching children to program computers seems to be one way to harness that power.

To teach young children how to program computers, Papert and his associates have developed a simple computer language, **Logo**, which is powerful enough to let children explore the world of differential equations or move to an understanding of HyperCard, a Macintosh courseware package (Yoder, 1992) but simple enough to enable children with no mathematical sophistication whatsoever to explore the world of plane geometry. For this purpose, Logo (which runs on most personal computers) introduces the turtle—a little triangular creature on the computer monitor that can be moved by means of ordinary words rather than the more abstract and complex terminology of most computer languages. For example, the child simply types FORWARD 50 to make the turtle move straight ahead 50 little turtle-steps, dragging a "pen" behind it so that you can see its path; FORWARD 50 RIGHT 90 FORWARD 50 makes it go ahead 50 steps, then turn to the right and go forward another 50 steps at a right angle to the first path. It is only a short child-step from here to the design of a complete square and but one small additional step to learn that all the instructions required for making this square can be shortened because they involve repetition (REPEAT 4 FORWARD 50 RIGHT 90) and can be given a collective name—such as SQUARE. Subsequently, when the child types SQUARE, the turtle draws a square. The child has easily and painlessly created a simple program.

As the child learns new instructions and continues to "play turtle," the programs can become more complex and the designs of plane geometry more intricate. Playing turtle simply involves imagining how the turtle will respond to all the possible combinations of instructions. Thus can a child learn to program the computer to draw a cartoon figure, a house, a tree—anything. Thus, too, can the child learn geometry, mathematics, the systematic and clear thinking required to write programs, and other aspects of what has come to be called **computer literacy**.

Logo has been used in a wide variety of school situations. Some of its important uses have been to investigate learners' problem-solving strategies (Lowenthal, Marcourt, & Solimando, 1998; Clements et al, 1997) and to compare self-guided discovery with teacher-guided instruction (Lee & Thompson, 1997). The evidence indicates that the use of Logo can contribute significantly to the development of spatial skills in children (Storey & Kennedy, 1997), as well as the development of *metacognition* and **cognitive strategies** (Kramarski & Mevarech, 1997). (Recall that metacognition involves an awareness of mental processes.)

Computer Applications Evaluated

Computers have enormous advantages for certain purposes in schools. Among these advantages are their staggering memory capacities, the overwhelming rapidity and accuracy with which they can deliver information, their

---

Logo Papert's computer language, designed for young children to allow them to learn programming skills as easily and painlessly as they might learn an exciting new game. The program uses a "turtle"—a small creature that can be instructed (that is, programmed) to move in different ways, tracing various geometric designs as it moves.

computer literacy The minimal skills required for effective interaction with computers. Does not require knowing how a computer functions internally or how to program one.

cognitive strategy A process involved in learning and remembering. Cognitive strategies include identifying problems, selecting approaches to their solution, monitoring progress in solving problems, and using feedback. Cognitive strategies are closely related to metacognition and metamemory.

problem-solving and computation capabilities, and the versatility of their presentation modes.

Computers also present advantages that are not directly related to their role in assisting instruction, but related instead to the cognitive processes that computer use can foster. As Papert (1993) notes, computers are intellectual tools that require a degree of explicitness and precision in the use of language—and, therefore, in thinking—not found in ordinary conversation. Computers do not understand ambiguous statements; they are not programmed to guess or to read between the lines. Instead, they respond logically and rationally. As a result, to be intelligent in a computer society—to be truly computer literate—requires learning how to be completely explicit, context free, repeatable, logical, and rational. This type of communication is quite different from our natural, spoken language, which tends to be highly implicit, specific to context, idiosyncratic, and intuitive.

Better or Not? Because of the important differences between computers and other instructional media such as teachers, texts, and television, Salomon and Gardner (1986) caution against attempting to evaluate computer-related instruction by asking such naive and largely uninformative questions as "Does it teach better than . . . ?" The important point for evaluations is the recognition that computers do things that are different from other instructional methods and do them differently as well. For example, computers allow us to teach programming and perhaps to foster the types of cognitive processes involved in programming. Thus, when children learn Logo, they also learn something about learning. And subsequent assessments reveal that children who become skilled in Logo also increase their mastery of metacognitive skills (Kramarski & Mevarech, 1997).

Even very young children can learn to program computers, argue Lachs and Dylan (1998), who taught primary school students relatively complex computer authoring skills involving multimedia presentations. Similarly, Jones (1998) successfully used computers to teach kindergarten children narrative writing skills. Research has scarcely begun to investigate what the eventual benefits of an early and intelligent introduction to computers might be.

Not surprisingly, the research is in general agreement that most of the many forms of computer-assisted or computer-based instruction lead to some positive changes in learners (for example, Schofield, Eurich-Fulcer, and Britt, 1994). But computers can't replace teachers at all; rather, they provide an additional resource.

Revolution or Not? So are we in the midst of a computer revolution in education and in society at large? *Revolution* implies sudden, dynamic, sweeping changes that ultimately transform significant aspects of our lives. Looking back through the ages, social historians have no difficulty identifying and naming revolutions: the agricultural revolution, the industrial revolution, the French Revolution. We recognize these revolutions clearly; sometimes we even think we understand them.

But recognizing current social change—or predicting future change—is more difficult. We are each too much a part of our culture to easily sense change. Perhaps we are too much a part of the change itself.

Certainly, computer use is proliferating in schools, and some insist that we are in the midst of a revolution. Computers, Papert (1993) tells us, have very rapidly become a fundamental part of our culture. They are more than simply tools that we can use for various purposes; they change our very way of thinking and acting.

But others point out that the use of computers in schools is still largely based on vague notions of their potential rather than on tried and proven practices. And, as Mergendoller (1998) points out, the enthusiasm with which many school jurisdictions embraced the computer a decade or so ago has resulted in a large number of schools that now have badly outdated computer equipment. As a consequence, and because many children have not had access to computers at home, measures of computer literacy are often disappointingly low. Nor have computers and their instructional potential been well integrated into the curriculum of most schools. As we have seen, in elementary schools, instructional use of computers is largely limited to drill and practice sorts of exercises; in high schools, computers are mainly word-processing tools.

Only during the last few years have computers become sufficiently compact and affordable to be widely available. And the potential of the Internet is just now being felt in schools—especially because the vast majority of classrooms still don't have Internet access.

Change in education is seldom rapid—especially from the perspective of those who are part of it. In the end, history might look back and judge that, yes, this was a sudden and most dramatic revolution that produced a truly marvelous outcome. The ultimate contributions of computer-based instructional systems may be even greater than we can yet imagine. All the caterpillars might yet decide they really do want to go up in that thing called a butterfly.

It is also possible that historians will look back and say, "There was no revolution of any kind back there near the end of the 20th century. There was only the rather slow proliferation of that primitive tool they called the computer. Of course, now it's obsolete."

OTHER INDIVIDUALIZED INSTRUCTIONAL PROGRAMS

The instructional use of computers can potentially be an extremely effective way of adapting instruction for individual learners. There are also a variety of other instructional methods developed specifically to individualize instruction.

Some of these clearly reflect the influence of psychological theory on education, very much like programmed instruction. Among these, perhaps no others have received greater attention than Bloom's suggestions for mastery learning; Keller's outline for a personalized system of instruction (PSI), sometimes called the Keller plan; and individually prescribed instruction (IPI).

Basic Assumptions

Each of these approaches shares a single fundamental assumption: *There are faster learners and slower learners* (Bloom, 1976).

This is vastly different from saying that there are gifted and less gifted learners (or that there are good learners and bad learners). This assumption says, in effect, that aptitude is primarily a function of the speed with which a student acquires information, concepts, or skills. As long as all students receive identical instruction, the correlation between aptitude and achievement will be high. In other words, with identical instruction, faster students will achieve more, and slower students will achieve less. However, if each student is presented with optimal learning conditions, the relationship between aptitude and achievement decreases dramatically because most learners now reach the same level. Using Bloom's terminology, all learners, provided they are given optimal instruction, will achieve *mastery* of important objectives.

A second important assumption of most individualized instructional systems is that learning requires constant evaluation—not for grading the learner but for guiding the learning/instruction process. This type of evaluation, termed **formative evaluation**, should not be

---

formative evaluation An evaluation undertaken before and during instruction, designed primarily to assist the learner to identify strengths and weaknesses. Formative evaluation is a fundamental part of the process of instruction.

confused with the more formal evaluation provided at the end of a unit or course, **summative evaluation**. Summative evaluation is intended primarily to provide a grade, whereas formative evaluation is an essential diagnostic tool in the teaching process. In both Bloom's and Keller's systems, for example, the attainment of a good grade is not the most important criterion; mastery of course objectives is.

Mastery Learning and Outcome-Based Education

Bloom's **mastery learning model** is based largely on Carroll's (1963) model of school learning. Simply stated, this model specifies that the degree of learning is primarily a function of the time spent learning relative to the amount of time required to learn. The amount of time required is, in turn, a function of both aptitude and quality of instruction received. (See Figure 10.4.)

Carroll's emphasis is on providing all learners with both high-quality instruction and the time required to learn. His objective is "equality of opportunity," which contrasts with Bloom's objective of "equality of attainment" (Carroll, 1989, p. 30).

Bloom's basic notion is that it is possible to analyze any learning sequence to specify specific

objectives and to teach so that most, if not all, students will attain these objectives. Although the teaching methods suggested by Bloom are much the same as those ordinarily used by teachers, they differ in two important respects: First, they are directed specifically toward the mastery of previously identified objectives, and second, they make extensive use of formative evaluation to diagnose learners' difficulties, to suggest modifications in instructional strategies, and to identify subject areas needing more time. A third important characteristic of Bloom's mastery learning is that it requires the use of a great variety of systematic and deliberate corrective procedures in conjunction with formative evaluation (Bloom, 1987). Among these corrective procedures are study sessions; individualized tutoring; reteaching; students helping each other in small, cooperative groups; and a selection of alternative instructional materials in a variety of forms, such as programs, films, and audiotapes. (See Table 10.1.)

One final characteristic of Bloom's mastery learning is the provision that classes typically progress from one unit to another as a group. This is accomplished by providing enrichment for students who master course objectives first. Thus, the pace of progress through the curriculum is determined largely by those who require the longest time to reach mastery. Ultimately, all students who have mastered course objectives are given "A's"; those who have not succeeded are given "I's" (for incomplete, but meaning "mastery in the making"). No students fail in this system.

Closely related to Bloom's mastery learning is an individualized instructional approach that is generally called **outcome-based education (OBE)** (Evans & King, 1994b). Like mastery

---

summative evaluation The type of evaluation that occurs at the end of an instructional sequence and that is designed primarily to provide a grade.

mastery learning model An instructional approach described by Bloom. A learning sequence is analyzed into specific objectives, and progress requires that each learner master sequential objectives.

$$\text{Degree of learning} = f\left(\frac{\text{time spent}}{\text{time needed}}\right)$$

FIGURE 10.4 Carroll's model of school learning: How much a child learns is a function of how much time is spent learning relative to how much time is required. Theoretically, given optimal instruction and adequate learning time, all learners can achieve mastery.

---

outcome-based education (OBE) An outgrowth of mastery learning. An individualized instructional program designed to bring about important learning outcomes defined in terms of the skills and knowledge that the learner will need upon completion of a course of study.

TABLE 10.1 Basic Elements of Bloom's Mastery Learning	
Underlying Assumptions	1. There are *faster* learners and *slower* learners (not better learners and poorer learners). 2. Learning requires constant *formative* evaluation, designed specifically to guide the teaching/learning process.
Broad Characteristics of Teaching Methods	1. Instruction is directed toward the attainment of specific, explicit, and previously identified objectives. 2. Instruction is guided by the results of formative evaluation. 3. Numerous corrective instructional procedures are provided in the form of study sessions, cooperative student groups, individualized tutoring, reteaching, and alternative instructional materials.

learning, outcome-based education is directed toward the mastery of important learning objectives. The basic difference between these two approaches is that mastery learning derives its objectives from the material to be learned; in contrast, OBE determines the skills and knowledge that students will need after graduation and is directed toward bringing about these outcomes (O'Neil, 1993; Brandt, 1994).

Keller's Personalized System of Instruction (PSI)

Fred Keller was a very important figure in the early history of conditioning theory and behaviorism. In fact, he is said to have been the founder of scientific psychology in Brazil (Dinsmoor, 1996). But he is perhaps best remembered for his **personalized system of instruction (PSI)** (Keller, 1968). PSI, also called the Keller plan, is an elaboration of Bloom's mastery learning. Originally developed for teaching introductory psychology at the college level, PSI has since been used in a variety of college courses (for example, Pear and Novak, 1996). And, in combination with computers, PSI has also been used very successfully from kindergarten through twelfth grade (Conard, 1997).

Essentially, a PSI approach requires that a course be broken down into small units, that appropriate instructional materials be developed for each of these units, and that students be allowed to take as much time as necessary to learn each unit. Whenever students feel they are ready, they are given a short unit quiz, the quiz is marked immediately, and they are then told whether they need to spend more time studying the same unit or whether they can proceed to the next unit. At the end of the course, an examination covering all material is presented (see Table 10. 2).

personalized system of instruction (PSI) An instructional approach developed by Keller, based in part on Bloom's mastery learning. Course material is broken down into small units, study is largely individual, a variety of study material is available, and progress depends on performance on unit tests. This is sometimes termed *the Keller plan*.

TABLE 10.2 Main Elements of Keller's Personalized System of Instruction (PSI)
▲ Directed toward mastery
▲ Objectives to be mastered clearly specified
▲ Self-paced instructional system
▲ Material is carefully sequenced and broken into small steps
▲ Repeated testing is employed
▲ Learner is given immediate feedback following testing
▲ Emphasis is on credit for success, not penalty for errors
▲ Lectures are used for motivation, as a reward

Unlike mastery learning, the Keller plan does not advocate the use of traditional instructional methods, nor does it rely as heavily on corrective procedures, although alternative learning materials are available. Instead, the onus of mastering a unit rests largely on the student. In many cases, the unit in question corresponds to a chapter in a textbook and to a programmed version of the same material. And, in many PSI programs, computers are used extensively (for example, Greer, 1997). Tutoring often occurs after a student proctor marks the unit quiz, but it is not an essential part of the course. Nor, indeed, is the traditional lecture. In fact, students attend lectures only after they have successfully completed specified units. Lectures are intended to serve as reinforcement for success rather than as a basis for it (Sherman, 1992).

Keller's PSI, like Bloom's mastery learning, is designed to provide experiences of success for all learners. And although both approaches recognize important individual differences among learners, they contradict the ancient belief that there are good and bad learners. Learners are faster or slower, perhaps, but not better or poorer. Accordingly, each approach attempts to provide learning experiences that will optimize the attainment of specific objectives for each learner. Those objectives might be either behavioral or performance objectives or a specified score on a quiz.

The advantages claimed for approaches such as these center on the attention that each pays to individual differences in rate of learning. Traditional approaches to instruction and evaluation make it almost inevitable that some of those who learn more slowly than their age/grade peers will fail, whereas these highly individualized approaches ensure that almost all students will eventually succeed.

Another advantage of mastery approaches may be increased student motivation. As Guskey (1997) notes, repeated exposure to a mastery approach should lead students to the expecta-tion that they will succeed if they work hard enough. It follows that students who are externally oriented can, as a result, eventually become more internally oriented and consequently more willing to accept challenges (see Chapter 11).

Evaluation of Individualized Instruction

Do individualized approaches to instruction work? In a word, yes. But to say that they always work better than more conventional approaches (or even most of the time) would require more convincing evidence than we now have.

Investigations of Keller's PSI and of Bloom's mastery learning primarily in elementary schools have found these approaches to be quite effective, both for reaching course goals and in terms of general attitudes toward course work. In a review of studies that investigated the effectiveness of mastery approaches, Slavin (1987) found several studies with positive results—and several others showed no advantage for mastery learning. Bloom (1987) suggests that results are usually positive when students make full use of the "corrective feedback" process that is part of formative evaluation.

Kulik, Kulik, and Bangert-Drowns (1990) analyzed 108 investigations of mastery learning. Their conclusion: In general, mastery learning increases achievement, most notably for weaker students. In fact, average increases for all groups were from approximately the 50th to the 70th percentile. Mastery learning also has positive effects on students' attitudes toward school. On the other hand, self-paced mastery programs are associated with lower completion rates in college courses.

Kulik, Kulik, and Cohen (1979) also analyzed 75 studies that compared Keller's PSI with conventional approaches (see Figure 10.2 for one comparison). They concluded: "The analysis establishes that PSI generally produces superior student achievement, less variation in achieve-

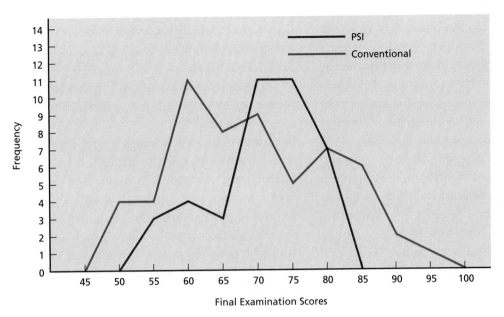

FIGURE 10.5   Distribution of final examination averages for 48 PSI and 48 conventional classes (PSI = personalized system of instruction). From J.A. Kulik, C. C. Kulik, and P.A. Cohen, "A Meta-Analysis of Outcome Studies of Keller's Personalized System of Instruction," *American Psychologist, 34*, 307–318. Copyright 1979 by the American Psychological Association. Reprinted with permission of the authors.

ment, and higher student ratings in college courses, but does not affect course withdrawal or student study time in these courses" (p. 307).

Lest we run off madly selling another educational panacea, we should note that PSI and mastery learning have their faults and weaknesses as well and that not all evaluations are as positive and as optimistic as that of Kulik and associates. For example, some critics have observed that an emphasis on the mastery of objectives that all (or most) learners can achieve might, in fact, penalize the fast learner (M. Arlin, 1984). At best, such a system does not maximize the faster learner's achievement; at worst, it leads to boredom, destroys motivation, and renders the assignment of grades meaningless because all who work long enough obtain As. Furthermore, we cannot completely discount the possibility that undue emphasis on specifiable objectives might restrict the teaching/learning process and prevent the occurrence of important incidental learning—and that it

might, in fact, lead to an extrinsically motivated, performance-based orientation rather than a mastery orientation. These approaches also require considerable effort from schools and teachers with respect to systematizing and simplifying instruction. And they demand that schools and teachers make a conscious effort to specify their immediate goals and sometimes also their long-range goals.

In spite of these potential disadvantages, these approaches can provide important experiences of success for learners who might otherwise lack them by making it possible for learners of all aptitudes to master units and courses.

ATTRIBUTE–TREATMENT INTERACTION

Approaches such as Keller's PSI and Bloom's mastery learning are based on the assumption that all learners can achieve the same instructional goals—that each is capable of mastery. However, they also recognize that some people learn faster than others and that some need more assistance. Even approaches that try to minimize the importance of differences in learners' characteristics must, in the end, recognize that these differences are sometimes quite important.

Other programs, such as learning styles approaches, are based directly on a recognition of differences among learners. Such programs require information about the relationship between learners' characteristics and specific instructional methods—or what is termed **attribute–treatment interaction** (Cronbach & Snow, 1977).

The basic premise of attribute–treatment research is simple: Specific instructional methods are better for students with one particular characteristic, whereas other instructional methods might be better for students with other characteristics. In other words, an attribute–treatment interaction exists whenever the effectiveness of instruction (the treatment) is shown to depend, at least in part, on the learner's characteristics. The ultimate goal of attribute–treatment research is to identify the best combinations of attributes and treatments.

Findings and Conclusions

Researchers have looked at numerous student characteristics (including age, gender, anxiety, dependence, conformity, various dimensions of intellectual abilities, and many others) and have attempted to identify the best instructional methods for students with specific characteris-

tics (lectures, small group interaction, programs, computers, demonstrations) (Ross, Rakow, & Bush, 1980; Whitener, 1989).

Although findings from ATI studies are by no means clear and simple, researchers have advanced several tentative conclusions. One of the most replicated findings is the interaction between anxiety and the degree to which an instructional method is structured or requires active learner participation. Specifically, very anxious students do better with instructional approaches that do not require a high degree of student interaction but are instead more "teacher centered" (see, for example, Snow & Swanson, 1992 and Figure 10.6). Similarly, there appears to be an interaction between general ability and structure. Students of lower ability do relatively better with structured approaches (such as programmed instruction) that use small steps together with frequent responses and reinforcement (Swing & Peterson, 1982). This interaction takes place in part because highly structured approaches reduce information processing requirements—that is, they demand fewer cognitive strategies from the learner (Resnick, 1981). Recall that mastery learning tends to be more effective with low-ability students.

In conclusion, then, at least two separate interactions between lesson structure and student attributes have been uncovered by research:

▲ Highly structured approaches benefit students of lower ability.
▲ Highly structured approaches are better for more anxious students.

Some Cautions Simple summaries of complex studies tend to make the results seem far clearer and more definite than they actually are. In fact, the results of research on attribute–treatment interaction are highly inconsistent and often contradictory. This means that no very valuable suggestions can yet be derived from this research

---

attribute–treatment interaction The relationship among students' characteristics (attributes), teaching methods (treatments), and outcomes. These relationships are sometimes quite complex. Thus, a given treatment (instructional method, for example) may be more effective for students with certain attributes than it is for others with different attributes.

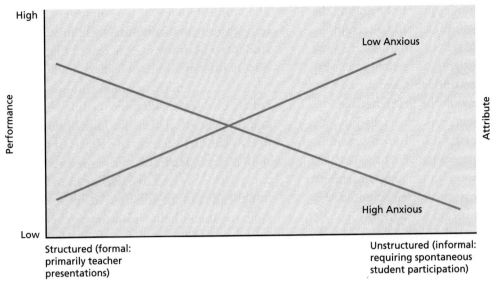

FIGURE 10.6 A schematic representation of an attribute–treatment interaction—specifically, an interaction between anxiety and degree of structure in teaching method: Anxious students tend to perform better with more structured approaches, but the opposite is true of students who are less anxious.

and applied directly to classroom practice. Besides, as Gagné and Dick (1983) observe, the most powerful variables related to school achievement continue to be intellectual ability and previous school achievement. Consequently, the most fruitful approach to matching instruction to students' characteristics is probably one that takes these two variables into account. And that is what happens, at least to a small degree, when students are sorted into groups on the basis of age, achievement and sometimes ability.

We should not be misled into thinking, however, that these two variables—achievement and ability—account for most of the variation in observed student achievement. In fact, they account for only about 25 percent of the variation; some of the remaining 75 percent is linked to other factors such as home background, the type and quality of instruction, and personality characteristics, particularly as they are reflected in motivation and attitudes. Teachers don't control all of these variables.

MAIN POINTS

1. North American schools are increasingly multicultural. Multicultural education seeks to look after the needs of children from all backgrounds. Adapting instruction for cultural diversity is a difficult and controversial task.

2. Language programs may be geared toward teaching minority children the dominant school language, or they might be directed toward teaching a second language to speakers of the dominant language. Language

immersion programs appear to be among the most effective means of learning a second language. Bilingual school programs are a controversial and highly researched phenomenon. Learning a second language sometimes has a negative effect on the first language (subtractive bilingualism), especially for minority children who learn the dominant language as a second language. For native speakers of the dominant language, learning a second language is most often an additive experience that results in a relatively high level of proficiency in both languages.

3. Tracking (ability grouping) is highly pervasive. Between-class ability grouping is controversial, and detracking is a common feature of school reform—largely because tracking can have negative effects on members of lower-ability groups and sometimes no effect on other groups. Within-class grouping is quite common and much less controversial.

4. Learning styles approaches attempt to tailor a variety of instructional features—instructional method, teaching mode, curriculum, evaluation, and rewards—to individual students' strengths and weaknesses.

5. Programmed instruction involves the sequential arrangement of information in small steps (frames); each of these requires learners to make a response that is then reinforced through immediate feedback (knowledge of results). A linear program (Skinner) requires all learners to progress through the same material in exactly the same sequence and to construct their own responses; a branching program (Crowder) requires learners to select an answer and then directs them to the next frame on the basis of that answer. Those who make errors are provided with further help.

6. The optimistic view of the computer revolution suggests that computers will provide students with immediate access to high-quality information; can lead to smaller, friendlier, and more personal schools; can reduce problems with basic reading, writing, and mathematical skills; and might do a great deal to counter the negative effects of television. A more pessimistic view suggests that computers may lead to a decline in computational and reading skills; might encourage violence; might help widen the gap between the haves and the have-nots; might lead us to rely on computer systems that rely for their expertise on information rather than on wisdom; and might depersonalize schools. Some resist the apparent revolution.

7. Computers are used in schools to teach computer literacy; as tools to manage instructional programs (data storage and analysis, for example), obtain information (databases and the Internet), provide career information, and for word processing and computation; for drill and practice instructional exercises; for simulations, including possibilities opened up by virtual reality; for computational purposes; as sophisticated teaching machines or audiovisual aids to present programs, sometimes in integrated learning systems; and as intelligent tutoring systems (ITS) where the computer modifies its interactions on the basis of its analysis of the student. Students can also be taught to program computers, with resulting cognitive benefits.

8. Bloom's mastery learning is based on the assumption that most learners are capable of mastering important school objectives but that some people require more time and more nearly optimal instruction than others. This "no-fail" program breaks the curriculum into small units that must be mastered before the student proceeds.

9. Keller's personalized system of instruction (PSI), closely related to Bloom's mastery learning, places the onus for attainment of unit and course objectives primarily on the students. Students are allowed to repeat unit quizzes until they reach a specified performance criterion and then progress on to the next unit.

10. Evaluations of these approaches to individualizing instruction indicate that they typically have positive effects on achievement and attitudes. They are sometimes associated with higher student attrition, however.

11. Attribute–treatment interactions exist when there is a consistent relationship between the effectiveness of an instructional approach and some identifiable characteristic (or grouping of characteristics) of the learners. The clearest example of an attribute–treatment interaction involves anxiety and instructional structure (highly anxious students often do better with structured approaches like programmed instruction).

12. A bear always faces the front of its tracks.

Applied Questions

▲ How has multicultural education been part of your schooling?

▲ What are some arguments for and against ability grouping?

▲ Can you create brief examples of branching and linear frames in one of your areas of expertise?

▲ Describe how you think computers might be used most effectively in the classroom.

▲ How can some of the principles of mastery learning be used in a traditional classroom?

Internet Activity

Use InfoTrac College Edition or other World Wide Web sources to research the following topic: Current attitudes and practices in multicultural education. Write up your findings. (See the inside back cover of this text for suggestions about where to begin.)

Sample search terms: Multicultural education

Study Terms

Suggested Readings

Excellent insight into the meaning of multiculturalism and multicultural education is provided by the annual editions of a periodical entitled *Multicultural Education.* These editions consist of highly readable articles culled from popular journals and magazines rather than from more technical research publications:

Multicultural Education. Guilford, CT: Dushkin

The book by Sharp is a comprehensive survey of the things teachers should know about computers and their uses in schools. And the Geisert and Futrell book is a very clear and practical introduction to the use of computers in schools.

Sharp, V. (1999). *Computer education for teachers* (3rd ed.). New York: McGraw-Hill.

Geisert, P. G., & Futrell, M. K. (1995). *Teachers, computers, and curriculum: Microcomputers in the classroom* (2nd ed.). Boston: Allyn & Bacon.

For those who are still at the stage of learning *about* computers and the Internet (rather than learning *with* them), the first of the following two booklets is as simple and clear an explanation of what the Internet is all about as you are likely to find. The second is also brief but a more detailed introduction to the Internet; it includes a variety of resources and suggestions for using the Internet in the classroom.

Rivard, J. D. (1997). *Quick guide to the internet for educators.* Boston, MA: Allyn and Bacon.

Kurland, D. J., Sharp, R. M., & Sharp, V. F. (1997). *Introduction to the internet for education.* Belmont, CA: Wadsworth.

Guskey's book provides an excellent summary and explanation of mastery learning, together with practical suggestions for applying the model in the classroom.

Guskey, T. R. (1997). *Implementing mastery learning* (2nd ed.). Belmont, CA: Wadsworth.

Seals are the staple food of the polar bear. Infant seals are particularly easy to capture when they are still in the aglos (calving dens). The aglo is a small ice cave hollowed out by a mother seal and accessible only from the water. It is covered with a 3- to 5-foot layer of snow and a thick cover of ice. The polar bear can scent aglos from a remarkable distance. Having found one, the bear rapidly excavates the overburden of snow with quick blows of paws and then attempts to break through the ice by rearing up and smashing downward with both front paws. If the ice is too thick, the bear may move back a short distance, run toward the aglo, leap high in the air, and come thundering down with all four paws, crashing noisily through the ice. It is then a simple matter to reach inside and pull out the squirming infant (Perry, 1966).

PART FIVE

Let such teach others who themselves excel.

Alexander Pope,
Essay on Criticism

More Effective Instruction

Let them teach who themselves excel . . . is a far cry from saying "those who can, do; and those who can't, teach." That is not to say that only the most excellent of students can be good teachers. But it does say that those who cannot understand the concepts they teach, those whose command of language is labored and imprecise, those who struggle to solve simple problems, might be better advised to learn—or to *do*—than to teach. And even those who themselves excel will soon discover that being an effective teacher requires more than a quick and elegant grasp of subject matter. Among other things, effective teachers need exceptional management, motivational, and assessment skills. These are the topics of the three chapters that make up Part Five.

Persons attempting
to find a motive in
this narrative will
be prosecuted;
persons attempting
to find a moral in it
will be banished;
persons attempting
to find a plot in it
will be shot.

Mark Twain,
Huckleberry Finn, Introduction

Motivation
and Teaching

PREVIEW

My grandmother, an astute observer of human affairs, spent much of her knitting and quilting time in quiet contemplation of human motives. "Why do geese go south and ravens stay?" she would mutter as her needles clicked. "Why did Réné go out in the storm?" "Why does Frank study so hard and Lucille won't do zip?" "Why doesn't Robert want to go to school anymore?" This chapter might have been of some value to her, although the questions it examines are surely no more important than the questions she asked. But it does provide some answers for why we do or don't do things and some suggestions for teachers, whose role in motivating students can hardly be overstated.

FOCUS QUESTIONS

▲ How valid and useful are instinct-based and hedonistic explanations of human behavior?

▲ What is arousal theory? What are its educational implications?

▲ How are extrinsic and intrinsic motivation related?

▲ What is Maslow's humanistic theory of motivation?

▲ What is self-efficacy? attribution theory?

Most of the time I was a pretty decent student in high school—although I spent a lot of time looking through the windows, hoping to see a bear. The nun who taught us, Sister Ste. Mélanie, didn't much care about that.

I spent a lot of time looking at girls, too—which had never alarmed any of the grown-ups, who recognized and dismissed my condition as one of chronic puppy love. But about halfway through that first year of high school, I discovered the incomparable Clarisse. When the good sisters first noticed me turning my mongrel eyes on Clarisse, they apparently decided it was no longer just a canine thing, and they were cautious and watchful rather than amused. I later discovered that Sister Ste. Mélanie even spoke of it with my grandmother, with whom I was living at the time.

By then I was absolutely smitten with a doglike devotion to this wonderful creature. I followed her around the schoolyard constantly, at what I thought was a discreet distance. I stared at her while she ate her lunch, trying to be inconspicuous, sometimes imagining myself to be a cucumber sandwich or a pickle. And I gazed longingly at her back when she stood at the chalkboard conjugating copulative verbs. That's when I first noticed that she had trouble with her verbs. Me, I knew copulative verbs inside out.[1]

---

[1] **PPC:** Are you sure it was "copulative" verbs, not transitive or intransitive or something? I mean, is this just for effect? And is it maybe going too far?

Author: I've checked my original notes. It was definitely copulative verbs.

"I'll help you with your grammar," I finally blurted out the line I had been rehearsing all morning. "At my grandma's after school."

"'kay," she nodded, making me so happy I almost died.

At lunchtime, between spoonfuls of pea soup, I casually outlined my plan for my grandmother, informing her that some girl who was having trouble with her verbs would be coming over and we'd go to my room where I'd teach her, which would be excellent practice, wouldn't it, for when I was a teacher, and at the same time it would help her, which is surely a fine and noble thing to do and . . .

"No!" my grandmother announced very firmly. "No, that wouldn't be right. Right here in the kitchen would be fine."

"All I want is a quiet place with no distractions so that I can teach her some verbs," I insisted.

"I won't distract you at all," my grandmother said. "And it's not that I don't trust you. It's just not right. People would wonder about your motives."

"My motives are just to help . . ."

"Your motives, like everybody else's," my grandmother interrupted, "are selfish. Everybody's motives are selfish. All of what I call our creature motives, like for food and drink and you-know-what, they're selfish. I'm not saying, mind you, that you-know-what is your motive for helping Clarisse."

Of course, I protested that you-know-what had nothing to do with my motives. But my grandmother disagreed at length, citing many convincing instances of behaviors whose motives might seem obvious and scrupulously moral but where careful examination revealed baser and far more selfish motives.

"But there are, of course, exceptions," she concluded generously.

"Me! I'm one!" I insisted.

"I don't think so," she said. "I think you have an ulterior motive."

MOTIVES: EXPLANATIONS FOR BEHAVIOR

Ulterior motives—a strange and wicked disorder from which I think I still suffer. You see, **ulterior motives** are, by definition, hidden and unknown; they do not show themselves. More than once I have wished that my true motives had been more obvious—more apparent to others.

In this chapter we look not at **motives** that are ulterior but those that are more obvious. Motives are what move us; they are the **causes** of what we do. Causes are agents or forces that produce an effect or an action. As Dweck (1986) notes, motives are the causes of all our goal-directed activity.

But motives are more than causes; they are also reasons for behavior, in the sense that **reasons** are explanations. Thus, motives explain the *why* of our behavior, whereas learning theories are more concerned with the *how* and the *what*.

From the teacher's point of view, the most important motives are those that have to do with learning and achievement. Teachers need to be especially concerned with why some students expend a great deal of effort in achievement situations and others do not.

Keith and Cool (1992) tried to determine some of the factors that most contributed to the achievement scores of more than 25,000 students. Not surprisingly, the strongest determining factor they found was ability. But two other factors also had strong effects: motivation and quality of instruction. "It appears," conclude Keith and Cool, "that students enrolled in a high-quality school and curriculum are more highly motivated by that curriculum. . . . Students with high academic motivation take more academic course work . . . and do more homework . . . and as a result, achieve at a higher level" (1992, p. 215).

The importance to the teacher of understanding motivation and the factors that affect it cannot be overemphasized. In many cases, motivation—or lack of motivation—clearly makes the difference between success and failure. Unfortunately, research reviewed by Anderman and Maehr (1994) indicates that there is often a significant decline in motivation during the middle grades of school. This decline is evident in negative attitudes and behaviors not especially conducive to high achievement. To the extent that this is true, it becomes even more urgent

ulterior motive A hidden motive. A reason for behavior that is not what it seems. Ulterior motives often involve an element of deception (as when my grandmother accused me of having ulterior motives when I said I wanted to help Clarisse with her verbs).

motive A cause of behavior. Our motives explain why we engage in some behaviors but not in others. They initiate behavior and direct it.

cause An agent or force that produces an effect or a result. A cause is one aspect of motivation.

reason An explanation for or defense of an action. In psychology, reasons are often treated as motives.

Teachers need to understand why some students put a great deal of effort into achievement situations and others don't—and why some activities are more likely than others to capture and maintain student interest.

that teachers understand student motivation and take steps to maintain it at a high level.[2]

This chapter explores various explanations for human behavior, with special emphasis on how schools and teachers can affect students' motivation. Initially, it touches briefly on some historical approaches to motivation, then it moves to a series of more detailed discussions of contemporary views of motivation, organized according to the major models discussed in earlier chapters: behaviorism, humanism, and cognitivism. Keep in mind that these divisions are artificial and therefore somewhat misleading. As we study them, we sometimes feel compelled to judge them and choose only one among them. But different theories are simply reflections of different worldviews and different underlying emphases and metaphors. None are correct or incorrect; rather, something of each can be useful for our various purposes.

HISTORICAL VIEWS OF HUMAN MOTIVATION

History presents us with a rich assortment of past beliefs about human motivation and student learning. Not all of these beliefs are relevant to our current views.

Instincts

One of the first views of human motivation—that concerning **instincts**—may be more rele-

---

instinct A complex, species-specific, relatively unmodifiable pattern of behaviors such as migration or nesting in some birds and animals. Less complex inherited behaviors are usually referred to as reflexes.

---

[2] **PPC:** Perhaps the bear should underline the importance of motivation for the classroom teacher.
Author: Yes. In the words of the bear's longtime mentor, Yogi Berra, "If the people don't want to come out to the park, nobody's gonna stop them." How the dickens can you stop somebody who doesn't want to do something? asks the bear.

vant to our understanding of animals than of people.

When my hunting dog, Zoe, gave birth to her first litter, 4-year-old Laurier watched bug-eyed as the bitch eased each little pup in turn from its sac, nipped its umbilical cord close to its belly, ate the afterbirth, and nudged the pup toward her nipples. "Where'd she learn to do that?" he asked. But Zoe hadn't really learned; somehow, she already knew. How to birth pups was one of the instincts with which she was born.

A Definition Biologists inform us that instincts are innate, complex, species-specific, relatively unmodifiable behavior patterns. What do these terms mean?

Innate: Instinctual behaviors are not learned but are genetically determined. That is, they are either present at birth or develop naturally later as a result of appropriate experiences.

Complex: Behaviors such as blinking in response to air blown in the eye, sucking behavior, and other simple behaviors of which we are capable at birth are not instincts; they are **reflexes**. Reflexes are very simple, unlearned, automatic, stimulus–response links. Instincts are more complex groupings of behaviors such as those involved in courting or nesting among some birds.

Species specific: Instincts are general within species. Thus, *all* wild ducks are characterized by a migratory instinct, and *all* bears (except for polar bears) by the urge to den up in winter.

---

reflex A simple, unlearned stimulus–response link such as salivating in response to food in one's mouth or blinking in response to air blowing in one's eye. For Piaget, behavioral reflexes such as looking, reaching, grasping, and sucking are especially important for early intellectual development.

Relatively unmodifiable: Because instincts are largely innate, they are not much affected by the environment—although, in the absence of some environmental experiences, instinctual behaviors can be changed somewhat. For example, female rats reared in a deprived environment do not exhibit the maternal and nesting instincts characteristic of female rats reared normally.

Human Instincts There are many examples of instinctual behavior patterns among animals; most have to do with nesting, migration, and mating—all behaviors related to survival. The question is whether people engage in behavior that can be similarly explained in terms of instincts.

Some early theorists thought so. For example, Bernard (1924) listed some 6,000 human instincts, ranging from the common ones (sexual, maternal) to remote inclinations, such as the tendency "to avoid eating apples that grow in one's own garden" (p. 212).

But these are not instincts at all. As we saw, instincts are more complex than this; they are general to all members of the species (which is not the case with the tendency to avoid eating apples from one's garden); and they are relatively unmodifiable (again, not the case with eating apples). But even if these were instincts, they would not be particularly valuable because naming an instinct neither explains a behavior nor predicts it. At best, the reasoning process is entirely circular: If we make love, an instinct theorist might reason, it's obvious that we have an instinct for doing so. Why, then, do we make love? Well, because we have this instinct, you see. How do we know that this instinct exists? Well, because people make love. And so on, *ad infinitum*.[3]

Currently, the notion of instinct is applied more often to animal than to human behavior, although a related phenomenon, **imprinting**, is sometimes linked to some features of infant development. Imprinting is the appearance of complex behaviors, apparently as a result of exposure to an appropriate object or event (releaser) at a **critical period** in the animal's life. For example, newly hatched ducklings will follow the first moving object they encounter and become attached to it. Fortunately, this object is usually the mother duck. However, Konrad Lorenz (1952) reports the case of a greylag goose that imprinted on him and followed him around like a dog. Much to his embarrassment, when it matured it insisted on foisting its affections on him during mating season.

There do not appear to be critical periods in an infant's life during which it must be exposed to appropriate experiences to have some behavior imprinted, although researchers such as Bowlby (1982) suggest that the first six months of an infant's life might be a **sensitive period** during which a parent or other caregiver must be present for the infant to develop strong attachment bonds.

Psychological Hedonism

A second historical explanation of human motivation is psychological hedonism, the belief that we act to avoid pain and to obtain pleasure.

---

[3] **PPC:** Some of my students don't know any Latin at all and they get very frustrated when the bear uses Latin expressions like this. Could he substitute another term?

Author: Yes, said he, I know other expressions, *ergo* I can, and i.e., (which stands for *id est*), he added, grinning sagely. I might have used *ad nauseam*, which would, *de facto*, not have changed things much *per se*.

---

imprinting Unlearned, instinctive behaviors that are not present at birth but become part of an animal's repertoire after exposure to a suitable stimulus during a critical period. The "following" behavior of young ducks, geese, and chickens is one example.

critical period A period in development when exposure to appropriate experiences or stimuli will bring about specific learning much more easily than at other times.

sensitive period A period when specific experiences have their most pronounced effects. For example, the first six months of life may be a sensitive period for the infant's formation of attachment bonds to the mother or primary caregiver.

Unfortunately, **psychological hedonism** is a vague and useless explanation for human behavior unless we can specify those conditions that are pleasurable and painful. That is, even if it is true that the pain/pleasure principle governs our activities, we can predict and control these activities only if we know what gives pleasure and what gives pain.

Need–Drive Theories

Need–drive theories offer one way to define pain and pleasure. **Needs** are states of deficiency or lack within an organism. **Drives** are the energies or tendencies to react which are aroused by needs. For example, we have a need for food; this need gives rise to a hunger drive; eating reduces the drive. According to behavioral psychologists like Hull, this is a very important explanation for behavior; it is labeled **drive reduction**.

If we assume that satisfying our needs is pleasant and that a state of need is unpleasant, the relationship between need theory and psychological hedonism is obvious: Identifying and describing needs makes clear the nature of pain and pleasure. A list of needs is a list of conditions that are pleasant when satisfied and unpleasant

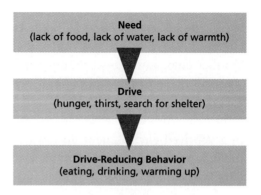

FIGURE 11.1 The drive-reduction model of motivation: A need (lack) leads to a drive (urge), which in turn leads to a behavior whose goal is to remedy the lack. This model is useful for explaining many physiologically based behaviors but does not effectively explain why some students work hard to learn their subjects and others go hiking instead.
From Guy Lefrançois, *Theories of Human Learning: What the Old Man Said* (4th ed.) Copyright © 2000 Wadsworth. Used by permission.

when unsatisfied. Liking for food, and the lengths to which humans and animals will go to obtain food, is perhaps the best available example of psychological hedonism (Mehiel, 1997).

Needs can be divided into two broad categories: psychological and physiological. **Physiological needs** include the need for food, water, sleep and rest, activity, and sex. **Psychological needs** include the need for affection, belonging, achievement, independence, social recognition, and self-esteem. These needs are more closely related to mental functioning. One important difference between these two categories is that psychological needs are never completely satisfied, whereas physiological needs can be. Also, psychological needs are probably more often learned than are physiological needs. (See Figure 11.1.)

---

psychological hedonism The belief that humans act primarily to avoid pain and to obtain pleasure.

need–drive theory A motivation theory that attempts to explain human behavior on the basis of the motivating properties of needs. Such theories typically assume that humans have certain learned and unlearned needs, which give rise to drives, which in turn are responsible for the occurrence of behavior.

need Ordinarily refers to a lack or deficit in the human organism. Needs can be either unlearned (for example, the need for food or water) or learned (the need for money).

drive The tendency toward a certain behavior that is brought about by an unsatisfied need—for example, the hunger drive is related to the need for food.

drive reduction The satisfaction of a need by eliminating the drive associated with it. For example, satisfying the need for water by drinking, thus eliminating the thirst drive.

---

physiological need A basic biological need, such as the need for food and water.

psychological need A human need other than those dealing with basic physical requirements such as food, sex, water, and temperature regulation (physiological needs). Psychological needs described by Maslow include the need to belong, to feel safe, to love and be loved, to maintain a high opinion of oneself, and to self-actualize.

"Mother" Lorenz

Summary and Implications of Historical Approaches to Motivation

From the teacher's point of view, the most useful explanations of motivation are those that provide us with the greatest insight about the circumstances under which students will be most interested in doing certain things—and least interested as well.

Explanations such as those based on instincts may be valuable explanations for a bear's habit of denning up in the winter, but they tell us little about why Frank will study all night before his science exam or why Sam will watch television instead and will then have to explain that he forgot all about the exam.

Nor does psychological hedonism tell us much about Sam or Frank. True, the belief that we do things that we expect will lead to pleasant outcomes—and that we avoid behaviors that lead elsewhere—does little violence to our naive convictions about human behavior. But, as we have seen, this belief by itself explains little; we need to know what is pleasant and what is unpleasant.

Theories about needs and drives begin to spell out some of the conditions and outcomes

that we find pleasant or unpleasant. We know that people who are hungry and thirsty will go to extraordinary lengths to obtain food and drink. People who are lonely can also go to staggering lengths to ease their solitude.

Teachers must be aware of their students' needs. It is clear, for example, that certain basic biological needs must be satisfied for the teaching/learning process to be effective. A hungry or thirsty student is almost certain to find concentration difficult. By the same token, a hungry teacher is a sad sight as well and is probably seldom as effective as a well-fed one. Other basic needs, such as the need for sex, are not likely to present a serious problem for younger students; the same cannot be said about adolescents or about teachers—young or old.[4]

Because most children's basic needs are adequately taken care of in our society, teachers aren't often called upon to walk around with a bag of cookies and a jug of milk. Psychological needs are quite another matter. Recall that these include the need for affection, belonging, achievement, social recognition, and self-esteem. One useful exercise that a prospective teacher might consider is to imagine what a "bag" filled with the wherewithal to satisfy these needs would look like. Teachers who, through their actions, can give each student a sense of accomplishment and belonging are probably carrying such a bag.

MAGNITUDE OF MOTIVATION: AROUSAL THEORY

How motivated a student is (in other words, how much effort a student is willing to make) is a function of three things, claim Brehm and Self

---

[4] ***PPC:*** And old bears? What can be said of their sexual needs?
Author: Actually, quite a lot. Much has been said by Marian Engel in the novel *Bear* (Toronto: McClelland and Stewart). But little of that is directly relevant to this so very serious textbook.

(1989): internal states such as needs or desires, potential outcomes, and the student's estimate of the likelihood that a specific behavior will lead to a given outcome. In this view, motivation is both physiological and psychological. And because it is physiological, they claim, it can be measured. That is, the physiological changes that accompany increasing motivation are changes in the **sympathetic nervous system**, the part of the nervous system responsible for changes that accompany emotion. These changes are evident in increasing **arousal**.

What Is Arousal?

Arousal is both a psychological and a physiological concept. Psychologically, it refers to alertness or attentiveness. In a sense, it is an individual's degree of wakefulness. At the lowest levels of arousal, the individual is asleep (or in a coma) and is totally inattentive; at higher levels of arousal, the individual is intensely aware and alert; at still higher levels of arousal, the individual might be in a state of panic or shock.

Accompanying these psychological states—ranging from sleep to panic—are underlying physiological changes evident in the functioning of the sympathetic nervous system. At the lowest levels of arousal, respiration and heart rate, brain-wave activity, conductivity of the skin to electricity, and so on, are all at low

---

sympathetic nervous system The part of the nervous system that instigates the physiological responses associated with emotion.

arousal As a physiological concept, arousal refers to changes in functions such as heart rate, respiration rate, electrical activity in the cortex, and electrical conductivity of the skin. As a psychological concept, arousal refers to degree of alertness, awareness, vigilance, or wakefulness. Arousal varies from very low (coma or sleep) to very high (panic or high anxiety).

levels. But with increasing arousal, respiration and heart rate can increase, the skin's electrical conductivity increases as a function of perspiration, and brain-wave activity changes predictably.

Sources of Arousal

The main sources of arousal are the **distance receptors**—hearing and vision—but arousal can be affected by any other source of stimulation, including activity of the brain. Some properties of stimuli—meaningfulness, intensity, unexpectedness, novelty, and complexity (Berlyne, 1960)—make them more arousing than others. Therefore, the amount of stimulation is probably less critical for determining level of activation than is the nature of the stimulation.

Arousal and Motivation

Increasing arousal, claim Brehm and Self (1989), is more or less equivalent to increasing motivation—more or less because the relationship is not completely linear. That is, at very low levels of arousal, motivation tends to be low and behavior ineffective. In fact, at the lowest level of arousal—sleep—there is little or no response to external stimulation. Try asking a sleeping person where Moose Jaw is. *Nada.* Ask her again just as she is waking up. "What the #$@#%##?" says she. But as she becomes more fully awake, she may respond correctly (if she knows the answer). However, in your zeal to observe the relationship between arousal and behavior, if you set your subject's house on fire, awaken her with a bucket of cold water, inform her that her house is on fire, and then ask her where Moose Jaw is, you

---

distance receptors The senses that receive stimulation from a distance (for example, hearing and vision).

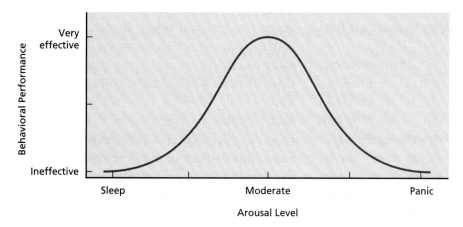

FIGURE 11.2 The relationship between performance and arousal level: Behavior is least effective with very low or very high levels of arousal.

will probably observe the ineffectiveness of behavior that accompanies excessive arousal.[5]

This inverted U-shaped relationship between arousal and behavior is shown in Figure 11.2. What this illustrates, in effect, is that motivation (and the effectiveness of behavior) increases along with increasing arousal until an optimal level is reached; following this, further increases in arousal will result in decreasing motivation and decreasing effectiveness of behavior (Watters, Martin, & Schreter, 1997).

The relationship between arousal and motivation can be summarized by two assumptions:

Assumption 1 *For any given activity, for an individual there is a level of arousal at which performance will be optimal.* Certain activities can best be performed under conditions of relatively high arousal, whereas others are best performed under conditions of lower arousal. Activities involving routine, habitual responses such as counting one's fingers or driving a car, do not ordinarily require a high level of arousal. On the other hand, intense, concentrated activities such as taking examinations require higher levels of arousal.

As we saw, people under great stress often engage in inappropriate behavior. There are the tragic examples of panic-stricken people in crowds trampling one another to death in their haste to escape danger (Schultz, 1964). There are also the studies of Marshall (cited by Bruner, 1957b), who found that fewer than one-quarter of the infantrymen in combat during World War II actually fired their rifles when under heavy fire. Fortunately, the enemy probably did no better.

Assumption 2 *An individual behaves so as to maintain the level of arousal that is most nearly optimal for ongoing behavior.* In other words, if the arousal level is too low, the individual will try to increase it; if it's too high, steps will be taken to lower it. For example, when people experience great fear, their first reaction may be to flee the object of their fear. The effect is to reduce

---

[5] ***PPC:*** By the way, just exactly where is Moose Jaw? It always frustrates me when an author asks a question but doesn't answer it. Besides, this might be important to somebody.

Author: Moose Jaw is in southern Saskatchewan—which is important to the people who live there. Apparently, it was once important to Al Capone, as well. He is rumored to have used it as a base for running whiskey across the U.S.–Canadian border during Prohibition. In fact, one of the cellars he reportedly used as a whiskey storage room is located under present-day Charlotte's, a restaurant on Main Street. My dad lives about four blocks from Charlotte's. In his old age, he dreams about as-yet undiscovered Capone tunnels.

arousal level. When people are bored, their level of arousal is probably too low. They may then engage in more stimulating activity: reading, sports (participating or observing), or if they are students, daydreaming. The effect should be an increase in arousal level. In support of this notion, Hughes (1997) reviews research which indicates that organisms seem to have a "need" for sensory change. This belief has long been used as an explanation for exploratory behavior, for risk taking, for curiosity—in fact, for learning (see, for example, Berlyne, 1960). In this connection MacIver, Reuman, and Main (1995) report evidence that the level of student boredom in schools is closely related to instructional procedures. Specifically, schools that emphasize memorization, drill, and repeated practice are more likely to have students who are acutely bored.

When Arousal is Too Low: Boredom

And bored students are less likely to be effective learners. In fact, like effective behavior, the most effective learning takes place under conditions of optimal arousal. Low levels of arousal are characterized by low attentiveness—and less effective learning. As a teacher, you can illustrate this point. Prepare a good lesson full of content, write it out, and read it to your class very slowly in a soothing monotone. Then deliver the same lesson to another, comparable class in your usual, "today" kind of style. Test the relative retention of your two classes. Little wonder that common synonyms for the term *motivating* include expressions such as "interesting," "captivating," "arousing," "moving," "useful," "involving," "stimulating," "compelling," "attention-getting," "challenging," and "curiosity-whetting."

When Arousal Is Too High: Anxiety

One manifestation of increasing arousal is **anxiety**—a feeling characterized by varying degrees of fear and worry. Research on anxiety and its relationship to learning (and more specifically to performance on tests) dates back more than 40 years but has been quite sporadic and unsystematic. However, in recent years there has been a marked upsurge in research on the nature of anxiety, its relationship to performance, and techniques that can be used to reduce it. Much of this research is of a psychiatric nature, because anxiety is implicated in many mental disorders. But some of it deals specifically with school learning and especially with **test anxiety**.

Test Anxiety Sarason (1980) was among the first to show that anxiety related to test taking decreases test performance. Zeidner (1998) later summarized much of the research on test anxiety. The conclusion is clear, claims Zeidner: General test anxiety causes poor overall performance. And more specific anxieties, like *math* anxiety or *computer* anxiety may be associated with poorer performance in those specific subjects (Kazelskis, 1998; Shermis & Lombard, 1998).

Not only is test anxiety associated with poorer performance, but it is also related to lower self-esteem. Research also indicates that besides their poorer performance on tests, highly anxious students do not profit as much from instruction. Some of these very anxious students, explain Birenbaum and Nasser (1994), simply have poorer study skills; others lack test-taking skills. As a result, anxiety appears to have a detrimental effect on test taking and on learning as well. This observation is apparently true for a wide variety of instructional methods. However, highly anxious students tend to learn

---

anxiety A feeling of apprehension, worry, tension, or nervousness.

test anxiety A characteristic evident in a fear of taking tests and an expectation of poor performance. Test anxiety can significantly impair test performance.

better with more structured instructional approaches, such as programmed learning, computer-assisted instruction, and teacher-directed lessons where student interaction is not expected or required. Thus, high anxiety does not always mean poorer test performance—although it often does (see J. H. Mueller, 1992a, b).

Reducing Test Anxiety There are a wide variety of approaches to reducing test anxiety in students. Most of these are aimed at changing students' attitudes about their personal competence—which is hardly surprising given that expected failure is one of the most important contributors to test anxiety (Zohar, 1998). Accordingly, these approaches often take the form of attempting to develop learning/thinking strategies. Also, students have successfully been taught relaxation techniques to reduce their anxiety (King et al., 1998). And, in one intriguing approach, Drake, Freed, and Hunter (1998) succeeded in reducing test anxiety by allowing students to use "crib sheets" while taking their tests.

There are a variety of things that classroom teachers can do to prevent or reduce test anxiety. These include changing instructional and evaluation procedures with a view to increasing the expectation of success and thereby reducing the expectation of failure. Also, teachers can reduce time pressure on students by providing more time for assignments and tests and perhaps by teaching students simple time management strategies. Teachers can also try to prevent failure by changing the difficulty level of assignments and tests, matching them more carefully to students' skill levels.

Hembree's (1988) review of 562 test-anxiety studies indicates that many of these approaches are effective for reducing test anxiety and that improved performance typically follows anxiety reduction. In light of these findings, Hembree argues that tests such as intelligence or standardized achievement measures—and even teacher-made examinations—consistently underestimate the abilities of test-anxious students—at least after fifth grade. Before this, test anxiety is not ordinarily a significant factor in test performance.

The implications of these findings are twofold: First, steps should be taken to reduce test anxiety for very anxious students, both through treatment programs and through changes in test-taking directions. And second, research is needed to discover ways to prevent test anxiety from developing in the first place.

Arousal Theory: Some Implications for Teaching

The relevance of arousal theory for education depends on the teacher's control over variables that affect arousal. With respect to test anxiety, as we have just seen, the teacher does have control over several important variables. Thus, teachers can sometimes modify instructional and testing procedures or use specific techniques designed to reduce test anxiety.

Teachers also have some control over arousal in the course of daily classroom activities. According to arousal theory, all students in a class should ideally be working at a relatively moderate level of arousal. Students who are asleep, nearing sleep, or just waking up are at levels of arousal too low for most classroom activities; those who show signs of panic and impending flight are at too high a level. The really central question for teachers is how to keep arousal level optimal.

We saw that the primary sources of arousal are the distance receptors, vision and hearing, but that all other sources of stimulation also have some effect. Furthermore, arousal is less affected by the amount than the intensity, meaningfulness, novelty, and complexity of stimulation (Berlyne, 1960). There are other factors as well. Degree of risk or personal involvement is directly related to arousal level, as illustrated by the arousing effects of risk-taking behavior.

Teachers control a significant part of the stimulation to which students are exposed. The intensity, meaningfulness, and complexity of what teachers say, what they do, how they look, and what they write all directly affect the attention (arousal) of their students. Thus, teachers can keep students at an uncomfortably high level of arousal by overemphasizing testing, making tasks unrealistically difficult, using threats, or presenting material that is too complex—and students might reduce their arousal by withdrawing attention and effort. Teachers can also keep students at too low a level of arousal by boring them—and again students may cease to pay attention.

Sadly, boredom is likely a far more serious problem in most classes than overexcitement. There are ways to avoid being boring. Most of them have to do with the intensity, meaningfulness, novelty, and complexity of what teachers say and do—and *how* they say and do it. See the case entitled "The Emperor Comes to Class" for an illustration of a novel, intense, complex—in short, arousing—approach to a history lesson.

◻ A BEHAVIORISTIC VIEW OF MOTIVATION

Motivational theories can be categorized much as can approaches to learning: behavioristic, humanistic, or cognitive. Recall that behavior-

The Emperor Comes to Class

THE SITUATION: Boris Randolph, a good teacher, as recollected by Elizabeth, teacher-in-training

He had a wealth of knowledge of history, and he would allow ten minutes at the beginning of each class for questions on any topic relating to history, not just the specific time frame we were dealing with in class. After an extensive unit on Napoleon, he presented to us a man who was dressed as the Emperor Napoleon. We were given the entire class period to question "Napoleon" about his life, his career, and the state of France and Europe during his reign. The gentleman who disguised himself as Napoleon was a history professor at the local university so he was able to correctly answer our questions. This man also came to us as Adolf Hitler, Joseph Stalin, and Otto von Bismarck.

ism is concerned with how the consequences of behavior regulate and control actions; that humanism is concerned with the autonomy, the dignity, and the worth of the self; and that cognitivism deals with how we know, think, and remember. Accordingly, behavioristic approaches emphasize **extrinsic motives** (external motives) such as those involving praise and reward; humanistic approaches emphasize the importance of **intrinsic motives** (internal motives) such as those related to the need to be autonomous, to develop competence, to actualize potential; and cognitive approaches emphasize the individual's need to know and understand.

Reinforcement and Praise

Psychological hedonism—the **pain/pleasure principle**—is a simple summary of the most basic behavioristic motivational principle: We behave to obtain pleasure and to avoid pain. However, as we saw earlier, pain and pleasure are subjective emotional evaluations that violate behaviorists' determination to be objective. Instead, behaviorists attempt to identify situations (stimuli) that have the effect of increasing the probability of a behavior. These are termed **reinforcers**. Reinforcers can then be used in various ways to bring about desirable behaviors and sometimes to eliminate those that are less desirable.

Recall from Chapter 4 that reinforcement can be either positive or negative. Positive reinforcement increases the probability of a behavior when it follows as a consequence of the behavior (a food reward given for an action, for example). Negative reinforcement also increases the probability of a response, but it does so as a function of being *removed* as a consequence of behavior (for example, detention terminates following an apology).

Positive and negative reinforcement (and sometimes punishment as well) are used in virtually all classrooms, even by the most humanistic or cognitively oriented teachers. Teachers praise and admonish students, they give high and low grades, they smile and frown. These and

---

extrinsic motive A motive associated with external sources of reinforcement—like food, money, or sex.

intrinsic motive A motive associated with internal sources of reinforcement—like satisfaction.

pain/pleasure principle A common expression for psychological hedonism—the belief that we are motivated to seek pleasure and avoid pain.

---

reinforcer A stimulus that causes reinforcement.

a thousand other indicators of approval or disapproval are examples of reinforcement. When reinforcement is used judiciously and systematically, it can have profound effects on behavior. (See Chapter 12 for a detailed discussion of the systematic use of reinforcement in the classroom.)

But we are not simply hungry rats in an experiment, Weiner (1984) informs us. If we look into a classroom, we will see that behavior is not simply driven by external rewards like candy bars or gold stars or high marks. Rather, behavior is *informed*. That is, it is driven by cognitions and by emotions.

It is not surprising that current applications of reinforcement theory in the classroom take students' thinking into account. As Stipek (1988) notes, the most powerful reinforcers for students are stimuli such as **praise**, the effectiveness of these stimuli clearly depend on a student's interpretations of the teacher's behavior.

Praise   Praise is not like food in an empty belly, warm and pleasurable even in the absence of learning. Rather, it is a complex event that says not only "you have done well" but also "you have behaved in a socially approved manner." Praise—and its absence, too—give students fundamentally important information with which to build their notions of self. Praise says things about how worthwhile and competent we are. And, as we see shortly, these are fundamentally important concepts for human motivation.

But teachers do not always use praise well. Brophy (1981) notes that much teacher praise is determined not so much by students' actual behavior as by the teacher's perception of what students need. As a result, praise is often used too infrequently to be effective, or else it is used too often to be meaningful. Praise used in these ways is not clearly contingent (dependent) upon a specific desired behavior, as a good reinforcer is, nor is it sufficiently credible to be very rewarding. (See Table 11.1 for a summary of Brophy's suggestions.)

Praise alone, note Hitz and Driscoll (1994), is not always entirely effective. But it can become very effective when it is designed to increase the student's self-esteem. For example, if praise is accompanied by constructive encouragement, it has long-term effects and more powerful ones than might a simple "good work!" Furthermore, note Hitz and Driscoll, encouragement should be specific rather than vague and general. And of course praise should be sincere. Hitz and Driscoll also caution that teachers should avoid labeling students or making comparisons among them.

For what should teachers praise their students? Their efforts, claim Mueller and Dweck (1998), rather than their abilities or intelligence. As we see later, children who are praised for effort are more likely to develop a view of intelligence as something malleable, something that they can work to improve. Those who are praised (or not praised) for their ability are more likely to view intelligence as fixed and unchangeable. When these children fail, they will subsequently be less persistent in school tasks, will enjoy them less, and will achieve less.

Extrinsic and Intrinsic Motivation   Praise, like little gold stars, hugs, and high marks, provides *extrinsic motives* for behavior. Those who are extrinsically motivated engage in behaviors for the external rewards they expect to follow. By contrast, those who are intrinsically motivated respond to internal sources of reinforcement such as personal satisfaction and a sense of accomplishment. Evidence shows that those who respond to *intrinsic motives* are more committed, enjoy their activities more, and are more persistent in the face of failure (Agbor-Baiyee, 1997).

---

praise Positive verbal comments or other signs of approval. For example, most of what my grandmother said to or about me (heh! heh!).

TABLE 11.1
Guidelines for Effective Praise

EFFECTIVE PRAISE	INEFFECTIVE PRAISE
1. Is delivered contingently	1. Is delivered randomly or unsystematically
2. Specifies the particulars of the accomplishment	2. Is restricted to global positive reactions
3. Shows spontaneity, variety, and other signs of credibility; suggests clear attention to the student's accomplishment	3. Shows a bland uniformity that suggests a conditioned response made with minimal attention
4. Rewards attainment of specified performance criteria (which can include effort criteria, however)	4. Rewards mere participation without consideration of performance processes or outcomes
5. Provides information to students about their competence or the value of their accomplishments	5. Provides no information at all or gives students information about their status
6. Orients students toward better appreciation of their own task-related behavior and thinking about problem solving	6. Orients students toward comparing themselves with others and thinking about competing
7. Uses students' own prior accomplishments as the context for describing current accomplishments	7. Uses the accomplishments of peers as the context for describing students' current accomplishments
8. Is given in recognition of noteworthy effort or success at tasks that are difficult for this student	8. Is given without regard to the effort expended or the meaning of the accomplishment (for this student)
9. Attributes success to effort and ability, implying that similar successes can be expected in the future	9. Attributes success to ability alone or to external factors such as luck or ease of task
10. Fosters endogenous attributions (students believe that they expend effort on the task because they enjoy the task or want to develop relevant skills)	10. Fosters exogenous attributions (students believe that they expend effort on the task for external reasons—to please the teacher, win a competition or reward, and so on)
11. Focuses students' attention on their own task-relevant behavior	11. Focuses students' attention on the teacher as an external authority figure who is manipulating them
12. Fosters appreciation of and desirable attributions about task-relevant behavior after the process is completed	12. Intrudes into the ongoing process, distracting attention from task-relevant behavior

Source: From J. Brophy, "Teacher Praise: A Functional Analysis," *Review of Educational Research*, *51*, No. 1, 5–32 (p. 26). Copyright 1981 by the American Educational Research Association. Reprinted by permission of the publisher.

Interest, note Wigfield, Eccles, & Rodriguez (1998), is closely related to intrinsic motivation. That is, those who engage in activities not because of the external rewards that might result but because of something more internal can be said to have greater interest in that activity. One of the important objectives of schools is to foster interest in specific subjects and in learning in general. As we see in Chapter 12, there is evidence that extrinsic rewards can be very useful for this purpose, especially in the early stages of learning (Lens & Rand, 1997).

Although extrinsic reinforcers (in the form of praise and otherwise) are used extensively by virtually all teachers, some teachers object to its systematic and deliberate use because they sense that there might be something mechanistic and

---

interest Involvement in or concern about something. This concept is related to intrinsic sources of motivation, reflected in knowledge about an activity or object and the placement of high value upon it.

dehumanizing about the systematic application of rewards and punishments (of extrinsic reinforcement, in other words) to shape behavior. Others object because they fear that students who are trained to respond too readily to extrinsic reinforcers might become too dependent on them. And some humanists fear that such students will never learn to listen to their own motives—to their intrinsic and fundamentally human urge to excel, to become someone worthwhile and actualized.

A HUMANISTIC VIEW OF MOTIVATION

Praise is quite different from extrinsic rewards like tiny gold stars and good grades. At its simplest level, praise is a verbal affirmation that the student has done well; at a more complex level, praise is an informative event that says much about the outcome of the student's efforts and also about the value and uniqueness of the student. Thus, praise might do much to increase the student's reliance on intrinsic (or internal) motivation (Fair & Silvestri, 1992). In this sense, praise is more humanistic than gold stars.

Humanistic psychology's concern with intrinsic motives is most clearly apparent in Maslow's (1970) theory of human needs and especially his concept of self-actualization.

Basic Needs and Metaneeds

Maslow proposes two general need systems: **basic needs** and **metaneeds**.

---

basic need Maslow's term for a lower-level need, such as the physiological needs or the need to belong, to love, and to have high self-esteem. Also termed *deficiency needs*.

metaneeds Maslow's term for higher needs. Concerned with psychological, self-related functions rather than with biology. These include the need for truth, beauty, justice, and to self-actualize. Also termed *growth needs*.

Basic Needs These basic needs include

physiological needs: the basic biological needs—for example, the need for food, water, and temperature regulation

safety needs: needs that are manifested in people's efforts to maintain sociable, predictable, orderly, and therefore nonthreatening environments

needs for love and belongingness: the need to develop relationships involving reciprocal affection; the need to be a member of a group

self-esteem needs: the need to cultivate and maintain a high opinion of oneself; the need to have others hold one in high esteem.

These self-esteem needs, notes Rowan (1998), are really two very distinct needs. That is, the esteem we receive from others is quite different from our own self-esteem. He argues that we need both. That is, we need to have others rate us well and approve of us; we also need to develop feelings of adequacy, of self-confidence, of being worthwhile.

These needs are hierarchical; high-level needs will be attended to only after low-level needs are satisfied (see Figure 11.3). When people lack food, they are not likely to be concerned with love or self-esteem. History provides striking examples of the potency of low-level needs. In the 1933 famine in eastern (Soviet) Ukraine, for example, where at least 4.5 million people died, more than half of the victims were infants. In the words of one survivor ("Ukrainian Famine Survivors," 1983):

> All you think about is food. It's your one, your only, your all-consuming thought. You have no sympathy for anyone else. A sister feels nothing for her brother; a brother feels nothing for his sister; parents don't feel anything for their children. You become like a hungry animal. You will throw yourself on food like a hungry animal. That's what

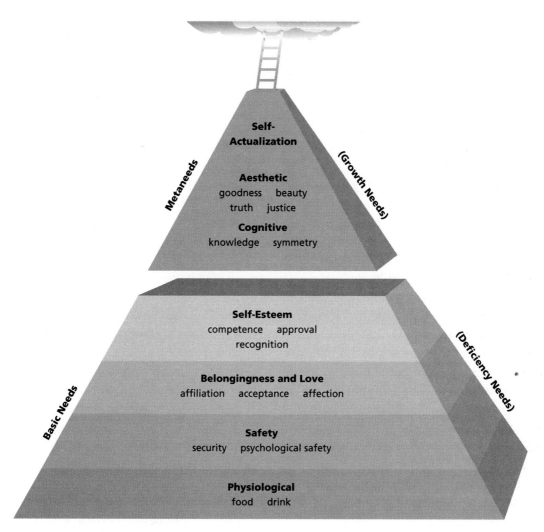

FIGURE 11.3 Maslow's hierarchy of needs: The open pyramid indicates that self-actualization is a never-ending process, not an ultimate, achievable goal.

you're like when you're hungry. All human behavior, all moral behavior collapses.

Metaneeds Maslow's basic needs are also termed **deficiency needs** because they motivate (lead to behavior) when the organism has a deficiency with respect to a need (for example, lacks food or water). The metaneeds are termed **growth needs** because they motivate behaviors that do not result from deficiencies but from a natural human tendency toward growth. The growth needs will be attended to only after the basic needs are reasonably satisfied.

---

deficiency need Maslow's expression for a basic need, so called because it motivates the person to act when a related deficiency is sensed—for example, a deficiency of food leads to eating, a deficiency of self-esteem leads to behaviors intended to increase esteem.

growth need Another expression for Maslow's metaneeds. So called because these needs motivate behavior not as a result of deficiencies but because of an intrinsic need to grow, to become, to actualize oneself. These include cognitive, aesthetic, and self-actualization needs.

The metaneeds include aesthetic and cognitive urges associated with such virtues as truth and goodness, the acquisition of knowledge, and the appreciation of beauty, order, and symmetry. The highest need in Maslow's system is our tendency toward *self-actualization.*

Self-actualization is a difficult concept, explain Leclerc and associates (1998)—one that is not yet fully clarified almost 50 years after its original formulation. Their survey of 26 "experts" indicates a general consensus that self-actualization is a process rather than a state. It is a process of growth—of becoming—evident in the unfolding and fulfillment of self. Interestingly, it is a process that is similar in many ways to the ideals of Chinese Taoism and Zen Buddhism (Chang & Page, 1991).

Most humanistic psychologists consider self-actualization absolutely central to the healthy experience of being human. But, laments Maslow (1991) in one of his posthumously published papers,[6] there are relatively few truly self-actualized people. Why? One reason is that growth requires will and effort and perhaps a great deal of sacrifice. And many of us, notes Maslow, suffer from the **Jonah complex.** Like that biblical character, we deliberately avoid the commitment and the effort required for our personal growth and development. Instead, we choose to struggle along, eating and drinking and satisfying our other needs. And in the end, we are somehow less human than we might have been. And perhaps less happy as well, notes Umoren (1992), who argues that our well-being is closely tied to how well we satisfy our high-level needs.

We should emphasize that self-actualization is not a single, unchanging goal toward which our development strives; rather, it is an ongoing process. Depiction of Maslow's theory as a triangle, which is how it is typically represented in textbooks, is misleading, says Rowan (1998). "What is wrong with the triangle," he says, "is that it suggests that there is an end point to personal growth" (p. 88). We never reach that point, says Rowan; we never reach the ultimate. He suggests that something like a ladder would be a better representation than a triangle (the triangle was apparently not Maslow's idea). Figure 11.3 combines both a triangle and a ladder.

An interesting dimension of self-actualization as described by Maslow concerns **peak experiences.** These are profoundly moving experiences that, in many instances, come close to defining what is meant by self-actualization. For example, a peak experience might involve the successful culmination of one's lifework, a religious revelation, or a defining moment in a profoundly intimate human relationship. Toward the end of Maslow's career, says Hoffman (1998), he recognized the possibility and importance of peak experiences in childhood. These might include overwhelming experiences in places of scenic grandeur, episodes associated with the resolution of crises, survival following near-death experiences, or even intensely moving and unforgettable dreams.

For most children, school is not a peak experience.

Competence Motivation

Maslow omitted a very important human motive, says Rowan (1998): the need to feel competent.

Jonah complex A phrase used by Maslow to describe those who avoid and deny their personal capacity for growth and self-actualization.

---

[6] A series of Maslow's previously unpublished papers, most of them written in the 1960s, have now been published in the *Journal of Humanistic Education and Development* (vol. 29, no. 3, 1991).

peak experience A label introduced by Maslow to describe an intensely moving and unforgettable experience that has a profound effect on an individual's life. A peak experience might involve what is interpreted by the individual as a supernatural experience, a profound mystical revelation, a startling insight, or other events closely related to the process of self-actualization.

"How about that? I recently became my own person, too."
Drawing by Lorenz; © 1984 The New Yorker Magazine, Inc.

R. W. White (1959) argues that this is one of our most important intrinsic needs. **Competence motivation** is manifested in the child's struggle to perform competently and the feelings of confidence and worth that accompany successful performance. In the sense that competence motivation involves efforts directed toward the growth and development of potential, it can be seen as one aspect of self-actualization.

As we see later in this chapter, notions of competence are basic to what cognitive theorists describe as **self-efficacy**—notions about how competent and effective we are in dealing with our environments (Bandura, 1986). In effect, White's theory of competence motivation says that the desire for a positive evaluation of one's effectiveness—in other words, high self-efficacy—is a fundamentally important human motive.

White believes that competence motivation is an especially important concept for understanding species such as ours because humans are born with so few innate competencies. Unlike the young of many nonhuman species, our infants cannot run or hide, they cannot feed themselves; they have little recognition of enemies or of danger. Perhaps even more important, infants know few of the signals, gestures, and sounds they need to master to understand the world and to communicate competently. To be human is to learn a thousand competencies; it's hardly surprising that we should be motivated to be competent.

Competence motivation, suggests White, explains a tremendous range of behaviors that

competence motivation White's phrase for our innate need to achieve competence and to feel competent. According to White, competence motivation has especially important adaptive value for a species that is born with little innate competence.

self-efficacy A term that refers to judgments we make about how effective we are in given situations. Judgments of self-efficacy are important for determining our choices of activities and influencing the amount of interest and effort we expend.

We have an innate need, says R. W. White, to be and feel competent. This drive for competence largely explains why some students strive to learn a second language, why some students spend hours practicing shooting baskets—and why others become so good at drawing on sidewalks.

are engaged in by children. The drive for competence—for mastery—explains curiosity and information-seeking behavior. Competence motivation is evident in the repetitive, circular reactions of Piaget's infant (see Chapter 3); it also explains why schoolchildren practice skills over and over again until they achieve competence.

Educational Implications of Humanistic Orientations

Humanistic approaches to motivation emphasize internal or intrinsic factors that affect behavior. The drive to achieve competence is an internal drive—an intrinsic motive. As we saw in Chapter 7, humanistic schools are child-centered rather than teacher- or subject-centered. Their emphasis is on affective growth and on the development of a healthy self-concept. However, humanistic concerns need not be incompatible with more traditional values that emphasize curriculum content and the development of basic skills.

In Chapter 7, we saw three educational alternatives that illustrate humanistic concerns: open education, learning styles schools, and cooperative learning. These alternatives put into practice some of the educational implications of humanistic approaches to motivation.

Perhaps the greatest contribution of humanistic approaches to instructional practice is embodied less in specific recommendations for the nitty-gritty of classroom practice than in teachers' attitudes toward students. Humanistic educators are concerned individuals who place great value on the personal development of their students. Accordingly, self-actualization is one of the most important goals of humanistic instruction—as is the concomitant development of positive feelings about the self and about personal effectiveness and competence (self-efficacy). As an example, consider the case entitled "A Leaf Has a Soul."

COGNITIVE VIEWS OF MOTIVATION

Again, we must realize that our psychological categories are seldom as neat as we would like; the real world is not as simple as the models we invent to represent it. For example, aspects of R. W. White's competence motivation theory are every bit as cognitive as they are humanistic, and in some ways they are behavioristic as well. And some of the theories we consider in this section have behavioristic and humanistic overtones.

Some of the earliest accounts of motivation viewed the human organism as a passive being—unmoved and unmoving in the absence of external or internal conditions that define needs, drives, and arousal levels; that trigger instinctual or primitive learned behavior; or those that are clearly associated with pain or pleasure. In other words, early psychology has, inadvertently or otherwise, described an organism that is highly reactive but considerably less active. Hence arose the contention that older theories have painted an overly passive and mechanistic picture of human beings.

Newer approaches are clearly more cognitive and social. We are now seen not as victims of internal or external prods moving us willy-nilly through our daily activities but as organisms whose ongoing activity is largely mediated by conscious evaluation, anticipation, and emotion. Bolles (1974), agreeing with one of Freud's basic beliefs, points out that there are no unmotivated behaviors. Thus, motivation is not a special force that should be isolated and classified just as needs are; it is simply a characteristic of ongoing behavior. And perhaps the single most important feature of human motivation is our ability to delay gratification. So much of our behavior is motivated by our anticipation of distant outcomes. To analyze human behavior in terms of conditions that seem relevant to the behavior of very young children is often fruitless for older children and

CASES FROM THE CLASSROOM

A Leaf Has a Soul

THE SITUATION: Miss Cook, eighth-grade English; a good teacher, as recollected by Eleanor, teacher-in-training

Miss Cook sensed I was shy and never called upon me to answer any questions in class. We had been told to write an assignment on personification. My topic had been a leaf that had a soul and how it was tossed by the wind.

After returning our papers, Miss Cook asked if I would kindly share my writing with the class. She asked with such quiet respect, and with such gentleness, I could not refuse. I read the paper in a shaky voice, and she thanked me. As I was walking out of the class, she suggested I keep a diary and think about a career in writing. I did both and find on thinking back that the experience of being in Miss Cook's English class affected a large portion of my life.

adults. For example, a promise of $20 tomorrow instead—all you have to do is wait—is unlikely to satisfy the 3-year-old who wants $1 so he can buy some ice cream *now*. We adults, on the other hand, would be more than happy to forgo $1 today in exchange for $20 tomorrow. We have learned to delay gratification by virtue of some uniquely human abilities involved in thinking, imagining, and verbalizing. Through a study of these ongoing cognitive processes social cognitive theorists such as Bandura search for understanding and for explanations of human behavior.

The clear emphasis of theories such as Bandura's is on our cognitive and information processing capacities and how these affect our behavior (Grusec, 1992). Among other things, Bandura looks at what is termed **self-referent thought**—thought that concerns our selves and our own mental processes. Metacognition, as we saw in Chapter 5, is one aspect of self-referent thought. Another that has important implica-

tions for motivation relates to our personal estimates of our effectiveness and competency, or what is termed *self-efficacy*.

Self-Efficacy

Self-efficacy, Bandura informs us, has to do with our own estimates of our personal effectiveness. "Perceived self-efficacy," he writes, "refers to beliefs in one's capabilities to organize and execute the courses of action required to produce given attainments" (1997, p. 3). The most efficacious people are those who are most competent. Accordingly, self-efficacy has two related components: The first has to do with the skills—the actual competencies—required for successful performance; the second concerns the individual's personal estimates of competence.

Personal estimates of competence are extremely important in education. As Zimmerman, Bandura, and Martinez-Pons put it, "Numerous studies have shown that students with a high sense of academic efficacy display greater persistence, effort, and intrinsic interest in their academic learning and performance" (1992, p. 664). Our beliefs about how likely we are to succeed in a given subject or endeavor (our

---

self-referent thought Thought that pertains to the self. Self-referent thought concerns our own mental processes (for example, thoughts that evaluate our abilities or monitor our progress in solving problems).

notions of self-efficacy for that subject or activity) profoundly influence what we choose to do, how much effort we are willing to put into it, and how persistent we will be. For example, following a study of 246 students at the end of their eighth and tenth years of school, Marsh and Yeung (1997) found that positive self-concepts in specific subjects (the extent to which students expect to do well) were among the best predictors of what students subsequently choose to study. In fact, this research showed academic self-concept to be a better predictor of future course selections than actual grades in various subjects. Accordingly, teachers must understand the origins of judgments of self-efficacy. Much of what teachers do—and can do—affects self-efficacy.

The Development of Self-Efficacy Judgments

Children's beliefs about their competence and effectiveness appear to change systematically during the school years. Children begin with global notions of whether they are "smart" or "not smart," explains Harter (1988). But there appears to be a definite, general bias in the direction of "smart." Thus, very young elementary school children frequently have highly optimistic notions of their competence. For example, Wigfield, Eccles, and Rodriguez (1998) reviewed research which indicates that a majority of first graders rank themselves near the top of their classes with respect to things like reading ability. But with increasing experience, most children's notions of self-efficacy change in two ways: First, they become more differentiated; that is, rather than simply seeing themselves as "smart" or "dumb," children now begin to develop notions of self-worth and self-competence in several areas: athletic, social, and academic. Second, their estimates of their own competence tend to decline, and in the end, progressively become more highly correlated with actual success as reflected in school grades.

Bandura (1997) identifies four important influences on a person's judgments of self-

efficacy (or personal competence): actual (*enactive*) experience, vicarious experience, verbal persuasion, and the influence of emotional states.

Enactive influences are evident in the results of the individual's own actions. Whether a person is habitually successful in a given task clearly influences personal judgments of competence. Those who are never successful are less likely to have positive evaluations of self-efficacy than are those who most often succeed. It does not follow, however, that success is invariably attributed to personal competence and inevitably results in judgments of high self-efficacy. As we see shortly, some individuals habitually attribute their successes to good fortune or to other factors over which they have no control, rather than to their own competence and effort. By the same token, these individuals take little personal blame for their failures, attributing them instead to bad luck. (For more information, see the section on attribution theories later in this chapter.)

A second influence on self-efficacy judgments is *vicarious* (secondhand). This has to do with observing the performance of others. Clearly, if we see that others around us always produce nicer paintings than we do, we are not likely to develop high evaluations of our artistic competence. Similarly, children who always receive the poorest grades—or the highest—are being provided with comparative information that might be highly instrumental for determining their judgments of personal worth.

Bandura (1981) suggests that the most important comparisons for forming judgments of personal competence are those that children make with their peers. It is not particularly helpful to my self-concept to beat the trousers off a 12-year-old at racquetball; it would be considerably more informative (and unlikely) for me to trounce the local open-class champion.

Vicarious sources of influence on self-judgments are most important in competitive school situations—which means, of course, that they are important in *most* school situations because, as we saw earlier, most are competitive. In more cooperative settings, however, comparisons with peers are not nearly as important.

Verbal persuasion can sometimes be an important source of information about competence. Those who lack confidence—and whose self-efficacy judgments are therefore presumably low—can sometimes be persuaded to do things they would otherwise be reluctant to do. Implicit in the persuasion ("come on, Emily, play your bandura[7] for us") is a positive judgment ("you play your bandura so well, Emily"). As Bandura (1997) notes, "it is easier to sustain a sense of efficacy . . . if significant others express faith in one's capabilities than if they convey doubts" (p. 101).

A fourth source of influence on judgments of self-efficacy relates to emotions and has to do with *physiological states* (arousal). As we saw earlier in this chapter, arousal refers to alertness or vigilance and ranges from sleep or comatose states to states of high, intense alertness or even panic.

High arousal, Bandura (1997) suggests, can affect self-judgments in various ways. For example, great fear might lead to judgments of low personal competence. A mountain climber overcome by fear might decide that he is incapable of continuing—as might a person about to speak in public. In contrast, great fear might lead a hiker to judge that she is capable of outrunning a bear.

In summary, our feelings of competence are a combined function of the results of our behavior (enactive influence: our successes and failures tell us much about how competent we are); our comparisons with others (vicarious influence: our performance is as good as, better than, or poorer than that of others); the persuasions of others (persuasory influence: when others persuade us, their behavior tells us positive things about our

TABLE 11.2 Main Sources of Information Affecting Judgments of Self-Efficacy	EXAMPLES OF INFORMATION THAT MIGHT LEAD JILL TO FORM POSITIVE ESTIMATES OF SELF-EFFICACY
Enactive (actual experience)	She wins a scholarship to attend agricultural college.
Vicarious (second-hand experience; modeling)	She learns that Ronald worked harder than she did but wasn't given a scholarship.
Persuasory (the effect of others' confidence—or doubt)	Her teacher tells her she should enroll in the advanced program for gifted farmers.
Emotive (the influence of physiological states)	She was tense before her pest control exam but felt exhilarated afterward.

competence); and the intensity of arousal (emotive influence: judgments of competence can be raised or lowered by the intensity of an immediate emotional reaction). (See Table 11.2 for a summary of influences on self-efficacy.)

Implications of Self-Efficacy Our personal judgments of our own effectiveness—our notions of self-efficacy—are extremely important determiners of what we do and don't do. Hence they are very valuable for understanding human motivation. In fact, as the Marsh and Yeung (1997) study shows, measures of self-efficacy are sometimes better predictors of behavior than are relevant skills. That's because under most circumstances, children—or adults—don't attempt to do things that they expect to do badly. "Efficacy beliefs," Bandura explains, "influence how people feel, think, motivate themselves, and behave" (1993, p. 118).

---

[7] *PPC:* I don't get this. Are you trying to make fun of Albert Bandura?
Author: Not really. A bandura is an ancient, many-stringed Ukrainian musical instrument. It looks a little like what we might imagine an angel's harp looks like.

Judgments of self-efficacy affect not only what we choose to do, and sometimes where we choose to do it, but also the amount of effort we are willing to expend when faced with difficulties. The stronger an individual's perceptions of efficacy, the more likely it is that individual will persist and the greater the effort expended will be. But if notions of self-efficacy are not entirely favorable, difficult activities may be abandoned after very little effort and time, or might not be undertaken at all—or they might be undertaken secretively and in private.[8]

Those with the most favorable judgments of self-efficacy are also more likely to accept risks than are those who are less confident of their effectiveness. For example, in a study of fifth and sixth graders, Meyer, Turner, and Spencer (1997) found that those with the highest self-efficacy ratings were also those most likely to seek and accept challenges. Those with lower estimates of self-efficacy were more likely to avoid challenges and also reacted more negatively to failure.

Not surprisingly, self-efficacy is closely linked with athletic functioning, notes Bandura (1997). Children whose sense of personal effectiveness in athletics is high are certainly far more likely to engage in competitive athletics—and to persist in the face of failure—than are those who, from the very beginning, doubt their ability to function well. Coaches have long known that self-confidence (another label for self-efficacy) is an essential ingredient for high-level athletic accomplishment. Teachers may well have known (or suspected) the same with respect to high levels of academic achievement, but teachers have not always acted as though this were true.

Self-efficacy judgments have also been shown to be related to goals. Zimmerman, Bandura, and Martinez-Pons (1992) show that students set their academic goals in relation to notions of their self-efficacy for academic achievement. Children who do not see themselves as effective learners set lower goals for themselves than do those who have higher estimates of self-efficacy. Goals are especially important, says Bandura (1986), because they set the criteria for personal failure or success. Reaching them, or failing to, is therefore accompanied by strong emotional reactions. Hence, the goals that learners set for themselves are powerful sources of motivation.

Judgments of efficacy also motivate our behavior by influencing our thoughts and our emotions. Those whose judgments of personal competence are low are far more likely to evaluate themselves negatively and to suffer from poor self-esteem. There is considerable evidence, notes Bandura (1997), that those with stronger feelings of self-efficacy are both physically and psychologically healthier. High self-efficacy, he notes, provides individuals with the tools necessary to deal effectively with most situations that life presents. Anxiety and phobias, he notes, are perhaps the most common manifestations of human distress and unhappiness. For example, a tremendous number of individuals suffer from social anxiety—that is, shyness or fear of speaking publicly. It is as though these individuals are afraid of being judged, afraid of what others will think of them. It follows, notes Bandura, that those with the greatest confidence in their personal effectiveness are least likely to be overwhelmed by social anxieties and phobias.

The importance of positive self-evaluations for achievement—that is, of expectations of high achievement—is highlighted in a study that examined the math and verbal achievement of nearly 700 sixth- and ninth-grade Norwegian students (Skaalvik & Rankin, 1995). For this study, the investigators developed scales that

---

[8] **PPC:** Can the bear illustrate this?

Author: Yes. For example, if a bear (or a student) did not consider himself a very good diver—that is, if he had a low estimate of self-efficacy with respect to this skill—he might, on a kick-in-the-rump sort of hot day, choose to dive into the pond where no one could see him. Similarly, students who have highly positive self-efficacy judgments with respect to their reading skills might enthusiastically volunteer to read out loud in class. Those with less positive judgments might prefer to read privately.

looked specifically at how students perceived their abilities in mathematics and verbal arts. Not surprisingly, the researchers found a high positive relationship between strong expectations of success and actual achievement. And, as they note, high expectations of success are one manifestation of high self-efficacy.

In conclusion, highly favorable judgments of personal competence (high self-efficacy), together with accompanying positive evaluations of the self (positive self-esteem), can be extremely important positive influences on a child's achievement in school—and on that child's happiness as well. By the same token, low self-efficacy judgments can have highly negative effects.

Attribution Theories

Success and failure clearly affect our judgments of personal competence—of self-efficacy. But we are not simple, highly predictable creatures, you and I: We don't necessarily react to our failures or successes in exactly the same way. **Attribution theory** recognizes that we attribute the outcomes of our behavior to a variety of causes. Some believe that they do well because they are intelligent; others are convinced that they are simply lucky. Our attributions, notes Weiner (1994), depend very much on our personalities—specifically, on one aspect of our personalities: our **locus of control**. Locus (place) of control refers to the causes to which we attribute our behaviors. Some of us are internally oriented; others are externally oriented. Furthermore, claims Weiner (1992), some people accept responsibility for the outcomes of their behaviors and others don't. And some attribute the causes of behavior to highly stable factors—that is, to factors that don't change much, like how difficult a task is. Others are more likely to attribute the causes of behavior to highly unstable factors—that is, to factors that are subject to change, like the amount of effort an individual expends on a task.

These three factors, *locus of control*, *personal responsibility*, and *stability*, are the cornerstones of Weiner's theory of motivation. These factors are extremely important in the attempt of cognitive motivational theory to understand the achievement-oriented behavior of students (or their lack of effort to achieve).

Locus of Control If I have an **internal orientation**, I might attribute my successes and failures to my ability, to my effort, or to a combination of the two. Note that these are factors *within* the individual. But if I have an **external orientation**, I am more likely to attribute my performance to factors that are *outside*, like luck or the difficulty of the task. As we see later, students who are internally oriented also tend to be more achievement oriented and more driven toward mastery of school tasks (Hill & Huntley, 1998). They are also more likely to be liked by teachers and to be judged more likely to succeed (Schraw & Aplin, 1998).

Personal Responsibility If I attribute the outcomes of my behaviors to external factors like luck or how difficult tasks are, I am attributing them to causes over which I have no control and for which I therefore have no responsibility. But

---

attribution theory A cognitive motivational theory concerned with predictable consistencies in what people interpret as the causes of the outcomes of behavior.

locus of control An aspect of personality evident in the individual's consistent tendency to attribute behavioral outcomes to a specific class of causes—causes over which the individual does, or does not, have control.

---

internal orientation A tendency to attribute the outcomes of behavior to factors within the individual (such as effort or ability).

external orientation A tendency to attribute the outcomes of behavior to factors outside the individual (such as luck or the difficulty of a task).

there are other external causes which can be controlled. If, for example, I attribute the outcomes of my behavior to an external cause like the interference of my friends, I may well have some degree of control over this cause. That is, I can do things such as avoid my friends, pay no attention to them, make them into enemies, make new friends, or all of the foregoing. Because I accept that I have some control over this cause, I also accept personal responsibility for the outcomes of my actions.

Similarly, some internal attributions are under my control and are therefore associated with a high level of personal responsibility. Effort, for example, is an internal cause which I can control. On the other hand, intelligence, also an internal cause of behavior, can be viewed as either controllable or not. As we see shortly, it all depends on your implicit theory of intelligence.

Stability and Instability of Causes The causes to which people attribute the outcomes of their behaviors can be highly stable and unchanging. The difficulty of a subject is one such possible attribution. If I attribute my failure in an educational psychology course to a stable cause like the tremendous complexity of the subject, I will not expect to do any better in the future than I have in the past. But if, on the other hand, I attribute my failure to an unstable cause like the difficulty of the exam, I can at least hope that the instructor will devise a less difficult examination next time.

The three dimensions of possible causes to which our successes and failures can be attributed give rise to eight different possibilities. These are illustrated in Table 11.3. Figure 11.4 summarizes the characteristics of four of the most important possible attributions that students can make when analyzing the outcomes of their efforts in school. That is, they can decide that they have done well or poorly because of effort, ability, luck, or the difficulty of the task

Causal Attributions

	Internal	External
Unstable	Effort (controllable)	Luck (uncontrollable)
Stable	Ability (uncontrollable)	Difficulty (controllable)

FIGURE 11.4 Four important possible attributions for success and failure: Our explanations for why we succeed or fail can be internal or external; they can also involve causes that are either stable or unstable, controllable or uncontrollable.

(or the lack of each of these). Clearly, performance can also be attributed to other causes (mood, illness, or fatigue, for example), but these are more personal, variable, and not easily amenable to scientific investigation.

Development of Attribution Tendencies The tendency to attribute success and failure to either internal or external causes seems to be a relatively predictable and stable personality characteristic. However, it is less apparent in children younger than nine, who have not yet differentiated between such factors as ability and effort. Schlangen and Steinsmeier-Pelster (1997) report that these children think that "amount of knowledge" is intelligence; they believe that smart people are those who work hard (and consequently succeed). At about nine or ten, children begin to consider ability as a separate factor that contributes to success. But even at this age, smartness is still equated with hard work. By age 11, however, children typically share our intuitive notions about the distinctions among ability, luck, effort, and task difficulty.

Performance versus Mastery Goals Children, Dweck (1986) informs us, seem to behave as though they subscribed intuitively to one of two

TABLE 11.3	
The Eight Classes of Causal Attributions in Weiner's Motivational Theory	
CHARACTERISTICS OF CAUSAL ATTRIBUTIONS	ILLUSTRATION (Rick's explanation of why he failed his educational psychology test)
Internal-unstable-controllable (high responsibility)	He spent the previous night at his girlfriend's house instead of studying.
Internal-unstable-uncontrollable (low responsibility)	He had sprained his wrist and couldn't write rapidly enough to complete the test.
Internal-stable-controllable (high responsibility)	He refuses, as a matter of principle, to study for any school subject.
Internal-stable-uncontrollable (low responsibility	He has a learning disability that makes it almost impossible for him to do well on multiple-choice tests.
External-unstable-controllable (high responsibility)	There didn't happen to be enough questions about all the stuff he knew so well.
External-unstable-uncontrollable (low responsibility)	The course outline assigned the wrong chapters to study.
External-stable-controllable (high responsibility)	Left-handed, red-headed males never do well at this university.
External-stable-uncontrollable (low responsibility)	Educational psychology is bleeping tough.

Source: Based on Weiner's theory of motivation, 1992.

views of intelligence: the **entity theory** or the **incremental theory**. If they subscribe to the entity theory, they behave as though they believe that intelligence is fixed and unchanging. Accordingly, their achievement goals are **performance goals**; that is, they will be moved to obtain favorable judgments about their competence (about their ability) and to avoid unfavorable judgments. On the other hand, if they subscribe to the incremental theory, they behave as though they believe that intelligence is malleable. Accordingly, the goals of their achievement-oriented behavior will be **mastery goals** (also termed *learning goals*) rather than performance goals; that is, they will focus on effort and attempt to increase their competence.

Dweck's analysis of attribution research strongly suggests that students whose basic orientation is toward performance goals (those who view intelligence as being fixed) need extremely high confidence in their ability to be willing to accept challenges. Students whose confidence is lower are more likely to be characterized by what

entity theory Dweck's label for the belief that ability is a fixed, unchanging entity. Associated with performance goals—that is, with doing well to be judged positively by others.

incremental theory Dweck's label for the belief that ability is malleable through work and effort. The theory is associated with mastery goals—that is, with increasing personal competence.

performance goal A goal directed toward performing well rather than toward mastering a subject and increasing one's competence.

mastery goal A goal directed toward increasing one's personal competence.

Dweck describes as "helplessness," primarily because they see failure as a direct reflection of their ability. As Harju and Eppler (1997) explain, these students are most likely to be characterized by pessimism and external motivation.

In contrast, students who are oriented toward mastery (those who view intelligence as malleable) are far more likely to seek challenges and to be persistent. That is, when students view ability as a function of effort, they are more likely to strive toward high achievement because for them the cost of failure is not as high as it is for those who see ability as fixed and unchangeable (Dweck & Leggett, 1988; Mueller & Dweck, 1998). (See Table 11.4.) These students, note Harju and Eppler (1997), tend to be optimistic and internally motivated.

Attribution and Achievement Motivation The implications of attribution theory for understanding students' behavior become clearer when they are considered in relation to what is termed **achievement motivation**. Some individ-

---

achievement motivation A need that, if high, is evident in a strong desire to achieve, to excel, to reach a high level of excellence. Achievement motivation can also be low.

uals behave as though they have a strong need to achieve, to be successful, to reach some standard of excellence; others behave as though they are more afraid of failing than desirous of success (McClelland et al., 1953). Research indicates that individuals who score high on measures of achievement motivation also tend to be high achievers in school (Atkinson & Raynor, 1978).

Other relevant findings are that high-need achievers are typically moderate risk takers. They attempt tasks that are moderately difficult, thus providing themselves with a challenge while keeping their probability of their success fairly high (McClelland, 1958; Thomas, 1980). In contrast, individuals with a low need to achieve typically attempt tasks that are either quite difficult or quite easy. Why?

The answer may lie in attribution theory. As a low-need achiever, if I attempt a very difficult task and fail, I can attribute my failure to the difficulty of the task, a factor over which I have no control; hence, I will assume no personal responsibility and experience no negative affect (emotion). If I am successful, there is again little positive affect because my success is due to external factors over which I have no control. If I am a high-need achiever and also a moderate risk taker, however, I

TABLE 11.4
Achievement Goals and Achievement Behavior

THEORY OF INTELLIGENCE	GOAL ORIENTATION	CONFIDENCE IN PRESENT ABILITY	BEHAVIOR PATTERN
Entity theory (Intelligence is fixed.)	*Performance goal* (Goal is to gain positive judgments and avoid negative judgments of competence.)	*If high*	*Mastery oriented* (Seeks challenge; extreme persistence)
		If low	*Helpless* (Avoids challenge; low persistence)
Incremental theory (Intelligence is malleable.)	*Learning goal* (Goal is to increase competence.)	*If high or low*	*Mastery oriented* (Seeks challenge that fosters learning; persistence)

Source: Adapted from Dweck (1986).

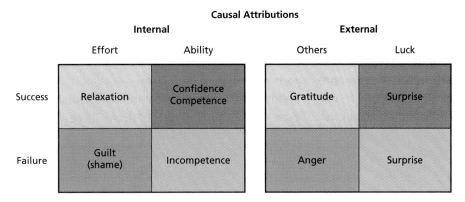

FIGURE 11.5 Relations between causal attributions and feelings associated with success and failure

can attribute success to my skill or effort; similarly, I can also attribute failure to personal factors. In either case, there is considerably more emotional involvement in the outcomes of the performance (see Figures 11.5 and 11.6).

It seems reasonable to suppose, then, that high-need achievers will tend to be internally oriented, whereas low-need achievers will more likely attribute their performance to external factors. This supposition is, in fact, borne out by research (Mueller & Dweck, 1998; Wittrock, 1986).

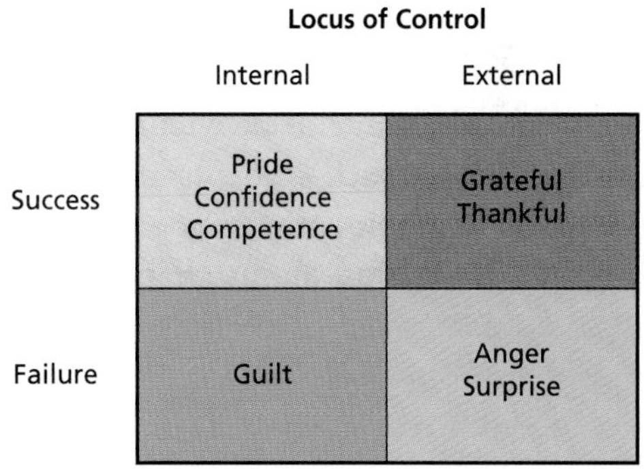

FIGURE 11.6 Relations between locus of control and feelings associated with success and failure

CLASSROOM APPLICATIONS OF COGNITIVE VIEWS

Cognitive approaches to understanding motivation have a wealth of educational implications. This is not surprising because many of these approaches have been developed specifically to understand achievement in the classroom.

Changing Attributions and Achievement Motivation

We know that attributions are related to motivation and performance and that internally oriented individuals typically manifest higher

achievement motivation and set themselves more realistic goals. There are indications, as well, that students with high achievement motivation are more satisfied with school and are less bored (Duda & Nicholls, 1992). One important question for educators is whether externally oriented individuals can be made more internally oriented.

Several attribution-changing programs have been developed and investigated. As Weiner (1994) notes, the major objective of most of these programs is to move students in the direction of effort attributions; that is, the programs attempt to lead students to the understanding that their successes and failures ought to be attributed to their personal efforts. Attributing failure to lack of ability, notes Miserandino (1998), is detrimental to future motivation and achievement. She found that basketball players who were told their misses were due to lack of effort rather than lack of ability subsequently improved significantly more than those whose misses were attributed to lack of ability.

Mueller and Dweck (1998) make much the same point with respect to the effects of praise. Contrary to popular opinion, they claim that praising students for their ability does not have beneficial effects on their motivation. In fact, the results of six separate studies reported by these authors indicate just the opposite. Students who are praised for their intelligence tend to develop performance goals; such students are moved to achieve to display their competence and to avoid unfavorable judgments about their ability. In contrast, students who are praised for their effort rather than their intelligence tend to develop learning goals; they focus on performance to *increase* their ability.

A program developed by McCombs (1982) attempts to develop motivation not only by changing students' attributions to internal causes like effort, but also by teaching cognitive strategies and metacognitive skills. As students become more adept at the management of these skills and strategies (as they learn more about learning) it follows that they will also begin to realize that they can exercise a great deal of control over learning and achievement—that it isn't just a matter of luck and faith. In most school-related tasks, luck should have little bearing on performance, although some students will invoke that "lady" repeatedly in any case: They blame luck when they have studied the wrong sections, inadvertently misaligned their answer sheets, or had the misfortune of being presented with inferior teachers. Teachers can exercise some control over the other three major categories to which performance outcomes can be attributed (effort, ability, and task difficulty), but luck can only be left to chance.

Not surprisingly, repeated failures are likely to have a negative effect on self-concept and on feelings of competence, and individuals who have failed more than they have succeeded will be reluctant to attribute their failures to lack of ability. Indeed, it is reasonable to predict that repeated failures will contribute to external attribution and corresponding feelings of powerlessness. By the same token, repeated successes in tasks of moderate or extreme difficulty (rather than tasks too absurdly simple) are most likely to lead to positive self-concepts, feelings of competence, acceptance of personal responsibility for performance, and high achievement drives.

The key phrase undoubtedly is "personal responsibility." To the extent that students accept personal responsibility for their performance they will be emotionally involved, success will enhance their self-concepts, motivational forces will be largely intrinsic rather than extrinsic, and the problems of classroom management (discussed in the next chapter) will become interesting pedagogical problems rather than discipline problems.

Changing Achievement Goals

Goal theory, another emphasis in cognitive explanations of motivation, examines how an individual's goals affect behavior. An achievement goal, says Ames (1992), is a pattern of beliefs and attributions that produces an intention to do or accomplish something. Goal theory is based on two important observations, which have been mentioned earlier in this chapter:

1. Students who believe that the outcomes of their behaviors result from personal effort tend to develop mastery goals—goals that focus on the intrinsic value of the learning. (Recall that Dweck also labeled these "learning goals.") Such students focus on developing skills,

understanding their work, becoming more competent—in short, mastering what they study. Mastery goals are associated with a high need for achievement, with risk taking, and with positive attitudes toward learning (see Fuchs et al, 1997).

2. Students who believe that behavioral outcomes are a function of ability rather than effort develop performance goals. Their focus is on doing better than others, achieving public recognition, and succeeding according to external norms. Learning and understanding are secondary for these students; doing well (performing) is all-important. Performance goals are associated with the avoidance of challenging tasks, use of short-term learning strategies, and negative affect following failure.

These two goal orientations are strongly influenced by whether students perceive classrooms as being oriented toward mastery. And that perception, says Ames (1992), is affected by at least three aspects of the classroom experience: tasks, evaluation, and authority. An analysis of these three factors provides numerous suggestions for teacher behaviors that might enhance student motivation. (Some of these are summarized in Table 11.5.)

1. *Tasks.* "Embedded in tasks," says Ames (1992), "is information that students use to make judgments about their ability, their willingness to apply effortful strategies, and their feelings of satisfaction" (p. 263). There are at least three important motivational dimensions of tasks: variety, challenge, and meaningfulness.

   Variety, notes Blumenfeld (1992), is associated with sustained motivation. And when tasks are defined in terms of specific, short-term goals, students are more likely to decide they can accomplish them with reasonable effort (to see themselves as efficacious). Similarly, tasks that are personally involving are less likely to lead students to compare their

---

TABLE 11.5
Instructional Strategies Designed to Promote a Mastery Orientation

▲ Present students with a variety of tasks with short-term goals that can be accomplished with reasonable effort.

▲ Assign work that is personally involving—hence, less likely to lead to comparisons with other students.

▲ Emphasize competence and mastery in your evaluation procedures.

▲ Avoid comparative evaluations.

▲ Focus on the processes of learning and on comprehension.

▲ Avoid the social comparisons implicit in singling out students for public praise.

▲ Give students meaningful choices regarding important issues like curriculum, methods and pace of studying, and evaluation.

▲ Encourage students to set meaningful, competence-oriented goals.

▲ Reward students for effort and improvements rather than for performance and product.

▲ Emphasize individual progress in evaluations.

---

performance with that of others—and less likely to lead to performance goals.

2. *Evaluation.* One of the surest ways to develop a performance orientation is to use evaluation procedures that emphasize ability and that underline comparisons among students. When the focus in classrooms is on students' products and on correctness and memorization, rather than on the processes of learning and comprehension, students soon become performance oriented. Unfortunately, as MacIver, Reuman, and Main (1995) point out, our traditional evaluation practices are, in fact, based largely on comparing the performance of a given student to that of other students.

   Social comparisons are among the most obvious performance-oriented evaluation procedures. They are evident, says Ames (1992), in our practice of making public the highest and lowest scores, of singling out students' papers and performances, of displaying students' achievements. The effects on those who do not compare favorably can be devastating.

Evaluation practices such as criterion-referenced assessment or portfolios, described in Chapter 13, avoid the most direct forms of social comparison and might contribute significantly to the development of more intrinsically motivated, mastery goals.

3. *Authority*. The extent to which teachers give students meaningful choices is directly related to students' mastery orientation. Research reviewed by Ames (1992) suggests that teachers who provide students with meaningful opportunities for autonomy are more likely to foster mastery orientations. Teachers who are highly controlling and who make all important decisions themselves encourage performance goals. Ames notes that in most contemporary classrooms students have few opportunities to make meaningful decisions regarding curriculum, methods and pace of studying, or assessment.

A Review of the Cognitive View

Why do some learners set challenging but attainable goals for themselves and others not? Why do some persist in the face of difficulty while others don't? How can teachers keep students interested?

Big questions, these, with no short or simple answers. But we have too little space here to be long-winded and no wish to be complex. So what follows is only a little bit of an answer squeezed from the contemporary cognitive view we have just reviewed.

A Cognitive View of the Learner This view insists that the learner is first of all a reflective, thinking being (that is, a cognitive being). In this view, motivation boils down to the individual learner's decisions about goals, how these decisions result from and interact with some of the learner's beliefs, and how the learner's behavior is guided by both beliefs and goals. In a sense, it is as though the learner evaluates the self in terms of wishes, inclinations, and abilities and evaluates goals in terms of likely rewards. And, as we have seen, for some learners, intrinsic rewards (often associated with mastery or learning) are more important than external rewards (often associated with performance or product).

The Importance of Self-Evaluation We asked what is important. The cognitive view suggests that the student's self-evaluation is one important factor. Believing that we are bright and capable—and loved because we are lovable—is fundamentally important to each of us. Most of our lives, Kegan (1982) says, we struggle to be meaningful—to mean something to others. If we

Drawing by Benard Schoenbaum; © 1989
The New Yorker Magazine. Inc.

mean nothing, that is then the measure of our personal worth.

The Role of the Teacher Do teachers affect students' self-evaluations? Clearly, yes. Much of what teachers do—and can do—both directly and indirectly influences students' perceptions of their competence and meaningfulness. But the classroom factors that contribute to these evaluations do not mold them in simple ways. As Marshall and Weinstein (1984) put it, influences are complex and interactive. Often students' self-evaluations are based partly on comparisons with other students. But many factors (in complex interaction) are involved in the final evaluation. For example, in most competitive situations, success increases self-evaluations of ability; failure has the opposite effect. But if children are each given different tasks, there are fewer opportunities for comparison than if all work on identical tasks. In much the same way, whole-class direct-instructional procedures often provide more opportunity for direct comparisons than do small-group approaches such as those used in cooperative learning.

Students' self-evaluations also clearly depend on the outcomes of their behaviors and on the responses of teachers and others. Other things being equal, success generally leads to positive self-evaluations. And teachers' responses to students are typically loaded with information. Gestures, attention, facial expressions, grades, and verbal comments are just a few sources of information that tell the student either "gee, you're pretty dumb, kid" (or worse) or "hey, way to go!"

The Importance of Outcomes Unfortunately, not everyone can do very well. In fact, not everyone is equally competent. But Marshall and Weinstein (1984) state that the outcome of social comparisons need not always be negative for low achievers. If teachers and students alike see competence and intelligence as a matter of

Social comparisons, such as those implicit in the act of singling out the class valedictorian (who also happens to be class president) are a clear form of performance-oriented evaluation. Some argue that social comparisons of this nature can be quite devastating for other close competitors who are not so honored.

accumulating skills and knowledge through effort (Dweck's incremental theory), rather than as a fixed, unchangeable quality (entity theory), low achievers need not suffer from unfavorable comparisons. Teachers who hold these views, claim Marshall and Weinstein, will favor non-competitive learning, flexible grouping, mastery-oriented learning, and comparisons of students' current performance with their own previous performance instead of comparisons with the performance of others.

MAIN POINTS

1. Motivation looks at the "why" of behavior. Among historical explanations of motivation are instinct theory (complex, unlearned patterns of behavior common to an entire species account for behavior); psychological hedonism (people behave to obtain pleasure and avoid pain); and need theories (the urge to satisfy physical and psychological needs drives behavior).

2. Increasing arousal is defined by physiological changes (for example, in respiration and heart rate) accompanied by increasing alertness or wakefulness and ranges from very low (sleep, boredom) to very high (anxiety, panic). Amount, intensity, meaningfulness, unexpectedness, and complexity of stimulation are directly related to the level of arousal. People try to maintain an optimal level of arousal for maximally effective behavior.

3. One responsibility of teachers is to maintain moderate levels of arousal in students. Overly high arousal, sometimes manifested in anxiety, often has a detrimental effect on students' learning and performance. In particular, test anxiety has repeatedly been shown to decrease grades. Very anxious students do better when exposed to instructional methods that are more structured, less demanding of public interaction, and consequently less anxiety arousing.

4. Behavioristic approaches to motivation stress the importance of positive and negative extrinsic reinforcers. One very important reinforcer is praise; the effectiveness of praise depends largely on the student's interpretation of the situation (hence, praise has important cognitive connotations). Praise should be used systematically, deliberately, and intelligently.

5. Humanistic approaches emphasize intrinsic (internal) motives such as those relating to autonomy, competence, and self-actualization. Humanistic educators are especially concerned with the personal development of students and the enhancement of positive self-concepts. Maslow's humanistic theory presents a hierarchical arrangement of need systems, with physiological needs at the lowest level (basic needs) and the need for self-actualization at the highest (metaneeds). R. W. White believes that an intrinsic need to develop competence motivation is an important human motive.

6. Cognitive theories describe humans as active, exploring, evaluating organisms capable of delaying gratification and of explaining the outcomes of their own behaviors (as contrasted with the more passive view of traditional theories).

7. Bandura suggests that ideas of self-efficacy (personal effectiveness) are important for determining which behaviors will be undertaken (children are least likely to attempt activities when they expect failure) and the amount of effort that will be expended

(greater if success is anticipated). Judgments of self-efficacy are affected by enactive influences (successful outcomes increase positive judgments), vicarious influences (comparisons with others), persuasory influences (persuasion by others), and emotive influences (high arousal can increase or decrease judgments of self-efficacy).

8. Weiner's attribution theory says that individuals tend to attribute their successes or failures to internal (ability and effort) or external (difficulty or luck) causes. Some of these imply a high level of responsibility; others don't. Similarly, some causes imply a high degree of personal control; others don't.

9. Mastery-oriented learners try to increase their competence; performance-oriented learners focus on achievement. Dweck suggests that children who subscribe to the entity theory (intelligence is fixed) tend to be oriented toward performance goals. Children who subscribe to the incremental theory (intelligence increases with effort) are more likely to be oriented toward mastery (learning) goals.

10. Students whose need for achievement is strong are typically more internally oriented (have an internal locus of control) and are consequently more likely to accept personal responsibility for the outcomes of their efforts. Achievement orientation can be modified by specific training programs that invite children to take risks, make predictions, modify predictions, establish realistic goals, and assume personal responsibility for the results of their behaviors.

11. Attribution-changing programs attempt to move students in the direction of making more effort attributions—that is, attributing successes and failures to the results of personal effort rather than to causes over which the individual has no control.

12. Most cognitively oriented, motivation-driven classroom interventions attempt to foster the development of mastery rather than performance goals by manipulating factors such as tasks (variety, personal meaningfulness and surmountable challenges foster commitment and persistence); evaluation (social comparisons encourage performance orientations); and authority (opportunities for meaningful autonomy enhance commitment and mastery goals).

Applied Questions

▲ Using library resources, describe some historical approaches to explaining human behavior.

▲ Outline a lesson where the teacher makes deliberate use of the educational implications of arousal theory.

▲ Do you think that excessive use of external rewards might reduce intrinsic motivation? Why or why not?

▲ Illustrate how human needs are hierarchical. What educational implications can you draw from this observation?

▲ List several teacher attitudes and behaviors that are likely to contribute to the development of mastery (learning) oriented students.

Internet Activity

Use InfoTrac College Edition or other World Wide Web sources to research the implications of test anxiety in schools: Write up your findings. (See the inside back cover of this text for suggestions about where to begin.)

Sample search terms: test anxiety

Study Terms

achievement motivation **430**

anxiety **412**

arousal **410**

attribution theory **427**

basic need **418**

cause **405**

competence motivation **421**

critical period **407**

deficiency need **419**

distance receptors **410**

drive **408**

drive reduction **408**

entity theory **429**

external orientation **427**

extrinsic motive **415**

growth need **419**

imprinting **407**

incremental theory **429**

instinct **406**

internal orientation **427**

interest **417**

intrinsic motive **415**

Jonah complex **420**

locus of control **427**

mastery goal **429**

metaneeds **418**

motive **405**

need–drive theory **408**

need **408**

pain/pleasure principle **415**

peak experience **420**

performance goal **429**

physiological need **408**

praise **416**

psychological hedonism **408**

psychological need **408**

reason **405**

reflex **406**

reinforcer **415**

self-efficacy **421**

self-referent thought **423**

sensitive period **407**

sympathetic nervous system **410**

test anxiety **412**

ulterior motive **405**

Suggested Readings

For a summary of just about everything you might want to know about test anxiety and research related to its causes, its effects, and its alleviation (at least up to 1998), see:

Zeidner, M. (1998). *Test anxiety: The state of the art.* New York: Plenum.

For a fascinating account of the effect of high arousal on human behavior, see:

Schultz, D. P. (1964). *Panic behavior.* New York: Random House.

For those interested in theories of human personality, Ewen's book presents a clear and useful introduction. Of particular relevance to this chapter is Part IV, which deals with humanistic and existential psychology and includes a chapter on the theory of Abraham Maslow:

Ewen, R. B. (1998). *An introduction to theories of personality* (5th ed.). Mahwah, NJ: Lawrence Erlbaum.

Cognitive theories of motivation are presented clearly at a sophisticated level in the following book:

Weiner, B. (1992). *Human motivation: Metaphors, theories and research.* Newbury Park, CA: Sage.

The Hamilton and Ghatala book presents practical educational applications of many of the theories discussed in this chapter. Especially relevant here is the ninth chapter, which examines the practical implications of various motivational theories. Bandura's book is an excellent summary of his views on the nature and importance of self-efficacy; the Ames and Ames' collection of articles, and especially the more recent Ames article, look specifically at the application of cognitive motivational concepts to the classroom:

Hamilton, R., & Ghatala, E. (1994). *Learning and instruction*. New York: McGraw-Hill.

Bandura, A. (1997). *Self-efficacy: The exercise of control*. New York: W. H. Freeman.

Ames, R., & Ames, C. (eds.). (1984). *Research on motivation in education (Vol. I): Student motivation*. New York: Academic Press.

Ames, C. (1992). Classrooms: Goals, structures, and student motivation. *Journal of Educational Psychology, 84,* 261–271.

The brown bear (**Ursus arctos**) is still found in small numbers in very limited mountainous areas of western Europe, in Russia, Asia, India, northern China, and North America. It is no longer found in the British Isles (Southern, 1964).

Oh wad some power
   the giftie gie us
To see oursels as
   others see us!
It wad frae monie
   a blunder free us
An' foolish notion.

Robert Burns, *To a Louse*

Classroom Management

PREVIEW

It may not surprise you to know that one of the principal reasons for teachers' unhappiness and premature retirement is discipline problems. This chapter, one of the more practical chapters in this text, outlines a variety of strategies and principles that can be effective in preventing and correcting disruptive behavior. This chapter looks also at the application of behavior modification in the classroom. The single most important point is that here, as in medicine, prevention is far more valuable than correction.

FOCUS QUESTIONS

▲ Why is good classroom management essential for effective teaching?

▲ What are the principal characteristics of each of the following management models:

Roger's humanistic model

Marlow's caring model

Kounin's teacher with-it-ness

Dreikurs' logical consequences

Skinner's behavior modification

Canter's assertive discipline

▲ What are some strategies for preventive classroom management?

One day when I was having trouble concentrating in school, I amused myself by sharpening my pencil as pointed as it would get without breaking the lead. Then I used it to try to make a hole in my rubber eraser, pounding it against the eraser with my ruler. My dad, our teacher, didn't appreciate the distraction and told me to stop—which I did for a while, but then I forgot. Maybe his day wasn't much better than mine because it seems like there weren't all that many warnings before he called me to the front of the class, pulled out the strap from the top right-hand drawer, and whacked me once on each hand.

That straightened me right out for most of the year—especially after the Doré brothers got into a fight during afternoon recess and my dad stood them in front of the whole school, bloody noses and all, each of them already crying, and he strapped them one after the other, and after that we corrected our spelling test from the morning period.

That double strapping actually straightened everybody out for a long time. But there was once, later that year, when my dad kept me in after school and ordered me to scrub the inside walls of the outhouse. It seems that someone had chosen to be offended by a tiny bit of graffiti penciled above the small hole (there was a larger hole, too). For a long time, I was convinced that God does watch

all transgressors and reports directly to their teachers, but later I remembered that the spelling test we had been given that afternoon had contained most of the words found in the graffiti. In those days, I spelled turkey "t-e-r-k-e-e."[1]

That was my last major punishment that year other than the time I had to write "I will not squirt ink on Louise" 150 times. It later occurred to me that this might be a nice title for a popular song.

CLASSROOM MANAGEMENT AND DISCIPLINE

It would be misleading to say that I was a discipline problem in my father's school. Problems imply something requiring a solution. In my dad's school, misbehaviors weren't so much problems as simply occasions that almost automatically called for discipline.

Misbehaviors tended not to persist.

Today's schools are vastly different from my father's school. Still, when researchers looked at the metaphors that pre-service teachers use to describe the roles of students and teachers, they found that the single most salient feature of the classroom was classroom management and control (Fry & Fleeners, 1997). That is, many teachers have reduced their understanding of teacher–class interaction to a complex, control-oriented process. Significantly, however, many beginning teachers don't feel adequately prepared to handle the realities of day-to-day classroom management, report Martin and Baldwin (1996) after interviewing and questioning 107 teachers. They suggest that without proper assistance and support, beginning teachers are far

---

[1] ***PPC:*** As a matter of academic interest, what was the graffiti?
Author: Luc Doré is a bird

And he is a terkee

I don't know if you herd

He is full of peapea.

(Hey, I was only in second grade.)

more likely than experienced teachers to suffer stress and perhaps **teacher burnout**.[2]

Negotiated Order Theory

Teachers have always been very concerned with **discipline** and **classroom management**—as was clear in my father's school. Classroom management is a general term referring to all of the actions that teachers take to organize instruction and classrooms to use time (the teacher's and the learners') effectively and happily, and to maximize learning. Discipline is a more specific term referring to actions that teachers (and sometimes learners) take to prevent or reduce the incidence of misbehavior, or to respond to behavior problems once they occur.

Classroom management and discipline, note Hogelucht and Geist (1997), can be usefully viewed as an example of the application of **negotiated order theory**. That is, teachers and students essentially *negotiate* and communicate to each other regarding the boundaries of acceptable and unacceptable behavior. They negotiate the consequences of nonadherence to these rules, and sometimes the consequences of exemplary behavior as well. Thus, when teachers voice dissatisfaction with events in the classroom, they are in effect voicing disapproval with current classroom order. In much the same way, student misbehavior is often a call for renegotiation of the rules of classroom order.

The challenge for beginning teachers is to find the easiest and most effective ways of negotiating and maintaining classroom order, the most effective ways of managing classrooms. Clearly, both the boundaries of acceptable and unacceptable behavior have changed dramatically over the years—as have the methods teachers use to maintain order and to promote learning and growth in the classroom. In my father's time, strapping was a normal part of most teachers' strategies. At other times and in other places, authorities have advocated highly permissive, nonpunitive techniques. What has remained constant, however, is the importance of classroom management for determining teaching success and happiness.

Importance in Teaching

As Doyle notes, some educators view management and discipline as a prerequisite to instruction—something to "get out of the way so that teaching can occur" (1986, p. 394). Not so. Neither classroom management nor classroom discipline can be taken care of and then put aside so that instruction and learning can take place. Rather, both are centrally involved in the ongoing process of teaching.

---

teacher burnout A general label for a condition marked by a teacher's profound negative reaction to teaching. One possible effect of high stress. Sometimes evidenced by cynicism, unhappiness, chronic absenteeism, and perhaps a decision to change careers.

discipline The control aspects of teaching. Refers to actions that teachers take to minimize behavior problems and their responses to problems when they do occur.

classroom management A comprehensive term for a variety of teacher actions designed to facilitate teaching and learning in the classroom. Classroom management includes disciplinary actions, daily routines, seating arrangements, and the scheduling of lessons.

---

[2] *PPC:* Many of my students get pretty nervous and scared when they read something like this. Is the bear going to tell students how to avoid burnout?

Author: Yes. Most of this chaper, says the bear, quite seriously, is full of good advice for preventing fires so that there will be no burnout. Also, scattered here and there through the chapter are wonderful, metaphoric fire extinguishers to be used to prevent a total burnout if a fire actually does start.

---

negotiated order theory A sociological theory which maintains that the smooth functioning of social groups depends on implicit or explicit agreement among members of the group with regard to the boundaries of acceptable behavior and the consequences of going beyond these boundaries. Typically, much of this agreement is negotiated informally but eventually finds its way into the rules or laws that govern the group.

Significantly, the most successful teachers appear to be those who deliberately use classroom management strategies—those who have a management plan (Jack et al., 1996). And it's probably accurate, says Bear (1998), that the ultimate goal of all classroom management plans and disciplinary strategies is to develop **self-discipline** among learners; the short-term goal is to maintain the sorts of conditions in the classroom that are most conducive to learning.

What is the best approach to classroom management? Unfortunately, there is no simple answer—no recipe that, when carried out, will always prevent or eliminate behavior problems and also lead to a high level of learning and, ultimately, to an admirable level of self-discipline in all learners. But, says Bear (1998), there is strong evidence that the most effective teachers use three different types of strategies: First are a variety of classroom management strategies designed to maintain a positive classroom climate that are highly effective in avoiding behavior problems; second are some specific operant learning strategies that are useful for short-term management of behavior problems; third are problem-solving, conflict resolution strategies geared toward achieving the long-term goal of self-discipline.

Much of the remainder of this chapter is a systematic summary and evaluation of classroom management strategies that fit within these three general groupings.

Control and Permissiveness in Today's Classrooms

First, to put the subject of this chapter into perspective we look briefly at the environment in which teaching, learning, and classroom management take place.

---

self-discipline The control of one's self. Implies adherence to personal standards of conduct rather than blind conformity to externally imposed rules.

Diversity in the Classroom Just as the "average student" is an abstraction that does not exist in the real world, there is no "average class." Every class is unique. Each has its special blend of personalities that interact with one another, and with the personality and style of the teacher, to create its own dynamic ecology—that is, its own ever-changing environment. Some classrooms are filled with obedient and compliant children; others are riddled with violence. Each day, note McCaslin and Good (1992), some 135,000 children in the United States bring guns to school! Thousands of others have been suspended or are on detention; thousands more are in institutions for juvenile offenders.

Some classes are a complex mix of different ethnic groups, abilities, language skills, and varying interests; others are a homogeneous collection of majority-group children. Some include only children of highly similar abilities and interests; others are inclusive classes, characterized by an unpredictable mix of special needs.

Commonality in the Classroom Yet, says Doyle (1979), certain characteristics are descriptive of most classes. These need to be taken into account in the business of teaching students and managing classes. Specifically, claims Doyle, the events that occur in classes are:

multidimensional: They can include a variety of individuals participating in many different activities and working toward separate goals.

simultaneous: Seldom is only one thing happening at a time. Even when teachers are engaged in direct, whole-class instruction, they can recognize different degrees of attentiveness among individual students and different behaviors (or misbehaviors) that may require them to interrupt the instructional process. As teachers phrase questions, they must also make decisions about who will answer, assess the pace of the lesson relative to time constraints, and constantly monitor individual students for signs of inattention or potentially disruptive behaviors.

immediate: Many of the events that occur simultaneously in the classroom require a teacher's immediate response. Decisions must be made and implemented rapidly if the flow of classroom activity is to remain smooth and purposeful.

unpredictable: Given the immediacy, the multidimensionality, and the simultaneity of classroom events, their course at any given moment is highly unpredictable.

To manage an environment as complex and unpredictable as a classroom—and one that demands a continuous, rapid sequence of immediate decisions—requires a special set of managerial skills. Unfortunately, these managerial skills are not simple recipes that can be memorized and applied as needed. Rather, they are a complex set of skills whose effective use depends to a great extent on the personal philosophies and teaching styles of teachers, on their knowledge and understanding of pedagogical principles, and on the composition of their classes. It is not a simple task.

But it is not a completely overwhelming task either—although it might seem that way to the beginning teacher. Expert teachers do not need to consciously analyze all the elements present simultaneously in the classroom; they don't need to deliberately and sequentially monitor and appraise the immediate activities of each student, responding when necessary and all the while maintaining a wonderful pedagogical flow, never failing to recognize and capitalize on those brief, unpredictable opportunities that recent jargon labels "teachable moments." Expert teachers, Kagan (1988) tells us, do all these things, many of them unconsciously. Such teachers develop sequences of routines and strategies that become almost automatic.

Can the classroom management skills and strategies used by expert teachers be learned? In a word, yes.

New Methods for New Philosophies? But, explains Brophy (1998), many of the classroom management principles still current in education were developed during the 1970s and '80s (or even earlier). And during much of that time, classrooms were largely teacher-centered. In these classrooms, teachers were given most of the responsibility for controlling student activity—that is, controlling the behavior of their students and directing their learning.

But now, although direct instructional techniques are still an integral part of most classrooms, student-centered constructivist classrooms give students far more responsibility for learning and also for managing their own behavior. Are the time-tested classroom management strategies still valid? Yes, says Brophy (1998), although some of the details of their implementation may occasionally need to be changed to accommodate the greater autonomy of today's students.

The Tension between Control and Permissiveness Most parents and teachers like to think of themselves as liberal and permissive rather than conservative and restrictive. Most would choose to be democratic rather than autocratic. And most describe their classrooms as student-centered rather than teacher-centered.

Is control necessary in the student-centered classroom? Is it ethical? Does it violate our commitment to value the autonomy, the self-direction, of each child?

There are no simple answers. If there were, there would be little controversy, and behaviorists and humanists would have much less disagreement.

Consider, first, that control of children's behavior is an essential responsibility of parenting. Part of a successful socialization process requires that children be prevented from engaging in behaviors that might be injurious to themselves or to others. Thus, parents do not permit their children to play with their dinner as it is cooking on the stove, to insert knives in electrical outlets, to jump off ladders, or to discharge firearms in the garage. Parenting also teaches a variety of socially appropriate behaviors, values and morals—"shoulds" and "should nots." It is less by accident than by virtue of parental control that children learn not to deface walls, steal other people's property, or kill the neighbor's dog. In short, certain standards of behavior are learned at least partly as a function of parental control. Whether such control involves reinforcement, punishment, models, reasoning, or a combination of these and other strategies cannot hide the fact that control is being exercised.

Control in the Classroom The classroom situation has historically been viewed as being very similar to that of parenting. Legally, teachers have been considered to be acting **in loco parentis**—in the place of parents. And, to some extent, they are still urged to act in all ways as might a wise, judicious, and loving parent. However, the legal concept of *loco parentis* has weakened considerably, explain Hoover and Kindsvatter (1997). Now, if the courts are called upon, they typically grant students much the same basic rights and freedoms as adults have—namely rights relating to freedom (to act and to speak without fear of retribution); equality (a fair distribution of opportunities, benefits, and requirements); and justice (fair treatment). Partly because of this, classroom management advice now frequently contains admonishments such as "do it by the book," "get it in writing," "always keep a copy," "never hit a student" and so on (see Sesno, 1998, for an explanation of these and 93 other one-line pieces of advice).

This, of course, doesn't imply that students must be allowed to do as they please for fear their rights and freedoms might be violated. In fact, control of student behavior may be absolutely necessary in some situations—as, for example, when Johnny insists on repeatedly setting fire to the library.[3] Teachers, by virtue of their position and by virtue of their duties, have a responsibility to exercise control over student behavior. Indeed, it is reasonable to insist that the exercise of control is one of the teacher's most important duties because, as Evertson and Harris (1992) point out, without classroom control, instruction may be totally ineffective. However, we are not speaking here of the fear-enforced control that was characteristic of some of yesterday's schools. Control can be achieved, or at least facilitated, in a variety of gentle ways, and some of these can be learned. Love, empathy, warmth, genuineness, and honesty can go a long way toward ensuring a classroom climate conducive to learning and development. In spite of these highly desirable qualities, however, discipline problems are common in classrooms. That teachers should judiciously administer rewards and punishment in an effort to maintain an effective educational environment does not mean that they care less for their students. Indeed, it might well indicate that they care more.

---

in loco parentis A Latin expression meaning, literally, "in the place of parents." Teachers are said to have rights and responsibilities *in loco parentis* to the extent that society charges them with the care and education of children.

[3] **PPC:** It might be worth noting that Johnny is not the only one who feels compelled to burn books. Here, for example, a group of parents recently decided that a whole raft of books used in high school English courses should be banned. And they actually had a bonfire in front of the school board offices.

Author: Fear of fire is one reason why the bear became so insistently politically correct in the last edition. But the choirboy thing didn't sit well on his defiant shoulders.

Organizing Models of Classroom Management

The advice that various experts give teachers about how to manage their classrooms and discipline their students varies enormously—which is not always very reassuring, especially for beginning teachers. Much of this variation stems from fundamentally different philosophical orientations. That is, these experts often have very different notions about what the causes of misbehavior are and very different notions about what sort of intervention is most effective and most appropriate.

At one extreme are management models that recommend the least amount of intervention possible: for example, open schools and humanistic approaches like that of Carl Rogers. At the other extreme are the more restrictive behavior modification models that make extensive use of systematic rewards and punishments. And in between are various models that try to balance permissiveness with restrictiveness and offer a variety of suggestions about how this might be accomplished.

Proponents of all of these approaches are unanimous in their belief that in the classroom, as in medicine, prevention should be valued more highly than correction. And it is reassuring, notes S. Black (1994b), that research is paying increasing attention to **preventive strategies**—the methods teachers use to prevent the occurrence of discipline problems. Perhaps

---

preventive strategy An instructional strategy designed to prevent discipline problems. Preventive strategies are an intrinsic part of good classroom management.

Models of classroom management range from highly permissive, where the teacher tries to intervene as little as possible, to highly directive, where the teacher assumes primary responsibility for establishing and enforcing rules of conduct. But even where there are clear rules, as in this classroom, classroom management can still be quite democratic and humanistic.

the most important (though not entirely surprising) finding of this research is that the degree of order in a classroom depends far less on the frequency and insistence with which the teacher acts to maintain or restore order than on the nature of ongoing classroom activity. As Black points out, teachers who are most effective at managing classrooms are those who design engaging and motivating lessons, who communicate goals and expectations clearly to their students, and who use unobtrusive and subtle techniques for maintaining students' attention and on-task behavior. These teachers, claims Black (1994b), can "throw away the hickory stick."

The second most important finding of this research concerns the timing of a teacher's interventions. The most successful classroom managers are teachers who seem to anticipate most accurately when misbehaviors are likely to occur and intervene early to prevent them. Also, the most effective interventions are subtle, brief, and often almost private, and as a result they do not interfere with ongoing classroom activities.

Preventive strategies are part of effective classroom management. That is, they depend on the arrangement of classroom activities to facilitate teaching and learning. There is a great deal of advice about the best ways of doing this, and much of it is based on the collective experience of successful teachers and on the systematic observations of teachers in their classrooms. For whatever it's worth, this chapter presents a distillation of such advice. Bear in mind, however, that your personality is one of the most important factors in the classroom situation. Students find reasons to like or to dislike teachers in the combination of elusive and abstract qualities that define personality. Unfortunately, though, desirable personality characteristics cannot easily be acquired if you don't already have them— nor can less desirable ones be simply thrown away like a worn-out pair of jeans. Not every-

body should be a teacher. For example, if you don't really care for children and they don't like you very much either, please . . .[4]

The remainder of this chapter describes several of the most representative classroom management and discipline models, loosely classified in terms of their principal orientation and the degree of permissiveness and restrictiveness that they advocate. Table 12.1 summarizes these and also previews much of what follows.

HUMANISTIC MODELS OF CLASSROOM MANAGEMENT

Humanistic models of classroom management reflect a strong emphasis on the uniqueness and dignity of every individual student. These are highly learner- rather than teacher-centered. They recommend a minimal amount of classroom intervention, active student participation, the development of a supportive environment, and a strong emphasis on self-development. Important models of humanistic classroom management include those of Carl Rogers and Michael Marland.

Freedom to Learn: Carl Rogers

The clear goal of humanistic teachers, claims Carl Rogers (Rogers & Freiberg, 1994), is to develop self-discipline in students. Broadly defined, self-discipline is "knowledge about oneself and the actions needed to grow and develop as a person" (p. 221). That, says Rogers, is the goal of most teachers, but not all take the right path.

And what is the right path? Simply put, it is among the most nondirective of classroom man-

---

[4] **PPC:** Perhaps the author should finish the sentence. Those who should take it to heart the most probably won't bother finishing it.
Author: Those of you who didn't bother finishing this sentence, well . . .

TABLE 12.1
Models of Classroom Management

	INSTRUCTIONAL PHILOSOPHY	THEORETICAL UNDERPINNING	BELIEFS ABOUT CAUSES OF MISBEHAVIOR	PRINCIPAL RECOMMENDATIONS	ADVOCATES
Most permissive— least directive	Highly learner-centered (constructivist)	Humanistic	Poor self-concept	Minimal intervention; teacher should provide supportive environment, encourage self-development	Carl Rogers Michael Marland
	Relatively learner-centered (high student participation but teacher direction)	Democratic	Inappropriate goals; faulty understanding of consequences; illogical assumptions and conclusions	Teacher should be democratic rather than autocratic; set reasonable limits; use techniques of reasoning and logic to identify goals; point out logical consequences of behaviors; use class meetings for rule setting and discussion	Jacob Kounin Rudolf Dreikurs
Least permissive— most directive	Highly teacher-centered; direct instruction	Behavioristic	Misbehaviors are learned; failure to learn appropriate alternative behaviors	Behavior modification techniques such as reinforcement, modeling, punishment	B. F. Skinner Lee Canter

agement models. Rogers, like Maslow, believed that all students have a basic desire to grow, to develop, to *become*. Ideally, the role of parents and teachers is to provide the sort of supportive environment that facilitates and fosters growth—an environment that accepts children unconditionally, values them for who they are, and fosters their growth. In this model, the teacher is a facilitator rather than a director, and students are active and fundamentally important participants in the teaching/learning process. A scenario based on Rogers' description of such a classroom is summarized in the case entitled "So Where's the Teacher?"

Unfortunately, Rogers does not provide a list of specific classroom management techniques that teachers can learn and apply to their classrooms. Doing so would, in a sense, violate his belief in the autonomy of students. This does not mean that he advocates the total permissiveness that sometimes characterized the open classrooms that were briefly popular in the early 1970s (see Chapter 7). As we saw, Rogers argues that students should be helped to become self-disciplined. And what is most important for helping students to grow and become self-disciplined is the atmosphere of trust, warmth, and acceptance that teachers foster.

The Rogerian school is clearly a student-centered school. In this school, the role of the teacher is nondirective or, (to use Rogers' term) facilitative, and students are self-motivated and require a minimum of direction. Common instructional techniques include inquiry approaches, group projects, and self-assessment. At the other extreme, are teacher-centered

So Where's the Teacher?

THE SITUATION: A day in Ms. Wilcox's classroom

Early one morning, Ms. Wilcox, history teacher, phones in to say she's sick and won't be able to come to school. The principal's wife answers the phone but forgets to pass on the message.

In her class, Ms. Wilcox has set up a program called Consistency Management. This program gives students responsibility for the conditions that they have decided are necessary for the classroom to work for them. These conditions are expressed in a series of jobs for which different students volunteer. When necessary, Ms. Wilcox has helped students to learn these jobs, which rotate to different students every three weeks.

Now that Ms. Wilcox is sick, various students in each class simply assume their normal responsibilities. Some serve as student facilitators, essentially teaching lessons, presenting projects, leading discussion groups, sending in attendance slips, and doing other routine and not-so-routine things.

During the final period of the day, someone in the office needs to have Ms. Wilcox sign a form. But they can't find her anywhere. So self-disciplined are her students that her absence has gone absolutely unnoticed all day long.

Source: Based on Rogers & Freiberg (1994).

schools; here teachers are highly directive, and students are controlled through external rewards and punishments. Common instructional techniques in teacher-centered schools include lecturing, questioning, drill and repetition, and teacher demonstrations.

Between these two extremes, according to Rogers and Freiberg (1994), are schools where the teacher's role is somewhere between facilitative and directive. Common instructional techniques in such schools include cooperative learning approaches and guided discovery. Figure 12.1 summarizes these distinctions.

Rogers is not highly prescriptive with respect to the specifics of what teachers should and should not do to manage their classrooms, but

TEACHER-CENTERED	
TEACHER'S ROLE	**INSTRUCTIONAL TECHNIQUES**
Highly directive	lecturing
Teacher directs student behavior and controls through external rewards and punishments	questioning
	drill and practice
	demonstration
Semidirective/semifacilitative	discussion
	cooperative groups
Teacher and students cooperate in designing the classroom and in establishing its important activities	guided discovery
	contracts
	role playing
Nondirective/facilitative	projects
	inquiry
Teacher encourages student autonomy and self-discipline	self-assessment
STUDENT-CENTERED	

Source: Based on C. R. Rogers and H. J. Freiberg, *Freedom to Learn* (4th ed.), 1994. New York: Merrill. Reprinted by permission of Prentice-Hall.

FIGURE 12.1 Teacher-centered versus student-centered discipline and learning

some instructional recommendations are implicit in his general description of the techniques and language of facilitative, nondirective teaching. Specifically, nondirective teachers:

are reflective. They reflect important aspects of learners' behavior and conversation to encourage them to think about their own thoughts. (For example, the teacher says, "What I sense you're saying is . . .")

provide support for learners. Communicate unconditional regard and support.

encourage self-assessment. For example, "How do you feel about your acting?"

develop responsibility in students. "What do you think you should do?"

foster self-actualization. Provide opportunities for learning and growth. Encourage the development of special talents.

Caring for Children: Michael Marland

Michael Marland (1975) also describes a variety of classroom management strategies and recommendations that are clearly humanistic; however, his are more specific than those suggested by Rogers and can be summarized in terms of five distinct recommendations.

1. Caring for Children Most important, says Marland, is to truly care for children. More than that, teachers must let children know that they are cared for—for example, by learning their names and getting to know as much as possible about each one.

2. Setting Rules Classroom management and discipline would be much simpler if we could just give teachers a clear and simple list of **rules** (prescriptions typically relating to what behavior is not permitted) and **routines** (customary ways of

doing things) that should govern all students in all classrooms—complete with prescribed consequences for violation of, or adherence to, these rules and routines.

But it's not quite so simple. Rules for student conduct are not and should not be fixed and absolute, says Marland. Instead, they must be relative to the teacher, to the situation, and to students. Still, research suggests some generally valid observations. For example, effective classroom management depends to a large extent on the successful establishment of rules and routines early in the school year (Doyle, 1986). However, because rules and routines are highly relative to situations, they are not usually established formally. That is, teachers seldom give students a list rules. Instead, students tend to learn most rules indirectly, often when infractions of rules occur. Many rules are never made explicit but are simply implied by the teacher's interventions.

In contrast, many routines are taught explicitly and directly. Particularly in the elementary grades, such routines are indispensable to the smooth operation of the class and govern the activities of both teachers and students. Routines specify where books and supplies are to be kept, how questions are to be asked and answered, how games are to be played, where reading circles are to be placed, and dozens of other details of classroom activity. The establishment of such routines is an important aspect of classroom management, and it provides a context for greatly facilitating learning.

Like rules, routines need to be established early in the school year. As Doyle (1986) observes, the most successful classroom managers are those

---

rule A prescribed method or procedure, often relating to behavioral conduct. For example, "smoking is not permitted on school property." Violation of rules often implies negative consequences.

routine A habitual or customary way of doing things. For example, selected students always distribute books at the beginning of the reading lesson.

who, in a sense, hover over activities at the beginning of the year, guiding and directing students until procedures have become routine and the routines have been learned and accepted by all students. Although rules and routines need to be predictable and consistent, they do not necessarily have to be enforced inflexibly. Even in the remarkably teacher-directed, isolated, one-room school that I attended, the "no talking" and "no leaving your desk without permission" rules could occasionally be bent and sometimes even broken.

I remember this happening one day when a bear ambled across the schoolyard and the teacher (my father) allowed the entire class to crowd up against the windows and watch. Later that day, he delivered a marvelous lesson on how bears socialize in the woods beyond the river, how they den up in the winter to dream of wild blueberries, and what their cubs look like when they are first born.

For days after that, I kept looking out the window, hoping to see a bear. Even now, years later, when I'm bored and tired I sometimes catch myself looking for a bear through my window. . . .

But there are few places for bears here.

Giving Legitimate Praise Praise, claims Marland (1975), is one of the most powerful of the teacher's tools. Teachers need to arrange situations so that they can make frequent but legitimate use of praise. However, they must be careful to observe two simple guidelines concerning the use of praise and criticism:

1. Praise, given its effect on self-esteem and self-concept, should be public. On occasion, it should be communicated to parents and other interested adults as well.

2. Criticism, in contrast, also because of its effects on self-esteem and self-concept, should be given privately.

Also, both praise and criticism should be specific rather than general. As we saw in Chapter 11, research clearly demonstrates that praise and punishment not contingent on behavior or not clearly related to a specific behavior are much less likely to be effective. Thus, Marland (1975) suggests that students should not be admonished in general terms such as "behave yourself" or "be good." Instead, students should be directed to engage in a specific behavior and given a reason for that behavior. For example, the teacher might say, "please put down your water pistol and your hunting knife because you are disturbing the class." Presumably, the rule relating to the inadvisability of disturbing the class has already been explained and justified and the penalties for repeated infraction of that rule has been made explicit.

Using Humor The effectiveness of humor is often overlooked by teachers who do not consider themselves spontaneously humorous. And teacher training programs have not gone out of their way to encourage prospective teachers to learn how to make others laugh or, perhaps most important, how to laugh at themselves. Potentially explosive confrontations can often be avoided by turning aside an implied student challenge with a skillful and humorous parry.

Shaping the Learning Environment True to his humanistic orientation, Marland (1975) suggests that a personalized classroom climate is most conducive to the avoidance of management problems and to a high degree of student involvement and learning. For example, there is something impersonal and cold about the traditional, dominating position of the teacher's desk at the front and center of the class. Of course, certain definite advantages are inherent in this traditional placement; there must be a focal point for students' attention, and it is consider-

A City Class

THE SITUATION: Mrs. Fitzsimmons, a good teacher, as recollected by George, teacher-in-training

In third grade, Mrs. Fitzsimmons designed a "city" in which my fellow students and I could actively take part. Every two weeks we elected a mayor, who was given privileges such as opening the "city gate" so the students could come into the classroom. Along the outside edges of the classroom we set up stores, restaurants, offices, and a zoo with large cardboard boxes, assigning students to each vocation. The currency in "our city" was silver-painted bottle caps with numbers; merchandise in the store was brought from home. If we behaved well all day and our lessons were completed, we were given time to transact in "our city," which was a learning experience in itself. By rewarding good behavior there was peer pressure to pay attention. As we got older, extra-credit assignments were given to those who had completed their work and could be a distraction in the classroom.

ably easier for students to look to the front to see their teacher than it is for them to look to the rear. My 11th-grade teacher moved her desk to the back of the room—not because she was experimenting with ways to personalize the classroom environment but because she could more easily watch those among us who had already dedicated our lives to mischief. We suspected as well that she had become tired of being bombarded with our crude, elastic-propelled spitballs.

Marland's advice that the learning environment be personalized goes beyond a search for a more personal arrangement of desks. It includes, as well, advice relating to decorative touches that are often more visible in the early grades rather than the later ones (posters, charts, wall hangings, student art and writing). And his advice also includes the general notion that discipline problems will be minimized in warm, personal environments where all students are accepted as capable.

The case entitled "A City Class" is one example of a personally meaningful classroom environment, which also involves the use of some reinforcement principles for classroom management and learning.

Strengths and Weaknesses of Humanistic Models

The major strength, and the major appeal, of humanistic models of classroom management is their attention to the uniqueness and worth of the individual. Their emphasis on the development of personal responsibility, the importance of the teacher's attitudes toward children, and the development of a climate of trust and love in the classroom are also among their strengths. In one study, 42 experienced teachers were exposed to a humanistic program designed, among other things, to improve classroom management skills. Among the results of this program were a significant reduction in the amount of stress reported by teachers, a more humanistic orientation toward classroom management, and an increase in feelings of personal power and responsibility (Hall, Hall, & Abaci, 1997).

The principal weakness of these management models from the beginning teacher's point of view is that they don't present enough specific recommendations for teacher behaviors that might be used to correct discipline problems. Although Marland's theory relating to setting rules and using praise and humor offers many very useful suggestions, in general, these models are more useful for preventing discipline problems than for correcting them.

DEMOCRATIC MODELS OF CLASSROOM MANAGEMENT

Like humanistic approaches to classroom management, democratic models respect the individuality and the rights of learners and emphasize the importance of their voices. Students are thus given opportunities to participate in important classroom management decisions. As a result, democratic models are relatively learner-centered. At the same time, however, the models typically advocate a greater degree of teacher direction. Teachers are expected to set reasonable limits for student conduct, to use reason and logic to identify rules and goals, and to determine appropriate consequences for infractions of rules. Models proposed by Kounin and Dreikurs are important examples of democratic classroom management.

Teacher With-it-ness and Desists: Jacob Kounin

Kounin (1970) argues that what successful teachers do to prevent misbehavior is probably more important than whatever they might do to handle misbehavior once it has occurred. Following a detailed analysis of teachers' behavior in actual classrooms, he describes a handful of specific behaviors that appear to be closely related to successful classroom management, and he identifies several teacher behaviors that are more likely to lead to student misbehaviors.

With-it-ness The most successful teachers, says Kounin (1970), seem to be more aware than less successful teachers of what is going on in their classrooms, who is responsible for infractions of rules, and when intervention is necessary. These teachers are more *with it*. **With-it-ness** is important for maintaining order in the classroom. Teachers who are with-it know what is going on and are more likely to be respected by their students.

An important part of being with-it, explains Kounin (1970), involves the successful use of **desists**—when teachers instruct learners to stop engaging in an off-task behavior. Teachers who are most with-it are those whose "desists" are on target and on time (neither too early nor too late). Teachers who are less with-it tend to instruct the wrong students to desist, or else they tend to deliver their desist requests either after an off-task behavior has been going on for some time or too far ahead of its occurrence.

Effective desists share several other important characteristics, says Kounin. These are summarized in Table 12.2.

The Ripple Effect Highly effective teachers seem to be more aware of what Kounin calls the **ripple effect**—the tendency of the effects of a teacher's behavior to spread to other students to whom the behavior is not directed. For example, a teacher's desists directed toward me ("Stop eating your pencil, Guy, or I'll just have to strap you. Again.") always seemed to ripple over and work on Luc Doré, who would immediately stop doing whatever he had been doing. He feared the strap even more than I did.

---

with-it-ness Kounin's expression for a quality of teacher behavior manifested in the teacher's awareness of all the important things happening in a classroom. Teachers who are with-it make more effective use of desists.

desist To stop, to refrain from. In education, desists are teacher behaviors intended to make a student stop (desist from) some ongoing or impending misbehavior. Desists can take the form of threats, simple requests, orders, pleas, and so on.

ripple effect Kounin's term for the tendency of the effects of teacher desists to spread to students other than those to whom they were directed.

TABLE 12.2
Characteristics of Effective Desists

The most effective desists (instructions to stop engaging in off-task behavior):

1. Clearly provide enough information for the student to understand specifically what is required. (For example, the desist, "quit that!" is not nearly as clear as "Edward, stop writing on the window.")

2. Suggest an alternative, on-task behavior rather than simply requesting cessation of the off-task behavior. (For example, the teacher continues "please return to your seat, Edward.")

3. Praise on-task behavior while ignoring concurrent off-task activities. (For example, again directed at Edward: "Edward, could you write those words in your notebook as neatly as you did yesterday? You have such a nice notebook.")

4. Provide descriptions of desirable behaviors or of relevant classroom rules. ("Hey, Edward, the caretaker gets very upset when someone writes on the window because he has to clean them.")

5. Provide timely desists (before the misbehavior spreads or intensifies).

6. Provide desists that are on target (directed toward the principal wrongdoer).

After Kounin, 1970.

The ripple effect seems to apply not only to punishment but to the more positive aspects of learning as well. For example, Clarke and Stephens (1996) report a study where a new assessment procedure in mathematics in one grade had a marked effect on how teachers taught mathematics in earlier grades and also on how students learned. In this case, the effect had "rippled" to both teachers and students.

Overlapping Classrooms, as we noted earlier, are characterized by multiple sequences of events occurring simultaneously. Successful teachers, says Kounin, are able to deal with several matters occurring at one time—a situation termed **overlapping**. Overlapping occurs in two different kinds of situations: when a desist is required in the course of a lesson or when something intrudes on the flow of the lesson. Both situations are illustrated in the case entitled "In the Counting House." The bathroom request is a

mild intrusion but one that would have been disruptive had Kightly interrupted himself to say, "Yes, okay, you can go to the bathroom, Sam." And the interception of the Evelyn West note is a nondisruptive desist—again, a situation that would have been clearly disruptive had Kightly stopped in mid-sentence and said, "Evelyn West! Would you like to read that note out loud to the class?" The guiding principle when dealing with overlapping, notes Kounin (1970), is that the ongoing flow of classroom activities should be interrupted as little as possible.

Smoothness and Momentum Successful teachers keep the pace of classroom activity flowing smoothly. This means that the teacher must be able to deal with overlapping and also that transitions between classroom activities occur smoothly. Kounin reports that a normal school day contains an average of more than 33 major changes in learning activities (not including nonacademic transitions such as going to recess or lunch). These include transitions from one subject to another and transitions from one major activity to another within lessons (say, from listening to reading, from reading to writing, from individual work to group activity).

---

overlapping Kounin's term for the simultaneous occurrence of two or more events in the classroom, each requiring the teacher's attention. Good class managers can handle overlapping events without disrupting the flow of classroom activities.

In the Counting House

THE PLACE: Walnut Creek Elementary

THE SETTING: Dennis Kightly's sixth-grade class

THE SITUATION: Mr. Kightly is reading a passage from Charles Dickens' *A Christmas Carol*

"... At length the hour of shutting up the counting-house arrived. With an ill-will Scrooge dismounted from his stool, and tacitly admitted the fact to the expectant clerk in the Tank, who instantly snuffed his candle out, and put on his hat.

"'You'll want all day to-morrow, I suppose?' said Scrooge...."
While the very with-it Mr. Kightly is reading, he notices that Sam Taylor, who today has a touch of the galloping something, has raised his hand tentatively in the beginning of the signal that means, "Sorry but I gotta go quick." At the same time, he sees that Evelyn West has just completed a note and is reaching to pass it to her cousin, Mary West.

"'If quite convenient, sir...'"
Mr. Kightly continues, at the same time nodding almost imperceptibly to Sam, who immediately lurches, bent over, from his desk.

"'It's not convenient,' said Scrooge, 'and it's not fair. If I was to stop half-a-crown...'"
By now Mr. Kightly has reached Evelyn's desk. He intercepts the message in mid-air, returns to his desk, and drops it in the wastebasket without missing a beat.

"'... for it, you'd think yourself ill-used...'"

Reading from Charles Dickens, *A Christmas Carol* 1843/1986, p. 23.

Good teachers, says Kounin, provide smooth transitions that maintain the momentum of classroom activities. In fact, reports Kounin, **jerky transitions** and lesson interruptions are among the principal causes of students' inattentiveness, restlessness, and misbehavior. Kounin describes several major causes of lesson slowdown or interruption, or jerky transitions. These are summarized in Table 12.3.

Maintaining Focus The most important factor for determining classroom order is not the frequency or strength of teachers' interventions as much as the nature of ongoing classroom activity.

There are a large variety of classroom activities. These include seat work, student presentations, small group activities, discussions, recitations, demonstrations, lectures, giving instructions, tutoring, and so on. In elementary school, an activity typically lasts between 10 and 20 minutes; in the higher grades, activities often last somewhat longer. Between activities are transitions, also sometimes considered a type of activity.

After an extensive study of student involvement and classroom activity, Gump (1969) found that small-group activities led by the teacher brought about the greatest involvement. In contrast, student presentations elicited the least student involvement—at least on the part of nonpresenters. Subsequently, several researchers have reported that involvement is least when students are doing seat work and greatest when teachers are actively leading the class (see, for example, Burns, 1984; Ross, 1984). Accordingly, disruptions and misbehaviors are most likely to occur during seat work, during student presentations, and during transitions.

---

jerky transition Kounin's expression for a disruptive and abrupt change in learning activities in the classroom.

TABLE 12.3
Types and Examples of Jerky Classroom Transitions

JERKY TRANSITION LABEL	EXPLANATION	EXAMPLE
Stimulus-boundedness	The teacher's attention is interrupted by an extraneous stimulus.	Mr. Kightly stops his reading when he sees Evelyn West writing her note. "That reminds me," he says, "I want each of you to write a note to your parents about . . ."
Thrusts	The teacher interrupts students' activities without prior signal and without consideration for their readiness.	"Make sure you put your names on your papers," says Mr. Kightly, while the students are in the process of finishing their tests.
Dangles	The teacher interrupts an ongoing activity and then returns to it again.	"Hey, put your pencils down for a minute, I want to read you this bulletin from the office. You can finish your tests later."
Truncations	The teacher does not return to the original activity after being interrupted.	"You can finish the tests after recess. I'm going to read you some more of *A Christmas Carol* first."
Flip-flops	The teacher makes a transition from one activity to a second and then flip-flops back to the first activity, as though he has changed his mind.	"*A Christmas Carol* was shorter than I thought. Okay, you can finish your tests now."
Overdwelling	The teacher spends far more time than necessary on some aspect of a lesson or perhaps with some aspect of a student's behavior (or, more often, misbehavior), causing lesson slowdown.	"Well, we haven't finished the Christmas unit like we were supposed to, so we'll continue in January."
Fragmentation	The teacher breaks down an activity (or a group of students) so that individuals are required to wait unnecessarily, resulting in a lesson slowdown.	"I want you to take your turns; only one student at a time at the whiteboard, the rest of you wait. Now it's your turn, Bobby."

Kounin (1970) describes three ways successful teachers attempt to maintain students' focus on ongoing activities:

1. Develop ways of making each student accountable—usually by having each individual in the class demonstrate a product, competence, or understanding: Other ways of making students accountable are to require that they answer questions in unison and to ask that they engage in a meaningful activity (like taking notes or making specific observations) while another student is making a presentation.

2. Use *group-alerting cues*, which are signals designed to maintain attention or alertness: Asking questions at random and keeping children in suspense about who will be called on next are common group-alerting cues. Interspersing questions that require a single individual to answer with questions that require a group answer is another.

3. Alter the format of classroom activities to maintain focus and prevent boredom: Lesson formats that require only one student to perform at a time (as with reading, for example)

often lead to inattentiveness on the part of other students. One lesson format to counteract this requires other students to perform a related task while one student is reading (for example, answer a question, think of a question, listen for an answer).

Logical Consequences: Rudolf Dreikurs

Dreikurs & Grey (1968) and Dreikers, Gunwald, and Pepper (1982) describe a well-known, though sometimes complex, democratic model of classroom management. Their model is closely based on the work of Alfred Adler, a personality theorist.

Goals: Adler's Theory Among other things, Adler believed that all human behavior is clearly motivated by the individual's desire to reach certain goals. Hence, to understand the behavior of students, it's important to know what these goals are, how children are likely to interpret them, and what behaviors are most likely to lead to the fulfillment of these goals.

There are four principal classes of goals that drive a child's behavior, says Adler: These are manifested in the child's need for gaining attention, exercising power, obtaining revenge, and appearing inadequate.

These goals, explains Adler, are hierarchical. That is, children (or students) first do things designed to gain attention. If that fails, they may try to obtain power, perhaps asserting themselves and becoming rebellious and defiant. If this goal, too, is not reached, the child may then strongly desire and try to obtain revenge. Finally, if all else fails, the child may try to appear helpless and inadequate.

Mistaken Assumptions The teacher must know, explains Dreikurs, that children often make mistakes in their assumptions about what sorts of behaviors are most likely to lead to the goals that they seek. In fact, the cornerstone of Dreikurs'

model of classroom management is the belief that all student misbehaviors result from these mistaken assumptions.

As an illustration, the most important of children's goals revolve around finding a place, gaining status—in other words, obtaining attention. Among the many acceptable ways to get attention are to achieve at a high level or to display socially adaptive behaviors. Unfortunately, many children assume that the way to gain the attention they want is to misbehave, to be disruptive and lazy, to ask for favors, to throw things, to cry, to yell and fight, and on and on.

Similarly, when children don't get all the attention they want, they may enter into a power struggle with authorities. If they fail to establish their will—that is, to obtain power—they may become frustrated and respond with even more inappropriate behavior. Such children can become stubborn, argumentative, and rebellious.

When frustrated children realize that they have little power, revenge becomes the next goal, says Adler. In an effort to exact revenge for the perceived injustices of a system that denies them both attention and power, children may become vicious and sullen and take steps to hurt others, or perhaps hurt animals.

Finally, in accordance with the fourth of Adler's hierarchical goals, a thoroughly frustrated child may begin to feel hopeless and give up. One manifestation of this, notes Adler, is the appearance of behaviors designed to make the child seem helpless and inadequate. Children may thus engage in patently stupid behaviors and show signs of a deep-seated inferiority complex.

How should teachers respond to misbehaviors of this nature?

Responding to Attention-Seeking Behavior Ignore the child's attention-seeking misbehavior, advises Dreikurs (Cassel & Dreikurs, 1972). Teachers who become visibly annoyed and impatient, or who react in any way to a child's bid for attention, are simply reinforcing that behavior. Hence, do not punish, nag, placate, advise, or admonish the attention seeker. But, says Dreikurs, the teacher should make a point of paying special attention to this child at other times when the child is not misbehaving. It's especially important that the teacher be aware when students are working well, or paying close attention to the teacher, so that the teacher can reward them with attention for desirable behaviors.

Responding to Power-Seeking Behavior When a child becomes stubborn and argumentative and shows other signs of wanting to dominate, and when the teacher has determined that power is the underlying goal, the most important rule, says Dreikurs, Gunwald, and Pepper (1982), is neither to fight nor give in. This contradicts the common belief that teachers should be firm in the face of student challenges, that they should meet an attempted show of strength with an even greater show of strength. Not so, claim Dreikurs and associates. Struggling for power with students simply leads to greater feelings of hostility. Instead, the teacher should

- ▲ recognize that the child does have legitimate power
- ▲ grant the child power where appropriate
- ▲ avoid a power struggle
- ▲ ask for the student's help when possible
- ▲ respect the child
- ▲ reach an agreement, perhaps using *logical consequences* (discussed shortly)

Responding to Revenge-Seeking Behavior A child's desire for revenge, according to Dreikurs, rises primarily from a frustrated struggle for power. The most important rule for teachers responding to revenge seeking is simple: Never show that you have been hurt. Because the objective of revenge is to hurt someone, admitting or showing hurt is an effective way of reinforcing revenge-seeking behavior. Among specific responses that Dreikurs recommends is to do the unexpected. Vengeful and rebellious students always know how to respond to expected teacher reactions, explains Dreikurs. But an unexpected reaction can sometimes defuse the situation before a serious problem results. Another possibility is to enlist the help of one or more members of the class in an effort to befriend the vengeful student. The objective is to persuade the student that others like him or her.

Responding to Displays of Inadequacy Among children's actions that attempt to project inferiority and inadequacy are unexpectedly stupid actions, failure to accept challenges, giving up easily, asking to be left alone, and refusing to participate. Students who manifest feelings of inadequacy are often excessively ambitious, notes Dreikurs, and find it difficult to succeed at the level they desire. Others are simply overly competitive and don't respond well to less than being first. And some are simply hypersensitive to pressure and give up rather than respond to it.

The most important rule for responding to displays of inadequacy, says Dreikurs, is to encourage the child's efforts even when they result in mistakes. The objective is to make children feel worthwhile, to lead them to realize that you have not given up on them. It's especially important, argues Dreikurs, for the teacher to remain supportive and constructive. And it's often useful to enlist the help and cooperation of other students in this endeavor.

Teaching Children to Apply Logical Consequences A student's misbehaviors can have two sorts of consequences, explains Dreikurs: **Natural consequences** are simply the natural, uncontrived outcomes of behavior. For example, a natural consequence of not getting up when the

---

natural consequences Dreikurs' phrase for the ordinary consequences of behavior—or, more specifically, misbehavior. Natural consequences are the effects and outcomes of behavior; they are not arranged or contrived.

alarm clock goes off is to miss school. Similarly, a natural consequence of not studying for an examination is to do worse than otherwise, and perhaps to fail.

In contrast to natural consequences, **logical consequences** are contrived (Dreikurs & Grey, 1968). That is, they are consequences of behaviors (or more often, of misbehaviors) that have been arranged by teachers and, in this democratic classroom management system, by students as well. Unlike natural consequences, these are outcomes that would not normally follow the behavior, although they are intended to seem natural and logical. Nor are logical consequences like punishment. Punishment, Dreikurs notes, is an expression of authority that often involves moral judgments and sometimes anger as well. Furthermore, punishment is rarely related directly to a specific misbehavior but tends to be general. The parent who spanks Albert for frying up the

goldfish would also be likely to spank Albert if he were to make holes in the kitchen window.

Punishment, claims Dreikurs, might have been acceptable decades ago. But now it's outdated and ineffective. Far more effective is the practice of setting up logical consequences with students—consequences that have been explained, understood, and agreed upon in advance by students. The main objective of these consequences is to bring about good behavior, not to punish. Thus, Albert and his father might agree that a logical consequence of his frying the goldfish would be for Albert to walk to the market and buy replacement goldfish, or for him to buy—and pay for—a nice fillet of trout and fry that up. Similarly, a logical consequence of his making holes in the window would be that he arrange to have the window repaired.

Table 12.4 presents several examples of possible logical consequences for specific misbehaviors; some of these are based on work by Dreikurs, Grunwald, and Pepper (1982). The logical consequences described in the table do not involve punishment in the usual sense of the word. Rather, these consequences are logical outcomes of the misbehaviors that are agreed upon and understood by the students.

---

logical consequences Dreikurs' phrase for a disciplinary tactic that involves contriving or inventing consequences for children's misbehavior in an attempt to modify that behavior. Unlike natural consequences, which follow naturally from a misbehavior, logical consequences are arranged, explained, discussed, and agreed upon by teachers and students.

TABLE 12.4
Examples of Logical Consequences

MISBEHAVIOR	LOGICAL CONSEQUENCE
Sandy writes her name on her desk.	She may either clean the desk or pay the caretaker to do so.
William scribbles his assignment in nearly illegible pencil on a wrinkled and torn scrap of paper.	The teacher will not read or grade the assignment until it has been rewritten.
Jane gets into a hair-pulling fight with Melissa after school.	Jane and Melissa are required to work out a schedule that prevents them from leaving school simultaneously until they have developed a written plan explaining why they fought and how they will avoid doing so in the future.
Susan disrupts the class by repeatedly speaking to Sarah out loud.	Susan and Sarah are invited to communicate only at recess or outside of school, or to work out a seating arrangement that will prevent them from disrupting the class.

Strengths and Weaknesses of Democratic Models

Among the main strengths of democratic models of classroom management is their humanistic-like respect of students' rights, reflected in part by their attempt to include students in discussions of rules, or the consequences of misbehaviors. Systems such as Kounin's and Dreikurs' also provide teachers with specific and sometimes very useful recommendations for preventing management problems and for responding to them. "A management system based on Kounin's principles," write McCaslin and Good, "provides expectations and understandings around which there is generally shared meaning between teachers and students, although teacher behaviors will be interpreted variously by individual students. The system allows the class to function in a relatively smooth and predictable way" (1992, p. 13).

One of the strengths of Dreikurs' model of logical consequences is that because of the role it gives students in establishing the consequences of their misbehaviors, it tends to promote a high degree of autonomy and responsibility. And, as Edwards (1993) notes, it also promotes respect between teachers and students.

Unfortunately, however, it can be very difficult for teachers to establish the motives that underlie children's misbehaviors. Furthermore, it may be overly simplistic to try to ascribe all misbehaviors to one of four classes of goals and mistaken assumptions. And, perhaps most important, it simply isn't always possible to arrive at clear, well-understood, and acceptable logical consequences for all misbehaviors and for all students. Unfortunately, the theory says little about what the teacher should do if Melissa simply refuses to stop fighting with Jane—blast the consequences, be they natural or logical. And the theory has no concrete advice to offer Albert's father if Albert agrees to replace the goldfish, but then fries them up again the next day.[5]

For more concrete advice about how to prevent misbehaviors, and how to deal with them democratically rather than autocratically, see Table 12.5.

---

[5] ***PPC:*** Frying of goldfish is perhaps too far-fetched an illustration to be very meaningful.
Author: The truth is that the illustration was not fetched from very far at all. And Albert, one of my second cousins, swears to this day that fried goldfish is as tasty as any wild trout.

TABLE 12.5
Webster's Principles of Nonautocratic Order

1. Teachers must make sure that all students understand the rules and standards and the reasons for their existence.
2. The first violation of a rule should lead to a warning, a discussion of alternative ways of behaving, and clarification of the consequences of repeated infractions.
3. Teachers should endeavor to discover the causes underlying misbehavior.
4. Whenever possible, teachers should address students in private regarding their misbehavior.
5. Sarcasm, ridicule, and other forms of discipline that can lead to public humiliation should be avoided.
6. When teachers make mistakes (if they ever do), they should apologize.
7. The punishment should fit the crime. Minor infractions should not bring about harsh punishment.
8. Extra classwork and assignments, academic tests, and other school-related activities should never be used as a form of punishment.

Source: Webster (1968), p. 50.

BEHAVIORISTIC MODELS OF CLASSROOM MANAGEMENT

Behavioristic models of classroom management are highly teacher directed. They are based on the belief that misbehaviors are either learned or result from failure to learn appropriate alternative behaviors. They recommend the judicious and systematic use of behavioral consequences to minimize classroom management problems—and to correct them when they do occur. Models based on Skinnerian operant conditioning, and the model of assertive discipline proposed by Canter, are two important examples of behavioristic models of classroom management.

Behavior Modification: B. F. Skinner

The main emphasis of the highly learner-centered classroom management models considered so far has been preventive. In contrast, the principal emphasis of those aspects of behavior modification considered in this section is *corrective*.

The immediate objective of corrective discipline is to change or eliminate a particular behavior. Reinforcement and punishment are among the most common elements of corrective discipline. Not surprisingly, then, strategies of corrective discipline often use principles of conditioning theory (described in Chapter 4). Collectively, these strategies define behavior modification, which is sometimes also called behavior management or behavioral intervention. **Behavior modification** refers specifically to strategies based on behaviorist learning theory.

Presland (1989) describes the most common sequence for a behavioral intervention program for an individual student as follows:

---

behavior modification Changes in the behavior of an individual; also refers to psychological theory and research concerned with the application of psychological principles in attempts to change behavior.

1. *Defining the problem.* Often a written list is developed of behaviors that are too frequent (speaking out in class) or too infrequent (volunteering answers for questions). The student might be involved in this step.

2. *Measuring the problem.* The teacher attempts to determine how serious (frequent or infrequent) the behavior actually is, perhaps by counting occurrences.

3. *Determining antecedents and consequences.* What conditions precede the behavior? What are its apparent consequences? In other words, how is it triggered and what reinforces it?

4. *Deciding how to change antecedents and consequences.* Are there existing consequences that serve to reinforce a too-frequent behavior? Are there new consequences that might reinforce an infrequent behavior? For example, one of the consequences of undesirable behavior might be increased teacher attention. This might serve to maintain the behavior. If so, teacher inattention might have the opposite effect. Similarly, increased teacher attention for less frequent but more desirable behaviors might increase their frequency.

5. *Planning and implementing the intervention.* Having determined which behaviors are in need of change and having identified certain antecedents (stimuli) and consequences (potential reinforcers) associated with them, it's now possible to devise a program designed to modify the behavior in question. The program should specify, often in contract with the student, how antecedents and consequences will be used and how the student will be involved.

6. *Following up.* Following the program's implementation, the teacher (and student) evaluate its effectiveness and determine whether additional or different intervention is desirable.

Systematic Reinforcement Programs Applying positive reinforcement as a corrective strategy often involves rewarding behaviors that run counter to those that present a problem. The teacher focuses on reinforcing the opposite behavior, instead of focusing on eliminating undesired responses. For example, if a teacher's attention reinforces Sally's disruptive behavior, one reinforcement strategy that might be effective is to pay attention when she is not being disruptive and to ignore her when she is.

Teachers have at their disposal a wide variety of potent reinforcers; some of these are praise, smiles, grades, and attention. When these social reinforcers prove ineffective, more elaborate reinforcement systems can be established. One example is the **token system** whereby students earn points or tokens for good behavior and sometimes lose them for less desirable behavior. Tokens can later be exchanged for tangible rewards.

Extrinsic Reinforcement Tokens are one example of **extrinsic reinforcement**. As we saw in Chapter 4, extrinsic reinforcement includes all sources of reinforcement that come from outside rather than from within an individual. Among the extrinsic reinforcers most commonly used in the classroom are attention, praise, tokens, stars, grades, and promotion. Another important and apparently quite effective source of reinforcement is defined by the **Premack principle** (Premack, 1965), which states that behavior that

ordinarily occurs frequently can be used to reinforce less frequent behavior. Parents and teachers use this principle constantly: A child is allowed to play outside after eating supper; a student is permitted to read a library book after completing an assignment.

Bijou and Sturges (1959) identify five distinct categories of extrinsic reinforcers:

consumables—like food and drink

manipulatables—things that can be manipulated like toys

visual and auditory stimuli—like green lights and gold stars and one-armed-bandit buzzers that mean, "Well done! You win!"

social stimuli—like smiles, hugs, and pats on the head

tokens—like plastic disks that can be used to buy other rewards

It is potentially valuable to consider how each of these reinforcers might be used in the classroom. Consumables are relatively inconvenient. A teacher walking around a classroom with a bag of cookies, dispensing them as she observes desirable student behavior, might occasion some concern among parents. But manipulatables, objects such as toys or trinkets, can be used successfully, particularly with young children. Reinforcing auditory and visual stimuli are less likely to be readily available to teachers. Such reinforcers are signals that have been given reinforcing properties. For example, if a teacher told students that he would ring a bell every time he was happy with them, the bell would be an auditory reinforcer. This should not be confused with social reinforcers, which take the form of praise, approval, or simply attention; these are by far the most prevalent and powerful reinforcers available to teachers. In this connection, also keep in mind that peer approval is often as powerful or even more powerful as a reinforcer than teacher approval.

---

token system A behavior modification system. Tokens are issued as rewards for desirable behaviors. These tokens can be accumulated and later exchanged for other rewards.

extrinsic reinforcement External reinforcement rather than reinforcement from within—for example, high grades, praise, or money.

Premack principle The recognition that behaviors that are frequently chosen by an individual (and are therefore favored) can be used to reinforce other, less frequently chosen behaviors. (For example, "You can watch television when you have finished your homework.")

Intrinsic Reinforcement Unlike extrinsic reinforcement, **intrinsic reinforcement** is not under a teacher's direct control. Recall that intrinsic reinforcement includes all sources of reinforcement that come from within rather than from outside—things like satisfaction and a sense of accomplishment. The teacher can nevertheless structure learning situations in ways that are more likely to lead to intrinsic satisfaction. Presenting students with tasks that are too difficult is not likely to lead to satisfaction with learning. Likewise, excessively simple tasks are not self-reinforcing. As we saw in Chapter 11, teachers can foster an intrinsic (mastery) orientation by manipulating tasks (personal involvement in challenging but achievable tasks); type of evaluation (social comparisons foster a performance orientation and a reliance on extrinsic sources of reinforcement like grades); and use of authority (providing students with opportunities for meaningful autonomy—say, in determining questions worth investigating—fosters an intrinsic orientation).

Effects of Extrinsic Rewards on Intrinsic Motivation A teacher's use of external rewards, especially in the early grades, is another potential source of influence on intrinsic motivation. If rewards are initially administered for behaviors related to learning, it follows that the process of learning can acquire the characteristics of a generalized reinforcer. In fact, it is customary for structured teaching programs based on reinforcement principles to use external rewards only in the initial stages of the program (see, for example, Walker & Shea, 1999). It is assumed that intrinsic reinforcement will eventually suffice to maintain the behavior.

There is a possibility, however, that the excessive use of reinforcement can have harmful effects on subsequent motivation (Lepper,

Keavney, & Drake, 1996). In one representative experiment, Lepper and Greene (1975) asked two groups of children to solve several geometric puzzles. One group was told that they would be allowed to play with some attractive toys as a reward; the other group was also allowed to play with the puzzles but was not led beforehand to expect a reward. Later, the children were observed unobtrusively to see whether any of them spontaneously played with the puzzles, which were freely available in the classroom. As is shown in Figure 12.2, significantly more of those who had not expected a reward continued to be motivated to play with the puzzles.

Why? Lepper and Greene (1975) suggest that the most reasonable explanation is a cognitive one. It is important for us to try to make sense of our behaviors—to understand why we do things. Typically, we resort to two classes of explanations for our behaviors: extrinsic or intrinsic causes. That is, we generally recognize that we do things for certain external rewards (money, prestige, being allowed to play with toys); for internal rewards (satisfaction, sense of accomplishment,

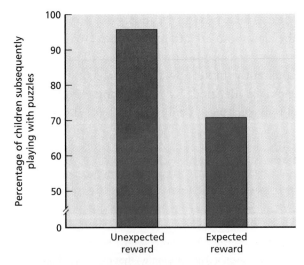

FIGURE 12.2 Significantly more of the children who had not expected a reward showed intrinsic interest by subsequently playing with the geometric puzzles. Based on data from M. R. Lepper and D. Greene (1975), "Turning Play into Work: Effects of Adult Surveillance and Extrinsic Rewards on Children's Intrinsic Motivation," *Journal of Personality and Social Psychology, 31,* 479–486.

---

intrinsic reinforcement Reinforcement that comes from within the individual rather than from outside (satisfaction, for example). Also termed *internal reinforcement.*

personal interest); or sometimes for both internal and external rewards. When external rewards are large and obvious, our motivation becomes largely extrinsic, but when we expect no great extrinsic rewards, we must look to intrinsic causes. Thus, children who expect reinforcement can understand and justify their behavior in terms of extrinsic factors; those who do not expect external rewards must justify their behavior in terms of such things as the pleasure and enjoyment associated with it. Children who do not expect rewards are subsequently more motivated (intrinsically motivated) to continue an activity. To the extent that this observation is true, the indiscriminate and excessive use of external rewards can clearly be dangerous.

These findings have not always been replicated, however. A meta-analysis of 96 studies that specifically examined to what extent extrinsic rewards might reduce intrinsic motivation concludes that, in general, "reinforcement does not harm an individual's intrinsic motivation" (Cameron & Pierce, 1994, p. 363). Hence, it would be premature to advise teachers to abandon the use of extrinsic reinforcers for fear that they might reduce interest (intrinsic motivation). Clearly, extrinsic reinforcers can be extremely useful for teachers. But teachers should take care to ensure that these are not used excessively, and they should also pay attention to the development of intrinsic motivation. As we saw in Chapter 11, children who are intrinsically motivated tend to be mastery oriented. Not only do these children achieve at a higher level but their emphasis is also on learning and understanding, rather than on simply performing and competing (Sweet, Guthrie, & Ng, 1998).

Seven Principles for Using Reinforcement Michael (1967) describes seven principles to keep in mind when attempting to control behavior through its consequences. Some of these principles have been discussed earlier, but all are important enough to bear repeating.

1. *The consequences of behavior, whether rewarding or punishing, are defined only in terms of their effect on the learner.* Teachers should not always assume that a stimulus they consider pleasant for a student will strengthen behavior. Peer attention, for example, is generally strongly reinforcing; for a very inhibited student, however, peer attention may be quite punishing. One useful concept in relation to this first principle (that reinforcement is highly individualistic) is the **reinforcement menu**, introduced by Addison and Homme (1966). A reinforcement menu is based largely on the Premack principle; it is a list of potentially reinforcing activities. Students are allowed to select from this list following behavior that merits reinforcement. Table 12.6 presents one example of a reinforcement menu. Interestingly, however, research with very young children (between 2 and 6 years old) indicates that the rewards selected by experimenters are sometimes more effective than rewards children are allowed to select for themselves (Baer et al., 1992).

reinforcement menu A list of activities, objects, or other consequences from which students may select reinforcers.

TABLE 12.6
A Reinforcement Menu*

REWARD	COST
1. One free period in the library	10
2. One free period in class	10
3. One day off from cleanup duty	5
4. Lunch with Ms. Clements (the teacher)	15
5. Lunch prepared by Ms. Clements	25
6. Extra help with one subject	2
7. Get to choose the game for gym	10
8. Get to sit anywhere in class for one day	3

*Members of a fifth-grade class were allowed to purchase activities from this menu, using points earned in school-related activities.

2. *The effects of reinforcement are automatic.* The teacher need not explain to students that if they learn well, they will receive some specific reinforcement that will then lead them to study even harder. If students do learn and are consequently reinforced, they will probably study even harder without ever having discussed this marvelous phenomenon with their teacher.

3. *Reinforcement or punishment should be closely related to the desirable (or undesirable) behavior.* As Pica and Margolis (1993) point out, teachers must have short-range goals clearly in mind so they can reinforce behavior that matches those goals. And students need to understand why they are being reinforced (or punished).

4. *Reinforcement should be consistent.* This does not mean that reinforcement must be given for every correct response. It does mean, however, that a specific behavior should not be reinforced once and punished the next time.

5. *Consequences should closely follow behavior.* Delayed reward or punishment is much less effective than immediate consequences. Adherence to this principle is clearly one of the major strengths of programmed instruction where learners receive immediate knowledge of results (discussed in Chapter 10). Another implication of this principle is that the period of time between giving a quiz and returning the results should be kept as short as possible.

6. *Use enough reinforcement to affect behavior.* Michael (1967) argues that teachers often underestimate the amount and potency of reinforcement necessary for behavioral change. This is particularly true during the early stages of learning.

7. *Set up students' work in small steps that can be individually reinforced.* Programmed instruction (see Chapter 10) can meet this requirement much more easily than can a classroom teacher who is responsible for a relatively large number of students.

Modeling Another behavior modification technique, **modeling**, is often used unconsciously by teachers who inadvertently serve as models for students. In much the same way, students also serve as models for each other. The deliberate and systematic use of models is perhaps rarer, but it can be highly effective.

---

modeling Learning through observation (or imitation).

Recall from Chapter 4 that one effect of models is the suppression or reappearance of previously suppressed deviant behavior. This effect, the **inhibitory-disinhibitory effect**, apparently occurs as a result of seeing a model being punished or rewarded for deviant behavior.

The inhibitory effect is common in schools. It is, in fact, what Kounin (1970) calls the ripple effect. When a teacher selects for punishment one offender from among a group of offenders, the hope is that the effects of the punishment will spread to the remainder of the group. This is why leaders are often punished for the transgressions of their followers.

Extinction Animal studies indicate that responses maintained by reinforcement can usually be eliminated through the complete withdrawal of reinforcement, a phenomenon labeled **extinction**. But this is not always true. For example, many pigeons that have been taught to peck at a disk for their food will stop pecking when food is no longer provided as a consequence of disk pecking. But other pigeons will continue to peck at the disk indefinitely, even when pecking no longer leads to reinforcement. Why?

A humanist might simply insist that to be a pigeon is to peck and that a fully actualized pigeon gets enormous intrinsic satisfaction from pecking at disks and remains unmoved by the crass material rewards that might move other pigeons. Others might argue that pigeons have a biological predisposition for pecking. Whatever the explanation, it remains true that not all behaviors can be extinguished through the removal of reinforcement. Furthermore, many disruptive behaviors in the classroom are rein-

forced by peers rather than by teachers. To the extent that teachers are not in control of relevant reinforcers, there is little that they can do to remove them.

More optimistically, some disruptive behaviors appear to be maintained by teacher attention; in these cases, it should be a relatively simple matter to cease paying attention. However, the matter might not be quite so simple if the behavior in question is highly disruptive of class activities. But there are other alternatives; the most common of these is punishment.

Punishment Punishment can take a variety of forms. Recall from Chapter 4 that there are, in principle, two distinct types of punishment: The first involves the presentation of a noxious (unpleasant) stimulus (castigation; presentation or Type I punishment); the second involves the removal of a pleasant stimulus (penalty; removal or Type II punishment).

Specific punishments used on a schoolwide basis, notes Bacon (1990), include expulsion, suspension, and physical punishment. Classroom teachers are more likely to use facial gestures of disapproval, reprimands, detention, unpleasant activities, time-outs, and, occasionally, physical punishment (see the case entitled "The Old Bag's Chair Trick").

Punishment in schools, and in the home, remains a highly controversial subject. For example, one survey of teachers and parents found that although there was very high agreement about the effectiveness of rewards in schools, there was very strong disagreement about the effectiveness of punishment (Miller, Ferguson, & Simpson, 1998).

---

inhibitory-disinhibitory effect The type of imitative behavior that results either in the suppression (inhibition) or appearance (disinhibition) of previously acquired deviant behavior.

extinction The cessation of a response as a function of the withdrawal of reinforcement.

punishment Involves either the presentation of an unpleasant stimulus or the withdrawal of a pleasant stimulus, as a consequence of behavior. Punishment should not be confused with negative reinforcement.

The Old Bag's Chair Trick

THE SITUATION: Mrs. Neigel, a bad teacher, as recollected by Rhonda, teacher-in-training

In fourth grade, I left my chair (we sat at tables) to retrieve my eraser from another student. When I returned to my chair, the teacher was standing behind my chair and proceeded to shout at me to sit down. As I sat down, she pulled my chair away from me and, you guessed it, I landed on the floor. She did this twice. The third time I managed to sit on the chair but before she returned to the blackboard, she smacked me across the face. Being a fourth grader, I was very frightened and extremely humiliated. The class was shocked. At the time, I thought she was an old bag, and I wished I wasn't in her class.

Many object passionately to the use of punishment—especially physical punishment. Yet most surveys indicate that punishments such as spanking are an extremely common child-rearing technique. Flynn (1998) reports following a survey of 207 single college students that spanking is viewed as highly acceptable, especially for preschoolers and young children, but less acceptable for children aged 11 years or more. Whipple and Richey (1997) summarized five surveys that looked at frequency of physical punishment in abusive and nonabusive homes. They calculated that *nonabusive* parents may spank their children as many as 5 times in a single 24-hour period. Significantly, however, abusive parents spanked their children even more often.

There is a need to re-examine the effectiveness of various forms of punishment.

Corporal Punishment Corporal punishment, also termed *physical punishment*, is the use of physical force to bring about pain. It is often associated with fear and humiliation.

Although physical punishment is no longer nearly as common as it was some decades ago,

Gregory (1997) reports that it is still used in many schools. In fact, it has been used consistently in North American schools throughout history (Ryan, 1994)—and, in at least some school systems, most students approve of its use (see, for example, Anderson & Payne, 1994).

Interestingly, courts as high as the U.S. Supreme Court have affirmed the rights of schools to use corporal punishment, providing it is not grossly excessive. In contrast, some apparently milder forms of punishment such as suspension and expulsion present schools with much clearer legal liabilities because several courts have ruled that to suspend students is to deprive them of their right to an education.

McFadden and associates (1992) looked at 4,391 discipline files from nine Florida schools. These schools had clear written rules concerning violations and disciplinary options. For example, they identified 25 classes of infractions ranging from serious (assault, possession of weapons), which were quite rare, to mild (bothering others). They found that seven categories of violations accounted for more than 80 percent of all misbehaviors. And the most common punishment for misbehaviors requiring counselor or principal intervention was in-school suspension; second most common, strikingly, was corporal punishment; third, suspension from school.

---

corporal punishment Punishment that uses physical force to inflict pain.

McFadden and associates (1992) also report marked race and gender bias in the application of corporal punishment. Not only did males account for more offenses than females but physical punishment was administered for a higher proportion of these offenses. Similarly, some 45 percent of all African American students referred were punished physically, but only 22 percent of the white students and 23 percent of the Hispanics were punished. Gregory (1997), in a more recent survey, reports the same gender and ethnic bias in a massive survey of more than 43,000 U.S. public schools.

The Case against Punishment Punishment often doesn't work, and this is one of the important objections to its use. In the McFadden and associates (1992) study just described, for example, punishment seemed to have little effect on recidivism (repetition of offenses). The large majority of the students referred for punishment in these schools were repeat offenders. As McFadden and colleagues put it, "punishments may actually serve to increase the frequencies of the very behaviors they are intended to eliminate" (1992, p. 145). In effect, those who punish violence with violence provide a model of aggression for children—a model that might be interpreted to mean that aggressiveness is permissible under certain circumstances.

A second objection to the use of physical punishment is that it likely places children at risk for physical abuse—and parents at risk for becoming child abusers (Whipple & Richey, 1997). There are also some obvious ethical and humanitarian objections to corporal punishment. In the abstract, violence, especially directed toward children, is shocking. And from a theoretical point of view, although punishment may be highly effective for drawing attention to socially undesirable behavior, it fails to illustrate suitable alternatives. (Punishment used in conjunction with reasoning and other corrective measures is not subject to the same objections.)

The Case for Punishment Most of these objections apply to corporal punishment and much less to verbal punishment. The forms of punishment that involve the removal of pleasant stimuli (for example, loss of privileges) are not subject to the same practical and philosophical objections and should be considered legitimate methods for teachers to use to maintain the degree of control essential for humane and personal teaching.

A case can be made for punishment based on several studies demonstrating that punitive methods can be effective in suppressing disruptive and sometimes dangerous behaviors, or self-injurious behavior (McGlynn & Locke, 1997). Some situations demand immediate and decisive intervention and do not lend themselves to the more gentle strategies of reinforcement, modeling, and reasoning. A child caught lighting matches and touching them to the draperies may be reasoned with and physically removed, but if he persists in burning the curtains at every opportunity, punishment may well be in order.

Although reinforcement, modeling, and reasoning have proved highly effective for promoting desirable behaviors, it is often unlikely that a child will learn to recognize unacceptable behaviors by simply generalizing in reverse from situations that have been reinforced. In many cases, then, punishment of specific behaviors can be highly instructive. And there is little evidence that punishment administered by a loving parent disrupts the emotional bonds between parent and child or routinely leads to emotional problems for the child (Dinsmoor, 1998).

One objection to the use of punishment is that it often does not work—although it might serve to suppress behavior or reduce its frequency, it does not lead to the elimination (extinction) of a response. Consider, however, that a punisher's intent is clearly to *suppress* a behavior; complete elimination is, in fact, absolutely irrelevant. If Timmy has been punished for burning curtains, we do not dare hope that he will, as a result, have forgotten how to burn curtains. But we are justified in hoping that he will refrain from doing so in the future.

This section is not meant to minimize the dangers of punishment. Several important points need to be made: The most important is that the majority of researchers and theorists remain virtually unanimous in their rejection of *corporal* punishment. Not only is physical punishment a humiliating violation of the person but it also presents an extremely undesirable model. If your task were to teach children that the best way to obtain what they want is by force, excessive use of physical punishment might well be your best teaching method.

If we do reject physical punishment (in practice, the rejection is far from complete), a variety of alternatives remain. The least objectionable ones are those involving the withdrawal of reinforcement and include three distinct types of punishment: reprimands, time-outs, and response cost.

Reprimands Reprimands can be either mild or harsh; they can be verbal or nonverbal, and they can be administered by teachers, parents, or peers. A simple "no" is a verbal reprimand; a shake of the head is a nonverbal reprimand.

Reprimands are the most common form of punishment, both in the home and in school. This is not particularly surprising because reprimands are simply expressions of disapproval. As such, they are available to anyone in power, and they are extremely easy to administer. Furthermore, given our social natures, reprimands can influence us as they cannot influence most animals.

Researchers have compared the frequency of praise and of reprimands administered by teachers. In a large-scale survey, M. A. White (1975)

found that the proportion of praise and reprimands changes markedly through school. Praise is more frequent than reprimands during first and second grade; in subsequent grades, reprimands are more common. The actual rate of reprimands through the remaining elementary and junior high school grades was approximately one every two minutes but dropped to about half that rate in high school. In college, it drops even more drastically. White also found that reprimands are somewhat more common with respect to students of lower ability. Merrett and Wheldall (1992) found that boys tended to be reprimanded more often than girls in secondary school, although not in primary school.

Research suggests that the effectiveness of reprimands depends on some of their characteristics. In general:

1. *Effective reprimands identify the undesirable behavior and provide specific rationales for doing (or not doing) something.* These are more effective than reprimands that simply express disapproval. For example, it is more effective to say, "Robert, please do not stick out your tongue because you distract the other children and you confuse me when I'm trying to explain something" than to say, "Don't do that, Robert!"

2. *They are consistent.* Acker and O'Leary (1996) provide evidence that inconsistent reprimands can actually lead to increases in misbehavior. In one study, they instructed mothers to respond to their toddler's inappropriate demands for attention (while the mothers were on the phone) by reprimanding half of the child's demands and providing positive attention to the other half. Not surprisingly, this behavior resulted in an increase in the toddlers' inappropriate demands and more crying and other displays of negative affect.

3. *They are given at a close distance.* In a study conducted by Van Houten and colleagues (1982), students were reprimanded from a dis-

---

reprimand A common mild punishment that takes the form of an expression of disapproval. Reprimands are often verbal ("you shouldn't do that") but can also be nonverbal (a head shake).

tance of either 1 meter or 7 meters (approximately 3¼ feet or 23 feet). The tone and intensity of the reprimands were kept constant. Reprimands from a distance of 1 meter were most effective.

4. *They are given softly.* (O'Leary & Becker, 1968; O'Leary et al., 1974). However, as Van Houten and Doleys (1983) note, soft reprimands are generally given in closer proximity to the student. It is also possible that, at close proximity, the teacher will reinforce the reprimand by means of eye contact and other nonverbal gestures that have been found to increase the effectiveness of reprimands.

5. *They consist of simple, unobtrusive squelches such as "shh," "wait," "no," or simply a look or a gesture.* Reprimands such as these have the advantage of minimizing class disruption.

Reprimands of the types discussed in this section, especially when they provide rationales for doing or not doing something, are as much a form of reasoning as of punishment. Unfortunately, this approach is clearly not always appropriate or effective for some of the most severe instances of disruptive behavior. In fact, the most effective forms of reprimands and reasoning, argue Larzelere and associates (1998) following a longitudinal study of misbehavior among preschoolers, is combined with punishment on at least some occasions. The largest increases in disruptive behavior in this study involved children whose parents often used reprimands but never backed them up with other punishment.

One of the reasons that reprimands might sometimes need to be accompanied by other forms of punishment is that, in many instances, reprimands are a form of attention that serves to reinforce misbehavior. In one study, for example, investigators found that a 4-year-old autistic child's destructive behavior was clearly being reinforced by repeated verbal reprimands. The child was

successfully treated by eliminating the reprimands and instead focusing reinforcement on alternate, acceptable behaviors (Fisher et al., 1996).

Students who engage in crimes such as physical violence, robbery, drug use and sale, rape, and vandalism in schools are likely to sneer at gentle reprimands. For these behaviors, more drastic measures are clearly warranted and, often, schoolwide security systems must be put in place (Myles & Simpson, 1994). In most cases, these misbehaviors occur in corridors, lunchrooms, washrooms, and playgrounds rather than in the classroom, and they are sufficiently rare in most schools that when they occur, they are usually dealt with by school administrators—although there are now chilling indicators that school violence may be rising dramatically (see, for example, Bachus, 1994; Natale, 1994). Still, the most common misbehaviors that classroom teachers must deal with on a daily basis are truancy, tardiness, inattentiveness, talking, and forgetting books and assignments. For these misbehaviors, a simple reprimand might suffice—or perhaps a time-out or response-cost procedure would work.

Time-Outs With a **time-out** procedure, students are removed from a situation in which they would ordinarily expect reinforcement and are placed where they cannot be reinforced. For example, if students like to be involved in classroom activities, being removed from the classroom for a time-out is a form of punishment.

Brantner and Doherty (1983) distinguish among three time-out procedures that classroom teachers might use. In **isolation**, the child

---

time-out A procedure where students are removed from situations in which they might ordinarily be rewarded. Time-out procedures are widely used in classroom management.

isolation A time-out procedure where a child is removed from an area of reinforcement (typically the classroom, although sometimes the playground or other areas) and isolated somewhere else.

is physically removed from the area of reinforcement (typically, the classroom; perhaps also the playground, the lunchroom, or the library) and isolated in a different place. Although isolation is not entirely uncommon in schools, it is somewhat controversial because it violates our more humanistic values. It reminds us of the types of seclusion that have sometimes been used with criminals.

In an **exclusion** time-out procedure, misbehaving children are not isolated but simply excluded from ongoing activities. A common exclusion procedure in a school might require a child to sit at the back of the room, facing in the opposite direction or perhaps sitting behind a screen.

A third, relatively mild, time-out procedure is labeled **nonexclusion**. With nonexclusion, the misbehaving child is removed from the ongoing activity (from the immediate source of reinforcement) and is required to observe others engaging in the activity. The child might, for example, be asked to stand apart from a game (or at the side of the class) and simply watch.

Time-out procedures are relatively common in some classrooms. They can be quite effective, conclude Marlow and associates (1997) following a study of noncompliant children in a school setting. But the effectiveness of these procedures can be increased even more when they are combined with what is termed **time-in** procedures. Time-in refers to a procedure where children are

systematically included, physically touched, and praised (in contrast with time-out where children are typically excluded and sometimes physically isolated).

Although time-out procedures are often effective for controlling classroom misbehaviors, they sometimes don't work at all. This is especially true, note Taylor and Miller (1997), when they are used with several students at one time; in these cases, time-out can become a source of attention that serves to reinforce misbehavior. These authors suggest that teachers must understand the function of the student's misbehavior to know how best to respond to it. Clearly, behaviors designed to obtain attention are not likely to be extinguished by time-out procedures.

Response Cost When students have been given tangible reinforcers for good behavior but stand to lose some of these reinforcers for disruptive behaviors, the loss is referred to as **response cost**. This too constitutes a mild form of punishment—similar to preventing a child who has misbehaved from watching television. Response-cost systems are frequently used in token reinforcement programs. As an example, in an experiment conducted by Truchlicka, McLaughlin, and Swain (1998), three adolescent special education students significantly improved their spelling following a procedure where they were given tokens for correct performance but lost tokens for incorrect responses. Similarly, Munson and Crosbie (1998) report a study where college students were initially given 5 cents for each frame they completed in a Skinnerian program. Subsequently, some lost 5 cents for each error that they made (response cost), while others were not punished for their errors. Results indicate that those in the

---

exclusion A time-out punishment procedure whereby a child is not removed from the situation but is excluded from ongoing activities, often by being required to sit behind a screen, in a corner, or facing away from the class.

nonexclusion The mildest form of time-out procedure; the child is not allowed to participate in ongoing activity but is required to observe.

time-in A reinforcement procedure, sometimes used in combination with time-out procedures. Time-in involves *including* children and exposing them to reinforcers such as praise and physical contact (in contrast with *time-out* which involves excluding and not reinforcing).

---

response cost A mild form of punishment whereby tangible reinforcers that have been given for good behavior are taken away for misbehavior. Response-cost systems are often used in systematic behavior management programs.

response-cost condition performed approximately 10 percent better than the other group.

Among the relative advantages of response-cost procedures for classroom management is that they do not remove the child from the learning situation (as time-out procedures typically do). Also, they are usually combined with a reinforcement procedure (use of tokens, for example) and can therefore benefit from the many advantages of reinforcement.

Assertive Discipline: Lee Canter

Another highly behavioristic management program is the well-known **assertive discipline** model advocated by Lee Canter (Canter & Canter, 1992). This model is based on the premise that teachers (and school systems) have become too permissive, too lenient. They have paid too little attention to the rights and responsibilities of teachers. Teachers possess three important classes of these rights and responsibilities:

▲ To establish rules and directions that clearly define the limits of acceptable and unacceptable student behavior
▲ To teach students to follow these rules and directions consistently throughout the school day and school year
▲ To ask for assistance from parents and administrators when support is needed in handling the behavior of students (Canter & Canter, 1992, p. 5)

These rights and responsibilities are extremely important, argues Canter, because they provide a blueprint for the kind of classroom environment that the teacher will establish. And

they dovetail, as well, with the rights of students—specifically, the rights to a teacher who:

▲ Will set firm and consistent limits
▲ Will provide consistent positive encouragement to motivate students to behave properly
▲ Will tell them what behaviors they must engage in to enable them to succeed in the classroom
▲ Will take the time to teach them how to manage their own behavior (Canter & Canter, 1992, p. 13)

The responsibility for putting these rights and responsibilities into effect is clearly the teacher's, says Canter. Hence the teacher needs to be assertive.

A Classroom Discipline Plan Assertive teachers bear the right and the responsibility to provide students with the best learning environment possible. Doing that, Canter insists, requires a classroom discipline plan, the purpose of which is not only to make the management of students easier, but also to protect their rights. Such a plan also increases the likelihood of parental and administrative support.

A classroom discipline plan specifies three things: (1) the rules that students must follow, (2) the positive recognition they will receive for following the rules, and (3) the consequences of not following the rules.

Rules need to be clear and observable, rather than vague. For example, "don't push or pull other students when you're in line" is a clear, simple rule. In contrast, "don't fool around," is vague, difficult to interpret, and difficult to enforce. Important and general rules include admonitions such as "follow the teacher's directions," "no profanity," "no teasing or bullying," "no eating during class," "walk, don't run, in the classroom."

Rules, and the consequences for following or not following them, clearly need to be different

---

assertive discipline The take-charge, aggressive, classroom management model advocated by Canter, based squarely on the notion that not only should teachers reinforce desirable behaviors, but they should also punish those that are undesirable.

at varying grade levels. Also, students should be involved in the formulation of the rules, and, of course, be fully aware of the consequences for rule infractions. Important positive consequences described by Canter include praise, notes sent home and phone calls, special privileges, awards, classwide recognition, and other tangible rewards.

Belief in the importance of a classroom discipline plan is shared by several theorists. For example, Hoover and Kindsvatter (1997) argue that all teachers must take the time to reflect upon and articulate a clear classroom management plan—what they call a *personal discipline plan*. The development of this plan is guided by answers to questions such as: What are student's democratic rights? What are my discipline-related rights and responsibilities as a teacher? What discipline-related beliefs will guide my discipline plan? What aspects of my character and personality need to be taken into consideration? What are some promising features of other plans (those of my colleagues, of different theorists)?

The discipline plan itself, note Hoover and Kindsvatter (1997), specifies the techniques and strategies that will be used in each of the four major aspects of classroom discipline:

▲ Establishing a positive classroom climate
▲ Maintaining order during class
▲ Intervening when order needs to be restored
▲ Correcting the behavior of serious or chronic misbehavers

Hoover and Kindsvatter's approach, like Canter's, is based on a recognition of both students' and teachers' rights and responsibilities. And, also like Canter's, their approach tends to be more assertive than passive (more proactive than reactive) and more behavioristic than humanistic.

Consequences for Misbehaving Assertive discipline plans clearly specify the consequences of misbe-

havior. My father had a discipline plan: The consequences of misbehaving in his school were clear. First, you would receive a warning. Second, you might get another warning often accompanied by a verbal reprimand, the strength of which depended on the severity of the transgression and the age of the transgressor. And third would be what we thought of as a real consequence: sometimes an unpleasant task like cleaning one of the little outhouses in the yard but, more often, a strapping. Parents supported this classroom management model wholeheartedly. And they didn't even know it was a form of assertive discipline.

The consequences that the Canter model speaks of are somewhat more gentle than those in vogue in the isolated community where I was schooled. But they are, nevertheless, clearly a form of punishment. Teachers should follow three guidelines when setting up consequences, advises Canter:

1. Consequences should be something students do not like, but they should not be physically or psychologically harmful.[6]

2. Consequences should be a choice.

3. Consequences do not have to be very severe to be effective.

Among the consequences that Canter advocates are most of those we have discussed in connection with the use of punishment in behavior modification programs: time-outs, response cost, detention, and being sent to the principal's office. The model of assertive discipline also recommends that parents be called upon to help to

---

[6] ***PPC:*** It might be worth pointing out that whether a specific form of punishment is psychologically harmful may depend more on the context in which it is given than on the specific nature of the punishment. A "strapping" in the author's school was apparently a socially accepted—even *expected*—form of punishment and is far less likely to have been psychologically harmful than it might be now in a relatively punishment-free contemporary school.
Author: Yes.

discipline their children. Teachers are advised to occasionally make tape recordings of the misbehaviors of children so that these can later be played for administrators and parents who might be skeptical when faced with the possibility that Angela, such a model little girl, would actually use profanity in public.

In summary, Canter (Canter & Canter 1992) describes four steps for establishing and implementing a program of assertive discipline in school: (1) establish rules and expectations, (2) identify misbehavior, (3) use punishment to enforce rules and expectations, and (4) implement a system of positive consequences for desired behaviors.

This program also provides many specific teacher suggestions concerning how to respond in various situations, how to implement consequences, how to deal with student anger, and how to handle the 5 to 10 percent of students who are truly difficult.

Strengths and Weaknesses of Behavioristic Models

One of the principal strengths of behavior modification is that it provides very specific recommendations for managing classrooms. Although all teachers make use of reinforcers and reprimands almost intuitively, most teachers can benefit from a clearer understanding of the types of available reinforcers, how reinforcement can be applied in the classroom, and when and how negative consequences such as reprimands are most effective. Behavior modification offers the well-informed teacher a wide array of detailed programs and concrete recommendations involving the systematic use of extrinsic and intrinsic reinforcers, as well as the use of models, token reinforcement systems, and even punishment in its various forms.

Canter's assertive discipline, too, provides teachers with a clear and workable set of proce-

dures for establishing and maintaining classroom order. To a large extent, it legitimizes the use of punishments that might be shunned by more humanistic models. His model is also clear and simple and has the advantage of involving both parents and administrators in the management of students. Furthermore, one of the sources of the appeal of Canter's model is its insistence on the rights and responsibilities of both teachers and students.

But the more liberal and humanistic educators argue that behavior modification smacks too much of behavior control. It pays too little attention to the dignity and worth of the student. More than this, it fails to recognize the value of autonomy and self-direction—opting, instead, for externally imposed control and direction. Also, some of its more aversive methods of control—those involving the use of punishment and negative reinforcement—can be highly ineffective and can also have negative consequences, evidenced by undesirable behaviors and personality characteristics.

☐ SOME PRACTICES FOR YOUR CLASSROOM MANAGEMENT PLAN

Preceding sections have dealt with several specific models of classroom management and discipline. First were the highly humanistic, student-centered approaches of Rogers and Marland. These were followed by a series of models described as democratic (those of Kounin and Dreikurs). Finally, we looked at the more authoritarian and assertive models of Skinner and Canter. In the remaining sections, we deal with a handful of more general approaches and strategies for maintaining classroom order and solving discipline problems. Most of these approaches share elements of one or more of the models already considered.

Reasoning

Reasoning, for example, which is one of the most important alternatives to the more direct forms of corrective intervention, is a fundamental component of humanistic and democratic approaches to classroom management.

Essentially, to reason is to provide a rational explanation; hence, reasoning as a corrective strategy involves presenting children with reasons for not engaging in deviant behavior or reasons for engaging in an alternative behavior. There is a fundamental difference between saying to a student, "don't snap your fingers because you are distracting the others and making it difficult for them to study," and saying, "don't snap your fingers or you will have to stay after school." The first statement uses reasoning; the second involves a threat of punishment. However, the first statement, while appealing to reason, might also be interpreted as implying a threat, depending on the child's prior experience with the teacher attempting the correction. If children have learned through experience that the likely consequences of not acceding to the wishes of authority, no matter how reasonably those wishes might be phrased, is some form of punishment, the effectiveness of reasoning might well be due to the implied threat.

Reasoning is considerably more appealing to parents and teachers than most other disciplinary alternatives. It somehow seems more humane to approach children on an intellectual level than to deal with them from our positions of power as dispensers of rewards and punishments. And, happily, research and good sense both confirm our suspicions that reasoning can

be an effective means of controlling or correcting student behavior (Vasquez-Levy, 1993).

Effectiveness of Different Reasons Researchers have investigated the comparative effectiveness of various kinds of reasons that might be given children to prevent them from engaging in some behavior. In a typical experiment, children are asked not to play with a toy and are then left alone with that toy; they have no reason to believe that they will be admonished if they do play with the toy. Investigators give the children specific reasons for not playing with the toy.

The evidence sugggest that rationales that stress the object ("the toy might break") are more effective for younger children than more abstract rationales relating to rights of possession ("you should not play with toys that belong to others"). But for older children (beyond age 6 or so), rationales that arouse empathy and emphasize the consequences of their behavior for other people ("other-oriented induction") are more persuasive than rationales that emphasize the consequences to the child. In other words, if the experimenter says, "do not play with that toy because you will make the child it belongs to unhappy," subjects are more likely not to play with the toy than if the experimenter says, "do not play with that toy because it might break and that would make you unhappy" (Walters & Grusec, 1977).

It follows from these observations that it is probably wise to provide younger children with specific, concrete reasons for requests that are made of them. After children have reached school age, however, more abstract rationales that are other directed and that consequently arouse empathy for others appear to be most effective.

Why Reason? Besides humanitarian and ethical considerations that clearly favor reasoning over punishing, reasoning is preferable to punish-

---

reasoning As a disciplinary strategy, the process of providing a rationale for doing or not doing certain things. Can be used as both a corrective and a preventive classroom management tactic. Forms an important part of humanistic and democratic approaches to classroom management.

ment for several practical reasons. First, a punishing agent provides a model of aggressiveness for the learner. In effect, the punisher's activities signify that one acceptable method of dealing with difficult situations is through the assertion of punitive power. Reasoning provides a rather different model. To reason with a child—to provide a rationale for acceptable behavior—is to say, in effect, that one way to cope with a difficulty is the deliberate application of thought.

A second advantage of a reasoning strategy is that such an approach lends itself naturally to the description of alternative acceptable behaviors. In other words, reasoning need not be restricted to providing rationales for why a behavior should *not* be engaged in but can also be used to explain why certain behaviors should be undertaken. Various forms of altruistic and prosocial behavior (cooperation, sharing, helping) cannot easily be taught by punitive means but instead lend themselves more readily to the use of models, reasoning, reinforcement, or a combination of these.[7]

Developing Morality in Students

The most effective and comprehensive management systems for classrooms, argue Smith and Misra (1992), are those that concentrate on reaching the academic and social goals that schools set for children. In other words, these are systems where the emphasis is on antecedent conditions that are designed to prevent or minimize disruptions and on consequences that reinforce appropriate behavior rather than punishing less appropriate behavior.

This philosophy is reflected in much of this chapter, which has emphasized preventive strategies, rather than **corrective strategies**. With proper attention to the aspects of teacher–learner interaction that are conducive to enthusiasm, warmth, and caring, the hope is that seriously disruptive behavior will be infrequent and the need for corrective action will therefore be rare. As a result, the teacher may have more time and energy to address the larger but sometimes less visible problems of social adjustment, self-discipline, and the development of *morality*.

Rules and regulations in a classroom exist not only to ensure the order necessary for teaching and learning, but also to foster the development of morality and of self-discipline in students. It is probably somewhat presumptuous of schools to assume that the development of high moral standards, the internalization of values, and the development of principles and ideals will result incidentally from the experiences that life provides for children and that nothing can, or should, be done deliberately to foster their development.

Many researchers and theorists (most notably, the more humanistically oriented theorists) argue that wise and sensitive teachers can accomplish much by way of the development of **character**—that is, values, moral strength, principles, and virtues.

Unfortunately, science finds these terms vague and ill-defined and, as a consequence,

---

[7] ***PPC:*** I don't think the bear should leave students with the impression that reasoning always works, that it's always the best approach to classroom management.

Author: The bear agrees. As was pointed out earlier, reasoning *in combination with* other approaches (such as reprimands) offers a powerful classroom management technique. But sometimes, especially for severe misbehaviors, reasoning can be quite ineffective. In the words of the bear's friend and mentor, Yogi Berra, "There are some people who, if they don't already know, you can't tell 'em."

---

corrective strategies Strategies designed to correct discipline problems. These often involve the systematic use of rewards and punishments.

character An inclusive and ill-defined term signifying those aspects of human personality that include the individual's values, moral strength, principles, virtues, and vices. Character relates to what we think of as the goodness or moral strength of the individual.

character is a rare term in today's social sciences. Otherwise, these sciences might have more advice to offer the teacher who is concerned with issues other than classroom management and the curriculum-bound teaching/learning process.

Conflict Management and Values Education

Humanistic approaches to education are less reluctant to tackle big words like *character* and *morality*. These approaches are more concerned than the behavioristic approaches with children's social and emotional needs and with helping them to develop social skills that are useful and necessary for effective interaction with others. Among other things, humanistic approaches present educators with a handful of values clarification and conflict management programs developed for use in schools.

As we saw in Chapter 7, **values education** refers to general programs developed to teach values in schools. Closely related are **values clarification programs** which are intended to encourage students to actively reflect on questions of personal morality (Colby, James, & Hart, 1998).

There are many approaches to teaching values and morality in schools. These are often tied in with the curriculum in health education or environmental studies (Fien, 1997). They include simply discussing moral dilemmas of the kind used by Kohlberg (1980) in his investigations. Role-playing situations where students act out situations involving moral or ethical questions are also effective, as are modeling procedures and direct teaching (Stoll & Beller, 1993).

Stories of real or fictitious individuals of high moral character can also lead to important insights about morality (Hart, 1998).

Another approach to teaching morals involves programs in **conflict management**. One of the better-known conflict management programs is that developed by Palmares and Logan (1975). They provide an extensive curriculum, both audiovisual and textual, intended to teach children a variety of methods they can use to resolve conflicts. Although many of these methods are learned incidentally and used spontaneously by most children, others experience difficulty in acquiring these social skills. For these children, the program should prove particularly effective.

Among the conflict resolution skills taught by the program are negotiating, compromising, taking turns, explaining, listening, apologizing, soliciting intervention, using humor, and invoking chance (for example, flipping a coin). In this program, 17 specific strategies are developed; 14 of these are primarily positive and clearly useful in adult interaction as well, and 3 are more negative although they too might occasionally be resorted to (violence, flight, and tattling).

This program, and variations of it, have been used extensively in several situations. For example, Beekman and Holmes (1994) developed a program that teaches parents five approaches that can work for resolving parent–child conflicts: collaborating, compromising, accommodating, avoiding, and directing. Similarly, S. Black (1994a) describes how trained students who are confident, caring, and intelligent can serve as **mediators** to intervene between a group

---

values education Instructional programs and strategies designed to teach specific values (notions of right and wrong), thereby promoting good behavior and developing good "character."

values clarification program A program designed to encourage learners to examine their personal beliefs about right and wrong, with a view to improving and clarifying their awareness of their own morality.

---

conflict management A program designed to teach individuals acceptable ways of resolving conflicts. Common conflict management techniques include negotiating, compromising, taking turns, explaining, listening, apologizing, mediating, using humor, and invoking chance.

mediator A student who is specially trained to intervene between two or more other students who are in conflict.

Helping children learn the many ways of resolving conflicts is one of the teacher's important reponsibilities. Among conflict resolution skills that can be taught and learned are negotiating, compromising, taking turns, listening, explaining, apologizing, using humor—perhaps even giving up the ball on occasion.

of other students who are in conflict. And Rubin (1994) also describes how negotiators (or mediators) can help to resolve conflicts.

Ten Procedures for Preventive Classroom Management

Classroom management skills must include strategies and ideas for resolving conflict. But perhaps far more important, they also need to include strategies and ideas for *preventing* them in the first place.

Grossnickle and Sesko (1990) provide a list of ten procedures that they consider to be an important basis for classroom management. Many of these have been mentioned earlier in this chapter but are worth repeating in this simple, organized form:

1. *Establish clear behavioral guidelines.* Expectations, standards, and rules should be clear to teachers, students, and parents. Preferably, they should be written out and distributed to all concerned.

2. *Adopt a teamwork approach.* Teachers, administrators, and parents are a team and should all work together to support, follow, and enforce agreed-upon management procedures.

3. *Design a complete discipline ladder.* This is a clear description of available corrective disciplinary measures and the order in which they are to be invoked (for example, first an in-class warning, followed, in order and if necessary, by an after-class conference, a phone call to parents, referral to the principal, help from counselors . . .).

4. *Teach self-management and self-discipline.* This is a gradual process but an essential function of schools.

5. *Invite good discipline.*

6. *Focus on students' success and self-esteem.*

7. *Implement firm, fair, and calm enforcement.*

8. *Plan lessons thoroughly.*

9. *Continually monitor the classroom environment.*

10. *Minimize problems early.*

Sadly, this isn't a recipe which, when followed step-by-step, will invariably lead to a well-managed, problem-free classroom, conducive to learning and growth. But it does suggest many of the proper ingredients.

MAIN POINTS

1. The expression "classroom management" refers to the arrangement of classroom activities to facilitate teaching and learning; "discipline" relates to the interventions made necessary by student behaviors that disrupt (or threaten to disrupt) classroom activities.

2. Classrooms are characterized by tremendous student and teacher diversity, multidimensionality of classroom events (many individuals, many activities, many goals); simultaneity (many events occurring at any one time); immediacy (events requiring instant teacher decisions and action); and unpredictability (the course of classroom events cannot easily be predicted). Hence, managing classes requires special pedagogical and information processing skills (vigilance and with-it-ness), which may eventually become automatic.

3. Despite some valid ethical and humanitarian objections to control, to the extent that teachers act *in loco parentis* and care for their students, discipline may be necessary— within the bounds of student rights.

Preventive strategies are essential to effective classroom management.

4. Rogers' and Marland's humanistic management models recommend minimal teacher intervention and advocate highly supportive, student-centered schools directed toward the development of self-discipline in students.

5. Kounin and Dreikurs present more democratic models of classroom management. These are mainly concerned with students' rights and voices but prescribe more teacher direction than do humanistic models. Kounin describes these important characteristics of successful classroom management: with-it-ness (timely, noninterruptive, on-target desists); overlapping (responding effectively to potential classroom disruptions without interrupting ongoing activity); smoothness and momentum (as opposed to jerky transitions, lesson slowdowns, and interruptions caused by stimulus-boundedness, thrusts, dangles, truncations, flip-flops, overdwelling, or fragmentation); maintaining focus (making students accountable, using group-

alerting cues, and using lesson formats that involve all students).

6. Dreikurs' logical consequences model interprets child misbehavior in terms of need for attention, power, revenge, or perhaps to appear inadequate. This model provides procedures for determining student motives and suggests specific teacher responses for behaviors related to each motive. It also advises setting up logical consequences as outcomes of misbehaviors—outcomes accepted as just by students and intended to encourage good behavior rather than to punish misbehavior.

7. Behavioristic classroom management applies conditioning principles in the classroom. Skinnerian behavior modification typically involves specific steps: Define the problem, measure it, determine response antecedents and consequences, decide how these can be changed, plan and implement intervention, and follow up (evaluate and terminate or perhaps modify the program).

8. Systematic reinforcement programs in schools typically use positive reinforcement, sometimes in the form of tokens or a combination of teacher praise and other tangible rewards (such as the Premack principle that calls for a desirable activity to be used as a reinforcer).

9. Extrinsic reinforcers include consumables, manipulatables, visual and auditory stimuli, social stimuli, tokens, and items on reinforcement menus (lists of rewards from which students select). The teacher's attention is extremely important. Principles governing the use of reinforcement in the classroom include these: Reinforcement is individualistic (defined only in terms of its effects on the individual); its effects are automatic; reinforcement and punishment should be consistent, should be closely related to the relevant behavior, and should occur as soon as possi-

ble; the amount of reinforcement required should not be underestimated; and students' work should be organized so that it is possible to reinforce small steps frequently.

10. Models provide children with standards of appropriate behavior. On occasion, punished models may serve to inhibit deviant behaviors as well. Perhaps the most important classroom model is the teacher.

11. Extinction involves an attempt to eliminate undesirable behavior through the withdrawal of reinforcement. Punishment involves the presentation of an unpleasant stimulus or the removal of a pleasant stimulus as a consequence of behavior. Among objections to the use of *corporal* punishment are claims that it does not always work, that it presents an undesirable model of violence, that it might have undesirable emotional side effects, and that it could lead to maladaptive behaviors through the introduction of frustration. Research indicates that punishment can suppress undesirable behaviors and that it can be particularly appropriate when it is necessary for a child to learn about behaviors that are not permitted.

12. Common punishments include reprimands (expressions of disapproval, generally verbal but sometimes nonverbal); time-outs (the removal of a student from a reinforcing situation—includes isolation [physical removal], exclusion [removal of the child from ongoing activities but not from the classroom], and nonexclusion [removal of the child from the ongoing activity to a place where the child continues to observe the activity]); and response cost (loss of previously earned reinforcers).

13. Canter's assertive discipline argues against permissiveness and advocates that teachers establish classroom discipline plans that

include clear rules, ways of teaching students to follow those rules, and provisions for involving parents in disciplining children.

14. Reasoning, often used in combination with other disciplinary measures, appears to be a highly effective and humane way of handling classroom problems. Concrete reasons appear to be more effective with younger children; abstract reasons that arouse empathy work better with older children and can be important for developing higher levels of moral orientation.

15. Besides maintaining classroom order, teachers should also attend to the development of social and affective skills in children. Humanistic educators suggest that teachers pay attention to students' emotional and moral development, perhaps by using specific values clarification and conflict management programs and techniques.

Applied Questions

▲ Why is good classroom management so important? Write an essay outlining your answer.
▲ List specific instructional strategies relating to each of the following management models:

     Rogers' humanistic model
     Marland's caring for children model
     Kounin's teacher with-it-ness
     Dreikurs' logical consequences
     Skinner's behavior modification
     Canter's assertive discipline

▲ If you wanted to develop a series of lessons to incorporate strategies for preventive classroom management, what would you come up with?

Internet Activity

Use InfoTrac College Edition or other World Wide Web sources to research the current use of physical punishment in homes and schools. Write up your findings. (See the inside back cover of this text for suggestions about where to begin.)

Sample search terms: corporal punishment

Study Terms

assertive discipline **473**
behavior modification **462**
character **477**
classroom management **443**
conflict management **478**
corporal punishment **468**
corrective strategies **477**
desist **454**
discipline **443**
exclusion **472**
extinction **467**
extrinsic reinforcement **463**
inhibitory-disinhibitory effect **467**

in loco parentis **446**
intrinsic reinforcement **464**
isolation **471**
jerky transition **456**
logical consequences **460**
mediator **478**
modeling **466**
natural consequences **459**
negotiated order theory **443**
nonexclusion **472**
overlapping **455**
Premack principle **463**
preventive strategy **447**

Suggested Readings

There are many books that present strategies relating to classroom management and discipline. The first of the following six books presents a reflective approach to classroom management; Sesno's little book is nontechnical and entertaining, but presents highly practical advice for teachers; the book by Hoover and Kindsvatter presents a thoughtful and easily read description of a wide range of ideas for classroom management; Walker and Shea's book is a clear and quite practical application of behavior management based on conditioning; Canter's book presents his methods of assertive discipline; and Kerr and Nelson's book presents detailed suggestions for dealing with children identified with *serious emotional disturbance* (SED) or *emotional and behavior disorders* (EBD):

Kauffman, J. M., Mostert, M. P., Trent, S. C., & Hallahan, D. P. (1998). *Managing classroom behavior: A reflective case-based approach* (2nd ed.). Needham Heights, MA: Allyn & Bacon.

Sesno, A. H. (1998). *97 savvy secrets for protecting self and school: A practical guide for today's teachers and administrators.* Thousand Oaks, CA: Corwin.

Hoover, R. L., & Kindsvatter, R. (1997). *Democratic discipline: Foundation and practice.* Upper Saddle River, NJ: Merrill.

Walker, J. E., & Shea, T. M. (1999). *Behavior management: a practical approach for educators* (7th ed.). Upper Saddle River, NJ: Merrill.

Canter, L., & Canter, M. (1992). *Lee Canter's assertive discipline: Positive management for today's classroom.* Santa Monica, CA: Lee Canter & Associates.

Kerr, M. M., & Nelson, C. M. (1998). *Strategies for managing behavior problems in the classroom* (3rd ed.). Upper Saddle River, NJ: Prentice Hall.

Bears are extremely confident and capable climbers, particularly when young. With increasing weight, however, they trust only the stoutest of branches, although a fall is not likely to prove disastrous. Polar bears, for example, can climb an almost sheer ice wall and will then routinely jump down from heights of 15 to 20 feet. And this in spite of their ponderous weights. One bear reportedly dived more than 50 feet into the water to escape hunting dogs and then set off in the direction of the closest land mass—an impressive 22 miles away (Perry, 1966; Matthews, 1969).

All animals are
equal, but some
animals are more
equal than others.

George Orwell, *Animal Farm*

Instructional
Objectives and
School Assessments

PREVIEW

In spite of the intuitive appeal of "schools without failures," "schools without tests," and other hypothetical situations where everyone is highly motivated, absolutely dedicated, and deliriously happy, the nitty-gritty of classroom practice sometimes (perhaps frequently) requires assessment. This chapter describes the various methods by which students' (and sometimes teachers') performances can be measured and evaluated, why assessment is important, some of the abuses and misuses of assessment procedures, and some current trends in educational assessment.

FOCUS QUESTIONS

▲ What is the difference between measurement and evaluation?

▲ What are the most useful kinds of instructional objectives?

▲ What are the characteristics of good measuring instruments?

▲ What are standardized tests, and what are their uses?

▲ How are criterion-referenced and norm-referenced evaluation different?

▲ What are performance-based assessments?

When I reached twelfth grade, they sent me to Collège Nôtre Dame—not the Notre Dame of academic, football, or hockey fame, but just a small, all-boys residential French Catholic high school (grades 8 through 12) up in Prince Albert. The school, which was staffed and run by the Brothers of the Sacred Heart, had been established for bright French Catholic students who had no easy access to a local high school. Eventually, it became home to an assortment of problem students sent to the Collège to be straightened out. Also, the school included a relatively large number of lads who were destined for the priesthood. I qualified on almost all counts.

There were about 80 of us in Nôtre Dame the year I attended. Rules and routines governed all aspects of our existence. On a typical day we would get up at 6:00, be in the chapel for mass at 6:30, have breakfast at 7:15, and begin classes at 8:00. School days (which included Saturdays) classes lasted until 4:00, with short breaks in the morning and afternoon and a brief lunch break. We had 30 minutes of free time before dinner followed by 90 minutes of organized sports, the nature of which depended on the season. Following this, there would then be an hour of study time before bed. By 9:00, the lights went out.

In most of our classes at Nôtre Dame, there were no more than five or six students. As a result, much of the instruction took the form of one-on-

one tutoring. Quizzes and tests were not a normal part of our classroom fare; we had tests only at Christmas and at the end of the year. But at least once a week, one of the Brothers would call each of us in for a discussion of our goals and our progress.

"You need to do better, Guy," was how most of the Brothers opened their discussions with me. This could have meant that with my startling intelligence and astonishing command of languages, the Brothers expected an uncommon display of genius from me.

"When the tests come," I promised, "I'll do awful good." And, in the meantime, I continued to dream of other things.

But when the tests came, they asked unexpected questions. Brother Alphonse called me into his office.

"Guy," said he, "You didn't do awful good. You got just a 61, here, on your Latin."

MEASUREMENT AND EVALUATION IN SCHOOLS

A statement such as, "You need to do better, Guy," implies **evaluation**. To evaluate is to judge certain qualities—to place a value on them, like "good" or "bad." A statement such as "you got just a 61, here," illustrates **measurement**.[1]

---

evaluation In contrast to measurement, evaluation involves making a value judgment—deciding on the goodness or badness of performance. It also denotes the highest level of intellectual skill in Bloom's taxonomy of educational objectives; there it is defined as the ability to render judgments about the value of methods or materials for specific purposes, making use of external or internal criteria.

measurement The application of an instrument to gauge the quantity of something, as opposed to its quality. Assessing quality involves evaluation, not measurement.

---

[1] *PPC:* Not to be too personal, but how did you get to where you are with grades like that?

Author: That was just one test, one grade, following a long term filled with difficult adjustments and much homesickness. On the next test, I scored . . . I forget. Besides, hardly anybody speaks Latin anymore.

Measurement involves the use of an instrument (for example, a ruler, a tape measure, or a test) to assess a specific quantity. In general, measuring is a more precise and more objective procedure; evaluating is less precise and more subjective. The term **assessment** is often used as a general term for the process of appraising student performance and can include elements of both measurement and evaluation.

Both measurement and evaluation are important parts of the instructional process. As we saw in Chapter 1, instruction can be described as a sequence of procedures conducted before teaching, during teaching, and after teaching (see Figure 13.1). In the before-teaching phase, assessment may be involved in placing students, selecting instructional procedures, and determining students' readiness. Plans for final assessment should also be made at this stage. During the teaching phase, assessment might be used to determine whether the goals are being met, as a basis for modifying instructional procedures, or as a learning tool. And in the after-teaching phase, assessment is used not only to determine the extent to which instructional goals have been met but also to gauge the effectiveness of instructional strategies and to re-evaluate students' placement and readiness. Measurement is being used when actual tests are administered; it is essentially a *quantitative* process. Evaluation is being used when teachers make decisions concerning the adequacy of instructional procedures, the readiness of students, and the extent to which curriculum goals are being met; it is a more *qualitative* process.

Evaluation isn't necessarily based on measurement. In fact, a great deal of educational assessment is not. The countless value judgments made by teachers about the abilities of

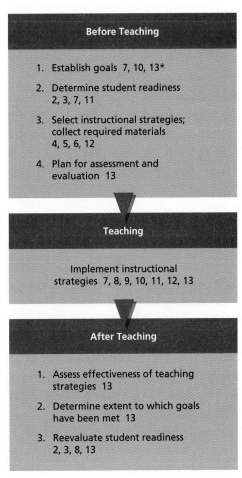

The Instructional Process

Before Teaching

1. Establish goals 7, 10, 13*
2. Determine student readiness 2, 3, 7, 11
3. Select instructional strategies; collect required materials 4, 5, 6, 12
4. Plan for assessment and evaluation 13

Teaching

Implement instructional strategies 7, 8, 9, 10, 11, 12, 13

After Teaching

1. Assess effectiveness of teaching strategies 13
2. Determine extent to which goals have been met 13
3. Reevaluate student readiness 2, 3, 8, 13

*Chapters containing relevant information

FIGURE 13.1 The three-stage model of the teaching process described in Chapter 1

students, their motivation, their persistence, their pleasantness, and so on are often examples of evaluation without measurement. Also, important assessment procedures such as **portfolios** often do not involve tests. In fact, some argue that one of the educational reforms most in need of implementation would involve replacing multiple-choice tests with forms of assessment that look at the student's performance in more

---

assessment A judgmental process intimately involved in the teaching/learning process. A general term for the process of appraising student performance. May include elements of both measurement and evaluation.

portfolio In educational assessment, a collection of actual samples of students' performance and achievements.

realistic, real-life situations (see, for example, Wiggins, 1998). This type of assessment is often called **performance assessment** or **authentic assessment**. These topics are covered later in this chapter.

In this chapter, as in most other educational writing, the terms *assessment* and *evaluation* are used interchangeably to include one or more of the following: subjective valuations, measurement with tests, or appraisal by another means.[2]

Formative and Summative Evaluation: A New Emphasis

The main purposes of educational assessment have always been to gauge student progress, to measure learning, to evaluate the learner's qualifications, and to guide decisions about student placement. As we saw in Chapter 10, these are the purposes of **summative evaluation**. Summative evaluation is intended mainly to provide a grade. In a sense, it *summarizes* the effects of learning and instruction.

Summative evaluation represents what are still valid and very useful functions of measurement and evaluation. But there is an important new emphasis in educational assessment, note Delandshere and Petrosky (1998). This emphasis

insists that the primary purpose of educational assessment is to support learning and teaching rather than to rank individuals and assign numbers to represent their accomplishments. This function of educational assessment is represented by **formative evaluation**. The principal purpose of formative evaluation is to provide both learners and instructors with guidance designed to improve the teaching/learning process.

The Importance of Educational Assessment

Evaluation is a central component of learning and teaching—as made clear in the teaching model presented in Figure 13.1. Sadly, however, teacher education programs often devote very little time to educational assessment. As a case in point, a survey of 397 teachers revealed that almost half of them thought that their training in assessment was inadequate and that they had been forced to learn through trial and error (Wise, Lukin, & Roos, 1991). Interestingly, however, even those who had learned through trial and error thought they actually knew quite a lot.[3]

Prevalence Not surprisingly, assessment procedures occupy a significant portion of classroom time. Gullickson (1985) reports that an average of 5 to 15 percent of class time is actually spent on tests. (In lower elementary grades, the percentage is closer to 5; in high school, it is closer to 15.)

---

performance assessment Assessment that looks at the actual performance of students in situations as close to real life as possible.

authentic assessment Refers to assessment procedures designed to allow students to demonstrate their ability to apply learning in real-life situations. Often contrasted with assessment based solely on objective tests, especially of the multiple-choice variety. Also termed *performance assessment*.

summative evaluation The type of evaluation that occurs at the end of an instructional sequence and that is designed primarily to provide a grade.

---

[2] *PPC:* It strikes me that there is a Yogi Berrism that the bear could have used to illustrate the difference between measurement and evaluation—when he said, "A nickel ain't worth a dime anymore." Can the bear explain that?
Author: No. Can you?

---

formative evaluation An evaluation undertaken before and during instruction, designed primarily to assist the learner to identify strengths and weaknesses. Formative evaluation is a fundamental part of the process of instruction.

---

[3] *PPC:* The bear should perhaps point out that this is most often a form of self-delusion and that teachers who are not well trained in assessment will never know important concepts and procedures.
Author: That is correct. It's a common and easy deception, well expressed by my grandmother's admonition that "you never know what you don't know." It follows that poorly trained teachers might well remain unaware of deficiencies in their knowledge.

Besides time spent actually writing, going over, and correcting tests, a tremendous range of other evaluative activities fills school days: asking students questions; commenting on students' responses and presentations; evaluating performances in subject areas such as art, drama, music, and writing; conducting informal observations of ongoing student work; correcting and grading homework assignments; evaluating written work; carrying out informal assessments of attitudes and effort; and many more. In fact, the bulk of the teacher's evaluations, especially in the lower elementary grades, is based on informal observation and on grading assignments and performance rather than on test results.

How Evaluation Procedures Influence Learning and Instruction How do these evaluative procedures affect students? Profoundly. In fact, it is difficult to overestimate the influence of evaluation on students' behavior. Ramsden (1988a) argues that students' beliefs about assessment are among the most important influences on learning. He explains that the types of assessments used determine what students study and how they learn. This is the reasoning that, in the early 1980s, was partly responsible for the development of a broad instructional approach sometimes labeled **measurement-driven instruction**. Measurement-driven instruction is instruction geared specifically toward increasing student performance on specific achievement measures.

One of the clear effects of measurement-driven instruction is an increase in students' grades. Unfortunately, however, it also has some negative effects, among which Cizek (1993b) includes a "dumbing down" and a "narrowing" of the curriculum. Our most common approaches to evaluation also encourage a passive form of

learning where rote memorization of facts and formulas is heavily rewarded. In other words, there are two broad approaches to learning: a surface approach that emphasizes memorization of unrelated facts and a deep approach that involves a deliberate and active search for underlying principles and concepts and attempts to discover relationships. Because our tests emphasize the simple, surface components of curriculum content and largely ignore the more complex, deeper aspects of knowledge, the surface components are what students learn. And teachers whose instructional methods are most clearly measurement driven may well be most responsible for developing surface learners.

How do we change surface approaches to deep ones? How do we induce learners to pay attention to relationships and principles, and how do we encourage them to achieve understanding instead of memorization?

This text provides several possible answers. For example, programs exist with the express goals of teaching thinking, developing cognitive strategies, imparting learning/thinking skills, or developing metacognitive awareness. And there are cognitive learning theories, such as those described by Bruner and by Ausubel, that emphasize meaningfulness and comprehension while de-emphasizing "meaningless rote learning." These theories provide several recommendations for helping students attend to the underlying structures of knowledge, relationships, and meaningfulness.

But perhaps, in Elton and Laurillard's words, "the quickest way to change student learning is to change the assessment system" (1979, p. 100) because in the final analysis students try to learn what teachers test, not what teachers suggest is important. It is not sufficient to pay lip service to the importance of complex cognitive processes such as synthesizing or evaluating, or what Bruner calls "going beyond the information given." If teacher-made tests and final examinations ask students only to repeat what they have

---

measurement-driven instruction A general approach to instruction wherein the overriding objective is to increase student performance on specific achievement measures.

read in textbooks or heard in class, that is what students will learn.

The point is clear: Teachers must evaluate students on the right things; that is, they must evaluate students on what they consider most important—the things they want students to learn.

A second point should also be clear: Evaluation needs to be fair, consistent, and reliable. Whenever possible, it should be based on the best measurements available, although it will often result from informal observation as well. And it must reflect the goals of the instructional process.

INSTRUCTIONAL GOALS AND ASSESSMENT

Educational goals tell the teacher what to teach and also which behaviors need to be evaluated. We cannot assess the effectiveness of our instructional procedures unless we know what they are intended to accomplish, and we cannot determine what they have accomplished without some form of assessment.

As we saw in Chapter 1, the desired outcomes or objectives of education can be expressed in broad terms such as "the goal of education is to develop decent, worthwhile citizens" or "the goal of education is to empower students." Among the broad educational goals advanced by a former president of the United States is the following statement:

> By the year 2000, American students will leave grades four, eight, and twelve having demonstrated competency in challenging subject matter including English, mathematics, science, history, and geography; and every school in America will ensure that all

---

educational goal An intended or desired outcome of the educational process. Often expressed in terms of instructional objectives that can range from highly general to very specific.

For frequently updated information on educational goals and Project 2000, see:
http://www.ed.gov/legislation/GOALS2000/TheAct/

---

students learn to use their minds well, so that they may be prepared for responsible citizenship, further learning, and productive employment in our modern economy. (George Bush, cited in R. Walker, 1990, p. 16)

This statement of educational goals forms part of what is titled the *Educate America Act.* The declared purpose of this act is to provide guidelines for educational reform with a view to improving teaching and learning. It describes several general educational goals initially slated for accomplishment by the year 2000. The most important of these are summarized in Table 13.1.

Although general statements of objectives such as these are useful for guiding the development of curriculum and influencing the behavior of administrators and students, they are not nearly as useful in the day-to-day business of teaching as are more specific instructional objectives.

Instructional objectives are statements about the type of performance that can be expected of students once they have completed a lesson, a unit, or a course. Objectives do not describe the course itself but describe instead the intended performance of students. Because performance implies behavior, the phrase "behavioral objectives" is sometimes used interchangeably with "instructional objectives."

Teachers' Accountability and Instructional Objectives

In recent years a renewed emphasis on the use of instructional objectives in schools has become

---

instructional objective A goal or intended result of instruction. Objectives can be either short-range or long-range. Also termed *behavioral objectives.*

TABLE 13.1
Educational Goals:
A Summary of Goals 2000 from the Educate America Act

GOALS	SOME CHANGES AND IMPLIED REFORMS
School readiness: All children will start school ready to learn.	Access for all children to appropriate preschool programs, adequate parenting, proper nutrition and health care
School completion: The high school graduation rate will increase to at least 90 percent.	A dramatic reduction in dropout rate, especially for students from minority backgrounds
Student achievement and citizenship: All students will leave grades 4, 8, and 12 having demonstrated competency over challenging subject matter and having learned to use their minds well.	A significant increase in the academic performance of all students at the elementary and secondary level; an increase in the percentage of students who are competent in more than one language
Teacher education and professional development: The teaching force will have access to programs for the continued improvement of their professional skills.	Increased access to preservice teacher education and continuing professional development activities
Mathematics and science: U.S. students will be first in the world in mathematics and science achievement.	System-wide strengthening of mathematics and science education, including the metric system of measurement, especially in the early grades
Adult literacy and lifelong learning Every adult will be literate and will possess the knowledge and skills necessary to compete in a global economy and exercise the rights and responsibilities of citizenship.	Provision of opportunity for all workers to acquire the knowledge and skills needed to adapt to emerging new technologies; increase in the number of quality programs designed to serve the needs of the growing number of part-time and midcareer students
Safe, disciplined, and alcohol- and drug-free schools: Every school will be free of drugs, violence, and the unauthorized presence of firearms and alcohol and will offer a disciplined environment conducive to learning.	The development and implementation by local educational agencies of policies to ensure that all schools are free of violence and the unauthorized presence of weapons; the development of a sequential, comprehensive drug and alcohol prevention program in kindergarten through twelfth grade
Parental participation: Every school will promote partnerships that will increase parental involvement and participation in promoting the social, emotional, and academic growth of children.	Deliberate efforts to actively engage parents and families in a partnership which supports the academic work of children at home and shared educational decision making at school

apparent. This emphasis stems not only from the recognition of their importance in teaching but also from a growing concern with what is called "teacher accountability" (MacIver, Reuman, & Main, 1995). This phrase implies that teachers should somehow be held accountable for their performance in the classroom—accountable perhaps to students and perhaps to parents but most certainly to the administrative authorities who hire and fire them.

Evaluating Teachers' Competence Implicit in the notion that teachers should somehow be held accountable for the results of their teaching is the assumption that if they are rewarded for effective teaching, they will work harder and become more effective. The practical implication of these beliefs is that many school jurisdictions have looked for ways to evaluate **teacher competence**—and ways to reward teachers.

Establishing a reward system is, in fact, far easier than determining how to evaluate competence. For example, Lunde and Barrett (1996) describe a university-based reward system that uses rewards such as **merit pay**, promotion, tenure, nominations for teaching awards, and development leaves. Henderson (1996) suggests that nonfinancial motivators such as appreciation, empowerment, and opportunities for professional development can also be quite effective.

Fortunately for teachers, there is no easy way to assess teachers' performance or competence. Part of the problem, note Milanowski, Odden, and Youngs (1998) is that we don't know precisely what competent teaching is or what the differences are between competent and less competent teachers. These authors analyzed tests now being developed to assess teaching skills. They conclude that more work needs to be done on assessment instruments. As a result, formal on-the-job evaluations of teacher competence

---

teacher competence A phrase used to describe the measurable performance of teachers—often assessed through the achievement of students.

merit pay A monetary incentive used to reward teacher competence.

tend to be rare (Shuler, 1996). And where assessments were attempted on a wide scale (in Texas, for example; see Millman & Darling-Hammond, 1990) one of the results was significant demoralization of teachers. Many of them objected to the implicit questioning of their competence and to the largely negative portrayal of teachers' competence widely disseminated by the media.

Nevertheless, teacher training institutions do, in fact, assess teacher competence—as do state or provincial teacher certification authorities (Holden, 1996). They do so when they decide to license a teacher (or, heaven forbid, not to). And, as Klein (1998) points out, an increasing number of jurisdictions are requiring teachers to write (and pass) one or more tests as a condition of employment. These tests are not simply paper-and-pencil tests (such as multiple-choice tests) but also include performance tests (where prospective teachers might be asked to make a presentation, for example).

But the significance of teacher accountability and teacher competence for you as a teacher is hardly limited to whether some authority decides, at some point in time, that you are competent to *begin* teaching. Being a thoughtful, dedicated, *reflective* teacher bent on self-improvement requires constant and systematic reflection upon and evaluation of your performance and effectiveness. Wiggins (1998) suggests that teachers should avail themselves of opportunities for peer review as well as self-review. To this end, he suggests that teachers videotape and analyze their own or others' instructional procedures, or that they observe other teachers and be observed by them.

It's easy to understand the administration's and the public's wish to monitor teachers' behavior and to assess their responsiveness to parental and administrative expectations. One manifestation of this wish to evaluate teachers is found in the widespread requirement that teachers specify instructional objectives for their courses. Whether instructional objectives are met can

provide one index of a teacher's effectiveness. But this is not the best reason for using instructional objectives; their contribution to good teaching and learning is even more important.

Mager's Instructional Objectives

To be useful, says Mager (1962, 1984), instructional objectives must specify clearly what the learner should be able to do following instruction. One useful instructional objective is a statement of the instructor's goals in *behavioral terms*—that is, worded in terms of the actual, observable performance of the student. This type of **behavioral objective** serves as a description of course goals and as a guide for instructional strategy. And, equally important, because it describes specific, observable behaviors as goals of the instructional process, it also serves as a guide for assessing students' and teachers' performance.

Characteristics of Good Behavioral Objectives

Consider the following statements of instructional objectives:

1. The student should understand evolutionary theory.

2. The student should be able to state the two Darwinian laws of evolution and give examples of each.

Mager argues that the second objective is more useful than the first for several reasons. The second objective specifies exactly what students must do to demonstrate that they have reached the course goal, it provides the teacher with specific guidelines for determining whether course goals have been reached, and it suggests

---

behavioral objective A phrase used to describe an instructional objective that can be expressed in terms of specific, observable, measurable behaviors. Mager's instructional objectives are behavioral objectives.

what must be taught if course goals are to be reached.

In contrast, the first statement, because of its use of the ambiguous term *understand* and the global phrase "evolutionary theory," does none of these things. It is clearly open to misinterpretation. Similarly, terms such as *know*, *appreciate*, and *master* are rarely found in the kind of objectives Mager recommends—unless, of course, the nature of knowing, appreciating, or mastering is also clearly spelled out. For example, President Bush's phrase "use the mind well" needs to be made more specific to be useful. We need to know what is involved in using the mind well.

A second quality of meaningful instructional objectives is that they often establish specific criteria of acceptable performance. Consider the following statements:

1. The learner will be able to translate a simple passage from French to English.

2. The learner will be able to translate a simple passage from French to English without use of a dictionary. The passage will be taken from the prescribed text, and the translation will be considered correct if there are no more than 5 errors for each 100 words of text and acceptable if the translation is completed in no more than 20 minutes for each 100 words.

The second statement is more precise than the first, and again it is more useful for both the instructor and the learner. It specifies the nature of the expected behavior and the constraints under which it is to be performed to be considered acceptable.

Writing good instructional objectives is a time-consuming task. However, carefully prepared objectives can be of tremendous assistance to teachers for planning instructional strategies and evaluating their own performance and also that of their students. If statements of behavioral objectives are given to each student at the begin-

ning of courses, units, or lessons, they can also be of tremendous value to the learner. For example, Aboderin and Thomas (1996) found that high school students who were given specific objectives did significantly better on subsequent achievement tests than did students who were not given objectives. And in this study involving some 730 students, it made little difference whether the objectives were given prior to text material, interspersed within the material, or even at the end. In Mager's words, "If you give each learner a copy of your objectives, you may not have to do much else" (1962, p. 53).

Gronlund's General and Specific Objectives

Not all educators agree that Mager's approach to instructional objectives is the best. Recent decades have seen a marked shift away from a behavioral orientation in psychology and education—an orientation that emphasizes measurable outcomes that could be expressed in Mager-type behavioral objectives. The behavioral orientation, notes Winn (1990), has gradually been replaced by a more cognitive orientation—an orientation that emphasizes understanding and other outcomes that are more difficult to measure—and one that is reflected in a movement from the more objective multiple-choice assessment to performance and portfolio assessment (discussed later).

Emphasis on precise, performance-oriented objectives is both appropriate and effective for simple skills and for content areas that can be described in terms of specific items of information, Gronlund (1995) claims. But such emphasis is considerably less appropriate for more complex subjects and more advanced cognitive behaviors. As Nahl-Jakobovits and Jakobovits (1993) point out, performance objectives do not recognize the importance of affective outcomes. The most effective teachers, they argue, are those who integrate the great variety of objectives they have for their students.

Accordingly, Gronlund suggests that teachers express main objectives in general rather than specific terms. Each main objective should then be elaborated in terms of more specific learning outcomes or, in many cases, in terms of actual examples of behaviors that would reflect the primary objective. These examples can then be used as a basis for what is termed *performance* or *authentic assessment*.

The former U.S. president's admonition that schools should "ensure that all students learn to use their minds" is a highly general objective. However, the extent to which it has been accomplished (or is being accomplished) can be ascertained far more easily if we can describe specific examples of performances or products that illustrate "using the mind." There is an important difference between these examples of behaviors and Mager's instructional objectives. Mager's objectives specify actual behaviors that constitute instructional objectives in and of themselves. What Gronlund recommends, however, are not objectives per se but are instead examples of the types of evidence that a teacher can look for to determine whether the primary objective has been attained. For instance, the primary objective might be the development of a certain attitude; specific behaviors would serve as evidence of attainment of that attitude. (Figure 13.2 summarizes the differences between these two viewpoints.)

Examples of Mager- and Gronlund-Type Objectives

To illustrate and clarify the preceding passage, consider the following objectives for a poetry unit. Objectives based on Mager's approach might include such statements as these:

1. The student should be able to name the titles and authors of five poems in the unit.

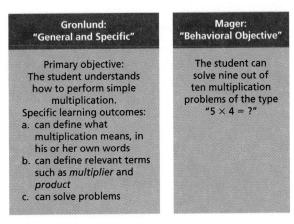

FIGURE 13.2 Types of instructional objectives

2. The student should be able to recite, with no more than three errors, ten consecutive lines from a single poem in the unit.

Gronlund's objectives might begin with a general, affective objective (#1 below) and then elaborate further with specific behavioral examples (2 and 3):

1. The student should develop knowledge and appreciation of, and liking for, the Romantic poets.

2. The student chooses to read (or write) poetry during a free reading period.

3. The student attempts to evaluate poetry as either good or bad (or to compare different poems).

In summary, each of these approaches to the formulation of instructional objectives has advantages and disadvantages. Mager's approach emphasizes specificity and objective behaviors and is particularly useful for simple skills and factual content areas. Gronlund's suggestions are useful for more complex subject areas and for high-level intellectual processes and can also be used to formulate specific objectives. There is clearly room for each in the conscientious teacher's repertoire.

Bloom's Taxonomy of Educational Objectives

Objectives are desired outcomes. School-related objectives include both the specific instructional objectives of teachers and the wider objectives of curricula, programs, principals, and communities—things like "using the mind" and "being responsible citizens." Questions relating to the wider objectives of education have traditionally been in the domains of philosophy, politics, and economics rather than psychology, and such objectives are seldom evaluated directly in schools—although perhaps they should be. Most classroom evaluation relates to the teachers' more specific objectives.

As an aid to teachers trying to sort out the most useful and appropriate objectives for their instructional efforts, Bloom and his associates have provided exhaustive lists of cognitive and affective educational objectives (referred to as a **taxonomy of educational objectives**) (Bloom et al., 1956; Krathwohl, Bloom, & Masia, 1964). The usefulness of lists such as these is that they can serve as guides for determining the goals for a lesson or course. As Ross (1993) notes, they can also be used as a model in designing educational computer-based programs such as those that use **hypertext**, an organizational method that allows the user to move freely among related topics. The taxonomy of objectives for the **cognitive domain**, for example, describes a class of objectives, a list of educational objectives that correspond to this class, and test questions that illustrate it (see Table 13.2). The six hierarchical classes of objectives in that domain are, from the lowest to the highest level: knowledge (factual information); **comprehension** (obtaining meaningfulness); **application** (using information, applying it in practical situations); **analysis** (breaking something down into components to arrive at comprehension); **synthesis** (understanding by looking at the larger organization); and *evaluation* (arriving at value judgment, weighing value).

---

taxonomy of educational objectives An exhaustive list of possible educational outcomes that can serve as a guide for compiling instructional objectives. The best-known taxonomy of educational objectives is Bloom's, which provides objectives in both the cognitive and the affective domains.

hypertext A basic organizational mode for computer-based information that allows the user to jump from topic to topic and back again.

cognitive domain Bloom's expression for the area of educational activity and educational objectives relating to acquiring information, understanding, analyzing, synthesizing, and so on.

comprehension The lowest level of understanding in Bloom's hierarchy of educational objectives. Comprehension is defined as the ability to apprehend the meaning of communication without necessarily being able to apply, analyze, or evaluate it.

application An educational objective described by Bloom. Consists primarily of the ability to use abstractions in concrete situations.

analysis The process of breaking something down into its component parts. As an intellectual activity, it consists primarily of examining the relationships among ideas in an attempt to understand them better. It is a relatively high-level intellectual skill in Bloom's taxonomy of educational objectives.

synthesis Putting together of parts to form a whole; complementary to analysis; a high-level intellectual ability in Bloom's taxonomy of educational objectives.

TABLE 13.2
Bloom's Cognitive Domain, Defined and Illustrated

CLASS OF OBJECTIVES	EXAMPLE
1. Knowledge (items of factual information)	Who wrote *A Midsummer Night's Dream*?
2. Comprehension (understanding, obtaining meaning from communication)	What was the author trying to say?
3. Application (using information, principles, etc., to solve problems)	Given what you know about the authenticity of the first quarto and about weather conditions in England in the summer of 1594, when do you think the play was written?
4. Analysis (arriving at an understanding by looking at individual parts)	Find the most basic metaphors in Act I and explain their meaning.
5. Synthesis (arriving at an understanding by looking at the larger structure or by combining individual elements)	Identify the four themes in *A Midsummer Night's Dream* and discuss how they contribute to the central action.
6. Evaluation (arriving at value judgments)	Do you agree with the statement that *A Midsummer Night's Dream* is Shakespeare's first undisputed masterpiece? Explain your answer.

Bloom and associates also list objectives in the **affective domain**. These deal with the learner's emotional reactions—that is, with motivational aspects of behavior including such things as interest, involvement, commitment, and positive or negative evaluation. See Bloom's handbook of objectives (Bloom et al., 1956) for a more detailed consideration of Bloom's taxonomy of educational objectives.

In an earlier section we noted the importance of what teachers test—how what they test determines what and how students learn. We also noted that schools tend to evaluate students on the basis of how many textbook- and teacher-presented facts they remember rather than on the basis of how much they understand, how cleverly they generalize and extrapolate, or how elegantly they formulate hypotheses and generate new concepts. Research on Bloom's taxonomy corroborates this unhappy finding. Fleming and Chambers (1983) analyzed more than 8,800 questions used primarily in high school tests. Nearly 80 percent dealt only with knowledge of facts and specifics—the lowest level in Bloom's taxonomy (see the box entitled "Remembering and Thinking").

Gagné's Learning Outcomes

Closely related to Bloom's taxonomy of educational objectives are what Gagné terms **learning outcomes**—the new capabilities that result from learning. There are five major domains of such learned capabilities: intellectual skills, verbal information, attitudes, motor skills, and cognitive strategies. These five domains represent, in effect, all the possible outcomes of the learning process.

---

affective domain Bloom's expression for the grouping of educational goals that relate to affect (emotion) and that are evident in behaviors relating to motivation, interest, and values.

learning outcomes Gagné's phrase for the new learning or capabilities that result from instruction and learning. According to his model, there are five major classes of possible outcomes of learning (intellectual skills, verbal information, attitudes, motor skills, and cognitive strategies).

Remembering and Thinking

The six classes of objectives described by Bloom and associates (1956) fall into two broad classes: those that involve remembering and those that require thinking. Only the knowledge objectives fall into the first category (knowledge of specifics, knowledge of ways and means of dealing with specifics, and knowledge of the universals and abstractions in a field). All these objectives emphasize remembering.

Most teachers want to teach for understanding (comprehension, application, and so on) as well as for recall. Yet few clearly know the precise skills involved in intellectual activities such as comprehension, application, synthesis, analysis, or evaluation. The two most frequently confused skills are comprehension and application.

Comprehension is the lowest level of understanding, implying no more than the ability to apprehend the substance of what is being communicated without necessarily relating it to other material. It can be tested by using items that require students to translate (change from one form of communication to another, express in their own words); interpret (explain or summarize); or extrapolate (predict consequences or arrive at conclusions).

Application, on the other hand, requires that learners be able to use what they comprehend—abstract from one situation to another. Application cannot be tested simply by asking students to interpret or translate; they must also be required to abstract the material to see its implications.

One final point: Your instructional objectives (what you want from your students) are communicated directly and effectively to your students through your measurement devices. Even if you emphasize repeatedly that you want to teach for comprehension and other high-level skills, you will probably be unsuccessful unless you construct achievement tests that reflect these objectives. In the final analysis, your students will study what you test.

Like Bloom's taxonomy of educational objectives, Gagné's learning outcomes can serve as a guide for formulating instructional objectives—as illustrated in Table 13.3. Also, much of the practical usefulness of Gagné's instructional theory derives from his analysis of the conditions most conducive to learning the capabilities represented by each of the five domains. Knowledge of these conditions can be valuable in suggesting appropriate instructional strategies, as also shown in Table 13.3 (Gagné, Briggs, & Wager, 1992).

Calvin and Hobbes   by Bill Watterson

Calvin and Hobbes © Watterson. Distributed by Universal Press Syndicate. Reprinted with permission. All rights reserved.

TABLE 13.3
Gagné's Major Learning Outcomes as Instructional Objectives with Suggestions Relevant for Instruction

OUTCOMES OF LEARNING	ILLUSTRATIVE INSTRUCTIONAL OBJECTIVE	INSTRUCTIONAL CONDITIONS THAT FACILITATE OUTCOMES
1. Intellectual skills		
High-order rules	Learner determines how to calculate the area of a trapezoid.	Review of relevant rules; verbal instruction to aid in recall of rules; verbal instructions to direct thinking
Rules	Learner discovers characteristics common to all mammals.	Learner is made aware of desired learning outcome; relevant concepts are reviewed; concrete examples are provided
Concepts	Learner classifies objects by size and color.	Examples presented; learner engaged in finding examples; reinforcement
Discriminations	Learner distinguishes among printed letters.	Simultaneous presentation of stimuli to be discriminated; reinforcement (confirmation); repetition
Simple types of learning (signal learning; stimulus–response learning; chaining)	Learner is conditioned to respond favorably to school.	Reinforcement; models; positive experiences in various school contexts
2. Verbal information	Learner writes down Gagné's five major learning domains.	Information that organizes content (advance organizers); meaningful context; instructional aids for retention and motivation
3. Cognitive strategies	Learner devises personal strategy for remembering components of basic information processing model.	Frequent presentation of novel and challenging problems; discussion and direct teaching of cognitive strategies
4. Attitudes	Learner chooses to read educational psychology text rather than a novel.	Models; reinforcement; verbal guidance
5. Motor skills	Learner types a summary of this chapter.	Models; verbal directions; reinforcement (knowledge of results); practice

BLUEPRINTS FOR TEACHER-MADE TESTS

We should emphasize at the outset that a test—whether it is a **teacher-made test** or a **standardized test**—is not like other common measuring instruments, such as rulers, scales, and thermometers. Rulers measure whatever they measure directly; our psychological and educational instruments measure indirectly.

In effect, a student's test performance consists of a sample of behaviors (selected from many potential behaviors) that (we assume) represents knowledge, ability, or attitude. We then

---

teacher-made test Any of the wide variety of tests written, developed, or organized by teachers, usually for the purpose of evaluating students or assessing the effectiveness of instruction.

standardized test A professionally developed—rather than teacher-made—test that provides the user with norms (standards) and typically indicates the average or expected performance of groups of subjects of certain grades or ages.

use this sample of behaviors as a basis for making inferences. The inferences we make about knowledge, ability, or other student characteristics are never based on direct measurement; they are simply inferences—educated bits of speculation based on nothing more than a sample of behavior. Hence, the question of precisely which behaviors to sample is extremely important.

As you probably know, the business of preparing tests, exams, and quizzes is often a pretty haphazard process. Teachers have a general idea of the sorts of things they want their students to learn, so they sit down near the end of the unit or term and fashion a compilation of questions that they hope will measure reasonably accurately some of the things they intended to teach. Some teachers are better than others at putting together appropriate questions. Many, however, could be helped considerably by learning more clearly the characteristics of good and bad test items (discussed later in this chapter) and by systematically attempting to blueprint their tests even before they begin to teach the relevant series of lessons.

A **test blueprint** is, in effect, a table of specifications for a test. It details the topics to be

tested, the nature of the questions to be used, how many questions will relate to each topic, and the sorts of cognitive processes to be sampled. Test blueprints need not be developed only by the teacher; they can also involve the collaboration of the students. Constructing the blueprint can do a great deal to clarify instructional goals, both for the teacher and for students. It can also contribute in important ways to the teacher's selection of instructional strategies and to the students' monitoring of their own learning processes.

Detailed test blueprints that take into consideration differences among possible learning outcomes can be based on systems such as Bloom's taxonomy or Gagné's learning outcomes. A typical test blueprint based on portions of Bloom's taxonomy, for example, takes the form of a table that lists all relevant topics and all classes of objectives and specifies the number of items for each topic relating to each class of objectives (see Table 13.4). One alternative to this, as Popham (1999) suggests, is to use simpler classifications that teachers and students might find easier and more useful. For example, items might be divided simply in terms of whether they involve mere recall or go beyond recall.

There are various other ways to devise test blueprints; some of these are easier and more useful in certain subjects. In physical education classes, for example, Bloom's taxonomy and

---

test blueprint A table of specifications for a teacher-made test. A good test blueprint provides information about the topics to be tested, the nature of the questions to be used, and the objectives (outcomes) to be assessed.

TABLE 13.4
A Simple Test Blueprint, Based on Bloom's Taxonomy,
Cognitive Domain, for Chapter 6 of This Text

Chapter 6 Topics	NUMBER OF ITEMS BY CLASS OF OBJECTIVES					
	Knowledge	Comprehension	Application	Analysis	Synthesis	Evaluation
Bruner's theory	3	4	3	2	2	1
Ausubel's theory	3	3	2	2	2	1
Other models	4	3	3	2	2	3
Totals	10	10	8	6	6	5

other similar classifications are not entirely relevant, so teachers might simply make a list of the skills that students are expected to acquire. This list of skills, together with an indication of the criteria that will be used as evidence of skill mastery, can serve as a test blueprint. Unfortunately, this kind of test blueprint in physical education classes is rare. Most often, teachers rely on informal, intuitive evaluation. And although there is clearly a need for such evaluation, it is seldom as impartial as more formal evaluation. Nor does it serve nearly as well as a guide to instruction.

CHARACTERISTICS OF A GOOD MEASURING INSTRUMENT

Probably the most important characteristic of a good test from the students' point of view is that it be fair (Shohamy, 1997). Essentially, this means that the test should reflect instructional objectives as they are understood by students— that is, it should reflect what was to be learned (and, presumably, what was actually taught). Also, as Elder (1997) notes, language difficulties such as those faced by minority-language students sometimes make tests seem grossly unfair. And, of course, if the test reveals weaknesses in underlying abilities *when no such weaknesses exist*, it is, by definition, unfair. Elder cautions, however, that what seem to be the effects of language problems can occasionally be indications of real differences.

From a measurement point of view, good measuring instruments have two important qualities: validity and reliability.

Validity

A test is valid if it measures what it is intended to measure; many tests don't, or else they measure many other things as well and are consequently not very dependable. **Validity** is the most important characteristic of a measuring instrument. If

a test does not measure what it purports to, the scores derived from it are of no value whatsoever.

Face Validity There are several different ways to measure or estimate validity—several indexes of validity (see Figure 13.3). The first, **face validity**, is the extent to which the test appears to measure what it is supposed to measure. This is probably the easiest type of validity to determine; if a test looks valid, it at least has face validity. Face validity is especially important for teacher-made tests. Students should know just by looking at a test that they are being tested on the appropriate things. A mathematics test that has face validity will consist of items that look like math items.

In some circumstances, however, test makers carefully avoid any semblance of face validity. Tests designed to measure personality characteristics such as honesty or openness, for example, are likely to be highly invalid if they appear to measure what they are actually intended to measure. Because we know that dishonest people might well lie to us, we are not likely to obtain an accurate measure of their honesty if we let them know what we are measuring. Better to deceive them, lie to them, to determine what liars and scoundrels they really are.

Content Validity A second important index of the extent to which a test measures what it purports to measure, **content validity**, is assessed by analyzing the content of test items in relation to the

---

validity The extent to which a test measures what it intends to measure. For example, an intelligence test is valid to the extent that it measures intelligence and nothing else. Educational and psychological tests are limited by their frequently low validity.

face validity The extent to which a test appears to be measuring what it is intended to measure.

content validity Test validity determined by a careful analysis of the content of test items and a comparison of this content with course objectives.

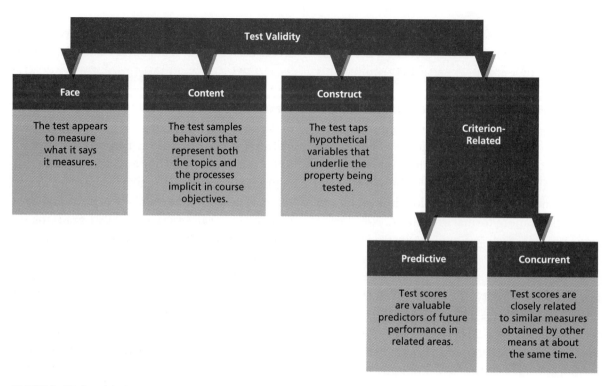

FIGURE 13.3 Types of test validity: determining whether a test measures what it purports to measure

objectives of the course, unit, or lesson. Content validity is perhaps the most crucial kind of validity for measurements of school achievement. A test with high content validity includes items that sample all important course objectives (both content [product] and process objectives) in proportion to their importance. Thus, if the objectives of an instructional sequence include the development of cognitive processes, a relevant test will have content validity only to the extent that it samples these processes. And if 40 percent of the course content (and, consequently, of the course objectives) deals with knowledge (rather than with comprehension, analysis, and so on), 40 percent of the test items should assess knowledge.

Determining the content validity of a test is largely a matter of careful, logical analysis. As Oosterhof (1994) notes, one of the main advantages of preparing a test blueprint (table of spec-

ifications) of the kind described earlier is that it ensures content validity (providing, of course, that the test maker follows the blueprint).

Tests and test items do not possess validity as a sort of intrinsic quality; that is, a test is not generally valid or generally invalid. Rather, it is valid for certain purposes and with certain individuals and invalid for others. For example, if the following item is intended to measure comprehension, it does not have content validity:

How many different kinds of validity are discussed in this chapter?

a. 1   b. 2   c. 3   d. 5   e. 10

If, on the other hand, this item were intended to measure knowledge of specifics, it would have content validity. And an item such as the following might have content validity with respect to measuring comprehension:

Explain why face validity is important for teacher-constructed tests.

However, this last item measures comprehension only if students have not been explicitly taught an appropriate answer. That is, it is possible to teach principles, applications, analyses, and so on as *specifics*, so that questions of this sort require no more than recall of knowledge. What an item measures is not inherent in the item itself but in the relationship between the material as it has been taught to the student and what the item requires.

Construct Validity A third type of validity, **construct validity**, is conceptually more difficult than either face or content validity. It is somewhat less relevant for teacher-constructed tests but extremely relevant for many other psychological measures (personality and intelligence tests, for example).

In essence, a construct is a hypothetical variable—an unobservable characteristic or quality, often inferred from theory. For example, a theory might specify that individuals who are very intelligent should be reflective rather than impulsive—reflectivity being evident in the care and caution with which the individual solves problems or makes decisions, and impulsivity being apparent in the individual's haste and failure to consider all aspects of a situation. One way to determine the construct validity of a test designed to measure intelligence would then be to examine how well it correlates with measures of reflection and impulsivity. (See Chapter 8 for a discussion of correlation.)

Criterion-Related Validity One of the main uses of tests is to predict future performance. Thus, we assume that all students who do well on year-end fifth-grade achievement tests will do reasonably well in sixth grade. We also predict that those who perform poorly on these tests will not do well in sixth grade, and we might use this prediction as justification for allowing them to fail fifth grade. The extent to which our predictions are accurate reflects **criterion-related validity**. One component of this form of validity, which we just described, is labeled **predictive validity** and is easily measured by looking at the relationship between test performance and subsequent performance. Thus, a college entrance examination designed to identify students whose chances of success in college are good has predictive validity to the extent that its predictions are borne out.

Concurrent validity, a second aspect of criterion-related validity, is the relationship between a test and other measures of the same behaviors. For example, the most accurate way to measure intelligence is to administer a time-consuming and expensive individual test; a second way is to administer a quick, inexpensive group test; a third, far less consistent approach, is to ask teachers to informally assess intelligence on the basis of what they know of their students' achievement and effort. Teachers' assessments are said to have concurrent validity to the extent that they correlate with the more formal measures. In the same way, the group test is said to have concurrent validity if it agrees well with measures obtained in other ways.

Reliability

Good measuring instruments are not only valid; they are also *reliable*. A reliable test is one that measures whatever it measures consistently. An intelligence test that yields a score of 170 for a

---

construct validity An estimate of test validity based on the extent to which test results agree with and reflect the theories that underlie the test.

criterion-related validity A measure of the extent to which predictions based on test results are accurate (predictive validity) and how well the test agrees with other related measures (concurrent validity).

student one week and a score of 80 the next week is probably somewhat unreliable (unless something quite dramatic happened to the student during the week).

Types of Reliability A test that is highly unreliable cannot be valid. Put another way, if a test measures what it purports to, and if what it measures does not fluctuate unpredictably, no matter how often it is given, the test should yield similar scores (unless, of course, the test is simple enough that the student learns and remembers appropriate responses from one testing to the next). Hence, one way to assess *reliability* is to look at the correlation between results obtained by giving the test twice or by giving two different forms of the same test to the same individuals. These are called **repeated-measures reliability** and **parallel-forms reliability**.

Another way to determine reliability, called **split-half reliability**, is to administer the test and then divide it into two halves for scoring. If all items are intended to measure the same things, the scores on the two halves should be similar.

Factors that Affect Reliability One factor that contributes to the reliability of a test is the stability of what is being measured. Clearly, if a characteristic fluctuates dramatically over time, measurements of that characteristic will also

fluctuate. However, most of what we measure in psychology and education is not expected to fluctuate unpredictably. That is, although we expect change in many characteristics, we can often predict the nature of the change. Students are expected to read better, understand more clearly, solve more problems, and generally improve cognitively throughout the course of their schooling. Tests that are valid and reliable should reflect these changes.

A second important factor, particularly with respect to teacher-constructed, multiple-choice, or true–false tests, is chance. As an example, consider a test consisting of 20 true–false items. The chance of getting any single item correct, if the student knows next to absolutely nothing, is one out of two. Hence, unless Lady Luck is looking pointedly in the other direction, the average score of a large class of hypothetical know-nothings should be about 50 percent. And some of the luckier individuals in this class may have astoundingly high scores. But a subsequent administration of this or a parallel examination might lead to startlingly different results.

One way to increase test reliability is obvious: Make tests longer. Of course, this does not mean that short objective tests must be avoided. In the long run, the effects of chance tend to even out; 100 short tests, taken all together, make up one long, sometimes highly reliable test. The most important admonition is simply that the teacher should not place undue confidence in the results of only a handful of short tests where the effects of chance cannot easily be controlled.

Another way of increasing the reliability of multiple-choice tests is to use a preponderance of items of moderate difficulty, rather than throwing in several very difficult or very easy items (Feldt, 1993). Other things being equal, using items that are either very easy or very difficult tends to result in less consistent patterns of responding.

---

repeated-measures reliability An estimate of the consistency (reliability) of a test based on the degree of agreement among scores obtained from different presentations of the same test.

parallel-forms reliability A measure of test consistency (reliability) obtained by looking at the correlation between scores obtained by the same individual on two different but equivalent (parallel) forms of one test.

split-half reliability An index of test reliability (consistency) derived by arbitrarily dividing a test into parallel halves (odd- and even-numbered items, for example) and looking at the agreement between scores obtained by each individual on the two halves.

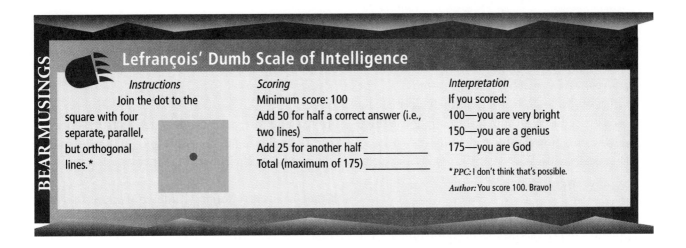

Lefrançois' Dumb Scale of Intelligence

Instructions
Join the dot to the square with four separate, parallel, but orthogonal lines.*

Scoring
Minimum score: 100
Add 50 for half a correct answer (i.e., two lines) _____
Add 25 for another half _____
Total (maximum of 175) _____

Interpretation
If you scored:
100—you are very bright
150—you are a genius
175—you are God

*PPC: I don't think that's possible.
Author: You score 100. Bravo!

Although a test cannot be valid without also being reliable, it can be reliable without being valid. Consider the box entitled "Lefrançois' Dumb Scale of Intelligence." This intelligence test has been demonstrated to be extremely reliable (as well as extremely democratic). In other words, it is extremely consistent: Testees obtain the same scores repeatedly. Bright people usually score 100; geniuses, 150; and God, 175. Unfortunately, however, the test is desperately invalid.

STANDARDIZED TESTS

A test is a collection of tasks (items or questions) assumed to be a representative sample of the behaviors that the tester wishes to assess. Given that human beings vary in countless ways, there are many types of tests and examples of each type. A few examples of psychological tests (creativity and intelligence) were given in Chapter 8. These tests are called *standardized tests*. They are so called because they provide standards (also called "norms") by which to judge the performance of individual students. Thus, intelligence tests are typically standardized so that average performance is reflected in a score close to 100. The norms for intelligence tests also tell us what

distribution of scores we might expect for a large group.

A large collection of tests that is particularly important for classroom teachers is **standardized achievement tests**. These professionally developed tests are available for virtually every school subject and are designed to provide teachers, school administrators, and parents with information about the relative performance of individual students, classes, or schools. The indication of relative performance is typically derived by comparing students' test results to the norms provided with the test. Hence, almost all standardized tests include the testing material itself and a manual that specifies the objectives of the test (what it is designed to measure), the age and grade levels for which it is appropriate, the samples on which it was standardized, and tables for converting the students' raw scores to scores that can be compared directly with the test norms.

Many school jurisdictions make routine use of achievement tests. One study reports that

---

standardized achievement test A professionally developed and normed test that is designed to measure achievement and to provide some basis for judging the relative quality of that achievement, given the student's age and grade placement.

students between first and fifth grades can expect to take an average of 1½ standardized achievement tests per year (Levin, 1983). Unfortunately, teachers don't often use the results of these tests to modify their instructional procedures, although they might use them to make decisions about student placement.

Uses of Standardized Tests

The main purpose of standardized tests, says Popham (1999), has always been to compare the performance of a single test taker to the average or expected performance of a comparable group—namely, the group on which the test was standardized. This permits schools and teachers to use tests for at least five distinct reasons (R. L. Linn, 1986).

The first reason is for placement in special education programs. As we saw in Chapter 8, intelligence tests, which are a common form of standardized *ability* test, are widely used for this purpose. However, legal challenges of their fairness have often been successful, especially when it could be shown that a test was biased toward a certain group. These legal challenges have resulted in the modification of some tests to reduce their biases, the translation of tests into different languages, and the use of a variety of assessment procedures in addition to intelligence tests. Recall that Public Law 94-142 mandates each of these changes.

The second use of standardized tests is to certify students' achievement. Minimum competency tests are a clear example of this use, as are the variety of standardized entrance examinations used to decide whether to accept an applicant for a course of study and the standardized final examinations used to determine success or failure following a course.

Besides these two principal uses, standardized tests are being used in some jurisdictions to determine the competency of teachers, to evalu-ate schools (through the performance of students), and for instructional diagnosis.

Using Standardized Test Norms

To use and interpret standardized tests, it is necessary to know about the types of scores and norms that are used with them.

Grade-Equivalent Norms Grade-equivalent scores are the most common among the various norms that are typically provided with standardized tests. These norms allow teachers to convert a **raw score** on a test to a grade equivalent (raw score means the actual, untransformed score on the test). Thus, students who take a standardized reading test will typically have their scores converted to a grade-equivalent score, meaning, essentially, that this student is reading at a grade level of 3, or 3.5, or 5, or whatever.

Several cautions are in order when interpreting grade-equivalent scores. First—and this applies to all standardized tests—it is extremely important to make sure that the test is suitable for the children being tested and that the norms are appropriate. Just as intelligence tests are often biased against groups for whom they were not normed, so too achievement tests are often biased against students whose school curriculum is different from that of the norming population or whose social, language, and ethnic backgrounds are different.

Once you have determined that an achievement test is suitable and that grade-equivalent

---

grade-equivalent score A score that has been converted to a grade equivalent using standardized test norms. It allows the user to conclude that the testee has performed at a level comparable to that of average children at a specified grade level.

raw score The actual numerical score that a testee obtains on a test; the testee's score before it is converted to a grade- or age-equivalent score, an IQ, or some other norm.

scores are therefore meaningful, it is important to know precisely what their meaning is. A grade-equivalent reading score of 5 obtained by a fourth-grade student does not indicate that the student should be in fifth grade. In fact, the raw score that corresponds to this grade-equivalent score is simply the average score of a large number of fifth-grade students. A few fifth-grade students will have scored either much higher or much lower. Similarly, many fourth-grade students in the norming group will have raw scores as high as some of the fifth-grade students. Hence, an achievement test does not separate cleanly among different grade levels; it does not give us an absolutely accurate index of what grade level a student should be. Furthermore, achievement tests given at different times of the year can produce markedly different results. For example, scores obtained immediately after summer vacation are often much lower than scores obtained just before the end of the previous term.

Age-Equivalent Norms Most achievement tests designed for use in schools provide grade-equivalent scores, although many also provide one or more of a variety of other types of norms, including age equivalents (and norms such as Z-scores, T-scores, percentiles, and stanines, explained in the box entitled "Norms and the Normal Distribution"). **Age-equivalent scores,** as the label implies, are norms expressed in terms of ages rather than grades. Such norms make provisions for converting raw scores to age equivalents that can be interpreted to mean that a student is functioning at a level comparable to the average for a specific age group. Age-

equivalent scores are more common for intelligence tests and other measures of ability or aptitude than they are for achievement tests. This is true largely because it is more meaningful to say that a person is intellectually at the level of a 4-year-old or a 9-year-old than to say that someone reads at a 4-year-old or a 9-year-old level. When interpreting age-equivalent scores, observe the same cautions as when interpreting grade-equivalent scores. The most important caution is that these scores represent averages; hence, there is a wide range of scores within most groups. Because standardized tests are far from completely valid or reliable, we should also be careful not to rely on them too heavily.

Some Pros and Cons of Standardized Tests There is ongoing controversy concerning the use of standardized tests in schools. On the one hand, many educators feel that the tests are unfair, biased, unreliable, and often invalid—that they are excellent examples of "science and technology run amok" (Wigdor & Garner, 1982). On the other hand, many argue that in spite of their weaknesses, standardized tests are more likely to be valid, reliable, objective, and fair than other forms of evidence upon which teachers and educators base their judgments.

During the middle of the 20th century, the antitesting movement seemed to be becoming dominant. Increasing numbers of school jurisdictions began to abandon the use of standardized tests; their use seemed incompatible with the cry for equity (R. L. Linn, 1986). But the pendulum now seems to have swung in the opposite direction once more. One important reason for this most recent swing was the publication of the report "A Nation at Risk" (National Commission on Excellence in Education, 1983). Among other things, the report put forth a cry for excellence rather than simply for equity and raised the frightening possibility that U.S. schoolchildren might be seriously deficient in basic reading,

---

age-equivalent score A score converted to age equivalents using standardized test norms. Such norms allow test users to interpret the subject's performance in terms of the average performance of a comparable group of children of a specified age.

Norms and the Normal Distribution

BEAR MUSINGS

If you threw 100 coins onto a table 1,000 times and recorded the number of heads and tails that came up each of the 1,000 times, a figure representing your tallies would probably look very much like the one in this box (here, the "0" represents 50 heads and 50 tails, and the scale on either side represents an increasing proportion of heads or tails).

This figure shows a **normal curve**—a mathematical abstraction to which the majority of the observations that concern us in the social sciences and in education conform. When we know that a set of observations, such as test scores, is distributed normally, we also know what a graphic representation of these scores would look like if we had enough of them. We know that most of the scores would cluster around the **mean** (arithmetical average) and that there would be fewer and fewer scores as we got farther and farther away from the mean.

Thus, if we knew the average, we might have some idea of what a score meant. But we would have an even better idea of its meaning if we also knew the **standard deviation**, which tells us how scores are distributed around the

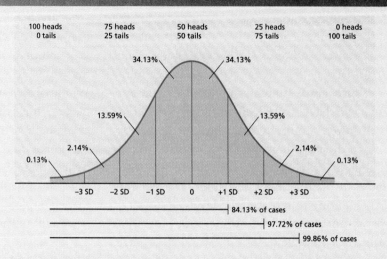

mean. Knowing the standard deviation allows us to determine how unusual a score is, because we know that approximately 66 percent of all observations will fall within 1 standard deviation of the mean, and approximately 95 percent will fall within 2 standard deviations of the mean. Hence, those who score higher than 2 standard deviations above a mean will be in the top 2.5 percent of the population.

To interpret a test score (providing we can assume that a large collection of such scores would be normally distributed), it follows that we especially need

to know the mean and the standard deviation. This is, in fact, what most manuals accompanying standardized tests tell us when they describe test norms.

Test norms can take a variety of forms, including age and grade equivalents or simply means and standard deviations. They can also be expressed as **percentiles**, **Z-scores**, **T-scores**, or **stanines**.

Percentiles indicate the percentage of scores that falls below a given point. Thus, the 75th percentile is the point at or below which 75 percent of all observations fall. If a student scores at the

---

normal curve A mathematical function that can be represented in the form of a bell-shaped curve. Many naturally occurring events are normally distributed; the vast majority of the events, or scores, cluster around the middle of the distribution, around the mean or median, with progressively fewer scores farther away from the average.

mean The arithmetic average of a set of scores. In distributions that are skewed (top- and bottom-heavy), the mean is not the best index of central tendency; that is, it is not necessarily at the middle of the distribution.

standard deviation A mathematical measure of the distribution of scores around their mean. In a normal distribution,

approximately two-thirds of all scores fall within 1 standard deviation on either side of the mean, and almost 95 percent fall within 2 standard deviations of the mean.

percentile The point at or below which a specified percentage of scores fall. For example, the 50th percentile is the point at or below which 50 percent of all scores fall. A score of 50 percent is not necessarily at the 50th percentile.

Z-score A standardized score with a mean of 0 and a standard deviation of 1. Hence, a Z-score of +3 is very high; a score of −3 is very low.

T-score A standardized score with a preset mean of 50 and a standard deviation of 10. A T-score of 70 is therefore quite

50th percentile on a standardized test, that student's score is exactly in the middle. Note that a score corresponding to the 40th or the 35th percentile is not a failing score; it is simply the score at or below which 40 or 35 percent of the observations fall.

Z-scores, T-scores, and stanines are all standard scores with a predetermined mean and standard deviation. They are used to simplify interpretation of test results. Because raw scores on different tests vary a great deal, as do means and standard deviations, simply knowing that a person has a score of 112 or 23 or 1,115 is meaningless unless we know what the mean and standard deviation are for a comparable group on that test. But when these raw scores are transformed into one of the standard scores, they become meaningful.

Z-scores are standard scores with a mean of 0 and a standard deviation of 1; T-scores have a mean of 50 and a standard deviation of 10; and a stanine score uses a mean of 5 and a standard deviation of 2. The meaning of these standard scores, relative to each other, is depicted in the figure here. As you can see, a T-score of 80 would be an extremely high score (3 standard devia-

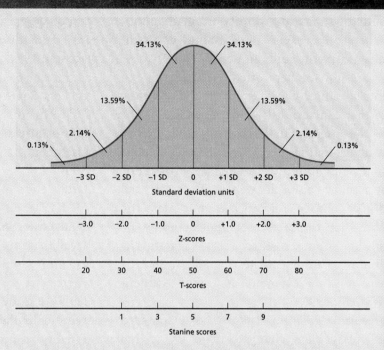

tions above the mean is above the 99th percentile); the equivalent Z-score would be 3. There is no exactly equivalent stanine score because the highest score possible on this 9-point scale is 9, which is 2 standard deviations above the mean.

Converting raw test scores to one of these standard-score scales is usually extremely simple because virtually all

tests that use them provide transformation tables. These tables typically allow you to read the standard-score equivalent directly, once you know the student's raw score and age or grade. And if you know the mean and standard deviation for these standard scores, they will be meaningful. Otherwise, they are just numbers.

---

high because 70 is 2 standard deviations above the mean, and only about 2.5 percent of all scores ordinarily fall beyond that point.

stanines Standard scores that make use of a 9-point scale with a mean of 5 and a standard deviation of 2.

minimum competency testing A global term for the administration of batteries of tests designed to determine whether students, or teachers, have reached some minimum level of competency in basic areas such as language and mathematics.

writing, and arithmetic skills. The report lent support to the concept of **minimum competency testing**, a general term for batteries of tests, often administered statewide, to determine whether students have achieved a minimum standard of competency.

Some object to the wide-scale use of standardized tests for other reasons. First, as Haladyna, Nolen, and Haas (1991) point out, raising educational achievement is equated too often with raising test scores. M. L. Smith's interviews of teachers indicate that when the results of standardized tests are made public, teachers often experience "feelings of shame, embarrassment, guilt, and anger" (1991, p. 9). As a result, teachers often prepare their students specifically to take a given test—a practice that can seriously undermine the validity of the test. Furthermore, note Nolen, Haladyna, and Haas (1992), although teaching to a test might improve students' marks, it does not actually raise achievement. In fact, it typically encourages memorization of specifics rather than the growth of understanding and thinking. Some research also suggests that minimum competency testing fails to increase measured achievement in many students (Winfield, 1990).

Sternberg (1992) suggests that standardized tests have changed little since their appearance in the early 1900s—except that they are a little easier to administer, somewhat more reliable, perhaps more attractively packaged. But they still measure pretty much the same things they've always measured: basic memory and some analytical abilities. We need alternatives, he claims, that also measure the more creative and pragmatic facets of intelligence and that begin to tap how people think and learn. As S. Black (1994c) notes, in the main, standardized tests measure only language and mathematical skills: They usually omit the other five of Gardner's seven intelligences (discussed in Chapter 8).

One other objection to standardized competency testing, claim Paris, and associates (1991), is that it may have a progressively more negative effect on students. In their surveys of large numbers of students, they found that many of them, especially the low achievers, became increasingly more anxious about tests. As a result, some cheated, and some simply stopped trying.

TEACHER-MADE TESTS

Standardized tests are widely used in most school systems; more than 80 percent of these are standardized achievement tests (García & Pearson, 1994). But a majority of the tests used in the classroom are constructed by classroom teachers. Some of these tests are highly representative of course objectives, are at an appropriate level of difficulty, and are used reasonably and wisely. But in many other cases, as McDougall (1997) phrases it, the "state-of-the-practice" is hardly "state-of-the-art."

Teacher-made tests can be used for a variety of purposes; only one of these is to assign grades. Recall that this is *summative* evaluation. Perhaps far more important is *formative* evaluation where tests are used to determine whether students are ready to begin a unit of instruction, to indicate to the teacher how effective instructional procedures are, to identify learning difficulties, to determine what students know and what they don't know, to motivate students to learn—and as a learning experience. In short, formative evaluation is the use of assessment to improve teaching and learning.

Teacher-made tests are often of the paper-and-pencil variety, although sometimes a sample of nonverbal behavior might be used for assessment. For example, in physical education, art, drama, and some workshop courses, students are sometimes asked either to produce something or to perform. Increasingly, performance-based assessment may also be required in other subjects such as mathematics, where teachers are interested in examining the processes by which students arrive at their answers rather than simply the products (more about performance assessment later in this chapter).

At present, the dominant form of classroom assessment continues to be teacher-made, written tests that are typically **objective tests** or **essay tests**. An essay test requires a written response of some length for each question. Objective tests, however, normally require little writing, and the scoring procedure is highly uniform (hence, objective).

The four major types of objective test items are completion, matching, true–false, and multiple choice. Examples of each are given in Figure 13.4.

Essay versus Objective Tests

Objective tests like the kind just described and more subjective essay tests can be used to measure almost any significant aspect of students' behavior. However, some course objectives are more easily assessed with one type of test than with another. Several major differences between essay and objective tests are given here. These differences can serve as a guide when deciding which to use in a given situation. Often, a mixture of both can be used to advantage (see the box entitled "To Be Objective or Subjective?"):

1. It is easier to tap high-level processes (analysis, synthesis, and evaluation) with an essay examination. That is, essay examinations can more easily be constructed to allow students to organize knowledge, to make inferences from it, to illustrate it, to apply it, and to extrapolate from it. However, good multiple-choice items can measure much the same things as free-response items (Thissen, Wainer, & Wang, 1994).

2. In some instances, essay examinations may be more appropriate than objective tests for assessing meaningful performance in real-life situations (Breland, 1999).

---

objective test A label used for a test in which the scoring procedure is simple, clear, and objective. Includes multiple-choice, completion, matching, and true–false formats.

essay test A tests that requires testees to construct responses of varying lengths in sentence, paragraph, or essay form.

1. *Completion*
   Test blueprints are often based on _____ taxonomy. Predictive and concurrent validity are two types of _____ validity.

2. *Matching*
   _____ Z-scores   1. mean = 50; standard deviation = 10
   _____ T-scores   2. mean = 0; standard deviation = 1
   _____ stanine   3. mean = 5; standard deviation = 2

3. *True–False*
   a. A good achievement test should result in a grade-equivalent score of between 4 and 5 for an average fourth-grade class.
   b. Content validity can be determined by making a careful, logical analysis of the relationship of test items to course objectives.

4. *Multiple Choice*
   The extent to which a test appears to measure what it s intended to measure defines:
   a. content validity
   b. face validity
   c. construct validity
   d. test reliability
   e. criterion-related validity

FIGURE 13.4   The four major types of objective test items

3. The content of essay examinations is often more limited than the content of the more objective tests. Because essay exams usually consist of fewer items, the range of abilities or of information sampled may be reduced. The objective question format, in contrast, permits coverage of more content per unit of testing time.

4. Essay examinations allow for more divergence. Students who do not like to be restricted in their answers often prefer essays over more objective tests. And some students, note Bridgeman and Morgan (1996) typically do very well on one type of test but not well at all on another.

5. Constructing an essay test is considerably easier and less time-consuming than making up an objective examination. In fact, an entire test

with an essay format can often be written in the same time it would take to write no more than two or three good multiple-choice items.

6. Scoring essay examinations usually requires much more time than scoring objective tests. This is especially true when tests can be scored electronically (as objective tests are in most universities and in an increasing number of schools). The total time involved in making and scoring a test is less for essay examinations than for objective tests if classes are small (20 students or fewer, perhaps) but is considerably less for objective tests as the number of students increases (see Figure 13.5).

7. The reliability of essay examinations is much lower than that of objective tests, primarily because of the subjectivity involved in the scoring. In one study, 300 essays were rated by 53 judges on a 9-point scale (Educational Testing Service, 1961). Slightly more than one-third of the papers received all possible grades; that is, each of these papers received the highest possible grade from at least one judge, the lowest possible grade from at least one other, and every other possible grade from at least one judge. Another 37 percent of the papers each received eight of the nine different grades; 23 percent received seven of the nine.

Other studies have found that a relatively poor paper that is read after an even poorer one will tend to be given a higher grade than if it is read after a good paper; that some graders consistently give moderate marks whereas others give extremely high and low marks, although the average grades given by each might be similar; that knowledge of who wrote the paper tends to affect scores, sometimes beneficially and sometimes to the student's detriment; and that if the first few answers on an essay examination are particularly good, overall marks tend to be higher than if the first few answers are poor.

There are a variety of methods for increasing the scorer's reliability on essay examinations; not the least of these is simply being aware of possible sources of unreliability.

Suggestions for Constructing Tests The advantages of a particular type of test can often be increased if the test is constructed carefully. By the same token, the disadvantages can also be made more severe through faulty item construction. Essay examinations, for example, are said to be better for measuring "higher" mental processes. Consider the following item:

List the kinds of validity discussed in this chapter.

If the tester's intention is to sample analysis, synthesis, or evaluation, this item has no advantage over many objective items. However, an item such as the following might have an advantage:

Discuss similarities and differences among three of the different types of validity discussed in this chapter.

Following are several specific suggestions for the construction of essay tests and of multiple-choice tests, the most preferred among objective-item forms.

Essay Tests

The following suggestions are based in part on Gronlund (1995):

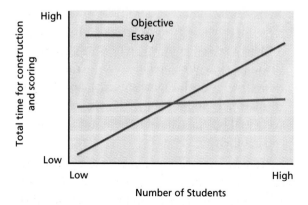

FIGURE 13.5 The relationship between class size and total time required for test construction and scoring for two types of test

To Be Objective or Subjective?

BEAR MUSINGS

The question is purely rhetorical. Not only does it have no answer, but it deserves none. Very few teachers will ever find themselves in situations where they must always use either one form of test or the other. Some class situations, particularly where size is a factor, may lend themselves more readily to objective test formats; in other situations, essay formats are better; sometimes a combi-nation of both may be desirable. The important point is that each has advan-tages and disadvantages. Good teach-ers should endeavor to develop the skills necessary for constructing the best possible items in a variety of for-mats without becoming passionate advocates of one over the other.

Good teachers also need to keep in mind that there are types of assess-ment other than the usual objective or essay tests, or standardized tests. Many of these alternatives are assessments of students' *performances* rather than simply products. They might involve keeping portfolios of students' work, writing anecdotal records, or looking for other evidence of the quality of stu-dents' learning and thinking. The choice of assessment procedure, cautions Boodoo (1993), should be determined by the purposes of the assessment.

1. Essay questions should be geared toward sampling processes not easily assessed by objective items (for example, analysis, synthesis, or evaluation).

2. As with all tests, essay questions should relate directly to the desired outcomes of the learning procedure. This should be clearly understood by the students as well.

3. To be scored easily, questions should be specific. If the intention is to give marks for illustrations, the item should specify that an illustration is required.

4. A judicious sampling of desired behavior should make up the substance of the items.

5. If the examiner's intention is to sample high-level processes, sufficient time should be allowed for students to complete the questions.

6. The weighting of various questions, and the time that should be allotted to each, should be specified for the student.

7. The questions should be worded so that the teacher's expectations are clear to both the stu-dent and the teacher.

There are ways to make the scoring more objective as well. One is to outline model answers before scoring the test (that is, write out an answer that would receive full points). Another is to score all answers for one item before going on to the next; this should increase uniformity of scoring. A third suggestion is sim-ply that the scorer be objective. For example, if poor grammar in a language arts test results in the loss of 5 points on one paper, grammar that is half as bad on another paper should result in the loss of $2\frac{1}{2}$ points.

Multiple-Choice Items A multiple-choice item consists of a statement or series of statements (called the stem) and three to five alternatives, only one of which is the correct or best solution. The other alternatives are referred to as *distrac-tors*. Each of the distractors is a response that should appear plausible if students do not know the answer. If students do know the correct answer, distractors should, of course, appear less plausible. Listed here are several suggestions for writing multiple-choice items. Most involve common sense (which makes them no less valid):

1. Both stems and alternatives should be clearly worded, unambiguous, grammatically correct, specific, and at the appropriate level of difficulty. Stems should also be clearly meaningful by themselves (Hoepfl, 1994).

2. Don't use no double negatives. They are very confusing and should be avoided. Are single negatives highly recommended? Not—says Tamir (1993), especially with items requiring a high degree of cognitive reasoning.

3. Test items should sample a representative portion of subject content, but they should not be taken verbatim from the textbook. This is defensible only when the intention is clearly to test memorization.

4. All distractors should be equally plausible so that answering correctly does not become simply a matter of eliminating highly implausible distractors. Consider the following example of a poor item:

   $10 + 12 + 18 =$

   a. 2,146   b. 7,568,482   c. 40   d. 1

   Highly implausible distractors, note Wolff and Wogalter (1998), can inflate scores dramatically.

5. Unintentional cues should be avoided. For example, ending the stem with *a* or *an* often provides a cue.

6. Qualifying words such as *never, always, none, impossible,* and *absolutely* should be avoided in distractors (though not necessarily in stems). They are almost always associated with incorrect alternatives. Words such as *sometimes, frequently,* and *usually* are most often associated with correct alternatives. In stems, both kinds of qualifiers tend to be ambiguous.

7. Provide students with feedback following testing. Going over and explaining test items leads to more learning, Snowman (1993) reports, than simply giving students more time to study.

Reporting Test Results

The main purpose of assessment, today's educators insist, is not so much to audit students but rather to support and assist teaching and learning. But this insistence, note Delandshere and Petrosky (1998), may represent more of a shift in rhetoric than in actual practice. In fact, much of educational assessment continues to be *summative* (it summarizes student progress and achievement) rather than *formative* (directed specifically toward improving teaching and learning).

No matter what the purposes of assessment, results typically need to be reported to students and parents. The feedback that students receive about their learning can be of tremendous value in guiding and motivating their efforts. It can also be highly reinforcing in this achievement-oriented society.

Making Scores Meaningful   Although raw scores can be reported directly to the student, they might not be very meaningful. A score of 40 on a test with a maximum possible score of 40 is different from a score of 40 on a test in which the ceiling is 80.

The traditional way to give meaning to test scores is to convert them either to a percentage or to a letter grade that has clearly defined (though arbitrary) significance. And if students are also told the mean (arithmetical average) and the range of scores (low and high scores), the scores become even more meaningful.

The mean is called a measure of **central tendency** because it indicates approximately the center of a distribution of scores. Two other common measures of central tendency are the

---

central tendency   The tendency for the majority of scores in a normal distribution to cluster around the center of the distribution. Measures of central tendency include the mean, the median, and the mode.

median and the **mode**. The median is the exact midpoint of a distribution. It is the 50 percentile—the point above and below which 50 percent of all scores lie. The mode is simply the most frequently occurring score; as such, it is not particularly valuable for educational and psychological testing. It is of considerable interest to shoe and clothing manufacturers, however, because they are not interested in manufacturing average or median sizes but those that occur most often.

A measure of central tendency is not nearly as valuable by itself as it is when combined with

a measure of variability (see box entitled "Norms and the Normal Distribution"). And the most useful measure of variability for normally distributed observations is the standard deviation. If students are sufficiently sophisticated, the standard deviation could be reported as an important dimension of test scores. A formula for computing the standard deviation is presented in Table 13.5.

---

median The midpoint or 50th percentile of a distribution; the point at or below which 50 percent of all scores fall.

mode The most frequently occurring score(s) in a distribution.

CRITERION-REFERENCED TESTING

Ochawa is a small kingdom hidden in a steamy jungle somewhere. One of its borders is a great river, which describes a serpentine half-circle

TABLE 13.5
Formulas for Summarizing Test Scores

	INDIVIDUAL	TEST SCORE	$\bar{X}$	$(X - \bar{X})$	$(X - \bar{X})^2$
SCORES ON TEST	Bill	37	33	4	16
	Joan	36	33	3	9
	Evelyn	35	33	2	4
	Renée	35	33	2	4
	Otis	33	33	0	0
	Sam	33	33	0	0
	Jose	33	33	0	0
	Rita	32	33	−1	1
	Odetta	30	33	−3	9
	Guy	26	33	−7	49
	Sums (Σ)	330	330	−0	92
	N = 10				

FORMULAS

$$\text{Mean } (\bar{X}) = \frac{\Sigma\,(sum)\,X}{N\,(number\ of\ scores)} = \frac{330}{10} = 33$$

Mode = 33 (most frequently occurring score)

Median = 33 (fiftieth percentile)

$$SD\left(\frac{standard}{deviation}\right) = \sqrt{\frac{\Sigma(X - \bar{X})^2}{N}} = \sqrt{\frac{92}{10}} = \sqrt{9.2} = 3.03$$

around most of its perimeter; the other border consists of an impenetrable row of mountains. So the inhabitants of Ochawa are trapped by the river on one side (they're afraid to try to cross it) and by the mountains on the other (although they can climb the mountains to their very tops, the other side is an unbroken row of sheer cliffs with a vertical drop of no less than 8,000 feet at any point). In Ochawa are many extremely ferocious, people-eating beasts. Fortunately, all are nocturnal. I say "fortunately" because, although the human inhabitants of Ochawa live on the mountainsides well beyond where the predators can climb, every day they must descend the mountain to find food.

Testing in Ochawa

In Ochawa a test is given to all able-bodied men, women, and children each day of their lives. It is a simple test. Before nightfall, each must succeed in climbing the mountain to a point beyond the reach of their predators. Failure to do so is obvious to all because the individual who fails simply does not answer roll call that evening. Success is equally obvious.[4]

This test is quite different from the ordinary testing practices of most schools. Passing the test doesn't require that individuals be the first to reach safety; it doesn't even require that they be among the first 90 percent to do so. Nor do they need to climb higher than everyone else. In fact, they will be just as successful if they are among the very last to reach safety. They will be just as alive as the first (and maybe less hungry).

Testing in Schools

Consider the situation in most of our schools. Assume that all students are expected to attain a certain level of performance in a variety of subjects—a level of performance that we will denote by the symbol X. Reaching X is analogous to climbing the cliff before the snarling beasts grab you.

Now, in the course of the school year, teachers prepare some tests that allow them to determine, quite accurately, that certain individuals usually do better than others. These students are, in effect, comparable to the people in the aforementioned kingdom who typically reach safety first, or who climb higher than the others. They are the students that the teacher can rightly assume have reached (or even gone beyond) X.

But when assessing students' performance and reporting grades, teachers don't often ask themselves which students have reached X and which haven't. Instead, they compare each child to the average performance of all children and make judgments on that basis about the relative performance of their students. Thus, in a very advanced class, students who have in fact reached X but who fall well below average performance may be assigned mediocre marks. In a less advanced class, the same students might be assigned much higher grades. This illustrates what is labeled **norm-referenced testing**. Norm-referenced tests are therefore tests in which the student's performance is judged and reported in terms of a standard or norm that is derived from typical student performance on the test. In other words, the results of such a test are based on comparisons among students. Such testing is highly compatible with competitive approaches to teaching but adapts poorly to more cooperative approaches.

With a second alternative, students are not compared one to the other; instead, their perfor-

---

[4] **PPC:** Where is this place? I want to send some of my students there.
Author: Why?

---

norm-referenced testing A test where the student is competing against the performance of other students rather than in relation to a pre-established criterion of acceptable performance.

mance is judged only in relation to a criterion—hence, **criterion-referenced testing**. In the jungle example, the criterion is simply the ability to climb beyond the reach of predators; success is survival, and failure is death.

Criterion-referenced testing can be used in schools and is in fact used extensively with mastery learning, PSI, and other forms of individualized instruction (see Chapter 10). For this reason, criterion-referenced tests are sometimes called *mastery tests* (Aiken, 1998). Criterion-referenced testing allows teachers to determine whether a particular student has reached a predetermined level or standard without having to compare that student to any other.

What is required for criterion-referenced testing is that teachers be able to specify what is involved in achieving X. That is, they must be able to specify the criteria of success in terms of specific behaviors. Often, these behaviors are students' responses to test items. Hence criterion-referenced testing typically involves careful analysis of items in light of clear instructional objectives. One of the great benefits of this, claims Popham (1994), is increased clarity of objectives, test items, and their interpretation—and perhaps increased effectiveness of instruction as well.

Which Approach Is Best? It is misleading to emphasize the difference between criterion-referenced and norm-referenced tests because the tests can be identical. The difference between the two lies in how teachers use the tests rather than in the nature of the tests themselves. With criterion-referenced testing, each student's performance is compared to a criterion; with norm-referenced testing, an individual's performance is compared to that of other students. Individual differences are far less important in criterion-referenced testing. Indeed, the objective is to have all students succeed.

Literature on educational testing has sometimes been preoccupied with a minor controversy surrounding the relative merits of these two approaches to testing. Advocates of criterion-referenced testing point to the inherent justice of their approach: No student need consistently fail for performing less well than others after a predetermined period of time. When students reach the criterion, they will have succeeded. Indeed, at that point they will be as successful on that particular task as all other students. And students who have more to learn at the outset of instruction will not fail simply because they start at a different place and consequently lag behind others in the beginning. If they reach the mountain heights before the beasts, they will survive just as surely as will those who climbed first, fastest, and highest. Criterion-referenced testing argues strongly for the individualization of instruction and evaluation. It fosters cooperation rather than competition, it encourages students to work toward the goals of the system rather than against other students, and it forces teachers to make those goals explicit. Also, as we see shortly, criterion-referenced testing is closely related to performance assessments (O'Leary & Shiel, 1997).

But criterion-referenced testing has certain limitations, as critics have been quick to point out. It is relatively simple to specify that after taking typing lessons for six weeks a student should be able to type 30 words per minute with no more than two errors, but it is considerably more difficult to determine precisely what a student should know or understand after sitting in a social studies class for six weeks. A criterion-referenced test is clearly appropriate in the first instance but is more difficult to apply to the second. Among other things, teachers are required to specify their standards and criteria with a

---

criterion-referenced testing A test in which the student is judged relative to a criterion rather than relative to the performance of other students. The teacher decides beforehand what specific performance is expected and tests to see whether the student has reached this criterion.

clarity that is not always easily achieved (Cizek, 1993a).

A second limitation is that some students are able to go beyond the criteria, given sufficient motivation to do so. Some educators fear that exclusive reliance on criterion-referenced testing can thwart students' initiative and stifle their motivation.

One advantage of norm-referenced testing is that it provides both students and those who would counsel them with valuable information concerning the likelihood of their success in academic situations where they will, in fact, be required to compete with others. For this reason, norm-referenced tests are highly useful for assessing students with disabilities (Gronna, Jenkins, & Chin-Chance, 1998). But, as we saw in Chapter 8, they can also be grossly unfair to minority groups (Samuda, 1998).

What should you do while the controversy rages around you? Nothing dramatic—this isn't exactly a war, so you don't have to take sides. Simply use both types of test. There are situations where norm-referenced tests are unavoidable and also highly useful. There are also many situations where justice and good sense dictate that you should establish definite criteria for success. Your students' learning—and your teaching—will benefit from your wisdom.[5]

PERFORMANCE-BASED ASSESSMENTS

Recent literature on educational assessment contains ever-increasing references to what are often termed *new approaches* to assessment. And although many of these approaches have been around for a long time, their popularity has increased dramatically in recent years (Wiggins, 1998). Collectively, these approaches to assessment are termed *performance-based assessment* (or simply *performance assessment.*) They are sometimes referred to as *authentic assessment.*[6]

Essentially, performance-based assessment attempts to determine students' competence by looking at examples of what they do—that is, by looking at their real-life performance. Performance assessments are said to be *authentic* to the extent that they make use of tasks that, in Wiggins' words, "teach students how adults are actually challenged in the field" (1998, p. xi). As R. L. Linn (1994) puts it, performance assessment requires that actual levels or standards of performance be expressed in terms of concrete examples and explicit definitions. The assumption is that performance assessment requires a level of understanding and an ability to apply learning that is not always evident in more conventional forms of assessment. Farr and Tone (1994) point out that a conventional, multiple-choice test might determine that carpentry students know the difference between a ball-peen, sledge, or claw hammer, but it would not demonstrate that the students actually know how to build a house. In their words, "There's a big difference between naming hammers and pounding nails in a wall" (p. viii).

The increasing popularity of performance-based assessment, note Ryan and Greguras (1998), is based largely on its promise that it can provide more authentic, direct appraisals of student competence and that it will therefore have

---

[5] ***PPC:*** The use of this term—wisdom—strikes me as somewhat overly optimistic for many of my students. Does the bear really believe this?

Author: The bear is optimistic as well as a kind and generous soul. He has known wise teachers.

[6] ***PPC:*** I've never liked the expression "authentic assessment" because it implies that every other type of assessment must, by definition, be unreal or not authentic. It's an emotionally loaded label that, basically, is meaningless.

Author: The bear, even when he pretended to be a choirboy, would not have put it quite so strongly, although he agrees that a term other than *authentic* would have been preferable. Terwilliger (1997) made much the same point, giving rise to a series of often strongly worded and emotional rebuttals (see *Educational Researcher,* 1998, vol. 6).

clearly positive consequences for learning and teaching. In fact, educational literature repeatedly claims that one principal component of current educational reform is increasing use of performance-based assessment.

Examples of Performance-Based Testing

Besides teaching reading, writing, arithmetic, and other related things, one of the purposes of your instructional procedures may be, in the former president's words, to teach students to use their minds well. If that is what you really want to do, then, as we have argued several times in these pages, you need to change your assessment procedures so that what is being assessed is not limited to items of information well remembered—or forgotten—but includes actual evidence of minds working well. Phrased another way, if cognitive strategies training programs (see Chapter 5) and new theories of motivation (Chapter 11) deliver their promise of empowering students to become autonomous, reflective, thinking learners, then we absolutely need assessment procedures based on new assumptions and new models.

Current testing practices, says G. Grant (1991), deal with behaviors that are easy to measure rather than with those that are more abstract. These practices encourage individual accomplishment and competitiveness rather than group accomplishment and cooperation. They are evident in the predominant role that ranking plays in reporting assessments, in the widespread use of one-correct-answer-only objective tests, in assessment procedures that consider only individual learning rather than group performance, and in the view of tests as scientific measuring instruments like thermometers or altimeters (Wolf et al., 1991).

But there is clearly a shift in the assumptions that underlie current testing practices and in our view of the learner (Hoffman et al., 1998). As

Delandshere and Petrosky (1998) note, assessment is now viewed as a tool for improving teaching and learning rather than simply a measure of student progress. Accordingly, it has become far more important to try to assess how students might perform in situations that are more realistic—that is, closer to real life—than objective, multiple-choice tests tend to be.

Performance-based assessment, although far from new—provides a clear alternative to objective tests. These include a variety of procedures and approaches; the most important of which are described here.

Developmental Assessments Developmental **assessments** are a form of performance-based assessment that attempt to document evidence of progressive accomplishments. They look at actual accomplishments rather than at relative accomplishments. That is, they look at characteristics of a student's actual behavior rather than accomplishments relative to other, comparable students.

Developmental assessments typically use detailed, performance-based lists of expected or desired behaviors as a guide for interpreting a student's progress. The most common approach to developmental assessments takes the form of checklists that present detailed, sequential lists of accomplishments or capabilities in any of a variety of areas. In some school systems, checklists have completely replaced more traditional, grade-oriented assessments (see Figures 13.6 and 13.7).

Less rigorous approaches to developmental assessment have long been common in elementary schools where, as McClean (1992) notes, tests are not nearly as common as they become

---

developmental assessment A performance-based assessment that looks at the student's performance in relation to developmental or course-based expectations rather than in relation to the performance of other students. Often uses checklists of expected (desired) behaviors.

INDIVIDUAL STUDENT PROGRESS REPORT
FULTONVALE ELEMENTARY SCHOOL

Name: Magee, Wayne
Grade: 02 **Homeroom:** 55
Teacher: Ms. A Sanders

Term: _____
Program Type: Regular _____
Modified _____

The checks (✔) in the columns show your child's development at this time
Any items not checked do not apply. The skills and behaviors observed are:

	Not yet apparent . . .		
		Is developing . . .	
			Developed as expected . . .

	NYA	ID	DE
PERSONAL & SOCIAL DEVELOPMENT			
Reflects positive attitudes about self		✔	
Works independently		✔	
Concentrates on tasks		✔	
Organizes materials and space		✔	
Makes effective use of time		✔	
Works and plays cooperatively		✔	
Respects the rights and properties of self and others		✔	
Follows class/school rules and routines		✔	
ATTITUDES TOWARD LEARNING			
Demonstrates initiative		✔	
Accepts new challenges		✔	
Demonstrates commitment to completing tasks		✔	
THINKING SKILLS AND LEARNING STRATEGIES			
Demonstrates critical thinking skills (organizes, reasons logically, plans, asks questions, evaluates . . .)		✔	
Demonstrates creative thinking skills (generates varied ideas, elaborates, shows originality . . .)		✔	
Demonstrates decision-making and problem-solving strategies		✔	
LANGUAGE LEARNING			
Language is developed and used in all subjects. It is an essential component of all learning.		✔	
Applies reading skills	✔		
Applies writing skills	✔		
Applies listening skills		✔	
Applies talking skills		✔	
MATHEMATICS			
Participates in mathematical activities		✔	
Understands the concepts		✔	
Applies problem-solving strategies		✔	
Computes accurately		✔	
SOCIAL STUDIES			
Participates in class activities and discussions		✔	
Understands the concepts		✔	
Applies skills and strategies related to responsible citizenship		✔	
SCIENCE			
Participates in class activities and discussions		✔	
Understands the concepts		✔	
Applies scientific process skills and strategies		✔	
HEALTH		✔	
Participates in class activities and discussions			
Understands the concepts		✔	
Applies skills and strategies related to personal well-being		✔	
PHYSICAL EDUCATION			
Participates in physical education activities		✔	
Demonstrates personal competency in motor skills and physical activities		✔	
Cooperates in group/team activities		✔	
ART			
Participates in art activities		✔	
Applies skills and concepts		✔	
MUSIC			
Participates in musical activities		✔	
Demonstrates an understanding of musical skills and concepts		✔	

COMMENTS:

Wayne continues to demonstrate a positive attitude and is eager to learn. He works diligently and his homework is usually completed in the alloted time. He takes pride in his work and enjoys sharing ideas that might enrich and extend the activities. He is enthusiastic and shows initiative and originality when encountering new activities. At times these ideas are counterproductive as the method he chooses is labor intensive, but he perseveres and adapts.

Wayne continues to demonstrate an increased fluency and an increased sight-word vocabulary base. However, Wayne is not an independent reader. His daily reading fluency is inconsistent. He has a good knowledge of the many word-recognition skills but the transfer and application of these skills is not consistent. Wayne's oral/verbal story fluency far exceeds his written ability. His spelling skills greatly inhibit his writing. Often, Wayne can't reread his own written stories with his inconsistent spelling patterns. His stories are very creative, imaginative, and interesting. It is frustrating to him when he cannot make the written words flow like his thoughts.

Wayne has a good understanding of the math concepts studied this term. he can apply these concepts in problem-solving situations. Wayne computes accurately, but he relies on manipulation rather than memory with his addition and subtraction facts to 18.

Wayne continues to demonstrate personal competency and good sportsmanship. He cooperated in the team activities involved in our Floor Hockey unit and is enjoying the individualistic focus in our Gymnastics unit.

A special thank-you to Mrs. Magee for her help Mondays in the computer room. Thanks AS

Parent/Guardian Signature: _____

FIGURE 13.6 A sample checklist report card. Used by permission of Strathcona County Schools.

Friendly

Sharing

Exciting

School

Fort Saskatchewan Elementary School
9802 – 101 Street
Fort Saskatchewan, Alberta
T8L 1V4
Office: (403) 998-7771
Child Safe: (403) 998-0484

INTERIM REPORT CARD

Date:

Dear Parents:
This interim report card is designed to give you a general indication of
your child's progress in school. If you have any questions, please call.
PLEASE RETURN TO YOUR CHILD'S HOME ROOM TEACHER by Wed., Oct. 21

STUDENT'S NAME: **GRADE:**

	Satisfactory Development	Requires Further Development
Showing a positive attitude toward school		
Developing good work habits		
Language learning		
Math		

TEACHER COMMENTS:

Teacher's Signature:

PARENT COMMENTS:

Parent/Guardian's Signature:

FIGURE 13.7 A sample checklist interim report card. Used by permission of Strathcona County Schools.

later. Instead, elementary teachers rely more on observation and relatively informal evaluation. That is, they make informal judgments about the competency of their students based on their observations of their students' actual performance.

Sampling Thinking Performances   Sampling thinking **performances** is a form of performance-based assessment that requires students to answer questions, solve problems, write, or do other things in actual rather than contrived circumstances. The objective is to sample performance that provides evidence of competency in the skills involved in cognition. Sampling performance is what happens when a novice driver takes a road test or a singer completes an audition. In these cases, the objective is to demonstrate the ability to perform the activity being assessed, by actually performing it. In much the same way, argue Wolf and associates (1991), if we want to assess a student's ability to think, we must sample actual performances of thought.

Exhibitions   Exhibitions are public displays of performance. They differ from other performance-assessment procedures in that they underline the social nature of thinking and learning. Common examples of exhibitions include oral examinations by expert or peer committees, musical recitations, and science fairs. This form of assessment requires students to synthesize their knowledge, to extrapolate from it, and to explain and demonstrate this knowledge in social situations.

---

sampling thinking performance An approach to performance-based assessment; students are given an opportunity to perform real-life activities that require and illustrate the use of specific cognitive processes.

exhibition A performance-based assessment procedure that requires the public display of competence. Exhibitions are most common in the visual or performing arts and in oral examinations for graduate degrees. They underline the social nature of thinking.

Portfolios   Portfolios are ongoing records of achievement or performance. They are collections of actual samples of a student's work, often gathered by the students themselves. In the primary grades, for example, portfolios might consist of drawings (preferably with the student's story/explanation written on the back, often by the teacher); samples of the student's writing; records of simple computations; perhaps tests and quizzes that tap meaningful processes. In later grades, portfolios include not only samples of early and later work but also a more systematic and structured range of work representing various subjects and cognitive processes. McClean (1992) suggests that a useful approach is to have students compile ongoing working portfolios. This active portfolio contains works in progress as well as earlier work. From this working portfolio, teachers and students select samples to be placed in a more permanent cumulative portfolio.

Portfolios can also be used in higher education. They are especially useful, note Smith and Tillema (1998), as reflective learning tools. That is, they can be used to provide insight into the learner's own thought processes and to provide evidence of change and progress. Hansen (1998) points out that one of their great benefits is that they can be used to involve the learner more actively in the learning process.

Portfolios such as these provide teachers and students with a continuous body of physical evidence about important changes in students. Thus, portfolios are useful not so much for assessing current attainment as for identifying acquisitions, detecting interests and special skills, and perhaps pointing out weaknesses. A well-organized portfolio is, in a sense, a biography of the learner's mind, a history of change and progress.

Portfolios provide teachers with a basis for assessment of changes in performance and thus provide a means for students to develop increasing awareness and understanding of their own

What I Want to Be When I Grow Up

THE SITUATION: Carolyn White, a good teacher, as recollected by Lillian, teacher-in-training

My eighth-grade language arts teacher, Mrs. White, was able to make writing weekly essays the highlight of the week. Each week we would write an essay on something about us. For example, we wrote on topics such as: "what I want to be when I grow up," "a hard decision I had to make," "my best friend," and so on. Then, after the teacher had corrected each essay, we wrote a final copy and put it into our "dossier," which was a book-style collection of all our writing. This idea made writing fun as well as enabling us to learn a lot about ourselves. Also, Mrs. White would go through the dossier when she made up our report cards and base her evaluation and her comments on the dossier. Then, at the end of the year, she gave us our dossiers back to keep. Mine is among my prized possessions now.

changing thought processes. Thus, the purpose of using portfolios is not simply to assess performance but, perhaps even more important, to provide ongoing occasions for learning (Porter & Cleland, 1995). In this connection, portfolios have been found to be especially valuable for gifted children because they can have important motivational consequences (Hadaway & Marek-Schroer, 1994). The use of portfolio assessment, and the creation of portfolios, can also result in significant changes in teaching styles (Valencia & Place, 1994).

Portfolios kept by teachers of their own performance can also be useful for improving teaching. Athanases (1994) reports a case where a teacher kept a portfolio of her instruction over a one-year period. The portfolio included samples of lessons as well as reflections on their effectiveness, thoughts about how they might be changed, and so on. (See the case entitled "What I Want to Be When I Grow Up.")

Summary and Assessment of Performance Assessment

Performance-based assessment attempts to assess students by examining their performance in situations as close to real-life as possible. There are four steps involved in performance assessment, explain Williams, Hetrick, & Suen (1998):

1. Clarify the reasons for the assessment.

2. Clarify the performance to be assessed.

3. Design exercises to be used in the assessment.

4. Develop a plan to evaluate the performances.

All of this sounds simpler than it sometimes is. Still, there is obvious growing interest in performance assessment. This interest, says Moss "... reflects the growing consensus among educators about the impact of evaluation on what students learn and what teachers teach, about the role that multiple-choice assessments have played in narrowing the curriculum to reflect the form and content of these tests, and about the potential power of carefully designed performance assessments to document and encourage critical, creative, and self-reflective thought" (1992, pp. 229–230).

It isn't yet clear that performance-based assessment delivers all these promises or that it is always the best alternative.

Performance-Based Assessment: Pros Emphases on learning how to learn and on autonomous, reflective, independent, creative thinking are incompatible with current testing practices in many ways. To the extent that our assessments demand the sort of linear thinking that is evidenced by acceptance and reproduction of single correct answers, they foster a type of teaching and learning that does not result in minds that work well but in minds that reproduce well.

Performance-based assessment appears to have several distinct advantages:

▲ It is better attuned to our changing educational emphases.
▲ It can be more equitable than more traditional approaches.
▲ It provides more ways of viewing competence and even excellence.
▲ It might expose social and intellectual skills that more traditional measures would overlook.
▲ It bases assessment on a wider range of evidence than has been customary.
▲ To the extent that it is more "authentic," it might be more relevant to competency in the real world.

Performance-Based Assessment: Cons But these new forms of assessment are clearly more cumbersome, more time-consuming, and in most cases less exact. That is, they require more time, more effort, more knowledge—in short, more resources—from teachers (Stecher & Herman, 1997). As a result, they are not often used for very large-scale assessments. Also, they are not as easily quantifiable as more objective measures and are therefore not as useful for educational decisions that require comparison. That is, they provide a less certain basis for answering such questions as "which 120 of these 500 college applicants should be admitted?" or "which one of these 120 should be given the Earnest Q. Honest Memorable Scholarship?" This is espe-

cially true, note Gearhart and Herman (1998), when evaluating portfolios that were produced with the support and help of peers, teachers, and parents. In such cases, it is often very difficult to determine exactly how much each individual student contributed to the portfolio. In the words of Gearhart and Herman (1998), "Whose work is it?"

Performance-based assessment suffers from relatively lower standards of reliability and validity than more conventional assessment procedures. This is partly because performance measures often cannot be quantified. Also results on performance-based tasks are usually interpreted by teachers who, notes Marzano (1994), are prone to being influenced by students' overall performance in other areas.

Ewell (1991) notes that these approaches to assessment also generate a tremendous volume of material and information but no simple way to interpret or summarize it. There is perhaps little hope for these approaches unless we can develop clear and effective procedures for collecting and displaying samples of performances and clear criteria for understanding their meaning.

SOME LEGAL ISSUES IN EDUCATIONAL ASSESSMENT

Assessment is a fundamental part of the teaching/learning process with important potential benefits for both teacher and learner. But tests are not always appropriate for all purposes, nor are they always used or interpreted fairly. With the increasing use of tests, especially standardized tests, and with increasing concern for privacy, individual rights, and fairness, some ethical issues implicit in the administration and use of tests have become matters of political and social concern.

Tests are often seen as a threat, as a violation of privacy, and as unjust. Unfortunately, these concerns are not entirely unfounded. For example, personality tests can invade privacy when they probe into matters that would not ordinarily be publicly revealed; tests can be threatening when school placement, job opportunities—indeed, success and failure—depend upon their results; and they can be patently unjust when used for unintended purposes or with groups for whom they were not designed. And, as McGill-Franzen and Allington (1993) point out, when the results of standardized tests are made public or are used as a basis for rewarding teachers or funding school programs, they can easily lead to a variety of unethical practices, including narrowing the curriculum so that teachers teach more directly to the tests and flunking or reclassifying students who don't do well on these tests to improve the reported results.

Because of concerns such as these, testing in schools, and the uses to which test results have been put, have been widely attacked and have led to many court cases. The end result has been a further clarification of the characteristics of good educational assessment.

The Three Requirements of Educational Assessment

Good educational assessment has three important characteristics. As we saw earlier, good measuring instruments need to be valid (they should measure what they are intended to measure) and they must be reliable (they need to measure accurately and consistently). They should also be *free from bias.*

Test bias, explains Popham, "refers to qualities of an assessment instrument that offend or unfairly penalize a group of examinees because of examinees' gender, ethnicity, socioeconomic status, religion, or other such group-defining characteristics" (1999, p. 67). For example, African Americans, and women, as a group, tend to score lower than whites or males on the Scholastic Assessment Test (SAT). This may be

an example of test bias (Aiken, 1998), and the use of such tests may be unfair.

The use of standardized tests like the SAT (and a variety of intelligence tests) as screening instruments for placement of students in special classes has typically resulted in a preponderance of minority-group students and those from lower socioeconomic levels being placed in these classes. This has led to court challenges. In some cases, the courts have outlawed the use of tests for screening and placement of students, ruling that they are discriminatory. In other cases, however, courts have ruled that the tests are not discriminatory when they are used with other mandated assessment procedures, (see, for example, Aiken, 1998).

Individuals with Disabilities Education Act (IDEA)

One of the results of these various court cases was the passage of Public Law 94-142 in 1975, later amended to become the *Individuals with Disabilities Education Act (IDEA)*. Recall from Chapter 9 that this law attempts to ensure fair treatment of children with disabilities. Among other things, it guarantees that all children will be educated in the "least restrictive environment"—a provision that is directly reflected in the principle of *inclusive* classrooms (that is, inclusion of children with special educational needs into the regular classroom). The law also guarantees free and appropriate educational services for all children and an individualized educational plan (IEP) for children with special needs. Most relevant for this chapter, it specifies that each child has a right to *nondiscriminatory evaluation and due process of law.* The courts have typically interpreted this to mean that children must be tested in their dominant language, that important educational decisions cannot fairly be based on the results of a single test, and that educational decisions can be challenged in a court of law.

The Right to Privacy and to Competent Teachers

Another very important piece of legislation that relates directly to educational assessment is the **Family Educational Rights to Privacy Act**. This law (Public Law 93-380) affects all schools funded by the U.S. Office of Education. Among other things, the law stipulates that:

▲ Parents of children younger than 18 must be given the right of access to education records kept by schools and relating to their own children.

▲ Parents have the right to challenge the accuracy and appropriateness of the information in their children's records.

▲ Parents have the right to limit public access to these records and to receive a list of individuals and agencies that have been given access to them.

▲ Parents have the right to be notified if and when the records are turned over to a court of law.

▲ All these parental rights become the student's rights after the age of 18 or after the student enters a postsecondary educational institution.

It's also reassuring (at least to students) that most educational jurisdictions have legislation or policies intended to ensure that all students have access to competent teachers. These policies typically make provisions for discharging incompetent teachers. Incompetence may be manifested in deficits and malpractices relating directly to instruction; it may also be evident in

---

Family Educational Rights to Privacy Act Public Law 93-380, which guarantees parents right of access and challenge with respect to the school records of their children and also guarantees the privacy of such records.

malpractices relating to assessment. For example, many jurisdictions *require* a minimum amount of assessment, sometimes at specific times and for specific purposes. And some specifically prohibit the assignment of lower grades, or even zeros, as a form of punishment when these grades do not truly represent the student's achievement or ability.

CONCLUDING THOUGHTS ON EDUCATIONAL ASSESSMENT

In most schools, far more emphasis is placed on the use of assessment for grading (summative evaluation) than on its instructional roles for identifying strengths and weaknesses, suggesting remediation, and so on (formative evaluation). This situation, suggests Wiggins (1998), needs to be rectified. Evaluation must be used more often to provide students with feedback about their performance. This feedback should emphasize progress toward important educational goals and should occur in the course of learning rather than only at the end of a unit. In Wiggins' words, evaluation needs to be more *educative.*

Our evaluation procedures are often weak not only in terms of how test results are used but, perhaps far more important, also in terms of what we choose to evaluate. Although class evaluation has a profound effect on what students learn, many teachers spend little time and effort in developing good assessment procedures or attempting to ensure that what they test is really what they want students to learn. As we saw, one result is that a great deal of class evaluation emphasizes the lowest level of cognitive objectives—specifically, knowledge of specifics. Accordingly, schools teach students to remember isolated facts rather than to understand, to look for relationships, and to go beyond the information given.

The solution? At least in part, the solution lies in changing evaluation procedures. If we want to teach students to think, to evaluate, to be critical, and to solve problems, we need to stop loading our tests with items that ask for a simple regurgitation of text- and teacher-sanctified facts. We can tell our students what our grand goals are, but unless our tests reflect what we say, our students will not believe us.

We have to change our attitudes toward measurement, insist Wolf and associates (1991). First, instead of ranking students, we need to develop sequential criteria of accomplishments—in other words, we must move to criterion- rather than norm-referenced assessment. Second, we have to change our notion that high reliability is an essential aspect of educational assessment. Portfolio-based assessments, for example, can vary considerably from one assessor to another. And third, we have to stop insisting that we need a single summary number to describe—and compare—students.

Old Wine

Are these new approaches to assessment really new? After all, observation of students' performance, anecdotal records, cumulative files including samples of student work, exhibitions such as science fairs, evaluation in social situations such as oral examinations, and various other performance-based approaches to assessment have been around for a long time.

Is this old wine in new bottles, new labels and all?

Is it just our assumptions, our emphases, and our goals that are changing? Or are they, too, just old wines now being rebottled? It's interesting to read what William James wrote in his "Talks to Teachers" almost a century ago:

> No elementary measurement, capable of being performed in a laboratory, can throw light on the actual efficiency of the subject; for the vital thing about him, his emotional and moral energy and doggedness, can be measured by no single experiment, and becomes known only by the total results in the long run . . . Be patient, then, and sympathetic with the type of mind that cuts a poor figure in examination. It may, in the long examination which life sets us, come out in the end in better shape than the glib and ready reproducer, its passions being deeper, its purposes more worthy, its combining power less commonplace, and its total mental output consequently more important. (James, 1915, pp. 135–143; quoted in Wolf et al., 1991, p. 51)

Old wine is often better than new wine.

MAIN POINTS

1. Measurement is the use of an instrument (a ruler, a thermometer, a test) to gauge the quantity of a property or behavior. Evaluation involves making a decision about quality, goodness, or appropriateness. Assessment includes aspects of both. Summative evaluation involves the use of assessment primarily to summarize and assign a number to what students have accomplished; formative evaluation is geared toward improving teaching and learning. What teachers assess is important in determining what students learn.

2. Educational goals can be broad statements relating to the general purpose of education (like Goals 2000). To be useful, instructional objectives should specify both what the learner must do and the criteria of acceptable performance. They can be highly performance

oriented and specific (Mager) or both general and specific (Gronlund).

3. Bloom's taxonomy can be valuable for setting up educational objectives and designing tests to determine the extent to which these goals have been reached. Gagné's learning outcomes can also be used as a guide for setting up instructional objectives.

4. A test blueprint is a table of specifications for a test. It should specify topics or behaviors to be sampled as well as the number or proportion of items that will relate to each.

5. Good measuring instruments need to be valid (measure what they purport to measure) and reliable (measure consistently). A test cannot be valid without also being reliable; however, it can be reliable without being valid. Aspects of validity include face validity (the test appears to measure what it says it measures), content validity (judged by analyzing test items to determine whether they sample appropriate content), construct validity (how well the test reflects underlying hypothetical variables), and criterion-related validity (the measure agrees with other current measures [concurrent validity] or predicts future performance [predictive validity]).

6. Reliability can be measured by looking at correlations between repeated presentations of the same test (repeated-measures reliability), between different forms of the same test (parallel-forms reliability), or between halves of a single test (split-half reliability).

7. Standardized tests are professionally developed instruments—usually measures of intelligence, personality, or achievement—that provide norms or standards for judging individual performance. Common uses of standardized tests are for special education placement, to certify students' achievement,

to judge the competency of teachers, to evaluate schools, and for instructional diagnosis.

8. Standardized achievement tests typically provide one or more of the following norms: age-equivalent scores (provide a comparison to average like-aged performance), grade-equivalent scores (provide comparison to expected performance for different grades), or percentiles (indicate percentage scoring below given point). Scores may be transformed to standard scores such as Z-scores (mean = 0, standard deviation = 1); T-scores (mean = 50, standard deviation = 10); or stanines (mean = 5, standard deviation = 2).

9. Teacher-made paper-and-pencil tests are either objective (true–false, completion, matching, or multiple-choice) or in essay form. Essay tests are better for tapping higher mental processes, allow for more divergence, and are less time-consuming to prepare; they are also more limited in content, less reliable, and more time-consuming to score.

10. Good essay examinations should sample processes not easily measured with objective tests. Questions should be specific and clearly worded, sufficient time should be allowed for answering, and relative weightings of different questions should be clear. Good multiple-choice items have clear, meaningful stems; distractors of approximately equal plausibility; and no double negatives, absolute qualifiers (always, never), or other unintentional cues (a, an, singulars, plurals).

11. One way to give meaning to raw scores on achievement tests is to convert them to percentage scores or letter grades. The average score, the range of scores, the class distribution, and the standard deviation are also

useful. Measures of central tendency include the mean (arithmetic average); the mode (most frequently occurring score); and the median (fiftieth percentile, midpoint).

12. Schools have traditionally used norm-referenced tests (judging performance in relation to the performance of other students). Criterion-referenced tests compare performance to a pre-established criterion rather than the performance of other students. Critics claim that current testing practices emphasize ranking, are geared toward providing numerical summaries of students, and encourage a reproductive rather than productive approach to teaching and learning.

13. One alternative is performance-based assessment, which might include developmental assessment (for example, progressive, criterion-specific checklists); sampling thinking performances (assessment of the actual performance of a thoughtful activity such as solving a math problem); evaluating exhibitions (public displays of samples of meaningful achievements and processes); or evaluating portfolios (actual collection representing ongoing records of samples of performance).

14. Performance-based assessment is more compatible with current emphases on developing autonomous, reflective thinkers. It may be more equitable, and it is geared toward learning (formative evaluation) rather than simply assessing achievements (summative evaluation). But it is time-consuming, difficult, and inexact.

15. Educational assessment should be valid, reliable, and free from bias. The *individuals with disabilities act* specifies that all learners have a right to nondiscriminatory evaluation and due process of law. The privacy of school records is guaranteed by legislation, as is parental access to such records. The competence of teachers is less easily guaranteed.

Applied Questions

▲ Illustrate how measurement and evaluation might be involved in the assessment of student performance in the classroom.

▲ Write instructional objectives to illustrate the approaches of Mager and Gronlund.

▲ Define reliability and each of the following kinds of validity: face, content, construct, and criterion-related (predictive and concurrent).

▲ If you were to debate the system-wide use of standardized achievement tests, what would be some pros and cons?

▲ Evaluate the relative merits of criterion-referenced and norm-referenced evaluation.

▲ What are portfolios, and why might they be used to evaluate student performance?

Internet Activity

Use InfoTrac College Edition or other World Wide Web sources to discover examples of how performance assessment and portfolios are currently being used in schools. (See the inside back cover of this text for suggestions about where to begin.)

Sample search terms: performance assessment

Study Terms

affective domain **497**

age-equivalent score **507**

analysis **496**

application **496**

assessment **487**

authentic assessment **488**

behavioral objective **493**

central tendency **514**

cognitive domain **496**

comprehension **496**

construct validity **503**

content validity **501**

criterion-referenced testing **517**

criterion-related validity **503**

developmental assessment **519**

educational goal **490**

essay test **511**

evaluation **486**

exhibition **522**

face validity **501**

Family Educational Rights to Privacy Act **526**

formative evaluation **488**

grade-equivalent score **506**

hypertext **496**

instructional objective **490**

learning outcomes **497**

mean **508**

measurement **486**

measurement-driven instruction **489**

median **515**

merit pay **492**

minimum competency testing **509**

mode **515**

normal curve **508**

norm-referenced testing **516**

objective test **511**

parallel-forms reliability **504**

percentile **508**

performance assessment **488**

portfolio **487**

raw score **506**

repeated-measures reliability **504**

sampling thinking performance **522**

split-half reliability **504**

standard deviation **508**

standardized achievement test **505**

standardized test **499**

stanines **509**

summative evaluation **488**

synthesis **496**

taxonomy of educational objectives **496**

teacher competence **492**

teacher-made test **499**

test blueprint **500**

T-score **508**

validity **501**

Z-score **508**

Suggested Readings

Wiggins' book is a useful and practical discussion of assessment for teachers. It is based on the assumption that testing should be *educative*: that is, it should be designed to teach rather than simply to measure. Popham's book is a briefer and clear explanation of those things teachers should know about assessment. It covers most of the topics discussed in this chapter. And the Aiken book includes coverage of standardized measures of achievement and ability as well as teacher-constructed tests:

Wiggins, G. (1998). *Educative assessment: Designing assessments to inform and improve student performance.* San Francisco: Jossey-Bass.

Popham, W. J. (1999). *Classroom assessment: What teachers need to know.* (2nd ed.). Boston, MA: Allyn and Bacon.

Aiken, L. R. (1998). *Tests and examinations: Measuring abilities and performance.* New York: John Wiley.

Those interested in the reform movement advocating that teachers' pay should be brought into line with their competency and performance might want to look at the following brief book:

Odden, A., & Kelley, C. (1997). *Paying teachers for what they know and do: New and smarter compensation strategies to improve schools.* Thousand Oaks, CA: Corwin Press.

The three following books are useful sources for information about performance-based approaches to assessment—especially the use of portfolios:

Farr, R., & Tone, B. (1998). *Portfolio and performance assessment: Helping students evaluate their progress as readers and writers* (2nd ed.). Fort Worth: Harcourt Brace.

Seidel, S., Walters, J., Kirby, E., Olff, N., Powell, K., Scripp, L., & Veenema, S. (1998). *Portfolio practices: Thinking through the assessment of children's work.* Washington, DC: National Education Association.

Yancey, K. B., & Weiser, I. (Eds.). (1997). *Situated Portfolios: Four perspectives.* Logan, Utah: Utah State University Press.

Purring among suckling young has been reported in the black bear. Growling among adult bears has also been reported (Ewer, 1973).

What we call the beginning is often the end
And to make an end is to make a beginning
The end is where we start from.
We shall not cease from exploration
And the end of all our exploring
Will be to arrive where we started
And know the place for the first time.

T. S. Eliot, *Little Gidding*

Epilogue and a Growing Footnote

During the spring when I was writing the first edition of **The Bear**, I spent many weekends out in the wilds chasing bears. Eventually, one caught up with me.

By then, I had figured out which way bear tracks point, and I knew that bears persistently point in the same direction, which is toward the front of their tracks. So when I found bear tracks I followed them, and followed them, and followed them. And after a while, I came across people tracks, which I recognized as well, and dang if they weren't following exactly the same bear tracks I was following. So I followed both the bear tracks and the people tracks for quite a long time. And then I came across more bear tracks and more people tracks, the meaning of which I now sat on a rock to figure out.

And then the bear showed up, nose to the ground. He was following my tracks—my tracks following his tracks, following my tracks . . . in a huge circle through the muddy swamp. *What we call the beginning is often the end*, says T. S. Eliot. *And the end of all our exploring will be to arrive where we started and know the place for the first time.*

And he wasn't even writing about bears.

So the next week, when I got to a chapter on programmed instruction—in those years it was a much bigger part of the text than it is now—I thought I'd illustrate the complexities of branching programs by writing a program on tracking bears, or bear tracking. It seemed to me that there is something strikingly sensible about a bear that persistently faces the front. There must surely be a lesson for teachers here, I explained to my grandmother. She looked skeptical.

Still, in that first edition, the bear was largely whimsy—although not entirely purposeless whimsy. A bear scrambling through the pages of a serious textbook was a bit of a jolt. It broke the tedium of uninterrupted academic content, and it sometimes made readers smile—or even laugh. And it didn't seem to detract from the serious "nuts and bolts" of the chapters, judging by the hundreds of students and professors who wrote letters after they read that first edition.

Over the years, the bear has become something more than whimsy, something more than a break from the tedium. At the same time, the bear has become less literal: He has become a metaphor. A metaphor is not, of course, a real thing; it's an invention. The bear metaphor was as much the invention of readers of earlier editions as it was mine. Some of these readers have decided that the bear is a metaphor for a teacher, or perhaps for teaching. Others have reached different conclusions. All are correct.

Much like that first bear that long-ago spring, we have now come full circle. And, in the manner of that wonderful design, we are ready to go back to the beginning, perhaps finally ready to understand its meaning. Maybe now we can see the tracks more clearly, recognize them without having to see who, or what, is actually standing in them. . . .

Remember that somewhere near the very beginning, you were given a word of caution: A science of humanity tends to dehumanize, we warned. It transforms living, breathing beings into "organisms"; it reduces our enormously complex behavior to stimuli and responses and the activity of our minds to inventions, to hypothetical structures. At the beginning we said that students are more than all this. At the end we say again that they are much more. Psychology has only just begun to understand; the last word has not been said or written.

Yet something has been said in the pages of this text. On 13 occasions, that something was reduced to a set of statements that were called "Main Points." Here, in this epilogue, all those main points are distilled into a single, final, all-embracing Main Point. This, reader, is what this text has been all about (blare of trumpets):

*A bear always faces the front.**

And that, I assure you, is true even of bears who have been going in circles—that not being nearly as pointless as I once thought. The relevance of the bear's customary posture for teaching can't easily be explained in anything shorter than a full-length book. Because this book is now concluding, suffice it to say that a teacher should try to behave as sensibly as a bear who persistently faces the front of its footprints. Teaching is both an art and a science. To reiterate a comment made in Chapter 1, where science fails, art should be used. The point is that there is much that is sensible in both the art and the science.

---

*When I wrote the first edition of this book in 1972, I had no doubt that this statement was absolutely true, but by 1975 I realized that it is only a very stupid bear who doesn't occasionally look backward. Accordingly, the second edition loudly proclaimed, "A bear ~~always~~ *usually* faces the front." Truth is a precarious luxury. By 1979 the bear had been approached from the rear so often that he had finally smartened up and now spent a lot of time facing backward. Accordingly, the title of the third edition announced with considerable assurance: "A bear ~~always usually~~ *sometimes* faces the front." How fickle truth! Perhaps more pertinent, how fickle bears! In 1982, with inflation rampant and the world situation tensing, we knew that the sagest of bears only very *rarely* faces the front. And a mere three years later, by 1985, it had finally happened: Confused by the awesome uncertainties of those years, though still moved by poetic visions of a peaceful and happy world, the bear looked boldly in all directions except, as the title page so unabashedly proclaimed, the front: "A bear ~~always usually sometimes rarely~~ *never* faces the front." But by 1988 things had changed again. In a cunning about-face, the bear began once more to face the front, only occasionally casting a furtive, sidelong glance in other directions. Until 1991. By then the bear had begun to sniff some new winds of change, winds that carried the stench of methane gases. After all these years, he thought he had begun to recognize the enemy: wild cows! He saw evidence of their passage in dried-up stream beds and in the taste of dead clover. He followed their spoor along the Saskatchewan River Valley and into the decimated boreal forests of the North. He watched them stealing trucks and playing cards while they slurped whisky and smoked cigars. He heard them blare out their country songs. He was not impressed, and he was very uneasy. Accordingly, in 1991, the bear absolutely *would not commit himself.* No way! But by 1994, the bear had had enough of sitting on his duff, looking here and there. Driven by a burning resolve to teach wild cows better values, the bear hurled himself headlong into the environmental crusades. Now, as the title insisted, he began to look to the future ("A bear ~~always usually sometimes rarely never always faces the front will not commit himself just now~~ faces the future.") Hah! That didn't last very long. People are suspicious and a little frightened of those too steadfastly focused on the future. In a moment of weakness, the bear decided he really wanted to be loved. So, in 1997, he became *politically correct,* for crying out loud.

But he hated himself, because being politically correct means trying to look like you're multicultural and multilingual and multicolored and outstandingly cool—even if you're not. And it means saying the right things and the nice things about everybody and everything. To be absolutely honest, the bear doesn't think and feel nice things about everything and everybody. Besides, he quickly discovered that being politically correct can be awful uncomfortable because it means spending a lot of time sitting on pointed fences.

That just wasn't the real bear. As my grandmother said so long ago, "There's more dog meat than choirboy in your bear."

Well, it's the new millennium, by jumpin' jickerybobs! The bear will no longer pretend to be a choirboy.

If it's to be dog meat, dog meat it is!

A bear ~~always usually sometimes rarely never always faces the front will not commit himself just now faces the future is politically correct~~ is not a choirboy!

GLOSSARY

This glossary defines the most important terms used (and **boldfaced**) in the text. In each case, the meaning given corresponds closely with its usage in the text. For more complete definitions, consult a standard psychological dictionary, which can be found in most libraries.

ability grouping Grouping students on the basis of ability for instructional purposes. See *within-class grouping*; *between-class grouping*.

acceleration One approach used for the education of the gifted. Acceleration programs attempt to move students through the conventional curriculum more rapidly than normal. See also *enrichment*.

accommodation Modification of an activity or ability in the face of environmental demands. In Piaget's description of development, assimilation and accommodation are the means individuals use to interact with and adapt to their world. See also *adaptation, assimilation*.

achievement motivation A need that, if high, is evident in a strong desire to achieve, to excel, to reach a high level of excellence. Achievement motivation can also be low.

acquisition metaphor A model of teaching marked by a view of learning as being largely a process of *acquisition* and accumulation by learners. See *participation metaphor*.

action research A highly subjective approach to educational research typically involving single cases or episodes. A common tool in reflective teaching. See *reflective teaching*.

adaptation Changes in an organism in response to the environment. Such changes are assumed to facilitate interaction with that environment. Adaptation plays a central role in Piaget's theory. See also *accommodation, assimilation*.

additive bilingualism A phrase used to describe situations where learning a second language has a positive effect on the first language and on general psychological functioning. See *subtractive bilingualism*.

advance organizer Introductory information given to learners to help them understand, learn, and remember new material.

affective domain Bloom's expression for the grouping of educational goals that relate to affect (emotion) and that are evident in behaviors relating to motivation, interest, and values. See also *cognitive domain*.

affective learning Changes in attitudes or emotions (affect) as a function of experience.

age-equivalent score A score converted to age equivalents using standardized test norms. Such norms allow test users to interpret the subject's performance in terms of the average performance of a comparable group of children of a specified age. See also *grade-equivalent score, standardized test*.

aggression In human beings, a much-studied characteristic that is generally defined as the conscious and willful inflicting of pain on others.

analysis The process of breaking something down into its component parts. As an intellectual activity, it consists primarily of examining the relationships among ideas in an attempt to understand them better. It is a relatively high-level intellectual skill in Bloom's taxonomy of educational objectives.

animism Attributing lifelike qualities to inanimate objects—as young children are wont to do.

anxiety A feeling of apprehension, worry, tension, or nervousness.

application An educational objective described by Bloom. Consists primarily of the ability to use abstractions in concrete situations.

arousal As a physiological concept, arousal refers to changes in functions such as heart rate, respiration rate, electrical activity in the cortex, and electrical conductivity of the skin. As a psychological concept, arousal refers to degree of alertness, awareness, vigilance, or wakefulness.

Arousal varies from very low (coma or sleep) to very high (panic or high anxiety).

articulation A cognitive apprenticeship technique. Learners are encouraged to put their conclusions, descriptions, and principles into words.

artificial intelligence (AI) Describes models, procedures, devices, or mechanisms intended to simulate or duplicate some of the intelligent functions of human mental activity.

assertive discipline The take-charge, aggressive, classroom management model advocated by Canter, based squarely on the notion that not only should teachers reinforce desirable behaviors, but they should also punish those that are undesirable.

assessment A judgmental process intimately involved in the teaching/learning process. A general term for the process of appraising student performance. May include elements of both measurement and evaluation. See also *evaluation, measurement.*

assimilation The act of incorporating objects or aspects of objects into previously learned activities. To assimilate is, in a sense, to ingest or to use something that was previously learned. See also *accommodation, adaptation.*

associative learning A simple type of learning where one event comes to be associated with another because of past experience. Both classical and operant conditioning are forms of associative learning. See *classical conditioning; operant conditioning.*

attention deficit hyperactivity disorder (ADHD) A disorder marked by excessive general activity for a child's age, attention problems, high impulsivity, and low frustration tolerance. Also termed *hyperactivity.*

attribute–treatment interaction The relationship among students' characteristics (attributes), teaching methods (treatments), and outcomes. These relationships are sometimes quite complex. Thus, a given treatment (instructional method, for example) may be more effective for students with certain attributes than it is for others with different attributes.

attribution theory A cognitive motivational theory concerned with predictable consistencies in what people interpret as the causes of the outcomes of behavior. See also *external orientation, internal orientation, locus of control.*

authentic assessment Refers to assessment procedures designed to allow students to demonstrate their ability to apply learning in real-life situations. Often contrasted with assessment based solely on objective tests, especially of the multiple-choice variety. Also termed *performance assessment.* See also *performance assessment.*

autoinstructional device Any instructional device that is effective in the absence of a teacher. Common examples are workbooks and computers.

autonomy Piaget's label for the second stage of moral development, characterized by a reliance on internal standards of right and wrong as guides for action and for judging the morality of an action. See also *heteronomy.*

aversive control The control of human behavior, usually through the presentation of noxious (unpleasant) stimuli, in contrast to techniques of positive control, which generally use positive reinforcement.

avoidance learning A conditioning phenomenon usually involving aversive (unpleasant) stimulation. The organism learns to avoid situations associated with specific unpleasant circumstances. See also *escape learning.*

babbling The relatively meaningless, highly repetitive sounds that young infants make in the early stages of language learning.

basic gender identity The individual's implicit understanding of the fundamental characteristics of masculinity and femininity.

basic need Maslow's term for a lower-level need, such as the physiological needs or the need to belong, to love, and to have high self-esteem. Also termed deficiency needs. See also *deficiency need, growth need, metaneeds.*

bear (a literal bear) A bobtailed, omnivorous, quadrupedal mammal that walks on the soles of its feet inventing poetic images and humming wonderful love songs. See also *bear (the metaphoric dog-meat kind of bear).*

bear (the metaphoric dog-meat kind of bear) A today kind of bear. A bear who has abandoned old prejudices and attitudes and deep-seated, ethnically based convictions of rightness and goodness. A tolerant and multicultural and multilingual and outstandingly cool bear. A good and wise bear—but also a bear who is no longer perched so uncomfortably on a pointed fence. This is a bear who has discarded his politically correct phase. Now, he doesn't give two hoots about the potential political consequences of committing himself to one side or the other. If you ask him, he sees himself as counter something or other. As the grandmother put it, there's a lot more dog meat than choir boy in this bear. See also *bear (a literal bear), wild cow.*

behavior The activity of an organism. Behavior can be either overt (visible) or covert (invisible or internal).

behavior management The systematic application of psychological principles in attempts to change behavior. See *behavior modification.*

behavior modification Changes in the behavior of an individual; also refers to psychological theory and research concerned with the application of psychological principles in attempts to change behavior.

behavioral objective A phrase used to describe an instructional objective that can be expressed in terms of specific, observable, measurable behaviors. Mager's instructional objectives are behavioral objectives. See also *expressive objectives.*

behaviorism A general term for theories of learning primarily concerned with the observable components of behavior (stimuli and responses).

behavioristic theories See *stimulus–response* (S–R) *theory*.

belief The acceptance of an idea as accurate or truthful. Beliefs are often highly personal and resistant to change. See also *law, model, principle, theory*.

between-class grouping The assignment of learners to ability groups or tracks that function in separate classrooms.

biofeedback Information that we obtain about our biological functioning. In a specialized sense, biofeedback refers to information that subjects receive about the activity of their nervous system when they are connected to one of various sensors or instruments designed for that purpose. See also *neurofeedback*.

biographical inventories Checklists or questionnaires designed to summarize the events and accomplishment of an individual's life.

brainstorming A technique popularized by Osborn and used to produce creative solutions for problems. A brainstorming session usually involves a small group of people who are encouraged to produce a wide variety of ideas, which are later evaluated. See also *Gordon technique*.

branching program Programmed material that, in contrast to a linear program, presents a variety of alternative routes through the material. Such programs typically make use of larger frames than do linear programs, and they frequently use multiple choices. Also termed *Crowder programs*. See also *frame*.

CAI One of many acronyms related to the application of computer technology to education. Specifically, CAI refers to computer-assisted instruction, the use of computers for instructional rather than administrative purposes.

capability A capacity to do something. To be capable is to have the necessary knowledge and skills.

case study An investigation that involves specific actions, episodes, or individuals. Case studies generally involve one single participant or event or no more than a small number of individual cases.

category A term used by Bruner to describe a grouping of related objects or events. In this sense, a category is both a concept and a percept. Bruner also defines it as a rule for classifying things as equal. See also *coding system*.

cause An agent or force that produces an effect or a result. A cause is one aspect of motivation. See also *reason*.

central tendency The tendency for the majority of scores in a normal distribution to cluster around the center of the distribution. Measures of central tendency include the mean, the median, and the mode. See also *mean, median, mode*.

cerebral palsy Label for a collection of congenital problems associated with brain damage and manifested in motor problems of varying severity and occasionally other problems such as convulsions or behavior disorders.

character An inclusive and ill-defined term signifying those aspects of human personality that include the individual's values, moral strength, principles, virtues, and vices. Character relates to what we think of as the goodness or moral strength of the individual.

chunking A memory process whereby related items are grouped together into more easily remembered chunks (for example, a prefix and four digits for a phone number rather than seven unrelated numbers).

circles of knowledge A generic term sometimes used to describe a variety of small-group learning approaches. These approaches stress face-to-face interaction, peer help, and rewards for cooperative, group activities rather than for individual activity. Such approaches are highly cooperative rather than competitive or individualistic.

classical conditioning Also called "learning-through-stimulus substitution" because it involves the repeated pairing of two stimuli. Eventually a previously neutral (conditioned) stimulus comes to elicit the same response (conditioned response) that was previously elicited by the first stimulus (unconditioned stimulus). This was the type of conditioning first described by Pavlov. See also *conditioning, operant conditioning*.

classification The act of grouping items in terms of common properties. Classification involves abstracting the properties of objects or events and making judgments concerning their similarities or differences from other objects or events.

classroom climate A vague expression that describes the general ambience of a classroom. Factors that contribute to classroom climate include the teacher's customary ways of interacting with students (teaching styles), physical features of the classroom, relationships and interactions among learners, and personal and decorative touches.

classroom management A comprehensive term for a variety of teacher actions designed to facilitate teaching and learning in the classroom. Classroom management includes disciplinary actions, daily routines, seating arrangements, and the scheduling of lessons.

claustrophobia A disorder whose principal symptom is fear of enclosed or confined spaces.

client-centered therapy A type of patient–counselor relationship. The counselor (therapist or psychiatrist) is not directive in the sense of telling clients how they should behave but rather attempts to allow patients to express themselves and discover their own ways of dealing with their own behavior. This therapeutic approach is generally contrasted with directive therapy. Also termed *person-centered therapy*. See also *counseling, directive therapy*.

coaching A technique sometimes used in cognitive apprenticeship approaches to instruction. The learner's cognitive behavior is guided by an expert.

cocktail party phenomenon An expression to describe sensory memory. The fleeting and unconscious availability for processing of stimuli to which the individual is not paying attention.

coding system A Brunerian concept; refers to a hierarchical arrangement of related categories. See also *category, hierarchies of classes.*

cognition To cognize is to know. Hence, cognition deals with knowing, understanding, problem solving, and related intellectual processes.

cognitive apprenticeship An instructional model wherein parents, siblings, other adults, and especially teachers serve as a combination of model, guide, tutor, mentor, and coach to foster intellectual growth among learners.

cognitive assessment system Naglieri and Das' test of intellectual functioning designed to identify cognitive deficits in challenged learners. It provides measures for each of the processes described by the PASS model of intellectual functioning. See *PASS.*

cognitive domain Bloom's expression for the area of educational activity and educational objectives relating to acquiring information, understanding, analyzing, synthesizing, and so on. See also *affective domain.*

cognitive learning Learning concerned primarily with acquiring information, developing strategies for processing information, decision-making processes, and logical thought processes.

cognitive strategy A process involved in learning and remembering. Cognitive strategies include identifying problems, selecting approaches to their solution, monitoring progress in solving problems, and using feedback. Cognitive strategies are closely related to metacognition and metamemory. See also *knowledge acquisition components, learning/thinking strategy, metacognition, metamemory, performance components.*

cognitive structure The organized totality of an individual's knowledge. Also termed *mental structure.* See also *knowledge.*

cognitivism Theories of learning primarily concerned with such topics as perception, problem solving, information processing, and understanding.

cohort A group of individuals born within the same specified period of time. For example, the cohort of the 1950s includes those born between January 1, 1950, and December 31, 1959, inclusive.

collaborative learning See *cooperative learning.*

combined schedule A combination of various types of schedules of reinforcement.

communication The transmission of a message from one organism to another. Communication does not necessarily involve language because some nonhuman animals can communicate, usually through reflexive behaviors. See also *language.*

comparative organizer A concept or idea that serves to facilitate the learning of new material by making use of the similarities and differences between the new material and previous learning.

competence motivation White's phrase for our innate need to achieve competence and to feel competent. According to White, competence motivation has especially important adaptive value for a species that is born with little innate competence.

competitive learning One of the most common instructional approaches in North America. It involves students working against each other to see who is best. In competitive learning, student rewards are inversely related to the performance of others. See also *cooperative learning, individualistic learning.*

comprehension The lowest level of understanding in Bloom's hierarchy of educational objectives. Comprehension is defined as the ability to apprehend the meaning of communication without necessarily being able to apply, analyze, or evaluate it.

computer literacy The minimal skills required for effective interaction with computers. Does not require knowing how a computer functions internally or how to program one.

computer simulation Mimicking or modeling certain actions, procedures, or phenomena using computers. For example, computers might be used to simulate (copy the actions of) weather patterns or chemical reactions.

computer-assisted instruction (CAI) The use of computer facilities to help in instruction.

concept A collection of perceptual experiences or ideas that are related because they possess common properties.

concept map See *conceptual model.*

conceptual change movement Literally, cognitive changes such as might be evident in greater understanding, knowledge, and awareness. More specifically, this expression refers to instructional approaches designed to foster mental reorganization rather than simply to increase the number of facts learned.

conceptual model A verbal or graphic representation of concepts and important relationships that exist among them. Designed to assist the learner in developing a clear and useful mental representation. Also termed a *concept map.*

concrete operations The third of Piaget's four major stages, lasting from age 7 or 8 to approximately age 11 or 12, and characterized largely by the child's ability to deal with concrete problems and objects or objects and problems that are easily imagined.

concurrent validity See *criterion-related validity.*

conditioned response (CR) A response elicited by a conditioned stimulus. In some obvious ways, a conditioned response resembles, but is not identical to, its corresponding unconditioned response. See also *neutral stimulus*.

conditioned stimulus (CS) A stimulus that initially does not elicit any response or that elicits a global, orienting response but that, as a function of being paired with an unconditioned stimulus and its response, acquires the capability of eliciting that same response. For example, a stimulus that is always present at the time of a fear reaction may become a conditioned stimulus for fear.

conditioning A type of learning describable in terms of changing relationships between stimuli, between responses, or between both stimuli and responses. See also *classical conditioning, operant conditioning*.

conflict management A program designed to teach individuals acceptable ways of resolving conflicts. Common conflict management techniques include negotiating, compromising, taking turns, explaining, listening, apologizing, mediating, using humor, and invoking chance.

confluence model Zajonc's term for the hypothesis that the intellectual climate of the home, determined principally in terms of the numbers and ages of family members, contributes in important ways to the development of children's intelligence. According to this model, children born into a relatively adult environment (firstborn and only children, for example) should, on average, have an intellectual advantage over those born in a less adult environment (later-born children, children in large families, children in single-parent homes).

confluent education A highly humanistic approach to education that attempts to integrate the affective and cognitive aspects of learning and teaching; sometimes described as part of the *human potential movement*. See *human potential movement*.

connectionism A theory that explains learning as the formation of bonds (connections) between stimuli and responses. The term is attributed to Thorndike.

conservation A Piagetian term for the realization that certain quantitative attributes of objects remain unchanged unless something is added to or taken away from them. Such characteristics of objects as mass, number, area, and volume are capable of being conserved.

construct validity An estimate of test validity based on the extent to which test results agree with and reflect the theories that underlie the test. See also *content validity, criterion-related validity, face validity, reliability, validity*.

constructivism A general term for student-centered approaches to teaching such as discovery-oriented approaches, reciprocal learning, or cooperative instruction—so called because of their assumption that learners should build (construct) knowledge for themselves. See *constructivist approaches*.

constructivist approaches A general label for instructional methods that are highly learner-centered and that reflect the belief that meaningful information is constructed by students rather than given to them. Often contrasted with *direct instruction*, constructivist approaches are reflected in discovery learning, cognitive apprenticeship, and humanistic approaches to teaching. See *direct instruction; progressive education*.

constructive memory An alternate label for long-term memory, meant to emphasize the extent to which remembering involves reconstructing experiences. With the passage of time, we tend to remember less and less accurately.

content A term used by Guilford to describe the content of a person's intellect. Intellectual activity (operations) involves content and results in products. See also *convergent thinking, creativity, divergent thinking, operation, product*.

content validity Test validity determined by a careful analysis of the content of test items and a comparison of this content with course objectives. See also *construct validity, criterion-related validity, face validity, reliability, validity*.

context Refers to all of the developmentally important characteristics of the environment in which development occurs—for example, culture, cohort influences, the family, historical events, and educational experiences.

contiguity The occurrence of things both simultaneously and in the same space. Contiguity is frequently used to explain the occurrence of classical conditioning. The simultaneity of the unconditioned and conditioned stimulus is assumed to be sufficient to explain the formation of the link between the two.

continuous reinforcement A reinforcement schedule in which every correct response is followed by a reinforcer. See also *fixed schedule, intermittent reinforcement, interval schedule, random schedule, ratio schedule, schedule of reinforcement*.

conventional Kohlberg's second level of morality, reflecting a desire to establish and maintain good relations with others (law and order; obedience).

convergent thinking A term used by Guilford to describe the type of thinking that results in a single, correct solution for a problem. Most conventional tests of intelligence measure convergent rather than divergent thinking. See also *content, creativity, divergent thinking, operation, product*.

cooperative learning An instructional method where students work together in small groups so that each member of the group can participate in a clearly assigned, collective task. Also termed *collaborative learning*. See also *competitive learning, individualistic learning*.

corporal punishment Punishment that uses physical force to inflict pain.

corrective strategies Strategies designed to correct discipline problems. These often involve the systematic use of rewards and punishments.

correlation A statistical relationship between variables. See also *variable.*

correlative subsumption The type of learning that takes place when new information requires an extension of what was previously known and therefore could not have been derived directly from it. See also *derivative subsumption, subsumption.*

counseling The act of giving advice. See also *client-centered therapy, directive therapy.*

craft knowledge Knowledge of the specifics of teaching. The science of teaching and a sort of practical wisdom that includes general information about teaching along with specific information about teaching particular subjects and lessons to students with identifiable characteristics.

creativity Generally refers to the capacity of individuals to produce novel or original answers or products. The term *creative* is an adjective that can be used to describe people, products, or processes. See also *convergent thinking, divergent thinking.*

criterion-referenced testing A test in which the student is judged relative to a criterion rather than relative to the performance of other students. The teacher decides beforehand what specific performance is expected and tests to see whether the student has reached this criterion. See also *norm-referenced testing.*

criterion-related validity A measure of the extent to which predictions based on test results are accurate (predictive validity) and how well the test agrees with other related measures (concurrent validity). Also termed *predictive validity.* See also *construct validity, content validity, face validity, reliability, validity.*

critical period A period in development when exposure to appropriate experiences or stimuli will bring about specific learning much more easily than at other times. See also *imprinting.*

crystallized abilities Cattell's term for intellectual abilities that are highly dependent on experience (verbal and numerical abilities, for example). These abilities do not appear to decline significantly with advancing age. See also *fluid abilities.*

culture Signifies the customs, beliefs, achievements, art, and literature that is particular to a distinct group of people.

database A source of information accessible by computers. Common databases include library cataloguing systems or abstracts of current journal articles. Databases are often organized by topics. For example, PSYCHINFO is a vast database that contains summaries of an enormous number of articles published in journals relevant to psychology.

declarative knowledge All the facts, information, and experiences that are part of what we know. Also termed *declarative memory.* See also *procedural knowledge.*

declarative memory Explicit, conscious long-term memory, in contrast with implicit (or nondeclarative) memory. Declarative memory can be either semantic or episodic. Also termed *explicit memory.* See also *episodic memory, semantic memory.*

deferred imitation The ability to imitate people or events in their absence. Deferred imitation is assumed to be crucial in the development of language abilities.

deficiency need Maslow's expression for a basic need, so called because it motivates the person to act when a related deficiency is sensed—for example, a deficiency of food leads to eating, a deficiency of self-esteem leads to behaviors intended to increase esteem. See also *basic need, growth need, metaneeds.*

dependent variable The variable (measurement, outcome, behavior) that reflects the effects of manipulations of the independent variable(s) in an experiment. The "then" part of the if-then equation implicit in an experimental hypothesis. See *independent variable; hypothesis.*

derivative subsumption The type of subsumption (or learning) that takes place when new material can be directly derived from what is already known. See also *correlative subsumption, subsumption.*

desist To stop, to refrain from. In education, desists are teacher behaviors intended to make a student stop (desist from) some ongoing or impending misbehavior. Desists can take the form of threats, simple requests, orders, pleas, and so on. See also *with-it-ness.*

detracking An educational reform movement based on the desire to rid educational systems of homogeneous grouping practices. See *homogeneous groups; tracking; ability grouping.*

development The growth, maturational, and learning processes occurring from birth to maturity. See also *growth, maturation.*

developmental arithmetic disorder A learning disability evident in specific problems in developing arithmetic skills in the absence of other problems such as mental retardation.

developmental assessment A performance-based assessment that looks at the student's performance in relation to developmental or course-based expectations rather than in relation to the performance of other students. Often uses checklists of expected (desired) behaviors.

developmental reading disorder A learning disability manifested in reading problems of varying severity—sometimes evident in spelling difficulties. Also termed *dyslexia* or *specific reading disability.*

dialectical thinking Thinking that recognizes, accepts, and attempts to resolve conflicts. Dialectical thinking is thought to be more characteristic of adults than of children or adolescents.

differential reinforcement of successive approximations The procedure of reinforcing only some responses and not others. Differential reinforcement is used to shape complex behaviors. See also *shaping*.

direct instruction A phrase used to describe teacher-directed approaches to teaching—in contrast with more student-centered approaches such as reciprocal teaching and cooperative learning (often included among *constructivist approaches*). See *constructivist approaches*.

direct reinforcement The type of reinforcement that affects the individual in question directly rather than vicariously. See also *vicarious reinforcement*.

direct teaching style A relatively authoritarian approach to teaching. Teachers are considered the primary source of information. See also *indirect teaching style*.

directive therapy A type of counselor–client relationship in which the counselor takes the major responsibility for directing the client's behavior. See also *counseling*.

discipline The control aspects of teaching. Refers to actions that teachers take to minimize behavior problems and their responses to problems when they do occur.

discovery learning The acquisition of new information or knowledge largely as a result of the learner's own efforts. Discovery learning is contrasted with expository or reception learning and is generally associated with Bruner, among others. It is an important instructional tool of the constructivist classroom. See also *reception learning, constructivist approaches*.

discriminated stimulus (S^D) A stimulus that is perceived by the organism. In operant conditioning, the discriminated stimulus elicits the response.

discrimination Processes involved in learning that certain responses are appropriate in specific situations but inappropriate in other, similar situations. Generalization is an opposite process. See also *generalization*.

disinhibition The appearance of a suppressed behavior. See also *inhibitory-disinhibitory effect*.

disposition An inclination or tendency to do (or not to do) something; an aspect of motivation. See also *motives*.

dissociability A term used by Ausubel to indicate the ease with which material that is to be recalled can be separated (dissociated) from other related material that is also stored in memory.

distance education An educational delivery system that involves little or no face-to-face contact but wherein instructional material is presented at a distance, often using one or more of a combination of computers, electronic networking facilities, telephone conferencing, facsimile transmitters, radio, television, film, videocassette recordings, or other communication media.

distance receptors The senses that receive stimulation from a distance (for example, hearing and vision).

distinct society A metaphor used to describe the Canadian cultural scene where, theoretically, two distinct cultures coexist; neither has been assimilated to the other as would happen in *melting pot societies*. See *melting pot societies*.

distortion One explanation for memory loss. Describes a process where the features of an experience are insufficiently bound together so that the person recollecting the experience cannot easily tell what happened when.

divergent thinking An expression used by Guilford to describe the type of thinking that results in the production of several solutions for one problem. Divergent thinking is assumed to be closely related to creative behavior, and the term is used interchangeably with the term *creativity*. See also *convergent thinking, creativity*.

diversity of training Bruner's expression relating to his belief that exposure to information under a wide range of circumstances is conducive to discovering relationships among concepts.

dizygotic Resulting from two separate eggs and forming fraternal (nonidentical) twins. See also *monozygotic*.

drive The tendency toward a certain behavior that is brought about by an unsatisfied need—for example, the hunger drive is related to the need for food. See also *need, need–drive theory*.

drive reduction The satisfaction of a need by eliminating the drive associated with it. For example, satisfying the need for water by drinking, thus eliminating the thirst drive.

dual-language immersion programs Immersion programs which include children who are native speakers of the dominant language and children who are learning the dominant language as a second language.

dynamic assessment Psychological assessment that attempts to measure the individual's ability to change (that is, to learn). May take the form of tests that gauge the extent to which testees profit from opportunities to learn new material.

echoic memory Neisser's term for sensory memory involving auditory stimulation—the fleeting availability for processing of auditory stimuli to which the individual is not paying attention.

educable mentally retarded (EMR) A label for those who are mildly retarded—having approximately an IQ between 50 and 70. See *mild retardation*.

educational goal An intended or desired outcome of the educational process. Often expressed in terms of instructional objectives that can range from highly general to very specific. See also *instructional objective*.

educational psychology A science concerned primarily with the study of human behavior in educational settings.

Applies existing psychological knowledge to instructional problems and develops new knowledge and procedures.

egocentric speech Vygotsky's intermediate stage of language development, common between ages 3 and 7; during this stage children often talk to themselves in an apparent effort to control their own behavior. See also *inner speech, social speech*.

egocentrism A way of functioning characterized by an inability to assume the point of view of others. A child's early thinking is largely egocentric.

eidetic image A particularly vivid type of visual image in memory. In many ways, it is as though the individual were actually able to look at what is being remembered—hence the synonym *photographic memory*.

elaboration A long-term memory process involving changing or adding to material, or making associations to make remembering easier. See also *organization, rehearsal*.

electroencephalograph (EEG) A graphlike representation of changes in electrical potential that occur in the brain.

elicited response A response brought about by a stimulus. This expression is synonymous with the term *respondent*. See also *operant, respondent, unconditioned response*.

eliciting effect Imitative behavior where the observer does not copy the model's responses but simply behaves in a related manner. See also *imitation, inhibitory-disinhibitory effect, modeling effect*.

emergentism An explanation that views language learning as the result of a gradual learning process involving social interaction, where understanding of grammar gradually emerges, rather than being prewired. See *hopeful monsters; nativism*.

emitted response A response not elicited by a stimulus but simply emitted by the organism. An emitted response is, in fact, an operant.

empower To enable; to give power to. One of the most important goals of education is to empower students by providing them with both specific information and learning/thinking strategies and by helping them to develop the feelings of personal power that accompany the realization that one is competent and worthwhile.

enactive A term used by Bruner to describe young children's representations of their world. The term refers specifically to the belief that children represent the world in terms of their personal actions. See also *iconic, symbolic*.

encoding A process whereby we derive meaning from the environment. To encode is to represent in another form. At a mental level, encoding involves the process of abstracting—representing something as a concept or a meaning.

encounter group See *growth group*.

English as a Second Language (ESL) An expression used to describe programs designed specifically for nonnative English speakers.

enrichment An approach to the education of gifted children. Enrichment involves providing students with additional and different school experiences rather than simply moving them more rapidly through the conventional curriculum. Also termed the *revolving door model*. See also *acceleration*.

entity theory Dweck's label for the belief that ability is a fixed, unchanging entity. Associated with performance goals—that is, with doing well to be judged positively by others. See also *incremental theory, mastery goal, performance goal*.

environmentalism The belief that whatever a child becomes is determined by experience (the environment) rather than by genetic makeup.

epilepsy A seizure disorder, sometimes genetic in origin, varying in severity; it is often treatable or controllable with drugs.

episodic memory A type of declarative, autobiographical (conscious, long-term) memory consisting of knowlege about personal experiences, tied to specific times and places. See also *semantic memory*.

equilibration A Piagetian term for the process by which we maintain a balance between assimilation (using old learning) and accommodation (changing behavior, learning new things). Equilibration is essential for adaptation and cognitive growth.

escape learning A conditioning phenomenon whereby the organism learns the means of escaping from a situation, usually following the presentation of aversive (unpleasant) stimulation. See also *avoidance learning*.

essay test A test that requires testees to construct responses of varying lengths in sentence, paragraph, or essay form. See also *objective test*.

ethnic Refers to the sharing of beliefs, values, history, or other characteristics, as might happen with distinct cultural or language groups.

evaluation In contrast to measurement, evaluation involves making a value judgment—deciding on the goodness or badness of performance. It also denotes the highest level of intellectual skill in Bloom's taxonomy of educational objectives; there it is defined as the ability to render judgments about the value of methods or materials for specific purposes, making use of external or internal criteria. See also *assessment, measurement*.

exceptionality A term used to describe a significant deviation from the average in terms of physical, intellectual, or emotional behaviors, abilities, or skills. It is a two-dimensional concept because it can indicate either significant superiority or significant handicaps. See also *special education teacher, special needs*.

exclusion A time-out punishment procedure whereby a child is not removed from the situation but is excluded from ongoing activities, often by being required to sit behind a screen, in a corner, or facing away from the class. See also *isolation, nonexclusion, time-out.*

executive model A view of the teacher as a master teacher (executive) responsible for arranging the teaching/learning situation, delivering lessons, and teaching learners prescribed skills and information. See also *liberationist model, therapist model.*

exemplary model A good example. A teacher, for example.

exhibition A performance-based assessment procedure that requires the public display of competence. Exhibitions are most common in the visual or performing arts and in oral examinations for graduate degrees. They underline the social nature of thinking.

existentialism A philosophical movement characterized by a preoccupation with existence. Existential philosophers often describe the human condition in terms such as *abandonment, loneliness, despair,* and *alienation.* These feelings are assumed to arise from our lack of certain knowledge about our origins and our eventual end. Hence the label *existentialism,* because the only knowable reality is existence.

experiment A deliberately controlled arrangement of circumstances under which a phenomenon is observed.

experimental analysis of behavior A phrase typically associated with Skinner's system. The term reflects his emphasis on the objective analysis of the variables involved in behavior—specifically, what the organism does, the circumstances under which the action occurs, and the consequences of the action (whether behavior occurs again under similar circumstances).

expert teachers Teachers who, by virtue of experience, training, and other intangible skills, share characteristics that make them better, more effective teachers than novices. In Sternberg's prototypical model of teaching expertise, these characteristics relate to knowledge, efficiency of problem solving, and insight for solving educational problems.

explicit memory See *declarative memory.*

exploration A cognitive apprenticeship procedure that requires learners to apply or generalize what they have learned, to investigate and test the potential applications of their learning.

expository organizer An idea or concept that serves as a description (exposition) of concepts that are relevant to new learning.

expository teaching An instructional technique strongly advocated by Ausubel. The teacher bears the responsibility of organizing and presenting information in relatively final form. Expository teaching is associated with reception learning rather than discovery-oriented approaches and is essentially another label for direct instruction. See also *reception learning, direct instruction.*

external orientation A tendency to attribute the outcomes of behavior to factors outside the individual (such as luck or the difficulty of a task). See also *attribution theory, internal orientation, locus of control.*

extinction The cessation of a response as a function of the withdrawal of reinforcement. See also *forgetting.*

extinction rate The lapse of time between the cessation of a response and the withdrawal of reinforcement.

extrinsic motive A motive associated with external sources of reinforcement—like food, money, or sex. See also *extrinsic reinforcement.*

extrinsic reinforcement External reinforcement rather than reinforcement from within—for example, high grades, praise, or money. See also *intrinsic reinforcement.*

face validity The extent to which a test appears to be measuring what it is intended to measure. See also *construct validity, content validity, criterion-related validity, reliability, validity.*

fact Something that observation leads us to believe is true or real. Ideally, the observations that determine our facts are sufficiently objective and repeatable to assure us that they accurately reflect how things actually are.

fading A technique used in cognitive apprenticeship programs. It involves the gradual withdrawal of supports (scaffolds) for the learner as these become progressively less necessary. See also *scaffolding.*

fading theory The belief that the inability to recall long-term memories increases with the passage of time as memory traces fade. Also termed *decay theory.*

Family Educational Rights to Privacy Act Public Law 93-380, which guarantees parents right of access and challenge with respect to the school records of their children and also guarantees the privacy of such records.

Feuerstein's Instrumental Enrichment (FIE) A detailed and comprehensive program designed to teach cognitive strategies and to make learners more aware of their own strategies.

filial piety A fundamental virtue in many oriental cultures. In effect, it says that people should always, under all circumstances, and at all ages, display the highest devotion and complete obedience to their parents, and that the welfare of parents always comes first. (My kids are occidental.)

fixed schedule A type of intermittent schedule of reinforcement. The reinforcement occurs at fixed intervals of time (an interval schedule) or after a specified number of trials (a ratio schedule). See also *continuous reinforcement, intermittent reinforcement, interval schedule, random schedule, ratio schedule, schedule of reinforcement.*

flashbulb memories Unusually vivid and relatively permanent recollections of the details surrounding first hearing some emotionally significant news.

flexibility A factor tapped by production measures of divergent thinking (creativity). It is evident in the ability or propensity to switch from one class of responses or solutions to another. See also *fluency, originality*.

fluency A factor thought to be involved in creativity and evident in the production of a large number of responses or solutions in a problem situation. See also *flexibility, originality*.

fluid abilities Cattell's term for intellectual abilities that seem to underlie much of our intelligent behavior but are not highly affected by experience (for example, general reasoning, attention span, and memory for numbers). Fluid abilities are more likely to decline in old age. See also *crystallized abilities*.

Flynn effect A label used to denote that there are gains in measured IQ over generations.

foreclosure Marcia's term for the adoption of a ready-made identity.

forgetting The cessation of a response as a function of the passage of time, not to be confused with extinction. See also *extinction*.

formal operations The last of Piaget's four major stages. It begins around age 11 or 12 and lasts until age 14 or 15. This stage is characterized by the child's increasing ability to use logical thought processes.

formal teaching style An approach to teaching that emphasizes competition, individual work, discipline, order, achievement, and external motivators. See also *informal teaching style*.

formative evaluation An evaluation undertaken before and during instruction, designed primarily to assist the learner to identify strengths and weaknesses. Formative evaluation is a fundamental part of the process of instruction. See also *summative evaluation*.

frame A unit of information presented in programmed instruction. A frame presents information and usually requires the student to make a response.

fraternal twins Twins whose genetic origins are two different eggs. Such twins are as genetically dissimilar as non-twin siblings. See also *identical twins*.

full inclusion The inclusion of all special needs children in regular classrooms regardless of the nature and severity of their handicaps.

g The abbreviation for general intelligence—a basic intellectual capability sometimes assumed to underlie all manifestations of intelligence.

gender identity disorder A label for the relatively rare condition where individuals don't feel comfortable with their anatomical sex—where they feel themselves to *be* the other sex and have strong preferences for that alternative.

gender roles Attitudes, personality characteristics, behavior, and other qualities associated with being male or female. Gender roles define masculinity and femininity. Also termed *sex roles*. See also *sex typing*.

gender schemas Notions about the characteristics associated with being male or female.

gender schema theory A cognitive gender typing theory that recognizes the usefulness of elements of both cognitive explanations (the child's growing understanding of the nature and meaning of gender) and social learning explanations (the influence of models and reinforcements) to account for the shaping of gender roles.

gender typing Learning behavior appropriate to the sex of the individual. The term refers specifically to the acquisition of masculine behavior by a boy and feminine behavior by a girl.

general intelligence See *g*.

generalization The transference of a response from one stimulus to a similar stimulus (stimulus generalization) or the transference of a similar response for another response in the face of a single stimulus (response generalization). A child who responds with fear in a new situation that resembles an old, fear-producing situation is showing evidence of stimulus generalization. Also termed *transfer*. See also *discrimination*.

generalized reinforcer A stimulus that is not reinforcing before being paired with a primary reinforcer. Generalized reinforcers are present so often at the time of reinforcement that they come to be reinforcing for a wide variety of unrelated activities. Stimuli such as social prestige, praise, and money are generalized reinforcers for human behavior. See also *primary reinforcer*.

giftedness Exceptional general ability. See *talented and gifted; talent*.

global before local A phrase used to describe a sequencing principle in cognitive apprenticeship. Refers to the recommendation that learners should be given some notion of what the final performance, the final task, the final global rendition will be before being asked to work on the individual subtasks that make up the whole.

grade-equivalent score A score that has been converted to a grade equivalent using standardized test norms. It allows the user to conclude that the testee has performed at a level comparable to that of average children at a specified grade level. See also *age-equivalent score, standardized tests*.

group investigation A collaborative instructional technique where students identify topics and related sources of information, form groups on the basis of shared interests, assign responsibility for collecting material, gather and study relevant material alone and in groups, prepare group reports, and present these to the class.

group test A type of test usually used to measure intelligence that may be given to large groups of subjects at one time. It is typically of the paper-and-pencil variety. See also *individual test*.

growth The quantitative, physical aspects of development. See also *development, maturation.*

growth group A general label for group process approaches to therapy and sometimes to instruction. These typically involve the use of techniques designed to foster communication, openness, self-discovery, sharing, conflict resolution, and so on, usually in small group settings. Also termed *sensitivity groups* or *encounter groups.*

growth need Another expression for Maslow's metaneeds. So called because these needs motivate behavior not as a result of deficiencies but because of an intrinsic need to grow, to become, to actualize oneself. These include cognitive, aesthetic, and self-actualization needs.

guided discovery A reflective teaching technique. Students are given much of the responsibility for finding relationships and organizing knowledge, but teachers are careful to provide the necessary guidance to ensure that discovery and learning occur.

hardware The physical components of a computer, including the monitor, controller, keyboard, chips, cards, circuits, drives, printer, and so on. See also *software.*

hedonistic Relating to the pain–pleasure principle—the tendency to seek pleasure and avoid pain.

herd behavior A type of imitative behavior involving large groups of individuals.

heterogeneous group An instructional group whose members represent a wide range of skills, abilities, interests, aspirations, and so on. See *homogeneous group.*

heteronomy Piaget's label for the first stage of moral development, marked by reliance on outside authority. See also *autonomy.*

hierarchies of classes Arrangements of concepts or classes in terms of their inclusiveness. At the top of the hierarchy is the concept (class) that is most inclusive (for example, writing instruments); below this highly inclusive concept are those included in it (for example, pens, typewriters, pencils). See also *coding system.*

holistic education A comprehensive term for educational approaches that attempt to remedy what is seen as the failure of traditional education to educate the whole brain. Advocates of holistic education believe that the right hemisphere—speculatively linked with art, music, and emotion—is neglected by curricula that stress reason, logic, language, science, and mathematics.

holophrase A sentencelike word uttered by young children early in the course of learning a language. A holophrase is a single word that the child uses to convey as much meaning as an adult would convey with a much longer phrase.

homogeneous group An instructional group whose members are highly similar in terms of the criteria that define the group (for example, ability, race, gender, or vocational aspirations). See *heterogeneous group.*

hopeful monsters Deacon's label for explanations that resort to what is sometimes termed *Deus ex machina*—a "God in a machine." Such explanations rely on an assumed but unseen and unprovable entity, organ, or feature to explain what cannot easily be explained otherwise.

human potential movement A label sometimes used to describe the combination of approaches in education, therapy, and other helping professions that stem from a humanistic orientation and reflect the conviction that the goal of each of these endeavors should be to foster the fullest development of each individual. See *self-actualization, confluent education.*

humanism A philosophical and psychological orientation primarily concerned with our humanity—that is, with our worth as individuals and those processes that are considered to make us more human. See *humanistic psychology.*

humanistic psychology A branch of psychology whose primary concern is with the development of the self and with the uniqueness of the individual. Sometimes referred to as *third-force* psychology; the other two forces are behaviorism and Freudian theory. See *humanism.*

hyperactivity A common term for attention deficit hyperactivity disorder. See also *attention deficit hyperactivity disorder (ADHD).*

hypertext A basic organizational mode for computer-based information that allows the user to jump from topic to topic and back again.

hypothesis An educated guess that can be tested. A prediction, generally based on observation, intuition, or theory, which must then be verified experimentally. A hypothesis can usually be expressed as an "if-then" statement.

iconic A term that refers to a developmental stage in children's representation of their world. The term is used by Bruner to describe an intermediate stage of development characterized by a representation of the world in terms of relatively concrete mental images. See also *enactive, symbolic.*

iconic memory Neisser's term for sensory memory involving visual stimulation—the fleeting availability for processing of visual stimuli to which the individual is not attending.

identical twins Twins whose genetic origin is one egg. Such twins are genetically identical. See also *fraternal twins.*

identity A logical rule that specifies that certain activities leave objects or situations unchanged. See also *reversibility.*

identity In Erikson's theory, a term closely related to self. Identity refers to the individual's self-definition, a sort of personal sense of who and what one is. To achieve identity is to arrive at a clear notion of who one is. One of the important tasks of adolescence is to select and develop a strong sense of identity.

identity achieved Marcia's term for individuals who have experienced a crisis and made a commitment, thus achieving a sense of identity.

identity diffusion An expression for a stage in early adolescence. During this stage the adolescent has a vague and changing sense of identity with no firm vocational commitment and an ambiguous belief system.

imitation Copying behavior. To imitate a person's behavior is simply to use that person's behavior as a pattern. Piaget also terms this *internal representation*. Bandura and Walters describe three different effects of imitation. See also *eliciting effect, inhibitory-disinhibitory effect, modeling effect, observational learning*.

implicit memory See *nondeclarative memory*.

imprinting Unlearned, instinctive behaviors that are not present at birth but become part of an animal's repertoire after exposure to a suitable stimulus during a critical period. The "following" behavior of young ducks, geese, and chickens is one example. See also *critical period*.

in loco parentis A Latin expression meaning, literally, "in the place of parents." Teachers are said to have rights and responsibilities *in loco parentis* to the extent that society charges them with the care and education of children.

inclusion See *mainstreaming*.

inclusive classroom A classroom that contains one or more children with special needs in addition to more average children.

incremental theory Dweck's label for the belief that ability is malleable through work and effort. The theory is associated with mastery goals—that is, with increasing personal competence. See also *entity theory, mastery goal, performance goal*.

independent variable The variable that is manipulated in an experiment to determine whether doing so causes changes in the dependent variable: the "if" part of the if-then equation implicit in an experiment. (See *dependent variable; hypothesis*.)

individual test A test, usually used to measure intelligence, that can be given to only one individual at a time. See also *group test*.

individualistic learning A common instructional approach where students work independently and at their own pace. Student rewards are independent of the performance of other students. See also *competitive learning, cooperative learning*.

individualized educational plans (IEPs) Individualized instructional programs tailored to a child's specific pattern of needs and abilities. IEPs may be used for gifted, learning-disabled, retarded, or average children. Also termed *individualized program plans* or *IPPs*.

individualized instruction Instructional procedures that lend themselves to deliberate and systematic adaptation to the individual needs, interests, and abilities of students.

individualized program plans (IPPs) See *individualized educational plans (IEPs)*.

Individuals with Disabilities Education Act (IDEA) See *Public Law 94-142*.

informal teaching style A teaching approach that grants students a relatively high degree of freedom and autonomy and emphasizes individual growth and fulfillment rather than academic achievement and external rewards. See also *formal teaching style*.

information processing (IP) Relates to how information is modified (or processed), resulting in knowledge, perception, or behavior. It is a dominant model of the cognitive approaches and makes extensive use of computer metaphors.

inhibition With imitative learning, the suppression of a previously acquired behavior. This sometimes occurs when a learner observes a model being punished for the behavior. See also *inhibitory-disinhibitory effect*.

inhibitory-disinhibitory effect The type of imitative behavior that results either in the suppression (inhibition) or appearance (disinhibition) of previously acquired deviant behavior. See also *eliciting effect, imitation, modeling effect, observational learning*.

inner speech Vygotsky's final stage in the development of speech, attained at around age 7, and characterized by silent "self-talk," the stream-of-consciousness flow of verbalizations that give direction and substance to our thinking and behavior. Inner speech is involved in all higher mental functioning. See also *egocentric speech, social speech*.

insight The perception of relationships among elements of a problem situation. A problem-solving method that contrasts strongly with trial and error.

instinct A complex, species-specific, relatively unmodifiable pattern of behaviors such as migration or nesting in some birds and animals. Less complex inherited behaviors are usually referred to as reflexes.

instruction The arrangement of external events in a learning situation to facilitate learning, retention, and transfer.

instructional objective A goal or intended result of instruction. Objectives can be either short-range or long-range. Also termed *behavioral objective*.

integrated learning system (ILS) A computer-based learning/instructional system that includes both hardware and software, often with links to external databases, and is designed to guide students through part or all of a curriculum. See also *intelligent tutor system (ITS)*.

intelligence quotient (IQ) A simple way to describe intelligence by assigning it a number that represents the ratio of mental to chronological age, multiplied by 100. Average IQ is therefore 100 and is based on a comparison between an individual's performance and that of other comparable people.

intelligent tutor system (ITS) A computer-based learning system that takes into account the individual learner's strengths and weaknesses and modifies its presentations accordingly. See also *integrated learning system (ILS)*.

interest Involvement in or concern about something. This concept is related to intrinsic sources of motivation, reflected in knowledge about an activity or object and the placement of high value upon it.

intermittent reinforcement A schedule of reinforcement that does not present a reinforcer for all correct responses. Also termed *partial reinforcement*. See also *continuous reinforcement, fixed schedule, interval schedule, random schedule, ratio schedule, schedule of reinforcement*.

internal orientation A tendency to attribute the outcomes of behavior to factors within the individual (such as effort or ability). See also *attribution theory, external orientation, locus of control*.

Internet The label for a worldwide, amorphous, changing web of computer linkages, mainly via telephone lines and satellites. The Internet uses the computing resources of many universities and industries and can be accessed by virtually anyone with a computer and a telephone, cable, or satellite link (modem). The Internet makes inexpensive electronic communication possible worldwide. Also termed *World Wide Web*.

interval schedule An intermittent schedule of reinforcement based on the passage of time. See also *continuous reinforcement, fixed schedule, intermittent reinforcement, random schedule, ratio schedule, schedule of reinforcement*.

intrinsic motive A motive associated with internal sources of reinforcement—like satisfaction. See also *intrinsic reinforcement*.

intrinsic reinforcement Reinforcement that comes from within the individual rather than from outside (satisfaction, for example). Also termed *internal reinforcement*. See also *extrinsic reinforcement*.

introjected values Rogers' phrase for values that do not result from direct experience but that are, in a sense, borrowed—sometimes from the reactions of others to the individual, sometimes from observations of how others appear to be, sometimes from the individual's unrealistic fantasies about the self.

intuitive thinking One of the substages of Piaget's preoperational thought, beginning around age 4 and lasting until age 7 or 8, marked by the child's ability to solve many problems intuitively and also by the child's inability to respond correctly in the face of misleading perceptual features of problems. See also *preconceptual thinking, preoperational thinking*.

isolation A time-out procedure where a child is removed from an area of reinforcement (typically the classroom, although sometimes the playground or other areas) and

isolated somewhere else. See also *exclusion, nonexclusion, time-out*.

jargon The unique, technical vocabulary of a discipline—sometimes useful but not always essential.

jargon shock My tongue was in my cheek in Chapter 3, but I'm glad you checked here. See *jargon*.

jerky transition Kounin's expression for a disruptive and abrupt change in learning activities in the classroom.

jigsaw A cooperative instructional technique. Individual members of groups are given the responsibility for mastering different aspects of specific tasks and teaching them to other members of their group. The key feature of jigsaw is that successful performance depends on the various contributions of each member.

Jonah complex A phrase used by Maslow to describe those who avoid and deny their personal capacity for growth and self-actualization.

knowledge base The storehouse of concepts, information, associations, and procedures that we accumulate over time.

knowledge of results Knowledge about the correctness or incorrectness of a response. Knowledge of results is usually immediate in programmed instruction.

language acquisition device (LAD) Chomsky's label to describe the neurological something in our brains that corresponds to grammar and that is intended to explain how we can learn, understand, and use language.

language immersion An approach to teaching a second language that involves placing the learner in an environment where only the second language is used.

language The use of arbitrary sounds in the transmission of messages from one individual or organism to another. Language should not be confused with communication. See also *communication*.

lateral thinking A term coined by de Bono to describe a way of thinking that leads to creative solutions.

lateralization A term that refers to the division of functions and capabilities between the two hemispheres of the brain.

law A statement that is accurate beyond reasonable doubt. See also *belief, model, principle, theory*.

law of effect A Thorndikean law of learning that states that the effect of a response leads to its being learned (stamped in) or not learned (stamped out).

law of exercise A Thorndikean law of learning that states that bonds (connections) become more strengthened the more often they are repeated (exercised). Thorndike rejected this law later in his career.

law of multiple responses One of Thorndike's laws based on his observation that learning involves the emission of a variety of responses (multiple responses) until one (presumably an appropriate one) is reinforced. Because of this law Thorndike's theory is often called a theory of trial-and-error learning.

law of prepotency of elements A Thorndikean law of learning that states that people tend to respond to the most striking (prepotent) of the various elements that make up a stimulus situation.

law of readiness A Thorndikean law of learning that takes into account that certain types of learning are difficult or impossible unless the learner is ready. In this context, readiness refers to maturational level, previous learning, motivational factors, and other characteristics of the individual that relate to learning.

law of response by analogy A Thorndikean law to explain transfer. An analogy is typically an explanation, comparison, or illustration based on similarity. In Thorndike's system, response by analogy refers to responses that occur because of similarities between two situations.

law of set or attitude A Thorndikean law of learning that recognizes that we are often predisposed to respond in certain ways as a result of our experiences and previously learned attitudes. This subsidiary law acknowledges the influence of culture and experience in determining our attitudes and, therefore, our most likely responses in a given situation.

learning Changes in behavior due to experience; does not include changes due to motivation, fatigue, or drugs.

learning disability A depression in the ability to learn specific things (for example, reading or arithmetic), where the learning difficulties are not related to mental retardation or emotional disturbance.

learning outcomes Gagné's phrase for the new learning or capabilities that result from instruction and learning. According to his model, there are five major classes of possible outcomes of learning (intellectual skills, verbal information, attitudes, motor skills, and cognitive strategies).

Learning Potential Assessment Device (LPAD) Feuerstein's measure of intelligence, developed to provide a dynamic rather than passive measure of intelligence—a measure of how the child can profit from experience rather than simply a measure of the effects of past experiences. Assessment procedures allow the examiner to coach, to provide hints and clues, to direct, and to help.

learning style A unique and important learner variable manifested in differences in biological rhythms (morning versus evening people), perceptual strengths (visual versus auditory learners), sociological preference (whole-group versus small-group instruction), attention span (long or short), and a wealth of personality variables (dependence or independence, for example).

learning styles approach An individualized instructional system that is designed specifically to cater to the learning style of each student. See also *learning style.*

Learning Styles Inventory (LSI) An instrument used to assess student learning styles. Identifies individual students' preferences for different approaches to teaching and learning, and attempts to assess the relative effectiveness of different learning environments and approaches with specific students.

learning/thinking strategy A process involved in learning and thinking; another expression for "cognitive strategy," introduced to emphasize that the strategies involved in cognition (knowing) are also involved in learning and thinking. See also *cognitive strategy, knowledge-acquisition components, metamemory, performance components.*

learning together A cooperative instructional technique where groups of four to six students work together on a jointly assigned task using small-group interaction skills. In learning together, each member of the group is individually responsible for mastering the material.

levels of processing An information-processing theory, attributed to Craik and Lockhart, maintaining that memory is a function of the level of information processing. At the lowest level, a stimulus is simply recognized as a physical event (and is available momentarily in short-term sensory memory); at a much deeper level, a stimulus is interpreted in terms of its meaning (and is available in long-term memory).

liberationist model This model views the teacher's role as one of freeing students' minds by providing them with the tools and attitudes necessary for learning. See also *therapist model, executive model.*

linear program The presentation of programmed material so that all learners progress through the same material in the same order. Linear programs typically make no provisions for individual differences in learning; however, the material is broken up into very small steps (frames). See also *branching program, frame.*

link system A mnemonic system wherein items to be remembered are linked to one another using visual images. See also *loci system.*

loci system A mnemonic system wherein items to be remembered are associated with visual images of specific places. See also *link system.*

locus of control An aspect of personality evident in the individual's consistent tendency to attribute behavioral outcomes to a specific class of causes—causes over which the individual does, or does not, have control. See also *attribution theory, external orientation, internal orientation.*

logical consequences Dreikurs' phrase for a disciplinary tactic that involves contriving or inventing consequences for children's misbehavior in an attempt to modify that behavior. Unlike natural consequences, which follow naturally from a misbehavior, logical consequences are arranged, explained, discussed, and agreed upon by teachers and students. See also *natural consequences.*

Logo Papert's computer language, designed for young children to allow them to learn programming skills as easily and painlessly as they might learn an exciting new game. The program uses a "turtle"—a small creature that can be instructed (that is, programmed) to move in different ways, tracing various geometric designs as it moves.

long-term memory A type of memory whereby, with continued rehearsal and recoding of sensory information (processing in terms of meaning, for example), material will be available for recall over a long period of time.

macroculture The type of culture that results from the melding of aspects of a variety of different cultures over time.

magnetic resonance imaging Popularly referred to as MRI, a powerful medical diagnostic tool that makes use of computer-enhanced images of magnetic fields in the body to reveal details about physical and neurological structure and functioning. Highly useful for brain and memory research.

mainstreaming The practice of placing students in need of special services in regular classrooms rather than segregating them. Also termed *inclusion* or *inclusive education*.

mastery goal A goal directed toward increasing one's personal competence. See also *entity theory, incremental theory, performance goal*.

mastery learning model An instructional approach described by Bloom. A learning sequence is analyzed into specific objectives, and progress requires that each learner master sequential objectives.

mastery of specifics A Brunerian term for the learning of details. Mastery of relevant specifics is necessary for acquiring concepts and discovering relationships among them.

maturation The process of normal physical and psychological development. Maturation is defined as occurring independently of particular experiences. See also *development, growth*.

mean The arithmetic average of a set of scores. In distributions that are skewed (top- and bottom-heavy), the mean is not the best index of central tendency; that is, it is not necessarily at the middle of the distribution. See also *central tendency, median, mode*.

measurement The application of an instrument to gauge the quantity of something, as opposed to its quality. Assessing quality involves evaluation, not measurement. See also *assessment, evaluation*.

measurement-driven instruction A general approach to instruction wherein the overriding objective is to increase student performance on specific achievement measures.

median The midpoint or 50th percentile of a distribution; the point at or below which 50 percent of all scores fall. See also *central tendency, mean, mode*.

mediator A student who is specially trained to intervene between two or more other students who are in conflict.

melting pot societies Geographical or political entities composed of a variety of cultures that are gradually assimilated to the dominant culture. The end result is that individual cultures are no longer identifiable, and the dominant culture becomes a *macroculture*. See *macroculture; pluralistic societies, distinct society*.

memory The effects that experiences are assumed to have on the human mind. Refers to the storage of these effects.

menarche A girl's first menstrual period, an event that transpires during pubescence.

mental age A measure or estimate of intellectual functioning expressed in terms of age. Thus an average 7-year-old has a mental age of seven.

mental retardation A significant general depression in the ability to learn, usually accompanied by deficits in adaptive behavior.

mental structure The organized totality of an individual's knowledge. See also *cognitive structure*.

mentor An individual engaged in a one-on-one teaching/learning relationship where the teacher (mentor) serves as a fundamentally important model with respect to values, beliefs, philosophies, and attitudes, as well as a source of more specific information. See also *tutor*.

merit pay A monetary incentive used to reward teacher competence. See also *teacher competence*.

metacognition Knowledge about knowing. As we grow and learn, we develop notions of ourselves as learners. Accordingly, we develop strategies to recognize our limitations and allow us to monitor our progress and take advantage of our efforts. See also *cognitive strategy, learning/thinking strategy, metamemory*.

metamemory The knowledge we develop about our own memory processes—our knowledge about how to remember, rather than simply our memories. See also *cognitive strategy, metacognition*.

metaneeds Maslow's term for higher needs. Concerned with psychological, self-related functions rather than with biology. These include the need for truth, beauty, justice, and to self-actualize. Also termed *growth needs*.

méthode clinique Piaget's experimental method involving an interview technique where questions are determined largely by the subject's responses. The flexibility of this method distinguishes it from ordinary interview techniques.

microculture Within a pluralistic society, identifiable minority groups who share a distinct culture different from that of the majority culture.

mild retardation A classification of mental retardation identified by degree and usually defined in terms of an IQ range between 50 and about 70. Also termed *educable*, children with mild retardation are capable of adequate social adaptation and achievement at about the sixth-grade level.

minimum competency testing A global term for the administration of batteries of tests designed to determine whether students, or teachers, have reached some minimum level of competency in basic areas such as language and mathematics.

misconception The result of conceiving wrongly, of misunderstanding. Misconceptions in fields such as science and mathematics are common among children (and sometimes adults as well), and often interfere with learning.

mnemonic device A systematic aid to remembering, like rhymes, acrostics, or visual imagery systems. See also *link system, loci system.*

modal model of memory A widely used model of human memory that draws distinctions among sensory storage, short-term memory, and long-term memory. First developed by Atkinson and Schriffin.

mode The most frequently occurring score(s) in a distribution.

model A representation, usually abstract, of some phenomenon or system. Alternatively, a pattern for behavior that can be copied by someone. See also *belief, law, principle, theory.*

modeling Learning through observation (imitation). See *observational learning, imitation.*

modeling effect A type of imitative behavior that involves learning a novel response. See also *eliciting effect, imitation, inhibitory-disinhibitory effect, observational learning.*

moderate retardation A degree of mental retardation defined in terms of an IQ range between 35 and 55. Those with moderate retardation can achieve at about the second-grade level and can profit from training in social and occupational skills.

monozygotic Twins resulting from the division of a single fertilized egg. This process results in identical twins. See also *dizygotic.*

morality The ethical aspect of human behavior. Morality is intimately bound to the development of an awareness of acceptable and unacceptable behaviors. It is therefore linked to what is often called *conscience.*

morpheme A combination of phonemes that make up the meaningful units of a language.

moratorium Erikson's term for the social function of the hiatus between childhood and adulthood. In Marcia's description, moratorium individuals are those who have not yet made a commitment and who are in a state of crisis (conflict) as they examine and experiment with various identities.

motive A cause of behavior. Our motives explain why we engage in some behaviors but not in others. They initiate behavior and direct it. See also *disposition.*

motor learning Learning that involves muscular coordination and physical skills. Such common activities as walking and driving a car involve motor learning.

multicultural education Educational procedures and curricula that are responsive to the various cultures and languages of students, with the goal of assuring that all children experience high-quality education.

multiculturalism Having to do with many cultures.

naive theory An expression used to describe psychological theories based on intuition and folk belief rather than on science. Also termed *implicit theory.*

nativism An explanation for language learning, such as Chomsky's, that assumes that language learning depends on a pre-existing neurological organ or pattern in the brain corresponding to a universal language grammar. Nativism is a *hopeful monster* type of explanation. See *hopeful monsters; emergentism.*

natural consequences Dreikurs' phrase for the ordinary consequences of behavior—or, more specifically, misbehavior. Natural consequences are the effects and outcomes of behavior; they are not arranged or contrived. See also *logical consequences.*

nature Genetic influences; heredity. See *nurture; nature-nurture controversy.*

nature-nurture controversy A long-standing argument over whether genetics (nature) or environment (nurture) is more responsible for determining human development.

need Ordinarily refers to a lack or deficit in the human organism. Needs can be either unlearned (for example, the need for food or water) or learned (the need for money). See also *drive, need–drive theory.*

need–drive theory A motivation theory that attempts to explain human behavior on the basis of the motivating properties of needs. Such theories typically assume that humans have certain learned and unlearned needs, which give rise to drives, which in turn are responsible for the occurrence of behavior. See also *drive, need.*

need state Bruner's expression describing the arousal level of an organism.

negative correlation The type of relationship that exists between two variables when high values in one are associated with correspondingly low values in the other.

negative reinforcer A stimulus that has the effect of increasing the probability of occurrence of the response that precedes it. Negative reinforcement ordinarily takes the form of an unpleasant or noxious stimulus that is removed as a result of a specific response. See also *positive reinforcer, reinforcement, reinforcer, reward.*

negotiated order theory A sociological theory which maintains that the smooth functioning of social groups depends on implicit or explicit agreement among members of the group with regard to the boundaries of acceptable behavior and the consequences of going beyond these boundaries. Typically, much of this agreement is negotiated informally but eventually finds its way into the rules or laws that govern the group.

neonate A newborn infant. The neonatal period terminates when an infant regains birth weight (about two weeks after birth).

net-generation (N-Gen) A phrase coined by Tapscott to describe the current generation of children in North America; reflects their command of digital media and, especially, the World Wide Web.

neurofeedback Refers to information that subjects are given about the functioning of their nervous systems. Unlike biofeedback, which refers to feedback relating to all biological systems, neurofeedback relates specifically to information about brain functioning (EEG feedback). See also *biofeedback*.

neutral stimulus A stimulus that does not initially lead reliably to a predictable response. For example, neutral stimuli are not associated with emotional responses until learning has occurred; at this point they are referred to as conditioned (rather than neutral) stimuli. See also *conditioned response*.

nondeclarative memory Refers to unconscious, nonverbalizable effects of experience such as might be manifested in acquired motor skills or classical conditioning. Also termed *implicit* or *procedural memory*. See also *declarative memory, episodic memory, semantic memory*.

nonexclusion The mildest form of time-out procedure; the child is not allowed to participate in ongoing activity but is required to observe. See also *exclusion, isolation, time-out*.

normal curve A mathematical function that can be represented in the form of a bell-shaped curve. Many naturally occurring events are normally distributed; the vast majority of the events, or scores, cluster around the middle of the distribution, around the mean or median, with progressively fewer scores farther away from the average.

norm-referenced testing A test where the student is competing against the performance of other students rather than in relation to a pre-established criterion of acceptable performance. See also *criterion-referenced testing*.

nurture The effects of experience, as opposed to the effects of heredity (nature). See *nature; nature-nurture controversy*.

object concept Piaget's expression for the child's understanding that the world is composed of objects that continue to exist apart from his or her perception of them.

objective test A label used for a test in which the scoring procedure is simple, clear, and objective. Includes multiple-choice, completion, matching, and true–false formats. See also *essay test*.

obliterative subsumption Ausubel's term for forgetting. The incorporation of new material into pre-existing cognitive structure so that the new material eventually becomes indistinguishable—in other words, becomes obliterated (reaches zero dissociability, in Ausubel's terms). See also *correlative subsumption, derivative subsumption, subsumption*.

observational learning A term used synonymously with the expression "learning through imitation." See also *imitation*.

one-shot taste aversion learning A powerful disinclination toward eating or drinking certain substances, acquired after a single pairing of the substance with subsequent nausea or illness. Taste aversions are easily learned, are highly resistant to extinction, and demonstrate biological predispositions.

open education A student-centered alternative to traditional education that emphasizes personal growth, independence, and cooperation and is not committed to the curriculum-bound, pass–fail, age-locked, grade-locked system of the traditional school. Also termed *open classroom*.

operant Skinner's term for a response not elicited by any known or obvious stimulus. Most significant human behaviors appear to be operants (for example, writing a letter or going for a walk). See also *respondent, unconditioned response*.

operant conditioning A type of learning that involves an increase in the probability that a response will occur as a function of reinforcement. Most of Skinner's experimental work investigates the principles of operant conditioning. See also *classical conditioning, conditioning*.

operation In Piaget's system, a term that remains relatively nebulous but essentially refers to a thought process. An operation is an action that has been internalized in the sense that it can be "thought" and is reversible in the sense that it can be "unthought."

operation As used by Guilford, a term that describes major kinds of intellectual activity, such as remembering, evaluating, and divergent and convergent thinking. See also *content, convergent thinking, creativity, divergent thinking, product*.

operational definition A concrete or behavioral definition of an abstract term. That is, a definition that permits an abstract concept to be observed and measured or evaluated.

organization A memory strategy involving grouping and relating material to maintain it in long-term memory. See also *elaboration, rehearsal*.

originality A measure of creativity evident in the production of novel (unexpected or statistically rare) responses or solutions in a problem situation. See also *flexibility, fluency*.

outcome-based education (OBE) An outgrowth of mastery learning. An individualized instructional program designed to bring about important learning outcomes defined in terms of the skills and knowledge that the learner will need upon completion of a course of study.

overlapping Kounin's term for the simultaneous occurrence of two or more events in the classroom, each requiring the teacher's attention. Good class managers can handle overlapping events without disrupting the flow of classroom activities.

pain/pleasure principle A common expression for psychological hedonism—the belief that we are motivated to seek pleasure and avoid pain. See also *psychological hedonism*.

paradoxical effect Literally, a surprising or contradictory effect. This phrase is used to describe the apparently sedating effect that some stimulants (such as Ritalin) have on children who suffer from excessive activity (hyperactivity).

parallel-forms reliability A measure of test consistency (reliability) obtained by looking at the correlation between scores obtained by the same individual on two different but equivalent (parallel) forms of one test. See also *split-half reliability*.

participation metaphor A model of teaching characterized by the view that *participation* is the basis of learning. Teachers who subscribe to the participation metaphor are greatly concerned with the processes of learning. See *acquisition metaphor*.

PASS The Das model of intellectual functioning, based on a three-unit model of information processing: attending (involving arousal and paying attention); processing (successive or simultaneous processing); and planning (metacognitive components, that is, involved in monitoring and controlling cognitive activity). See also *planning, simultaneous processing; successive processing*.

peak experience A label introduced by Maslow to describe an intensely moving and unforgettable experience that has a profound effect on an individual's life. A peak experience might involve what is interpreted by the individual as a supernatural experience, a profound mystical revelation, a startling insight, or other events closely related to the process of self-actualization. See *self-actualization*.

pedology A Soviet discipline of child development, very popular in the Soviet Union in the 1930s, that used Western tests for psychoassessment. Vygotsky and Luria were pedologists. In the mid-1930s, the Soviet government decreed that pedology was a "bourgeois pseudoscience" and ordered that it no longer be written about, researched, or even discussed, thus wiping out all pedology centers and putting all pedologists out of work.

peer-assisted learning (PAL) A form of tutoring in which the tutors are typically school peers rather than older students or adults. See *mentor, tutor*.

penalty The type of punishment that involves losing or giving up something pleasant.

percentile The point at or below which a specified percentage of scores fall. For example, the 50th percentile is the point at or below which 50 percent of all scores fall. A score of 50 percent is not necessarily at the 50th percentile.

perception The translation of physical energies into neurological impulses—that is, stimuli into sensations—that can be interpreted by the individual.

performance Actual behavior. The inference that learning has occurred is typically based on observed changes in performance.

performance assessment Assessment that looks at the actual performance of students in situations as close to real life as possible. See also *authentic assessment*.

performance goal A goal directed toward performing well rather than toward mastering a subject and increasing one's competence. See also *entity theory, incremental theory, mastery goal*.

performance-based assessment A global expression for assessment procedures that try to determine what students know and are capable of, on the basis of their actions. Performance-based assessment looks at samples of actual behavior in real-life situations. Also termed *authentic assessment*. See also *authentic assessment*.

personality The set of characteristics that we typically manifest in our interactions with others. It includes all the abilities, predispositions, habits, and other qualities that make each of us different.

personalized system of instruction (PSI) An instructional approach developed by Keller, based in part on Bloom's mastery learning. Course material is broken down into small units, study is largely individual, a variety of study material is available, and progress depends on performance on unit tests. This is sometimes termed *the Keller plan*. See also *individualized educational plans (IEPs)*.

person-centered therapy See *client-centered therapy*.

phenomenal field The feelings, perceptions, and awareness that an individual has at any given moment. See also *phenomenology*.

phenomenology An approach concerned primarily with how individuals view their own world. Its basic assumption is that each individual perceives and reacts to the world in a unique manner and that this phenomenological worldview is important for understanding the individual's behavior. See also *phenomenal field*.

phoneme The simplest unit of language, consisting of a single sound, such as a vowel.

phonology The structure of speech sounds of a language.

physiological need A basic biological need, such as the need for food and water.

planning In the Das model of intelligence, this is the intentional or conscious aspect; in other terms, metacognitive strategies. See also *PASS, simultaneous processing, successive processing*.

pluralistic societies Societies composed of many different cultures.

portfolio In educational assessment, a collection of actual samples of students' performance and achievements.

positive control Control of human behavior, usually through the presentation of pleasant stimuli. This is in contrast to techniques of aversive control, which generally use negative reinforcement.

positive correlation The type of relationship that exists between two variables so that high or low scores on one are associated with correspondingly high or low scores on the other.

positive reinforcer A stimulus that, when added to a situation, increases the probability that a response will recur. This usually takes the form of a pleasant stimulus (reward). See also *negative reinforcer, reinforcement, reinforcer, reward.*

positron emission tomography Also referred to as a *PET scan.* A medical diagnostic technique and research tool that can be used to provide computer-enhanced images of body structures and of neurological functioning. A powerful tool for brain and memory research.

postconventional Kohlberg's third level of morality, reflecting an understanding of social contract and more individualistic principles of morality.

pragmatics The implicit language rules that govern practical things such as when to speak and how to take turns in conversation.

praise Positive verbal comments or other signs of approval. For example, most of what my grandmother said to or about me (heh! heh!).

preconceptual thinking The first substage in the period of preoperational thought, beginning around age 2 and lasting until age 4, so called because the child has not yet developed the ability to classify. See also *intuitive thinking, preoperational thinking.*

preconventional The first of Kohlberg's three stages of moral development, based on hedonistic or obedience-oriented judgments.

predictive validity See *criterion-related validity.*

Premack principle The recognition that behaviors that are frequently chosen by an individual (and are therefore favored) can be used to reinforce other, less frequently chosen behaviors. (For example, "You can watch television when you have finished your homework.")

preoperational thinking The second of Piaget's four major stages, lasting from around age 2 to age 7 or 8. It consists of two substages: intuitive thinking and preconceptual thinking. See also *intuitive thinking, preconceptual thinking.*

PREP program A cognitive strategies training program based on the PASS model of intellectual functioning. It seeks to identify specific deficiencies and problems in cognitive processing and to remedy them by providing learners with tasks designed to develop processing skills. See also *PASS, planning, simultaneous processing, successive processing.*

presentation punishment A label for the kind of punishment that results from presenting an aversive stimulus (such as a frozen boot) following a behavior. So called because it involves presenting an aversive stimulus. Also called Type I punishment. See *removal punishment.*

preventive strategy An instructional strategy designed to prevent discipline problems. Preventive strategies are an intrinsic part of good classroom management.

primary reinforcer A stimulus that is reinforcing in the absence of any learning. Such stimuli as food and drink are primary reinforcers because, presumably, an organism does not need to learn that these are pleasant. See also *generalized reinforcer.*

principle A statement relating to uniformity or predictability. Principles are far more open to doubt than laws but are more reliable than beliefs. See also *belief, law, model, theory.*

principle of opposite control Describes the tendency for sensations and movements on either side of the body to be controlled by the opposite cerebral hemisphere.

proactive inhibition The interference of earlier learning with the retention of subsequent learning. See also *retroactive inhibition.*

procedural knowledge Knowing how to do something; knowing procedures and facts (declarative knowledge). Also termed *procedural memory.* See also *declarative knowledge.*

process disorder A type of learning disability that involves a deficit in a basic psychological process such as perceiving, remembering, or paying attention. In practice, process disorders are difficult to separate from other specific learning disabilities such as developmental reading or arithmetic disorder. See also *developmental arithmetic disorder; developmental reading disorder.*

processing The intellectual or cognitive activities that occur as stimulus information is reacted to, analyzed, sorted, organized, and either stored in memory or forgotten.

prodigy An individual characterized by a distinct form of giftedness—marked by a highly focused talent or ability, such as musical or artistic talent, for example.

product A term used by Guilford to describe the result of applying an operation to content. A product can take the form of a response. See also *content, convergent thinking, creativity, divergent thinking, operation.*

profile A description of individual patterns of strengths, weaknesses, or abilities.

profound retardation A degree of mental retardation defined in terms of a measured IQ below 20 or 25 and marked by limited motor development and a need for nursing care.

programmed instruction An instructional procedure that makes use of the systematic presentation of information in small steps (frames), in the form of a workbook or another device. Programs typically require learners to make responses and provide immediate knowledge of results.

progressive education An educational reform movement closely associated with John Dewey and identified primarily by child- rather than teacher-centered instructional approaches. Constructivist approaches to instruction (such as discovery learning) are essentially examples of progressive education movements under new labels. See *constructivist approaches, direct instruction.*

prompt A device used in programmed instruction to help to ensure that the student will answer correctly. These can take a variety of forms.

psychological hedonism The belief that humans act primarily to avoid pain and to obtain pleasure.

psychological need A human need other than those dealing with basic physical requirements such as food, sex, water, and temperature regulation (physiological needs). Psychological needs described by Maslow include the need to belong, to feel safe, to love and be loved, to maintain a high opinion of oneself, and to self-actualize. See also *self-actualization.*

psychology The science that examines human behavior (and that of other animals as well).

psychometrics Refers to the measurement of psychological functions and characteristics.

psychosexual A term used to describe psychological phenomena based on sexuality. Freud's theories are psychosexual because they attribute development to sexually based forces and motives.

psychosocial Pertaining to events or behaviors that relate to the social aspects of development. Erikson's theory is psychosocial; it deals with the resolution of social crises and the development of social competencies (independence or identity, for example).

puberty Sexual maturity.

pubescence Changes of adolescence leading to sexual maturity.

Public Law 94-142 A 1975 U.S. education act that guarantees special students a free and appropriate education, nondiscriminatory evaluation, due process, an individualized educational plan (IEP), and education in the least restrictive environment. Amended in 1990 by the Individuals with Disabilities Education Act (IDEA). See also *individualized educational plans (IEPs).*

punishment Involves either the presentation of an unpleasant stimulus or the withdrawal of a pleasant stimulus, as a consequence of behavior. Punishment should not be confused with negative reinforcement.

race A biological term referring to an attempt to classify humans in groups distinguishable in terms of their genetic ancestry; often identifiable on the basis of physical, mental, or personality characteristics. The concept is unclear, contradictory, and not very useful.

racism The belief that identifiable groups of humans inherit different physical, mental, and personality characteristics.

radical acceleration model Stanley's acceleration program for gifted children, designed specifically for very high achievers in mathematics. Also termed a *compression* or *compaction program*, it attempts to compress the mathematics curriculum so that it can be covered in a fraction of the time that would ordinarily be required.

random schedule A type of intermittent schedule of reinforcement which can be of either the interval or the ratio variety and is characterized by the presentation of rewards at random intervals or on random trials. Although both fixed and random schedules can be based on the same intervals or on ratios, one can predict when reward will occur under a fixed schedule, whereas it is impossible to do so under a random schedule. Also termed *variable schedule.* See also *continuous reinforcement, fixed schedule, intermittent reinforcement, interval schedule, ratio schedule, schedule of reinforcement.*

rate of learning A measure of the amount of time required to learn a correct response or, alternatively, a measure of the number of trials required before the correct response occurs.

ratio schedule An intermittent schedule of reinforcement that is based on a proportion of correct responses. See also *continuous reinforcement, fixed schedule, interval schedule, intermittent reinforcement, random schedule, schedule of reinforcement.*

raw score The actual numerical score that a testee obtains on a test; the testee's score before it is converted to a grade- or age-equivalent score, an IQ, or some other norm.

reason An explanation for or defense of an action. In psychology, reasons are often treated as motives. See also *cause.*

reasoning As a disciplinary strategy, the process of providing a rationale for doing or not doing certain things. Can be used as both a corrective and a preventive classroom management tactic. Forms an important part of humanistic and democratic approaches to classroom management.

reception learning A type of learning that involves primarily instruction or tuition rather than the learner's own efforts. Teaching for reception learning, often associated with Ausubel, usually takes the form of expository or didactic methods; that is, the teacher structures the mater-

severe retardation A level of mental retardation defined in terms of an IQ range between 20 and 40. Severely retarded people can learn to communicate and, with systematic training, to take care of simple hygiene.

sex typing The learning of behaviors according to the gender of an individual in a given society; the acquisition of masculine and feminine gender roles. See also *gender roles.*

shaping A technique whereby animals and people are taught to perform complex behaviors that were not previously in their repertoires. The technique involves reinforcing responses that become increasingly closer approximations of the desired behavior. Also termed *the method of successive approximations* or *the method of differential reinforcement of successive approximations.* See also *differential reinforcement of successive approximations.*

short-term memory A type of memory wherein material is available for recall for only a matter of seconds. Short-term memory primarily involves rehearsal rather than more in-depth processing. It defines our immediate consciousness. Also termed *primary memory* or *working memory.*

short-term sensory storage The phrase refers to the simple sensory recognition of such stimuli as a sound, a taste, or a sight. Also termed *sensory memory.*

siblings Offspring whose parents are the same. In other words, brothers and sisters.

simultaneous processing One of four major components of the PASS model of intelligence. Involves cognitive processing wherein important elements of the stimulus situation are reacted to simultaneously—as in perceptual recognition, for example. See also *PASS, planning, successive processing.*

Skinner box Various experimental environments used by Skinner in his investigations of operant conditioning. The typical Skinner box is a cagelike structure equipped with a lever and a food tray attached to a food mechanism. It allows the investigator to study operants (for example, bar pressing) and the relationship between an operant and reinforcement.

social cognitive theory A label for Bandura's theory. It attempts to explain human social learning through imitation, using principles of operant conditioning while recognizing the importance of intellectual activities, such as imagining and anticipating. Hence, the theory serves as a transition between purely behavioristic and more cognitive approaches.

social learning The acquisition of patterns of behavior that conform to social expectations—learning what is acceptable and what is unacceptable in a given culture.

social speech In Vygotsky's theorizing, the most primitive stage of language development, evident before age 3. During this stage the child expresses simple thoughts and emotions out loud. The function of social speech is to control the behavior of others. See also *egocentric speech, inner speech.*

socialization The complex process of learning both those behaviors that are appropriate within a given culture and those that are less appropriate. The primary agents of socialization are home, school, and peer groups.

software Computer instructions; programs. Also termed *courseware.* See also *hardware.*

special education teacher A teacher whose training and/or functions deal specifically with the education of exceptional children. See also *exceptionality.*

special needs A phrase used to describe individuals whose social, physical, or emotional exceptionalities require special treatment and services for them to develop their potential. See also *exceptionality.*

spiral curriculum Bruner's term for a curriculum that revisits the same topics repeatedly, often at different grade levels, at different levels of abstraction and generality, depending on the interests and background knowledge of the learners.

split-half reliability An index of test reliability (consistency) derived by arbitrarily dividing a test into parallel halves (odd- and even-numbered items, for example) and looking at the agreement between scores obtained by each individual on the two halves. See also *parallel-forms reliability.*

stand-alone computer A computer system that is complete by itself because it includes a processing unit, a monitor, and an input device (keyboard)—in contrast with several computer terminals linked to a central computing system.

standard deviation A mathematical measure of the distribution of scores around their mean. In a normal distribution, approximately two-thirds of all scores fall within 1 standard deviation on either side of the mean, and almost 95 percent fall within 2 standard deviations of the mean.

standardized achievement test A professionally developed and normed test that is designed to measure achievement and to provide some basis for judging the relative quality of that achievement, given the student's age and grade placement. See also *standardized test.*

standardized test A professionally developed—rather than teacher-made—test that provides the user with norms (standards) and typically indicates the average or expected performance of groups of subjects of certain grades or ages. See also *age-equivalent scores, grade-equivalent scores.*

stanines Standard scores that make use of a 9-point scale with a mean of 5 and a standard deviation of 2.

stereotype A strong, relatively unexamined belief typically generalized to a class of superficially similar situations or individuals.

stimulus (*pl.* stimuli) Any change in the physical environment capable of exciting a sense organ.

stimulus–response (S–R) theory A learning theory with primary emphasis on stimuli and responses and the relationships between them. Such theories are also termed *behavioristic theories.*

Strategies Program for Effective Learning/Thinking (SPELT) A program designed to involve students in the learning process and to foster the development of cognitive strategies—an *embedded* program that is taught as an integral part of regular courses.

student-centered teaching Rogers' expression for an approach to teaching based on a philosophy of self-discovered learning. The approach requires that the teacher genuinely care for students as individuals and that students be allowed to determine for themselves what is important in their lives.

student teams–achievement divisions (STAD) A cooperative instructional technique where students are assigned to heterogeneous groups of four to six (including high- and low-ability students and different ethnic groups) to work on certain tasks. Afterward, they are given quizzes (to be answered individually, without cooperation) and rewarded by *team* on the basis of the group's performance on the quizzes. See also *teams–games–tournaments (TGT).*

subsumer The term used by Ausubel to describe a concept, an idea, or a combination of concepts or ideas that can serve to organize new information. Cognitive structure is therefore composed of subsumers.

subsumption Ausubel's term for the integration of new material or information with existing information. This term implies a process whereby a new stimulus becomes part of what is already in cognitive structure. See also *correlative subsumption, derivative subsumption, obliterative subsumption.*

subtractive bilingualism A phrase used to describe a situation in which learning a second language has a generally negative effect, often evident in lower proficiency in both languages. See also *additive bilingualism.*

successful intelligence Sternberg's view that intelligence involves a balance among selecting and shaping environments and adaptation to achieve personal goals and those of society. See *triarchic theory of successful intelligence.*

successive processing Cognitive processing where elements of a stimulus situation need to be responded to sequentially—as in solving some logical problems or executing motor tasks. This is an important element in the PASS model of intelligence. See also *PASS, planning, simultaneous processing.*

summative evaluation The type of evaluation that occurs at the end of an instructional sequence and that is designed primarily to provide a grade. See also *formative evaluation.*

superstitious schedule A fixed-interval schedule of reinforcement in which the reward is not given after every correct response but rather after the passage of a specified period of time. This schedule is called superstitious because it leads to the learning of behaviors that are only incidentally related to the reinforcement.

symbolic The final stage in the development of children's representations of their world. The term is used by Bruner to describe the representation of the world in terms of arbitrary symbols. Symbolic representation includes representation in terms of language and also in terms of theoretical or hypothetical systems. See also *enactive, iconic.*

symbolic model A model other than a real-life person. Any pattern for behavior may be termed a symbolic model if it is not a person. For example, books, television, and written instructions can provide symbolic models.

sympathetic nervous system The part of the nervous system that instigates the physiological responses associated with emotion.

syntax The arrangement of words to form sentences.

synthesis Putting together of parts to form a whole; complementary to analysis; a high-level intellectual ability in Bloom's taxonomy of educational objectives.

tacit knowledge Nondeclarative knowledge. Knowledge that cannot be easily or completely verbalized but that is implicit (such as how to ride a bicycle).

talent Exceptional ability in a specific field such as music or literature. See *talented and gifted; giftedness.*

talented and gifted A phrase used to describe an advantageous combination of intelligence, creativity, and motivation that results in the potential for superior achievement in one or more fields. See *talent; giftedness.*

task analysis The process of analyzing what is to be learned in terms of a sequential series of related tasks. Task analysis provides the teacher with information about important skills and knowledge that might be prerequisite for what is to be taught.

taxonomy of educational objectives An exhaustive list of possible educational outcomes that can serve as a guide for compiling instructional objectives. The best-known taxonomy of educational objectives is Bloom's, which provides objectives in both the cognitive and the affective domains.

teacher burnout A general label for a condition marked by a teacher's profound negative reaction to teaching. One possible effect of high stress. Sometimes evidenced by cynicism, unhappiness, chronic absenteeism, and perhaps a decision to change careers.

teacher competence A phrase used to describe the measurable performance of teachers—often assessed through the achievement of students. See also *merit pay.*

Teacher Effectiveness Training (TET) Gordon's humanistic training program for teachers. It emphasizes good teacher–learner relationships, honest interpersonal communication, and conflict resolution.

teacher expectations A phrase used to describe the often unconscious expectations that teachers have regarding the likely achievement and behavior of students. Teacher expectations often reflect biases related to variables such as gender, ethnicity, and social class.

teacher-made test Any of the wide variety of tests written, developed, or organized by teachers, usually for the purpose of evaluating students or assessing the effectiveness of instruction. See also *standardized test*.

teaching style A customary way of teaching. Teaching styles are often described as either teacher centered (also labeled *formal* or *direct instruction*) or learner-centered (*informal* or *constructivist*). See *formal teaching style; informal teaching style; direct instruction; constructivist approaches*.)

teams–games–tournaments (TGT) A cooperative instructional technique identical to student teams–achievement divisions (STAD) except that instead of being given quizzes at the end, students play tournaments of competitive games that center around content-relevant questions. See also *student teams–achievement divisions*.

technology of teaching A Skinnerian phrase for the systematic application of the principles of behaviorism (especially of operant conditioning) to classroom practice.

test anxiety A characteristic evident in a fear of taking tests and an expectation of poor performance. Test anxiety can significantly impair test performance.

test blueprint A table of specifications for a teacher-made test. A good test blueprint provides information about the topics to be tested, the nature of the questions to be used, and the objectives (outcomes) to be assessed.

test of divergent thinking A creativity test. These are usually open-ended, production tests designed to measure factors such as fluency, flexibility, and originality.

theory A body of information pertaining to a specific topic, a method of acquiring and dealing with information, or a set of explanations for related phenomena. See also *belief, law, model, principle*.

theory of multiple intelligences Gardner's belief that human intelligence consists of seven distinct and largely unrelated areas of talent or capability: logical-mathematical, linguistic, musical, spatial, bodily kinesthetic, interpersonal, and intrapersonal.

therapist model A primarily humanistic view of the teacher's role—namely, that of facilitating healthy growth and self-actualization. See also *liberationist model, executive model*.

third-force psychology A general expression for humanistic approaches to psychology such as those exemplified by

the work of Carl Rogers and Abraham Maslow. The first two forces are psychoanalysis and behaviorism (S–R psychology).

third wave Toffler's expression for the computer revolution (the first two waves of monumental change are the agricultural and the industrial revolutions).

time-in A reinforcement procedure, sometimes used in combination with time-out procedures. Time-in involves *including* children and exposing them to reinforcers such as praise and physical contact (in contrast with *time-out* which involves excluding and not reinforcing). See *time-out*.

time-out A procedure where students are removed from situations in which they might ordinarily be rewarded. Time-out procedures are widely used in classroom management. See also *exclusion, isolation, nonexclusion, reprimand, response cost*.

token system A behavior modification system. Tokens are issued as rewards for desirable behaviors. These tokens can be accumulated and later exchanged for other rewards.

tracking A general term for the formation of groups on the basis of any one or more of a variety of student characteristics such as ability, interests, social class, ethnic membership, language background, and vocational aspirations.

transductive reasoning The type of reasoning that proceeds from particular to particular rather than from particular to general or from general to particular. One example of transductive reasoning is the following: Cows give milk. Goats give milk. Therefore goats are cows.

transfer A general term for the application of old learning to a new situation. Also termed *generalization*. See *generalization*.

transitional bilingualism This describes a situation in which a minority language is gradually replaced by the dominant language, essentially disappearing within a few generations.

trial-and-error learning A Thorndikean explanation for learning based on the idea that when placed in a problem situation, an individual will emit a variety of responses but will eventually learn the correct one as a result of reinforcement. Trial-and-error explanations for learning are sometimes contrasted with insight explanations.

triarchic theory of successful intelligence Sternberg's model of successful intelligence as involving analytical, creative, and practical abilities. See *successful intelligence*.

T-score A standardized score with a preset mean of 50 and a standard deviation of 10. A T-score of 70 is therefore quite high because 70 is 2 standard deviations above the mean, and only about 2.5 percent of all scores ordinarily fall beyond that point.

tutor A teacher involved in a one-on-one teaching situation. Tutors are frequently other students or else other teachers or experts. See also *mentor*.

ulterior motive A hidden motive. A reason for behavior that is not what it seems. Ulterior motives often involve an element of deception (as when my grandmother accused me of having ulterior motives when I said I wanted to help Clarisse with her verbs).

unconditioned response (UR) A response that is elicited by an unconditioned stimulus. See also *operant, respondent*.

unconditioned stimulus (US) A stimulus that elicits a response before learning. All stimuli that are capable of eliciting reflexive behaviors are examples of unconditioned stimuli. For example, food is an unconditioned stimulus for the response of salivation.

validity The extent to which a test measures what it intends to measure. For example, an intelligence test is valid to the extent that it measures intelligence and nothing else. Educational and psychological tests are limited by their frequently low validity. See also *construct validity, content validity, criterion-related validity, face validity, reliability*.

values clarification program A program designed to encourage learners to examine their personal beliefs about right and wrong, with a view to improving and clarifying their awareness of their own morality.

values education Instructional programs and strategies designed to teach specific values (notions of right and wrong), thereby promoting good behavior and developing good "character."

variable A property, measurement, or characteristic that is susceptible to variation. In psychological experimentation, qualities of human beings such as intelligence and creativity are considered variables. See also *correlation*.

variable schedule See *random schedule*.

vicarious reinforcement Reinforcement that results from observing someone else being reinforced. With imitative behavior, observers frequently act as though they are being reinforced when they are really not being reinforced; rather, they are aware, or simply assume, that the model is being reinforced. See also *direct reinforcement*.

virtual reality (VR) A computer-based simulation that typically involves a number of sensory systems (such as bodily sensations, visual images, and auditory signals) in order to produce a sensation of realism.

WASP Acronym for "white Anglo-Saxon Protestant." Frequently used to describe the main characteristics of the group that has historically been the most common in North America.

wild cow (almost literal) A bovine creature found in both forested and nonforested regions of the world. Wild cows are particularly unrestrained creatures, given to a great variety of social and solitary diversions, including playing cards, smoking cigars, and drinking whiskey. They also like to dance and to ice skate, and some are quite wonderful surfers. Sadly, they do not fly nearly as well as pigs. See also *bear, wild cow (metaphoric)*.

wild cow (metaphoric) Wild cows are a lot of the things that are wrong with this planet: starvation, pollution, illiteracy, preventable infant mortality, famine, terrorism, resource depletion, AIDS, murder, puny teacher salaries, and on and on. See also *bear, wild cow (almost literal)*.

within-class grouping Ability groups or tracks that are formed and function within the regular classroom. See *between-class grouping*.

with-it-ness Kounin's expression for a quality of teacher behavior manifested in the teacher's awareness of all the important things happening in a classroom. Teachers who are with-it make more effective use of desists. See also *desists*.

working memory See *short-term memory*.

zone of proximal growth Vygotsky's phrase for the individual's current potential for further intellectual development. Conventional measures of intelligence assess current intellectual development rather than the potential for future development. Vygotsky believed that the zone of proximal growth (future potential) might be assessed by the use of further questioning and hints and prompts while administering a conventional intelligence test.

Z-score A standardized score with a mean of 0 and a standard deviation of 1. Hence, a Z-score of $+3$ is very high; a score of -3 is very low.

BIBLIOGRAPHY

AAMD Ad Hoc Committee on Terminology and Classification. (1992). Mental retardation: Definition, classification, and systems of support (9th ed.). Washington, DC: American Association on Mental Retardation.

Aarnoutse, C., Brand-Gruwel, S., & Oduber, R. (1997). Improving reading comprehension strategies through listening. *Educational Studies, 23,* 209–227.

Aboderin, A. O., & Thomas, M. (1996). An evaluation of the influence of behavioural objectives on Nigerian students' cognitive achievement in biology. *Research in Science and Technological Education, 14,* 193–204.

Acker, M. M., & O'Leary, S. G. (1996). Inconsistency of mothers' feedback and toddlers' misbehavior and negative affect. *Journal of Abnormal Child Psychology, 24,* 703–714.

Adamson, G. (1983, January). The coin with more than two sides. *ATA Magazine,* 28–30.

Addison, R. M., & Homme, L. E. (1973). The reinforcing event (RE) menu. *Improving Human Performance, 2,* 145–150.

Agbor-Baiyee, W. (1997). A cyclical model of student career motivation. *College Student Journal, 31,* 467–472.

Agne, K., Greenwood, G. E., & Miller, L. D. (1994). Relationships between teacher belief systems and teacher effectiveness. *Journal of Research and Development in Education, 27,* 141–152.

Ahsen, A. (1977a). *Psych eye: Self-analytic consciousness.* New York: Brandon House.

——— (1977b). Eidetics: An overview. *Journal of Mental Imagery, 1,* 5–38.

Aiken, L. R. (1998). *Tests and examinations: Measuring abilities and performance.* New York: Wiley.

Airasian, P. W., & Walsh, M. E. (1997). Constructivist cautions. *Phi Delta Kappan, 78,* 444–449.

Akande, A. (1997). Creativity: The caregiver's secret weapon. *Early Child Development and Care, 134,* 89–101.

Alain, C., & Woods, D. (1997). Attention modulates auditory pattern memory as indexed by event-related brain potentials. *Psychophysiology, 34,* 534–546.

Alexander, P. A., & Judy, J. E. (1988). The interaction of domain-specific and strategic knowledge in academic performance. *Review of Educational Research, 58,* 375–404.

Alexander, P. A., Murphy, P. K., & Woods, B. S. (1996). Of squalls and fathoms: Navigating the seas of educational innovation. *Educational Researcher, 25,* 31–36, 39.

Ambert, A. N. (1991). *Bilingual education and English as a second language: A research handbook, 1988–1990.* New York: Garland.

American Psychiatric Association. (1994). *Diagnostic and statistical manual of mental disorders* (4th ed.). Washington, DC: American Psychiatric Association.

Ames, C. (1992). Classrooms: Goals, structures, and student motivation. *Journal of Educational Psychology, 84,* 261–271.

Amsel, A. (1989). *Behaviorism, neobehaviorism, and cognitivism in learning theory: Historical and contemporary perspectives.* Hillsdale, NJ: Erlbaum.

Anderman, E. M., & Maehr, M. L. (1994). Motivation and schooling in the middle grades. *Review of Educational Research, 64,* 287–309.

Anderson, C. W., & Smith, E. L. (1984). Children's preconceptions and content-area textbooks. In G. G. Duffy, L. R. Roehler, & J. Mason (Eds.), *Comprehension instruction: Perspectives and suggestions.* New York: Longman.

Anderson, J. R. (1983). *The architecture of cognition.* Cambridge, MA: Harvard University Press.

Anderson, S., & Payne, M. A. (1994). Corporal punishment in elementary education: Views of Barbadian school children. *Child Abuse and Neglect: The International Journal, 18,* 377–386.

Annett, J. M. (1996). Olfactory memory: A case study in cognitive psychology. *Journal of Psychology, 130,* 309–319.

Antil, L. R., Jenkins, J. R., Wayne, S. K., & Vadasy, P. F. (1998). Cooperative learning: Prevalence, conceptualizations, and the relation between research and practice. *American Educational Research Journal, 35,* 419–454.

Applegate, B., et al. (1997). Validity of the age-of-onset criterion for ADHD: A report from the DSM-IV field trials. *Journal of the American Academy of Child and Adolescent Psychiatry, 36,* 1211–1221.

Aranha, M. A. (1997). Creativity in students and its relation to intelligence and peer perception. *Revista Interamericana de Psicologia, 31,* 309–313.

Arlin, M. (1984). Time, equality, and mastery learning. *Review of Educational Research, 54,* 65–86.

Aronson, E., Blaney, N., Stephan, C., Sikes, J., & Snapp, M. (1978). *The jigsaw classroom.* Beverly Hills: Sage.

Artiles, A. J., Barreto, R. M., Pena, L., & McClafferty, K. (1998). Pathways to teacher learning in multicultural contexts: A longitudinal case study of two novice bilingual teachers in urban schools. *Rase: Remedial and Special Education, 19,* 70–90.

Artzt, A. F., & Armour-Thomas, E. (1998). Mathematics teaching as problem solving: A framework for studying teacher metacognition underlying instructional practice in mathematics. *Instructional Science, 26,* 5–25.

Athanases, S. Z. (1994). Teachers' reports of the effects of preparing portfolios of literacy instruction. *Elementary School Journal, 94,* 421–439.

Atkinson, J. W., & Raynor, J. O. (1978). *Personality, motivation, and achievement.* New York: Wiley.

Atkinson, R. C., & Shiffrin, R. M. (1968). Human memory: A proposed system and its control processes. In K. W. Spence & J. T. Spence (Eds.), *The psychology of learning and motivation* (Vol. 2). New York: Academic Press.

Aubrey, C. (1993). An investigation of the mathematical knowledge and competencies which young children bring into school. *British Educational Research Journal, 19,* 27–41.

Audette, B., & Algozzine, B. (1997). Re-inventing government? Let's re-invent special education. *Journal of Learning Disabilities, 30,* 378–383.

Aunapu, G., Monroe, S., Sachs, A., & Taylor, E. (1993) Intermarried . . . with children. *Time,* Special Issue, Fall, 64–65.

Ausubel, D. P. (1963). *The psychology of meaningful verbal learning.* New York: Grune & Stratton.

———(1977). The facilitation of meaningful verbal learning in the classroom. *Educational Psychologist, 12,* 162–178.

Ausubel, D. P., & Robinson, F. G. (1969). *School learning: An introduction to educational psychology.* New York: Holt, Rinehart & Winston.

Babad, E. Y. (1985). Some correlates of teachers' expectancy bias. *American Educational Research Journal, 22,* 175–183.

———(1993). Pygmalion—25 years after: *Interpersonal expectancies in the classroom.* In P. D. Blanck (Ed.), Interpersonal expectations: Theory, research, and application. Cambridge: Cambridge University Press.

Baber, W. L., Garrett, M. T., & Holcomb-McCoy, C. (1997). Vision: A model of culture for counselors. *Counseling and Values, 41,* 184–193.

Bacdayan, A. W. (1994). Time-denominated achievement cost curves, learning differences and individualized instruction. *Economics of Education Review, 13,* 43–53.

Bachus, G. (1994). Violence is no stranger to rural schools. *School Administrator, 51,* 18–22.

Bacon, E. H. (1990). Using negative consequences effectively. *Academic Therapy, 25,* 599–611.

Baddeley, A. D. (1997). *Human memory: Theory and practice* (Rev. ed.). East Sussex, UK: Psychology Press.

Baer, J. (1993–94). Why you shouldn't trust creativity tests. *Educational Leadership, 51,* 80–83.

Baer, R. A., Tishelman, A. C., Degler, J. D., Osnes, P. G., & Stokes, T. F. (1992). Effects of self- vs. experimenter-selection of rewards on classroom behavior in young children. *Education and Treatment of Children, 15,* 1–14.

Bainer, D. L., & Didham, C. (1994). Mentoring and other support behaviors in elementary schools. *Journal of Educational Research, 87,* 240–247.

Baltes, M. M., & Silverberg, S. B. (1994). The dynamics between dependency and autonomy: Illustrations across the lifespan. In D. L. Featherman, R. M. Lerner, & M. Perlmutter (Eds.), *Life-span development and behavior* (Vol. 12). Hillsdale, NJ: Erlbaum.

Banaji, M. R., & Crowder, R. G. (1989). The bankruptcy of everyday memory. *American Psychologist, 44,* 1185–1193.

Bandura, A. (1962). Social learning through imitation. In N. R. Jones (Ed.), *Nebraska Symposium on Motivation.* Lincoln: University of Nebraska Press.

———(1969). *Principles of behavior modification.* New York: Holt, Rinehart & Winston.

———(1977). *Social learning theory.* Morristown, NJ: General Learning Press.

———(1981). Self-referent thought: A developmental analysis of self-efficacy. In J. H. Flavell & L. Ross (Eds.), *Social cognitive development: Frontiers and possible futures.* Cambridge: Cambridge University Press.

———(1986). *Social foundations of thought and action: A social cognitive theory.* Englewood Cliffs, NJ: Prentice-Hall.

———(1993). Perceived self-efficacy in cognitive development and functioning. *Educational Psychologist, 28,* 117–148.

———(1997). *Self-efficacy: The exercise of control.* New York: W. H. Freeman.

Bandura, A., & Walters, R. (1963). *Social learning and personality development.* New York: Holt, Rinehart & Winston.

Banks, J. A. (1993b). The canon debate, knowledge construction, and multicultural education. *Educational Researcher, 22,* 5–14.

Banks, J. A., & Banks, C. A. M. (1997). *Multicultural education: Issues and perspectives* (3rd ed.). Boston, MA: Allyn & Bacon.

Bar, V., Zinn, B., Goldmuntz, R., & Sneider, C. (1994). Children's concepts about weight and free fall. *Science Education, 78,* 149–169.

Barkley, R. A., & Biederman, J. (1997). Toward a broader definition of the age-of-onset criterion for attention-deficit-hyperactivity-disorder. *Journal of the American Academy of Child and Adolescent Psychiatry, 36,* 1204–1210.

———(1998). "Definition of ADHD": Reply. *Journal of the American Academy of Child and Adolescent Psychiatry, 37,* 344–345.

Barnett, C., & Monda-Amaya, L. E. (1998). Principals' knowledge of and attitudes toward inclusion. *Rase: Remedial and Special Education, 19,* 181–192.

Barnett, W. S. (1993). Benefit-cost analysis of preschool education: Findings from a 25-year follow-up. *American Journal of Orthopsychiatry, 63,* 500–508.

Barrett, G. V., & Depinet, R. L. (1991). A reconsideration of testing for competence rather than for intelligence. *American Psychologist, 46,* 1012–1024.

Bartolome, L. I. (1994). Beyond the methods fetish: Toward a humanizing pedagogy. *Harvard Educational Review, 64,* 173–194.

Basadur, M., & Hausdorf, P. A. (1996). Measuring divergent thinking attitudes related to creative problem solving and innovation management. *Creativity research journal, 9,* 21–32.

Basseches, M. (1984). *Dialectical thinking and adult development.* Norwood, NJ: Ablex.

Baumrind, D. (1993). The average expectable environment is not good enough: A response to Scarr. *Child Development, 64,* 1299–1317.

Bear, G. G. (1998). School discipline in the United States: Prevention, correction and long term social development. *Educational and Child Psychology, 15,* 15–39.

Becvar, R. J., & Becvar, D. S. (1997). The client-therapist relationship: A comparison of second order family therapy and Rogerian therapy. *Journal of Systemic Therapies, 16,* 181–194.

Beekman, S., & Holmes, J. (1994). Resolving conflict with kids: Five approaches that can work for you. *PTA Today, 19,* 11–13.

Beitchman, J. H., Wilson, B., Brownlie, E. B., Walters, H., et al. (1996). Long-term consistency in speech/language profiles: I. Developmental and academic outcomes. *Journal of the American Academy of Child and Adolescent Psychiatry. 35,* 804–814.

Bellamy, C. (1997). *The state of the world's children: 1997.* New York: Oxford University Press.

Belmont, J. M. (1989). Cognitive strategies and strategic learning: The socio-instructional approach. *American Psychologist, 44,* 142–148.

Beltrame, J. (1998). California grapples with divisive language issue. *Edmonton Journal,* June 1, p. A12.

Bem, S. L. (1981). Gender schema theory: A cognitive account of sex typing. *Psychological Review, 88,* 354–364.

——— (1989). Genital knowledge and gender constancy in preschool children. *Child Development, 60,* 649–662.

Berlyne, D. E. (1960). *Conflict, arousal and curiosity.* New York: McGraw-Hill.

Bernard, L. L. (1924). *Instinct: A study in social psychology.* New York: Holt, Rinehart & Winston.

Bernhard, J. K. (1992). Gender-related attitudes and the development of computer skills: A preschool intervention. *Alberta Journal of Educational Research, 38,* 177–188.

Bielinski, J., & Davison, M. L. (1998). Gender differences by item difficulty interactions in multiple-choice items. *American Educational Research Journal, 35,* 455–476.

Bijou, S. W., & Sturges, P. S. (1959). Positive reinforcers for experimental studies with children—Consumables and manipulatables. *Child Development, 30,* 151–170.

Birenbaum, M., & Nasser, F. (1994). On the relationship between test anxiety and test performance. *Measurement and Evaluation in Counseling and Development, 27,* 293–301.

Black, S. (1994a). Handling anger. *Executive Educator, 16,* 27–30.

——— (1994b). Throw away the hickory stick. *Executive Educator, 16,* 44–47.

——— (1994c). Different kinds of smart. *Executive Educator, 16,* 24–27.

Bloom, B. S. (1964). *Stability and change in human characteristics.* New York: Wiley.

——— (1976). *Human characteristics and school learning.* New York: McGraw-Hill.

——— (1984). The 2 sigma problem: The search for methods of group instruction as effective as one-to-one tutoring. *Educational Researcher, 13,* 4–15.

——— (1987). A response to Slavin's mastery learning reconsidered. *Review of Educational Research, 57,* 507–508.

Bloom, B. S., Engelhart, M. B., Furst, E. J., Hill, W. H., & Krathwohl, D. R. (1956). *Taxonomy of educational objectives: Handbook I: Cognitive domain.* New York: Longman.

Blumenfeld, P. C. (1992). Classroom learning and motivation: Clarifying and expanding goal theory. *Journal of Educational Psychology, 84,* 272–281.

Blumenfeld, P. C., Marx, R. W., Soloway, E., & Krajcik, J. (1996). Learning with peers: From small group cooperation to collaborative communities. *Educational Researcher, 25,* 37–40.

Bolles, R. C. (1974). Cognition and motivation: Some historical trends. In B. Weiner (Ed.), *Cognitive views of human motivation.* New York: Academic Press.

Boodoo, G. M. (1993). Performance assessments or multiple choice? *Educational Horizons, 72,* 50–56.

Boone, D. E. (1995). A cross-sectional analysis of WAIS-R aging patterns with psychiatric inpatients: Support for Horn's hypothesis that fluid cognitive abilities decline. *Perceptual and Motor Skills, 81,* 371–379.

Boring, E. G. (1923). Intelligence as the tests test it. *New Republic, 35,* 35–37.

Borkowski, J. G., Milstead, M., & Hale, C. (1988). Components of children's metamemory: Implications for strategy generalization. In F. E. Weinert & M. Perlmutter (Eds.), *Memory development: Universal changes and individual differences.* Hillsdale, NJ: Erlbaum.

Borton, T. (1970). *Reach, touch, and teach: Student concerns and process education.* New York: McGraw-Hill.

Bossert, S. T. (1988). Cooperative activities in the classroom. In E. Z. Rothkopf (Ed.), *Review of research in education* (Vol. 15). Washington, DC: American Educational Research Association.

Botella, C., Banos, R. M., Perpina, C., Villa, H., Alcaniz, M., & Rey, A. (1998). Virtual reality treatment of claustrophobia: A case report. *Behaviour Research & Therapy, 36,* 239–246.

Bowden, C. L. (1994). Bipolar disorder and creativity. In M. P. Shaw & M. A. Runco (Eds.), *Creativity and affect.* Norwood, NJ: Ablex.

Bower, T. G. R. (1989). *The rational infant: Learning in infancy.* New York: Freeman.

Bowlby, J. (1982). *Attachment and loss (Vol. 1): Attachment* (2nd ed.). London: Hogarth.

Bozarth, J. D. (1997). Empathy from the framework of client-centered theory and the Rogerian hypothesis. In Robart, A. C., Greenberg, L. L., et al., (Eds.), *Empathy reconsidered: New directions in psychotherapy.* Washington, DC: American Psychological Association.

Braddock, J. H. II, & Slavin, R. E. (1993). Why ability grouping must end: Achieving excellence and equity in American education. *Journal of Intergroup Relations, 20,* 51–64.

Bradshaw, G. L., & Anderson, J. R. (1982). Elaborative encoding as an explanation of levels of processing. *Journal of Verbal Learning and Verbal Behavior, 21,* 165–174.

Bradshaw, J. L. (1989). *Hemispheric specialization and psychological function.* New York: Wiley.

Brand-Gruwel, S., Aarnoutse, C. A. J., & Van Den Bos, K. P. (1998). Improving text comprehension strategies in reading and listening settings. *Learning and Instruction, 8,* 63–81.

Brandon, P. R., Newton, B. J., & Hammond, O. W. (1987). Children's mathematics achievement in Hawaii: Sex differences favoring girls. *American Educational Research Journal, 24,* 437–461.

Brandt, R. (1994). On creating an environment where all students learn: A conversation with Al Mamary. *Educational Leadership, 51,* 24–28.

Bransford, J. D., & Johnson, M. K. (1973). Consideration of some problems in comprehension. In W. G. Chase (Ed.), *Visual information processing* (pp. 383–438). New York: Academic Press.

Brantner, J. P., & Doherty, M. A. (1983). A review of timeout: A conceptual and methodological analysis. In S. Axelrod & J. Apsche (Eds.), *The effects of punishment on human behavior.* New York: Academic Press.

Braun, C. (1976). Teacher expectations: Sociopsychological dynamics. *Review of Educational Research, 46,* 185–213.

Bray, M. A., Kehle, T. J., & Hintze, J. M. (1998). Profile analysis with the Wechsler Scales: Why does it persist? *School Psychology International, 19,* 209–220.

Brehm, J. W., & Self, E. A. (1989). The intensity of motivation. *Annual Review of Psychology, 40,* 109–131.

Breland, H. M. (1999). From 2 to 3 Rs: The expanding use of writing in admissions. In S. J. Messick (Ed.), *Assessment in higher education: Issues of access, quality, student development, and public policy.* Mahwah, NJ: Erlbaum.

Brewer, K. R., & Wann, D. L. (1998). Observational learning effectiveness as a function of model characteristics: Investigating the importance of social power. *Social Behavior and Personality, 26,* 1–10.

Bridgeman, B., & Morgan, R. (1996). Success in college for students with discrepancies between performance on multiple-choice and essay tests. *Journal of Educational Psychology, 88,* 333–340.

Brisk, M. E. (1991). Toward multilingual and multicultural mainstream education. *Journal of Education, 173,* 114–129.

Brody, L. E., & Mills, C. J. (1997). Gifted children with learning disabilities: A review of the issues. *Journal of Learning Disabilities, 30,* 282–296.

Bronfenbrenner, U. (1989). Ecological systems theory. In R. Vasta (Ed.), *Annals of child development* (Vol. 6). Greenwich, CT: JAI Press.

Brophy, J. E. (1981). Teacher praise: A functional analysis. *Review of Educational Research, 51*(1), 5–32.

———— (1998). Classroom management as socializing students into clearly articulated roles. *Journal of Classroom Interaction, 33,* 1–4.

Brophy, J. E., & Good, T. L. (1974). *Teacher–student relationships: Causes and consequences.* New York: Holt, Rinehart & Winston.

Brown, C. N. (1997). Gifted identification as a constitutional issue. *Roeper Review, 19,* 157–167.

Brown, G. I. (Ed.) (1971). *Human teachings for human learning: An introduction to confluent education.* New York: Viking Press.

Brown, H. D., & Kosslyn, S. M. (1993). Cerebral lateralization. *Current Opinion in Neurobiology, 3,* 183–186.

Brown, J. S., Collins, A., & Duguid, P. (1989). Situated cognition and the culture of learning. *Educational Researcher, 18,* 32–42.

Brown, R., & Kulik, J. (1982). Flashbulb memory. In U. Neisser (Ed.), *Memory observed: Remembering in natural contexts.* San Francisco, CA: W. H. Freeman.

Bruer, J. T. (1997). Education and the brain: A bridge too far. *Educational Researcher, 26,* 4–16.

Bruner, J. S. (1957a). On going beyond the information given. In *Contemporary approaches to cognition.* Cambridge, MA: Harvard University Press.

———— (1957b). On perceptual readiness. *Psychological Review, 64,* 123–152.

———— (1961a). The act of discovery. *Harvard Educational Review, 31,* 21–32.

———— (1961b). *The process of education.* Cambridge, MA: Harvard University Press.

———— (1966). *Toward a theory of instruction.* Cambridge, MA: Harvard University Press.

———— (1973). Organization of early skilled action. *Child Development, 44,* 1–11.

———— (1983). *Child's talk.* New York: Norton.

———— (1985). Models of the learner. *Educational Researcher, 14,* 5–8.

———— (1990a). *Acts of meaning.* Cambridge, MA: Harvard University Press.

———— (1990b). Metaphors of consciousness and cognition in the history of psychology. In D. E. Leary (Ed.), *Metaphors in the history of psychology.* New York: Cambridge University Press.

———— (1992). Foreword to the second edition. In S. Farnham-Diggory, *Cognitive processes in education* (2nd ed.). New York: HarperCollins.

———— (1997a). Celebrating divergence: Piaget and Vygotsky. *Human Development, 40,* 63–73.

———— (1997b). Will the cognitive revolutions ever stop? In D. M. Johnson & C. E. Emeling, (Eds.) *The future of the cognitive revolution.* New York: Oxford University Press.

Bruner, J. S., Goodnow, J. J., & Austin, G. A. (1956). *A study of thinking.* New York: Wiley.

Brunson, D. A., & Vogt, J. F. (1996). Empowering our students and ourselves: A liberal democratic approach to the communication classroom. *Communication Education, 45,* 73–83.

Buber, M. (1958). *I and thou.* New York: Scribner's.

———— (1965). *The knowledge of man* (M. Friedman, Ed.). New York: Harper & Row.

Bullock, M. (1985). Animism in childhood thinking: A new look at an old question. *Developmental Psychology, 21*, 217–255.

Burkam, D. T., Lee, V. E., & Smerdon, B. A. (1997). Gender and science learning early in high school: Subject matter and laboratory experiences. *American Educational Research Journal, 34*, 297–331.

Burks, L. C. (1994). Ability group level and achievement. *School Community Journal, 4*, 11–24.

Burns, D. E., Johnson, S. E., & Gable, R. K. (1998). Can we generalize about the learning style characteristics of high academic achievers? *Roeper Review, 20*, 276–281.

Burns, R. B. (1984). How time is used in elementary schools: The activity structure of classrooms. In L. W. Anderson (Ed.), *Time and school learning: Theory, research and practice*. London: Croom Helm.

Busch, B. (1993). Attention deficits: Current concepts, controversies, management, and approaches to classroom instruction. *Annals of Dyslexia, 43*, 5–25.

Bussey, K., & Bandura, A. (1992). Self-regulatory mechanisms governing gender development. *Child Development, 63*, 1236–1250.

Butcher, J. (1993). The content, structure and meaning of teachers' management schemata: Ordered trees of novice and expert teachers. Special Issue: International conference on teacher thinking: I. *Journal of Structural Learning, 11*, 299–318.

Buzzelli, C. A. (1992). Young children's moral understanding: Learning about right and wrong. *Young Children, 47*, 48–53.

Cadieux, A., Boudreault, P., & Laberge, J. (1997). The Otis-Lennon Ability Test as a predictor of grade repetition and academic performance. *Psychological Reports, 81*, 223–226.

Cahill, B., & Adams, E. (1997). An exploratory study of early childhood teachers' attitudes toward gender roles. *Sex Roles, 36*, 517–529.

Cahill, L., & McGaugh, J. L. (1998). Mechanisms of emotional arousal and lasting declarative memory. *Trends in Neurosciences, 21*, 294–299.

Calfee, R. (1981). Cognitive psychology and educational practice. In D. C. Berliner (Ed.), *Review of research in education* (Vol. 9). Washington, DC: American Educational Research Association.

Cameron, A. W. (1956). *A guide to eastern Canadian mammals*. Ottawa: Department of Northern Affairs and National Resources.

Cameron, J., & Pierce, W. D. (1994). Reinforcement, reward, and intrinsic motivation: A meta-analysis. *Review of Educational Research, 64*, 363–423.

Campbell, F. A., & Ramey, C. T. (1990). The relationship between Piagetian cognitive development, mental test performance, and academic achievement in high-risk students with and without early educational intervention. *Intelligence, 14*, 293–308.

Campbell, R. L. (1993). Epistemological problems for neo-Piagetians. *Monographs of the Society for Research in Child Development, 58*, 168–191.

Canivez, G. L., & Watkins, M. W. (1998). Long-term stability of the Wechsler Intelligence Scale for Children—Third Edition. *Psychological Assessment, 10*, 285–291.

Canter, L., & Canter, M. (1992). *Lee Canter's assertive discipline: Positive management for today's classroom*. Santa Monica, CA: Lee Canter & Associates.

Carey, S. T. (1987). Reading comprehension in first and second languages of immersion and Francophone students. *Canadian Journal for Exceptional Children, 3*, 103–108.

Carlson, S. L., & White, S. H. (1998). The effectiveness of a computer program in helping kindergarten students learn the concepts of left and right. *Journal of Computing in Childhood Education, 9*, 133–147.

Carpentieri, S. C., & Morgan, S. B. (1994). A comparison of patterns of cognitive functioning of autistic and nonautistic retarded children on the Stanford-Binet—fourth edition. *Journal of Autism and Developmental Disorders, 24*, 215–223.

Carroll, J. B. (1963). A model of school learning. *Teachers College Record, 64*, 723–733.

———— (1989). The Carroll model: A 25-year retrospective and prospective view. *Educational Researcher, 18*(1), 26–31.

———— (1997). Psychometrics, intelligence, and public perception. *Intelligence, 24*, 25–52.

Carroll, J. C., & Rest, J. R. (1982). Moral development. In B. B. Wolman, et al. (Eds.), *Handbook of developmental psychology*. Englewood Cliffs, NJ: Prentice-Hall.

Case, R. (1975). Gearing the demands of instruction to the developmental capacities of the learner. *Review of Educational Research, 45*, 59–87.

———— (1991). Stages in the development of the young child's first sense of self. *Developmental Review, 11*, 210–230.

Cash, J. R., et al. (1997). Effectiveness of cognitive apprenticeship instructional methods in college automotive technology classrooms. *Journal of Industrial Teacher Education, 34*, 29–49.

Cassel, P., & Dreikurs, R. (1972). *Discipline without tears*. Toronto: Alfred Adler Institute of Ontario.

Cattell, R. B. (1971). *Abilities: Their structure, growth and action*. Boston: Houghton Mifflin.

Cavell, M. (1996). Erik Erikson and the temporal mind. *Psychoanalysis and Contemporary Thought, 19*, 191–206.

Cermak, L. S., & Craik, F. I. (Eds.). (1979). *Levels of processing in human memory*. Hillsdale, NJ: Erlbaum.

Chan, D. W. (1998). Stress, coping strategies, and psychological distress among secondary school teachers in Hong Kong. *American Educational Research Journal, 35*, 145–163.

Chandler, P. S. (1994). The gender equity quiz. *Learning, 22*, 57.

Chang, R., & Page, R. C. (1991). Characteristics of the self-actualized person: Visions from the east and west. *Counseling and Values, 36*, 2–10.

Cherry, E. C. (1953). Some experiments on the recognition of speech with one and two ears. *Journal of the Acoustical Society of America, 25*, 975–979.

Chi, M. T. H., & Glaser, R. (1980). The measurement of expertise: Analysis of the development of knowledge and skill as a basis for assessing achievement. In E. L. Baker & E. S.

Quellmalz (Eds.), *Educational testing and evaluation: Design, analysis and policy.* Beverly Hills: Sage.

Chi, M. T. H., Glaser, R., & Farr, M. (Eds.) (1988). *The nature of expertise.* Hillsdale, NJ: Erlbaum.

Childs, G., & McKay, M. (1997). The influence of family background on teachers' ratings of children starting school. *Australian Journal of Psychology, 49*, 33–41.

Chomsky, N. (1972). *Language and mind* (Enl. ed.) New York: Harcourt Brace.

Cienkus, R. C., & Ornstein, A. C. (1997). Distance learning: Teaching by lecture/explanation. *High School Journal, 80*, 247–253.

Cizek, G. J. (1993a). Reconsidering standards and criteria. *Journal of Educational Measurement, 30*, 93–106.

——— (1993b). Rethinking psychometricians' beliefs about learning. *Educational Researcher, 22*, 4–9.

Clandinin, D. J., & Connelly, F. M. (1996). Teachers' professional knowledge landscapes: Teacher stories—stories of teachers—school stories—stories of schools. *Educational Researcher, 25*, 24–30.

Clarizio, H. F. (1992). Teachers as detectors of learning disability. *Psychology in the Schools, 29*, 28–34.

Clarke, D., & Stephens, M. (1996). The ripple effect: The instructional impact of the systemic introduction of performance assessment in mathematics. In M. Birenbaum & F. J. Dochy (Eds.), *Alternatives in assessment of achievements, learning processes and prior knowledge: Evaluation in education and human services.* Boston, MA: Kluwer Academic Publishers.

Clements, D. H. (1991). Enhancement of creativity in computer environments. *American Educational Research Journal, 28*, 173–187.

——— (1997). (Mis?)constructing constructivism. *Teaching Children Mathematics, 4*, 198–200.

Clements, D. H., Battista, M. T., Sarama, J., Swaminathan, S., & McMillen, S. (1997). Students' development of length concepts in a logo-based unit on geometric paths. *Journal for Research in Mathematics Education, 28*, 70–95.

Clements, S. D. (1966). *Minimal brain dysfunction in children: Terminology and identification* (NINDB Monograph No. 3). Washington, DC: U.S. Department of Health and Human Services.

Cohen, D. K. (1972). Does IQ matter? *Current, 141*, 19–30.

Cohen, E. G. (1994). Restructuring the classroom: Conditions for productive small groups. *Review of Educational Research, 64*, 1–35.

Cohen, G. (1996). *Memory in the real world* (2nd ed.). East Sussex, UK: Psychology Press.

Cohen, M. J., Riccio, C. A., & Gonzalez, J. J. (1994). Methodological differences in the diagnosis of attention-deficit hyperactivity disorder: Impact on prevalence. *Journal of Emotional and Behavioral Disorders, 2*, 31–38.

Cohen, S. (1993/1994). Television in the lives of children and their families. *Childhood Education, 70*, 103–104.

Cohn, M. M., & Kottkamp, R. B. (1993). *Teachers: The missing voice in education.* New York: State University of New York.

Colby, A., James, J. B., & Hart, D. (Eds.) (1998). *Competence and character through life.* Chicago, IL: University of Chicago Press.

Cole, M., & Wertsch, J. V. (1996). Beyond the individual-social antinomy in discussions of Piaget and Vygotsky. *Human Development, 39*, 250–256.

Collins, A., Brown, J. S., & Newman, S. E. (1989). Cognitive apprenticeship: Teaching the craft of reading, writing, and mathematics. In L. B. Resnick (Ed.), *Knowing, learning, and instruction: Essays in honor of Robert Glaser.* Hillsdale, NJ: Erlbaum.

Colom, R., Andres-Pueyo, A., & Juan-Espinosa, M. (1998). Generational IQ gains: Spanish data. *Personality and Individual Differences, 25*, 927–935.

Combs, A. W. (1982). *A personal approach to teaching: Beliefs that make a difference.* Boston: Allyn & Bacon.

——— (1988). Is there a future for humanistic or person-centered education? *Person-Centered Review: Special Issue: The person-centered approach in education, 3*, 96–103.

——— (1990). Toward a viable psychology of meaning. *Person-Centered Review. Special Issue: Fiftieth anniversary of the person-centered approach, 5*, 449–463.

Conard, C. J. (1997). Fairbanks System of Instruction at Fairbanks Country Day. *Behavior & Social Issues, 7*, 25–29.

Consejero, E. M., Cuevas, C. A., Guzman, J. I. N., & Cagigas, G. R. (1998).

Contat, M. (1974). *The writings of Jean-Paul Sartre.* (Compiled by M. Contat and M. Rybalka). Evanston, IL: Northwestern University Press.

Cooper, R. (1996). Detracking reform in an urban California high school: Improving the schooling experiences of African American students. *Journal of Negro Education, 65*, 190–208.

Corno, L., & Snow, R. E. (1986). Adapting teaching to individual differences among learners. In M. C. Wittrock (Ed.), *Handbook of research on teaching* (3rd ed.) (pp. 605–629). New York: Macmillan.

Craik, F. M., & Lockhart, R. S. (1972). Levels of processing: A framework for memory research. *Journal of Verbal Learning and Verbal Behavior, 11*, 671–684.

Crawford, M. A., Doyle, W., Leaf, A., Leighfield, M., Ghebremeskel, K., & Phylactos, A. (1993). Nutrition and neurodevelopmental disorders. *Nutrition and Health, 9*, 81–97.

Crockett, L. J., & Petersen, A. C. (1987). Findings from the Early Adolescence Study. In R. M. Lerner & T. T. Foch (Eds.), *Biological-psychosocial interactions in early adolescence: A life-span perspective.* Hillsdale, NJ: Erlbaum.

Cronbach, L. J., & Snow, R. E. (1977). *Aptitudes and instructional methods.* New York: Irvington.

Cropley, A. J. (1996). Recognizing creative potential: An evaluation of the usefulness of creativity tests. *High Ability Studies, 7*, 203–219.

Cross, T. L., Coleman, L. J., & Terhaar-Yonkers, M. (1991). The social cognition of gifted adolescents in schools: Managing the stigma of giftedness. *Journal for the Education of the Gifted, 15*, 44–55.

Crowder, N. A. (1961). Characteristics of branching programs. In D. P. Scannell (Ed.), *Conference on programmed learning.* Lawrence: University of Kansas, Studies in Education.

——— (1963). On the differences between linear and intrinsic programming. *Phi Delta Kappan, 44*, 250–254.

Cziko, G. A. (1992). The evaluation of bilingual education. *Educational Researcher, 21*, 10–15.

Daily Report Card, August 14, 1995. Education Commission of the United States and the National Education Goals Panel. Washington, DC.

Damon, W., & Colby, A. (1987). Social influence and moral change. In W. M. Kurtines & J. L. Gewirtz (Eds.), *Moral development through social interaction*. New York: Wiley.

Daniels, H., & Bizar, M. (1998). *Methods that matter: Six structures for best practice classrooms*. York, ME: Stenhouse Publishers.

Das, J. P. (1992). Beyond a unidimensional scale of merit. *Intelligence, 16*, 137–149.

Das, J. P., Kar, B. C., & Parrila, R. K. (1996). *Cognitive planning: The psychological basis of intelligent behavior*. Thousand Oaks, CA: Sage.

Das, J. P., Mishra, R. K., & Pool, J. E. (1995). An experiment on cognitive remediation of word-reading difficulty. *Journal of Learning Disabilities, 28*, 66–79.

Das, J. P., Naglieri, J. A., & Kirby, J. R. (1994). *Assessment of cognitive processes*. Boston: Allyn & Bacon.

Davydov, V. V. (1995). The influence of L. S. Vygotsky on education theory, research, and practice. *Educational Researcher, 24*, 12–21.

Deacon, T. W. (1997). *The symbolic species: The co-evolution of language and the brain*. New York: W. W. Norton.

Deal, L. V., & Haas, W. H. (1996). Hearing and the development of language and speech. *Folia Phoniatrica et Logopedica, 48*, 111–116.

DeFries, J. C., Plomin, R., & Fulker, D. W. (1994). *Nature–nurture during middle childhood*. Cambridge, MA: Blackwell.

Delandshere, G., & Petrosky, A. R. (1998). Assessment of complex performances: Limitations of key measurement assumptions. *Educational Researcher, 27*, 14–24.

Delgado-Hachey, M., & Miller, S. A. (1993). Mothers' accuracy in predicting their children's IQs: Its relationship to antecedent variables, mothers' academic achievement demands, and children's achievement. *Journal of Experimental Education, 62*, 43–59.

DeLong, G. R. (1993). Effects of nutrition on brain development in humans. *American Journal of Clinical Nutrition, 57*, 286s–290s.

Dennison, G. (1969). *The lives of children: The story of the First Street School*. New York: Random House (Vintage Books).

Deutsch, W. (1992). Teaching machines, programming, computers, and instructional technology: The roots of performance technology. *Performance and Instruction, 31*, 14–20.

DeVries, R. (1997). Piaget's social theory. *Educational Researcher, 26*, 4–18.

Dewey, J. (1933). *How we think* (rev. ed.). Lexington, MA: D. C. Heath.

Diamond, K. E., & LeFurgy, W. G. (1994). Attitudes of parents of preschool children toward integration. *Early Education and Development, 5*, 69–77.

Diaz, R. M. (1983). Thought and two languages: The impact of bilingualism on cognitive development. In E. W. Gordon (Ed.), *Review of research in education* (Vol. 10). Washington, DC: American Educational Research Association.

Dickens, C. (1843/1986). *A Christmas carol*. London: Octopus Books.

Dinkelman, T. (1997). The promise of action research for critically reflective teacher education. *Teacher Educator, 32*, 250–274.

Dinsmoor, J. A. (1996). Studies in the history of psychology: CVI. An appreciation of Fred S. Keller, 1899–1996. *Psychological Reports, 79*, 891–898.

——— (1998). Punishment. In W. T. O'Donohue, et al. (Eds.), *Learning and behavior therapy*. Boston, MA: Allyn & Bacon.

Douvan, E. (1997). Erik Erikson: Critical times, critical theory. *Child Psychiatry and Human Development, 28*, 15–21.

Dowell, H. H. (1997). The Ausubelian preschool program: Balancing child-directed and teacher-directed approaches. *Early Childhood News, 9*, 12–17.

Doyle, W. (1979). Making managerial decisions in classrooms. In D. Duke (Ed.), *78th yearbook of the National Society for the Study of Education: Part 2. Classroom management*. Chicago: University of Chicago Press.

——— (1986). Classroom organization and management. In M. C. Wittrock (Ed.), *Handbook of research on teaching* (3rd ed.). New York: Macmillan.

Drake, V. K., Freed, P., & Hunter, J. M. (1998). Crib sheets or security blankets? *Issues in Mental Health Nursing, 19*, 291–300.

Dreikurs, R., & Grey, L. (1968). *Logical consequences: A new approach to discipline*. New York: Hawthorne.

Dreikurs, R., Grunwald, B. B., & Pepper, F. C. (1982). *Maintaining sanity in the classroom: Classroom management techniques* (2nd ed.). New York: Harper & Row.

Duda, J. L., & Nicholls, J. G. (1992). Dimensions of achievement motivation in schoolwork and sport. *Journal of Educational Psychology, 84*, 290–299.

Dunn, R., & Griggs, S. A. (1988). *Learning styles: Quiet revolution in American secondary schools*. Reston, VA: National Association of Secondary School Principals.

Dunn, R., & Stevenson, J. M. (1997). Teaching diverse college students to study with a learning-styles prescription. *College Student Journal, 31*, 333–339.

Dunn, R., Dunn, K., & Perrin, J. (1994). *Teaching young children through their individual learning styles: Practical approaches for grades K–2*. Boston: Allyn & Bacon.

Dweck, C. S. (1986). Motivational processes affecting learning. *American Psychologist, 41*, 1040–1048.

Dweck, C. S., & Leggett, E. L. (1988). A social-cognitive approach to motivation and personality. *Psychological Review, 95*, 256–273.

Eagle, M. (1997). Contributions of Erik Erikson. *Psychoanalytic Review, 84*, 337–347.

Eby, J. W. (1998). *Reflective planning, teaching, and evaluation: K–12* (2nd ed.). Upper Saddle River, NJ: Merrill.

Educational Testing Service. (1961). Judges disagree on qualities that characterize good writing. *ETS Development, 9*, 2.

Edwards, C. H. (1993). *Classroom discipline and management*. New York: Macmillan.

Edwards, V., & Redfern, A. (1992). *The world in a classroom: Language in education in Britain and Canada*. Clevedon, UK: Multilingual Matters.

Eichenbaum, H. (1997). Declarative memory: Insights from cognitive neurobiology. *Annual Review of Psychology, 48,* 547–572.

Eilers, R. E., & Oller, D. K. (1988). Precursors to speech. In R. Vasta (Ed.), *Annals of child development* (Vol. 5). Greenwich, CT: JAI Press.

Eisenberg, N., Miller, P. A., Shell, R., McNalley, S., & Shea, C. (1991). Prosocial development in adolescence: A longitudinal study. *Developmental Psychology, 27,* 849–857.

Eisner, E. W. (1982). An artistic approach to supervision. In T. J. Sergiovanni (Ed.), *Supervision of teaching (ASCD 1982 Yearbook)*. Alexandria, VA: Association for Supervision and Curriculum Development.

Elder, C. (1997). What does test bias have to do with fairness? *Language Testing, 14,* 261–277.

Elias, G., & Broerse, J. (1996). Developmental changes in the incidence and likelihood of simultaneous talk during the first two years: A question of function. *Journal of Child Language, 23,* 201–217.

Ellzey, J., & Karnes, F. A. (1993). Comparison of scores on the WISC-R and the Stanford-Binet, fourth edition, for rural gifted students. *Rural Special Education Quarterly, 12,* 10–13.

Elton, L. R. B., & Laurillard, D. M. (1979). Trends in research on student learning. *Studies in Higher Education, 4,* 87–102.

Emde, R., Kubicek, L., & Oppenheim, D. (1997). Imaginative reality observed during early language development. *International Journal of Psycho-Analysis, 78,* 115–133.

Emerson-Stonnell, S., & Carter, C. (1994). Math mentor programs. *Gifted Child Today, 17,* 26–34.

Engel, M. (1976). *Bear.* Toronto: McClelland and Stewart.

Ennis, R. H. (1976). An alternative to Piaget's conceptualization of logical competence. *Child Development, 47,* 903–919.

———— (1978). Conceptualization of children's logical competence: Piaget's propositional logic and an alternative proposal. In L. S. Siegel & C. J. Brainerd (Eds.), *Alternatives to Piaget: Critical essays on the theory.* New York: Academic Press.

Erickson, M. T. (1992). *Behavior disorders of children and adolescents* (2nd ed.). Englewood Cliffs, NJ: Prentice-Hall.

Erikson, E. H. (1959). *Identity and the life cycle: Selected papers.* Psychological Issue Monograph Series, I (No. 1). New York: International Universities Press.

Erin, J. K., & Koenig, A. J. (1997). The student with a visual disability and a learning disability. *Journal of Learning Disabilities, 30,* 309–320.

Eshel, Y., & Grosberger, M. (1993). Active learning and its effect on the development of independence in pupils. *Megamot, 35,* 62–75.

Eshel, Y., & Klein, Z. (1995). Elementary school integration and open education: Long-term effects of early interventions. In G. Ben-Shakhar, A. Lieblich, et al., (Eds.), *Studies in psychology in honor of Solomon Kugelmass. Publications of the Hebrew University of Jerusalem, 36,* 155–171.

Evans, K. M., & King, J. A. (1994a). Outcome-based and gifted education: Can we assume continued support? *Roeper Review, 16,* 260–264.

———— (1994b). Research on OBE: What we know and don't know. *Educational leadership, 51,* 12–17.

Evans, R. I. (1989). *Albert Bandura: The man and his ideas— a dialogue.* New York: Praeger.

Evers, W. M. (1998). From progressive education to discovery learning. In W. M. Evers (Ed.), *What's gone wrong in America's classrooms?* Stanford, CA: Hoover Institution Press.

———— (Ed.) (1998). *What's gone wrong in America's classrooms?* Stanford, CA: Hoover Institution Press.

Evertson, C. M., & Harris, A. H. (1992). What we know about managing classrooms. *Educational Leadership, 49,* 74–78.

Ewell, P. T. (1991). To capture the ineffable: New forms of assessment in higher education. In G. Grant (Ed.), *Review of research in education* (Vol. 17). Washington, DC: American Educational Research Association.

Ewer, R. F. (1973). *The carnivores.* Ithaca, NY: Cornell University Press.

Eysenck, H. J. (1998). *A new look at intelligence.* New Brunswick, NJ: Transaction.

Fabricius, W. V., & Wellman, H. M. (1993). Two roads diverged: Young children's ability to judge distance. *Child Development, 64,* 399–419.

Facon, B., & Facon-Bollengier, T. (1997). Chronological age and Peabody Picture Vocabulary Test performance of persons with mental retardation: New data. *Psychological Reports, 81,* 1232–1234.

Fair, E. M. III, & Silvestri, L. (1992). Effects of rewards, competition and outcome on intrinsic motivation. *Journal of Instructional Psychology, 19,* 3–8.

Farnham-Diggory, S. (1992). *Cognitive processes in education* (2nd ed.). New York: HarperCollins.

Farr, R., & Tone, B. (1998). *Portfolio and performance assessment: Helping students evaluate their progress as readers and writers* (2nd ed.). Fort Worth: Harcourt Brace.

Feldman, D. H. (1993). Child prodigies: A distinctive form of giftedness. *Gifted Child Quarterly, 37,* 188–193.

Feldt, L. S. (1993). The relationship between the distribution of item difficulties and test reliability. *Applied Measurement in Education, 6,* 37–48.

Fennema, E., Carpenter, T. P., Jacobs, V. R., Franke, M. L., & Levi, L. W. (1998). A longitudinal study of gender differences in young children's mathematical thinking. *Educational Researcher, 27,* 6–12.

Fenstermacher, G. D., & Soltis, J. F. (1992). *Approaches to teaching.* New York: Teachers College Press.

Ferrington, G., & Loge, K. (1992). Virtual reality: A new learning environment. *The Computing Teacher, 20,* 16–19.

Fetterman, D. M. (1994). Terman's giftedness study. In R. J. Sternberg (Ed.), *Encyclopedia of human intelligence* (Vol. 2). New York: Macmillan.

———— (1998). Webs of meaning: Computer and internet resources for educational research and instruction. *Educational Researcher, 27,* 22–30.

Feuerstein, R. (1979). *The dynamic assessment of retarded performers.* Baltimore: University Park Press.

———— (1980). *Instrumental enrichment: An intervention program for cognitive modifiability.* Baltimore: University Park Press.

——— (1994). *Learning potential assessment device.* In R. J. Sternberg (Ed.), Encyclopedia of human intelligence (Vol. 2). New York: Macmillan.

Fien, J. (1997). Learning to care: A focus for values in health and environmental education. *Health Education Research, 12,* 437–447.

Fischer, C. S., Hout, M., Jankowski, M. S., Lucas, S. R., Swidler, A., & Voss, K. (1996). *Inequality by design: Cracking the bell curve myth.* Princeton, NJ: Princeton University Press.

Fisher, W. W., Ninness, H. A. C., Piazza, C. C., & Owen-DeSchryver, J. S. (1996). On the reinforcing effects of the content of verbal attention. *Journal of Applied Behavior Analysis, 29,* 235–238.

Flavell, J. H. (1985). *Cognitive development* (2nd ed.). Englewood Cliffs, NJ: Prentice-Hall.

Fleming, M., & Chambers, B. (1983). Teacher-made tests: Windows on the classroom. In W. E. Hathaway (Ed.), *New directions for testing and measurement: Vol. 19, Testing in the schools.* San Francisco: Jossey-Bass.

Flynn, C. P. (1998). To spank or not to spank: The effect of situation and age of child on support for corporal punishment. *Journal of Family Violence, 13,* 21–37.

Flynn, J. R. (1987). Massive IQ gains in 14 nations: What IQ tests really measure. *Psychological Bulletin, 101,* 171–191.

Follman, J. (1991). Teachers' estimates of pupils' IQs and pupils' tested IQs. *Psychological Reports, 69,* 350.

Frable, D. E. S. (1997). Gender, racial, ethnic, sexual, and class identities. *Annual Review of Psychology, 48,* 139–162.

Franchi, J. (1994). Virtual reality: An overview. *Techtrends, 39,* 23–26.

Franco, F., & Butterworth, G. (1996). Pointing and social awareness: Declaring and requesting in the second year. *Journal of Child Language, 23,* 307–336.

Fredericks, D. W., & Williams, W. L. (1998). New definition of mental retardation for the American Association of Mental Retardation. *Image—The Journal of Nursing Scholarship, 30,* 53–56.

Freiberg, H. J., & Driscoll, A. (1992). *Universal Teaching Strategies.* Boston: Allyn & Bacon.

Fridell, S. R., Zucker, K. J., Bradley, S. J., & Maing, D. M. (1996). Physical attractiveness of girls with gender identity disorder. *Archives of Sexual Behavior, 25,* 17–31.

Friedkin, N. E., & Thomas, S. L. (1997). Social positions in schooling. *Sociology of Education, 70,* 239–255.

Frisch, R. E., & Revelle, R. (1970). Height and weight at menarche and a hypothesis of critical body weights and adolescent events. *Science, 169,* 397–398.

Fry, P. G., & Fleeners, M. J. (1997). An analysis of pre-service teacher-class interaction metaphors. *Journal of Classroom Interaction, 32,* 23–28.

Fuchs, D., & Fuchs, L. S. (1995). What's "special" about special education? *Phi Delta Kappan, 76,* 542–546.

Fuchs, D., Fuchs, L. S., Mathes, P. G., & Simmons, D. C. (1997). Peer-assisted learning strategies: Making classrooms more responsive to diversity. *American Educational Research Journal, 34,* 174–206.

Fuchs, L. S., Fuchs, D., Karns, K., Hamlett, C. L., Katzaroff, M., & Dutka, S. (1997). Effects of task-focused goals on low-achieving students with and without learning disabilities. *American Educational Research Journal, 34,* 513–543.

Fuchs-Beauchamp, K. D., Karnes, M. B., & Johnson, L. J. (1993). Creativity and intelligence in preschoolers. *Gifted Child Quarterly, 37,* 113–117.

Gabrieli, J. D. E. (1998). Cognitive neuroscience of human memory. *Annual Review of Psychology, 49,* 87–115.

Gage, N. L. (1964). Theories of teaching. In E. R. Hilgard (Ed.), *Theories of learning and instruction: The sixty-third yearbook of the National Society for the Study of Education.* Chicago: University of Chicago Press.

Gagné, E. D. (1985). *The cognitive psychology of school learning.* Boston: Little, Brown.

Gagné, E. D., Yekovich, C. W., & Yekovich, F. R. (1993). *The cognitive psychology of school learning* (2nd ed.). New York: HarperCollins.

Gagné, R. M. (1985). *The conditions of learning* (4th ed.). New York: Holt, Rinehart & Winston.

Gagné, R. M., & Briggs, L. J. (1983). *Principles of instructional design* (3rd ed.). New York: Holt, Rinehart & Winston.

Gagné, R. M., & Dick, W. (1983). Instructional psychology. *Annual Review of Psychology, 34,* 261–295.

Gagné, R. M., Briggs, L. J., & Wager, W. W. (1992). *Principles of instructional design* (4th ed.). Fort Worth: Harcourt Brace Jovanovich.

Gallagher, J. J. (1960). *Analysis of research on the education of gifted children.* State of Illinois: Office of the Superintendent of Public Instruction.

——— (1994). Teaching and learning: New models. *Annual Review of Psychology, 45,* 171–195.

Galton, F. (1869). *Hereditary genius: An inquiry into its laws and consequences.* London: Macmillan.

Garcia, E. E. (1993). Language, culture, and education. In L. Darling-Hammond (Ed.), *Review of research in education* (Vol. 19). Washington, D.C.: American Educational Research Association.

García, G. E., & Pearson, P. D. (1994). Assessment and diversity. In L. Darling-Hammond (Ed.), *Review of research in education* (Vol. 20). Washington, DC: American Educational Research

Gardner, H. (1983). *Frames of mind: The theory of multiple intelligences.* New York: Basic Books.

——— (1993). Educating for understanding. *American School Board Journal, 180,* 20–24.

——— (1997). Six afterthoughts: Comments on "Varieties of intellectual talent." *Journal of Creative Behavior, 31,* 120–124.

——— (1998). Are there additional intelligences? The case for naturalist, spiritual, and existential intelligences, In J. Kane (Ed.), *Education, information, and transformation.* Englewood Cliffs, NJ: Prentice-Hall.

Gardner, H., & Hatch, T. (1989). Multiple intelligences go to school: Educational implications of the theory of multiple intelligences. *Educational Researcher, 18,* 4–10.

Gathercole, S. E. (1998). The development of memory. *Journal of Child Psychology and Psychiatry and Allied Disciplines, 39,* 3–27.

Gaynor, J. L. R., & Runco, M. A. (1992). Family size, birth-order, age-interval, and the creativity of children. *Journal of Creative Behavior, 26*, 108–118.

Gearhart, M., & Herman, J. L. (1998). Portfolio assessment: Whose work is it? Issues in the use of classroom assignments for accountability. *Educational Assessment, 5*, 41–55.

Gelman, R. (1982). Basic numerical abilities. In R. J. Sternberg (Ed.), *Advances in the psychology of human intelligence* (Vol. 1). Hillsdale, NJ: Erlbaum.

Gelman, R., Meck, E., & Merkin, S. (1986). Young children's numerical competence. *Cognitive Development, 1*, 1–29.

Genesee, F. (1985). Second language learning through immersion: A review of U.S. programs. *Review of Educational Research, 55*, 541–561.

George, P. S. (1993). Tracking and ability grouping in the middle school: Tentative truths. *Middle School Journal, 24*, 17–24.

George, P., Morgan, J., & Jenkins, T. (1997). Detracking Troup County: Providing an exemplary curriculum for all students. *Equity and Excellence in Education, 30*, 60–67.

Getzels, J. W., & Jackson, P. W. (1962). *Creativity and intelligence.* New York: Wiley.

Giangreco, M. F. (1997). Key lessons learned about inclusive education: Summary of the 1996 Schonell Memorial Lecture. *International Journal of Disability, Development, and Education, 44*, 193–206.

Gillespie, D. (1996). Narrative and reflective teaching practice. *Innovative Higher Education, 21*, 11–22.

Gilligan, C. (1982). *In a different voice: Psychological theory and women's development.* Cambridge, MA: Harvard University Press.

Giroux, A. (1992). Teaching moral thinking: A reconceptualization. *Journal of Educational Thought, 26*, 114–120.

Goldberg, M. (1996). Expanding the possibilities of the U.S. Survey through student-directed teaching and learning. *Oah Magazine of History, 10*, 43–47.

Goldman, W. P., & Seamon, J. G. (1992). Very long-term memory for odors: Retention of odor-name associations. *American Journal of Psychology, 105*, 549–563.

Goldschmid, M. L., & Bentler, P. M. (1968). *Conservation concept diagnostic kit: Manual and keys.* San Diego: Educational and Industrial Testing Service.

Good, T. L., & Marshall, S. (1997). Do students learn more in heterogeneous or homogeneous groups? In E. Dubinsky & D. Mathews (Eds.), *Readings in cooperative learning for undergraduate mathematics. MAA notes, No. 44.* Washington, DC: The Mathematical Association of America.

Goodenough, F. (1926). *Measurement of intelligence by drawings.* New York: Harcourt, Brace & World.

Gordon, T. (1974). *T.E.T.: Teacher effectiveness training.* New York: Peter H. Wyden.

Gould, S. J. (1981). *The mismeasure of man.* New York: Norton.

Gourgey, A. F. (1998). Metacognition in basic skills instruction. *Instructional Science, 26*, 81–96.

Grabe, M., & Grabe, C. (1998). *Integrating technology for meaningful learning* (2nd ed.). Boston, MA: Houghton Mifflin.

Grant, G. (1991). Introduction. In G. Grant (Ed.), *Review of research in education* (Vol. 17). Washington, DC: American Educational Research Association.

Grant, J. P. (1993). *The state of the world's children:1993.* New York: Oxford University Press.

Greer, R. D. (1993). Contingencies of the science and technology of teaching and prebehavioristic research practices in education. *Educational Researcher, 12*, 3–9.

Gregory, J. F. (1997). Three strikes and they're out: African American boys and American schools' responses to misbehavior. *International Journal of Adolescence & Youth, 7*, 25–34.

Gresham, F. M., & MacMillan, D. L. (1997). Social competence and affective characteristics of students with mild disabilities. *Review of Educational Research, 67*, 377–415.

Grippin, P. C., & Peters, S. C. (1984). Learning theories and learning outcomes: The connection. Lanham, MD: University Press of America.

Gronlund, N. E. (1995). *How to write and use instructional objectives* (5th ed.). Boston: Allyn & Bacon.

Gronna, S. S., Jenkins, A. A., & Chin-Chance, S. A. (1998). Who are we assessing? Determining state-wide participation rates for students with disabilities. *Exceptional Children, 64*, 407–418.

Gross, M. U. (1992). The use of radical acceleration in cases of extreme intellectual precocity. *Gifted Child Quarterly, 36*, 91–99.

Grossman, H. (1995). *Special education in a diverse society.* Boston: Allyn & Bacon.

Grossnickle, D. R., & Sesko, F. P. (1990). *Preventive discipline for effective teaching and learning.* Reston, VA: National Association of Secondary School Principals.

Grusec, J. E. (1992). Social learning theory and developmental psychology: The legacies of Robert Sears and Albert Bandura. *Developmental Psychology, 28*, 776–786.

Guffey, D. G. (1991). Ritalin: What educators and parents should know. *Journal of Instructional Psychology, 19*, 167–169.

Gugerty, L. (1996). Non-diagnostic intelligent tutoring systems: Teaching without student models. *Instructional Science, 25*, 409–432.

Guglielmi, R. S., & Tatrow, K. (1998). Occupational stress, burnout, and health in teachers: A methodological and theoretical analysis. *Review of Educational Research, 68*, 61–99.

Guild, P. (1994). Making sense of learning styles. *School Administrator, 51*, 8–13.

Guilford, J. P. (1950). Creativity. *American Psychologist, 5*, 444–454.

——— (1959). Three faces of intellect. *American Psychologist, 14*, 469–479.

——— (1967). *The nature of human intelligence.* New York: McGraw-Hill.

Gullickson, A. R. (1985). Student evaluation techniques and their relationship to grade and curriculum. *Journal of Educational Research, 79*, 96–100.

Gump, P. V. (1969). Intra-setting analysis: The third grade classroom as a special but instructive case. In E. Williams

& H. Rausch (Eds.), *Naturalistic viewpoints in psychological research*. New York: Holt, Rinehart & Winston.

Guri-Rozenblit, S. (1993). Differentiating between distance/open education systems: Parameters for comparison. *International Review of Education, 39*, 287–306.

Guskey, T. R. (1997). *Implementing mastery learning* (2nd ed.). Belmont, CA: Wadsworth.

Guthrie, E. R. (1935). *The psychology of learning*. New York: Harper & Brothers.

Gutiérrez, R., & Slavin, R. E. (1992). Achievement effects of the nongraded elementary school: A best evidence synthesis. *Review of Educational Research, 62*, 333–376.

Hadaway, N. L., & Marek-Schroer, M. (1994). Student portfolios: Toward equitable assessments for gifted students. *Equity and Excellence in Education, 27*, 70–74.

Haddon, F. A., & Lytton, H. (1968). Teaching approach and the development of divergent thinking abilities in primary schools. *British Journal of Educational Psychology, 38*, 171–180.

Haladyna, T. M., Nolen, S. B., & Haas, N. S. (1991). Raising standardized achievement test scores and the origins of test score pollution. *Educational Researcher, 20*, 2–7.

Hall, E., Hall, C., & Abaci, R. (1997). The effects of human relations training on reported teacher stress, pupil control ideology and locus of control. *British Journal of Educational Psychology, 67*, 483–496.

Hall, F. R., & Kelson, K. R. (1959). *The mammals of North America* (Vol. 2). New York: Ronald Press.

Hallahan, D. P., & Kauffman, J. M. (1994). *Exceptional children: Introduction to special education* (6th ed.). Boston: Allyn & Bacon.

Halpern, D. F., & Coren, S. (1990). Laterality and longevity: Is left-handedness associated with younger age at death? In S. Coren (Ed.), *Left-handedness: Behavioral implications and anomalies*. Amsterdam: Elsevier.

Hammer, D. (1997). Discovery learning and discovery teaching. *Cognition and Instruction, 15*, 485–529.

Hansen, C. B. (1998). Using reflective portfolios as a tool to teach writing to students with learning disabilities: A project for preservice teachers. *Reading & Writing Quarterly: Overcoming Learning Difficulies, 14*, 307–317.

Hany, E. A. (1997). Modeling teachers' judgment of giftedness: A methodological inquiry of biased judgment. *High Ability Studies, 8*, 159–178.

Harju, B. L., & Eppler, M. A. (1997). Achievement motivation, flow and irrational beliefs in traditional and nontraditional college students. *Journal of Instructional Psychology, 24*, 147–157.

Harrington, J., Harrington, C., & Karns, E. (1991). The Marland report: Twenty years later. *Journal for the Education of the Gifted, 15*, 31–43.

Harris, B. D. (1963). *Children's drawings as measures of intellectual maturity*. New York: Harcourt, Brace & World.

Hart, D. (1998). Can prototypes inform moral developmental theory? *Developmental Psychology, 34*, 420–423.

Harter, S. (1988). Developmental processes in the construction of self. In T. D. Yawkey, G. R. Adams, & J. E. Johnson (Eds.), *Integrative processes and socialization: Early to middle childhood*. Hillsdale, NJ: Erlbaum.

Harvey, M. L., Loomis, R. J., Bell, P. A., & Marino, M. (1998). The influence of museum exhibit design on immersion and psychological flow. *Environment & Behavior, 30*, 601–627.

Hativa, N., & Becker, H. J. (Eds.). (1994). Computer-based integrated learning systems: Research and theory. *International Journal of Educational Research, 21*, 1–119.

Hativa, N., & Lesgold, A. (1996). Situational effects in classroom technology implementations: Unfulfilled expectations and unexpected outcomes. In S. T. Kerr (Ed.), *Technology and the future of schooling: Ninety-fifth yearbook of the National Society for the Study of Education*. Chicago: University of Chicago Press.

Hauser, R. M., & Sewell, W. H. (1985). Birth order and educational attainment in full sibships. *American Educational Research Journal, 22*, 1–23.

Hay, D. F., Stimson, C. A., & Castle, J. (1991). A meeting of minds in infancy: Imitation and desire. In D. Frye & C. Moore (Eds.), *Children's theories of mind: Mental states and social understanding*. Hillsdale, NJ: Erlbaum.

Hebb, D. O. (1947). The effects of early experience on problem solving maturity. *American Psychologist, 2*, 306–307.

———— (1966). *A textbook of psychology* (2nd ed.). Philadelphia: Saunders.

Hedges, L., & Friedman, L. (1993). Gender differences in variability in intellectual abilities: A reanalysis of Feingold's results. *Review of Educational Research, 63*, 94–105.

Heiligenstein, E., & Anders, J. (1997). Pemoline in adult attention deficit hyperactivity disorder: Predictors of nonresponse. *Journal of American College Health, 45*, 225–229.

Heinbokel, A. (1997). Acceleration through grade skipping in Germany. *High Ability Studies, 8*, 61–77.

Hembree, R. (1988). Correlates, causes, effects and treatment of test anxiety. *Review of Educational Research, 58*, 47–77.

Henderson, N. (1996). Motivating your development staff. *Currents, 22*, 30–34.

Henker, B., & Whalen, C. K. (1989). Hyperactivity and attention deficits. *American Psychologist, 44*, 216–223.

Henshaw, A., Kelly, J., & Gratton, C. (1992). Skipping's for girls: Children's perceptions of gender roles and gender preferences. *Educational Research, 34*, 229–235.

Herrnstein, R. J., & Murray, C. (1994). *The bell curve: Intelligence and class structure in American life*. New York: Free Press.

Herschel, R. T. (1994). The impact of varying gender composition on group brainstorming performance in a GSS environment. *Computers in Human Behavior, 10*, 209–222.

Hess, R. D., & Azuma, H. (1991). Cultural support for schooling: Contrasts between Japan and the United States. *Educational Researcher, 20*, 2–8.

Heward, W. L., & Orlansky, M. D. (1992). *Exceptional children: An introductory survey of special education* (4th ed.). New York: Merrill.

Heyns, O. S. (1967, Feb. 4). Treatment of the unborn. *Woman's Own*, p. 18.

Higbee, K. L. (1977). *Your memory: How it works and how to improve it*. Englewood Cliffs, NJ: Prentice-Hall.

Hill, O. W., & Huntley, L. (1998). Internal-internal dimension of epistemic and personality factors and a measure of achievement motivation. *Psychological Reports, 82,* 1331–1334.

Hines, T. (1991). The myth of right hemisphere creativity. *Journal of Creative Behavior, 25,* 223–237.

Hitz, R., & Driscoll, A. (1994). Give encouragement, not praise. *Texas Child Care, 17,* 2–11.

Hodapp, R. M., & Dykens, E. M. (1994). Mental retardation's two cultures of behavioral research. *American Journal of Mental Retardation, 98,* 675–687.

Hoepfl, M. C. (1994). Developing and evaluating multiple choice tests. *Technology Teacher, 53,* 25–26.

Hoffman, E. (1998). Peak experiences in childhood: An exploratory study. *Journal of Humanistic Psychology, 38,* 109–120.

Hoffman, J. V., Worthy, J., Roser, N. L., & Rutherford, W. (1998). Performance assessment in reading: Implications for teacher education. In J. Osborn,& F. Lehr, (Eds.), *Literacy for all: Issues in teaching and learning.* New York: Guilford Press.

Hogan, K., & Pressley, M. (1997). Scaffolding scientific competencies within classroom communities of inquiry. In K. Hogan & M. Pressley (Eds.), *Scaffolding student learning: Instructional approaches and issues.* Albany, NY: State University of New York.

Hogelucht, K. S. B., & Geist, P. (1997). Discipline in the classroom: Communicative strategies for negotiating order. *Western Journal of Communication, 61,* 1–34.

Holden, P. (1996). Teacher competencies: A standard approach? *Literacy Broadsheet, 43,* 7–10.

Holland, J. L., Magoon, T. M., & Spokane, A. R. (1981). Counseling psychology: Career interventions, research, and theory. In M. R. Rosenzweig & L. W. Porter (Eds.), *Annual review of psychology* (Vol. 32). Palo Alto, CA: Annual Reviews.

Holland, R. W. (1994). Mentoring as a career development tool. *CUPA Journal, 45,* 41–44.

Hooper, S. R. (1992). The classification of developmental disorders: An overview. In S. R. Hooper, G. W. Hynd, & R. E. Mattison (Eds.), *Developmental disorders: Diagmostic criteria and clinical assessment.* Hillsdale, NJ: Erlbaum.

Hoover, R. L., & Kindsvatter, R. (1997). *Democratic discipline: Foundation and practice.* Upper Saddle River, NJ: Merrill.

Horn, J. L., & Donaldson, G. (1980). Cognitive development in adulthood. In O. G. Brim, Jr., & J. Kagan (Eds.), *Constancy and change in human development.* Cambridge, MA: Harvard University Press.

Houtz, J. C. (1990). Environments that support creative thinking. In C. N. Hedley & J. Houtz (Eds.), *Cognition, curriculum, and literacy.* Norwood, NJ: Ablex.

Howe, M. J. A. (1998). Early lives: Prodigies and non-prodigies. In A. Steptoe (Ed.) *Genius and the mind: Studies of creativity and temperament.* Oxford, UK: Oxford University Press.

Huber, G. L., Sorrentino, R. M., Davidson, M. A., Epplier, R., & Roth, J. W. H. (1992). Uncertainty orientation and cooperative learning: Individual differences within and across cultures. *Learning and Individual Differences, 4,* 1–24.

Huefner, D. S. (1994). The mainstreaming cases: Tensions and trends for school administrators. *Educational Administration Quarterly, 30,* 27–55.

Huesmann, L. R. (1997). Observational learning of violent behavior: Social and biosocial processes. In A. Raine, P. Brennan, et al. (Eds.), *Biosocial bases of violence. NATO ASI series: Series A: Life sciences, Vol. 292.* New York: Plenum.

Hughes, M., Nowicki, S., & Lohr, B. (1998). Call learning in black-capped chickadees (Parus atricapillus): The role of experience in the development of "chick-a-dee" calls. *Ethology, 104,* 232–249.

Hughes, R. N. (1997). Intrinsic exploration in animals: Motives and measurement. *Behavioral Processes, 41,* 213–226.

Hull, C. L. (1951). *Essentials of behavior.* New Haven, CT: Yale University Press.

Hunt, E. (1989). Cognitive science: Definition, status, and questions. *Annual Review of Psychology, 40,* 603–629.

Hunt, R. R., & Ellis, H. C. (1999). *Fundamentals of cognitive psychology.* New York: McGraw-Hill.

Huntington, D. D., & Bender, W. N. (1993). Adolescents with learning disabilities at risk? Emotional well-being, depression, suicide. *Journal of Learning Disabilities, 26,* 159–166.

Husén, T., & Tuijnman, A. (1991). The contribution of formal schooling to the increase in intellectual capital. *Educational Researcher, 20,* 17–25.

Hyde, J. S., & Jaffee, S. (1998). Perspectives from social and feminist psychology. *Educational Researcher, 27,* 14–17.

Iannaccone, C. J., & Hwang, Y. G. (1998). Transcending social skills oriented instruction within integrated classrooms. *Emotional and Behavioural Difficulties, 3,* 25–29.

Intons-Peterson, M. J. (1988). *Gender concepts of Swedish and American youth.* Hillsdale, NJ: Erlbaum.

Jack, S. L., Shores, R. E., Denny, R. K., & Gunter, P. L. (1996). An analysis of the relationship of teachers' reported use of classroom management strategies on types of classroom interactions. *Journal of Behavioral Education, 6,* 67–87.

Jacklin, C. N. (1989). Female and male: Issues of gender. *American Psychologist, 44,* 127–133.

Jackson, J. F. (1993). Multiple caregiving among African Americans and infant attachment: The need for an emic approach. *Human Development, 36,* 87–102.

Jacobi, M. (1991). Mentoring and undergraduate academic success: A literature review. *Review of Educational Research, 61,* 505–532.

Jacques, N., Wilton, K., & Townsend, M. (1998). Cooperative learning and social acceptance of children with mild intellectual disability. *Journal of Intellectual Disability Research, 42,* 29–36.

James, W. (1890). *The principles of psychology.* New York: Holt, Rinehart & Winston.

Janzen, T., Graap, K., Stephanson, S., Amarshall, W., & Fitzsimmons, G. (1995). Differences in baseline EEG measures for ADD and normally achieving preadolescent males. *Biofeedback and Self Regulation, 20,* 65–82.

Jaspers, K. (1962). *Kant / Karl Jaspers.* (Hannah Arendt, Ed.; Ralph Manheim, Trans.) New York: Harcourt, Brace & World.

Jaspers, K. (1963). *The future of mankind.* Chicago: University of Chicago Press.

Jensen, A. R. (1980). *Bias in mental testing.* London: Methuen.

———— (1998). *The g factor: The science of mental ability.* Westport, CT: Praeger.

Jimenez, M. (1992, Oct. 30). Surviving high school in the '90s. *Edmonton Journal*, pp. A1, A4.

Jiménez, R. T., García, G. E., & Pearson, P. D. (1995). Three children, two languages, and strategic reading: Case studies in bilingual/monolingual education. *American Educational Research Journal, 32,* 67–97.

John, K. R. (1998). Selected short-term memory tests as predictors of reading readiness. *Psychology in the Schools, 35,* 137–144.

Johnson, B. (1996). Constructivism and promoting the child's view. *Educational and Child Psychology, 13,* 68–76.

Johnson, D., & Johnson, R. (1975). *Learning together and alone.* Englewood Cliffs, NJ: Prentice-Hall.

Johnson, D. W., & Johnson, R. T. (1994). *Learning together and alone: Cooperative, competitive, and individualistic learning* (4th ed.). Boston: Allyn & Bacon.

Johnson, D. W., Johnson, R. T., Holubec, E. J., & Roy, P. (1984). *Circles of learning: Cooperation in the classroom.* Alexandria, VA: Association for Supervision and Curriculum Development.

Jonassen, D. H. (1993). Conceptual frontiers in hypermedia environments for learning. *Journal of Educational Multimedia and Hypermedia, 2,* 331–335.

Jones, E. H., & Montenegro, X. P. (1988). *Women and minorities in school administration: Facts and figures, 1987–1988.* Arlington, VA: American Association of School Administrators.

Jones, I. (1998). The effect of computer-generated spoken feedback on kindergarten students' written narratives. *Journal of Computing in Childhood Education, 9,* 43–56.

Jovanovic, J., & King, S. S. (1998). Boys and girls in the performance-based science classroom: Who's doing the performing? *American Educational Research Journal, 35,* 477–496.

Jurczak, P. M. (1997). The language and metaphor of Jean Piaget. *Educational Psychology Review, 9,* 311–318.

Justice, E. (1985). Categorization as a preferred memory strategy: Developmental changes during elementary school. *Developmental Psychology, 21,* 1105–1110.

Juvonen, J., & Bear, G. (1992). Social adjustment of children with and without learning disabilities in integrated classrooms. *Journal of Educational Psychology, 84,* 322–330.

Kagan, D. M. (1988). Teaching as clinical problem solving: A critical examination of the analogy and its implications. *Review of Educational Research, 58,* 482–505.

Kaiser, D. H., Zentall, T. R., & Galef, B. G. Jr., (1997). Can imitation in pigeons be explained by local enhancement together with trial-and-error learning? *Psychological Science, 8,* 459–460.

Kamii, C., & Warrington, M. A. (1997). Multiplication with fractions: A constructivist approach. *Hiroshima Journal of Mathematics Education, 5,* 11–20.

Kamps, D. M., Kravits, T., Gonzalez Lopez, A., Kemmerer, K., Potucek, J., & Harrell, L. G. (1998). What do the peers think? Social validity of peer-mediated programs. *Education and Treatment of Children, 21,* 107–134.

Kanchier, C. (1988). Maximizing potential of gifted and talented students through career education. *Agate, 2,* 6–13.

Kantor, H., & Lowe, R. (1995). Class, race, and the emergence of federal education policy: From the New Deal to the Great Society. *Educational Researcher, 24,* 4–11, 21.

Kaplan, S. L., & Alfonso, V. C. (1997). Confirmatory factor analysis of the Stanford-Binet Intelligence Scale: Fourth edition with preschoolers with developmental delays. *Journal of Psychoeducational Assessment, 15,* 226–236.

Karacostas, D. D., & Fisher, G. L. (1993). Chemical dependency in students with and without learning disabilities. *Journal of Learning Disabilities, 26,* 491–495.

Kauffman, J. M., Lloyd, J. W., & Riedel, T. M. (1995). Inclusion of all students with emotional or behavioral disorders? Let's think again. *Phi Delta Kappan, 76,* 522–530.

Kazelskis, R. (1998). Some dimensions of mathematics anxiety: A factor analysis across instruments. *Educational and Psychological Measurement, 58,* 623–633.

Kegan, R. (1982). *The evolving self: Problem and process in human development.* Cambridge, MA: Harvard University Press.

Keirouz, K. S. (1993). Gifted curriculum: The state of the art. *Gifted Child Today, 16,* 36–39.

Keith, T. Z., & Cool, V. A. (1992). Testing models of school learning: Effects of quality of instruction, motivation, academic coursework, and homework on academic achievement. *School Psychology Quarterly, 7,* 207–226.

Keller, F. S. (1968). Good-bye teacher. . . . *Journal of Applied Behavior Analysis, 1,* 79–89.

Kelly, G. J. (1997). Research traditions in comparative context: A philosophical challenge to radical constructivism. *Science and Education, 81,* 355–375.

Kendall-Tackett, K. A., & Eckenrode, J. (1996). The effects of neglect on academic achievement and disciplinary problems: A developmental perspective. *Child Abuse and Neglect, 20,* 161–169.

Kennedy, M. M. (1978). Findings from the follow-through planned variation study. *Educational Researcher, 7,* 3–11.

———— (1997). The connection between research and practice. *Educational Researcher, 26,* 4–12.

Keogh, B. K., Gallimore, R., & Weisner, T. (1997). A sociocultural perspective on learning and learning disabilities. *Learning Disabilities Research and Practice, 12,* 107–113.

Kiewra, K. A. (1997). Effects of advance organizers and repeated presentations on students' learning. *Journal of Experimental Education, 65,* 147–159.

King, N. J., Ollendick, T. H., Murphy, G. C., & Molloy, G. N. (1998). Utility of relaxation training with children in school settings: A plea for realistic goal setting and evaluation. *British Journal of Educational Psychology, 68,* 53–66.

Kirby, E. A., & Kirby, S. H. (1994). Classroom discipline with attention deficit hyperactivity disorder in children. *Contemporary Education, 65,* 142–144.

Kirby, P. C., & Paradise, L. (1992). Reflective practice and effectiveness of teachers. *Psychological Reports, 70* (special issue), 1057–1058.

Kirschenbaum, H. (1991). Denigrating Carl Rogers: William Coulson's last crusade. *Journal of Counseling and Development, 69,* 411–413.

Kirschenbaum, R. J. (1998). Dynamic assessment and its use with underserved gifted and talented populations. *Gifted Child Quarterly, 42,* 140–147.

Kitchener, R. F. (1996). The nature of the social for Piaget and Vygotsky. *Human Development, 39,* 243–249.

Klein, P. D. (1997). Multiplying the problems of intelligence by eight: A critique of Gardner's theory. *Canadian Journal of Education, 22,* 377–394.

Klein, S. P. (1998). Standards for teacher tests. *Journal of Personnel Evaluation in Education, 12,* 123–138.

Klein, S. S., & Ortman, P. E. (1994). Continuing the journey toward gender equity. *Educational Researcher, 23,* 13–21.

Klingner, J. K., Vaughn, S., & Schumm, J. S. (1998). Collaborative strategic reading during social studies in heterogeneous fourth-grade classrooms. *Elementary School Journal, 99,* 3–22.

Knitzer, J., Steinberg, Z., & Fleisch, B. (1990). *At the school house door: An examination of programs and policies for children with behavioral and emotional problems.* New York: Bank Street College of Education.

Kohl, H. R. (1969). *The open classroom: A practical guide to a new way of teaching.* New York: Random House (Vintage Books).

Kohlberg, L. A. (1964). Development of moral character and moral ideology. In M. L. Hoffman & L. W. Hoffman (Eds.), *Review of child development research* (Vol. 1). New York: Russell Sage Foundation.

———— (1969). Stage and sequence: The cognitive developmental approach to socialization. In D. Gosslin (Ed.), *Handbook of socialization theory and research.* Chicago: Rand McNally.

———— (1971). Stages of moral development as a basis for moral education. In C. Beck, E. V. Sullivan, & B. Crittendon (Eds.), *Moral education: Interdisciplinary approaches.* Toronto: University of Toronto Press.

———— (1980). *The meaning and measurement of moral development.* Worcester, MA: Clark University Press.

Kohlberg, L., & Candee, D. (1984). The relationship of moral judgment to moral action. In W. M. Kurtines & J. L. Gewirtz (Eds.) *Morality, moral behavior, and moral development* (pp. 52–73). New York: Wiley.

Kohn, A. (1993). Choices for children: Why and how to let students decide. *Phi Delta Kappan, 75,* 8–16, 18–21.

Kollins, S. H., Newland, M. C., & Critchfield, T. S. (1997). Human sensitivity to reinforcement in operant choice: How much do consequences matter? *Psychonomic Bulletin and Review, 4,* 208–220.

Korkman, M., & Pesonen, A. E. (1994). A comparison of neuropsychological test profiles of children with attention deficit-hyperactivity disorder and/or learning disorder. *Journal of Learning Disabilities, 27,* 383–392.

Korthagen, F. A. (1993). Two modes of reflection. *Teaching & Teacher Education, 9,* 317–326.

Kottkamp, R. B., Provenzo, E. F., Jr., & Cohn, M. M. (1986). Stability and change in a profession: Two decades of

teacher attitudes, 1964–1984. *Phi Delta Kappan, 67,* 559–567.

Kounin, J. S. (1970). *Discipline and classroom management.* New York: Holt, Rinehart & Winston.

Kozma, R. B. (1991). Learning with media. *Review of Educational Research, 61,* 2, 179–211.

Kramarski, B., & Mevarech, Z. R. (1997). Cognitive-metacognitive training within a problem-solving based Logo environment. *British Journal of Educational Psychology, 67,* 425–445.

Krathwohl, D. R., Bloom, B. S., & Masia, B. B. (1964). *Taxonomy of educational objectives, the classification of educational goals. Handbook II: Affective domain.* New York: McKay.

Krech, D., Rosenzweig, M., & Bennett, E. (1960) Effects of environmental complexity and training on brain chemistry. *Journal of Comparative and Physiological Psychology, 53,* 509–519.

———— (1962). Relations between brain chemistry and problem-solving among rats in enriched and impoverished environments. *Journal of Comparative and Physiological Psychology, 55,* 801–807.

———— (1966). Environmental impoverishment, social isolation, and changes in brain chemistry and anatomy. *Physiology and Behavior, 1,* 99–104.

Krechevsky, M., & Seidel, S. (1998). Minds at work: Applying multiple intelligences in the classroom. In R. J. Sternberg & W. M. Williams (Eds.), *Intelligence, instruction, and assessment.* Mahwah, NJ: Erlbaum.

Kristiansen, R. (1992). Evolution or revolution? Changes in teacher attitudes toward computers in education, 1970–1990. *Education and Computing, 8,* 71–78.

Kubitschek, W. N., & Hallinan, M. T. (1998). Tracking and students' friendships. *Social Psychology Quarterly, 61,* 1–15.

Kuhn, D. (1984). Cognitive development. In M. H. Bornstein & M. E. Lamb (Eds.), *Developmental psychology: An advanced textbook* (pp. 133–180). Hillsdale, NJ: Erlbaum.

Kulik, C. C., Kulik, J. A., & Bangert-Drowns, R. L. (1990). Effectiveness of mastery learning programs: A meta-analysis. *Review of Educational Research, 60,* 265–299.

Kulik, J. A., & Kulik, C. L. (1992). Meta-analytic findings on grouping programs. *Gifted Child Quarterly, 36,* 73–77.

Kulik, J. A., Kulik, C. C., & Cohen, P. A. (1979). A meta-analysis of outcome studies of Keller's Personalized System of Instruction. *American Psychologist, 34,* 307–318.

Kumar, V. K., Kemmler, D., & Holman, E. R. (1997). The Creativity Styles Questionnaire–Revised. *Creativity Research Journal, 10,* 51–58.

Kurland, D. J., Sharp, R. M., & Sharp, V. F. (1997). *Introduction to the internet for education.* Belmont, CA: Wadsworth.

Kurtines, W. M. & Gewirtz, J. L. (Eds.), *Morality, moral behavior, and moral development* (pp. 52–73). New York: Wiley.

Kurtz, P. (1997). *The courage to become: The virtues of humanism.* Westport, CT: Praeger/Greenwood.

Labouvie-Vief, G. (1980). Beyond formal operations: Uses and limits of pure logic in life-span development. *Human Development, 23,* 141–161.

———— (1986). Modes of knowledge and the organization of development. In M. L. Commons, L. Kohlberg, F. A.

Richards, & J. Sinnott (Eds.), *Beyond formal operations. 3: Models and methods in the study of adult and adolescent thought.* New York: Praeger.

Lachs, V., & Dylan, W. (1998). Making the computer dance to your tune: Primary school pupils authoring hypermedia. *Journal of Computing in Childhood Education, 9,* 57–77.

Lam, T. C. L. (1992). Review of practices and problems in the evaluation of bilingual education. *Review of Educational Research, 62,* 181–203.

Lambert, W. E. (1975). Culture and language as factors in learning and education. In A. Wolfgang (Ed.), *Education of immigrant students.* Toronto: Ontario Institute for Studies in Education.

Landry, R. (1987). Additive bilingualism, schooling, and special education: A minority group perspective. *Canadian Journal for Exceptional Children, 3,* 109–114.

Langdon, D. W., Rosenblatt, N., & Mellanby, J. H. (1998). Discrepantly poor verbal skills in poor readers: A failure of learning or ability? *British Journal of Psychology, 89,* 177–190.

Lawrence, M., & Veronica, M. (1997). Secondary school teachers and learning style preferences: Action or watching in the classroom? *Educational Psychology, 17,* 157–170.

Lawson, A. E. (1993). At what levels of education is the teaching of thinking effective? *Theory into Practice, 32,* 170–178.

Larzelere, R. E., Sather, P. R., Schneider, W. N., Larson, D. B., & Pike, P. L. (1998). Punishment enhances reasoning's effectiveness as a disciplinary response to toddlers. *Journal of Marriage & the Family, 60,* 388–403.

Leask, S. J., & Crow, T. J. (1997). How far does the brain lateralize? An unbiased method for determining the optimum degree of hemispheric specialization. *Neuropsychologia, 35,* 1381–1387.

Lechner, J. V., & Barry, N. H. (1997). Multicultural education through art, literature, and music: A study of preservice teachers' perceptions of appropriate materials and methods. *Journal of Research and Development in Education, 30,* 87–102.

Leclerc, G., Lefrançois, R., Dube, M., Hebert, R., & Gaulin, P. (1998). The self-actualization concept: A content validation. *Journal of Social Behavior and Personality, 13,* 69–84.

Lederhouse, J. N. (1997). Caught in the middle: Evangelical public elementary educators. *Anthropology and Education Quarterly, 28,* 182–203.

Lee, D. L., & Belfiore, P. J. (1997). Enhancing classroom performance: A review of reinforcement schedules. *Journal of Behavioral Education, 7,* 205–217.

Lee, E. S. (1951). Negro intelligence and selective migration: A Philadelphia test of the Klineberg hypothesis. *American Sociological Review, 16,* 227–233.

Lee, M. O. C., & Thompson, A. (1997). Guided instruction in logo programming and the development of cognitive monitoring strategies among college students. *Journal of Educational Computing Research, 16,* 125–144.

Lefrançois, G. R. (2000). *Psychological theories and human learning: What the Old Man said* (4th ed.). Belmont, CA: Wadsworth.

Leinhardt, G. (1990). Capturing craft knowledge in teaching. *Educational Researcher, 19,* 18–25.

Lens, W., & Rand, P. (1997). Combining intrinsic goal orientations with professional instrumentality/utility in student motivation. *Polish Psychological Bulletin, 28,* 103–123.

Lepper, M. R., & Greene, D. (1975). Turning play into work: Effects of adult surveillance and extrinsic rewards on children's intrinsic motivation. *Journal of Personality and Social Psychology, 31,* 479–486.

Lepper, M. R., Keavney, M., & Drake, M. (1996). Intrinsic motivation and extrinsic rewards: A commentary on Cameron and Pierce's meta-analysis. *Review of Educational Research, 66,* 5–32.

Lerner, J. W. (1995). *Attention deficit disorders: Assessment and teaching.* Pacific Grove, CA: Brooks/Cole.

Lerner, R. M. (1993). The demise of the nature-nurture dichotomy. *Human Development, 36,* 119–124.

Levin, B. (1983, March). Teachers and standardized achievement tests. *Canadian School Executive,* p. 11.

Levy, G. D. (1993). Introduction: An integrated collection on early gender-role development. *Developmental Review, 13,* 123–125.

Lewis, J. E. (1994). Virtual reality: Ready or not! *Technos, 3,* 12–17.

Lifshitz, H. (1998). Instrumental enrichment: A tool for enhancement of cognitive ability in adult and elderly people with mental retardation. *Education and Training in Mental Retardation, 33,* 34–41.

Liggitt-Fox, D. (1997). Fighting student misconceptions: Three effective strategies. *Science Scope, 20,* 28–30.

Lindholm, K. J., & Aclan, Z. (1991). Bilingual proficiency as a bridge to academic achievement: Results from bilingual/immersion programs. *Journal of Education, 173,* 99–113.

Linn, M. C., & Muilenburg, L. (1996). Creating lifelong science learners: What models form a firm foundation. *Educational Researcher, 25,* 18–24.

Linn, R. L. (1986). Educational testing and assessment: Research needs and policy issues. *American Psychologist, 41,* 1153–1160.

——— (1994). Performance assessment: Policy promises and technical measurement standards. *Educational Researcher, 23,* 4–13.

Litterst, J. K., & Eyo, B. A. (1993). Developing classroom imagination: Shaping and energizing a suitable climate for growth, discovery, and vision. *Journal of Creative Behavior, 27,* 270–282.

Loftus, E. F. (1979). *Eyewitness testimony.* Cambridge, MA: Harvard University Press.

Lohman, D. F. (1993). Teaching and testing to develop fluid abilities. *Educational Researcher, 22,* 12–23.

Lorenz, K. (1952). *King Solomon's ring.* London: Methuen.

Lou, Y., Abrami, P. C., Spence, J. C., Poulsen, C., Chambers, B., & d'Apollonia, S. (1997). Within-class grouping: A meta-analysis. In E. Dubinsky & D. Mathews (Eds.), *Readings in cooperative learning for undergraduate mathematics. MAA notes, No. 44.* Washington, DC: The Mathematical Association of America.

Lourenco, O., & Machado, A. (1996). In defense of Piaget's theory: A reply to 10 common criticisms. *Psychological Review, 103,* 143–164.

Lowenthal, F., Marcourt, C, & Solimando, C. (1998). Cognitive strategies observed during problem solving with LOGO. *Journal of Computer Assisted Learning, 14,* 130–139.

Lowther, D. L., Bassoppo-Moyo, T., & Morrison, G. R. (1998). Moving from computer literate to technologically competent: The next educational reform. *Computers in Human Behavior, 14,* 93–109.

Lubar, J. F., Swartwood, M. O., Swartwood, J. N., & O'Donnell, P. H. (1995). Evaluation of the effectiveness of EEG neurofeedback training for ADHD in a clinical setting as measured by changes in T.O.V.A. scores, behavioral ratings, and WISC-R performance. *Biofeedback and Self-Regulation, 20,* 83–99.

Lukas, K. E., Marr, M. J., & Maple, T. L. (1998). Teaching operant conditioning at the zoo. *Teaching of Psychology, 25,* 112–116.

Lund, D. E. (1994). Conceptions of intelligence in an academic community. *Journal of Educational Thought, 28,* 59–87.

Lunde, J. P., & Barrett, L. A. (1996). Decentralized/departmental reward systems. *New Directions for Teaching & Learning, 65,* 93–98.

Luria, A. R. (1968). *The mind of a mnemonist: A little book about a vast memory.* New York: Avon Books.

Lynch, E. W., Simms, B. H., von Hippel, C. S., & Shuchat, J. (1978). *Mainstreaming preschoolers: Children with mental retardation.* Washington, DC: Head Start Bureau, U.S. Government Printing Office.

Maccoby, E. E., & Jacklin, C. N. (1974). *The psychology of sex differences.* Palo Alto, CA: Stanford University Press.

——— (1980). Sex differences in agression: A rejoinder and reprise. *Child Development, 51,* 964–980.

MacIver, D. J., Reuman, D. A., & Main, S. R. (1995). Social structuring of the school: Studying what is, illuminating what could be. *Annual Review of Psychology , 46,* 375–400.

MacKay, A. (1982). *Project Quest: Teaching strategies and pupil achievement.* Occasional Paper Series, Centre for Research in Teaching, Faculty of Education, University of Alberta, Edmonton, Alberta, Canada.

MacWhinney, B. (1998). Models of the emergence of language. *Annual Review of Psychology, 49,* 199–227.

Maehr, M. L., & Maehr, J. M. (1996). Schools aren't as good as they used to be; they never were. *Educational Researcher, 25,* 21–24.

Mager, R. F. (1962). *Preparing instructional objectives.* Palo Alto, CA: Fearon.

——— (1984). *Preparing instructional objectives* (2nd ed.). Belmont, CA: Pitman Learning.

Maguire, E. A., Burgess, N., Donnett, J. G., Frackowiak, R. S. J., Frith, C. D., & O'Keefe, J. (1998). Knowing where and getting there: A human navigation network. *Science, 280,* 921–924.

Maker, C. J. (1993). Creativity, intelligence, and problem solving: A definition and design for cross-cultural research and measurement related to giftedness. *Gifted Education International, 9,* 68–77.

——— (1996). Identification of gifted minority students: A national problem, needed changes and a promising solution. *Gifted Child Quarterly, 40,* 41–50.

Mann, C. (1994). New technologies and gifted education. *Roeper Review, 16,* 172–176.

Manning, B. H., & Payne, B. D. (1996). Mental deliberations during teaching episodes: Novice teachers versus expert teachers. *Teacher Education Quarterly, 23,* 57–67.

Marcia, J. E. (1966). Development and validation of ego-identity status. *Journal of Personality and Social Psychology, 3,* 551–558.

——— (1980). Identity in adolescence. In J. Adelson (Ed.), *Handbook of adolescent psychology.* New York: John Wiley.

——— (1993). The relational roots of identity. In J. Kroger (Ed.), *Discussions on ego identity.* Hillsdale, NJ: Erlbaum.

Marfo, K., Mulcahy, R. F., Peat, D., Andrews, J., & Cho, S. (1991). Teaching cognitive strategies in the classroom: A content-based instructional model. In R. M. Mulcahy, R. H. Short, & J. Andrews (Eds.), *Enhancing learning and thinking.* New York: Praeger.

Markle, S. M. (1978). *Designs for instructional designers.* Champaign, IL: Stipes.

Markle, S. M., & Tiemann, P. W. (1974). Some principles of instructional design at higher cognitive levels. In R. Ulrich, T. Stachnik, & T. Mabry (Eds.), *Control of human behavior.* Glenview, IL: Scott, Foresman.

Marland, M. (1975). *The craft of the classroom: A survival guide to classroom management at the secondary school.* London: Heinemann Educational Books.

Marland, S. P. (1972). *Education of the gifted and talented.* Washington, DC: U.S. Government Printing Office.

Marlow, A. G., Tingstrom, D. H., Olmi, D. J., & Edwards, R. P. (1997). The effects of classroom-based time-in/time-out on compliance rates in children with speech/language disabilities. *Child & Family Behavior Therapy, 19,* 1–15.

Marques, L., & Thompson, D. (1997). Misconceptions and conceptual changes concerning continental drift and plate tectonics among Portuguese students aged 16–17. *Research in Science and Technological Education, 15,* 195–222.

Marsh, H. W., & Yeung, A. S. (1997). Coursework selection: Relations to academic self-concept and achievement. *American Educational Research Journal, 34,* 691–720.

Marshall, H., & Weinstein, R. (1984). Classroom factors affecting students' self-evaluations: An interactional model. *Review of Educational Research, 54,* 301–325.

Marso, R. N., & Pigge, F. L. (1997). A longitudinal study of persisting and nonpersisting teachers' academic and personal characteristics. *Journal of Experimental Education, 65,* 243–254.

Martin, J. R. (1996). There's too much to teach: Cultural wealth in an age of scarcity. *Educational Researcher, 25,* 4–10, 16.

Martin, N. K., & Baldwin, B. (1996). Helping beginning teachers foster healthy classroom management: Implications for elementary school counselors. *Elementary School Guidance and Counseling, 31,* 106–113.

Martinez, M. E. (1994). Access to information technologies among school-age children: Implications for a democratic society. *Journal of the American Society for Information Science, 45,* 395–400.

Martinsen, O. (1997). The construct of cognitive style and its implications for creativity. *High Ability Studies, 8,* 135–158.

Marton, F., & Saljo, R. (1984). Approaches to learning. In F. Marton, et al. (Eds.), *The experience of learning.* Edinburgh: Scottish Academic Press.

Marzano, R. J. (1993). How classroom teachers approach the teaching of thinking. *Theory into Practice, 32,* 154–160.

———— (1994). Lessons from the field about outcome-based performance assessments. *Educational Leadership, 51,* 44–50.

Masia, C. L., & Chase, P. N. (1997). Vicarious learning revisited: A contemporary behavior analytic interpretation. *Journal of Behavior Therapy and Experimental Psychiatry, 28,* 41–51.

Maslow, A. H. (1970). *Motivation and personality* (2nd ed.). New York: Harper & Row.

———— (1991). How we diminish ourselves. *Journal of Humanistic Education and Development, 29,* 117–120.

Massaro, D. W., & Cowan, N. (1993). Information processing models: Microscopes of the mind. *Annual Review of Psychology, 44,* 383–425.

Masur, E. F. (1993). Transitions in representational ability: Infants' verbal, vocal, and action imitation during the second year. *Merrill-Palmer Quarterly, 39,* 437–455.

Matson, J. V. (1991). Failure 101: Regarding failure in the classroom to stimulate creative behavior. *Journal of Creative Behavior, 25,* 82–85.

Matthews, L. H. (1969). *The life of mammals* (Vol. 1). New York: Universe Books.

Mayer, R. E. (1989). Models for understanding. *Review of Educational Research, 59,* 43–64.

Mayo, K. E. (1993). Learning strategy instruction: Exploring the potential of metacognition. *Reading Improvement, 30,* 130–133.

Mazzoni, G. (1998). Memory suggestibility and metacognition in child eyewitness testimony: The roles of source monitoring and self-efficacy. *European Journal of Psychology of Education, 13,* 43–60.

McCaslin, M., & Good, T. L. (1992). Compliant cognition: The misalliance of management and instructional goals in current school reform. *Educational Researcher, 21,* 4–17.

McClean, L. (1992). Student evaluation in the ungraded primary school: The SCRP principle. In D. J. Bateson (Ed.), *Classroom testing in Canada: Proceedings of the Second Canadian Conference on Classroom Testing, June 1 and 2, 1990.* Vancouver: University of British Columbia, Centre for Applied Studies in Evaluation.

McClelland, D. C. (1958). Risk taking in children with high and low need for achievement. In J. W. Atkinson (Ed.), *Motives in fantasy, action, and society.* Princeton, NJ: Van Nostrand.

———— (1973). Testing for competence rather than for "intelligence." *American Psychologist, 28,* 1–14.

McClelland, D. C., Atkinson, J. W., Clark, R. A., & Lowell, E. L. (1953). *The achievement motive.* New York: Appleton-Century-Crofts.

McClelland, J. L., McNaughton, B. L., & O'Reilly, R. C. (1995). Why there are complementary learning systems in the hippocampus and neocortex: Insights from the successes and failures of connectionist models of learning and memory. *Psychological Review, 102,* 419–457.

McCombs, B. L. (1982). Transitioning learning strategies research into practice: Focus on the student in technical training. *Journal of Instructional Development, 5,* 10–17.

McDonald, J. L. (1997). Language acquisition: The acquisition of linguistic structure in normal and special populations. *Annual Review of Psychology, 48,* 215–241.

McDonnell, A. P., Brownell, K., & Wolery, M. (1997). Teaching experience and specialist support: A survey of preschool teachers employed in programs accredited by NAEYC. *Topics in Early Childhood Special Education, 17,* 263–285.

McDougall, D. (1997). College faculty's use of objective tests: State-of-the-practice versus state-of-the-art. *Journal of Research and Development in Education, 30,* 183–193.

McEneany, J. E. (1990). Do advance organizers facilitate learning? A review of subsumption theory. *Journal of Research and Development in Education, 23,* 89–96.

McFadden, A. C., Marsh, G. E., II, Price, B. J., & Hwang, Y. (1992). A study of race and gender bias in the punishment of school children. *Education and Treatment of Children, 15,* 140–146.

McGill-Franzen, A., & Allington, R. L. (1993). Flunk' em or get them classified: The contamination of primary grade accountability data. *Educational Researcher, 22,* 19–22.

McGlynn, A. P., & Locke, B. J. (1997). A 25-year follow-up of a punishment program for severe self-injury. *Behavioral Interventions, 12,* 203–207.

McKerrow, K. (1997). Ability grouping: Protecting relative advantage. *Journal for a Just and Caring Education, 3,* 333–342.

McMann, N., & Oliver, R. (1988). Problems in families with gifted children: Implications for counselors. *Journal of Counseling and Development, 66,* 275–278.

Mednick, S. A. (1962). The associative basis of the creative process. *Psychological Review, 69,* 220–232.

Mehiel, R. (1997). The consummatory rat: The psychological hedonism of Robert C. Bolles. In Bouton, M. E., & Fanselow, M. S. (Eds.), *Learning, motivation, and cognition: The functional behaviorism of Robert C. Bolles.* Washington, DC: American Psychological Association.

Mensh, E., & Mensh, H. (1991). *The IQ mythology: Class, race, gender, and inequality.* Carbondale: Southern Illinois University Press.

Mercer, C. D. (1990). Learning disability. In N. G. Haring & L. McCormick (Eds.), *Exceptional children and youth* (5th ed.). Columbus, OH: Merrill.

Mergendoller, J. R. (1998). Moving from technological possibility to richer student learning. *Educational Researcher, 25,* 43–46.

Merrett, F., & Wheldall, K. (1992). Teachers' use of praise and reprimands to boys and girls. *Educational Review, 44,* 73–79.

Merritt, R. D., & Kok, C. J. (1997). Implications of the People–Male theory for the interpretation of the Draw-a-Person Test. *Personality Assessment, 68,* 211–214.

Meyer, D. K., Turner, J. C., & Spencer, C.A. (1997). Challenge in a mathematics classroom: Students' motivation and strategies in project-based learning. *Elementary School Journal, 97,* 501–521.

Meyer, M. M., & Fienberg, S. E. (Eds.). (1992). *The case of bilingual education strategies.* Washington, DC: National Academy Press.

Michael, J. (1967). *Management of behavioral consequences in education.* Inglewood, CA: Southwest Regional Laboratory for Educational Research and Development.

Milanowski, A., Odden, A., & Youngs, P. (1998). Teacher knowledge and skill assessments and teacher compensation: An overview of measurement and linkage issues. *Journal of Personnel Evaluation in Education, 12*, 83–101.

Miles, S. (1997). Exploration and discovery: Creating an enthusiastic, exciting classroom. *Early Childhood News, 9*, 36–40.

Milgram, S. (1963). Behavioral study of obedience. *Journal of Abnormal and Social Psychology, 67*, 371–378.

Miller, A., Ferguson, E., & Simpson, R. (1998). The perceived effectiveness of rewards and sanctions in primary schools: Adding in the parental perspective.

Miller, G. A. (1956). The magical number seven, plus or minus two: Some limits on our capacity for processing information. *Psychological Review, 63*, 81–97.

Miller, R. (1990). Beyond reductionism: The emerging holistic paradigm in education. *Humanistic Psychologist, 18*, 314–323.

Millman, J., & Darling-Hammond, L. (Eds.). (1990). *The new handbook of teacher evaluation: Assessing elementary and secondary school teachers.* Newbury Park, CA: Sage.

Miserandino, M. (1998). Attributional retraining as a method of improving athletic performance. *Journal of Sport Behavior, 21*, 286–297.

Moallem, M. (1997). The content and nature of reflective teaching: A case of an expert middle school science teacher. *Clearing House, 70*, 143–150.

Moffitt, A. R. (1971). Consonant cue perception by 20–24 week old infants. *Child Development, 42*, 717–731.

Molfese, V. J., DiLalla, L. F., & Bunce, D. (1997). Prediction of the intelligence test scores of 3- to 8-year-old children by home environment, socioeconomic status, and biomedical risks. *Merrill-Palmer Quarterly, 43*, 219–234.

Moloney, K., & Stacey, K. (1997). Changes with age in students' conceptions of decimal notation. *Mathematics Education Research Journal, 9*, 25–38.

Moore, K. D., & Hanley, P. E. (1982). An identification of elementary teacher needs. *American Educational Research Journal, 19*, 137–144.

Moss, P. A. (1992). Shifting conceptions of validity in educational measurement: Implications for performance assessment. *Review of Educational Research, 62*, 229–258.

Moynahan, E. O. (1973). The development of knowledge concerning the effects of categorization upon free recall. *Child Development, 44*, 238–245.

Mueller, C. M., & Dweck, C. S. (1998). Praise for intelligence can undermine children's motivation and performance. *Journal of Personality and Social Psychology, 75*, 33–52.

Mueller, J. H. (1992a). Anxiety and performance. In A. P. Smith & D. M. Jones (Eds.), *Handbook of human performance* (Vol. 3). London: Academic Press.

———— (1992, April 30). *Test anxiety, study behaviors, and achievement.* Paper presented at the annual meeting of the Western Psychological Association, Portland, Oregon.

Muffoletto, R. (1994). Schools and technology in a democratic society: Equity and social justice. *Educational Technology, 34*, 52–54.

Mulcahy, R. F. (1991). Developing autonomous learners. *Alberta Journal of Educational Research, 37*, 385–397.

Mulcahy, R. F., Marfo, K., Peat, D., Andrews, J., & Clifford, L. (1986). Applying cognitive psychology in the classroom: A learning/thinking strategies instructional program. *Alberta Psychology, 15*, 9–12.

Mulcahy, R. F., Peat, D., Andrews, J., Darko-Yeboah, J., & Marfo, K. (1990). Cognitive-based strategy instruction. In J. Biggs (Ed.), *Learning processes and teaching contexts.* Melbourne: Australian Council for Educational Research.

Munson, K. J., & Crosbie, J. (1998). Effects of response cost in computerized programmed instruction. *Psychological Record, 48*, 233–250.

Murnane, R. J., Singer, J. D., & Willett, J. B. (1988). The career paths of teachers: Implications for teacher supply and methodological lessons for research. *Educational Researcher, 17*, 22–30.

Murray, T. (1998). Authoring knowledge-based tutors: Tools for content, instructional strategy, student model and interface design. *Journal of the Learning Sciences, 7*, 5–64.

Myles, B. S., & Simpson, R. L. (1994). Understanding and preventing acts of aggression and violence in school-age children and youth. *Preventing School Failure, 38*, 40–46.

Naglieri, J. A. (1988). *DAP; draw a person: A quantitative scoring system.* New York: Harcourt Brace Jovanovich.

Naglieri, J. A., & Das, J. P. (1997). Cognitive assessment system. Chicago, IL: Riverside.

Nagy, P., & Griffiths, A. K. (1982). Limitations of recent research relating Piaget's theory to adolescent thought. *Review of Educational Research, 52*, 513–556.

Nahl-Jakobovits, D., & Jakobovits, L. A. (1993). Bibliographic instructional design for information literacy: Integrating affective and cognitive objectives. *Research Strategies, 11*, 73–88.

Natale, J. A. (1994). Your life is on the line. *Executive Educator, 16*, 22–26.

National Center for Education Statistics. (1989). *Digest of education statistics.* 1989 (25th ed.). Washington, DC: U.S. Department of Education.

National Commission on Excellence in Education. (1983). *A nation at risk: The imperative for educational reform.* Washington, DC: U.S. Government Printing Office.

Neisser, U. (1976). *Cognition and reality.* San Francisco: Freeman.

Nelson, C., & Pearson, C. (1991). *Integrating services for children and youth with emotional and behavior disorders.* Reston, VA: Council of Exceptional Children.

Newman, H. H., Freeman, F. N., & Holzinger, G. M. (1937). *Twins: A study of heredity and environment.* Chicago: University of Chicago Press.

Nickerson, R. S. (1988). On improving thinking through instruction. In E. Z. Rothkopf (Ed.), *Review of research in education* (Vol. 15). Washington, DC: American Educational Research Association.

Nicolopoulou, A. (1993). Play, cognitive development, and the social world: Piaget, Vygotsky, and beyond. *Human Development, 36,* 1–23.

Noble, K. D., & Smyth, R. K. (1995). Keeping their talents alive: Young women's assessment of radical, post-secondary acceleration. *Roeper Review, 18,* 49–55.

Nolen, S. B., Haladyna, T. M., & Haas, N. S. (1992). Uses and abuses of achievement test scores. *Educational Measurement: Issues and Practices, 11,* 9–15.

Norris, D., & Pyke, L. H. (1992). Entrepreneurship in open education. *Australian Journal of Adult and Community Education, 32,* 168–176.

Novak, J. D. (1993). Human constructivism: A unification of psychological and epistemological phenomena in meaning making. *International Journal of Personal Construct Psychology, 6,* 167–193.

Nunes, T., Carraher, D. W., & Schliemann, A. D. (1993). *Street mathematics and school mathematics.* New York: Cambridge University Press.

Nussbaum, J. (1979). Children's conception of the earth as a cosmic body: A cross age study. *Science Education, 63,* 83–93.

Oakes, J. (1997). Detracking: The social construction of ability, cultural politics, and resistance to reform. *Teachers College Record, 98,* 482–510.

Oakes, J., & Guiton, G. (1995). Matchmaking: The dynamics of high school tracking decisions. *American Educational Research Journal, 32,* 3–33.

Ochoa, S. H., Rivera, B., & Ford, L. (1997). An investigation of school psychology training pertaining to bilingual psycho-educational assessment of primarily Hispanic students: Twenty-five years after Diana v. California. *Journal of School Psychology, 35,* 329–349.

Ogbu, J. U. (1994). Understanding cultural diversity and learning. *Journal for the Education of the Gifted, 17,* 354–383.

O'Leary, K. D., & Becker, W. C. (1968). The effects of a teacher's reprimands on children's behavior. *Journal of School Psychology, 7,* 8–11.

O'Leary, K. D., Kaufman, K. F., Kass, R. E., & Drabman, R. S. (1974). The effects of loud and soft reprimands on the behavior of disruptive students. In A. R. Brown & C. Avery (Eds.), *Modifying children's behavior: A book of readings.* Springfield, IL: Charles C. Thomas.

O'Leary, M., & Shiel, G. (1997). Curriculum profiling in Australia and the United Kingdom: Some implications for performance-based assessment in the United States. *Educational Assessment, 4,* 203–235.

Olson, B., & Douglas, W. (1997). The family on television: Evaluation of gender roles in situation comedy. *Sex Roles, 36,* 409–427.

O'Neil, J. (1993). Making sense of outcome-based education. *Instructor, 102,* 46–47.

Onwuegbuzie, A. J. & Daley, C. E. (1998). Similarity of learning styles of students and a teacher in achievement in a research methods course. *Psychological Reports, 82,* 163–168.

Oosterhof, A. (1994). *Classroom applications of educational measurement.* New York: Macmillan.

Orford, E. (1998). Wrestling with the whirlwind: An approach to the understanding of ADD/ADHD. *Journal of Child Psychotherapy, 24,* 253–266.

Ornstein, A. C. (1993a). How to recognize good teaching. *American School Board Journal, 180,* 24–27.

Ozar, L. A. (1994). Diverse assessment—key to richer learning. *Momentum, 25,* 53–56.

Padilla, A. M. (1991). English only vs. bilingual education: Ensuring a language-competent society. *Journal of Education, 173,* 38–51.

Page, E. B., & Grandon, G. M. (1979). Family configuration and mental ability: Two theories contrasted with U.S. data. *American Educational Research Journal, 16,* 257–272.

Pajares, M. F. (1992). Teachers' beliefs and educational research: Cleaning up a messy construct. *Review of Educational Research, 62,* 307–332.

Palardy, J. M. (1991). Behavior modification: It does work, but . . . *Journal of Instructional Psychology, 19,* 127–131.

Palincsar, M. S., & Brown, A. L. (1984). Reciprocal teaching of comprehension—fostering and monitoring activities. *Cognitive Instruction, 1,* 117–175.

Pallas, A. M. (1993). Schooling in the course of human lives: The social context of education and the transition to adulthood in industrial society. *Review of Educational Research, 63,* 408–477.

Palmares, U., & Logan, B. (1975). *A curriculum on conflict management.* Palo Alto, CA: Human Development Training Institute.

Papalia, D. F. (1972). The status of several conservative abilities across the life-span. *Human Development, 15,* 229–243.

Papert, S. (1987). Computer criticism vs. technocentric thinking. *Educational Researcher, 16* (1), 22–30.

Papert, S. (1993). *The children's machine: Rethinking school in the age of the computer.* New York: Basic Books.

Paris, S. G., Lawton, T. A., Turner, J. C., & Roth, J. L. (1991). A developmental perspective on standardized achievement testing. *Educational Researcher, 20,* 12–20.

Parker, S. (1997). *Reflective teaching in the postmodern world: A manifesto for education in postmodernity.* Buckingham, PA: Open University Press.

Parker, W. D. (1998). Birth-order effects in the academically gifted. *Gifted Child Quarterly, 42,* 29–38.

Parnes, S. J. (1967). *Creative behavior workbook.* New York: Scribner's.

Parnes, S. J., & Harding, H. F. (Eds.). (1962). *A sourcebook for creative thinking.* New York: Scribner's.

Parse, R. R. (1998). *The human becoming school of thought: A perspective for nurses and other health professionals.* Thousand Oaks, CA: Sage.

Parshall, G. (1995, Sept. 25). A 'glorious mongrel.' *U.S. News and World Report.* p. 48.

Parsons, J. B. (1983). The seductive computer: Can it be resisted? *ATA Magazine, 63,* 12–14.

Pasch, M., Langer, G., Gardner, T. G., Starko, A. J., & Moody, C. D. (1995). *Teaching as decision making: Successful practices for the elementary teacher* (2nd ed.). White Plains, NY: Longman.

Patterson, C. H., & Purkey, W. W. (1993). The preparation of humanistic teachers for schools of the next century. *Journal of Humanistic Education and Development, 31,* 147–155.

Patton, J. R., & Polloway, E. A. (1990). Mild mental retardation. In N. G. Haring & L. McCormick (Eds.), *Exceptional children and youth* (5th ed.). Columbus, OH: Merrill.

Paulus, P. B., & Paulus, L. E. (1997). Implications of research on group brainstorming for gifted education. *Roeper Review, 19,* 225–229.

Pear, J. J., & Novak, M. (1996). Computer-aided personalized system of instruction: A program evaluation. *Teaching of Psychology, 23,*119–123.

Pearman, E. L., Huang, A. M., & Mellblom, C. I. (1997). The inclusion of all students: Concerns and incentives of educators. *Education and Training in Mental Retardation, 32,* 11–20.

Pease-Alvarez, L., & Hakuta, K. (1992). Enriching our views of bilingualism and bilingual education. *Educational Researcher, 2,* 4–6.

Peat, D., Mulcahy, R. F., & Darko-Yeboah, J. (1989). SPELT (Strategies Program for Effective Learning/Thinking): A description and analysis of instructional procedures. *Instructional Science, 18,* 95–118.

Peat, D., Wilgosh, L., & Mulcahy, R. (1996). Efficacy of cognitive strategy-based instruction for elementary students with learning disabilities: A retrospective study. *Canadian Journal of School Psychology, 12,* 135–142.

Pelham, W. E., Jr., Carlson, C., Sams, S. E., Vallano, G., Dixon, M. J., & Hoza, B. (1993). Separate and combined effects of methylphenidate and behavior modification on boys with attention deficit-hyperactivity disorder in the classroom. *Journal of Consulting & Clinical Psychology, 61,* 506–515.

Peloquin, S. M. (1996). Using the arts to enhance confluent learning. *American Journal of Occupational Therapy, 50,* 148–151.

Percy, R. L. (1990). The effects of teacher effectiveness training on the attitudes and behaviors of classroom teachers. *Education Research Quarterly, 14,* 15–20.

Pérez, B., & Torres-Guzmán, M. E. (1992). *Learning in two worlds: An integrated Spanish/English biliteracy approach.* New York: Longman.

Perez, S. A. (1994). Responding differently to diversity. *Childhood Education, 70,* 151–153.

Perry, P., Pasnak, R., & Holt, R. W. (1992). Instruction on concrete operations for children who are mildly mentally retarded. *Education and Training in Mental Retardation, 27,* 273–281.

Perry, R. (1966). *The world of the polar bear.* Seattle: University of Washington Press.

Petersen, A. C. (1988). Adolescent development. *Annual Review of Psychology, 39,* 583–607.

Peterson, C. (1997). Why am I teaching this? *Science Scope, 21,* 18–21.

Petrie, D., & Willis, C. (1998). Morality and sexual issues in older adolescent females. *Journal of Social Distress and the Homeless, 7,* 121–135.

Piaget, J. (1932). *The moral judgment of the child.* London: Kegan Paul.

——— (1954). *The construction of reality in the child.* New York: Basic Books.

——— (1960). *The child's conception of the world.* London: Routledge.

——— (1961). The genetic approach to the psychology of thought. *Journal of Educational Psychology, 52,* 275–281.

——— (1972). Intellectual development from adolescence to adulthood. *Human Development, 15,* 1–12.

Pica, L., Jr., & Margolis, H. (1993). What to do when behavior modification is not working. *Preventing School Failure, 37,* 29–33.

Pillay, H. (1998). An investigation of the effect of individual cognitive preferences on learning through computer-based instruction. *Educational Psychology, 18,* 171–182.

Pinard, A., & Laurendeau, M. (1964). A scale of mental development based on the theory of Piaget: Description of a project (A. B. Givens, Trans.). *Journal of Research and Science Teaching, 2,* 253–260.

Plewis, I. (1997). Inferences about teacher expectations from national assessment at Key Stage One. *British Journal of Educational Psychology, 67,* 235–247.

Plomin, R., Fulker, D. W., Corley, R., & DeFries, J. C. (1997). Nature, nurture, and cognitive development from 1 to 16 years: A parent-offspring study. *Psychological Science, 8,* 442–447.

Plucker, J. A. (1996). Gifted Asian-American students: Identification, curricular, and counseling concerns. *Journal for the Education of the Gifted, 19,* 315–343.

Polloway, E. A. (1997). Developmental principles of the Luckasson et al. (1992) AAMR definition of mental retardation: A retrospective. *Education and Training in Mental Retardation, 32,* 174–178.

Polloway, E. A., Patton, J. R., Smith, T. E. C., & Buck, G. H. (1997). Mental retardation and learning disabilities: Conceptual and applied issues. *Journal of Learning Disabilities, 30,* 297–308.

Popham, W. J. (1994). The instructional consequences of criterion-referenced clarity. *Educational Measurement: Issues and Practice, 13,* 15–18.

——— (1999). *Classroom assessment: What teachers need to know* (2nd ed.). Boston, MA: Allyn and Bacon.

Porter, C., & Cleland, J. (1995). *The portfolio as a learning strategy.* Portsmouth, NH: Boynton/Cook.

Prawat, R. S. (1991). The value of ideas: The immersion approach to the development of thinking. *Educational Researcher, 20,* 3–10.

Premack, D. (1965). Reinforcement theory. In D. Levine (Ed.), *Nebraska Symposium on Motivation.* Lincoln: University of Nebraska Press.

Presland, J. (1989). Behavioural approaches. In T. Charlton & K. David (Eds.), *Managing misbehaviour: Strategies for effective management of behaviour in schools.* London: Macmillan.

Presno, C. (1997). Bruner's three forms of representation revisited: Action, pictures and words for effective computer instruction. *Journal of Instructional Psychology, 24,* 112–118.

Purkey, W. W. (1984). *Inviting school success: A self-concept approach to teaching and learning* (2nd ed.). Belmont, CA: Wadsworth.

Purkey, W. W., & Novak, J. M. (1996). *Inviting school success: a self-concept approach to teaching, learning, and democratic practice* (3rd ed.). Belmont, CA : Wadsworth.

Qin, Z., Johnson, D. W., & Johnson, R. T. (1995). Cooperative versus competitive efforts and problem solving. *Review of Educational Research, 65*, 129–143.

Rafferty, C. D., & Fleschner, L. K. (1993). Concept mapping: A viable alternative to objective and essay exams. *Reading Research and Instruction, 32*, 25–34.

Raines, H. H. (1994). Tutoring and teaching: Continuum, dichotomy, or dialectic. *Writing Center Journal, 14*, 150–162.

Ramsden, P. (1988a). Studying learning: Improving teaching. In P. Ramsden (Ed.), *Improving learning: New perspectives*. London: Kogan Page.

Randhawa, B. S., & Pavelich, B. (1997). Evidence on validity for the Teaching Behavior Rating Scale. *Psychological Reports, 81*, 451–461.

Raphael, B. (1976). *The thinking computer: Mind inside matter*. San Francisco: Freeman.

Raskins, M. H., & Higgins, E. L. (1998). Assistive technology for postsecondary students with learning disabilities: An overview. *Journal of Learning Disabilities, 31*, 27–40.

Rayner, S., & Riding, R. (1997). Towards a categorisation of cognitive styles and learning styles. *Educational Psychology, 17*, 5–27.

Reay, D. A. (1994). *Understanding how people learn*. East Brunswick, NJ: Nichols.

Reed, E. W. (1997–98). Projects and activities: A means, not an end. *American Educator, 21*, 26–27.

Reffel, J. A. (1998). Cued vs. free recall in long-term memory of the fifty United States. *Current Psychology: Developmental, Learning, Personality, Social, 16*, 308–315.

Rehfeldt, R. A., & Hayes, L. J. (1998). The operant-respondent distinction revisited: Toward an understanding of stimulus equivalence. *Psychological Record, 48*, 187–210.

Reid, R. M., John, W., Vasa, S. F., & Wright, G. (1994). Who are the children with attention deficit-hyperactivity disorder? A school-based survey. *Journal of Special Education, 28*, 117–137.

Reiff, J. C. (1992). *Learning styles*. Washington, DC: National Education Association.

Renzulli, J. S. (1977). *The enrichment triad model: A guide for developing defensible programs for the gifted and talented*. Mansfield Center, CT: Creative Learning Press.

——— (1986). The three-ring conception of giftedness: A developmental model for creative productivity. In R. J. Sternberg & J. E. Davidson (Eds.), *Conceptions of giftedness*. Cambridge: Cambridge University Press.

Renzulli, J. S., & Reis, S. M. (1994). Research related to the schoolwide enrichment triad model. *Gifted Child Quarterly, 38*, 7–20.

Renzulli, J. S., & Smith, L. H. (1978). *The learning styles inventory: A measure of student preference for instructional techniques*. Mansfield Center, CT: Creative Learning Press.

Renzulli, J. S., Reis, S. M., & Smith, L. H. (1981). *The revolving door identification model*. Mansfield Center, CT: Creative Learning Press.

Resnick, L. B. (1981). Instructional psychology. *Annual Review of Psychology, 32*, 659–704.

Rhine, S. (1998). The role of research and teachers' knowledge base in professional development. *Educational Researcher, 5*, 27–31.

Rich, J. M. (1993). Discipline and moral development. *High School Journal, 76*, 139–144.

Rich, Y. (1993). Stability and change in teacher expertise. *Teaching and Teacher Education, 9*, 137–146.

Richards, R. (1994). Creativity and bipolar mood swings: Why the association? In M. P. Shaw & M. A. Runco (Eds.), *Creativity and affect*. Norwood, NJ: Ablex.

Riethmiller, R. J., & Handler, L. (1997). Problematic methods and unwarranted conclusions in DAP research: Suggestions for improved research procedures. *Journal of Personality Assessment, 69*, 459–475.

Robinson, A., & Clinkenbeard, P. R. (1998). Giftedness: An exceptionality examined. *Annual Review of Psychology, 49*, 117–139.

Robinson, N. M. (1992). Radical acceleration in the People's Republic of China: Early entrance to university. *Roeper Review, 14*, 189–192.

Robinson, N. M., Abbott, R. D., Berninger, V. W., & Busse, J. (1996). Structure of abilities in math-precocious young children: Gender similarities and differences. *Journal of Educational Psychology, 88*, 341–352.

Rogers, C. R. (1951). *Client-centered therapy: Its current practice, implications and theory*. Boston: Houghton Mifflin.

——— (1957). The necessary and sufficient conditions of therapeutic personality change. *Journal of Consulting Psychology, 21*, 195–203. (Reprinted in 1992, *Journal of Consulting and Clinical Psychology, 60*, 827–832.)

——— (H. Kirschenbaum & V. L. Henderson, Eds.). (1989). *The Carl Rogers reader*. Boston, MA: Houghton Mifflin.

Rogers, C. R., & Freiberg, H. J. (1994). *Freedom to learn* (4th ed.). New York: Merrill.

Rogers, C. R., & Skinner, B. F. (1956). Some issues concerning the control of human behavior: A symposium. *Science, 124*, 1057–1066. (Reprinted in 1990, *TACD Journal, 18*, 79–102.)

Rogers, K. B. (1998). Using current research to make "good" decisions about grouping. *NASSP Bulletin, 82*, 38–46.

Rojewski, J. W., & Schell, J. W. (1994). Cognitive apprenticeship for learners with special needs: An alternate framework for teaching and learning. *Remedial and Special Education, 15*, 234–243.

Rose, R. J. (1995). Genes and human behavior. *Annual Review of Psychology, 46*, 625–654.

Rosen, M. (1995). Gender differences in structure, means and variances of hierarchically ordered ability dimensions. *Learning and Instruction, 5*, 37–62

Rosenkoetter, L. I., Huston, A. C., & Wright, J. C. (1990). Television and the moral judgment of the young child. *Journal of Applied Developmental Psychology, 11*, 123–137.

Rosenshine, B., & Meister, C. (1994). Reciprocal teaching: A review of the research. *Review of Educational Research, 64,* 479–530.

Rosenshine, B., & Stevens, R. (1986). Teaching functions. In M. C. Wittrock (Ed.), *Handbook of research on teaching* (3rd ed.). New York: Macmillan.

Rosenthal, R. (1987). Pygmalion effects: Existence, magnitude, and social importance. A reply to Wineburg. *Educational Researcher, 16,* 37–41.

Rosenthal, R., & Jacobson, L. (1968a). *Pygmalion in the classroom: Teacher expectations and pupils' intellectual development.* New York: Holt, Rinehart & Winston.

———— (1968b, April). Teacher expectations for the disadvantaged. *Scientific American, 218,* 19–23.

Ross, A. O. (1980). *Psychological disorders of children: A behavioral approach to theory, research, and therapy* (2nd ed.). New York: McGraw-Hill.

Ross, R. P. (1984). Classroom segments: The structuring of school time. In L. W. Anderson (Ed.), *Time and school learning: Theory, research and practice.* London: Croom Helm.

Ross, S. M., Rakow, E. A., & Bush, A. J. (1980). Instructional adaptation for self-managed learning systems. *Journal of Educational Psychology, 72,* 312–320.

Ross, T. W. (1993, Fall–Winter). Bloom and hypertext: Parallel taxonomies? *Ed-Tech Review,* pp. 11–16.

Rost, D. H., & Hanses, P. (1997). Not achieving—not gifted? About the identification of gifted underachievers by teacher ratings. *Zeitschrift für Entwicklungspsychologie und Pædagogische Psychologie, 29,* 167–177.

Roth, W. M. (1993). Metaphors and conversational analysis as tools in reflection on teaching practice: Two perspectives on teacher–student interactions in open-inquiry science. *Science Education, 77,* 351–373.

Roth, W. M., & Bowen, M. (1993). Maps for more meaningful learning. *Science Scope, 16,* 24–25.

Rothenberg, R. (1989). The open classroom reconsidered. *Elementary School Journal, 90,* 69–86.

Rowan, J. (1998). Maslow amended. *Journal of Humanistic Psychology, 38,* 81–92.

Rowe, J. (1991). Perspectives on adoption. In E. D. Hibbs (Ed.), *Adoption: International perspectives.* Madison, CT: International Universities Press.

Rowatt, W. C., Nesselroade, K. P. Jr., Beggan, J. K., & Allison, S. T. (1997). Perceptions of brainstorming in groups: The quality over quantity hypothesis. *Journal of Creative Behavior, 31,* 131–150.

Roy, P., & Hoch, J. (1994). Cooperative learning: A principal's perspective. *Principal, 73,* 27–29.

Rubin, J. Z. (1994). Models of conflict management. *Journal of Social Issues, 50,* 33–45.

Rubin, K. H., Attewell, P. W., Tierney, M. C., & Tumolo, P. (1973). Development of spatial egocentrism and conservation across the life-span. *Developmental Psychology, 9,* 432–437.

Rudenberg, S. L., Jansen, P., & Fridjhon, P. (1998). The effect of exposure during an ongoing climate of violence on children's self-perceptions, as reflected in drawings. *South African Journal of Psychology, 28,* 107–115.

Rushton, J. (1988). Race differences in behaviour: A review and evolutionary analysis. *Journal of Personality and Individual Differences, 9,* 1009–1024.

Rust, F. O. (1994). The first year of teaching: It's not what they expected. *Teaching and Teacher Education, 10,* 205–217.

Ryan, A. M., & Greguras, G. J. (1998). Life is not multiple choice: Reactions to the alternatives. In M. D. Hakel (Ed.), *Beyond multiple choice: Evaluating alternatives to traditional testing for selection,* Mahwah, NJ: Erlbaum.

Ryan, E. R., Hawkins, M. J., & Russell, R. (1992). Education: An exchange of ideas among three humanistic psychologists. *Journal of Humanistic Education and Development, 30,* 178–191.

Ryan, F. J. (1994). From rod to reason: Historical perspectives on corporal punishment in the public school, 1642–1994. *Educational Horizons, 72,* 70–77.

Sadker, M., & Sadker, D. (1986). Sexism in the classroom: From grade school to graduate school. *Phi Delta Kappan, 68,* 512.

Sadker, M., Sadker, D., & Klein, S. (1991). In G. Grant (Ed.), *Review of research in education* (Vol. 17). Washington, DC: American Educational Research Association.

Sadler-Smith, E. (1997). "Learning style": Frameworks and instruments. *Educational Psychology, 17,* 51–63.

Salomon, G., & Gardner, H. (1986). The computer as educator: Lessons from television research. *Educational Researcher, 15,* 13–19.

Salomon, G., & Perkins, D. N. (1998). Individual and social aspects of learning. In P. D. Pearson & A. Iran-Nejad (Eds.), *Review of Research in Education, 23,* 1–24.

Samuda, R. J. (1998). *Psychological testing of American minorities: Issues and consequences* (2nd ed.). Thousand Oaks, CA: Sage.

Sanger, M. J., & Greenbowe, T. J. (1997). Students' misconceptions in electrochemistry: Current flow in electrolyte solutions and the salt bridge. *Journal of Chemical Education, 74,* 819–823.

Sarason, I. G. (1980). Introduction to the study of test anxiety. In I. G. Sarason (Ed.), *Test anxiety: Theory, research, and applications.* Hillsdale, NJ: Erlbaum.

Scarr, S. (1985). Constructing psychology: Making facts and fables for our times. *American Psychologist, 40,* 499–512.

Schacter, D. L., Norman, K. A., & Koutstaal, W. (1998). The cognitive neuroscience of constructive memory. *Annual Review of Psychology, 49,* 289–318.

Schank, R. C., & Abelson, R. P. (1977). *Scripts, plans, goals and understanding.* Hillsdale, NJ: Erlbaum.

Schlangen, B., & Steinsmeier-Pelster, J. (1997). Implicit theories of intelligence among schoolchildren. *Zeitschrift für Entwicklungspsychologie und Pædagogische Psychologie, 29,* 301–329.

Schmuck, R. A., & Schmuck, P. A. (1997). *Group processes in the classroom* (7th ed.). Madison, WI: Brown & Benchmark.

Schofield, J. W., Eurich-Fulcer, R., & Britt, C. L. (1994). Teachers, computer tutors, and teaching: The artificially intelligent tutor as an agent for classroom change. *American Educational Research Journal, 31,* 579–607.

Schraw, G. (1998). Promoting general metacognitive awareness. *Instructional Science, 26,* 113–125.

Schraw, G., & Aplin, B. (1998). Teacher preferences for mastery-oriented students. *Journal of Educational Research, 91,* 215–220.

Schultz, D. P. (1964). *Panic behavior.* New York: Random House.

Schwill, A. (1997). Fundamental ideas: Rethinking computer science education. *Learning and Leading with Technology, 25,* 28–31.

Scott, M. S., Duel, L. L. S., Jean-Francois, B., & Urbano, R. C. (1996). Identifying cognitively gifted ethnic minority children. *Gifted Child Quarterly, 40,* 147–153.

Sears, R. R., Maccoby, E. P., & Lewin, H. (1957). *Patterns of child rearing.* Evanston, IL: Row, Peterson.

Sehr, D. T. (1997). *Education for public democracy.* Albany, NY: State University of New York Press.

Semb, G. B., & Ellis, J. A. (1994). Knowledge taught in school: What is remembered? *Review of Educational Research, 64,* 253–286.

Semrud-Clikeman, M., & Hynd, G. W. (1992). Developmental arithmetic disorder. In S. R. Hooper, G. W. Hynd, & R. E. Mattison (Eds.), Developmental disorders: *Diagnostic criteria and clinical assessment.* Hillsdale, NJ: Erlbaum.

Serbin, L. A., Powlishta, K. K., & Gulko, J. (1993). The development of sex typing in middle childhood. *Monographs of the Society for Research in Child Development,* 58, No. 2.

Sesno, A. H. (1998). *97 savvy secrets for protecting self and school: A practical guide for today's teachers and administrators.* Thousand Oaks, CA: Corwin.

Sfard, A. (1998). On two metaphors for learning and the dangers of choosing just one. *Educational Researcher, 27,* 4–13.

Shabo, A., Guzdial, M., & Stasko, J. (1997). An apprenticeship-based multimedia courseware for computer graphics studies provided on the World Wide Web. *Computers and Education, 29,* 103–116.

Shaklee, B. D. (1992). Identification of young gifted students. *Journal for the Education of the Gifted, 15,* 134–144.

Shanahan, T. (1998). On the effectiveness and limitations of tutoring in reading. In P. D. Pearson & A. Iran-Nejad (Eds.), *Review of Research in Education, 23,* 217–234.

Shannon, T. A. (1994). Salmon's laws. *Executive Educator, 16,* 52–54.

Shapiro, S. B. (1995a). Training effects of one academic year on instructional values of MA students in confluent education and counseling psychology. *Psychological Reports, 76,* 225–226.

———— (1995b). Training effects of one academic year on the instructional values of MA students in confluent education and counseling psychology: A follow-up study. *Psychological Reports, 77,* 792–794.

———— (1995c). Training effects of one academic year on the instructional values of MA students in confluent education and counseling psychology: A second follow-up study. *Psychological Reports, 77,* 1305–1306.

———— (1997). The UCSB Confluent Education program: Its essence and demise. *Journal of Humanistic Psychology, 37,* 80–105.

———— (1998). *The place of confluent education in the human potential movement.* Lanham, MD: University Press of America.

Sharan, Y., & Sharan, S. (1992). *Expanding cooperative learning through group investigation.* New York: Columbia University, Teachers College Press.

Shepard, L. A., Smith, M. L., & Vojir, C. P. (1983). Characteristics of pupils identified as learning disabled. *American Educational Research Journal, 20,* 309–331.

Sherman, J. G. (1992). Reflections on PSI: Good news and bad. *Journal of Applied Behavior Analysis, 25,* 59–64.

Shermis, M. D., & Lombard, D. (1998). Effects of computer-based test administrations on test anxiety and performance. *Computers in Human Behavior, 14,* 111–123.

Shohamy, E. (1997). Testing methods, testing consequences: Are they ethical? Are they fair? *Language Testing, 14,* 340–349.

Shuler, S. C. (1996). Assessing teacher competence in the arts: Should Mr. Holland have gotten the gig? Introduction to the Symposium on Teacher Evaluations. *Arts Education Policy Review, 98,* 11–15.

Shulman, L. S. (1986). Paradigms and research programs in the study of teaching. In M. C. Wittrock (Ed.), *Handbook of research on teaching* (3rd ed.). New York: Macmillan.

Skaalvik, E. M., & Rankin, R. J. (1995). A test of the internal/external frame of reference model at different levels of math and verbal self-perception. *American Educational Research Journal, 32,* 161–184.

Skinner, B. F. (1948). *Walden II.* New York: Macmillan.

———— (1953). *Science and human behavior.* New York: Macmillan.

———— (1954). The science of learning and the art of teaching. *Harvard Educational Review, 24,* 86–97.

———— (1961). *Cumulative record* (rev. ed.). New York: Appleton-Century-Crofts.

———— (1965, October 16). Why teachers fail. *Saturday Review,* pp. 80–81, 98–102.

———— (1968). *The technology of teaching.* New York: Appleton-Century-Crofts.

———— (1969). *Contingencies of reinforcement: A theoretical analysis.* New York: Appleton-Century-Crofts.

———— (1971). *Beyond freedom and dignity.* New York: Knopf.

Slate, J. R., Jones, C. H., Sloas, S., & Blake, P. C. (1998). Scores on the Stanford Achievement Test-8 as a function of sex: Where have the sex differences gone? *High School Journal, 81,* 82–86.

Slavin, R. E. (1983). *Student team learning: An overview and practical guide.* Washington, DC: National Education Association.

———— (1987). Mastery learning reconsidered. *Review of Educational Research, 57,* 175–213.

———— (1993a). Ability grouping in the middle grades: Achievement effects and alternatives. *Elementary School Journal, 93,* 535–552.

———— (1995). *Cooperative learning: Theory, research, and practice* (2nd ed.). Boston: Allyn & Bacon.

Smedler, A. C., & Torestad, B. (1996). Verbal intelligence: A key to basic skills. *Educational Studies, 22,* 343–356.

Smith, G. P. (1995). Pavlov and appetite. *Integrative Physiological and Behavioral Science, 30,* 169–174.

Smith, K., & Tillema, H. (1998). Evaluating portfolio use as a learning tool for professionals. *Scandinavian Journal of Educational Research, 42,* 193–205.

Smith, K. E. (1997). Student teachers' beliefs about developmentally appropriate practice: Pattern, stability, and the influence of locus of control. *Early Childhood Research Quarterly, 12,* 221–243.

Smith, L. (1993). *Necessary knowledge: Piagetian perspectives on constructivism.* Hillsdale, NJ: Erlbaum.

Smith, M. A., & Misra, A. (1992). A comprehensive management system for students in regular classrooms. *Elementary School Journal, 92,* 353–372.

Smith, M. L. (1991). Put to the test: The effects of external testing on teachers. *Educational Researcher, 20,* 8–11.

Snow, R. E., & Swanson, J. (1992). Instructional psychology: Aptitude, adaptation, and assessment. *Annual Review of Psychology, 43,* 583–626.

Snowman, J. (1993). Research alive: How accurate is the conventional wisdom about classroom testing practices? *Midwestern Educational Researcher, 6,* 19–20.

Snyder, E. P., & Shapiro, E. S. (1997). Teaching students with emotional/behavioral disorders the skills to participate in the development of their own IEPs. *Behavioral Disorders, 22,* 246–259.

Soloman, G. (1992). Technology and the balance of power. *The Computing Teacher, 19,* 10–11.

Soloman, J. (1993). Four frames for a field. In P. J. Black & A. M. Lucas (Eds.), *Children's informal ideas in science.* New York: Routledge.

Sonnier, I. L. (Ed.). (1985). *Methods and techniques of holistic education.* Springfield, IL: Thomas.

——— (1991). Hemisphericity: A key to understanding the individual differences among teachers and learners. *Journal of Instructional Psychology, 18,* 17–22.

Sonnier, I. L., & Sonnier, C. B. (1992). The Sonnier model of educational management: Implementing holistic education. *Journal of Instructional Psychology, 19,* 135–140.

——— (1995). Nurturing hemispheric preference through affective education. *Journal of Instructional Psychology, 22,* 182–185.

Soper, J. D. (1964). *The mammals of Alberta.* Edmonton, Alberta: Hamly Press.

Southern, H. N. (1964). *The handbook of British mammals.* Oxford: Blackwell Scientific.

Soutter, A. (1996). A longitudinal study of three cases of gender identity disorder of childhood successfully resolved in the school setting. *School Psychology International, 17,* 49–57.

Sowder, J. T. (1998). Perspectives from mathematics education. *Educational Researcher, 27,* 12–14.

Sparzo, F. J. (1992). B. F. Skinner's contributions to education: A retrospective appreciation. *Contemporary Education, 63,* 225–233.

Spearman, C. E. (1927). *The abilities of man.* New York: Macmillan.

Speece, D. L., MacDonald, V., Kilsheimer, L., & Krist, J. (1997). Research to practice: Preservice teachers reflect on reciprocal teaching. *Learning disabilities Research and Practice, 12,* 177–187.

Springer, S. P., & Deutsch, G. (1989). *Left brain right brain* (3rd ed.). New York: Freeman.

Srebnik, D. S., & Elias, M. J. (1993). An ecological, interpersonal skills approach to drop-out prevention. *American Journal of Orthopsychiatry, 63,* 526–535.

Stanley, J. C. (1976). The case for extreme educational acceleration of intellectually brilliant youths. *Gifted Child Quarterly, 20,* 66–75.

Stanovich, K. E. (1992). Developmental reading disorder. In S. R. Hooper, G. W. Hynd, & R. E. Mattison (Eds.), *Developmental disorders: Diagnostic criteria and clinical assessment.* Hillsdale, NJ: Erlbaum.

Statistics Canada. (1992). *Earnings of men and women: 1990.* Ottawa, Ont.: Minister of Industry, Science and Technology.

——— (1996). The 1997 Canada Yearbook. Ottawa, Ont.: Minister of Industry.

Stecher, B. M., & Herman, J. L. (1997). Using portfolios for large-scale assessment. In G. D. Phye (Ed.), *Handbook of classroom assessment: Construction of Knowledge.* San Diego: Academic Press.

Steptoe, A. (1998). Mozart: Resilience under stress. In A. Steptoe (Ed.) *Genius and the mind: Studies of creativity and temperament.* Oxford, UK: Oxford University Press.

Stern, C. (1956). Hereditary factors affecting adoption. In *A Study of Adoption Practices* (Vol. 2). New York: Child Welfare League of America.

Stern, W. (1914). *The psychological methods of testing intelligence.* Baltimore: Warwick & York.

Sternberg, R. J. (1984a). A contextualist view of the nature of intelligence. *International Journal of Psychology, 19,* 307–334.

——— (1992). Ability tests, measurements, and markets. *Journal of Educational Psychology, 84,* 134–140.

——— (1995). Theory and measurement of tacit knowledge as a part of practical intelligence. *Zeitschrift für Psychologie, 203,* 319–334.

——— (1996a). *Successful intelligence: How practical and creative intelligence determine success in life.* New York: Simon & Schuster.

——— (1996b). Myths, countermyths, and truths about intelligence. *Educational Researcher, 25,* 11–16.

——— (1997a). The concept of intelligence and its role in lifelong learning and success. *American Psychologist, 52,* 1030–1037.

——— (1997b). *Thinking styles.* Cambridge: Cambridge University Press.

——— (1998a). Metacognition, abilities, and developing expertise: What makes an expert student? *Instructional Science, 26,* 127–140.

——— (1998b). Applying the triarchic theory of human intelligence in the classroom. In R. J. Sternberg & W. M. Williams (Eds.), *Intelligence, instruction, and assessment.* Mahwah, NJ: Erlbaum.

Sternberg, R. J., & Horvath, J. A. (1995). A prototype view of expert teaching. *Educational Researcher, 24,* 9–17.

Sternberg, R. J., & Kaufman, J. C. (1998). Human abilities. *Annual Review of Psychology, 49*, 479–502.

Stevens, R. J., & Slavin, R. E. (1995). The cooperative elementary school: Effects on students' achievement, attitudes, and social relations. *American Educational Research Journal, 32*, 321–351.

Stewart, D. W. (1993). *Immigration and education: The crisis and the opportunities.* New York: Lexington.

Stilwell, B. M., Galvin, M. R., Kopta, S. M., & Padgett, R. J. (1998). Moral volition: The fifth and final domain leading to an integrated theory of conscience understanding. *Journal of the American Academy of Child and Adolescent Psychiatry, 37*, 202–210.

Stinnett, T. A. (1997). "AAMR Adaptive Behavior Scale-School": Test review. *Journal of Psychoeducational Assessment, 15*, 361–372.

Stipek, D. J. (1988). *Motivation to learn: From theory to practice.* Englewood Cliffs, NJ: Prentice-Hall.

Stoll, S. K., & Beller, J. M. (1993), March 24–28). *The effect of a longitudinal teaching methodology and classroom environment on both cognitive and behavioral moral development.* Paper presented at the Annual Meeting of the American Alliance for Health, Physical Education, Recreation and Dance, Washington, DC.

Storey, V. E., & Kennedy, T. D. (1997). A comparison of the critical thinking skills and spatial ability of fifth grade children using simulation software or Logo. *Journal of Computing in Childhood Education, 8*, 345–363.

Strawitz, B. M. (1993). The effects of review on science process skill acquisition. *Journal of Science Teacher Education, 4*, 54–57.

Subhi, T. (1997). Who is gifted? A computerised identification procedure. *High Ability Studies, 8*, 189–211.

Swanson, H. L. (1993). An information processing analysis of learning disabled children's problem solving. *American Educational Research Journal, 30*, 861–893.

Swanson, H. L., O'Connor, J. E., & Cooney, J. B. (1990). An information processing analysis of expert and novice teachers' problem solving. *American Educational Research Journal, 27*, 533–556.

Sweet, A. P., Guthrie, J. T., & Ng, M. M. (1998). Teacher perceptions and student reading improvement. *Journal of Educational Psychology, 90*, 210–223.

Swing, S. R., & Peterson, P. L. (1982). The relationship of student ability and small-group interaction to student achievement. *American Educational Research Journal, 19*, 259–274.

Sykes, G., & Bird, T. (1992). Teacher education and the case idea. In G. Grant (Ed.), *Review of research in education* (Vol. 18). Washington, DC: American Educational Research Association.

Tamir, P. (1993). Positive and negative multiple choice items: How different are they? *Studies in Educational Evaluation, 19*, 311–325.

Tappan, M. B. (1997). Language, culture, and moral development: A Vygotskian perspective. *Developmental Review, 17*, 78–100.

Tapscott, D. (1997). Growing up digital: The rise of the Net generation. New York: McGraw-Hill.

Tavris, C., & Baumgartner, A. I. (1983, February). How would your life be different if you'd been born a boy? *Redbook*, p. 99.

Taylor, J., & Miller, M. (1997). When timeout works some of the time: The importance of treatment integrity and functional assessment. *School Psychology Quarterly, 12*, 4–22.

Terman, L. M. (1925). *Genetic studies of genius. The mental and physical traits of a thousand gifted children* (Vol. 1). Stanford, CA: Stanford University Press.

Terman, L. M., & Oden, M. (1959). *Genetic studies of genius: Vol. 5: The gifted group at mid-life.* Stanford, CA: Stanford University Press.

Terwilliger, J. (1997). Semantics, psychometrics, and assessment reform: A close look at "authentic" assessments. *Educational Researcher, 26*, 24–27.

Thissen, D., Wainer, H., & Wang, X-B. (1994). Are tests comprising both multiple-choice and free-response items necessarily less unidimensional than multiple-choice tests? An analysis of two tests. *Journal of Educational Measurement, 31*, 113–123.

Thomas, H., & Lohaus, A. (1993). Modeling growth and individual differences in spatial tasks. *Monographs of the Society for Research in Child Development*, Serial 237, Vol. 58, whole No. 9.

Thomas, J. W. (1980). Agency and achievement: Self-management and self-regard. *Review of Educational Research, 50*, 213–240.

Thomas, R. M. (1992). *Comparing theories of child development* (3rd ed.). Belmont, CA: Wadsworth.

——— (1996). *Comparing theories of child development* (4th ed.). Belmont, CA: Wadsworth.

Thompson, C., & Crutchlow, E. (1993). Learning style research: A critical review of the literature and implications for nursing education. *Journal of Professional Nursing, 9*, 34–40.

Thompson, D. W. (1997). Practice effects of advance organization with older adult subjects. *Educational Gerontology, 23*, 207–212.

Thorndike, E. L. (1898). Animal intelligence: An experimental study of the associative processes in animals. *Psychological Review Monograph Supplement, 2*, (8).

——— (1913a). *Educational psychology* (Vol. 1). *The psychology of learning.* New York: Teacher's College Press.

——— (1913b). *Educational psychology* (Vol. 2). *The original nature of man.* New York: Teachers College Press.

——— (1931). *Human learning.* New York: Appleton-Century-Crofts.

——— (1932). Reward and punishment in animal learning. *Comparative Psychology Monographs, 8* (39).

——— (1935). *The psychology of wants, interests, and attitudes.* New York: Appleton-Century-Crofts.

Thorndike, R. L., & Hagen, E. (1977). *Measurement and evaluation in psychology and education* (4th ed.). New York: Wiley.

Thorndike, R. L., Hagen, E., & Sattler, J. M. (1985). *Revised Stanford-Binet intelligence scale* (4th ed.). Boston: Houghton Mifflin.

Tillema, H. H., & Knol, W. E., (1997). Promoting student teacher learning through conceptual change or direct instruction. *Teaching and Teacher Education, 13*, 579–595.

Tiplady, B., Faineteau, H., Loganathan, A., Spiegelberg, M., Taylor, Z., & Wright, P. (1998). Effects of ethanol and temazepam on performance in memory and psychomotor tasks: A dose-response comparison. *Human Psychopharmacology, 13*, 285–291.

Tobin, J. J., Wu, D. Y. H., & Davidson, D. H. (1989). *Preschool in three cultures: Japan, China, and the United States.* New Haven, CT: Yale University Press.

Tochon, F. V. (1993). From teachers' thinking to macro-semantics: Catching instructional organizers and connectors in language arts. Special Issue: International conference on teacher thinking: II. *Journal of Structural Learning, 12*, 1–22.

Toffler, A. (1970). *Future shock.* New York: Random House.

——— (1980). *The third wave.* New York: Morrow.

Tomesen, M., & Aarnoutse, C. (1998). Effects of an instructional programme for deriving word meanings. *Educational Studies, 24*, 107–128.

Topping, K., & Ehly, S. (Eds.) (1998). *Peer-assisted learning.* Mahwah, NJ: Erlbaum.

Torrance, E. P. (1962). *Guiding creative talent.* Englewood Cliffs, NJ: Prentice-Hall.

——— (1966). *Torrance tests of creative thinking (Norms technical manual).* Princeton, NJ: Personnel Press.

——— (1974). *Torrance tests of creative thinking.* Lexington, MA: Ginn.

——— (1986). Teaching creative and gifted learners. In M. C. Wittrock (Ed.), *Handbook of research on teaching* (3rd ed.) (pp. 630–647). New York: Macmillan.

——— (1993). The beyonders in a thirty year longitudinal study of creative achievement. *Roeper Review, 15*, 131–135.

Torrance, E. P., & Sisk, D. A. (1997). *Gifted and talented children in the regular classroom.* Buffalo, NY: Creative Education Foundation Press.

Truchlicka, M., McLaughlin, T. F., & Swain, J. C. (1998). Effects of token reinforcement and response cost on the accuracy of spelling performance with middle-school special education students with behavior disorders. *Behavioral Interventions, 13*, 1–10.

Tsang, M. C. (1988). Cost analysis for educational policymaking: A review of cost studies in education in developing countries. *Review of Educational Research, 58*, 181–230.

Tulving, E. (1989). Remembering and knowing the past. *American Scientist, 77*, 361–367.

——— (1991). Concepts in human memory. In L. R. Squire, N. M. Weinberger, G. Lynch, & J. L. McGaugh (Eds.), *Memory: Organization and locus of change.* New York: Oxford University Press.

Tung, P., Lam, R., & Tsang, W. K. (1997). English as a medium of instruction in post-1997 Hong Kong: What students, teachers, and parents think. *Journal of Pragmatics, 28*, 441–459.

Turner, R. L., & Denny, D. A. (1969, February). Teacher characteristics, teacher behavior, and changes in pupil creativity. *Elementary School Journal*, pp. 265–270.

Tyler-Wood, T., & Carri, L. (1991). Identification of gifted children: The effectiveness of various measures of cognitive ability. *Roeper Review, 14*, 63–64.

U.S. Bureau of the Census. (1992). *Statistical abstracts of the United States, 1991* (112th ed.). Washington, DC: U.S. Government Printing Office.

——— (1994). *Statistical abstracts of the United States, 1994* (114th ed.). Washington, DC: U.S. Government Printing Office.

——— (1996). *Statistical abstracts of the United States: 1996* (116th ed.) Washington, DC: U.S. Government Printing Office.

——— (1997). *Statistical abstracts of the United States, 1997* (117th ed.). Washington, DC: U.S. Government Printing Office.

U.S. Department of Education. (1991). *Twelfth annual report to Congress on the implementation of PL 94–142: The education for all handicapped children act.* Washington, DC: U.S. Government Printing Office.

U.S. Office of Education. (1977, August 23). Implementation of part B of the Education of the Handicapped Act. *Federal Register, 42*, 42474– 42518.

Ukrainian famine survivors recall season in hell. (1983, October 20). *Edmonton Journal*, p. A1.

Ulrich, R. E., & Azrin, N. H. (1962). Reflexive fighting in response to aversive stimulation. *Journal of Experimental Analysis of Behavior, 5*, 511–521.

Umoren, J. A. (1992). Maslow hierarchy of needs and OBRA 1987: Toward need satisfaction by nursing home residents. *Educational Gerontology, 18*, 657–670.

Unruh, R. P., & Dupree, M. (1998). An examination of the CATM blocks and block pattern intervention. *Journal of Instructional Psychology, 25*, 134–138.

Uzgiris, I. C., & Hunt, J. (1975). *Assessment in infancy: Ordinal scales of psychological development.* Urbana: University of Illinois Press.

Valdés, G. (1998). The world outside and inside schools: Language and immigrant children. *Educational Researcher, 27*, 4–18.

Valencia, S. W., & Place, N. (1994). Portfolios: A process for enhancing teaching and learning. *Reading Teacher, 47*, 666–669.

Valli, L. (1992). Beginning teacher problems: Areas for teacher education improvement. *Action in Teacher Education, 14*, 18–25.

Valsiner, J. (1987). *Culture and the development of children's action: A cultural-historical theory of developmental psychology.* New York: Wiley.

Van der Veer, R. (1996). Vygotsky and Piaget: A collective monologue. *Human Development, 39*, 237–242.

Van Houten, R., & Doleys, D. M. (1983). Are social reprimands effective? In S. Axelrod & J. Apsche (Eds.), *The effects of punishment on human behavior.* New York: Academic Press.

Van Houten, R., Nau, P. A., MacKenzie-Keating, S., Sameoto, D., & Colavecchia, B. (1982). An analysis of some variables influencing the effectiveness of reprimands. *Journal of Applied Behavior Analysis, 15*, 65–83.

Vasquez-Levy, D. (1993). The use of practical arguments in clarifying and changing practical reasoning and classroom practices: Two cases. *Journal of Curriculum Studies, 25,* 125–143.

Von Glasersfeld, E. (1997). Homage to Jean Piaget (1896–1982). *Irish Journal of Psychology, 18,* 293–306.

Vosniadou, S., & Brewer, W. F. (1992). Mental models of the earth: A study of conceptual change in childhood. *Cognitive Psychologist, 24,* 535–585.

Voss, J. F., Wiley, J., & Carretero, M. (1995). Acquiring intellectual skills. *Annual Review of Psychology, 46,* 155–181.

Vygotsky, L. S. (1962). *Thought and language* (E. Hamsman & G. Vankan, Eds. and Trans.). Cambridge, MA: MIT Press.

———— (1978). *Mind in society.* Cambridge, MA: Harvard University Press.

———— (1986). *Thought and language* (A. Kozulin, Ed. and Trans.). Cambridge, MA: MIT Press.

———— (1991). *Pedagogicheskaia psikhologiia* [Pedagogical psychology, 2nd ed.]. Moscow: Pedagogika. (Original work published in 1926).

———— (1992). *Educational psychology* (M. O'Connor & R. Silverman, Eds.). Winter Park, FL: PMD Publications.

———— (1993). *The collected works of L. S. Vygotsky. Vol. 2: Fundamentals of defectology (abnormal psychology & learning disability).* New York: Plenum.

Vygotsky, L. S., & Luria, A. R. (1993). *Studies on the history of behavior: Ape, primitive man, & child* (V. I. Golod & J. E. Knox, Eds.). Hillsdale, NJ: Erlbaum.

Wade, R. C. (1994). Conceptual change in elementary social studies: A case study of fourth graders' understanding of human rights. *Theory and Research in Social Education, 22,* 74–95.

Wagner, M. E., Schubert, H. J. P., & Schubert, D. S. P. (1985). Effects of sibling spacing on intelligence, interfamiliar relations, psychosocial characteristics, and mental and physical health. *Advances in Child Development and Behavior, 19,* 196–198.

Wagner, P. A. (1994). Adaptations for administering the Peabody Picture Vocabulary Test-Revised to individuals with severe communication and motor dysfunctions. *Mental Retardation, 32,* 107–112.

Wagner, R. K., & Sternberg, R. J. (1984). Alternative conceptions of intelligence and their implications for education. *Review of Educational Research, 54,* 179–223.

Walker, H. (1979). *The acting-out child: Coping with classroom disruption.* Boston: Allyn & Bacon.

Walker, J. E., & Shea, T. M. (1999). *Behavior management: A practical approach for educators* (7th ed). Upper Saddle River, NJ: Merrill.

Walker, L. J., Pitts, R. C., Hennig, K. H., & Matsuba, M. K. (1995). Reasoning about morality and real-life moral problems. In M. Killen & D. Hart, (Eds.), *Morality in everyday life: Developmental perspectives.* New York: Cambridge University Press.

Walker, R. (1990, February 28). Governors set to adopt national education goals. *Education Week,* p. 16.

Wallach, M. A. (1985). Creativity testing and giftedness. In F. D. Horowitz & M. O'Brien (Eds.), *The gifted and talented: Developmental perspectives* (pp. 99–123). Washington, DC: American Psychological Association.

Wallach, M. A., & Kogan, N. (1965). *Modes of thinking in young children: A study of the creativity-intelligence distinction.* New York: Holt, Rinehart & Winston.

Wallick, M. D. (1998). A comparison study of the Ohio Proficiency Test results between fourth-grade string pull-out students and those of matched ability. *Journal of Research in Music Education, 46,* 239–247.

Walters, G. C., & Grusec, J. E. (1977). *Punishment.* San Francisco: Freeman.

Walters, R. H., & Llewellyn, T. E. (1963). Enhancement of punitiveness by visual and audiovisual displays. *Canadian Journal of Psychology, 17,* 244–255.

Walters, R. H., Llewellyn, T. E., & Acker, W. (1962). Enhancement of punitive behavior by audiovisual displays. *Science, 136,* 872–873.

Wang, M. C., Haertel, G. D., & Walberg, H. J. (1993). Toward a knowledge base for school learning. *Review of Educational Research, 63,* 249–294.

Ward, M. F. (1994). Attention deficit hyperactivity disorder. In R. J. Sternberg (Ed.), *Encyclopedia of human intelligence* (Vol. 1). New York: Macmillan.

Wasserman, E. A., & Miller, R. R. (1997). What's elementary about associative learning? *Annual Review of Psychology, 48,* 573–607.

Waterhouse, P. (1991). *Tutoring.* Stafford, UK: Network Educational Press.

Watson, J. (1998). Fostering reflection in pupils with learning difficulties. *International Journal of Disability, Development and Education, 45,* 9–16.

Watson, J. B. (1913). Psychology as the behaviorist views it. *Psychological Review, 20,* 157–158.

———— (1916). The place of a conditioned reflex in psychology. *Psychological Review, 23,* 89–116.

Watson, L. (1997). Children's misconceptions and conceptual change. *Australian Journal of Early Childhood, 22,* 12–16.

Watters, P. A., Martin, F., & Schreter, Z. (1997). Caffeine and cognitive performance: The nonlinear Yerkes-Dodson Law. *Human Psychopharmacology, 12,* 249–257.

Weber, G. (1996). *Episodic learner modeling, 20,*195–236.

Webster, S. W. (1968). *Discipline in the classroom: Basic principles and problems.* New York: Chandler.

Wechsler, D. (1958). *The measurement and appraisal of adult intelligence* (4th ed.). Baltimore: Williams & Wilkins.

Weiner, B. (1984). Principles for a theory of student motivation and their application within an attributional framework. In R. Ames & C. Ames (Eds.), *Research on motivation in education (Vol. 1): Student motivation.* New York: Academic Press.

———— (1992). *Human motivation: Metaphors, theories and research.* Newbury Park, CA: Sage.

———— (1994). Integrating social and personal theories of achievement striving. *Review of Educational Research, 64,* 557–573.

Weinstein, C. F., & Mayer, R. F. (1986). The teaching of learning strategies. In M. C. Wittrock (Ed.), *Handbook of research on teaching* (3rd ed.) (pp. 315–327). New York: Macmillan.

Weinstein, R. S. (1996). High standards in a tracked system of schooling: For which students and with what educational supports? *Educational Researcher, 25*, 16–19.

Weinstein, R. S., Madison, S. M., & Kuklinski, M. R. (1995). Raising expectations in schooling: Obstacles and opportunities for change. *American Educational Research Journal, 32*, 121–159.

Wellman, H. M. (1990). *The child's theory of mind.* Cambridge, MA: MIT Press.

Wellman, H. M., & Gelman, S. A. (1992). Cognitive development: Foundational theories of core domains. *Annual Review of Psychology, 43*, 337–375.

Whipple, E. E., & Richey, C. A. (1997). Crossing the line from physical discipline to child abuse: How much is too much? *Child Abuse & Neglect, 21*, 431–444.

Whitaker, P. (1994). Mainstream students talk about integration. *British Journal of Special Education, 17*, 13–16.

White, B. Y., & Frederiksen, J. R. (1998). Inquiry, modeling, and metacognition: Making science accessible to all students. *Cognition and instruction, 16*, 3–118.

White, M. A. (1975). Natural rates of teacher approval and disapproval in the classroom. *Journal of Applied Behavior Analysis, 8*, 367–372.

White, R. T., & Tisher, R. P. (1986). Research on natural sciences. In M. C. Wittrock (Ed.), *Handbook of research on teaching* (3rd ed.). New York: Macmillan.

White, R. W. (1959). Motivation reconsidered: The concept of competence. *Psychological Review, 66*, 297–333.

White, S. H., & Cahan, E. D. (1997). How developmental psychologists make their ideas clearer. *Human Development, 40*, 87–90.

Whitener, E. M. (1989). A meta-analytic review of the effect on learning of the interaction between prior achievement and instructional support. *Review of Educational Research, 59*, 65–86.

Wideen, M., Mayer-Smith, J., & Moon, B. (1998). A critical analysis of the research on learning to teach: Making the case for an ecological perspective on inquiry. *Review of Educational Research, 68*, 130–178.

Widener, A. J. (1998). Beyond Ritalin: The importance of therapeutic work with parents and children diagnosed ADD/ADHD. *Journal of Child Psychotherapy, 24*, 267–281.

Wigdor, A. K., & Garner, W. R. (Eds.). (1982). *Ability testing: Uses, consequences, and controversies, Part 1: Report of the Committee.* Washington, DC: National Academy Press.

Wigfield, A., Eccles, J. S., & Rodriguez, D. (1998). The development of children's motivation in school contexts. In P. D. Pearson & A. Iran-Nejad (Eds.), *Review of Research in Education, 23*, 73–118.

Wiggins, G. (1998). *Educative assessment: Designing assessments to inform and improve student performance.* San Francisco: Jossey-Bass.

Wilczenski, F. L. (1994). Changes in attitudes toward mainstreaming among undergraduate education students. *Educational Research Quarterly, 17*, 5–17.

Wilgosh, L. (1991). Underachievement and related issues for culturally different gifted children. *International Journal of Special Education, 6*, 82–93.

Williams, B. L., Hetrick, C. J., & Suen, H. K. (1998). Development of performance-based assessments. *American Journal of Health Behavior, 22*, 228–234.

Wilson, K., & Tally, W. (1990). The "Palenque" project: Formative evaluation in the design and development of an optical disc prototype. In B. Flagg (Ed.), *Formative evaluation for educational technologies.* Hillsdale, NJ: Erlbaum.

Wilson, L. (1988). Phase change: Larry Wilson on selling in a brave new world. *Training, 11*, 14.

Winder, R., & Borrill, J. (1998). Fuels for memory: The role of oxygen and glucose in memory enhancement. *Psychopharmacology, 136*, 349–356.

Windschitl, M. (1998). The WWW and classroom research: What path should we take? *Educational Researcher, 27*, 28–33.

Wineburg, S. S. (1987). The self-fulfillment of the self-fulfilling prophecy: A critical appraisal. *Educational Researcher, 16*, 28–37.

Winfield, L. F. (1990). School competency testing reforms and student achievement: Exploring a national perspective. *Educational Evaluation and Policy Analysis, 12*, 157–173.

Winn, W. (1990). Some implications of cognitive theory for instructional design. *Instructional Science, 19*, 53–69.

Winsten, S. (1949). *Days with Bernard Shaw.* New York: Vanguard Press.

Winter, S. (1996). Teachers' expectations toward disruptive students in Hong Kong. *Psychologia: An International Journal of Psychology in the Orient, 39*, 102–108.

Winzer, M. (1997). *Special education in early childhood: An inclusive approach.* Scarborough, Ont.: Prentice-Hall.

Wise, S. L., Lukin, L. E., & Roos, L. L. (1991). Teacher beliefs about training in testing and measurement. *Journal of Teacher Education, 42*, 37–42.

Wiske, M. S. (1994). How teaching for understanding changes the rules in the classroom. *Educational Leadership, 51*, 19–21.

Witt, S. D. (1997). Parental influence on children's socialization to gender roles. *Adolescence, 32*, 253–259.

Wittrock, M. C. (1986). Students' thought processes. In M. C. Wittrock (Ed.), *Handbook of research on teaching* (3rd ed.) (pp. 297–314). New York: Macmillan.

Wittrock, M. C. (1992). An empowering conception of educational psychology. *Educational Psychologist, 27*, 129–141.

Wolf, D., Bixby, J., Glenn, J., & Gardner, H. (1991). To use their minds well: Investigating new forms of student assessment. In G. Grant (Ed.), *Review of research in education* (Vol. 17). Washington, DC: American Educational Research Association.

Wolff, J. S., & Wogalter, M. S. (1998). Comprehension of pictorial symbols: Effects of context and test method. *Human Factors, 40*, 173–186.

Wolraich, M. L., & Baumgaertel, A. (1997). The practical aspects of diagnosing and managing children with attention deficit hyperactivity disorder. *Clinical Pediatrics, 36*, 497–504.

Wood, B. S. (1981). *Children and communication: Verbal and nonverbal language development* (2nd ed.). Englewood Cliffs, NJ: Prentice-Hall.

Wood, D., Bruner, J. S., & Ross, G. (1976). The role of tutoring in problem solving. *Journal of Child Psychology and Psychiatry, 17*, 89–100.

Wright, D. S., Gaskell, G. D., & O'Muircheartaigh, C. A. (1998). Flashbulb memory assumptions: Using national surveys to explore cognitive phenomena. *British Journal of Psychology, 89*, 102–121.

Wu, A. K. W., & Lee, M. C. (1998). Intelligent tutoring systems as design. *Computers in Human Behavior, 14*, 209–220.

Wynn, V. E., & Logie, R. H. (1998). The veracity of long-term memories—Did Bartlett get it right? *Applied Cognitive Psychology, 12*, 1–20.

Yerrick, R., Parke, H., & Nugent, J. (1997). Struggling to promote deeply rooted change: The "filtering effect" of teachers' beliefs on understanding transformational views of teaching science. *Science Education, 81*, 137–159.

Yoder, S. (1992). The turtle and the mouse . . . a tale. *The Computing Teacher, 20*, 41–43.

Yoshioka, H., Yoshida, A., Okano, S., Yamazoe, I., et al. (1995). Effects of early undernutrition and subsequent nutritional rehabilitation on brain development: I. The most critical period. *Developmental Brain Dysfunction, 8*, 66–72.

Zajonc, R. B. (1975, January). Birth order and intelligence: Dumber by the dozen. *Psychology Today*, pp. 37–43.

Zajonc, R. B., & Markus, G. B. (1975). Birth order and intellectual development. *Psychological Review, 82*, 74–88.

Zajonc, R. B., & Mullally, P. R. (1997). Birth order: Reconciling conflicting effects. *American Psychologist, 52*, 685–699.

Zeidner, M. (1998). *Test anxiety: The state of the art*. New York: Plenum.

Zern, D. (1997). The attitudes of present and future teachers to the teaching of values (in general) and of certain values (in particular). *Journal of Genetic Psychology, 158*, 505–507.

Zigler, E. (1994). Reshaping early childhood intervention to be a more effective weapon against poverty. *American Journal of Community Psychology, 22*, 37–47.

Zigler, E., & Hodapp, R. M. (1991). Behavioral functioning in individuals with mental retardation. *Annual Review of Psychology, 42*, 29–50.

Zimmerman, B. J., Bandura, A., & Martinez-Pons, M. (1992). Self-motivation for academic attainment: The role of self-efficacy beliefs and personal goal setting. *American Educational Research Journal, 29*, 663–676.

Zohar, D. (1998). An additive model of test anxiety: Role of exam-specific expectations. *Journal of Educational Psychology, 90*, 330–340.

NAME INDEX

SUBJECT INDEX